Mattias Karlsson

Relations of Power in Early Neo-Assyrian State Ideology

Studies in Ancient Near Eastern Records

General Editor:
Gonzalo Rubio

Editors:
Nicole Brisch, Petra Goedegebuure, Markus Hilgert, Amélie Kuhrt, Peter Machinist, Piotr Michalowski, Cécile Michel, Beate Pongratz-Leisten, D. T. Potts, Kim Ryholt

Volume 10

Mattias Karlsson

Relations of Power in Early Neo-Assyrian State Ideology

DE GRUYTER

ISBN 978-1-5015-1619-1
e-ISBN (PDF) 978-1-61451-691-0
e-ISBN (EPUB) 978-1-61451-968-3
ISSN 2161-4415

Library of Congress Cataloging-in-Publication Data
A CIP catalog record for this book has been applied for at the Library of Congress.

Bibliographic information published by the Deutsche Nationalbibliothek
The Deutsche Nationalbibliothek lists this publication in the Deutsche Nationalbibliografie; detailed bibliographic data are available on the Internet at http://dnb.dnb.de.

This volume is text- and page-identical with the hardback published in 2016.
Typesetting: Meta Systems Publishing & Printservices GmbH, Wustermark
Printing and binding: CPI books GmbH, Leck

♾ Printed on acid-free paper
Printed in Germany

www.degruyter.com

Preface

This book is a revised version of my doctor of philosophy thesis, presented at Uppsala University in 2013. The main title of my thesis was “Early Neo-Assyrian State Ideology”. While this thesis focused mainly on the propaganda of “only” two kings of the period, namely Ashurnasirpal II and Shalmaneser III, the present work deals with the propaganda of *all* the kings of the Early Neo-Assyrian Period (934–745 BCE), making it complete in a way. The present work also puts more stress on theories, notably gender theory.

I want to thank Gojko Barjamovic for recommending my work for the SANER-series. I also want to thank the editor of the series, Gonzalo Rubio, for accepting my manuscript. Since I started my revising work in late 2013, I have received written comments from Julian Reade for which I am thankful. I have also benefited from the critique and suggestions which the opponent on my doctoral defence, Eva Cancik-Kirschbaum, gave me. I am also in gratitude to Gonzalo Rubio and the anonymous peer-reviewers for reading and commenting on my initial draft. Finally, I want to thank Walter de Gruyter and its executive board for publishing my work, as well as its senior editorial director Michiel Klein-Swormink, its project editors Emily Hough and John Whitley, and its production editor Katja Brockmann.

Lastly, I want to take the opportunity to get the following preface, which was given as a postscript on a separate paper at the presentation of my thesis, in press. “*At the completion of this Ph.D.-project in Assyriology (branch of Semitic Languages) in September 2013, I would like to thank for all the critique I have received. I would like to thank especially Olof Pedersén (first adviser), Gojko Barjamovic (second adviser), and Jakob Andersson. I also would like to thank the scholars who acted as formal or informal opponents at the seminars which were based on my work, namely Gunnel Ekroth, Andreas Fuchs, Ulla Koch, and Saana Svärd. For giving me feedback on seminars or otherwise, I would like to thank Zack Cherry, Frands Herschend, Thomas Hertel, Gullög Nordquist, Sina Tezel, Andreas Winkler, and Rikke Wulff-Krabbenhöft. My apologies to anyone who may feel unjustly excluded from this enumeration. Naturally, all aspects of my thesis as well as any inaccuracies in the final manuscript are my own responsibility.*”

Contents

Preface — v

List of figures — xi

Abbreviations — xiii
Bibliographical abbreviations — **xiii**
Symbols and other abbreviations — **xiii**

1 Introduction — 1
1.1 Topic and background of the study — **1**
1.2 Aims of the study — **4**
1.3 Earlier research — **5**
1.4 General notes on the primary sources — **8**
1.4.1 Assyrian royal inscriptions and iconography — **8**
1.4.2 State ideology and propaganda — **10**
1.5 Method — **18**
1.6 Theory — **27**
1.7 Relations of power "in real life" — **31**
1.7.1 The geopolitical setting — **32**
1.7.2 The socio-economic setting — **37**

2 The primary sources of the study — 45
2.1 The major primary sources — **45**
2.2 The minor primary sources — **53**

3 The relationship between the great gods and the foreign lands — 59
3.1 Owners and masters of the world — **59**
3.2 Conquerors of the foreign lands — **66**
3.3 Summary — **73**

4 The relationship between the great gods and the king of Assyria — 75
4.1 Representative of the great gods — **75**
4.2 Priest and servant of the great gods — **93**
4.3 Master builder of the great gods — **103**

4.4 Warrior of the great gods — 113
4.5 Summary — 122

5 The relationship between the king of Assyria and the foreign lands — 125
5.1 Overcoming the foreign landscapes — 125
5.2 Pacifying the foreign animals — 133
5.3 Respecting the foreign deities — 140
5.4 Confronting the foreign elites and people — 147
5.4.1 Status and hierarchy — 147
5.4.2 Function and reciprocity — 158
5.4.3 Realized reciprocity: tribute — 173
5.4.4 Realized reciprocity: paternalism — 181
5.4.5 Differentiation of the foreign people and lands — 189
5.4.6 Alleged roles of ethnicity and nationalism — 202
5.4.7 Emphasis on the king and the ruling class — 211
5.4.8 Self versus Other: identity and alterity — 223
5.4.9 Gendered roles and relations — 228
5.5 Summary — 242

6 Ideological development within the reigns — 247
6.1 Introduction — 247
6.2 Ideology and regnal phases of Ashurnasirpal II — 249
6.3 Ideology and regnal phases of Shalmaneser III — 255
6.4 Ideology and regnal phases of the other kings — 262
6.5 Summary and reflections — 266

7 Local propaganda and regional politics — 269
7.1 Introduction — 269
7.2 Ashurnasirpal II and local propaganda — 272
7.3 Shalmaneser III and local propaganda — 278
7.4 The other kings and local propaganda — 283
7.5 Summary and reflections — 286

8 Ideological comparison between the reigns — 291
8.1 Introduction — 291
8.2 General comparison Ashurnasirpal II–Shalmaneser III — 294
8.3 Strategic comparison Ashurnasirpal II–Shalmaneser III — 301
8.4 The other kings and strategic comparisons — 306
8.5 Summary and reflections — 308

9 The development of Assyrian state ideology — 311
9.1 Introduction — 311
9.2 Early Neo-Assyrian propaganda in history: royal iconography and titulary — 314
9.3 Early Neo-Assyrian propaganda in history: textual narrative — 318
9.4 Summary and reflections — 325

10 Conclusion of the study — 327
10.1 Final conclusions and reflections — 327
10.2 Further research — 330

Bibliography — 331

Figures — 359

Appendices and indices — 379
1 List of the inscriptions — 381
2 List of the iconography — 401
3 Spatial distribution of the major primary sources — 407
4 Deity hierarchy in the texts — 409
5 Divine titles and epithets in the texts of Ashurnasirpal II — 413
6 Divine titles and epithets in the texts of Shalmaneser III — 425
7 Divine titles and epithets in the texts of the other kings — 433
8 Royal titles and epithets of Ashurnasirpal II — 447
9 Royal titles and epithets of Shalmaneser III — 463
10 Royal titles and epithets of the other kings — 473
11 List of the most common royal titles and epithets I — 485
12 List of the most common royal titles and epithets II — 489
13 Visual representations of Ashurnasirpal II — 493
14 Visual representations of Shalmaneser III and the other kings — 499
15 List of the most common royal visual representations — 503
16 Early Neo-Assyrian state ideology in history — 505

List of figures

Fig. 1: Map of the Near East in the Early Neo-Assyrian Period 361
Fig. 2: Map of the city Assur 362
Fig. 3: Map of the citadel of Kalhu 363
Fig. 4: Plan of the North-West Palace 364
Fig. 5: Plan of Fort Shalmaneser 365
Fig. 6: King in battle 1 366
Fig. 7: King in battle 2 366
Fig. 8: King as hunter 367
Fig. 9: King as libating priest 367
Fig. 10: Deities as warriors 1 368
Fig. 11: Deities as warriors 2 368
Fig. 12: "Display of strength" 369
Fig. 13: "Difficult path" 369
Fig. 14: King banqueting 370
Fig. 15: The sacred tree scene (king as venerating priest) 370
Fig. 16: Human and bird-headed genii 371
Fig. 17: Human-headed bull colossus 371
Fig. 18: King having his weapons ritually purified 372
Fig. 19: The statue of Ashurnasirpal II (king as priest (statue)) 373
Fig. 20: The Ninurta Stele (king as venerating priest) 373
Fig. 21: King receiving tribute 1 (The Black Obelisk) 374
Fig. 22: King receiving tribute 2 (The Black Obelisk) 374
Fig. 23: King receiving tribute 3 (The Black Obelisk) 375
Fig. 24: King receiving tribute 4 (The Black Obelisk) 375
Fig. 25: King as priest 1 376
Fig. 26: King as priest 2 376
Fig. 27: King receiving captives 1 377
Fig. 28: King receiving captives 2 377
Fig. 29: The Nabu Stele (king as venerating priest) 378
Fig. 30: Statue of a god or genie 378

Abbreviations

Bibliographical abbreviations

AEAD	see Parpola et al. 2007b
AHw	see von Soden 1959–81
CAD	see Gelb et al. 1956–2011
EAC	see Cohen 2011
MZL	see Borger 2003
RIMA1	see Grayson 1987
RIMA2	see Grayson 1991
RIMA3	see Grayson 1996
RINAP1	see Tadmor and Yamada 2011
RINAP3/1	see Grayson and Novotny 2012
RINAP3/2	see Grayson and Novotny 2014
RINAP4	see Leichty 2011

Symbols and other abbreviations

°	sic (= "actually written so")
*	form attested in variant writing of the "master text"
′	marking line order after lacuna
″	marking line order after lacunae
[ ]	marking reconstructed text
Ad2E	Ashur-dan II, epigraphic (source)
Ad2I	Ashur-dan II, iconographic (source)
Ad3E	Ashur-dan III, epigraphic (source)
Ad3I	Ashur-dan III, iconographic (source)
AE	Ashurnasirpal II, epigraphic (source)
AI	Ashurnasirpal II, iconographic (source)
An2E	Adad-narari II, epigraphic (source)
An2I	Adad-narari II, iconographic (source)
An3E	Adad-narari III, epigraphic (source)
An3I	Adad-narari III, iconographic (source)
An5E	Ashur-narari V, epigraphic (source)
An5I	Ashur-narari V, iconographic (source)
app(s).	appendix(es)
b.	bottom (e.g. of register)
D	D-stem
DN(N)	divine name(s)
e.	edge (e.g. of tablet)
eNA I	Early Neo-Assyrian period, 934–884 BCE
eNA II	Early Neo-Assyrian period, 883–824 BCE
eNA III	Early Neo-Assyrian period, 823–745 BCE
ex(s).	exemplar(s)
fig(s).	figure(s) (external reference)

Fig(s).	Figure(s) (internal reference)
GN(N)	geographical name(s)
Gt	Gt-stem
l.	left (e.g. of column)
lNA (I–II)	Late Neo-Assyrian period
MA (I–II)	Middle Assyrian period
N	N-stem
NN	unknown name
OA (I–II)	Old Assyrian period
obv.	obverse (of tablet)
PN(N)	personal name(s)
r.	right (e.g. of column)
rev.	reverse (of tablet)
RN(N)	royal name(s)
SE	Shalmaneser III, epigraphic (source)
SI	Shalmaneser III, iconographic (source)
S4E	Shalmaneser IV, epigraphic (source)
S4I	Shalmaneser IV, iconographic (source)
SA5E	Shamshi-Adad V, epigraphic (source)
SA5I	Shamshi-Adad V, iconographic (source)
t.	top (e.g. of register)
TN2E	Tukulti-Ninurta II, epigraphic (source)
TN2I	Tukulti-Ninurta II, iconographic (source)

1 Introduction

1.1 Topic and background of the study

The Neo-Assyrian empire was one of the great empires of the ancient world. At its maximal extent in the 7th century BCE, it comprised extensive areas of the Ancient Near East, including parts of present-day Turkey, Iran, and Egypt. A considerable amount of Neo-Assyrian royal inscriptions and iconography that legitimate the imperialism and right to rule of the kings has been preserved. This material can be classified as state ideology, conveying the official formulation of an imperial idea in a fundamentally propagandistic and indoctrinating manner (Liverani 1979; Garelli 1982).[1] The topic of this book – Neo-Assyrian state ideology – centres on the world view which is expressed in these sources, more precisely in the inscriptions and iconography of the ten kings of the formative Early Neo-Assyrian Period (934–745).[2] This study is thus not focused on the actual structure or workings of the empire but on the ideas behind it. The notion that "the history of Assyria was not only the history of the growth of an empire, but also the history of the growth of an imperial idea" (Beaulieu 2005: 49) is here recognized.

Nevertheless, before proceeding to describing the plan and realization of this study in detail, a brief historical background needs to be given. The Neo-Assyrian empire ultimately had its roots in the city state Aššur,[3] which in the third millennium BCE seems to have been an insignificant polity, being under some kind of authority of first the Sargonic state (2334–2154) and then the Ur III state (2112–2004) (Cancik-Kirschbaum 2008: 30–31).[4] The ethnical composition of this small, dependent polity is unclear, but it may have had an "Akkadian" character right from the start (Larsen 1976: 43).

With the Old Assyrian state (c. 2000–1500), a seemingly independent Assyrian polity had developed. This polity was not only governed by the ruler but also by an assembly of Aššur (*ālum*) consisting of free men. Eponyms (*limmum*), i.e. male representatives of "aristocratic" families, also seem to have played a role. The title of "king" (*šarrum*) was a prerogative of the god Ashur. The city state in question had a mercantile character, as attested by the trade

---

1 For the terms state ideology and propaganda, see the discussion in subsection 1.4.2.

2 For the aim formulation proper, see section 1.2. All dates given in this work follow the so-called middle chronology, worked out by Brinkman (1977: 335–48).

3 In this book, Aššur refers to the city state, Assur to the city, and Ashur to the god.

4 Michalowski (2009) argues, based on a discussion on the ruler Zarriqum, that Aššur, just like Nineveh (Zettler 2006), was semi-independent in the Ur III Period.

colonies (*kārum*) and stations (*wabartum*) in Anatolia, notably Kanesh.[5] This trade, in which tin and textiles were given in exchange for gold and silver, was in the hands of the aristocratic families of Aššur and their representatives in Anatolia. At one time, Aššur formed a part of the great, Habur-based, north-Mesopotamian state under the Amorite ruler Shamshi-Adad I (1813–1781). A period of which much is unknown due to the general lack of sources then followed (Larsen 1976: 109–223).

In the Middle Assyrian Period (c. 1500–1000),[6] Aššur developed from a city state to a territorial state, i.e. it now consisted of areas beyond the city of Assur and its hinterland. Some scholars, using a looser definition, even refer to the Middle Assyrian state as an empire.[7] A first step in this polity development was the gaining of independence from the Hurrite state of Mitanni with its centre in the Habur area. Under Ashur-uballit I (1363–1328), "Assyria" (*māt Aššur*) seeked recognition as one of the great powers in the Amarna correspondence (Liverani 1990). Under Adad-narari I (1305–1274) and Shalmaneser I (1273–1244), the land between the twin rivers in northern Mesopotamia was gradually conquered from the Hurrites and the Hittites. Cities such as Nineveh and Arbela now became part of the Assyrian state.

Under the authority of kings like Tukulti-Ninurta I (1243–1207) and Tiglath-pileser I (1114–1076), the power of the Assyrian state was consolidated, and even Babylonia was temporarily conquered. The major turning-point in Assyrian state ideology took place in the Middle Assyrian Period. The ruler went from "prince" (*rubû*) to "king of the universe" (*šar kiššati*) (Magen 1986: 13–19). Royal inscriptions switched emphasis from building to warfare, and a notion of a divinely ordered imperialism was formulated. The nobility continued to be influential (Kuhrt 1997: 362–63), but the power of the ruler, now sharing the title of "king" with Ashur, was strenghtened. In the 11th and 10th centuries BCE, the control of the Assyrian state over western territiories was weakened following Arameans migrating to the Habur and Balih areas. The sources from these centuries are very sparse.

Turning finally to the Neo-Assyrian Period (934–609),[8] it was with the Early Neo-Assyrian Period that Assyria began to evolve from a territorial to an

5 The idea of Lewy (1956) that there actually existed an Old Assyrian empire, consisting of the area covered by the trade, is generally refuted.

6 If not stated otherwise, the description in this and the next paragraph on the Middle Assyrian Period follows Cancik-Kirschbaum 2008: 40–59.

7 See e.g. Barjamovic (2013: 137–50) who uses the term "territorial empire". See also Liverani 1988 for a description of the Middle Assyrian state as a "network empire".

8 If not stated otherwise, the description in this and the following paragraphs on the Neo-Assyrian Period follows Cancik-Kirschbaum 2008: 59–100.

imperial state, carrying the idea of a "universal empire" (Barjamovic 2013: 137–50, 153). Ashur-dan II (934–912) repeatedly refers to fighting the Arameans and to reconquering lands. According to a common way of reckoning, this period starts with this king.[9] As is narrated by them in their respective royal annals, Adad-narari II (911–891) and Tukulti-Ninurta II (890–884) continued the political-military acts of reclaiming lands. In this study, I refer to this first phase of the Early Neo-Assyrian Period as eNA I.

Ashurnasirpal II (883–859), followed by his son Shalmaneser III (858–824), then came to power. The former is generally regarded as one of the most important kings of the Neo-Assyrian Period. His state ideology is extensive and pretentious, his army arguably conducted many and far-reaching military campaigns (e.g. to the Mediterranean), and he moved the capital away from Assur to Kalhu (modern Nimrud) where he commissioned the so-called North-West Palace and many temples. His son and successor Shalmaneser III kept Kalhu as his royal residence, carried out military campaigns in many directions, commissioned a plenty of royal inscriptions, as well as several temples and palaces, not the least the palace today known as Fort Shalmaneser in Kalhu. The end of this ruler's reign was turbulent, with a "civil war" breaking out in 826 BCE and still being unsettled at the king's death three years later. His field marshal, Dajjan-Ashur, is believed to have played a key role in the late phase of the said king's reign (Fuchs 2008). I refer to this second phase of the Early Neo-Assyrian Period as eNA II.

Three years into the reign of Shamshi-Adad V (823–811), the son of Shalmaneser III, this "rebellion" was finally put down. This king is also famous for his Babylonian campaigns. The grandson of Shalmaneser III, Adad-narari III (810–783), had a long reign, notable e.g. by his building of a new palace in Kalhu. He is believed to have been a minor at accession, and the queen-mother Sammuramat, who is often identified as the basis for the legend of the queen-ruler Semiramis, is supposed to have been influential at court. The reign of Adad-narari III has often been seen as a time of decline, although this understanding is not undisputed (Siddall 2013). The said king was followed by his three sons Shalmaneser IV (782–773), Ashur-dan III (772–755), and Ashur-narari V (754–745), concluding this first imperial phase. The sources from all these later reigns are comparatively modest, and a gradual weakening of centralized authority in the first half of the 8th century BCE can be detected, although warfare remained a vital ideological theme. Indicative of a political decentralization of a sort is the powerful position of the field marshal and provinicial

9 See e.g. Grayson (1991: 131) and Kuhrt (1997: 473). Other scholars, e.g. Roux (1992: 283), prefer to start from the reign of his successor Adad-narari II and 911 BCE.

governor Shamshi-ilu. In this study, I refer to this third phase of the Early Neo-Assyrian Period as eNA III.

From the perspective of the territorial size of states, the truly imperial state of Assyria was however realized only with the Late Neo-Assyrian Period (744–609) and the king Tiglath-pileser III (744–727) and the Sargonid kings of Sargon II (721–705), Sennacherib (704–681), Esarhaddon (680–669), and Ashurbanipal (668–627). Many different areas, peoples, and cultures formed a part of this imperial state, whose capital was transferred from Kalhu to Dur-Sharrukin by Sargon II and then finally to Nineveh by Sennacherib. The preserved propaganda pieces from these powerful rulers are very extensive and pretentious, and they often tell of the ambitious, religious and military projects of the empire. The Assyrian empire continuously expanded its borders, and the great lands and cultures of Egypt and Babylonia were placed under the Assyrian king's command. The disintegration of the empire was relatively sudden and is quite unclear to historians. In the final phase, a formidable military threat evolved, and through the combined strength of the armies of the Medes and the Babylonians, the Assyrian empire was defeated around 610 BCE. It however lived on in the ideologies and structures of the succeeding empires of the region (Seux 1980–83: 166; Lamprichs 1995: 405–406), notably the Persian one (Barjamovic 2012).

Neo-Assyrian state ideology then covers a period of over 300 years, and studies on this topic have consequently often been thematic or arranged as surveys (see s. 1.3). A case study, focusing on the state ideology of individual kings or of a certain phase within the time period, is another possible delimitation. In deciding the direction of such a case study, it seems easily defendable to focus on the ten kings and formative historical phase, marked by reconquests and initial empire building, of the Early Neo-Assyrian Period. During this early phase of the Assyrian imperial age, the decisive step to move away from the traditional capital Assur was taken, and the period is represented by rulers who are regarded by historians as much influential in Assyrian history, first and foremost Ashurnasirpal II and Shalmaneser III. There are in other words good reasons to centre on the Early Neo-Assyrian Period and the highlighted topic of Early Neo-Assyrian state ideology.

1.2 Aims of the study

The overarching aim of this study is to contribute to the description of Early Neo-Assyrian state ideology, both seen as an entity and as consisting of ten parts, i.e. subdivided into the ten reigns. It is to be noticed here that Ashurnasirpal II and Shalmaneser III combined are responsible for the vast majority of the preserved royal inscriptions and iconography from this time period. The proportions here are 73 %[10] and 79 % respectively (see apps. 1–3), which means that the propaganda of these two rulers to a large extent represent Early Neo-Assyrian state ideology available to Assyriologists. Nevertheless, a full coverage of the period is needed to give a complete picture.

There are of course many different aspects of a particular state ideology. In other words, the overarching aim then needs to be complemented with a more delimited, precise, and narrower one. The narrower aim of this study is to portray how the relationship between the Mesopotamian deities, the Assyrian king, and "the foreign lands"[11] is described and depicted in the inscriptions and iconography of the Early Neo-Assyrian kings. This narrower aim, addressed in chapters 3–5, should be understood as a means to fulfil the overarching one. It should be stated here that my usage of the terms "Assyrian" and "foreign" is strictly a pragmatic, practical one, and I do not intentionally refer to any alleged, ancient nationalities in using them. With regards to geography (see Fig. 1), these terms simply refer to lands and people inside and outside the borders which the Middle Assyrian kings established, and which, put crudely, consisted of the area between the Euphrates and the Tigris in northern Mesopotamia (Radner 2006–2008: 42–53).[12]

After the fulfilment of the narrower aim, some comparative or secondary aims[13] need to be addressed in order to fulfil the overarching aim in a more complete way. These comparative or secondary aims are to trace ideological developments within the reigns (see ch. 6), to trace the existence of local propaganda (see ch. 7), to compare the ideologies of Ashurnasirpal II and Shalmaneser III and the other kings of the Early Neo-Assyrian Period with one another (see ch. 8), and to place the identified Early Neo-Assyrian state ideology in the historical-ideological contexts of the Old, Middle, and Late Neo-Assyrian periods (see ch. 9). The fulfilment of these aims are intended to lead to a coherent fulfilment of the overarching aim of this work.

1.3 Earlier research

In this section, earlier research on Neo-Assyrian state ideology in general (i.e. surveys), according to themes, or through case studies on shorter historical

10 If not otherwise stated, percentage proportions on inscriptions are calculated from "texts" and not "exemplars". For these terms, see section 2.1. The exemplar number here is 87 %.

11 For the defining of these three units of analysis, see section 1.5.

12 For fuller notes on the geography of Assyria and the region, see subsection 1.7.1.

13 "Comparative" in the sense that they all, in one way or another, focus on comparisons, and "secondary" in the sense that they are all derived from the fulfilment of the narrower aim.

phases or on the sources of Ashurnasirpal II, Shalmaneser III, and other Early Neo-Assyrian kings is presented. Assyriology literature which uses the theoretical approaches of this study are briefly mentioned.[14]

General studies on Neo-Assyrian state ideology are to be found e.g. in the anthology edited by Larsen containing important contributions by e.g. Liverani (1979) regarding the written sources, and by Reade (1979a) on the visual sources. Studies on Assyrian royal inscriptions and their ideological character are found in the anthology edited by Fales (1981a–b), updated by himself in a subsequent article (Fales 1999–2001), as well as in the recent anthology edited by Eph'al and Na'aman (2009). Other vital and epigraphically based studies on Assyrian state ideology include those by Garelli (1982) and Tadmor (1997) who both highlight the issue of propaganda. An extensive, although not complete, study on Assyrian royal titles and epithets has been made by Cifola (1995). The ideological character of Neo-Assyrian state iconography has been investigated by e.g. Winter (1981) and Magen (1986).

Studies which focus on particular themes of Neo-Assyrian state ideology are many and diverse. Oded (1992) discusses the justifications for war in Assyrian royal inscriptions, Bär (1996) centres on the topic of foreign tribute, Shafer (1998) studies the phenomenon of Assyrian monuments in the periphery, and Weissert (1997) and C. Watanabe (1998) discuss the ideological role of the royal hunting. The topic of the nature of the Assyrian king – human or divine – as given in the sources has been frequently discussed. The aged but still relevant studies by Labat (1939) and Frankfort (1948) focus on the human nature of the king, while the works by Engnell (1943), Gadd (1948), and more recently Parpola (1999) identify a divine, or at least semi-divine, essence of the king. The external, religious policies of the Assyrian kings, mostly in relation to Israel and Judah, has also been a frequent topic. The works by Olmstead (1931) and Spieckermann (1982) identify a zealous Assyrian approach, while the studies by McKay (1973), Cogan (1974), and Holloway (2001) see a pragmatic and tolerant Assyrian attitude.

Moving on, the anthology edited by Hill *et alii* (2013a) centres on a dichotomy of cosmic/political orientations of Assyrian and Mesopotamian kingship, identifying three approaches in earlier research: the cosmic or political aspect is put before the other, the two aspects are separate but equal, or the focal point is on exploring the interaction between the two. It is claimed that studies on Assyrian and Mesopotamian kingship tend to focus on the political aspect

14 This presentation is nowhere from complete, but my hope is that it can give a fairly good idea of what has been done before. For two overviews of Neo-Assyrian studies in list form, see Mattila and Radner 1997, and Gaspa and Luukko 2008.

(Hill et al. 2013b: 4). Contrasting this identified pattern, Pongratz-Leisten (2015) highlights religion and ideology in imperial Assyria. Intertextuality between Assyrian royal inscriptions and various mythological texts has been investigated e.g. by Cancik-Kirschbaum (1995) and Maul (1999). The descriptions of the enemy in Assyrian royal inscriptions have been studied by Fales (1982) and Zaccagnini (1982), while Saggs (1982) has addressed the status and treatment of defeated foreigners.

As for works which are specifically dedicated to the study of Early Neo-Assyrian state ideology, the focal point tends to be on individual kings rather than on the time period as such. Most of these studies then highlight Ashurnasirpal II. The dissertation by Cifarelli (1995), containing (post-colonial) analyses both of the iconographic (emphasized) and epigraphic material, should be mentioned here. Ideology and iconography are focused on by e.g. Winter (1983), J. M. Russell (1998b), and Lumsden (2004) on the reliefs of the North-West Palace, and by e.g. Parpola (1993), Albenda (1994), and Porter (2003) in the debate on the possible meaning of the Assyrian "sacred tree" from the same building. Thorough studies, e.g. including the ideological dimensions, of the inscriptions of Ashurnasirpal II have been made by Liverani (1982a, 1992b) and De Filippi (1977). The classical article by Olmstead (1918) in which the author in question refers to the "calculated frightfulness" of the named king might also be mentioned. My own dissertation which highlights relations of power in the state ideology of Ashurnasirpal II (and Shalmaneser III) as conveyed in the royal inscriptions and iconography of the two rulers may also be mentioned here (Karlsson 2013).

Studies on Shalmaneser III are mostly concerned with his historical significance and/or contact with the west and the Israelite state. This is e.g. true of the articles by Elat (1975) and Grayson (2007), and of the monographs by Schneider (1991) and Yamada (2000). Although discussions on the ideological aspects of the sources are to some extent included in the named monographs, they nevertheless play a minor role there. Additionally, the two studies in question mainly use the epigraphic material. Articles which study ideology and the king's iconography include those by M. Marcus (1987) and Hertel (2004). The works by Schachner (2007, 2009) which present and discuss the king's iconographic material in Balawat and at the Tigris source respectively count as two other prominent secondary sources. The mostly historically focused articles on Shalmaneser III by Olmstead (1921), Lambert (1974a), and Tadmor (1975) might also be mentioned.

Also Adad-narari III has been the subject of at least one separate study, namely through the dissertation by Siddall which centres on the historical and ideological aspects of Adad-narari III's reign. It gives an outline, taking the analysis by Liverani (1979) as its starting point, of "early Neo-Assyrian royal ideology" between 934–810 BCE (Siddall 2013: 151–67), and continues with presenting yet another outline, still using the analysis by Liverani (1979), of the state ideology of the king in question (Siddall 2013: 171–87). Although not exclusively dedicated to the ideological aspect, Siddall makes use of both epigraphic and iconographic sources in his analysis.

Regarding scholars who have critically examined Assyriology literature on ancient Assyria and Assyrian state ideology from the perspectives of critical, gender, and post-colonial theories, the works by Bahrani (2001, 2003), which make use of all three approaches, stand out. The study by Chapman (2004) on the gendered language of warfare in Assyrian royal inscriptions, as well as in the Bible, at least indirectly criticizes the traditional neglect of gender studies in Assyriology. Also Holloway (2006b), Fales (2010), M. Marcus (1995a–b), and Winter (2010) belong to those who have critically examined scholarly literature in these areas – the former ones with post-colonial studies, and the latter ones mainly with gender studies.

In sum, the preceding paragraphs have shown that although research on Neo-Assyrian state ideology is quite substantial, a monograph which solely is dedicated to the *ideological* dimension of the sources of *all* Early Neo-Assyrian kings, and furthermore include, on an equal footing, analyses of the inscriptions and iconography in question, has not to my knowledge been published before. Additionally, thorough comparisons between the respective propaganda programmes of the Early Neo-Assyrian rulers are comparatively rare (Karlsson 2013; Siddall 2013). Last but not least, the two topics of ideology development within reigns (see s. 6.1) and locally formed propaganda (see s. 7.1) are also relatively rarely researched and focused on.

1.4 General notes on the primary sources

1.4.1 Assyrian royal inscriptions and iconography

In this subsection, the phenomena of Assyrian royal inscriptions and iconography of which the sources of the Early Neo-Assyrian kings form a part are generally discussed. The sources of this study, presented and discussed more fully in chapter two, cover almost every aspect which is brought up below. It also needs to be said that all the specific texts and monuments that are merely mentioned in chapter one will be presented in chapter two.

The primary sources consist in part of texts. The subgenres of Assyrian royal inscriptions are annals, summary inscriptions (also called "display inscriptions"), dedicatory texts, letters to/from a god, labels/tags, and captions/

epigraphs (Grayson 1981: 37).[15] The annals and summary inscriptions both sort under the heading of commemorative texts, but they tend to differ with regards to the arrangement of their narrative – the former chronologically and the latter geographically. This structure goes hand in hand with their varying length – long and short respectively – causing elaborations and summaries respectively (Kuhrt 1997: 476–77). An archetypal annalistic text consists of sections of divine names and epithets, signalling an invocation or dedication, and of the royal name and titulary, followed by a year-by-year narration in first person of the king's achievements at war, continued by a building inscription, a section of blessings and curses, and lastly by a dating (Renger 1997: 172).[16] As already noted, summary inscriptions arrange the warfare narration according to geographical principles, but they may otherwise contain much of the elements of annals. They tend to contain a prologue with an invocation of deities and/or a royal titulary, a geographically structured summary of events, a main section contextualizing the textual composition, and an epilogue with maledictions (Tadmor 1973: 141).

Moving on, dedicatory texts self-evidently focus on the dedication of a certain object (most often the inscribed one) to a deity or a king, while letters to/from a god are structured as royal/divine reports on military campaigns to a certain deity/king. Label texts may be written upon objects such as bricks and clay cones as a way of referring to the source and purpose of these objects, while caption texts serve to comment on accompanying iconography (Grayson 1987: 3–4). All these literary subgenres are not mutually exclusive and do frequently overlap, but they are nevertheless to a certain extent canonical, in that they were created within an established standard of form and content (Tadmor 1981, 1997). Royal hymns, prayers, decrees, and chronicles are also used in this study, although falling outside the definitions of the literary genre of royal inscriptions (Grayson 1987: 3).

Regarding the media and provenances of Assyrian royal inscriptions, inscriptions without any accompanying image can for example be attested on clay, stone, or metal tablets, prisms, and cylinders, and on clay bricks, clay cones, and clay hands. These kinds of inscribed objects were displayed or hidden, deposited behind walls or under thresholds and floors (J. M. Russell 1999), unprovenanced or excavated *in situ*, belonging to a certain public or private

---

15 For alternative identifications of genres within the corpus of royal inscriptions, see e.g. Ellis 1968: 94–124, Renger 1980–83: 71–75, and Schneider 1991: 10–42.

16 In his analysis of eNA I-annals, Schramm (1973: 12–17) adds the components of "filiation passage" and "legitimacy passage" before the warfare narration, and refers to the feature of "the call to a later prince" rather than specifically to blessings and curses.

archive or library (Pedersén 1985–86). Inscriptions are also integral parts of larger monuments such as statues, wall reliefs, and stelae.

The primary sources also consist of iconography. Images can be subdivided into non-narrative and narrative iconography (Cifarelli 1995: 233–35). The former category refers to images of a heraldic and iconic character, e.g. images displaying the king standing in isolation and in a fixed pose. These kinds of sources are often found on stelae, cliff reliefs, and statues. In contrast, narrative iconography conveys scenes in which temporal and logical sequences of events and actions are unfolded. This latter kind of iconography is predominantly found on palace or temple walls and door bands, through paintings *al fresco* or on glazed bricks, through reliefs on "obelisks", and through carvings or engravings on ivories, seals, and stone or metal vessels (J. M. Russell 1998–2001). The two categories occasionally overlap on the monuments. As will be discussed more fully below (see s. 2.1), there is often a correlation between form, i.e. narrative or non-narrative, and content, i.e. the motifs of royal iconography such as cult, warfare, tribute, and hunting. Also Assyrian royal *iconography* was created within certain recognized standards of form and content (Reade 1981a: 145, 154–55; Czichon 1992: 174–79).

As for the various contexts of the pieces of "art", many monuments, such as most obelisks and cliff reliefs, contain both image and text, and they were situated in cultural landscapes such as in temples, palaces, city squares, and city gates, as well as in natural landscapes, then often at geographical extremes such as on mountains and cliffs, or at sea shores and river sources. It is however quite common that pieces of iconography, especially seals and ivories, are without any clear provenance. As opposed to the texts, the iconography was more or less always visible in character, although some monuments were more "public" than others (see subs. 1.4.2).

1.4.2 State ideology and propaganda

In this subsection, the origins and nature of the primary sources will be discussed. I will argue that these are, in terms of contents and motives, primarily state *ideological* and only secondarily historical, religious, or literary, and that the royal inscriptions and iconography can be described as propaganda.

As noted by e.g. Cancik-Kirschbaum (1997: 69), the texts coming from ancient Assyria tend not to convey true political reflection. The philosophical dimension in question is indirectly expressed, and remains to be deduced, notably from studying the royal inscriptions and iconography. These sources can be understood as state ideology. The term state ideology refers to a coherent set of ideas which express the official (i.e. the elite's) world view on political matters. The term propaganda adds a purpose to this state ideology, namely to convince the ruled of the ruler's right to rule.[17] Propaganda is here a tool to channel the dominant ideology, in a "traditional relationship" between the two terms (Ellul 1965: 193–96). Not the least through the means of state ideology and propaganda, the discourse of the time is expressed, conveying the allowed frames of "correct thinking" (Foucault 1982). Ideology and propaganda are here seen as vital for shaping societies, and not just as reflections of the socio-economic order or as only one part of creating authority,[18] but they form political, military, and economic conditions.[19]

Beginning with the *state* character of the ideology, a discussion on the possible origins of the sources is crucial. The scholarly discussion revolves around how much the king himself had to do with the creative process, and how much of it was entrusted to the officials, scribes, and artisans. A commonly held view is that the king was active in the selection and planning, and that he finally authorized the material by approving the final draft (Winter 1997: 367–68). As noted by Roaf (2013: 353 n. 2), the kings did not write their royal inscriptions themselves. It was the scribes who did that, although certain kings could have showed some interest and given general instructions. In all this, the scribes must have practised strict self-censorship. A distinction between the "historical author", i.e. the scribe or artisan, and the "implied author", i.e. the king, may illustrate this creative process (Schneider 1991: 117–26). Still, the role of the literati in the production should not be underestimated (Tadmor 1997; Ataç 2010; Pongratz-Leisten 2013). In any case, the king should be understood as embracing the material in some way, not the least since it is clearly an idealized image of the king as always winning, strong, and majestic that is conveyed in the sources.[20]

17 This understanding of the sources largely corresponds with the ideology definition of Marx (1970) [1845–46] as complemented by the cultural and sociological aspects identified by Gramsci (1971) [1926–37] and Althusser (1971). As concluded by Liverani (1979: 299), the author of e.g. royal inscriptions was then "the Assyrian ruling class".

18 For the former approach, see Marx (1970) [1845–46]. For the latter, see Mann (1994) who identifies four different aspects of social power: ideology, the army, economics, and politics.

19 This is not to say that political, military, and economic tools were not also ways of ensuring dominance. It would be naïve to think that ideology and propaganda did all the work. As stated by Parker (2011), implementation and legitimacy (the latter in the sense of a ruler's just and lawful right or way of ruling) should also be regarded as crucial aspects of kingship.

20 A related discussion concerns how much room the individual king had to make a personal imprint on the material. It would be naïve to suppose that the ruler was completely bound up by tradition. As always, a balance between naivety and vulgar cynicism has to be found. For the idea of severe structural limitations, i.e. the opposite of free reins, see e.g. Pečirková 1993.

As for ideology, the old view regarding Assyrian royal inscriptions was that they are primarily a source of historical information. A prime example here is the idea of Olmstead (1916) that the texts are essentially historical, and that the most contemporary account of an event almost automatically is the most reliable. This way of looking at the sources, with little attention payed to underlying motives, was challenged by the so-called Italian school which shifted the focal point from the narration that the sources convey to the texts themselves, thereby emphasizing authorship, reader/audience, and political background (e.g. Liverani 1973). In other words, the texts are primarily ideological and only secondarily historical. A similar shift has occurred in the iconographic field where the development has gone from describing Assyrian royal narrative art as objective and historically orientated to recognizing their inherently political and ideological character (Groenewegen-Frankfort 1951; Winter 1981 resp.). In some sense "all art is ideological", lacking an "objective" history telling, but rather carrying ambitions to naturalize the relevant scenes of domination (Bahrani 2001: 37).

As argued by Winter (2010: 597–98), it is not tenable to keep "an innocent view of an automatic connection between the word and the world", but the material must be checked against other data and acknowledged as "fictional reality" or "inversion of reality" (Franke 1995: 32; Liverani 1995: 2353–54 resp.). A proof of the ideological and at least partly fictive contents of the primary sources is that they do not contain descriptions of Assyrian defeats (Tadmor 1975: 36; Reade 1983: 23), but convey a praising of the royal persona which never can be taken at face value (Grayson 1981: 46). Also, Assyrian soldiers are never depicted wounded or at a disadvantage in royal iconography (Collon 1995: 136). Several studies have also shown how ideological considerations were decisive in describing certain historical events, offering clearly biased stories (e.g. Gelio 1981; Tadmor 1981). As for the visual arts, Winter (1997: 372–76) has shown, based on a discussion of the term *ṣalmu*, that portrait likeness of the king was not a goal for the artisan, and Bahrani (2003: 121–25) similarly notes that mimical art was not aspired by people in Mesopotamia, and that the royal image in this sense can be regarded as a "performative image" conveying the notion of the ideal ruler rather than giving a mimetic portrayal (Schroer 2006b: 43).

This is not the same as to say that the sources are all completely fictional. A certain connection, seen e.g. in the use of the ideologically charged royal titles and epithets, between royal claims and actual reality must have existed (Liverani 1973: 188; Garelli 1982: 16). I would still argue that the reality in question must be a fairly distorted one. The stance made by Siddall (2013: 134–40) against cynicism and his view that the claims in the royal ideology mirror reality to a close degree should be met with scepticism. Although recognizing the top-down nature of ideology, and discussing alternative propaganda channels, Siddall (2013: 134–40) in his inspired rejecting of Marxist and Postmodern perspectives on ideology argues that ideology is primarily "an idealist phenomenon" and that it can be defined as "the system of thought, customs and beliefs of a culture". Two amazing claims are seemingly made here: Assyrian royal inscriptions and iconography were only secondarily political, and the pervading praises of the king in these sources were embraced by the whole Assyrian population. Despite the different views on the proximity between history and ideology, there is today a consensus that these sources are highly appropriate for a study on ideology.

After having stated that the material should be regarded as state ideology, the next issue to dicuss is propaganda. The term propaganda evokes images of totalitarian regimes of the 20th century CE, and may be seen as anachronistic by some if not qualified.[21] The political philosopher Ellul (1965: 61–87) brings up four distinctions in his classifying of propaganda. Firstly, there is *political* propaganda, i.e. when a government aims at certain goals, and *sociological* propaganda, i.e. when goals consciously or unconsciously are promoted and established through social interaction. Secondly, there is *agitational* propaganda, i.e. when goals are sought through stressing differences, and *integrational* propaganda, i.e. when goals are sought through stressing uniformity. Agitational propaganda is mainly associated with subversion and revolutionary movements, but it may equally well be used by governments as a way of creating an enemy image in times of crisis and war. Thirdly, Ellul refers to *vertical* propaganda, transmitted from leader to people, and to *horizontal* propaganda, transmitted inside a certain group. Fourthly, he sees the interrelated but separate concepts of *rational* and *irrational* propaganda. As will be made apparent below, Assyrian royal inscriptions and iconography contain elements of all of these categories.[22]

As stated by Tadmor (2011: 719–20), references to Assyrian royal inscriptions as propaganda should not be regarded as anachronistic since the relevant composition "serves the cult of the personality of the king", and/or "it propagates certain political ideas and tendencies". On this basic level of definition,

21 This evocation often serves to dismiss scholarly works that use the term as "anachronistic", as if saying that manipulative political leaders either did not exist in ancient times or that they existed but did not have the means to exercise any firm control over their subjects.

22 The irrational aspect may be seen in the dogma on Ashur's world dominion (see s. 3.1), and in the fervent, religious duty of the Assyrian king to implement it (see s. 4.4 and subs. 5.4.2).

propaganda implies a desire to manipulate and control other people's minds. Following this line of thought, Garelli (2000: 48) sees the palace decor as a way of glorifying the king, and Liverani (1995: 2361) talks of the power of ideology to determine actions, and of a core ambition of the royal inscriptions to celebrate and mobilize. In this sense, the inscriptions convey an "ideological grammar" which aimed at justifying inequalities of various kinds (Liverani 1979: 303). M. Marcus (1995a: 2487) and Pollock (1999: 173) likewise identify an aim of naturalizing a certain world view in order to reproduce domination. The apparent "realistic" impression of the art and texts of the Assyrian kings may here be understood as part of an agenda to naturalize relations of inequality. Pollock (1999: 173) also refers to the power of the dominant ideology to inspire loyalty and cohesion among the ruling class and the population. In this context, legitimacy was sought through "the creation of a particular view of how the world works".

The issue of recipient is of course vital in this discussion. Some scholars argue for a very restricted access to the material, especially when discussing prisms and cylinders which were often deposited behind walls. Gadd (1948: 60–64) and Schneider (1991: 52) talk of the annals as directed towards the deities only, Bachelot (1991: 116–20) and Reade (1979a: 338–39) refer to the iconography as mainly reaching out to the officials and courtiers of the palace,[23] while Galter (1998: 90–91) and Shafer (1998) identify posterity as the actual and intended recipients of text and image respectively. Ataç (2010: 201) argues that court scholars and master craftsmen were the intended viewers, as well as producers, of the reliefs in the North-West Palace. More often a relatively wide scope of recipients is identified, even if just the intended, as opposed to the potential, recipients are considered (Winter 1983: 27; J. M. Russell 1991: 266; Liverani 1995: 2354–55; Collins 2008: 27).

Indications of the relatively wide scope of recipients, and therefore indirectly of the propaganda dimension in its inherent dissemination aspect, are seen by Kuhrt (1997: 476) who argues that the existence of archival versions of the annals hints to a widespread dissemination, and likewise by Oppenheim (1960) who proposes the occurrence of a public recital of the letters to a god. Obviously, this oral transmission downsizes the problematic issue of illiteracy in the context of claiming the texts as propaganda.[24] The massproduced, in-

23 Having a similar approach, Barjamovic (2011: 59–60) highlights "court and elite integration" and "social contracts" between the king and various elites.

24 Despite the literary form and dialect of the relevant texts, these public recitals may have been fairly intelligble to their audiences. In this context, it should be noted that several textual passages of Ashurnasirpal II are written in the colloquial Neo-Assyrian (Deller 1957). Further-

scribed bricks and clay cones were also widely available. As for the iconography, Porter (2003: 59–79) has convincingly shown that the images of Assyrian kings were created with their potential recipients in mind, Liverani (1981: 231–51) has argued the same regarding varying annals editions in Assur and Nineveh, and J. M. Russell (1998b: 715) has suggested that the concentration of palace reliefs to public spaces implies a wish to persuade the human inhabitants and visitors of the palace. Everyone was in some way reached by the propaganda. The more technical, complex, and detailed propaganda such as royal inscriptions was addressed to the elite, while the coarser, i.e. visual, oral, ceremonial, and architectural, propaganda was directed towards the populace, Assyrian and foreign (Liverani 1990: 28–29).

This is not the same as to say that the material had a purely political goal. As Bahrani (2003: 166) notes, such a stance would be to reproduce the Orientalist notion of Oriental despotism.[25] Other goals, e.g. religious ones, must also be reckoned with, thereby avoiding positions of vulgar cynicism. The sources can not be reduced into "pure self-boast" but also display genuine religious beliefs (Albrektsson 1967: 42–45). Imperialism and religion went hand in hand in the Assyrian state of the Neo-Assyrian Period (Pongratz-Leisten 2015). Bahrani (2008: 241–42 n. 17) however takes a reversely extreme position when arguing that Assyrian palace reliefs were not propaganda, but were made for the "visual pleasure" of primarily the king and his courtiers. The images of war and violence are, in addition, seen as a way of glorifying war and victory, juxtaposing good and evil in a religious mode of thinking (Bahrani 2008: 219). However, to deny the strikingly propagandistic nature of the sources is not tenable. Rather, political and religious motives in the articulation of state ideology are not mutually exclusive.

The same can be said of the relationship between propaganda and literature. Although the elaborate language and style of royal inscriptions often tell of literary goals and ambitions, the notional frame of the compositions, conveying a one-sided praising of the people and groups in power, of course overarchs these features. In other words, the literary merits of the texts should here be understood as functional for the relevant praising.

It seems to be a trend in recent scholarship to object to the relevance of especially the term propaganda (e.g. Shafer 1998; Ataç 2010), not only in terms of the issue of religion or literature vs. politics referred to above, but also when

---

more, the overall message of the recital (the king is great, the deities are behind him, and the people should therefore obey the king's orders) should have been grasped by everyone.

25 See also her general discussion on representation and ideology (Bahrani 2008: 65–74). The related criticism by Ataç (2010: 87–89) derives from other perspectives.

focusing on who the recipients of the alleged propaganda were. Siddall (2013: 149) e.g. centres on the remote provenance of many texts, and is for that reason sceptical towards the idea of Assyrian royal inscriptions as propaganda, not seeing a contemporary audience beyond the palace. Parker (2011: 372–75), sharing a similar scepticism, nevertheless argues that in particular stelae, royal decrees, and royal buildings were means by which the king could convey propaganda to external recipients. Similarly, while the palace art aimed only at the elite of society, cylinder seals with their visual and textual programs could have functioned as an effective, widespread "propaganda" channel (Siddall 2013: 147). This school of thought claims, pointing to the actual finding-places, that this "propaganda" mainly was directed to the elites and to the Assyrian heartland (Parker 2011: 368).

There are several reasons for problematizing these restrictions. As noted by Fales (2009: 281–82), it is plausible to suggest that Assyrian propaganda was transmitted orally, through "words of mouth", by the people coming into contact with ideologically vital subjects and objects of various kinds. Additionally, there are cases of Assyrian royal inscriptions, on e.g. the Tell Fekhereye statue and the Sfire treaty, being translated into Aramaic, i.e. the everyday language of the Sargonid period (Machinist 1983b: 732–33; Fales 2007: 105–107 resp.). Furthermore, the reported, persuasive speech of the Assyrian chief eunuch in the local language at the gate of the besieged city of Jerusalem (see II Kings 18–19, Isaiah 36–37) was directed at a larger group of people, socially and ethnically (Siddall 2013: 149), although it is of course difficult to use this filtered imagery as firm evidence. It also seems that a dissemination of Assyrian royal inscriptions are reflected in the Hebrew Bible, with the formers' themes and messages mirrored negatively, turned against the Assyrian kings and state (Machinist 1983b: 729–31; Weissert 2011). Lastly, as noted by Siddall (2013: 144), the public atrocities described and depicted in the sources of this study, may be regarded as carrying propaganda of a sort. In other words, Assyrian propaganda was transmitted orally, textually, and visually well beyond the palace and temple walls of Assyria.

A wish to communicate with, impress, and persuade the contemporary world is apparent in the sources of the Early Neo-Assyrian kings. Monuments like the Kurkh monoliths and the Rassam and Black obelisks were all situated in relatively public spaces. The throne base, the glazed brick panel at the throne room, and the door bands on temple and palace gates were all placed at ideologically charged and comparatively public spaces. The cliff relief at Kenk Boğazı was situated at a busy border crossing area (Börker-Klähn 1982: 189). Last but not least, the grand North-West Palace, but also Fort Shalmaneser and the palace of Adad-narari III, were showpieces of the capital and the objects of conspicious consumption with the function of creating awe (J. M. Russell 1998b; Pollock 1999), each symbolizing the microcosm of the ordered world (Winter 1993; Liverani 1995: 2362). All these monuments share the dual propaganda characteristics of being widely available and having firmly rhetorical content. Simultaneously they were addressed to the deities. The rhetorical and partly available door bands of the Mamu temple, for example, may have been turned towards the cella, thus intended primarily for the god's eyes, although the poor archaeological context makes this argument difficult to affirm or reject.

The intention to impress and influence viewers and readers is in fact articulated in the texts themselves. The North-West Palace and the Sharrat-niphi temple were made "for the everlasting admiration of (foreign) rulers and princes" (*ana nanmar malkī u rubē ša dārâte*)[26] (AE35:8, AE32:10–11 resp.)[27]. The North-West Palace was the focal point of the huge feast, allegedly with divine statues and almost 70 000 mortals as guests, as told of in the Banquet Stele (AE30:102–54). As for this building, Ashurnasirpal II refers on the same stele to its reliefs when exclaiming that he depicted "praises of my heroism" (*tanattī qardūtija*) on the palace walls (AE30:30–31). Some restrictions of course apply. In a curse section it is prescribed that the successor or "future prince" (*rubû arkû*) "must not hand out the key, (for) there must not be open access" (*napṭartu lā irassipi° ina libbi lā erraba*) to the palace (AE17:v41–42). However, in the same curse section it is stated that scholars (*ummânu*) must be allowed to see and read the inscription, here that on the Ninurta Stele, and that none (including the people?) should be barred access to it (AE17:v62–66). Clearly then, the kings sought to impress and influence other human beings through their monuments of various kinds.

In what way, and to what degree, the ruled components of Assyrian society really believed in the claims made by their kings is difficult to say given the

---

26 The transcriptions of this study are rendered, e.g. in terms of Babylonian/Assyrian, according to the attestations. In case of attestations written in both dialects, and of logograms, Babylonian forms are given. (For the features of the Neo-Assyrian dialect, see Hämeen-Anttila 2000.) The grammar of von Soden 1995 is followed, but secondary vowel length is (in line with CAD) not indicated. Isolated Akkadian words are transcribed with endings in the nominative singular. Unconventional forms and possible scribal errors are marked by °. Forms attested only in variant writings, i.e. outside the master texts, are denoted by *. A word is within the reconstruction markers [ ] when the writing of it is significantly damaged, and when the relevant word can be safely reconstructed from undamaged attestations.

27 For the "coding" of the major primary sources exemplified here, see appendices 1–2. For practical reasons, eNA I and III-attestations are given in chapters 3–5 only when the relevant ideological phenomenon is unattested for both Ashurnasirpal II and Shalmaneser III.

lack of sources on this matter. It is reasonable to assume that opposition towards the dominant ideology was not uncommon among ordinary people (Richardson 2010). Opposition was expressed also within the Assyrian ruling class. Even though the royal propaganda to some extent self-indoctrinated the elite (Reade 1979a: 338–39), the frequent references to opposition within the elite show that the state ideology (or at least the court-sponsored version of it) was not embraced everywhere. The civil war at the end of Shalmaneser III's reign is one example of this, and so are the entries in the Eponym Chronicle that refer to revolts, e.g. in the time period 763–759 BCE (see Millard 1994). Clearly, the state ideology did not express any Assyrian *Volksseele*, and it can not safely be regarded as representative.

To conclude the discussion of this subsection, the primary sources of this study should be regarded as state ideology, conveying mainly political propaganda. Their function of fulfiling genuine religious needs aside, religious themes and motifs were considered to be powerful political tools in the aim of naturalizing asymmetrical relations of power. Opposing to recent trends in the field, I state that viewing the claims in Assyrian state ideology with scepticism and cynicism, and not seeing Assyrian state ideology as expressing an Assyrian *Volksseele* (but rather expressing the interests of those in power) are reasonable, sound, and non-elitist approaches.

1.5 Method

In this section, the methodology of this study is presented and discussed. It begins with notes on the methods of the analysis conducted primarily in chapters 3–5, focusing on definitions, delimitations, and analytical aspects. It concludes with a discussion centred on the methods relevant for chapters 6–9, then focusing on datings, classifications, and comparative issues.

Beginning with definitions, the identification of the main units of analysis of this study – the Mesopotamian deities, the Assyrian king, and the foreign lands – was made in a surveying stage of the research process, and should be regarded as a result of the tendency of the sources towards favouring the topics of royal imperialism and divine intervention. This tendency is e.g. reflected in the annals which centre on the narration of royal war conquests as well as on the royal titulary which often refers to the role of the deities.

Defining the term "Mesopotamian deities", these are the gods and goddesses who are recognized as "the great gods" (*ilāni rabûti*) in Assyrian royal inscriptions. This term, sometimes understood as referring to deities in general, refers to "the principal divinities of the pantheon", most often counted to seven or twelve in number in enumerations and invocations (Black and Green 1992: 99). The great gods are often enumerated in Assyrian royal inscriptions in this genre's components of "invocation of deities" and "concluding formulae" (see app. 4). As many as 23 deities are referred to as great gods in the texts of the Early Neo-Assyrian kings,[28] at least if viewing the different manifestations of deities as separate ones. The relevant entry in the epithet catalogue of Tallqvist (1938: 14–15) gives 24.[29]

Moving on, "the king of Assyria" (*šar māt Aššur*) may seem straightforward in identifying, but this agent in effect signifies the Assyrian ruling class (see subs. 1.7.2). Thus, this unit of analysis can also be represented by the high officials, even though the overwhelming majority of cases speak of the king, hence the name of this unit of analysis. As will be apparent in subsection 5.4.7, the king and his officials embodied the Assyrian state.

Regarding the term "foreign lands", the word "lands" (*mātāti*) as opposed to "the land (of Assyria)" (*mātu*) is here highlighted (Steiner 1982: 634, CAD M I: *mātu*).[30] The borders between the mutually exclusive *mātāti* and *mātu* naturally changed over time, but in Early Neo-Assyrian times the land between the Euphrates and the Tigris in northern Mesopotamia made up the latter, judging from the attested provincial structure of the Assyrian state (Radner 2006–08: 42–53). The geography, animals, deities, people/elites of the foreign lands as demarcated above are all featured in the primary sources, and these individually and combined make up my definition of the foreign lands. This identifying of the four animate or inanimate components of the foreign lands is reflected in the four-fold division of chapter five.

In the discussion chapters, the relevant three units of analysis (*ilāni rabûti, šar māt Aššur, mātāti*) will be treated as entities, but notes on important differentiations within these will be made continuously. Regarding the uniformity of

28 Adad (e.g. AE1:i77, SE42:12), Anu (e.g. AE17:i11, SE2:i3), Ashur (e.g. AE1:i76–77, SE42:12), Damkina (e.g. AE28:v9), Ea (e.g. AE28:v9, SE2:i3), Ea-sharru (e.g. AE30:58), Enlil (e.g. AE28:v9, SE2:i3), Gula (e.g. AE28:v9), Inanna (S4E2:8), Ishtar (e.g. AE1:i70, SE21:2), Ishtar-kakkabi (S4E2:8), Ishtar-belat-Kidmuri (e.g. AE30:58), Marduk (e.g. AE17:i11, SE10:i9), Nabu (e.g. AE30:58), Nergal (e.g. AE153:4, SE46:15), Ninlil (e.g. AE17:i11, SE14:14), Ninurta (e.g. AE28:v9, SE6:i8), Nusku (e.g. AE17:i11, SE14:14), Shala (e.g. AE28:v9), Shamash (e.g. AE19:3, SE21:2), Sharrat-niphi (e.g. AE28:v9), the Sibitti (e.g. AE30:58, SE95:1), and Sin (e.g. AE19:3, SE21:2). These are presented in subsection 1.7.2.

29 Adding the deities Mah, Ninmah, Ninhursanga, the Anunnaki, the Igigi, Bel, Laz, Ishum, Ber, and Anunitu, while leaving out some of the others enumerated above.

30 In some cases the foreign lands are referred to as "highlands" (*ḫuršāni*) and (less often) as "mountains" (*šadâni*). These terms are equated with *mātāti* since hilly landscapes are firmly associated with foreign lands in the Mesopotamian world view (Maul 1999: 213).

Mesopotamian deities, it is e.g. reasonable to assume that Ashur held a special place within the group of great gods. As for the uniformity of the foreign lands, the proposed Assyrian distinction between a fraternal relation to Babylonia, a respectful attitude towards the west, and contempt towards the northern and eastern regions (Reade 1979a: 333–34), emphasizes the need for differentiations. In light of the existence of words referring to these two units of analysis – *ilāni rabûti* and *mātāti* – I believe that a common treating, but acknowledging differentiations, is justified.

As made clear by the narrower aim of this study, it is the *relationship* between the three units of analysis which is the focal point. This relationship is studied on the basis of its status and function in terms of power. To exemplify what I mean by status, the royal title "king of the universe" (*šar kiššati*) is illustrative, while the royal epithet "righteous shepherd" (*rē'û kīnu*) can exemplify the functional aspect. The relevant title refers to the status of having universal dominion, while the relevant epithet alludes to shepherding which implies a royal function of protecting and providing. Admittedly, these two concepts often overlap in practice, but they can be maintained here at least as analytical constructs. The term *rôle* may incorporate both concepts in question. The immediate results of the analysis will consist of the identification of themes (epigraphy) and motifs (iconography) related to the aim of describing the relationship in terms of status and function.

The term power is here understood as relation-based, referring to the ability to influence or control the behaviour of other people. In contrast to Svärd (2012), who seems to be inspired by the theories of Weber (1978 [1922]) on informal social power and the shortcomings of the bureaucratic state, and who refers to "heterarchy" in discussing women and power in Neo-Assyrian palaces, I focus on hierarchical structures and on any given individual's *formal* chance of influencing political decisions. In other words, political power and formal hierarchy are the key concepts in my definition. This definition is only logical because this study does not highlight relations of power in real life, with its room for authority and agency, but in the world of *ideology*. Exemplifying how this definition works in the analysis, the statements that the deities give orders to the king and that a shepherd (the king) directs cattle (the people) indirectly but clearly express relations of power.

Leaving the field of definitions, at least for now,[31] and instead turning to a discussion on the actual analysis, this study rests on a basic philological and

31 The important definitions (i.e. text, exemplar, divine/royal title or epithet, royal visual representation, visual program, scene, and iconographic entity) which are directly related to the composition of the primary sources will be clarified below in section 2.1.

art historical analysis of the primary sources. As for the former, the methods developed by the Italian school after inspiration e.g. from the works of the literary critical theorist Barthes (1967) are adopted. This means that the text is regarded as a structure, containing signs which convey an underlying "ideological grammar". A cornerstone of this approach is the view that variations and literary structures are meaningful and not random, in this way highlighting the agenda of the author or patron. This methodology entails on the one hand a close reading of the text with attention paid to grammar and word semantics, and on the other hand observing the use of literary phenomena such as repetition, topicalization, juxtaposition, word play, metaphor, synonym, and intertextuality. Every single morpheme and literary phenomenon count in this type of textual analysis (e.g. Liverani 1973).

As for the basic art historical analysis, an art object (e.g. a soldier in a sculptured narrative scene) is both analysed as an individual image (the soldier in isolation), and as a component of a context or scene (the soldier is engaged in a certain battle). In a yet higher level of analysis, the whole scene (the king along with his army conquer an enemy city) forms the basis of interpretation, and if the relevant scene is a part of a visual program, the highest level is present. This approach involves careful studies of format, style, design, gesture, position, perspective, and proportion, but also of "outer contexts" whereby the work of art is understood from its historical and manufactural background. This interpretative process leads to "iconology" and a move towards a possible "intrinsic meaning or content" of the work of art (Panofsky 1972 [1939]: 14–15). Art can in a sense be described as a language, involving a similar kind of close reading. In line with this, Winter (1983: 24–26) has analysed scenes on the walls of the North-West Palace in terms of the lingustic elements subject, object, and predicate.

A contextual approach has often been adopted in the studying of Ancient Near Eastern sources, e.g. by Ross (2005) who centres on aspects like "the locus of production, iconography, medium, context, and composition" when interpreting the visual arts. Her approach is as much focused on context as it is on content, as is evidenced by her highlighting of the manufactural and historical-political backgrounds, the role of media, and the arrangement of the art. The same can be said of the methodology developed by Fales (1999–2001) for studying Assyrian royal inscriptions. He highlights the aspects of "chronology, geography, material/media, typology/function, and literary elements", leading to a "contextual evaluation of the chosen texts". All these aspects say something on the message(s) of the relevant text.

This study also takes the contextual approach as it makes a distinction between content and context. The identified themes and motifs – the content –

are contextualized in this type of approach. Several different contexts are recognized, namely frequency, sequence, clustering, typology, time, space, and visual/textual. The royal title "king of the universe" may again be used to exemplify. Its frequency states how often it is attested, its sequence refers to how prominent its place is in the ordering of titles, and its clustering shows which other titles it is attested with. Typology focuses on the issue if the title in question is attested only with certain types of monuments or types of inscriptions, time alludes to the possibility of a different use of the title within or between reigns, space refers to the role of the provenance of the monument on which the title was written, and the visual/textual context lastly centres on the question whether the motifs of the inscribed monument can aid in understanding the title. The same kind of contextualization is valid for analyses of iconographic motifs. Five of the seven contexts are naturally integrated into the discussions of chapters 3–5, while the remaining two contexts – time and space – are highlighted in the following chapters 6–9.

The last contextual aspect – visual/textual – expresses the intent to integrate text and image into a combined analysis. This approach is e.g. pursued by Winter (1997: 376–77) who regards images both as complements and parallels to texts, and by Zettler (1996) who claims the status of written documents as artefacts, and advocates a holistic approach. Bahrani (2003: 96–120, 168–69) similarly argues that word and image must be considered as a single unit and parts of a dialectic relationship, and further argues that a separation of the two was alien to the cultures of the Ancient Near East and rather reflects what she refers to as Western beliefs. As for this work, contextual data may not always be present or fruitful,[32] but the intention is nevertheless to make sure that the analysis is conducted in a holistic way.

Delimitation of the sources is an important part of any study. Here I distinguish between major and minor primary sources. The major primary sources of this study are naturally the inscriptions and iconography (i.e. the state ideology and propaganda) of the Early Neo-Assyrian kings. The criteria for classifying a certain source, whether textual or visual, as a major primary source centre on the four-fold aspects of dating, creator/patron, content, and recipient. A specific source has to be reasonably well-dated to either of the ten kings, the creator/patron must represent the state in a not far-fetched way, the content must be rhetorical in style, i.e. conveying a continuous narrative and not being mere lists, formulae or the like, and the recipients ought to be comparatively

32 The so-called Standard Inscription of the North-West Palace seems e.g. to have been applied to the palace walls regardless of what the surrounding motifs were (Paley 1976).

broad and numerous.[33] This means that comparatively mundane sources such as royal letters would qualify into the major primary sources of this study. A supplementary criterion concerns only minor art and brief texts of officials, i.e. sources which are very numerous. My standpoint here is that only those sources which incorporate the royal name (epigraphy) or the royal image (iconography) are major primary sources. This of course tells of the primary position of the king in the relevant unit of analysis.

As for the first criterion, the dating of the primary sources is a vital part of the methodology of this work. Only primary sources which can be reasonably well-dated are part of the source base proper of this study. Dating can be achieved through various means, e.g. by observing stylistic features on images and cuneiform signs (palaeography), by noting the mentioning of royal names, regnal years or eponyms, and by deducing from archaeological contexts.[34] In this way, the collection of major primary sources has been gathered and established (see apps. 1–2). Regarding some objects, datings are controversial and much debated, which is the case with the seated statue from Assur, the White Obelisk from Nineveh, the dedicatory text to Adad from Assur, and the Sultantepe inscription. In each of these cases, I have brought up and motivated my own datings in chapter two.

The dating of sources is often more problematic when it comes to establishing their temporal belonging *within* individual reigns, i.e. their internal chronology. The methodology for doing this responds to the needs of fulfiling the secondary aim which is addressed in chapter six. Turning at first to the dating of the preserved royal iconography, the stylistic indicators identified by Madhloom (1970: 7–117) for dating Neo-Assyrian monuments are of limited value in this context, and the internal dating of iconography thus becomes more dependent on texts. Admittedly, there is a danger in dating images on the basis of their accompanying texts, since these two types of sources need not have been created at the same time. Here it is interesting to note that the reliefs of the North-West Palace seem to antedate the accompanying Standard Inscription, unclear how much (Reade 1985: 206–207; J. M. Russell 1998–2001: 245). However, the two types of Ashurnasirpal II attested on the walls seem to have their origins in two teams of workmen rather than in variations according to time (Reade 1985: 205–206), the latter suggested by Paley (1976) in his referen-

33 Due to the present unsatisfactory state of our knowledge, the fourth and last criterion can not be viewed as an absolute necessity, but the first three are certainly indispensible.

34 The archaeological contexts are especially important when distinguishing between the image corpora of Ashurnasirpal II and Shalmaneser III as these seem to belong to the same stylistic phase of Assyrian art production (Strommenger 1970: 32–33).

ces to the "young" and "mature" king. All in all, different construction stages for text and image need not cross regnal phases, and I have generally posited relative simultaneity.

As for the dating of the preserved royal inscriptions, half (50 %) of the texts of Ashurnasirpal II can with reasonable certainty be dated to either the first (884/3–872) or the second half (871–859) of his reign (see app. 1).[35] Two ways of establishing an internal chronology in this context have been especially noted (Brinkman 1968: 392; De Filippi 1977; Reade 1985). Firstly, early texts state Carchemish of the land Hatti as the western border of the king's dominion, while later texts instead refer to Mt Lebanon and the Great Sea in the corresponding place.[36] Secondly, the northern limits of his kingdom span from the source of the river Subnat to the city of (or the interior of) Nirbu in the earlier texts, while the latter component is substituted by Urartu or the Tigris source in texts from the second half.[37] The classifying of the Kalhu Standard Inscription into two versions – A (with Nirbu) and B (with Urartu) – follows this logic (Paley 1976: 145–58). At other times, the texts can be dated with the aid of the latest mentioned eponym.

Regarding the dating of Shalmanser III's texts according to internal chronology, the situation is somewhat better, thanks to many firmly dated annals. Almost two thirds (59 %) of this king's text corpus can with reasonable certainty be dated to either of the three regnal phases of 859/8–847, 846–835, and 834–824/3 BCE (see app. 1).[38] Several undated and short texts from Assur can be dated with the aid of similar texts which are indeed dated. According to this principle, inscribed objects from the Ashur temple belong to the first phase, those from the Anu-Adad temple and the Tabira Gate to the medial phase, and those from the city walls and the other city gates may belong to the last phase (Grayson 1996: 120). This dating principle is highly plausible but of course not fixed, since a certain construction project naturally could have progressed over two or even three regnal phases.

---

35 An externally, rather than internally, based division of the reigns into phases seemed best, given the problems in identifying watershed points in the ten Early Neo-Assyrian reigns.

36 Carchemish was the focal point of early military campaigns, while the king's first visit to Mt Lebanon and the Great Sea occurred in a year somewhere between 874–867 BCE (Reade 1985: 204–205). Unfortunately, the interval in question crosses his two regnal phases, making the close at hand-dating to the second regnal phase not completely secure.

37 Nirbu was the target of a military campaign in 882 BCE, while Urartu was attacked somewhere between 864–860 BCE, and the king's visit to the sources of the Tigris seems to have taken place at a date between 865–861 BCE (Reade 1985: 205–206).

38 It is the temporal distribution of the sources and the fact that the reign of this king was so much longer that legitimates this unique dividing into *three* regnal phases.

Lastly, as for dating and the texts of the remaining Early Neo-Assyrian rulers, not even a third (29 %) of these texts can be reasonably well-dated within regnal phases (see app. 1). This troublesome situation is due largely to the relative scarcity of the often dating-supplied annals,[39] the proportional richness in label texts, and the substantial share of texts of high officials. The two latter types of texts are often difficult to use for internal chronology, since they tend to be short and not focusing on the king respectively.

Proceeding to the next step of aim fulfilment, the ideological comparisons between different phases will ideally be made both generally, taking all the internally dated sources as an entity, and strategically. Regarding the latter, important sources which are similar as to genre, type of monument, and provenance (cities and type of building or room), and which belong to different regnal phases, are compared with each other. To exemplify, two royal statues from Kalhu inscribed with annals – one from the medial phase, the other from the last phase – can be compared. They belong to the same genre (annals), type of monument (statues), and have the same provenance (Kalhu). These comparisons are allegedly as fair as possible. As obvious from the low number and degree of internally dated eNA I and III-propaganda, strategic comparisons are the only options for analysing these. In both kinds of comparisons, the dual aspects of quantity and quality of ideological themes or motifs in regnal phases are fundamental.[40]

Another secondary aim, met in chapter seven, centres on investigating whether there are any meaningful variations due to provenance, in terms of cities or regions. In other words, local propaganda will be traced. As a first step of this particular aim fulfiling, the major primary sources are classified as to whether they belong to the inner core (represented primarily by Assur, Kalhu, Nineveh, and Balawat), the outer core (the provinces distant from Assur), or to the periphery (the border areas or foreign lands).[41] This geographical division of course corresponds to the geopolitical situation of the time in which Early Neo-Assyrian kings had authority over the Assyrian heartland and over the more distant provinces situated between the twin rivers in northern Mesopotamia (Postgate 1992b, 2007). Although the distinction between inner and outer core does not come across in the state administrative sources, it can be clearly detected from a historical perspective (Radner 2011: 321–23). 95 % of the

39 This is at least true for the text corpus of Adad-narari III (representing almost 50 % of the total text corpora of eNA I and III) with its consistently non-annalistic texts.

40 For example, the attestation of a theme in a certain regnal phase can be proved both by pointing to its frequency and by pointing to its nature of being a good example. Quantitative and qualitative evaluations are pivotal also for the following comparisons of chapters 7–9.

41 It is the geopolitical setting under *Shalmaneser III* that is the basis for these definitions.

texts of this study have reasonably clear provenances (see app. 1). The remaining 5% resist classification either because the object in question completely lacks archaeological context, without the text being able to give any clear indication as to the provenance, or because a particular text or image is attested in several localities, without a possibility to infer which one is the original source, if such existed.[42]

After classifying these sources according to locality, the next step will be to examine ideological similarities and differences by general and strategic comparisons. As for the latter, it is crucial that comparisons are made through sources which are similar with regards to genre, type of monument, and building. A comparison between the commemorative text inside the Ninurta temple at Kalhu and that inside the Ishtar temple at Nineveh may e.g. be suitable. These two texts share genre (commemorative texts), type of monument (wall inscriptions), and closer provenance (temples), and the comparison should therefore be considered fair and valid. In the discussion on the eNA I and III-propaganda and variations due to provenance, it is because of the relative scarcity of major primary sources from the eight reigns in question only meaningful to make strategic and phase-based[43] comparisons.

Examinations of variation patterns due to locality have at least two other spatial levels beside those of cities or regions: type of building and type of room. A possibility here is to check if there are any ideological variations dependent on whether the relevant archaeological context is a temple or palace/citadel area. However, as noted by several scholars (e.g. Liverani 1979: 301; Pollock 1999: 186), the relevance of this kind of distinction rests on an anachronistic view on a separation between the Temple (the "sacral" sphere) and the Palace (the "profane" sphere). Moreover, this subject would most likely be too extensive to include in this study. It would also be possible to study variations based on in which room the inscribed or uninscribed object once was situated. In this study, such an ambition would be highly relevant when analysing the motifs on the walls of the many rooms and wings of the North-West Palace. Such a study has however been done already (J. M. Russell 1998b), making a renewed study somewhat redundant.

In the eighth chapter of this book, another secondary aim, this time concerning the differences and similarities between the propaganda of the ten Early Neo-Assyrian kings in general, and between Ashurnasirpal II and Shalmaneser III in particular, is addressed. In some ways, this chapter merely brings

42 A royal inscription could e.g. have been intended to be placed in several cities simultaneously. This seems to be the case for the text AE115 in its wide distribution.
43 In other words, the comparisons are based on phases (eNA I–III) and not on reigns.

together the results of the indirectly expressed comparisons made continuously in chapters three to five, but it also conducts a few strategic comparisons by which individual sources representative of one king are compared to those of others. Prime examples here are most-likely-to-be-similar comparisons between the images and texts of the Kurkh Monolith and the Kurkh Stele, the Rassam Obelisk and the Black Obelisk, and the two sets of door bands from the palaces and gates of Balawat. In the discussion on the eNA I and III-propaganda and variations due to individual reigns, it is because of the relative scarcity of major primary sources from the eight reigns in question only meaningful to make strategic and phase-based comparisons.

A final secondary aim of this study, addressed in chapter nine, focuses on placing the identified Early Neo-Assyrian state ideology into the context of its Old, Middle, and Late Neo-Assyrian equivalents.[44] Due to the need for delimitations, the relevant comparisons and contextualizations self-evidently have to be strategic and not general, and they naturally have to rely to a considerable extent on earlier research. Thus, all the royal motifs[45] of the Early Neo-Assyrian kings will be investigated, drawing from the data of Magen (1986), whether these are attested in earlier and/or later periods, and the most common (the ten sources combined) royal epithets of the Early Neo-Assyrian rulers will be investigated in the same way, this time by using the data collection of Seux (1967). Since there is no corresponding work on textual narrative themes over time,[46] earlier and later texts need to be surveyed in search for the selected themes. The relevant themes will be chosen from the premise that at least one characteristic theme of each section of chapters 3–5 has to be singled out. In the following survey, it is then investigated whether these themes are attested in earlier and/or later periods.

1.6 Theory

Theory is an integral part of research within the humanities. The issue therefore is not whether theory should be used or not,[47] but rather as to *which* particular theory should be used. In this section, the theories employed in this study will be presented, and the use of them will be motivated.

---

44 For the sake of fair comparisons, these three periods are then each subdivided into two phases, corresponding to generally acknowledged, historical watershed points.

45 For the terms of royal motif or royal visual representation, see section 2.1.

46 The excellent summaries of themes in Borger 1961 and Schramm 1973 are not suited for this study, since they have been derived from a different methodological framework.

47 Too often theory-orientated studies are dismissed as "biased". As long as there are criteria and the used theories are relevant for the study, there is no reason to speak of bias.

The criteria regarding the selection of these theories should naturally be based on the overarching aim of this study, which focuses on the power relationship between the Mesopotamian deities, the Assyrian king, and the foreign lands. In other words, theories which centre on relations of power, ethnical relations, and divine intervention are suitable for this study.

One theory that highlights power relations is social critical theory. It can be used in order to understand the primary sources and their combinatory aspects of power and communication, evolving into state ideology and propaganda. A focal point of this approach is the relationship between base and superstructure. The standpoint of Marx (1970 [1845–46]) in this regard – at least in his role of economist – is that the superstructure is merely a reflection of the base, but philosophers such as Althusser (1971) and Gramsci (1971 [1926–37]) have problematized this, and argued that it is in fact a genuine two-way relationship in which the conditions of the base constantly need to be reproduced by the superstructure, which in its turn is influenced by the mode of production in the base. Althusser here introduces the concept of "Ideological State Apparatuses" (ISAs), while Gramsci uses key concepts such as "hegemony" and "culture" in order to argue that ideology and culture are crucial in the ambition of achieving hegemony and establishing what common sense is in a given society. State ideology and propaganda are in other words important tools for (re)producing asymmetric relations of power. In this study, this branch of critical theory is employed in order to understand the nature and origins of the primary sources, and to understand the often expressed relations of antagonism and confrontation. It is of course only logical to apply a theory with a conflict perspective to this material.

Another theory which centres on power relations, and which additionally focuses on ethnical relations, is of course post-colonial theory. Established as a discipline (but drawing from several existing ones) by Said (1978), post-colonial theory highlights colonialism, power, and communication. Although Said focused on the creation and juxtaposition of "the Orient" and (what came to be termed) "the Occident" in European literature, this method of identifying and defining a deviating "Other" in contrast to a normal "Self" in a colonialist context is obviously relevant also for this study which deals with the relationship between the Assyrian deities or king and the foreign lands. The essence-based notion of an Other created in order to define oneself, according to the dichotomy of identity and alterity, and the idea of a close connection between knowledge and power are naturally linked to the concepts of subaltern (the Other being different and inferior), and epistemic violence (the Other being redefined by a coercive power) (Spivak 1988).

As for the use of this theory, the pivotal concepts of Self/Other and subaltern in a colonialist context will be highlighted. Taken as a whole, post-colonial theory mainly comes to use in identifying and discussing the Orientalist[48] discourse tied to descriptions of ancient Assyria, and in understanding the roles of antagonism which are often attested in the primary sources. As for the relevant discourse, the old notions on Oriental despotism, violence, and decadence are the starting points. Oriental despotism alludes to the remote and alone Oriental ruler who has all political power in his hands, while Oriental violence refers to the ferocity and zeal in the Oriental ruler's warfare. Oriental decadence, lastly, centres on a polity and culture as static and ignorant, and the Oriental ruler as living a luxurious life of extravagance in his palace and harem. All these Orientalist images owe much to the European stereotyping of the Ottoman state (Said 1978: 4; Solvang 2006).

A third theory which is much focused on power relations and relevant to use here is gender theory. This theory is diverse, and a qualification as to which one I use obviously needs to be made. In her study on women and gender in ancient Mesopotamia, Bahrani (2001: 14–25) talks of three "waves" of women, feminist or gender studies in scholarly literature.[49] The first wave (from the 1960's) centred on biological sex, and e.g. tried to discover women in ancient sources in order to "write women in to history". The second wave (from the 1970's) turned attention away from sex to gender, and employed concepts such as femininity and masculinity which were regarded as socially constructed. It also, not the least, focused on gender in the context of societal power structures. The third wave (from the mid 1980's) sharpened the emphasis on gender and power structures, and added the dimensions of non-positivism and relativism. Dichotomies based on gender, biological sex, and sexuality are also questioned. That is, there does not exist one single universally valid and fixed gender system.[50]

This work uses approaches both from the second and third waves as it centres on the fluent concept of gender as an integral part of discourses of power. A first step is nevertheless to observe the absence and presence of men and women (biological sex) in the sources. The overwhelming proportion of men in comparison with that of women in the sources is neither normal nor self-evident – although characterized as such in patriarchal gender systems of the past and the present – but it has to be focused on and explained in order

48 If not stated otherwise, I refer to the colonial discourse of Orientalism, identified in Said 1978, when I use the words Orientalist and Orientalism.

49 As pointed out by Bahrani herself, the following dates and characterizations are schematic.

50 As for the first wave, it is still thriving today, exemplified e.g. by the work of Macgregor (2012), while a prominent precursor of the second wave is de Beauvoir 1997 [1949]. The study by Butler (1990) is a good example of the third (postmodern) wave.

to get a fuller picture. To ignore the sex bias of the sources is hardly tenable, especially not when discussing relations of power.

Ultimately though, this study is more interested in the social roles (gender) which the participants take. This of course means that the notions of masculinity and femininity in the Neo-Assyrian context will be identified and discussed. Gender study will mainly be used with the aim of understanding the roles that the participants take in times of confrontation. It is my belief that this theory, not often used in Assyriology circles (M. Marcus 1995b; Winter 1996; Pollock 1999; Bahrani 2001), can provide new insights. The way gender was constructed in ancient Assyria will be discussed in subsection 5.4.9, although it can be stated already at this stage that masculinity seems to have been connected to warfare and political power, with emasculation or femininity representing the opposite poles or different spheres.

Social critical theory, post-colonial theory, and gender theory are merged in their respective emphasis on discourse, colonialism, and gender. Identity and alterity are often constructed by gendered language and art. "Women" is here seen as a construct, connected to relations of power, having sex and gender interwoven with e.g. ethnicity (Bahrani 2001: 3–4, 123–27). In this interweaving, an emasculation or feminization of the Other often takes place in colonial discourse (Cixous 1976; Sinha 1995). As noted by Winter (2010: 623 n. 72), Otherness is established in a border crossing context not just by distinguishing barbarism from civilization, but also by ascribing female characteristics to national groups. An example of how this works is the derogatory Roman description of Carthage as a gynecocracy – a state ruled by a woman, i.e. Dido. The rule of Cleopatra VII Philopator in Egypt would be another example. Rome feminized Carthage, the Greeks regarded Persia/Asia as female, and the Romans eventually looked upon Greeks as feminine (Sidebottom 2004: 6, 9, 12). Often, foreign warriors could be likened to women in order to degrade them (Chapman 2004: 48–50). By feminizing the Other, the colonial subjects become abnormal and subordinated.

The theory of patrimonialism also centres on power relations. Patrimonialism refers to a way of government which highlights a "father figure" who governs his polity as if it were his own paternal household. This hierarchical form of "traditional domination" is a projection of patriarchy unto a wider social arena. The leader is supreme and rules by his own legitimate authority and through his bureaucratic officials (often eunuchs) who are closely tied to him personally. A patrimonial state is also characterized by the absence of upper and middle classes (Weber 1978 [1922]; Schloen 2001). The idea behind the term should not be confused with the Orientalist idea of the all-powerful, remote, and alone Oriental despot, in this case the Assyrian king. Patrimonialism, as well as the terms royal autocracy and absolute monarchy, imply something dynamic and not essence-based, while the idea on Oriental despotism expresses the notions of something static and essence-based. Patrimonialism will be used in the context of understanding gender relations and in the context of describing the relative strength of the Assyrian king.

In its role of focusing on ethnical relations, the concept of ethnicity has a natural place in this section and in the discussion. References to "Assyrian" and "foreign" agents permeate the present study. At least three different ideas on ethnicity can be detected in scholarly literature: primordialism (ethnic groups are natural and fixed), perennialism (ethnic groups are natural but constantly changing), and social constructivism (ethnic groups are not a basic human condition, but constructed in social interaction) (Sollors 1989; Eriksen 1993). As noted by Cancik-Kirschbaum (2011), in Assyriological literature from especially the 19th, but also from the 20th century, "the Assyrians" are often referred to as a distinctive race and nation, easily separated from other ethnic groups. In this study however, the idea of *ethnos* as constructed is taken, while it will be demonstrated that this is what is actually expressed in the primary sources. Complementing this discussion, the related and modern concept of nationalism and the anachronistic use of it in describing ancient Assyria will also be brought up in this context.

A few concepts from the terminology of the history of religion should also be highlighted. This of course responds to the need for picturing the belief of divine presence and agency held in ancient Assyria, and relates to the criterion of divine intervention. More specifically, these concepts highlight the attributes of the divine as well as the forms of contact between the deities, the king, and the foreign lands. In this regard, the concepts of omnipresence (everywhere present), omnipotence (all-powerful), and omniscience (all-knowing) on the one hand, and transcendence (with divine and human spheres separated) and immanence (with divine and human spheres crossed) on the other are used (Jones 2005). The terms transcendence and immanence are then seen as general and universal terms, and not as restricted to their original setting of biblical theology (van der Toorn 2000).

1.7 Relations of power "in real life"

In order to understand the power relations which are given in the ideological sources, and which are discussed in chapters 3–9, the relations of power "in real life" need to be identified. In subsection 1.7.1 the geopolitical setting is described, and in subsection 1.7.2 other power relations such as those based on class, biological sex, and in some sense religion are discussed.

1.7.1 The geopolitical setting

In this subsection, the geopolitical setting of the Ancient Near East in the Early Neo-Assyrian Period will be described.[51] Following the geographic definitions employed in this work, the description moves from the inner core (the Assyrian heartland), via the outer core (the provinces distant from Assur), and to the periphery (the border areas and foreign lands). It starts from Assur and, moving from one region to a neighbouring one, ends in Egypt.

Historians refer to an Assyrian core, heartland, or triangle. The said triangle had Assur, Nineveh, and Arbela as its three nodes (Radner 2011: 321–23). This land was situated, roughly speaking, mainly on the eastern side of the Tigris and between and above two of that river's main tributaries Upper and Lower Zab (see Fig. 1). The city of Assur was located at the southern edge of this heartland, on the western bank of the Tigris. Its origins are obscure, but it was certainly in existence already in the third millennium BCE, having relations both to the states of the Sargonic dynasty and Ur III. It then served as the centre of the Old Assyrian city state, and as the capital[52] of the Middle Assyrian territorial state. The first three kings of the Early Neo-Assyrian Period and (initially) also Ashurnasirpal II ruled from this city. Assur remained the spiritual and cultural centre even after its loss of status of capital city. This can for example be seen in the circumstance that the caves of the Old Palace served as the burial place for Neo-Assyrian kings.

The city of Arbela was located quite a distance to the north-east of Assur, distant to the Tigris and between the Lower and Upper Zab. This old, still existing city was one of the most important ones of the Assyrian heartland. Military campaigns towards the east often started from here (e.g. SE6:iii58). At a distance to the west of Arbela, the city of Kalhu was situated just to the north of the mouth of the Upper Zab and on the eastern bank of the Tigris. This city was in existence already in the Middle Assyrian Period, then as a provincial centre (Postgate and Reade 1976–80: 320–21). It was Ashurnasirpal II who elevated it to the capital city of the Assyrian state. It remained its capital until Sargon II and this king's move to his specially built city of Dur-Sharrukin/Khorsabad in the late 8th century BCE. It may be noted here that Kalhu was practically the only city of the Assyrian heartland which stayed loyal to Shalmaneser III in the civil war at the end of this king's reign.

---

51 If not stated otherwise, this subsection follows the historical overview in Kuhrt 1997 and the maps presented in the "Helsinki Atlas" (Parpola and M. Porter 2001). Practically all of the toponyms presented below will recur in the following chapters of this study.

52 I use this term even though it is in some ways misleading, since the capital city in Assyria in practice was the city in which the Assyrian king was. The Assyrian king had fully equipped palaces both in the distant provinces and in the heartland (Roaf 2013: 336, 346).

The old city of Nineveh was located on the eastern bank of the Tigris, a short distance to the north-west of Kalhu. Its history of development can be traced back to prehistoric times. It was only during the Middle Assyrian Period that this city became "Assyrian". Nineveh often served as the starting point of military campaigns towards the west and north (e.g. AE1:i70, SE2:i29). Sennacherib made this city his capital, and it kept this status right until it was seized and sacked in 612 BCE. The city of Balawat, ancient Imgur-Enlil, was located between Kalhu and Nineveh. Both Ashurnasirpal II and Shalmaneser III highly appreciated this city, judging from their substantial building activities there. The status of Balawat is not totally clear, but it has been proposed that it functioned as a royal country residence or as a station and supply base for the army (Mallowan 1957: 79; J. Oates 1983 resp.). The city seems not to have been an outpost but situated at an important highroad which crossed the Assyrian heartland (D. Oates 1974: 173–74).

Moving on to the outer core of the Early Neo-Assyrian state, the area of steppe and wetlands now known as the Jezirah, situated to the west of the Assyrian heartland and reaching to the Euphrates, was established as a part of the land of Assyria in the Middle Assyrian Period. The Early Neo-Assyrian kings gradually reclaimed their authority over this land, which they themselves called Hanigalbat. Settlements and cities along the fertile Euphrates tributary Habur were frequent. The polities of Laqe and Bit-Halupe, the latter with its capital city Dur-Katlimmu, were important and situated close to the Euphrates. The established polity of Shadikanni was located further to the north, while the significant cities of Guzana and Nasibina were situated in either ends – west and east respectively – of the Habur triangle.

The significant Euphrates tributary Balih is located further to the west of the Habur, still in the Jezirah. Among its cities, the city Harran stands out. Shalmaneser III built sanctuaries at this site (Holloway 2001: 401), and the city was to become the seat of government of the last Assyrian king Ashur-uballit II (611–609) as he organized resistance in response to the Babylonian and Median invasions of the Assyrian heartland. The important city of Huzirina, present-day Sultantepe, was also situated at the Balih. According to Parpola and M. Porter (2001), the extensive and much discussed polity of Rasappa may have been located just to the south of Balih, although other scholars think that it was situated to the east of the Habur, at a clear distance from the Euphrates (Roaf 1990: 164; Jursa 2007). The first and last Early Neo-Assyrian kings did not control much of the Jezirah,[53] and the authority of Ashurnasirpal II in the

53 As already noted in section 1.1, the first kings struggled with Arameans over the right to land, while the last kings dealt with the effects of political decentralization.

area appears to have been rather weak, at least in comparison with that of Shalmaneser III (Liverani 2004: 220).

Turning to the description of the periphery, i.e. the border areas and the foreign lands, the highland polity of Urartu was situated at Lake Van and the city Turushpa, to the north of the Assyrian heartland. Urartu seems to have emerged as a power factor in the reign of Shalmaneser III who speaks of a campaign directed at this land (SE17:25). Ashur-narari V is described as defeated in an Urartean royal inscription (Grayson 1996: 246). Moving further southeast, the related polity Musasir was situated on the Zagros range. In the steppes and deserts of the highland landscapes of the eastern regions, several peoples were residing, among them the Medes and Manneans, but also those of Parsua and Zamua. The polities of Gilzanu and Hubushkia were powers of some significance, located by Lake Urmia. Further to the south, the Elamite culture manifested itself through various political formations, among them the city Susa which was situated in a lowland area not far away from actual Mesopotamia. At the foot of the Zagros, and close to the important Tigris tributary of Diyala, the polity Namri was located. Shalmaneser III repeatedly intervened in the affairs of this state (e.g. SE14:111–19). The nearby city of Der is highlighted by Shamshi-Adad V (SA5E4:6′–20′).

Turning further west of Der, Babylonia was situated between the twin rivers. This polity traditionally played an important role in Assyrian foreign affairs. Its kings ruled over e.g. the old city states of Babylon, Borsippa, Sippar, Nippur, and Uruk. Its population was not ethnically homogeneous but composed of "Akkadians"/Kassites, Suteans, Chaldeans, and Arameans. In the most southerly area of Mesopotamia, the Chaldeans – an ethnic group speaking a Semitic language – were settled. Their main tribes were Bit-Jakin, Bit-Dakkuri, and Bit-Amukani (Brinkman 1968: 246–88).

Ever since the later years of Adad-narari II, Babylonia and Assyria enjoyed peaceful relations with each other. Marriages between the two royal houses were made, and treaties which stipulated the refraining from violence as well as mutual assistance in times of trouble were in effect. Ashurnasirpal II never refers to any violence directly aimed at Babylonia and his ally Nabu-apla-iddina, although attacks on the state of Suhu, which was situated at Babylonia's north-western border along the Euphrates, are mentioned (e.g. AE1:iii16–26). The treaty was then renewed with the accession of Shalmaneser III to the throne. Following upon the death of Nabu-apla-iddina, a war of succession broke out between the appointed successor Marduk-zakir-shumi I and his brother Marduk-bel-usate. Shalmaneser III intervened, killed the latter, and reinstalled the former on the throne of Babylon.

The treaty was temporarily renewed after Shalmaneser III's death, when his appointed heir Shamshi-Adad V received assistance from Marduk-zakir-shumi I in order to put down a rebellion which had erupted in the late years of his father, and which was brought to an end only after six whole years. A treaty between these two rulers was established, with the Babylonians appearing to be the stronger part (Brinkman 1968). The on-the-surface friendly relations between the two royal houses were however brought to an end when Shamshi-Adad V successfully attacked Babylonia. His son Adad-narari III in his turn initiated a return to amicable relations after some initial hostilities between the two states, in a way closing the circle.

Moving a great distance to the north-west of Babylonia, the region just to the north of the Habur triangle was a strategically important, mountainous, border area. The city of Tushhan, directly controlled by the Assyrian king, and the lands of Katmuhu and Bit-Zamani are often spoken of by Ashurnasirpal II (e.g. AE17:ii5–48, AE17:iv1–2 resp.). The diffuse polity of "the lands of Nairi" is to be located to this area in this time period. To the north, the mountainous land of Shubria seems to have been beyond the control of the Assyrian king (Schachner 2009: 217–18). The sources of the twin rivers are situated in this region. Shalmaneser III proudly proclaims that he visited the sources of these river systems during his campaigns (e.g. SE14:92–93).

Further to the south-west of this area, the vital polities of Kummuh and Bit-Adini were situated at the Euphrates. The seizing of the latter's capital Til-Barsip in the early years of Shalmaneser III was an important step in the development of the Neo-Assyrian empire (Cancik-Kirschbaum 2008: 59–60). Along with e.g. the neighbouring city state Carchemish, it headed the first coalition against Shalmaneser III (e.g. SE1:53′–73′). The land to the west of the Euphrates was referred to as the land Hatti, alluding to the Neo-Hittite culture which developed in Syria after the collapse of the Hittite kingdom in the 12th century BCE. Control over the trans-Euphratic lands was uneven and fluctuating in the age of this early imperial phase (Cancik-Kirschbaum 2008: 59–60). Sam'alla, Patina/Unqi, and Bit-Agusi with its capital Arpad were important cities and/or polities in Early Neo-Assyrian times, as seen e.g. by the latest mentioned polity's loyalty oath to Ashur-narari V.

The peoples of this region consisted variously of Luwian-speaking Neo-Hittites and Aramaic-speaking peoples, the latter with a preference of forming polities containing the word "house" (*bītu*). During this time period, Carchemish was probably the most influential city with a Neo-Hittite profile, while Bit-Adini arguably was the most influential Aramaic polity. The Neo-Hittite influence was naturally stronger close to and beyond the Taurus mountains, in the Cilician polities of Que (beyond the Amanus range) and Gurgum, and in the Taurus polities of Enzi and Melid. Adad-narari III presents himself (alongside Shamshi-ilu and Sammuramat) as a lord of some treaties in the region, e.g.

involving Gurgum. Shalmaneser III frequently claims to have fought with south-eastern Anatolian rulers, notably Kate of Que, in the later phase of his reign (e.g. SE16:143′–51′). Somewhat further to the north-west, the diffuse but significant land Tabal was situated.

Turning considerably southwards, the important cities of Damascus and Hamath were situated firmly inland. The rulers of these polities headed the second and larger coalition against Shalmaneser III, a coalition which finally disintegrated only after four whole military confrontations, e.g. at Qarqar and the Orontes. Also Adad-narari III had much to do with the polity of Damascus, arguably conquering it. Moving beyond the two mountain ranges of Anti-Lebanon and Lebanon down to the coast, several kings of the period claim to have received tribute from the Phoenician city states located by or very near the sea (e.g. AE1:iii85–88, SE14:103–104). These include the polities of Arwad, Tyr, Sidon, Simurra, and Byblos. This area, especially the city of Byblos, was more influenced by the Egyptian than the Mesopotamian civilization (Kuhrt 1997). The Phoenician city states did *not* participate in the large, second coalition against Shalmaneser III. Moving further south, the Hebrew polities of Israel and Judah were in existence at this time period. The former was at first, under Ahab, an enemy to Shalmaneser III, taking part in the second coalition, but it later turned into a tributary state under Jehu. Adad-narari III in his turn saw to the submission of Samaria under Joash (e.g. An3E7:8–9). Along the coast and further to the south, the Philistean city states of Ashkelon, Ashdod, and Gaza were located.

The vital land of Egypt was at this time politically weak and fragmented, in its Third Intermediate Period. The Lower Egyptian kings of the 22nd dynasty (945–715) nominally ruled, from the delta, over the whole country, but considerable autonomy was, at least at times, enjoyed by Upper Egyptian high priest-kings residing in the old capital Thebes (Grimal 1994: 311–33). Nevertheless, Egypt was a factor to be reckoned with in the Levant, as evidenced for example by the Palestinian campaign of Sheshonq I (targeting e.g. Jerusalem) in 925 BCE (Grimal 1994: 322–23), and by the participation of Egypt in the Syrian-Palestinian coalition in the 9th century BCE.

This overview of the geopolitical setting in the Early Neo-Assyrian Period has shown that the Assyrian king was not "king of the universe" in real life. At times, he did not even control much of his heartland. There was a constant tension between "universal ideology" and "facts on the ground" in the Neo-Assyrian state, meaning that the wide territorial claims of the Assyrian rulers did not always match the political reality (Barjamovic 2012: 43). All this may be kept in mind when focusing on the discussion chapters of this book, presenting the Assyrian king's own view on power relations.

1.7.2 The socio-economic setting

This subsection focuses on aspects which are relevant to discuss for the understanding of the following chapters of this book, namely stratification according to social class (causing elites), sex (causing patriarchy), and religion (in terms of the socio-economic power of the temples). The theories of Orientalism and patrimonialism will naturally be included in the discussion.

Beginning with a discussion on class as the basis for social stratification, it is very clear that Mesopotamian society was highly unequal, with the ruler at one end of the scale and the workers and slaves at its other end. The ruler was however not alone at the top of the pyramid, but was rather a part of a ruling class, which governed the relevant polity (Liverani 2014).

It follows that, even if the propaganda say otherwise, not only the king was a powerful figure in the Neo-Assyrian society and state. An Assyrian ruling class, with the king as its head, is often identified as the main agent of ancient Assyrian society in scholarly literature. Parpola (2007a: 257) sees, in sociological terms, a "Neo-Assyrian ruling class" as an independent social entity. Despite its multi-ethnic and international composition it constituted a homogeneous whole. Liverani (1979: 299) uses the same term, but in a Marxist, essential sense. Similarly, Lamprichs (1995: 381) and Parker (2011: 364, 376) refer to "the elite" and "the people" of both the core and periphery in their describing the mechanisms of Neo-Assyrian imperialism.

Regarding the origins of this class or elite[54], the men behind the ruler functioned as an institution of power throughout Assyrian history (Grayson 1993). This is especially true for the Old Assyrian Period with the comparatively weak status of the ruler – not yet termed king – and strong statuses of noblemen and the heads of merchant houses. Several phenomena speak of the latter's privileged positions. Nobles and high officials erected their own stelae, as they did also in Middle Assyrian times, in the Row of Stelae in Assur (Reade 2004a), and they were in some way involved in the actual governing of their polity, something which is reflected e.g. in the city assembly and in the tradition of eponyms, the latter simultaneously referring to an office and to the dating system (Larsen 1976: 109–223). The custom of greatly rewarding, as well as emphasizing the roles of, high officials at the Middle Assyrian coronation likewise attests to the elevated status of the nobles (Müller 1937: 6). In other words, the nobility held considerable power both in the Old and Middle Assyrian periods (Kuhrt 1997: 362–63).

54 These two terms are used interchangeably in this study, and should be seen as synonyms.

In Neo-Assyrian times, a professional bureaucracy developed and gained power at the expense of the traditional nobility, thus changing the nature of the social stratification and of the composition of the elite.[55] This bureaucracy was often represented by what probably were "eunuchs" (*ša rēši*), portrayed as beardless in the iconography (Grayson 1995b; Tadmor 2002). A supposed conflict between the new bureaucracy and old nobility is often taken as the cause of the civil war at the end of Shalmaneser III's reign (Reade 1981a: 156–60). The first half of the 8th century BCE was a period in which the said bureaucracy enjoyed extensive power and autonomy. The field marshal Shamshi-ilu e.g. seems to have ruled the western provinces in his own right, even if paying formal allegiance to the king. Being a creation of the king, this "new elite" had separated from their maker to become an independent power factor (Grayson 1982: 273–79; Fuchs 2008: 78–93).

As for this new elite and its composition and roles, it consisted in part of intellectuals, court officials, and clergies of the temples, all of whom were directly appointed by the king (Pongratz-Leisten 2013: 292–93). Among these, the scholarly expertise or "literati" of the Neo-Assyrian court often stand out in the sources (Cancik-Kirschbaum 2008: 88–89; Tadmor 2011: 137, 143–46). The diviners e.g. had the power to influence state policy by their omen interpretations (Pongratz-Leisten 2013: 292). The new elite was also greatly involved in the military, which was a main sector of the Neo-Assyrian state. Sometimes referred to as the "great ones" (*rabânu*/*rabûtu*) in Neo-Assyrian sources, they formed a special powerful class, constituting a kind of "military aristocracy" (Larsen 1976: 293). During the Neo-Assyrian Period, the highest officials (i.e. the said great ones) were entrusted with the governance and exploitation of specific geographic regions, thus institutionalizing their great power (Grayson 1993; Mattila 2000: 137–47).

Evaluating the outline above, the Assyrian polity was not *de facto* an absolute monarchy, although it may have had this status *de iure* in the times of the strong kingship of the Neo-Assyrian Period. Assyrian kingship never evolved into an absolute monarchy *de facto*, since it constantly had counterweights such as nobles or royal eunuchs to appease (Labat 1939: 15–19; Oppenheim 1979: 133–37). The image of the all-powerful, remote, and alone Oriental despot, which belongs to the approach of Orientalism (Wittfogel 1977), is hardly applicable. The king could naturally not have ruled the state single-handed,

55 Another social history is presented by Faist (2010: 15, 17–18) who argues that many of the central features of state administration in Assyria of the first millennium BCE developed already in Middle Assyrian times. According to her, the break in terms of institutional development instead took place between the Old and Middle Assyrian periods.

but he was dependent on the support of other individuals and groups of people. Three components of the ruling class or elite were detected above: the king, and the new and old elites. The new elite, which developed in the Neo-Assyrian Period, and which largely were represented by eunuchs, resonates remarkably well with the theory of patrimonialism (see s. 1.6).

Turning to a discussion on social stratification based on biological sex, society in Mesopotamia was fundamentally patriarchal, with a built-in driving force towards a naturalization of male domination (Pollock and Bernbeck 2000: 163–64). Ancient Mesopotamia was a male-dominated society with not much room for women to gain and exercise power (Bottéro 2001b).

In analogy with this reasoning, Assyrian society has frequently been described as a patriarchy (e.g. M. Marcus 1995b; Kuhrt 1997: 363; Melville 2004: 37). Often Middle Assyrian sources, giving the image of Assyrian women as oppressed, have been referred to in such conclusions. The Middle Assyrian laws describe women as having no or few rights, and as being dependent on her husband, father, or father-in-law (Saporetti 1979: 10–14, 20). Assante (2007: 380) labels, largely on the basis of some Assyrian pornographic visual arts from the Middle Assyrian Period, the Assyrian society as "androcentric", i.e. focused on the male population. The Middle Assyrian palace edicts paint a picture of the seclusion of women. Using the term "harem" in its Ottoman sense would be to accept the Orientalist discourse (Solvang 2006), but a purpose of controlling women is clearly present (Melville 2004: 37). As for the Old Assyrian Period, it is apparent that the business and governing of the polity were male domains (Larsen 1976).

Turning to the Neo-Assyrian Period, the relative invisibility of women in the ideological sources is an indicator of continuity. M. Marcus (1995a: 2498) here interprets the absence of women in important royal iconography as serving to support the legitimacy of the patriarchal power structure by making women invisible. When women are indeed depicted in Assyrian state art, they are merely represented as passive, anonymous victims and captives. They are here wailing through hair tearing/dust strewing and ululation (?), or making gestures of submission (alternatively of horror and grief) in deportation rows or from the crenellations of city walls. In several of these depictions, women are portrayed as mothers, thus associated with the private, family sphere (Albenda 1987: 17–21). As noted by Schwyn (2006: 328–29), this may not so much reflect the artisans' impression of foreign gender structures than conveying Assyrian values. In other words, even if the depicted women are foreigners, the Assyrian gender system is illustrated.

As for the relative invisibility of (Neo-)Assyrian women, ordinary Assyrians of the female sex are basically absent from the state art, and those linked to the Assyrian ruling class are rarely portrayed. Ornan (2002: 461–65) has noted that not even Assyrian queens are often depicted in the state art. They are generally not referred to in the official inscriptions either, with the notable exceptions of Sammuramat and Naqi'a/Zakutu (Macgregor 2012: 82–85; Melville 1999 resp.), and they are rarely more than just named in the archival sources (Svärd 2012: 90–135). Perhaps telling of their peripheral status, the word for "queen" (*šarratu*) refers only to goddesses or foreign (ruling) queens (Melville 2004: 43, 51, CAD Š II: *šarratu*), and whether the term *sēgallu*, referring to Assyrian "queens" (AEAD: *sēgallu*, queen), was equivalent in terms of status seems far from certain. In reaction to this relative insignificance and invisibility in official Assyrian sources, Melville (2004: 37) speaks of a "male-oriented society", and talks about a view of the Assyrian political sphere as a "male sphere of influence".

The image of Assyrian women as powerless and as restricted to the private sphere may however be partly revised if looking at more mundane Neo-Assyrian sources (Svärd 2008; Macgregor 2012). Still, although Assyrian women occasionally are spoken of as seemingly acting in their own right, in their roles as priestesses, midwives, wet-nurses, mourners, singers, musicians, prostitutes, and sometimes as legal subjects, being able to dispose relatively freely of inheritance, dowry, investments, and sales (Svärd 2008; Macgregor 2012; Stol 2012), the overall impression must be that Assyrian society was a patriarchy. Women who stand out in a positive, empowered way in the sources may do this on account of their male family ties rather than because of any strong position of women in Assyrian society. Similarly, the highlighting of the "widow" (*almattu*) as a unique example of a free and independent woman (Saporetti 1979: 18–20; Démare-Lafont 2011: 241–45) is quite unconvincing given the overarching patriarchal structure (Stol 2012: 181–88). These alleged examples of "strong women" can not be viewed as atoms, standing in isolation, devoid of socio-political structures.

Evaluating the outline above, the society of the Early Neo-Assyrian state was clearly patriarchal, at least when defining patriarchy by focusing on political structures and formal hierarchies. The peripheral role of Assyrian women in the political arena tells of the prevailing power structures according to sex in Assyria. Patrimonialism, as an extended form of patriarchy and with paternal households and patrilinearity, was in fact a general feature of the Ancient Near East (Schloen 2001). At the same time, the anachronistic, Orientalist notions of the Oriental despot and passive harem women should not be applied to the Neo-Assyrian material (Solvang 2006). Although it would be unfair to say that Assyrian women, "high" and "low", were powerless and merely restricted to the private sphere, it would be equally unfair to give an idealized description of gender equality in ancient Assyria.

The temple institutions were important parts of Mesopotamian society. They were economically significant and employed or involved many people. Temples formed special and large households with estates, goods, and servants (e.g. peasants), and they were often excempted from taxes and state labour (Postgate 1992a: 109–36). The heterogeneous group of "the ministers of the cult" constituted a distinct social category, and the head of the temple was normally "the great priest" (sanga gal) (Bottéro 2001a: 119–25). The temples with their clergies had the potential to intervene in politics through the prestige which their patron deity gave them (Bottéro 2001a: 117).

All this is true of Assyria specifically, although the potential of being a power factor in politics should perhaps not be stressed. The uniquely strong priestly connection of the Assyrian king must have worked against the formation of the temples as separate institutions of power, commonly found in southern Mesopotamia (Müller 1937; Labat 1939: 15; Menzel 1981: 130–74; Fuchs 2005: 35). Presumably, most often the temples and the king must have worked together in their common goals of naturalizing unequal relations of power, having mutual interests (Pollock 1999: 173). It would however be naïve to believe that the temples and priests did not form elements to consider in the power politics also of the Assyrian state. The significant position of the great priest, here that of Ashur, can e.g. be detected by a preserved land grant to him from the time of Adad-narari III (An3E51).

A short presentation of these Assyrian temple institutions with their respective patron deities will conclude this subsection,[56] at the same time presenting the unit of analysis of "the great gods". Among the different cults and deities of ancient Assyria, the god Ashur naturally stands out. The origins of this god are unclear, but it has been suggested that he personified the hilly outcrop of the city Assur, i.e. the site where his temple subsequently was laid out (Lambert 1983). Telling of the close relationship between this god and the Assyrian state is the circumstance that the god, the city, and the land bear the same name. As opposed to many other Mesopotamian deities, Ashur seemingly only had a sanctuary in one city, i.e. in Assur. The southern god Enlil, who also was associated with kingship, was spoken of in Assyria both as an independent god and as a god merging with Ashur, depending on whether a relationship with the goddess Ninlil was expressed or not. This process of a syncretism between Ashur and Enlil was started already in the days of Shamshi-Adad I (Grayson 1987: 47; Chamaza 2002: 124–25).

---

56 If not stated otherwise, I follow Tallqvist 1938 (concerning divine epithets), and Black and Green 1992 or Bottéro 2001a: 44–58 (regarding the descriptions of individual gods and goddesses) in this schematic presentation of cults and deities of ancient Assyria.

The god Ninurta, associated with warfare and agriculture, was also a major recipient of the cult. He was the patron deity of Kalhu, and his temple and ziggurat were situated next to the North-West Palace. The weather god Adad was worshipped both inside and outside the borders of Assyria in various guises, and had as one of his many cult centres the north-eastern, Assyrian city of Kurba'il. The remote, impersonal, and southern sky god Anu was prominent in the hierarchy of deities, and e.g. shared a temple with Adad in Assur. The astral gods of Sin, the moon, and Shamash, the sun, were also vital components of the Assyrian pantheon and cult. The former is described as radiant and wise, while the latter was often connected to omens, dominion, and to the exercise of justice. There was a combined Sin-Shamash temple in Assur, and the moon god had an important sanctuary in the western city of Harran. The wisdom god Ea was also highly venerated, e.g. through a sanctuary dedicated to one of his aspects – Ea-sharru – in Kalhu.

Moving on, the warrior god Nergal was the main deity of the important core city Tarbisu. In company with Ninurta, he was associated with royal hunting. The god Nusku, often spoken of as the minister of Enlil, is also referred to as a great god in the sources, and is associated with wisdom. The group of male deities termed the Sibitti, "the seven", are represented through seven dots in emblems, and they too were provided with a temple in Kalhu. The Babylonian god Marduk is referred to in sections of invocations of deities, having dominion and wisdom as his main attributes. The Babylonian scribal god Nabu had a temple in Kalhu, commissioned by Adad-narari III. None of these two southern gods are represented by emblems on the stelae of Ashurnasirpal II and Shalmaneser III, but this changes with the reigns of Shamshi-Adad V and Adad-narari III. From thereon, Marduk and Nabu play a greater role in the Assyrian royal inscriptions than ever before.

As for goddesses, Enlil's spouse Ninlil, worshipped under the name of Mullissu in Assyria, is quite often referred to by the Early Neo-Assyrian kings (see apps. 4–7). The cult of the goddess Ishtar, a deity associated with warfare and love, was important. She was the tutelary deity of Nineveh and Arbela, and also had a temple with a long history in Assur. Also Ishtar of Nineveh could be identified as Mullissu in Neo-Assyrian times. One of Ishtar's forms was that of Sharrat-niphi, a goddess who was provided with a temple in Kalhu. Another form – Ishtar-belat-Kidmuri – was traditionally worshipped in Kalhu (Reade 2002: 199). Other forms of Ishtar, referred to as great gods in the sources, were Ishtar-kakkabi and Inanna. Also the mother goddess Damkina, the healing goddess Gula, and the grain goddess Shala are included among the great gods in the major primary sources.

After having presented all the deities who are called great gods in the major primary sources, there are two additional gods who need to be presented, due to their fairly prominent role in the said sources. Mamu, god of dreams, was dedicated a temple in Balawat by Ashurnasirpal II. Shulmanu, the local god of Dur-Katlimmu, should also be mentioned, not the least because his divine name forms a part of the royal name Shalmaneser. Allegedly, he functioned as an aspect of the god Ashur (Radner 1998: 51). Adad-narari III seems to have directly sponsored the cult of this god (e.g. An3E42).

In sum, this subsection has identified and presented three different relations of power in real life, namely power relations based on class, sex, and the religious sphere. The terms Orientalism, patrimonialism, ruling class/elite, and patriarchy were all integral to the discussion. The relevant power relationships in real life should all be kept in mind in the evaluating of the relations of power in the ideological sources, conducted in chapters 3–9.

2 The primary sources of the study

Preceding the discussion chapters 3–9, the primary sources of this study are presented in the two sections of this chapter. The major primary sources, i.e. the propaganda of the Early Neo-Assyrian kings, are focused on in section 2.1, while the minor primary sources are highlighted in section 2.2.

2.1 The major primary sources

In this section, the inscriptions and iconography of the Early Neo-Assyrian kings are discussed and presented. It begins with a brief discussion centred on the texts, i.e. on *what* genres have been preserved, *where* the texts have been found, and *when* they were composed (in terms of reigns and phases). A corresponding discussion focusing on the iconography then follows. The non-narrative material of divine epithets, royal titulary, and royal visual representations are introduced, and some crucial terms, such as exemplar and iconographic entity, are clarified. It ends with a presentation of the most important and representative propaganda of the Early Neo-Assyrian kings.

As indicated in subsection 1.4.1, the preserved propaganda from the Early Neo-Assyrian rulers are of many different literary (sub)genres. Taking appendix one as the starting point, there are of course commemorative texts with its dual components of annals and summary inscriptions. There are also dedicatory texts, letters to and from a god, label texts, and captions. Stepping outside the definitions of the overarching genre of royal inscriptions, there are in addition royal prayers, royal hymns, royal decrees, a royal chronicle, and loyalty oaths or treaties. There are in other words a wide range of literary genres attested in the major primary sources of this study. Inscriptions have been preserved on a wide range of materials, such as on tablets (mostly of clay), clay cones, bricks, but also on different large-scale monuments. There are in total 452 texts, or 1889 exemplars, preserved from the period.

Turning to the question *where* these inscriptions have been found, appendix three presents a clear picture. If counting from texts (and not exemplars), the cities of Assur and Kalhu both stand for around 30 % of the total number of texts. Nineveh and Balawat come next in terms of quantity, having 15 and 13 percent respectively. The remaining geographic entities of "the rest of the inner core", the outer core, and the periphery (border areas/foreign lands) each contribute with three percent. Four percent of the texts (1,5 % of the exemplars) are unprovenanced. The Assyrian heartland is in other words the provenance for as much as 90 % of the total text corpus from the period. This tendency is even stronger (97 %) if counting from exemplars.

Moving on to a discussion on *when* the preserved material were composed, appendix three can again be consulted. Taking the three phases of the Early Neo-Assyrian Period as the points of departure, the first phase represents just 9 % of the total, while the second phase (with the kings Ashurnasirpal II and Shalmaneser III) stands for as much as 73 % of the total, and the third phase conveys 18 % of the total. As hinted at in section 1.2, the said rulers then represent much of the whole period in terms of the propaganda. If counting by exemplars, the relevant tendency is even stronger (87 %).

In analogy with iconography (Cifarelli 1995: 233–35), the epigraphic material is both narrative and non-narrative. Textual narrative passages represent the former category, while divine and royal titles and epithets represent the latter. As has been generally recognized, divine and royal titularies are, due to their concise, program-based, and ideological nature, an extremely useful source when studying Mesopotamian state ideology (Tallqvist 1938; Hallo 1957; Seux 1967; Liverani 1981). This study also centres much on this type of source, as reflected not the least in appendices 5–7 where all the divine epithets of the period are listed, and in appendices 8–12 where all the royal epithets of the period are enumerated. Identifying and delimiting epithets were important tasks in the preparatory stages of this study.[57] In order to save space, I often use the term epithet to signify also titles, even though I am aware of the distinction made between the two terms (Hallo 1957).

As for terminology, I should clarify that the terms "text" or "inscription", which are synonyms in this study, are used in the same way as in RIMA and RINAP, i.e. the main publications of Assyrian royal inscriptions. Following this, one particular text can have several "exemplars", i.e. a certain inscription can be attested more than once, thus having exemplars. Both ways of counting – according to text or exemplar – the epigraphic material with titularies and narrative textual themes have their varying setbacks, but I think that it is less misleading to count a long, central text with only one exemplar, and a short, peripheral text with many exemplars once each than to favour the latter by

57 Often it is unclear where a particular epithet ends and another begins. In this study, a fairly minimalist principle is applied in the issue of distinguishing epithet units. Instead of recognizing extremely long epithet units, several grammatically separable epithet units are isolated. Furthermore, similes in noun form and statives in the 1 p. sg. are included. Divine epithets within royal epithets are ignored in the latter. Royal epithets on other rulers are excluded. In the context of epithet statistics, every exemplar of a text has been regarded as complete.

focusing solely on quantity. Put differently, the qualitative aspect of inscriptions are better accomodated by using the text-based approach of counting.[58] However, the study may in a way be regarded as exemplar-based insofar as variant writings, i.e. writings diverging from the "master texts" in RIMA and RINAP, are fully recognized.[59] The statistics on titles and epithets also incorporate the exemplar-based way of counting.

As indicated in subsection 1.4.1, the iconography of the Early Neo-Assyrian kings cover a wide range of the attested monuments and craftsmanships used to express Assyrian state ideology. Emanating from the relevant list in appendix two, there are monumental and miniature reliefs that were hewn on temple and palace walls, and reliefs also decorated strategically placed obelisks, stelae, a thronebase, and cliff walls. Sculpture in the round, which portray deities, genii, and kings, were made and placed in strategic areas. Iconography from the time period have also been preserved from embossings on door bands of palace and temple gates. Minor visual arts are attested through paintings on glazed bricks, an embossing on a weapon, reliefs on small "utensil" vessels, carving on ivories, and through engravings on cylinder seals. There are in other words a wide range of iconography attested in the major primary sources of this study. In terms of iconographic entities – a term that I will soon explain – the relevant number is 80.

Turning to the question of *where* the preserved iconography have been found, a look at appendix three is informative. As much as 54 % of the total number of entities have Kalhu as their provenance. The outer core and the border areas or foreign lands represent a sursprisingly great proportion, namely 10 and 13 percent respectively. The city Assur, in contrast, has only a share of 6 % of the total. Iconographic entities which originate in Nineveh and those which lack secure provenance count to 8 % and 5 % respectively. Balawat provides 4 % of the total, while the rest of the inner core stands for only 1 %. In sum, the emphasis on Kalhu, the relative scarcity of iconography from Assur and Nineveh, and the relatively great proportion of sources from outside the inner core (23 %) are noteworthy. If counting individual scenes and not iconographic entities, these 23 % will decrease significantly however, and Kalhu and Balawat will have completely dominant positions.

Moving on, as for the question of *when* the preserved iconography of the Early Neo-Assyrian kings were composed, appendix three can again be con-

58 It would e.g. in my opinion be absurd to count a routinely stamped label text (SE111, 77 exs.) 77 times while counting the important text on the Black Obelisk (SE14, 1 ex.) just once.
59 Variant writings are given in the footnotes (major variants) and at the end (minor variants) of these volumes. Forms which are attested only in variants are in my study indicated by *.

sulted. As indicated in section 1.2, the situation is similar to the one regarding the distribution of texts. The first phase conveys only 1 % of the total iconographic entities, while the second phase represents 79 % of the total, and the third phase stands for 20 % of the total amount. There is once again a very clear dominance of the second phase in terms of proportions. This dominance will only be heightened if counting from individual scenes.

The iconographic material consists of both narrative and non-narrative material (Cifarelli 1995: 233–35). The narrative (carrying continuous, narrative scenes) and non-narrative (carrying heraldic-iconic motifs) types of art are expressed in varying degrees. The aspects of type of material and choice of scene or motif are closely interrelated. The non-narrative part of the sources, which are important due to the central position of the king in these, are the so-called "royal visual representations" (with the short form "royal motifs"), which present the Assyrian king in various roles and stances (Magen 1986). They can be regarded as the visual equivalent of the royal titulary. Their valuable role in providing evidence for the propaganda of the period is not the least demonstrated by appendices 13–15. The relevant lists convey motifs telling of a rich and multifaceted view on Assyrian kingship.

Before the presentation of individual sources, three important terms pertaining to iconography need to be explained before proceeding. As for "iconographic entity", I for example count the monumental reliefs in the North-West Palace as one entity, not subdividing them according to location, choice of motifs, or the like. This dividing of the visual sources can provide a rough estimate for a reasonably fair statistical evaluation. An alternative is of course to count "scenes". However, it is often unclear where a scene starts and ends, and it is probably anachronistic to sever parts from what was meant to be a unity or program. Regarding the term "visual program", I simply mean iconographic entities which in their quantity of scenes are extensive enough to be qualified as carrying virtual programs of visual art.

In the following, a presentation of the individual sources and their find spots is given. It is structured geographically, moving from one locality to the next. The presentation is selective (based on importance and representativity) and not very detailed, thus having the character of a survey.[60] Following the context-based approach, images and texts are presented together. Important sources whose datings within the period are disputed will be discussed within the geographically structured presentation framework.

60 Simply to make it more reader friendly. For a detailed presentation of the propaganda of Ashurnasirpal II and Shalmaneser III, see Karlsson 2013: 36–53. The sources which will be used in the strategic comparisons of chapters 6–8 will be described in greater detail there.

The city Assur (see Fig. 2) is the find spot for much of the relevant propaganda. Although many of the Early Neo-Assyrian kings did not rule from the Old Palace of this city, they seem to have been buried there. Inscribed (with label texts) but undecorated sarcophagi of Ashurnasirpal II and Shamshi-Adad V have been excavated from under the floor, or in the "caves", of this building (AE115, SA5E9). As for the residential quarters of the palace, only the Standard Inscription of Assur (AE53) seems to have decorated the walls (Orlamünde 2011b: 447–50). Shalmaneser III had some statues representing himself as priest (see s. 4.2) made and placed at a city gate and in a temple (SI4, SI6, SI8).[61] The ones at the city gate have commemorative inscriptions preserved (SE25, SE40). Adad-narari II, Ashurnasirpal II, and Sammuramat all made and placed inscribed (with label texts) but undecorated stelae in the Row of Stelae (An2E9, AE108, An3E25). An uninscribed fragment of a door band from a gate of the Anu-Adad temple and the reign of Shalmaneser III, depicting tributaries, has been preserved (SI9).[62] Small fragments of texts (with captions) and images (of tributaries) of one obelisk dated to Shalmaneser III have been found (SI12, SE132–52).

Regarding the provenience of Assur and inscriptions which were not attached to monuments of art, many bricks, tablets, and cones dated to Shalmaneser III have been excavated from the temples of the city (notably those belonging to Ashur and Anu-Adad), and the city gates and walls (e.g. SE42, SE53 resp.). Several texts of the two editions of Shalmaneser III's annals which come from Assur are attested on various, undecorated media (SE6, SE9–11, SE13, SE15).[63] Also some royal prayers and hymns focusing on various deities (such as Enlil and Ninlil) have been preserved (AE171–73, SE154) on a few clay tablets excavated from Assur. The two literary subgenres of letter to or from a god, undoubtedly Ashur (Grayson 1996: 192), are attested from Assur and the reigns of Shalmaneser IV and Shamshi-Adad V respectively on two fragmentarily preserved clay tablets (S4E3, SA5E4).

Turning to Kalhu (see Fig. 3), much of the sources from the Early Neo-Assyrian kings derive from this city, not the least from the North-West Palace

---

61 As for the seated (and headless) statue of SI4, Reade (1986) argues for identifying the image as the deity Kidudu mentioned in the text, but it may rather be regarded as an image of the king (Strommenger 1970: 15; Magen 1986: 148). Another statue of Shalmaneser III has been found at the same city gate (SI6), making the latter interpretation probable.

62 This dating is likely due to the ambitious work of this king on this temple (Grayson 1996: 115), as proved e.g. by his dedicatory text to Adad (SE131). This text can be dated to Shalmaneser III due to text parallels and the said building profile of the king (Frahm 2009: 67).

63 Six different editions of Shalmanser III's annals have been recognized (Schramm 1973: 70–81). The main bearers of the two Assur editions are arguably SE6 and SE10.

(see Fig. 4). This building was decorated with monumental reliefs on its entrance façade and on the walls of the rooms of the palace (AI4),[64] not the least on those in the throne room. The reliefs depict the king at war, in hunt, receiving tribute, and in various priestly roles (see Figs. 6–10, 12–15). Genii and the "Assyrian sacred tree" also decorate much of the walls (see Figs. 15–16, 18), and colossi with human heads and bull or lion bodies were placed at entrances (see Fig. 17). The Standard Inscription (AE23), which is a summary inscription, accompany many relief decorations, placed in a band of cuneiform across the reliefs or between two relief registers. Some rooms of the palace have the Standard Inscription as their sole decoration. A few door bands depicting the king receiving tribute have also been found in the palace (AI15). Just outside the throne room, the Banquet Stele with its image of the king as shepherd (see subs. 5.4.4) and its text focusing on a great state banquet was found (AI20, AE30). The inscribed but undecorated sarcophagus of the queen of Ashurnasirpal II, Mullissu-mukannishat-Ninua, have been discovered under the floors of the palace, used as a burial place (SE98).

As for palaces and Kalhu, the nearby palace of Adad-narari III has not yielded any substantial evidence. In contrast, the review palace (*ekal māšarti*) of Shalmaneser III (see Fig. 5), located at the south-eastern edge of the citadel area and called Fort Shalmaneser by its excavators, has revealed a lot. A huge panel of glazed bricks, depicting a tree, a winged disk, and the king as priest and carrying a label text, were situated above the entrance to the throne room (SI18, SE114). A throne base of the palace, with reliefs depicting tributaries and a friendly meeting between Shalmaneser III and the Babylonian king, accompanied by some summary inscriptions and captions, has also been preserved (SI14, SE28, SE59–62). In a store room of Fort Shalmaneser, another statue of Shalmaneser III, the so-called Kurba'il Statue, was found, inscribed with an annalistic inscription (SI5, SE12). Several inscribed stone slabs and door sills of the palace, sometimes focusing on the mayor of the city, Shamash-bela-usur, as a dedicator, have been excavated (SE29–37). The earliest known edition of Shalmaneser III's annals is inscribed on one stone slab (SE1). Quite a few decorated pieces of ivory derive from Fort Shalmaneser or from Kalhu generally (AI25–28, SI19–24).

Kalhu did not only consist of palaces. There were e.g. several temples adjacent to the North-West Palace. In the Sharrat-niphi temple, two gateway lions and a statue of Ashurnasirpal II were found (AI11–12, see Fig. 19), along with accompanying commemorative inscriptions (AE28, AE32, AE39). In the Ninurta

64 Also, some garments and attires of individuals (king, attendants, genii) were decorated with profane and religious motifs (AI23, see Fig. 18). For a discussion, see Canby 1971.

temple, commissioned by Ashurnasirpal II, walls were decorated with reliefs depicting deities and genii in interaction (see Fig. 11), and colossi were placed at entrances (AI2, AI7). The very long annalistic inscription AE1 was inscribed on the temple walls and floors. It is one of the many "annals series" of Ashurnasirpal II that have been found in Kalhu.[65] An inscribed stele showing Ashurnasirpal II as priest and carrying a long annalistic inscription was found at an entrance (AI19, AE17, see Fig. 20). The building of the adjacent ziggurat is spoken of by Shalmaneser III (e.g. SE56). In the Nabu temple, another temple situated in the citadel, statues portraying genii from the time of Adad-narari III have been found, two of these with a dedicatory text (An3I8–10, An3E26, see Fig. 30). A stele of Shamshi-Adad V which depicts this king as priest and which contains his annals was situated at an entrance (SA5I1, SA5E1, see Fig. 29).

Turning to the remaining parts of Kalhu, the central part of the citadel, with its "Central Building" and "Centre Palace"/"Shalmaneser's Building",[66] have yielded some evidence, first and foremost the Black and Rassam Obelisk (SI11, AI16). While the latter is fragmentary (and belonging to Ashurnasirpal II), the former is complete. The Black Obelisk was commissioned by Shalmaneser III and mainly depicts tribute processions, accompanied by annals and some captions (SE14, SE87–91, see Figs. 21–24). Fragmentary reliefs (depicting genii and lions) and colossi from this area and phase are also preserved (AI3, AI9, SI1, SI3). In this central citadel area, yet another statue of Shalmaneser III was found (SI7). It has the latest of the three editions of Shalmaneser III's annals which come from Kalhu (SE1, SE8, SE16). An uninscribed bronze helmet, depicting Ashurnasirpal II being crowned, has also been found.[67] Several cylinder seals, having both images and texts, have Kalhu as their provenance (AI31–32, AI35–37, SI25).

Moving on to the city Nineveh, wall reliefs from the temples of Ishtar and Nabu have been found (AI1). The so-called Standard Inscription of Nineveh was found in connection with these (AE40). Paintings on glazed bricks have the local palace as their provenance (AI21). Ashurnasirpal II commissioned much work in this city, and he is here represented e.g. as hunting lions. Many

---

65 These are AE1, AE4, AE8–11, AE13, AE2, and AE3+5+7. Other annals series derive from Nineveh (AE15) and Assur (AE16) (Grayson 1991: 192). For a discussion on variants of the temple texts of Kalhu based on Layard's unpublished records, see Reade and Finkel 2002.

66 These buildings have variously been understood as temples and palaces, as exemplified in the interpretations of the Central Building (Meuszyński 1976: 43; Reade 2002: 196 resp.).

67 Whether this bronze helmet really had Kalhu as its provenance is not fully certain. For doubts concerning the authenticity of this source, see Berlejung 1996. Considering its good execution and its focus on genii, it can be seen as a genuine piece of Ashurnasirpal II.

royal decrees from the time of Adad-narari III have been found in the Niniveh state archives (An3E45–58).[68] A royal chronicle, called the "Synchronistic History" and dated to Adad-narari III, tells of the relationship between Assyria and Babylonia from the Middle Assyrian Period onwards (An3E59). Treaties and loyalty oaths have also been preserved, e.g. between Shamshi-Adad V and his Babylonian counterpart (SA5E15), and between Ashur-narari V and Mati'-ilu of Arpad (An5E2). Impressions from the royal seal, depicting the king stabbing a lion, have also been preserved from Nineveh (SI26, An3I11).[69] From the nearby city Tarbisu and its Nergal temple, an inscribed and decorated (with scenes of tribute and cult) stone vessel of the field marshal Bel-luballit has been found (SA5I2, SA5E12).[70]

Turning to the city Balawat, both Ashurnasirpal II and Shalmaneser III adorned gates of the local palace with door bands depicting the king in various roles and stances, i.e. as conducting warfare and hunt, receiving tribute, and engaged in cult activities (AI13, SI10, see Figs. 25–28). The door bands of Shalmaneser III are greater in size and better preserved. Both sets of bands are with commemorative inscriptions and captions (AE51, AE80–97, SE5, SE63–86). Ashurnasirpal II also decorated a gate of the temple of the local god Mamu with door bands, likewise fragmentarily preserved and accompanied by a fragmentary commemorative inscription and some captions (AI14, AE18, AE155–63). These mainly depict scenes of tribute. The building of the city and temple is also told of on two stone tablets (AE50).

Regarding the sources from the outer core, i.e. the provincial areas distant from Assur, there are three inscribed and decorated stelae to discuss. The stelae at Tell al-Rimah and Saba'a show Adad-narari III as a priest (An3I2–3), while the stele from Tell Abta notably depicts the royal eunuch Bel-Harran-beli-usur in the same position (S4I1). They all carry commemorative inscriptions (An3E6–7, S4E2). Further west, in Dur-Katlimmu a fragmentary relief (depicting attendants) from the local palace (AI5), and a fragmentary (showing the king's head) and inscribed (with a commemorative text) stele of Adad-narari III were found (An3I4, An3E8). Further north along the Habur, in Shadikanni some reliefs, colossi, and sculptured lions, which were executed in a local, provincial style, have been found from the local palace of the governor Mushezib-Ninurta (AI6, AI10), named in dedicatory and label texts (AE149–51). At the Balih city Sultantepe, there is a letter to god-like inscription preserved

68 This does not necessarily mean that the royal decrees as such originated from Niniveh.
69 Although it is, naturally, futile to look for the spatial belonging of the royal seal as such.
70 Its dating has now been established beyond doubt (Reade and Finkel 2008: 95; Fuchs 2008: 71–72). It was counted among Shalmaneser III's text corpus by Grayson (1996: 177).

on a clay tablet from a library and the time of Shalmaneser III (SE17), largely telling of divinely ordered warfare.[71]

Moving on to the propaganda from the border areas, the so-called Kurkh Monolith and Kurkh Stele[72] of Ashurnasirpal II and Shalmaneser III respectively were situated next to each other in the city Kurkh, ancient Tushhan (AI18, SI13). The two stelae depict the ruler as priest, and convey long annalistic inscriptions (AE19, SE2). The eroded and fragmentary Babil Stele, commissioned by Ashurnasirpal II and carrying a commemorative text, has also been preserved (AI17, AE20). Moving to the middle Euphrates, fragments of a locally produced stele of Tukulti-Ninurta II, depicting a god and the king's father (Börker-Klähn 1982: 181; J. M. Russell 1998–2001: 245) and bearing a short and much difficult text (Grayson 1991: 188), has been found at the city Terqa (TN2I1, TN2E21). At Kenk Boğazı, situated at upper Euphrates, a depiction of Shalmaneser III as priest has been found on the face of a cliff, along with a commemorative text (SI15, SE20).

As for the propaganda in the foreign lands, two depictions of Shalmaneser III, with accompanying inscriptions, are preserved on the cliff faces of the so-called Tigris tunnel, located at the sources of the Tigris river (SI16–17, SE21–24). Finally, three stelae from the time of Adad-narari III, but decorated only with moon standards and/or fragmentary images of powerful people, have been preserved (An3I5–7). The Antakya and Pazarcik stelae in their texts tell of prominent roles of Shamshi-ilu and Sammuramat in the context of establishing of boundaries (An3E2, An3E3 resp.). The Para Stele stood in the Phoenician island state Arwad (Börker-Klähn 1982: 198).

2.2 The minor primary sources

In this section, the most important minor primary sources, both epigraphic and iconographic, are presented and discussed. The four-fold criterion (see s. 1.5) is used as the basis in the structuring of this section, with relevant sources of unclear or other date brought up initially, and with those which lack clear propaganda dimension concluding the whole section.

---

71 A dating of this partly damaged text to Ashurnasirpal II has been proposed by Reade (1989), mainly on the basis of the mentioning of the name of this king in the text. Following Lambert (1961: 156) and Grayson (1996: 85), this text is here dated to Shalmaneser III because an eponym refers to this king's first field marshal, Ashurnasirpal II is referred to as in the past, and the order of the campaigning fits better with the former ruler.

72 In order to avoid confusion between these two monuments of Ashurnasirpal II and Shalmaneser III, I call the former king's monument "monolith" and the latter's "stele".

Among the minor primary sources, i.e. those which do not completely fulfil the criteria, are sources loosely dated to the 10th, 9th, or 8th century BCE. Beginning with major monuments in stone, the fragmentary obelisks from Nineveh and Assur, carrying tribute scenes, can only be loosely dated within the period (see Börker-Klähn 1982: figs. 139–45, 156–60; Orlamünde 2011a: pls. 11–26).[73] Another example is formed by the inscribed pieces of the statue of a 9th century BCE king, called statue S5 by Strommenger (1970: 18), excavated from the Ninurta temple. The four cliff reliefs in Karabur of southern Anatolia, depicting single deities in three of them and a eunuch in the fourth (see Börker-Klähn 1982: figs. 236–39), can be loosely tied to Shamshi-ilu or Tiglath-pileser III (Taşyürek 1975). A stone slab from Assur (see Börker-Klähn 1982: fig. 242), arguably depicting the same eunuch, is executed in the art style of Tiglath-pileser III (J. M. Russell 1998–2001: 251).

Regarding loosely dated stelae, a number of stelae with only a moon standard carved (see e.g. Börker-Klähn 1982: fig. 230) can not be more precisely dated than to the 8th century BCE (J. M. Russell 1998–2001: 251). The stele of the otherwise unattested governor of Duru, Mushezib-Shamash, showing him in a royal pose, but beardless and bare-headed, and without any divine emblems (see Börker-Klähn 1982: fig. 233) can not be dated more precisely than to the 8th century BCE either (J. M. Russell 1998–2001: 252). The remains of the stelae of two governors of the practically autonomous dynasty of Suhu and Mari by the middle Euphrates can be classified as minor not only because of their unprecise dating but also because of their non-Assyrian framework (see e.g. Cavigneaux and Ismail 1990: pl. 35:17). A curious circumstance is that these "governors" are actually depicted wearing the Assyrian royal crown on their heads (J. M. Russell 1998–2001: 252).

Moving on to other kinds of material, some fragmentary glazed bricks from Assur and Nineveh, lacking any royal motif, are also difficult to date (see Andrae 1923: pl. 6; Campbell Thompson and Hutchinson 1931: fig. 28 resp.). As for loosely dated minor art, much of the large quantity of carvings on ivory excavated from Kalhu can be dated only roughly to the 9th or 8th centuries BCE. These carvings convey scenes of tribute, cult, and warfare in which the king may or may not be present. Scenes depicting mythological creatures, sacred trees, animals, and decorative designs are also commonly conveyed (see Mallowan and Davies 1970: 1, figs. 6, 85, 94, 171).[74] Another type of minor art

73 As one consequence of this exclusion, the obelisk text A.0.99.1001 in RIMA1 has not been included in the text corpus of the major primary sources of this study.

74 The post-1970 findings of decorated ivory objects in the North-West Palace give no reasons for additions to the corpus of this study (see Herrmann, Laidlaw, and Coffey 2009).

which in many cases can not be more precise dated than to the 9th or 8th centuries BCE are cylinder seals from the Assyrian inner and outer core (see Collon 1987, 2001), showing mythological scenes, as well as tribute, royal warfare, cult, and hunt (Collon 1987: 75–89; Herbordt 1998–2001: 268–69). In many cases, the motifs on ivories and seals are not accompanied by texts or images of the king, adding to the difficulties. Also the fragmentary stone vessel found in Fort Shalmaneser, depicting some eunuchs (see Searight et al. 2008: fig. 606), belongs to the minor art which are difficult to date (Reade and Finkel 2008: 97). Finally, also some fragmentary royal inscriptions of this time period can not be attributed to a specific reign (see e.g. RIMA2: A.0.0.1013–26, RIMA3: A.0.0.1027–1101).

Turning to sources whose datings by scholars alternate between different time periods, the 290 cm high White Obelisk from Nineveh depicting tribute, royal warfare, cult, hunt, and banquets (see Börker-Klähn 1982: fig. 132) are in line with most scholars regarded as belonging to Ashurnasipal I (1049–1031) of the Middle Assyrian Period rather than to Ashurnasirpal II (e.g. Cifarelli 1995: 114–27).[75] It is mostly philologists who have dated this obelisk to the second king with this name (e.g. Grayson 1991: 254–55). The main argument here is that the shrine *bīt-natḫi*, which is mentioned in the text on the White Obelisk (see RIMA2: A.0.101.18:1, epigraph), is otherwise referred to only by Ashurnasirpal II. This circumstance may however be just another result of the hazardous preservation of the primary sources.

The dating to Ashurnasirpal I can be derived from various stylistic features such as the fact that also the king's officials wear fez-shaped hats. This clearly points to a Middle Assyrian date, since the officials and nobility of Neo-Assyrian times do not wear these headgears (Reade 2009: 248–49). Additionally, the coarse style which characterizes the reliefs on the White Obelisk is very different from the elegant style on the Rassam Obelisk. Since Nineveh, the provenance, was an important core city the coarseness of the reliefs can not simply be explained away as being "provincial art" from the time of Ashurnasirpal II. Rather, it may be understood as part of a chronologically determined art development, closely related to the "Broken Obelisk" of Ashur-bel-kala (1073–1056) (see Börker-Klähn 1982: fig. 131).

The wall paintings in the provincial palace of Til-Barsip conveying narrative scenes and ornamental motifs are, as noted e.g. by Reade (1979b: 76–80), most likely not from the 9th century BCE but from the Late Neo-Assyrian Period (see Thureau-Dangin and Dunand 1936). As Madhloom (1970: 23–26) convin-

75 Pittman (1997: 350) also dates it to the Middle Assyrian Period but to Tiglath-pileser I. As a consequence of my dating, text A.0.101.18 in RIMA1 of this monument is excluded.

cingly demonstrated on the basis of stylistic features such as chariots, armour, and clothing, the identified two phases of painting at the site (Thureau-Dangin and Dunand 1936: 45–49) seem in reality to have developed simultaneously in the 7th century BCE. Similarly, the sculptures from the provincial palace of Hadatu, modern Arslan-Tash, having guardian figures and slabs with scenes which illustrate the royal chariot, processions of soldiers, and the cavalry (see Thureau-Dangin 1931), may on stylistic grounds be dated to the Late Neo-Assyrian Period. As concluded by Madhloom (1970: 3), features of the chariot, armours, and dresses conclusively date these sculptures to the time of Tiglath-pileser III. The fragmentary wall paintings in Fort Shalmaneser, e.g. depicting a row of officials (see D. Oates 1959: pl. 29), may also date to the Late Neo-Assyrian Period. As observed by D. Oates (1959: 125), these paintings have the style of 7th century BCE art, and most likely belong to the time of Esarhaddon, a ruler well-known to have initiated building projects (e.g. a new palace) in Kalhu.

Concluding this discussion on controversial (in terms of dating) primary sources, the cliff relief at Eğil (see Börker-Klähn 1982: fig. 154) is most likely a monument of Sargon II (Wäfler 1976; Bartl 1999–2001), and not of Shalmaneser III as argued by Börker-Klähn (1982: 192–93). The relief in question shows a crowned king – a god according to Wäfler – standing on a plinth, making the standard ritual gesture of pointing with the index-finger (see s. 4.2) and holding an axe, while divine emblems hover in mid-air. A now erased figure stood face-to-face with the king/god. The provenance of this monument, an Urartean landscape, combined with the shape of the divine emblems, not of a 9th century BCE style, make a dating to Sargon II much more plausible. This king is known for his warfare against Urartu, and the emblems are very different from those on e.g. the Kurkh Stele (SI13).

Regarding sources which clearly are from other periods and furthermore may be questionable as to the criteria of creator/patron or content, texts such as the Middle Assyrian laws and palace decrees may be useful in order to understand the various power structures of Assyrian society, notably the gender system. The Middle Assyrian laws are written on 14 partly fragmentary clay tablets (see Driver and Miles 1935; Saporetti 1984), which were found in a private context in Assur (Pedersén 1985–86). Tablet A, the best preserved one, deals with the legal status of women. The palace decrees in their turn are preserved on nine fragmentary clay tablets from Assur, and they are made up of 23 decrees, from nine different rulers, which regulate the status and movement of women in the Middle Assyrian court (see Weidner 1956). Both of these text corpora seem to have been compiled in the reign of the Middle Assyrian king Tiglath-pileser I (Weidner 1956).

As for other sources which relate to the issues of sex and gender and which are also from another period and are, in this case, not very rhetorical in content, the queen tombs which were excavated from under the floors of the domestic quarters of the North-West Palace have ornamental iconography and brief texts (see Damerji 1999). Still, they belong to the later queens or "palace women" (*sēgallu*) of Tiglath-pileser III (Jaba), Shalmaneser V (Banitu), and Sargon II (Atalia). Moreover, the texts merely consist of label texts and the iconography is symbolic-decorative. Although Mullissu-mukannishat-Ninua was laid to rest in one of these tombs, her burial place seems to have contained secondary deposits (Fadhil 1990; Postgate 2008). The finds still say something of the status of Assyrian queens, and this issue will obviously be relevant in my discussing of Assyrian gender roles.

Turning to sources whose only setback is their dating to another period, the royal inscriptions and iconography of the Old, Middle, and Late Neo-Assyrian periods are highly relevant, since they need to be analysed in order to fulfil one of the secondary aims of this study.[76] Although not being royal inscriptions in the strict sense, the coronation ritual from Middle Assyrian times and the coronation hymn from the reign of Ashurbanipal are important sources (see Müller 1937; Livingstone 1989: text 11 resp.). They give, in a very poignant way, the bases for the legitimacy of the Assyrian king. The Late Neo-Assyrian royal creation myth is also highly relevant (Cancik-Kirschbaum 1995: 20). This text describes the divine creation of the world and underworld, and conveys the idea of kingship as a divinely ordained institution of creation (see Mayer 1987). The so-called Tukulti-Ninurta Epic is another useful minor primary source (see Machinist 1983a). This text describes the struggle between Tukulti-Ninurta I and his Babylonian counterpart Kashtiliash IV in highly rhetorical and ideological terms. Finally, the court poetry and literary miscellanea (see Livingstone 1989), prophecies (see Parpola 1995b), treaties and loyalty oaths (see Parpola and K. Watanabe 1988) from the Neo-Assyrian state archives in Sargonid Nineveh are also relevant, due to their official and rhetorical background and nature.

Other sources from the same archive are equally official but less rhetorical. These include first and foremost state/royal letters, mostly *to* the king (see e.g.

76 For the texts, see RIMA1–2 for the Old and Middle Assyrian texts, RINAP1 for Tiglath-pileser III and Shalmaneser V, Fuchs 1994 for Sargon II, RINAP3 for Sennacherib, RINAP4 for Esarhaddon, and Borger 1996 for the texts of Ashurbanipal. For the iconography, see Börker-Klähn 1982: figs. 130–32 for the Middle Assyrian images, Barnett and Falkner 1962 for Tiglath-pileser III and Esarhaddon, Albenda 1986 for Sargon II, Barnett, Bleibtreu, and Turner 1998 as well as Russell 1998a for Sennacherib, and Barnett 1976 for Ashurbanipal.

Parpola 1987). It also includes documents such as administrative and legal texts (see e.g. Fales and Postgate 1992; Kwasman and Parpola 1991 resp.), royal decrees (see Kataja and Whiting 1995), and omen literature, i.e. reports on astrology and liver omens (see Hunger 1992; Starr 1990 resp.). Only a small share of these texts come from the Early Neo-Assyrian Period (see s. 2.1).[77] The Neo-Assyrian Eponym Chronicle (see Millard 1994: texts B:1–10) is not as rhetorical as the Synchronistic History (see s. 2.1), since it merely gives notes on army movement, in addition to giving the name and title of the eponym, and it only rarely refers to some other event (revolts, solar eclipses, godnappings, cult measures) (Millard 1994: 4–5). The associated eponym lists and king lists, whether Assyrian or synchronistic (see Millard 1994: texts A:1–9; Grayson 1980–83: 101–25, texts 3.9–17 resp.), may also carry some weight in the analysis of the present study.

Other sources are minor just because of content, being not at all rhetorical. The decree, *de facto* a list, possibly from the time of Shalmaneser III, on the organization of and rations for the cultic personnel of the Ashur temple is one example (see Menzel 1981: 18–19, text 16). The so-called Nimrud Wine Lists are of the same type. Preserved from the reigns of Adad-narari III and Shalmaneser IV, they concern the wine rations of the royal household (see Kinnier Wilson 1972). Administrative and legal documents from the core city Shibaniba, probably dated to Shalmaneser III, are also minor (see Finkelstein 1953: 111–76, texts 68–90). The texts from the archive of the Governor's Palace of Kalhu, found from and established in the reign of Adad-narari III for Bel-tarsi-ilumma, are also minor because of their type, i.e. these are administrative, business, and legal texts (see Postgate 1973). The documents from Fort Shalmaneser concerning administrative and legal matters are not only excluded because of their type but also because of their datings to the late 8th century BCE or between 648–614 BCE (see Dalley and Postgate 1984). Lastly, the texts on the tablets from the Nabu temple of Kalhu are minor due to their types, i.e. mainly magical, medical, prayers, and instructions for scribes. The temple library in question seems to have been established in 798 BCE (see Wiseman and Black 1996).

77 As for the royal correspondence from Kalhu, the preserved texts from the North-West Palace are from the reigns of Tiglath-pileser III and Sargon II (see Saggs 2001).

3 The relationship between the great gods and the foreign lands

A direct relationship between the Mesopotamian deities and the foreign lands is not often expressed. Normally the Assyrian king, i.e. the link between the two agents, is described as interacting with the foreign lands on behalf of the deities (see s. 4.1). The descriptions and depictions which do portray this relationship will be discussed in the two sections of this chapter.

3.1 Owners and masters of the world

In the first section of this chapter, I will argue that the great gods are imagined as the owners and masters over the whole world both from a sphere separated from mankind (transcendence) and from a position in which the borders between the divine and human spheres are crossed (immanence). Their control over the universe implies a cosmic-mythological dominion, while their control over the world expresses a worldy-earthly dominion.

As illustrated by appendices 5–7, the divine titles and epithets, i.e. the main source, are mostly inward looking, concerned with the status and function of the individual deity *within* the divine sphere. Ashur is e.g. called "king of all the great gods" (*šar gimrat ilāni rabûti*) (e.g. AE17:i1, SE2:i1), Ninurta is referred to as the "first son (of Enlil)" (*aplu rēštu*) (e.g. AE1:i1–2), and Ninlil is spoken of as "mother of the great gods" (*ummi ilāni rabûti*) (e.g. AE8, SE11:5′–6′obv.). Obviously, these inward looking epithets are of limited value with respect to the aims of this study. The focal point here is on status and internal hierarchy, something which also can be expressed by the hierarchical institution of "the assembly of the gods" (Jacobsen 1976: 86–91; Bottéro 2001a: 48–55) and by the differentiated and varying power properties of the individual deities (Bottéro 2001a: 45–48). The relative order of individual deities in lists and enumerations also tells of the focus on internal hierachy in the divine sphere (see app. 4). Turning to iconography, the genii in the Nabu temple (e.g. An3I8) express hierarchies in the divine sphere, given their mere intercession function and humbly clasped hands (Strommenger 1970: 18). In analogy, the same inferior status may be given the lion and bull colossi and other genii from Kalhu (e.g. AI8, AI4:N5 resp.).

The relationship between the deities and the foreign lands is *indirectly* articulated by focusing on the deities as the heads of the universe, thereby having power over everything and everyone, the foreign lands included. The deities are here considered the rulers, owners, and creators of the universe (Bottéro 2001a: 77–90). Ashur is e.g. "the king of heaven and underworld" (*šar šamê u erṣetim*) (An5E2:vi6). Similarly, Enlil is described as "the one who draws the designs of heaven and underworld" (*muṣṣir eṣurāt šamê u erṣetim*) (e.g. SE2:i2), as well as "king of destinies and designs" (*šar šīmāti u gišḫurrī*) (AE98:1), the lastly mentioned word referring to a blueprint of cosmic scheme, i.e. to the plans of creation (CAD G: *gišḫurru*). Both the creation of the universe and the inhabited earth and the infusing of it with a certain divine world order are alluded to here (Jacobsen 1976: 165–91).

The Mesopotamian deities are in this context described as the holders of various "cosmic offices" (Jacobsen 1976: 84–86). The water god Ea is described as "the king of the (subterranean waters of) Abzu" (*šar Apzû*) (e.g. AE17:i3, SE2:i2), the moon god Sin is called "light of heaven and underworld" (*nannār šamê erṣeti*) (e.g. SE2:i2), the healing goddess Gula is described as "the great chief physician" (*azugallatu rabītu*) (An3E34:7), the god of skilled arts Nabu is "the scribe of the deities" (*tupšar ilāni*) (S4E2:3), and the weather god Adad is referred to as "the lord of abundance" (*bēl ḫegalli*) (e.g. AE47:4, SE14:7). All these divine epithets refer to the deities having a transcendent, cosmic-mythological dominion. Also the iconography refers to this type of dominion which is especially associated with the abstract and aloof heaven god Anu (Schneider 2011: 76–77). The god Ninurta was not just regarded as a warrior god but also as a god of agriculture, and the bird heads, giving his sacred symbol (Mallowan and Davies 1970: 16), which decorate the sickle and sceptre of Ashurnasirpal II probably allude to this particular deity and his cosmic office or domain (AI25, AI12 resp.).

Also the idea of the deities as supreme – in spirit, form, and skills – tells of this indirect authority. As for spirit, the majestic status of the deities is conveyed e.g. by the very common epithets "great lord" (*bēlu rabû*) and "great mistress" (*bēltu rabītu*).[78] Expressing their elevated and sublime statuses are the epithets which refer to deities as "exalted" (*ṣīru*) and "elevated" (*šaqû*),[79]

78 Attested for Adad (e.g. AE49:6′, SE12:8), Ashur (e.g. AE50:46, SE1:11), Enlil (e.g. AE98:2), Mamu (AE50:32), Marduk (e.g. SE5:v4), Nabu (An3E26:8), Nergal (SA5E12:3), Ninurta (e.g. AE1:i9, SE19:6obv.), Shulmanu (e.g. An3E42:2′), Sibitti (SE95:4), and Sin (An5E2:iv4)/Ishtar (AE56:19, SE38:1) and Sharrat-niphi (SE49:2, e.g. AE28:i1). Unsurprisingly, especially the main Assyrian god Ashur is referred to by this epithet.

79 Attested for Adad (e.g. AE17:i6), Anu (SE10:i1), Enlil (e.g. AE17:i8, SE6:i2), and Ninurta (SE19:2obv., e.g. AE1:i1)/Adad (SE12:1), Ishtar (SE17:2), Nabu (An3E26:1), Ninurta (SE5:v5), Shamash (SE6:i5), and Sin (e.g. AE17:i4–5, SE6:i4).

"foremost" (*ašarēdu*) and "unique" (*ēdiššû*),[80] "perfect" (*gitmālu*), "splendid" (*šarḫu*/*šitarḫu*/*šurruḫu*), and "famous" (*šūpû*),[81] "pre-eminent" (*etellu*), "capable" (*lē'û*), and "powerful" (*mugdašru*),[82] "all-powerful" (*dandannu*), "majestic" (*šagapīru*), and "all-mighty" (*kaškaššu*),[83] "greatest" (*šurbû*) and "supreme" (*šūturtu*).[84] These divine epithets express an idea of the deities being above everyone and everything. This kind of exaltation of the divine beings and their sublimity was a standard feature of religion in Mesopotamia (Bottéro 2001a: 58–61). In short, the deities belonged to another sphere. As noted by Bottéro (2001a: 61) and Schneider (2011), the hierarchy and separation of the deities in relation to humankind functioned as an important component of religious beliefs in Mesopotamia.

As for supremacy and form, the state of being "luminary" (*namrīru*) is associated with Ninurta, Adad, Ishtar-kakkabi, and above all Sin (SA5E1:i13, An3E6:3, S4E2:4, e.g. AE17:i4–5 resp.), and it refers to a heavenly radiance which these deities possess (Oppenheim 1943; Cassin 1968, CAD N I: *namrirrū*). The goddess Sharrat-niphi is also elevated by her looks, such as in the epithets of "shining appearance" (*zīmu namru*) (AE28:i2) and "she whose form is outstanding among the goddesses" (*ina ilāti šūturat nabnīssa*) (AE28:i2). This is also true of Ninurta whose limbs are described as "luxuriant" (*šummuḫu*) (e.g. SA5E1:i21), probably in the sense of being fit for battle. In iconography, the anthropomorphic deities can be depicted elevated by their standing on their sacred animals (e.g. An3I12), the divine emblems which hover in mid-air also express their elevation and different forms (e.g. AI20, SI13), and the same is the case of the wearing of horns by e.g. genii and colossi (e.g. AI4, AI8 resp.). As for the lastly mentioned form, Sin is "bearer of exalted horns" (*nāši qarnī ṣīrūti*) (S4E2:6). Form and (elevation) are also told of in Enlil's epithet "great mountain" (*šadû rabû*) (An3E44:5obv.), this god taking the shape of a mountain.

80 Attested for Adad (An3E6:2–3), Ishtar (e.g. AE17:i10, SE10:i5), Nergal (SA5E12:1), Ninlil (An3E34:13), Ninurta (e.g. AE1:i1, SE10:i4), and Shulmanu (SE:RN, S4E:RN)/Adad (An3E7:1). The former epithet is a part of the RN of Shalmaneser (*Šulmānu-ašarēd*).

81 Attested for Adad (SE131:1), Enlil (SE10:i2), Ishtar (AE28:i6), Nergal (e.g. AE17:i8, SE11:3′ obv.), Ninurta (SE19:3obv., e.g. AE1:i6), and Sibitti (SE95:1)/Nabu (An3E26:1) and Ninurta (AE169:3, SE19:3obv.)/Ninurta (e.g. SA5E1:i8).

82 Attested for Adad (An3E7:1), Ninurta (e.g. SA5E1:i23), and Sin (e.g. SE2:i2)/Ninurta (e.g. AE1:i2) and Sharrat-niphi (AE28:i3)/Adad (An3E7:1).

83 Attested for Nergal (e.g. SE14:10) and Ninurta (e.g. AE1:i1, SE6:i6)/Ninurta (e.g. SA5E1:i2)/ Adad (SE12:2, e.g. AE152:4), Nabu (An3E26:2), and Ninurta (e.g. SA5E1:i23).

84 These epithets in superlative form (von Soden 1995: 112) are attested for Adad (An3E7:1), Enlil (SE10:i2), Ninurta (AE167:1), and Sharrat-niphi (AE28:i3)/Ishtar (AE28:i6).

Another way of expressing the greatness and elevation of the deities was to describe their skills, being omnipotent and omniscient. As for the former attribute, "the great gods" are described as "the ones who decree destinies" (*mušimmū šīmāti*) (AE47:6, e.g. SE6:i8). Similarly, Nabu is "he who has acquired the tablet of destinies [of the deities]" (*āḫiz ṭuppi šīmāt* [*ilāni*]) (An3E34:6). The vital act of determining destinies, thus creating Order, was a prerogative of the deities (Bottéro 2001a: 92–94). The blessings and curses that often end Assyrian royal inscriptions refer to a role of the Mesopotamian deities as rewarding or punishing those who will deal with the inscribed artefact or monument (e.g. AE50:34–49, SE10:1l.e.). Also in these literary components, the theme of the omnipotent gods and goddesses comes across. The attribute of divine omnipresence is implicitly expressed here.

The quality of omniscience was similarly regarded as ultimately being a divine attribute. As shown by Pongratz-Leisten (1999) in her study on the theme of the wise Mesopotamian king, knowledge was considered having a divine origin. In the primary sources, Ea (SE2:i2) and Sin (e.g. AE8, SE15:6) are both referred to as "wise" (*eršu*), and the former god is also "lord of wisdom and intelligence" (*bēl nēmeqi ḫasīsi*) (e.g. AE17:i4, SE6:i3), while Marduk, Ninurta, and Ea are regarded as "the sage of the deities" (*apkal ilāni*) (e.g. AE17:i5, SE10:i8, e.g. AE1:i5 resp.), and Nusku is described as "the circumspect god" (*ilu multālu*) (e.g. AE17:i7, SE14:12). Furthermore, Ninurta is seen as "he who understands skills" (*karaš niklāti*) (e.g. SA5E2) and "he who is very wide of mind" (*ṣurru šumdulu*) (e.g. SA5E1:i22), Ea is described as "he who knows everything" (*mūdê mimma šumšu*) (SA5E15:7), and Nabu is portrayed as "he who has learned the scribal art" (*āḫizu šukāmi*), "sage in the skills" (*apkal niklāti*), "wise one" (*igigallu*), as well as "wide of understanding" (*rapšā uznī*) (An3E26:1–4).

The numinous character of the Mesopotamian deities in their belonging to another, more sublime reality could both be transcendent and immanent (Jacobsen 1976: 3). According to Jacobsen (1976: 5–6), the aspect of immanence characterized religious thought in Mesopotamia. In other words, the borders between the three dimensions of divinity, i.e. the cosmological, mythological, and political, were systematically crossed in Mesopotamia (Frahm 2013: 97–99). The relationship between the deities and the foreign lands was perceived of as *direct* by regarding the deities also as the owners and masters of the earth and as the lords of mankind, thus possessing more of an immanent, worldly-earthly dominion as well. The Mesopotamian deities were here believed to govern the whole world (Bottéro 2001a: 90–95). The metaphor of the deities as "rulers" arguably developed in the third millennium BCE, and it carried with it a notion of picturing the cosmos as a polity which was governed by the deities (Jacobsen 1976: 75–91). As for Assyria specifically, it was the Middle

Assyrian Period that introduced a theologization of the cult of Ashur which promoted the notion of the god Ashur as world ruler (von Soden 1963: 135; Chamaza 2002: 123–27).

As for the nature of this idea of inclusion, Bottéro (2001a: 96) identifies a universalist approach and argues that religion in Mesopotamia/Assyria was non-excluding in character and that the power of the deities was seen as universal. This religious universalism was, however, not zealously imposed. The frequent conflicts between Mesopotamia/Assyria and its neighbours had to do with conflicting interests such as the right to resources rather than with any cultural or religious issues. Thus, the ethnocentrism which inevitably accompanies the imposing of one society's cultural-religious ideals upon those of another was not of a xenophobic character. This kind of inclusive religious imperialism can be contrasted e.g. with the one in Egypt which rather focused on exclusion (Kuhrt 1997).[85] Anyway, the great gods of Mesopotamia/Assyria were thought of as deities also over the foreign lands.

This widespread authority and inclusive attitude is told of in the divine epithets. Anu (e.g. [AE20:2], SE2:i1), Ashur (e.g. AE40:9, [SE17:1]), and Enlil (An3E34:3) are described as "lord of all lands" (*bēl mātāti*), Shamash and Adad are "lord of all" (*bēl gimrī*) (SE6:i5, SE12:1 resp.),[86] and Marduk is "king of all" (*šar gimrī*) (SE5:v6). Shamash (e.g. AE17:i9, SE14:8) and, less commonly, Ninurta (e.g. SA5E1:i4) and Marduk (e.g. An3E34:5) are each "commander of all" (*muma"er gimrī*), while Enlil (e.g. AE17:i9, SE14:4–5) and Ea (SE2:i2*) both are referred to as "creator of all" (*bānû kullati*). Shamash is also "the light of all lands" (*nūr mātāti*) (S4E2:5).

Moving on, Ninurta is called "foremost in the quarters" (*ašarēd kibrāti*) and "the one who, like Shamash, oversee the quarters" (*ša kīma Šamši ibarrū kibrāti*) (e.g. AE1:i4, SA5E1:i11–12 resp.), while Ishtar is a goddess "whose name is called in the corners of all lands" (*ina kibrāt mātāti kalîšina nabû šumša*) (AE28:i6–7). Furthermore, Ashur is "the one who made my (the king's) kingship surpass the kings of the four quarters" (*mušarbû šarrūtija eli šarrāni ša kibrāt erbetti*) (e.g. AE1:i41), thereby indirectly alluding to his world dominion. In the Mesopotamian world view, the world was made up of four "quarters" (*kibrātu*). The attestations of these divine epithets in the context of royal imperialism make it unlikely that it is the mythical dimension of *mātāti* or *kibrātu* which is referred to here (see s. 3.2).

85 In order to realize the typically *Assyrian* features of the propaganda, comparative references to other regions and countries, notably Egypt, are made throughout this study.

86 The word *gimru* can refer to animate beings in a sense of totality. The plural form also carries the meaning of "the whole world" (AHw I/G: *gimrum*, CAD G: *gimru*).

The foreign lands and people are not just portrayed as *passive* subjects, but also as active ones, in this power relationship which were based on the notion that the Mesopotamian gods and goddesses were governing the whole of humanity, including foreigners, in a universalistic approach and ambition (Bottéro 2001a: 96–97, 103–105). In this relationship, the foreign people – just like people in Mesopotamia – were regarded as the servants of the deities, created to relieve the lower gods of their labour duties and menial tasks (Schneider 2011: 41–44). In line with this world view, the correct state of things was when the foreign lands were submissive and payed tribute to the Mesopotamian deities. Reliefs showing tribute delivering in the temples of Anu-Adad in Assur and in that of Mamu in Balawat allude to the fulfilment of these obligations towards the Mesopotamian deities (SI9, AI14 resp.).

The incorrect state of things was when the foreign lands were "unsubmissive" ([*lā kanšūte*]) or "insubordinate" (*lā māgirūte*) (e.g. [SE41:1], SE1:13 resp.) to Ashur and when they "withheld the tribute and tax of Ashur" (*bilta u maddattu ša Aššur iklû*) (e.g. SE20:8–9). These acts and attitudes were likened to sins and crimes (see subss. 5.4.2–3), and connect to the concepts of alterity and "the Other" (see subs. 5.4.8).[87] The kings repeatedly claim that they bring tribute or booty and captives back to Assyria, e.g. to the temples (e.g. AE1:iii45–46, SE1:38–40). The latter statement, focusing on booty and captives, of course speaks of the realization of the obligation by force. The idiomatic statement "I carried away his/their plunder" (*šallassu/sunu ašlula*) is ever present in the sources (e.g. AE1:ii58–59, SE6:iii49). Shalmaneser III explicitly states that he presented booty to Adad and Ishtar after returning home from some military campaigns (SE12:36, SE17:62 resp.).

The hierarchical and binding relationship between the Mesopotamian deities and the foreign lands was expressed e.g. in loyalty oaths where all deities mentioned in the oath document are called upon to protect and supervise the keeping of the agreement (AE175:9′). Although being attested from the Sargonid period, it is relevant to note here that vassal treaties of Esarhaddon are even marked with the seal of the god Ashur (see Collon 1987: figs. 559–61). The seals of Ashur and Ninurta are said to have been impressed on decrees issued by Adad-narari III (e.g. An3E45:1), thereby legitimizing the grants in question. More importantly, Mesopotamian deities are described as protecting overseas borders established by Adad-narari III in co-operation with Shamshi-ilu and Sammuramat (An3E2:4–6, An3E3:1–7 resp.).

87 This "Other" has in its associations with *mātāti* been regarded as gendered female in the context of understanding the imperialistic warfare of Assyrian kings (M. Marcus 1995b).

The Mesopotamian deities are occasionally described as having direct *functions* in relation to the foreign lands and people. Ashur e.g. acts as "the shepherd of all rulers" (*rē'û ša kal malikī*) (SE17:1), while Shamash is "the one who guides aright humankind" (*muštēšir tenēšēte*) (e.g. SE2:i3) as well as "the judge of the (four) quarters" (*dajjān kibrāti*) (e.g. AE1:i44, SE2:i3). The latter god is also "[he who secures justice for all living beings] ([*muštēšir šiknat napištim*]) and "judge of all cities" (*dajjān kiššat ālāni*) ([SA5E15:8–9], S4E2:5 resp.). The sun god Shamash was integrated into Assyrian royal ideology at the end of the Middle Assyrian Period, e.g. with an idea of his universal jurisdiction (von Soden 1963: 136). Possibly alluding to the same jurisdictional and earthly context, the great gods are "those who finalize decisions" (*gāmerūt purussê*) (e.g. An2E2:5, TN2E1:14).

As for further direct functions, Adad, whose cult was widespread in the west, is frequently described as contributing to the prosperity of the foreign lands. In this capacity he is referred to as "the one who makes the (four) quarters flourish" (*muṭaḫḫidu° kibrāti*), "the canal inspector of water courses" (*gugal nārāti*), and "the one who provides pasturage and watering for the people of all cities" (*nādin rîti u mašqīte ana nišē kal ālāni*) (AE148:6, AE148:5, AE148:2–3 resp.). As for the lastly mentioned epithet, Ninurta is similarly referred to as "the one who gives sceptre (and powers of) decisions to the totality of cities" (*nādin ḫaṭṭi u purussê ana napḫar kal ālāni*) (e.g. AE1:i4). In the same vein, Nabu is described as "he who has with him (the power to) depopulate and repopulate" (*ša šuddû šušubbu bašû ittišu*) (An3E26:5), while Marduk is praised as "the one who colonizes cities" (*mušēšib ālāni*) (S4E2:2). Once again, the clear context of worldly, royal imperialism makes the interpretations of references to mythical regions or Assyria proper unlikely. In any case, the notion of divine authority over the whole world and humankind is expressed in the written sources.

As for the direct, immanent, and divine function of bringing prosperity to earth, the sacred tree scene of the North-West Palace has by many scholars been understood as representing the artificial pollination of a date palm, and thus symbolizing the notions of fertility and prosperity (e.g. AI4:B21). The genii here hold a male date cluster whose seeds, with the aid of the water in the buckets, are sprinkled over the female plants of the tree, fertilizing these. The winged disk which hovers over the tree ensures the action, and the king's presence displays his commitment to this particular expression of the divine order (e.g. Winter 1983; Porter 2003).[88] The genii's position *behind* the king may be

88 The Assyrian sacred tree has also been understood as an icon of the cult (Albenda 1994; Giovino 2007), as a mystical illustration of Assyrian monotheism (Parpola 1993), and as an apotropaic symbol (Parker-Mallowan 1983; Russell 1998b). The theory of monotheism has been a result of "honorary transposition", reflecting the main role of the king in the scene rather than him being "pollinated". Porter (2003: 18–19) has convincingly shown that this interpretation of the scene fits well with actual pollination techniques, and the "cone" in the hands of the genii looks very similar to actual date palm clusters. The interpretation of pollination is strenghtened further by the image of the king as shepherd, holding a long staff, on either side of the sacred tree (AI4:B12, AI4:B14). This shepherding motif links the scene with fertility and prosperity even closer. In other rooms of the palace, especially in F, I, and L, human or bird-headed genii pollinate the sacred tree without the winged disk or the king being present (e.g. AI4:L10). The sacred tree scene is also attested in the minor art (see s. 4.2).

Summing up, I have argued that the great gods are imagined as the owners and masters over the whole world both from a sphere separated from mankind (transcendence) and from a position in which the borders between the divine and human spheres are crossed and integrated (immanence). Their control over the universe implies a cosmic-mythological dominion, while their control over the world expresses a worldy-earthly dominion.

3.2 Conquerors of the foreign lands

In this following section, a highlighted feature of the immanent dominion of the Mesopotamian deities will be identified and discussed. I will here argue that the great gods of Mesopotamia commonly are portrayed as directly engaged in imperialistic wars against unsubmissive foreign lands and people.

The deities are described as direct conquerors of the foreign lands in Assyrian royal inscriptions. Picking up on this, Weinfeld (1983) concludes that divine intervention was not only an idea of the Hebrews but a general idea of the Ancient Near East including Assyria. Similarly, Albrektsson (1967) notes that the idea that deities were in charge both of forces of nature and of historical developments (e.g. through warfare) was a general feature of the religious belief systems of the Ancient Near East. Weippert (1972: 476–84), studying the Assyrian sources, uses the term "holy war" in the sense that the deities, through e.g. omens, are the ones who decide about wars, they are present on

effectively confronted by Cooper (2000). An alternative term to polytheism has been brought up by Bottéro (2001a) who uses the term henotheism. More recently, Scurlock (2013: 173) means that the tree scene of SI18 is "a direct reference to Ishtar as a tree flanked by Dumuzi's goat", and Ataç (2013: 403–11), focusing on trees, genii, cones, and date palms, claims that the sacred tree was an embodiment of Abzu and the antediluvian cosmos.

military campaigns through divine standards, and they are regarded as the actual warriors in the primary sources. The earthly war was consequently given a theological meaning with the implication that the deities lead the army, the troops belong to them, and the army's enemies are their enemies. Assyrian royal inscriptions show that the Assyrian kings credit the support of their deities as the cause of their own victories. In other words, it was in reality the Assyrian deities who fought (Weeks 1983).

In some cases it seems plausible to presume that the deities' enemy in question embodies the mythical land which Mesopotamian gods fight against in various myths such as Angim, Lugal-e, the Anzu Myth (all Ninurta), the Gilgamesh Epic, and the Enuma Elish (Marduk).[89] In the first three myths Ninurta combats the demonic creatures of Asag and Anzu. Reliefs on the Ninurta temple of Kalhu seem to show the god in question engaged in a fight against a mythical creature, probably Asag (AI2). The horned god here fights with a pair of thunderbolts in his hands, making an identification with Adad equally possible. According to Meuszyński (1972), also "fish men" and the chaotic, primeval creature of Tiamat are fought against in these scenes. A seal from the 9th century BCE displays the same hybrid creature (Asag) being shot at with arrows directed by a god – probably Ninurta – who stands on his sacred animal while operating his bow (see Collon 1987: fig. 783). Mesopotamian seals often depict scenes of battle and contest from myths, epics, and legends (Collon 1987: 75). The scene on the one side of the Terqa Stele which depicts a god striking a seized snake with an axe is another example of the theme of battle in another, mythological sphere (TN2I1).

As will be shown in section 5.2, lions are in part associated with foreign lands and with forces of Chaos. In the Central Building of Ashurnasirpal II two types of genii are positioned between lions who stand on their hindlegs (AI3). Although the reliefs are broken, acts of taming or stabbing on the part of the genii may be posited. In reverse, the two lionesses outside the Sharrat-niphi temple of Kalhu (AI11) should be understood as fighting *against* Chaos in light of their functions of guarding the building from demons and malevolent spirits (Madhloom 1970: 100–101). Similarly, the names of the gateway lions which Shamshi-ilu commissioned and placed in Til-Barsip speak of a conquering and pacifying function (An3E34:19–24). The war goddess Ishtar is often illustrated on images holding bow and arrows, while standing on her sacred animal the lion (see e.g. Collon 1987: fig. 773).[90]

---

89 It may also be noted that the word in question ('kur') can, in addition to "(mythical enemy) land", also refer to the underworld (kur nu-gi-a/*māt lā târi*) (CAD M I: *mātu*).

90 Not only deities but also Assyrian kings are portrayed as lions or defeating lions in their and the deities' common ambition of conquering the wild and chaotic foreign lands (see s. 5.2).

Also the epigraphic evidence may sometimes allude to the mythical 'kur', e.g. when the god Enlil and the goddess Sharrat-niphi are called "he/she who shakes the highlands" (*munarriṭ/at ḫuršāni*) (AE98:1–2, AE28:i4 resp.). The word *ḫuršānu* may also carry mythical connotations, referring to hostile, enemy regions (AHw I/Ḫ: *ḫuršānu*, CAD Ḫ: *ḫuršānu* A). In the vast majority of cases however, the context of royal imperialism establishes an interpretation of worldly lands as the targets of the divine warfare in question.

Divine epithets refer to the deities as direct agents and warriors. These deities are mainly Adad, Ishtar, Nergal, Ninurta, the Sibitti, and Zababa, all largely defined by their violent natures (see apps. 5–7).[91] Ishtar is repeatedly described as "the mistress of battle and combat" (*bēlat qabli u tāḫāzi*) (e.g. AE29:25′, SE2:i3). She was regarded as a female deity who had crossed the border into a male sphere marked by violence, thus only seemingly diverging from the prevalent idea in Mesopotamia/Assyria of warfare as a domain of masculinity (Bahrani 2001: 146–50). Moving on, Ninurta is e.g. called "lord of battle and combat" (*bēl qabli u tāḫāzi*) (SE10:i4), "he who concentrates on battles" (*ḫāmim tuqmāte*) (e.g. AE1:i2), and "splendid and perfect warrior" (*qarrādu šarḫu gitmālu*) (SE19:3obv.). The lastly mentioned epithet is also used for Adad (An3E6:1–2). Nergal, as well as Ninurta, is "king of battle" (*šar tamḫāri*) (e.g. AE1:i6, SE11:3′obv. resp.), Zababa seems to be called "[great warrior]" ([*qarrādu rabû*]) ([SA5E15:16]), and the Sibitti are "perfect heroes" (*ālilū gitmālūtu*) (SE95:1), or simply engaged in "warriorhood" (*qardūtu*) (An5E2:vi20). The great gods in unison are "those whose attack implies battle and combat" (*ša tību-šunu tuqumtu šašmu*) (e.g. TN2E1:15).

The stating of the violent roles and attributes of the Mesopotamian deities is sometimes accompanied by mentioning, in general terms, their opponents. The names of some city gates in Assur, which are enumerated in one of Shalmaneser III's texts, convey the idea of divine warfare directed at certain opponents, i.e. "Ashur (is) the one who makes the obstinate submit" (*Aššur mukanniš šapṣūte*) (SE25:44),[92] and "Shamash (is) the slayer of the rebellious" (*Šamaš nēr multarḫi*) (SE25:45).[93] The opponents of the deities are also expressed in the Sibitti epithet of "they who cause enemies to fall" (*mušamqitū zajjāri*) (SE95:3), and in the Ninurta epithets of "destroyer of the evil ones" (*mu'abbit*

91 Also deities not profiled as warriors are described as such in the sources. Sin is violent in the epithet "[he whose] punishing role is made apparent for the deities" ([*ša*] *šēressu ina ilāni šūpât*) (SA5E15:10), and Nabu is spoken of as "martial" (*dāpinu*) (An3E26:1).

92 The word *šapṣu* alludes to the notion of the enemy as unsubmissive (CAD Š I: *šapṣu*).

93 Tellingly, the word *multarḫu* can also mean "arrogant" (CAD M II: *muštarḫu*), expressing the idea that the opponents of the Assyrian deities lack humility and piety (see subs. 5.4.8).

lemnūte) (e.g. AE1:i8), "destroyer of enemies" (*muḫalliq zā'irī*) (e.g. AE1:i8), "he who makes the insubordinate submit" (*mušakniš lā māgirī*) (e.g. AE1:i8), and "he who causes the evil ones/evildoer to fall" (*mušamqit lemnūte/targīgi*) (e.g. AE17:i6, AE1:i7 resp.). Adad is also "he who causes the evil ones to fall" (*mušamqit lemutti*) (An3E6:4), while Ishtar is "overthrower of the obdurate ones" (*sākipat ašṭūti*) (An3E34:7). All these epithets may simultaneously refer to divine warfare in transcendent (mythical) and immanent (worldly) spheres, but the overall context of royal imperialism arguably favours the latter interpretation.

The deities are sometimes explicitly described as conducting warfare upon the foreign lands, with or without their instrument the Assyrian king/army. In the textual narrative, the deities are e.g. told of as having destroyed the abodes of the kings of Hatti (SE17:9), while Nergal and the fire god Girru are portrayed as warriors in the earthly sphere in the same text (SE17:29). The idea of the deities owning weapons which they then, as in the just cited text, use themselves, or hand over to the Assyrian king (see s. 4.4) is an established theme (Bahrani 2008: 189–97). The deities are also invoked in royal prayers and curses to defeat his (the king's)/their enemies by violent means (e.g. AE26:69–72, SE12:35–36). Once again, the deities' enemies are connected to the notions of alterity and "the Other", in the sense of them setting themselves up against the divine Order (see subs. 5.4.8).

In epithets, Ashur and Shamash are "those who made all their (the enemy rulers') lands submit at his (the king's) feet" (*kullat mātātišunu ana šēpēšu ušeknišā*) and "the ones who cut down like marsh reeds difficult mountains and rulers hostile to him (the king)" (*šadâni šapṣūte u malkī nakrīšu kīma qān api uḫaṣṣiṣū*) (e.g. AE17:i18–19, AE1:i22–23 resp.), while Ashur and Ninurta are "the ones who made the difficult mountains and the rulers of all lands hostile to him (the king) submit at his feet" (*šadê šapṣūte u malkī nakrīšu kullat mātātišunu ana šēpēšu ušeknišā*) (e.g. AE1:iii128–29). The deities rather than the Assyrian king are pictured as the actual warriors also in the divine epithet describing Nergal "he who goes ahead of me" (*ālik pānija*) (AE154:14′), and in the epithet describing Ashur, Adad, Sin, Shamash, and Ishtar as "those who go in front of my troops" (*ālikūt maḫri ummānātija*) (AE19:4). Zababa and Palil are each "he who marches in the front" (*ālik maḫri*) (SA5E15:16, An5E2:vi19 resp.). Military units of the Assyrian army were actually referred to by the name of deities, i.e. Nergal, Adad, Ishtar, Sin, and Shamash (Larsen 1999: 153).[94] In line with the imperialistic ethos of the Neo-Assyrian state, the great gods were

94 This custom of naming army units after deities existed also in Egypt (Grimal 1994: 255), although the overall aims of their religious imperialism were different (Kuhrt 1997).

"those who have extended his (the king's) land" (*urappišū māssu*) (An3E6:9). All these attestations convey the idea of divine warfare in an immanent sphere.

The literary subgenres of letters to and from a god also highlight the deities as warriors and conquerors. In a letter from a god (SA5E4), probably Ashur, the 5th campaign of Shamshi-Adad V is referred to in terms of the god as the orchestrator of the events (Weidner 1933–34: 101–104). The god here says that the king wrote to him (in a letter to a god) about the king having defeated his enemies, but that this happened only because the god had decided so. Pongratz-Leisten (2013: 295–304) sees the presence of an actual, elaborate, and ceremonial dialogue between Ashur and the Assyrian king, consisting of seven steps in which reports, letters to a god, as well as letters from a god were main components. It is interesting to note that the relevant god explicitly stands behind massacres, plundering, enslaving, destruction of cities, cutting down of trees, and other such atrocities. Two fragmentary letters to a god have been preserved from this time period (An3E43, S4E3). In the one of Adad-narari III, a blood bath is told of for approval by the god. Clearly, Ashur and the other deities were perceived of as actual warriors.

The warring side of the deities is also expressed in the iconography. In the glazed brick panel of Fort Shalmaneser (SI18), the god in the winged disk, probably Ashur,[95] who is greeted and revered by the king is depicted wearing a dagger and possibly exuding a light or radiance of a sort (Reade 1963: 43–44). The "awe-inspiring radiance of Ashur" (*pulḫi melammē ša Aššur*) is often referred to in the context of pacifying or defeating unsubmissive enemies (e.g. AE17:iii20–21, SE2:i22–23). In the motif of the brick panel, goats encircle the sacred tree, and this animal may be associated with Ashur (Reade 2002: 175). Picking up on this identification, the presence of this god on military campaigns may be illustrated by the goats who adorn tents of the royal camp (AI4:B7t.). The winged disk of Ashur accompanies the Assyrian king in warfare, cult activities, army marches, and encountering scenes on the walls of the North-West Palace (AI4:B3t., AI4:B5t., AI4:B7b., AI4:B11t. resp.). The gesture of the king, e.g. using bow, is often mirrored by the gesture of the human-headed, horned figure in the winged disk (e.g. AI4:B11t.), in this manner expressing their common force and will.

95 The relative status of this god as the most important deity makes it quite likely that it is Ashur who is represented in the winged disk. For interpretations favouring Ashur, see e.g. Reade 1963, and Parpola 1993, and for interpretations favouring Shamash, i.e. the other major candidate, see e.g. Magen 1986, and Black and Green 1992. As noted by Black and Green (1992: 185–86), also Ninurta has been identified as the winged disk. Possibly, as pointed out by Reade (2002: 200), one identification does not have to exclude another.

Two types of birds, or one type of bird with two different functions, accompany the king in scenes of warfare in the reliefs of the said palace. The one kind of bird merely follows the king, flying over or resting on moving chariots (e.g. AI4:B8t.), while the other kind of bird does in fact attack enemy soldiers (e.g. AI4:B11t.). These birds may possibly represent Ninurta and/or the Anzu bird. As already noted, the warrior god Ninurta had a bird as his sacred animal, and the ferocious Anzu bird, the arch-enemy of Ninurta, is paradoxically equated with (in simile form) the Assyrian army by Ashurnasirpal II and Shalmaneser III (AE1:ii107, SE5:iii5). Additionally, the former ruler likens himself to a bird (*iṣṣūru*) in a textual passage which centres on royal warfare (AE1:ii36). The birds in question can of course simply be interpreted as birds of prey waiting to dig in on the corpses of the battlefield (Collon 1995: 136), but in light of the above argumentation and the parallelism of position and function to the winged disk of Ashur the understanding of these birds as mythological figures seems more plausible.

Two chariots containing two different "divine standards" (*urigallu*), one in each, accompany the royal chariot in the iconography of Ashurnasirpal II and Shalmaneser III (e.g. AI14:57–58, SI10:4), and they are occasionally depicted as employed in battle (e.g. AI4:B10–11t., SI10:9t.). These standards probably represent the gods Adad and Nergal (Deller 1992: 292–93). As will be argued in section 5.3, and as noted by Holloway (2001), this phenomenon of divine standards does not however justify anachronistic identifications of the Assyrian wars as ancient versions of the Crusades. Although from the Late Neo-Assyrian Period, it is relevant to mention that priests are seen offering to these chariots in the reliefs of Sennacherib (see Barnett et al. 1998: pls. 142, 346–47), telling of the sacred status of these warfare instruments.

Concluding this discussion on iconography and the warring deities, the much noted scene from the camp of Ashurnasirpal II where a man with a cone-shaped hat seemingly slaughters an animal may illustrate the high art of divination, i.e. extispicy, carried out by a priest (AI4:B7t.).[96] The will and plans of the deities were believed to be revealed in the entrails of the sacrified animal (Bottéro 2001a: 176–81). The state archival material clearly shows that it was customary for the Neo-Assyrian kings to consult the deities, notably the gods Shamash and Adad, by means of divination before embarking on a military campaign (Starr 1990; Hunger 1992). A solar eclipse, referred to in the Eponym Chronicle for year 763 BCE (see Millard 1994), was especially discouraging in

96 Another possibility, proposed by Reade (2005), is that the slaughtering may illustrate the preparations for a cultic meal. In any case, a secular setting seems quite unlikely.

this context. By signalling their consent to the king's war plans the deities became the official war initiators.

The deities and their warfare are described as "furious and merciless" (*ezzu lā pādû*) (e.g. AE1:i7), and "fierce" (*ekdu*, *mamlu*) as for Ninurta (e.g. AE1:i4, SA5E1:i5 resp.), and as "strong" (*gešru*/*gešertu*) regarding Adad, Ninurta, Sharrat-niphi, and "the great gods" (e.g. AE17:i6, SE6:i6, AE28:i1, S4E2:10 resp.). In two other epithets, Adad and Nabu are praised for their "strength" (*kubukku*, *dannūtu*) (An3E6:2, An3E26:6 resp.), and Ashur is described as "strong" (*dān*) in the royal name of Ashur-dan. The divine, supernatural force of warfare is even likened to a flood, alluding to the Deluge which divided Mesopotamian history into before and after the Flood, in the epithets of "he whose attack is a flood" (*ša tību̇šu abūbu*), "he who flattens the enemy land" (*sāpin māt nakri*),[97] and "he who rides the flood" (*rākib abūbi*), all three referring to Ninurta (e.g. AE1:i7, AE1:i7, SA5E2 resp.). Adad is "the flooder" (*ša rāḫiṣi*) (SE5:iii3, e.g. AE1:iii120), "the thunderer" (*šāgimi*) (SA5E1:iii69), and "he who rides the great storms" (*rākib meḫāni rabûti*) (An3E6:3–4). Ninurta is in his warfare enthusiasm called "the one who rejoices in battles" (*ša tuqmātū ittallu*) (e.g. AE1:i6). Similarly, Ishtar is called "she whose game is battle" (*ša mēlultaša tuqumtu*) and "she who perfects the rite(s) of warriorhood" (*ša paraṣ qardūte šuklulat*) (e.g. SE2:i3, SE14:13 resp.).[98] These divine epithets all serve to stress the idea of the fierce and inspired nature of the warfare of the Mesopotamian deities.

However, in contrast to these grim descriptions, warrior deities like Adad, Ninurta, and Ishtar, but also (although less sursprisingly) Nabu are in addition portrayed as possessing and showing "mercy" (*rēmu*) (AE148:6, AE28:i7, e.g. AE1:i9, An3E26:4 resp.). Moreover, Inanna and Nabu display "overlooking" (*saḫrītu*) or "relenting" (*tajjāru*), arguably of sins (S4E2:7, An3E26:7 resp.), while Sharrat-niphi and Ishtar are said to be sympathetic and benevolent to those who are submissive and worshipping (AE28:i5–6, S4E2:7 resp.). The mechanisms of this reciprocal idea of "good in response to good" and "evil in response to evil" will be discussed further in subsection 5.4.2. Earlier on, in section 4.4, it will be demonstrated that the Assyrian king is described in much the same way as the deities in the narrations of warfare, borrowing many of their potent attributes and qualities.

Summing up, I have argued that the great gods of Mesopotamia commonly are portrayed as directly engaged in imperialistic wars against unsubmissive

---

97 The verb *sapānu* is associated with the act of flooding (CAD S: *sapānu*), in this way associated with the historical watershed which the Deluge was believed to be.

98 Notably, both the words *mēlultu* and *parṣu* refer to cultic activities (CAD M II: *mēlultu*, CAD P: *parṣu*). War is then ritualized and given a religious meaning.

foreign lands and people. Attested both in texts (e.g. through letters from a god) and images (e.g. through the winged disk), this theme and motif then tell of the immanent dominion of the Mesopotamian deites.

3.3 Summary

The relationship between the Mesopotamian deities (i.e. the great gods) and the foreign lands is mostly indirectly expressed. Normally the Assyrian king acts as the link between the other two units of analysis in question. The great gods are of another nature, live in another sphere, having created mankind and the world, the foreign lands and peoples included. They are described as in charge of the universe with its dual components of heaven and underworld, having various cosmic offices related to their respective profiles. The deities here enjoy a cosmic-mythological type of dominion. Separated from the human world, they have a transcendent existence and kind of authority.

A direct relationship is pictured when the great gods are presented as having universal and earthly-worldly dominion, and in the theme of divine intervention through warfare, in this way assuring the Assyrian king's conquering of the foreign lands. As for the former direct contact, the foreign lands are e.g. described as generally owing tribute and submission to Ashur and the great gods, sometimes in an oath binding, treaty-based relationship. At other times, Shamash and several other deities are described as having direct authority and jurisdiction over the world, i.e. the four quarters.

As for the latter direct contact, winged disks who probably represent Ashur, divine birds who probably represent Ninurta and/or the Anzu bird, and divine chariots which contain standards representing Adad and Nergal are depicted as taking part in battle on the Assyrian king's side. The literary theme of divine warfare, expressed both in epithets and narrative passages, is common. The phenomenon of omens consulted before embarking on a military campaign, the naming of army units after deities, and the military orchestrating role of Ashur in the subgenre of letter from a god further emphasize the warring function of the deities. Being part of the human world, the great gods have an immanent existence and kind of authority.

4 The relationship between the great gods and the king of Assyria

In this chapter, the nature of the relationship between the Mesopotamian deities and the Assyrian king is identified and discussed. The bonds between these two units of analysis are much highlighted in the primary sources. In this context, the kings of the Early Neo-Assyrian Period each claim to be the representative, priest, servant, builder, and warrior of the great gods.

4.1 Representative of the great gods

As concluded in the previous chapter, the direct contact between the great gods and foreign lands is restricted to vaguely defined authority and divine warfare. Adding another agent to the equation, I will now argue that the Assyrian king functioned as a link between the other two agents. In this mediating position, the Assyrian king presents himself as the deities' (human) representative on earth, supported and protected by them.

The relationship between the king and the deities is much referred to in the sources of Assyrian kings, including those of the Early Neo-Assyrian Period (see e.g. apps. 8–12). This observation is commonly made in scholarly literature. Assyrian royal inscriptions describe a close connection between palace and temple, ruler and deities (Renger 1997: 172), the Mesopotamian kings consistently justified their authority through references to the divine sphere (Liverani 1995: 2360–61), and the topic of the king and the deities is an important element of Mesopotamian royal titles and epithets (Seux 1967: 18–27). Common to all these conclusions is the identifying of the Assyrian king as the deities' representative on earth. Speaking from a broader geographic horizon, the idea of kingship as divine rule, with the actual king as mere representative and instrument of the deities, was a general feature of the state ideologies in the Ancient Near East (Albrektsson 1967: 45–50).

The idea of the king as the link between deities and humans is e.g. expressed by the traditional title "vice-regent of Ashur" (*iššak Aššur*) (e.g. AE2:1, SE1:1), which is attested as often as 80 times[99] and heads a common epithet cluster which e.g. is part of the Standard Inscription (AE23:1). This frequent and prominent title refers to the king's traditional bond to the main god of

99 As a rule of thumb in this study, mentioning of the frequency of individual royal/divine epithets or of royal visual representations refers to the statistics given in appendices 5–16.

Assyria (Seux 1965a: 106–109). The title is claimed right from the start of Assyrian history (Larsen 1976: 149), expressing a deviation from the southern notion of kingship (Garelli 1981: 2–3). Ashurnasirpal II also twice refers to himself as "the vice-regent of Ashur and Ninurta" (*iššak Aššur u Ninurta*) (e.g. AE17:i37). This honorary inclusion of the latter god may be a reflection of this king's commitment to Kalhu, which was made into a main cult centre of this deity. Using an adjective instead of the divine name of Ashur, Adad-narari III was "exalted vice-regent" (*iššakku ṣīru*) (An3E6:7), while Shalmaneser III was "the prudent" (*pitqudu*) and "splendid (*šurruḫu*) vice-regent of Ashur" (SE2:i6*, e.g. SE57:3 resp.).

As the *iššakku* of Ashur the king was in a sense just "the ruler over a single city or city state under the sovereignty of a god" (Frankfort 1948: 227). Similarly, Seux (1965a: 109) argues that this title reflects the dual idea of subordination under a deity and authority over a city or land. The king was a mediator between two worlds (Maul 1999: 207),[100] an individual who united secular and spiritual power,[101] and as *iššakku* and "priest" (*šangû*) he was the "interlocutor" between humans and deities, and a "priest-king" who took care of the real king's, i.e. Ashur's, property (Novák 2002: 445 n. 15). In line with this idea of property management, the originally Sumerian title 'ensi' (*iššakku* in Akkadian) referred to a city or city state ruler, and alluded to responsibilities in the agricultural domain (Frankfort 1948: 227, CAD I–J: *iššakku*). The use by the Assyrian rulers of this title is part of a broader usage of it in Mesopotamia and beyond (Hallo 1957; Seux 1967: 110–16, 399).

Telling of the above Ashur emphasis, this god always heads the enumerations of deities in the texts of the kings of the period, at least whenever he is listed (see app. 4). The special role of Ashur is also seen in the circumstance that the epithet "my/his lord" (*bēlī/šu*) is mostly used in describing Ashur in the texts of the Early Neo-Assyrian rulers (e.g. AE1:i12, SE1:27, see apps. 5–7). Ashur is also referred to as "my god" (*ilī*) (e.g. An3E5:7, S4E1:20). The close and intimate relationship between Ashur and the Assyrian king may be expressed in an inscription where the former is addressed in the 2nd person singular (AE154:3). Ashur was quite naturally "the one who gives kingship" (*nādin šarrūti*) (An5E2:v5), and the likely recipient and sender of letter to and from a god (Pongratz-Leisten 2013). The Assyrian king in his turn was "he [whom] Ashur

100 However, this is a one-sided image of the royal propaganda. A direct link between deities and individuals is attested e.g. in seals of Neo-Assyrian officials, showing the seal owner independently addressing deities and sacred trees (see e.g. Collon 1987: figs. 773, 812, 866).

101 Telling of a fusion between sacred and secular aspects, the words for vice-regent and priest are frequently written with the same cuneiform sign (MZL: šid/sign 485/page 340).

greatly established [for the kingship] of Assyria" ([*ša ... ana šarrūt*] *māt Aššur rabîš ukinnûšu*) (Ad2E1:4). In other words, the Assyrian king was the representative of Ashur in particular.

Also the title of "governor" (*šakkanakku*) refers to the king as in the centre of a three-tiered relationship, having a mediating role. Shalmaneser III e.g. calls himself "governor of the great gods" (*šakkanakki ilāni rabûti*) (SE12:9), while Ashurnasirpal II, again highlighting the special role of Ashur, is once referred to as "the governor of Ashur" (*šakkanakki Aššur*) (AE40:9). This title was also (actually firstly) used to denote a group of high officials in various Near Eastern states, and thus clearly conveys the notion of representing a higher authority (Hallo 1957, CAD Š I: *šakkanakku*).

Not only the titles of *iššakku* and *šakkanakku* served to express the Assyrian king's role as a link between two spheres and as a representative of the great gods. Also the title "overseer" (*waklu*) can be understood in this way, taking its administrative association and late attestation into consideration. Carrying the notion of a society's legal-administrative head in the Old Assyrian Period (Larsen 1974, 1976), this title can be understood more figuratively in the Neo-Assyrian Period, conveying the theme of "royal administrator" (Siddall 2013). Adad-narari III is referred to by this ancient title no less than nine times in his many preserved decrees (e.g. An3E45:2).

Turning to other expressions of the mediating role in the sources of this study, the priestly dress and necklace of divine emblems which the king often wears on stelae allude to his status of a link between deities and humans (Hrouda 1965: 142–46). The mediating role is also illustrated in the mythological text (see s. 2.2) which tells of the world's creation and then proceeds to define the institution of kingship as pivotal for Creation (Cancik-Kirschbaum 1995: 20). This idea can also be seen through city planning, with Kalhu being dotted with palaces and temples, symbolizing the unique role of the king (Reade 2002: 141). Reflecting on royal correspondance, it is telling that the deities are the king's lords, while the king is the lord of the people (Pongratz-Leisten 2013: 295). In sum, the Early Neo-Assyrian kings are the great gods', primarily Ashur's, representatives on earth, occupying a status or function of mediator between the other two units of analysis.

The theme of the king as chosen by the deities is often articulated. This has been frequently noted in scholarly literature. Garelli (1979: 320–24) refers to divine choice as crucial for a king's legitimacy, Seux (1980–83: 166–67) states the importance of the idea of the king as chosen and invested by the deities in Mesopotamian royal ideology, and divine election is identified as constituting the traditional ground for legitimacy of rule beside that of royal descent by Tadmor (1981: 26–30). The actual process of divine election has been identified by Labat (1939: 44–48) who refers to onlooking, name uttering, and destiny determining as the three consecutive stages.

The theme of divine election is often expressed in the relevant primary sources. In an alternative first stage of the election process, the king is "conceived of" (*edû* D) in the hearts of the deities. It is here exclaimed that "the great gods of heaven and underworld conceived me (Ashurnasirpal II) in their just hearts" (*ilāni rabûti ša šamê u erṣetim ina kēni libbīšunu ūdûni*) (AE2:24). Adad-narari III is "the king in whose youth Ashur conceived and bestowed with a rulership without rival" (*šarru ša ina ṣeḫrūssu Aššur uttûšuma malkūt lā šanān umallû qātuššu*) (e.g. An3E8:1–2). The conceiving stage may also be alluded to when the ruler describes himself as "desired" (*ba"ītu, ḫišiḫtu*) by deities (CAD B: *ba'ītu*, AHw I/Ḫ: *ḫišiḫtum*, CAD Ḫ: *ḫišiḫtu*). The king is here "the desired one of the deities" (*ba"īt ilāni*) (AE40:9, e.g. SE1:3), "desired of the great gods" (*ḫišiḫtu° ilāni rabûti*) (AE173:4′), and "desired of Enlil" (*ḫišiḫti Ellil*) (e.g. AE172:9′). As for the last epithet, Enlil is much referred to in a king's divine election. This god had a traditional role of kingmaker, and was sometimes equated with Ashur from the Middle Assyrian Period onwards (Chamaza 2002: 124–25).[102]

Moving on to the better attested stages of divine election, the king is the blessed target of divine onlooking. The great gods "looked happily upon him (Shalmaneser III)" (*ḫadîš ippalsūšu*) (SE5:vi5), thereby acknowledging this king as their chosen one. Regarding Ashurnasirpal II, it is stated that "Ashur cast eyes and saw me (him), and my (his) authority and power came forth by his holy command" (*Aššur ... ina nīše īnēšu ēmurannimma malkūtī kiššūtī ina pîšu elli ūṣâ*) (AE30:20–21). The ruler is also described as being "called" (*nabû* N), i.e. elected, by the deities. Ashur is here "the lord who called your name" (*bēlu nābû šumika*) (e.g. AE1:i17). Moreover, in the address to future rulers, the successor to the Assyrian throne is described as "he whose name Ashur will call" (*ša Aššur šumšu ... inabbûšu*) (e.g. AE32:16). The ruling king was "he [whose] name Ashur called [since] earliest times" ([*ša ... ultu*] *ullâ Aššur šumšu ibbû*) (Ad2E1:2), or "he whose name the deities called from earliest times" (*ša ultu ullâ ilāni ibbū zikiršu*) (e.g. SA5E2). Destiny determining followed the divine blessing acts of conceiving, onlooking, and calling. This stage is implicitly expressed e.g. when the king claims that "[my (his) kingship, lordship, and power came forth] at the command of [the great] gods" (*ina pî ilāni* [*rabûti šarrūtī bēlūtī kiššūtī ūṣâ*]) (AE20:41).

---

102 Ashur is for example described bearing the typical Enlil epithet of "father of the great gods" (*abu ilāni rabûte*) (Ad2E4:1), arguably indicative of a syncretism of a kind.

Often the epithet "chosen one" (*nišītu*) is used to express the divinely elected status of the Assyrian king. Notably, *nišītu* refers to the act of onlooking and a deity's object of glance, i.e. choice (CAD N II: *nišītu*). The king is quite commonly called "chosen of Enlil" (*nišīt īnē Ellil*) (e.g. AE40:9–10, SE1:3). Ashurnasirpal II is in one inscription referred to as "chosen of your (Ishtar's) father Enlil" (*nišīt īnē abiki*) (AE46:1). In another epithet, the king is referred to as "chosen of Enlil and Ashur" (*nišīt īnē Ellil u Aššur*) (AE23:1). This attestation is highly noteworthy in that it not only distinguishes between the two gods but also places Ashur in a subordinate position. In line with the typical stress on Kalhu cults, Ninurta is also a part of the divine election process, namely through the epithet "chosen of Enlil and Ninurta" (*nišīt īnē Ellil u Ninurta*) (e.g. AE3:18, [SE16:1]).

The title of "designate" (*nibītu*) also refers to the state of being chosen as well as alluding to a stage of the election process (*nabû* N). In this context, the kings are described as "designate of Enlil and Ninurta" (*nibīt Ellil u Ninurta*) (AE2:1), "designate of the heroic Ninurta" (*nibīt Ninurta qardi*) (e.g. AE1:i21), "designate of [the deities]" (*nibīt* [*ilāni*]) (AE47:15), "designate of Sin" (*nibīt Sîn*) (e.g. AE1:i33), and "designate of Ashur" (*nibīt Aššur*) (Ad2E1:1). The penultimate epithet belongs to Ashurnasirpal II and is much centred on by him, e.g. in the annalistic inscription in the Ninurta temple (AE1). Last but not least, the common epithet of "appointee of Enlil" (*šakin Ellil*) (e.g. AE57:1, SE26:2) speaks of a stage and of a divinely chosen position in that it is based on a verbal adjective (thus passive) form of the verb *šakānu*, referring to the king "being placed" in power.

The handing over of insignia from the deities to the king was an ideologically much significant ritual in Mesopotamia (Berlejung 1996). The ruler is being granted insignia during the coronation. Various insignia, among them the royal garments, "the *simtu* of kingship", and "the 'me' of lordship", are described as being entrusted by the gods and goddesses to the kings of Assyria and Mesopotamia at the coronation ritual (Magen 1986: 19–28).

A unique embossing on a helmet from the time of Ashurnasirpal II shows him being given royal insignia by Ashur and Ishtar in the presence of bird-headed genii and the winged disk (AI24:22t.). The king is "[the one whose hands the deities] of heaven [and underworld] filled with the just [sceptre]" ([*ilāni*] *ša šamê* [*u erṣeti haṭṭa*] *eširtu* [*qātuššu*] *umallū*) (SE9:15–17), "[the one into whose grasp they (Ninurta and/or Ashur) granted] the exalted crown" (*agâ ṣīra* [*ušatmeḫū*]) (AE47:14), and "[the one who has been granted weapons], sceptre, crown, and [staff by DN]" ([*ša* DN *ušatmeḫu kakka*] *ḫaṭṭa agâ u* [*šibirra*]) (AE153:5). Similarly, Anu, Enlil, and Ea chose Ashurnasirpal II, and "granted weapons, sceptre, crown, and staff to his lordship" (*kakku ḫaṭṭu agâ u šibir-*

ru ušatmeḫū bēlūtī) (e.g. AE40:10–11). Shamash is additionally "lord of my (Adad-narari II's) crown" (*bēl kulūlija*) (An2E2:102). Otherwise, a leading role of Ashur in the coronation of the king is played in the sources, not the least in the coronation texts (see s. 2.2). As is commonly stated in the texts studied here, the king could then "greatly take a seat on the throne of my (his) kingship" (*ina kuṣṣi šarrūtī rabîš ūšibu*) (e.g. AE17:i63, SE1:14), in a process in which the great gods are "those who have established his throne" (*ušaršidū kussâšu*) (An3E8:3).

The granting of two particular divine insignia, namely the "staff" (*šibirru*) and "sceptre" (*ḫaṭṭu*), both of which are associated with the shepherding role (see subs. 5.4.4), is occasionally highlighted.[103] The successor is sometimes referred to as "the one whom Ashur will name for the shepherdship of Assyria" (*ša Aššur ana rē'ût māt Aššur inabbûšu*) (e.g. AE28:v13–14), and the ruling king is "[the one whose] hand you (Ashur) have granted the sceptre which herds the people" ([*ša*] *ḫaṭṭa murte'ât nišē tušatmeḫu qāta*) (AE154:3). Anu, Enlil, and Ea had jointly named the king for the shepherdship of Assyria (e.g. AE40:10), and Ashur had granted the ruler a sceptre in order for him "[to shepherd] the people" ([*ana rē'ût*] *nišē*) (SE5:i6).

The king is, by the acts of election and coronation, being granted a "regnal period" (*palû*). This concept is attested already in Sumerian times as 'bala', and means "period of office", "reign of king and dynasty", or just "dynasty" (CAD P: *palû*). Especially Shalmaneser III, who uses this term as a dating device in the narration of his military campaigns, refers to this concept. Additionally, Ashurnasirpal II claims that he is "the one whose reign you (Sharrat-niphi/Ninurta) established" (*tušaršidu palâšu*) (AE28:i14–ii1, e.g. AE1:i12 resp.). As in the Sumerian King List where the rule of dynasties and city states are outlined in consecutive order (see Jacobsen 1939), the deities are regarded as the ones who decide about successions of power.

After having identified the royal role of mediator and divine choice, the issue of the nature of the king in the state ideology naturally emerges.[104] In the older literature the notion of a deified Assyrian king dominates (e.g. Olmstead 1931: 452). Engnell (1943: 16, 31) states that "according to the Sumero-Accadian king ideology the monarch is of divine origin" who functioned as "the maintainer of the divine ideology" and as the representative, especially in the cult, of various divine characters. This idea of the Assyrian king as divine

---

103 The common divine granting of "radiance" (e.g. *melammu*) and "weapons" (*kakku*) will be discussed below and in section 4.4 respectively, focusing on royal deification and warfare.
104 The topic of royal deification in Mesopotamia is large, and my ambition here is restricted to draw conclusions on the basis of the propaganda of the Early Neo-Assyrian Period.

in essence, or at least as a being fundamentally apart from ordinary humans, has more recently been taken up by Parpola (1999) who, based on e.g. prophecies and external analogies, describes the Assyrian king as a "son of God" and sometimes also as a "saviour king", i.e. a Messiah. According to this school of thought, this royal ideology was gradually and intentionally diffused across the region.[105] A related school of thought centres on the cosmic role of the king, and is often inspired by the theory of Frazer (1894) who saw an idea of the ageing king who needed to be ritually killed or rejuvenated by ceremonies in order to preserve the fertility and prosperity of the land. The king and the divine nature are here in symbiosis.

On the other side in the debate is the scholarly mainstream with Labat and Frankfort as its early proponents. Labat (1939: 361–72) argues that the king was the representative of humankind to the deities and acted as a link in the three-tiered relationship in question, that the king was regarded as both quasi-divine and as a pious worshipper, and that this paradox regarding the king's nature was due to two parallel ideas, namely the divine origin of kingship and the impossibility for any king to attain divine status. The concepts of the religious character of kingship and the deification of kings must be separated – the former was standard while the latter was alien and deviating. He concludes by stating that a deification of the king in cult or among the populace never took place in Assyria. Frankfort (1948: 295–312) shares Labat's stance in his juxtaposition of a divine Egyptian king and a human Mesopotamian ruler. On point after point (union king-goddess, "son of DN", worship of kings in temples or of royal statues, divine determinatives[106], royal names in PNN), he discredits the idea of a divine Mesopotamian king.

Among today's scholars, Maul (1999: 206–13) states that the king was just a humble and pious servant, and that in reality Ashur was regarded as the true king. This last observation, made already by Seux (1980–83: 167–71), refers to the coronation texts which exclamate: "Ashur is king! Ashur is king!" (*Aššur šar Aššur šar*) (see Müller 1937: text 1:i29; Livingstone 1989: text 11:15), supposedly in order to remind the enthroned king of his subordinate status. The coronation also involved the slapping of the king's cheeks by the *šangû* priest, and the king's prostration in front of Ashur, all in the context of exclaiming that "Ashur is king!" (Pongratz-Leisten 2013: 292–93). Furthermore, the king (*māliku-amēlu*) is made by the same material, i.e. clay, as humans in the royal creation myth (Cancik-Kirschbaum 1995: 17). Michalowski (2008: 34, 41) claims that

105 At least according to Frahm (2006: 88–91, 2011b: 280–81) who critically refers to this school as "neo-diffusionist" who has identified a "pan-Assyrian" foreign policy.

106 For an explanation of the term divine determinative, see below in this section.

the phenomenon of royal deification in Mesopotamia has been highly overstated, and argues that it only occurred during exceptional historical circumstances. Consequently, he prefers to talk of *sacred*, rather than divine, kingship. Royal deification was regarded as haughty and abnormal in Mesopotamia (Schneider 2011: 119–23).

Nevertheless, there seems to be a trend of claiming the limited relevance of discussing royal deification in terms of the binary logic human/divine. Instead of "either or", the focal point is now on degrees and aspects. After discussing the words "shadow" (*ṣillu*) and "image" (*ṣalmu*) in relation to the binary logic human/divine, Machinist (2011: 413–24, 429–30) claims that, despite certain innovations (king as divinely connected or created, royal radiance, king as a representation of god) from the time of Tukulti-Ninurta I, there was always a crucial and decisive hesitation on the part of Assyrian kings throughout history to claim divine status. He concludes by stating that Assyrian *kingship* – not its holder – was considered divine. Similarly, Cooper (2008: 261–65) detects a general tendency in Mesopotamian history of resistance towards transgressing the fleeting boundaries between the human and divine with regards to royal ideology. Also Winter (2008: 80–86) refers to blurred boundaries between the divine and human, and goes on to claim that portraying the ruler as partly divine is a general feature of Mesopotamian state ideology. Focusing on the same discussion points as Machinist, she sees tendencies of royal deification in the Neo-Assyrian Period, taking Ashurnasirpal II as an example, but does not talk of royal deifications consistently employed. It was first and foremost *kingship* that was divine.

Another and related trend, centred on in the anthology edited by Hill, Jones, and Morales (2013a, 2013b: 4, 6), explores the interaction between the cosmic and political orientations of Mesopotamian kingship, instead of seeing "either or", or the two orientations as running parallel but separate. Also in this trend, degrees and aspects are highlighted. The cosmic sun similes (the theme of the king as sun) e.g. are here regarded as more than just metaphors. These were employed by Mesopotamian kings to claim at least partly divine status (Charpin 2013: 75–76). As the image of a god, incarnation tendencies are conveyed, most of all in relation to Shamash, and the Assyrian king is here "a kind of living image of the sun-god".[107] Cultic texts actually speak of a statue (?) named *ṣalam šarri* (written with a preceding divine determinative) which received offerings and prayers. Still, Assyrian kings never presented themselves as truly and fully divine (Frahm 2013: 102–12). Scurlock (2013: 155–59,

107 The Assyrian king was also associated with Saturn. Saturn and falling stars give another (than the sun) and more vulnerable image of the king's power (Frahm 2013: 109–12).

174) similarly argues that "Mesopotamian kings would qualify literally only as idols (*eidolon*)", and with divine power as incarnated, conditioned, and temporary. In the ruler's cosmic role, self-sacrifice (in the spirit of the god Tammuz who spent time in the underworld for the sake of those on earth) and good government were the focal points. The kings kept their fairly humble status and individuality in death.

Turning at last to the major primary sources, the related themes conveyed by the epithet "son of DN" (not attested for the Early Neo-Assyrian kings) and the mentioning of divine fashioning of the king's body (see below in this section) may be taken metaphorically rather than literally (Röllig 1981: 118–19; Cooper 2000: 440). As for the divine body fashioning, Ashurnasirpal II narrates that he commissioned a luxurious statue of himself in red gold, and placed it in front of Ninurta in the temple of the same god (AE30:76–78). The description is similar to the narrations where the same ruler describes his creating statues of deities (e.g. AE1:ii132–34). It is interesting that the only preserved statue of Ashurnasirpal II (AI12) is actually made in a red-yellow coloured type of limestone (Strommenger 1970: 13–15). It does not necessarily follow that the royal statue had the same status as the divine ones however. The age-old function of the private/royal statue in temples of representing a pious worshipper aside (see s. 4.2), a mere associating with the divine sphere seems more likely here, especially because of the general lack of evidence for royal deification which will be noted below.

The epithet "holy progeny" (*nabnītu ellutu*), which may refer to a divinely created being since the noun in question also refers to divine births (CAD N I: *nabnītu*), is attested only once (AE40:6). The deities are, in relation to Tukulti-Ninurta II, "those who changed my (the king's) figure to a lordly figure" (*nabnītī ana nabnīti bēlūti uštennū*) and "those who truly [took notice of me?] in my (the king's) mother's womb" (*ša ina šassūr ummī kīniš* [...]) (e.g. TN2E1:19, TN2E1:18 resp.). In narrative passages, this king and his predecessor and father Adad-narari II bring up the same ideological theme, claiming that the great gods created them and endowed them with outstanding physical and mental qualities (e.g. An2E2:5–7, TN2E1:18–21). On the same grounds as above, an associating with the divine rather than a real claim of deification seems like the most plausible interpretation. The words *binûtu*, *bukuru* and *ilittu*, also meaning "offspring" or the like, are on the other hand only given to deities and not to the king (see apps. 5–10 and the entries in CAD).

The Early Neo-Assyrian kings rather stress their human fathers and ancestors. Ashurnasirpal II e.g. consistently (89 times) describes himself as "son of Tukulti-Ninurta II" (*mār Tukultī-Ninurta*), and occasionally also as "grandson of Adad-narari II" (*mār māri Adad-nārārī*), and as "offspring of Ashur-dan II" (*liblibbi ša Aššur-dān*) (e.g. AE17:i28, AE17:i29, AE17:i31 resp.). The mortal-based patronym plays an important role in the propaganda, as evident e.g. in the fact that it is the most frequently attested epithet in the sources of Ashurnasirpal II and Shalmaneser III. This focus on patrilinearity, by the way, tells of political power as a masculine domain and of the king as "the hegemonic male" (see subss. 1.7.2, 5.4.9).

Engnell (1943: 37) takes the circumstance that some epithets are shared by deities and kings as conclusive evidence of the king's divine nature. Again, a metaphorical interpretation is a clear and preferable alternative. The metamorphic descriptions of the king as "Adad, the flooder" (*Adad ša rāḫiṣi*) (SE5:iii3, e.g. AE1:iii120), "impetuous flood" (*abūbu šamru*) (e.g. AE40:13), "arisen flood wave" (*edû gapšu*) ([SE5:i3], e.g. AE1:i13), one who flattens "like a flood" (*abūbāniš*) (e.g. SE12:18), "fierce dragon" (*ušumgallu ekdu*) (e.g. AE1:i19, [SE9:2]), "lion" (*labbāku*) (e.g. AE17:i36), and "wild bull" (*rīmu*) (SE2:ii52) in the context of narrating the king's military deeds may be understood as emphasizing outstanding personal qualities. If there were any explicit evidence for royal deification, these descriptions could be taken more seriously. These royal epithets also reflect a borrowing of attributes from the mythological sphere, displaying intertextuality.

Especially Ashurnasirpal II and Shamshi-Adad V, but also Shalmaneser III although to a lesser extent, describe themselves as having attributes and personal qualities which are also associated with deities. An examination of the reference works of Tallqvist (1938) and Seux (1967) identifies these as "merciless" (*lā pādû*), "wise" (*eršu*), "capable" (*lēʾû*), "exalted" (*ṣīru*), "magnificient" (*šarḫu*), "intelligent" (*ḫasīsu*), "strong" (*gešru*), "hero" (*ālilu*), "splendid" (*šitarḫu*), "brilliant" (*šarūru*), and "celebrated" (*nâdu*) – just to name a few. The attribute of "perfect" (*gitmālu*), so central for the idea of Parpola (1993) that the Neo-Assyrian king was "the perfect man" (*eṭlu gitmālu*), is not applied to the king.[108] The fact that the Early Neo-Assyrian kings used "divine" qualities in their describing of themselves and their deeds does not automatically prove that claims of royal deification is at hand. Rather, this usage may simply be seen as a way of stressing the bond between the king and the deities, which was considered to be vital for a king's legitimacy. To this end, qualities and attributes alluding to the divine were employed. As argued also by Cancik-Kirschbaum (2008: 104), the Assyrian king describes himself as receiving attributes from the Mesopotamian deities, but he does not present himself as a god.

108 Parpola's interpretation of the sacred tree scene has been effectively confronted in detail by Cooper (2000), and the latter's criticism need therefore not be repeated here.

A special kind of divine quality which the deities granted the king at coronation is "aura" or "radiance" (Oppenheim 1943: 31; Cassin 1968: 65–82). This divine radiance, variously called *melammu*, *šalummatu*, *namurratu*, *šurbatu*, and *rašabbatu*, is along with "fear" (*pulḫu*) often described as powerful and decisive in pacifying or defeating the king's enemies (see subs. 5.4.2). The royal epithets "he who is decked with radiance" (*āpir šalummate*) ([SE5:i3–4], e.g. AE1:i19–20) and "the brilliant one" (*šarūru*) (SE1:6) likewise states that the Early Neo-Assyrian kings claimed this radiant power. Also the narrative passage in which the great gods are said to have placed "royal radiance" (*melammē šarrūti*) on the king's head tells of this (An2E2:8–9). Adad-narari II portrayed himself as "awe-inspiringly radiant" (*namurrāku*) and "splendid" (*šurruḫāku*) (e.g. An2E2:15, An2E4 resp.), while Tukulti-Ninurta II saw himself as "fearful (inspiring)" (*palḫāku*), "terrifying" (*rašubbāku*), and "radiant" (*šalummāku*) (e.g. TN2E4, TN2E1:31, TN2E2 resp.). As noted by Cassin (1968: 65–82), royal radiance was however different in character, i.e. derived, temporary, and conditional, from divine radiance. The ten kings are not visualized with this attribute.

Divine descent or essence can consequently not be seen as proved from these examples of hyperbole of the Early Neo-Assyrian kings. Undoubtedly though, the authority of the king is often described in terms of divine powers. In this regard, the relevant rulers are occasionally described as having power over life and death. When the king conquers unsubmissive lands he can either show mercy or carry out brutal punishments (see subs. 5.4.2). A delegation from a defeated city e.g. addresses Ashurnasirpal II with the words: "As it pleases you, kill! As it pleases you, let live!" (*mā ḫadât dūku mā ḫadât balliṭ*) (AE1:i81). In the preserved royal decree of this king, the ruler is portrayed as the only person who can command capital punishment and demonstrates that his words are law (AE174:83:20′–21′). Violations of this law e.g. brings out the punishment of the cutting out of the violators' tongues (AE174:82:3rev.). In other words, the king is, in analogy with the deities, regarded as having power over life and death. But once again, metaphors and analogies can not be used as firm evidence for royal deification.

Evidence of a cult of the king in temples is not attested for any Assyrian king (Cancik-Kirschbaum 2008: 122). Nevertheless, Olmstead (1931: 452) in his days regarded the royal stele as expressing a cult of the king. The altar which was placed in front of the Ninurta Stele at the main entrance to the Ninurta temple is an element of this argumentation (AI19). It is however more reasonable to regard the stele rather as conveying messages of divine support, the honouring of the deities, and the celebration of divine kingship, because the king is actually worshipping the deities on these standard Assyrian stelae images, through the gesture of the pointed index-finger (Cogan 1974: 56–60; Reade 1979a: 340–44; Renger 1980–83: 74). According to this interpretation, the altar in question was meant to function as an offering table to the deities. Actually, the stele and the altar seem not to have originally functioned as a unit, since the former probably was brought from the nearby North-West Palace (Reade 2002: 169–71). Similarly, the luxurious royal statue mentioned above would have been a votive statue rather than an icon of the cult. As proposed by Machinist (2011: 423–24), Assyrian royal statues were votive in function, and they were venerated only in the sense of celebrating the king's role as mediator between the two spheres.

Furthermore, the image of a sacred and ceremonial union between the Assyrian king and a goddess, in a "sacred marriage", is not given by the sources, and nor are the possible deification alluding images of *ṣillu and ṣalam šarri*, discussed by Machinist (2011), mentioned in the sources of this study. Moreover, divine determinatives[109] are in reality not used in the writing of the names of the ten rulers. The one preceding Shalmaneser III's name refers to the god Shulmanu, while the accompanying simple name determinative[110] (denoting humans) refers to the king.[111] As for the writing of Ashurnasirpal II's name, the divine determinative is absent, even though the god Ashur is involved.[112] The best evidence in this discussion on the role of the divine determinative is however the writing of Tukulti-Ninurta II's name, made up of a suffixed noun followed by a DN. The former is preceded by the simple name determinative and the latter by the divine one. These are additional proofs of the absence of royal deification in this time period. The presence of a tension between (super)human claims and divine nature is there, but not to the extent that it seems justified to talk of deified kings.

The subordinate statuses of the Early Neo-Assyrian kings are clearly indicated by their constant referring of the deities as "my deities" (*ilānija*) (e.g. AE2:27, SE16:41), and "my lords" (*bēlīja*) (e.g. AE30:60, SE2:i33). It is first and foremost Ashur that is described as "my/his lord" (*bēlī/šu*) in the texts of the Early Neo-Assyrian kings (e.g. AE1:i12, SE1:27). Several gods and goddesses are

109 As for this feature, in the writing of names of deities a special cuneiform sign (an) with a determinative function preceded the spelling out of the name (MZL: an/sign 10/page 49).

110 For this cuneiform sign, see MZL: diš/sign 748/pages 417–18.

111 The same applies to the writing of Shalmaneser IV's name. Similarly, the name of Adad-narari (II and III) has a divine determinative because of the god and not the king. That Shamshi in the RN of Shamshi-Adad (V) really refers to the sun god can be seen in a writing of it with the logogram 'utu', giving the Sumerian name for the sun god (SA5E11:2).

112 The same trend can be observed from the writing of the RN of Ashur-dan (II and III).

consequently described as giving "orders" (*pû*, *qibītu*) to the king (e.g. AE1:i70, SE14:63). Also, words which denote instructing (e.g. *kullumu*) are used in this context (AE19:26). Obeying their orders, the king was simply "the servant" (*ardu*) of the deities (An3E43:2, [S4E3:10]).

Royal acts of praying (e.g. AE171, SE95:5–9) and "bowing down" (*šukênu*) (SE5:vi2) in relation to the deities, told of in narrative passages, also tell of the subordinate status of the king. As for the latter act, Ashurnasirpal II is depicted kneeling, while making the pointing gesture and catching water streams, in the miniature reliefs (AI23:C7,27a–b). Moreover, Shamshi-Adad V is depicted kneeling down in front of a divine symbol in reliefs on a stone vessel (SA5I2). This sentiment of fundamental submission is also expressed in Ashurnasirpal II's royal prayer to Ishtar (AE171). Tellingly, Tukulti-Ninurta II is "the prince who fears you (Ashur)" (*rubû pāliḫka*) (TN2E23:2), and Adad-narari III and Shalmaneser IV are each "he who fears your (Ashur's) great divinity" (*pāliḫ ilūtika rabûti*) (An3E43:2, [S4E3:10]). The cult images of Ninurta and Ishtar are called "your (the deity's) great divinity" (*ilūtika/ki rabûti*) (AE31:15, AE40:37 resp.). The king's duty to make divine statues thus indicates an essential hierarchy in terms of status.

The power relations given in curses state that the deities will punish a disregardful king. The latter will e.g. loose his power, suffer military defeats, have a short and bad life, and have his progeny destroyed (Lackenbacher 1982: 162–67). The deities similarly have the power in the blessing sections to convey rewards to future rulers who respect the monument in question (e.g. AE17:v45–54, SE25:34–36), and they are also called upon to defeat the enemies of the king (e.g. AE4:3′, SE12:35–36). As for the former, the theme of the giving of many days and years, in life/on the throne, features prominently (e.g. AE31:18, SE56:10–11). As for curses, the king was obliged to swear by god (*šumi ili izakkar*) when issuing decrees, here in favour of Nergal-erish (An3E9:19–21rev.), thus showing his humility and subordination.

Another clear indication of a belief in the human nature of the Assyrian king is to be found in the "social perspective" of the iconography, which depicts the ruler of equal size to his human surroundings. This perspective has largely been understood as conveying the idea of the king as human but a *primus inter pares*, i.e. "first among equals" (Groenewegen-Frankfort 1951: 173; Barnett 1960: 16; Reade 1979a: 331–32; Czichon 1992: 172–73). Highly noteworthy here is that the royal statues are commonly of natural or even diminished size (e.g. AI12, SI5). Except from on one side of the throne base, the ten kings are portrayed of equal size to those around them (SI14:4b). This exception may either be a mistake or a reflection of an idea simply about the special status of the king within the human community.

This idea may also be expressed in the officials' and courtiers' gesture of clasped hands in the king's presence (e.g. AI14:67–68, SI10:7b.). Even the crown prince or field marshal is depicted making this gesture of reverence and respect (e.g. AI4:D3, SI11:D2). The king is always the centre point of these compositions, surrounded by attendants, bodyguards, officials, and courtiers. Fly wisks, "napkins", and sunshades handled by the attendants signal and delimit the special space of the king (Collins 2010: 197). The king's divinely given authority and special status within the human community is also expressed through depicting him sitting or standing with the insignia crown and mace (e.g. AI17, SI16–17). As for iconography and royal deification, no Early Neo-Assyrian king is ever depicted with horns, or holding rod and rope, or standing on sacred animals – three standard divine attributes in Mesopotamian iconography (Black and Green 1992: 93–98).

To conclude this subdiscussion, there is not any tenable evidence in the sources which suggests that the ten kings were considered anything but human. Metaphors can not be used as solid proofs if considering the overall lack of explicit references to royal deification. Although it is surely legitimate to talk of degrees and aspects (these will then be low and peripheral respectively), the binary dichotomy human/divine is still valid. The special status of the king was propagated in other ways than through royal claims of deification. I would also argue that an identifying of *divine* Assyrian kings relates to the Orientalist discourse on the Oriental despot (see subs. 5.4.8).

The king is supported and protected by the deities in the fulfilment of his duties (Kuhrt 1997: 504–505). This divine aid was believed to be conveyed in many ways, e.g. by astrology, prophecies, dreams, and liver omens (Bottéro 2001a: 170–85). This kind of support was obviously of a guiding or commanding character. In the next step, the relevant divine support was believed to be manifested through the deities acting together with the Assyrian ruler. This help enabled the king to fulfil his/their wishes in various fields of action. The most common theme here seems to be that the Assyrian kings receive assistance on the battlefield (Pongratz-Leisten 2001: 230). The literary subgenre of letter *from* a god narrates the blessed consequences of this aid as received by the addressed king, and the "reversed" subgenre of letter *to* a god similarly presents the image of the king thanking the deity for his/her support during the campaign. The great gods are here "those who listen to his (the king's) petitions" (*šēmū taslītīšu*) (S4E2:8).

The supported and protected status of the king was also expressed through the phenomenon of "personal gods" which was a religious belief prevalent even in Sumerian times (Black and Green 1992: 148). The god Shulmanu has been identified as a manifestation of Ashur and as the protective, personal god of at least Shalmaneser I (Radner 1998: 49–53). Shulmanu is, in the text corpus of Shalmaneser III, never attested other than as a part of the king's name.[113] Ashurnasirpal II seems to have had a special attachment to Shalmaneser I among his forefathers, something which is conveyed e.g. through references to the said ruler as the original builder in the context of reconstruction projects, notably that of Kalhu (e.g. AE1:iii132). The god Shulmanu seems then to have been an important, if not personal, god of Ashurnasirpal II and Shalmaneser III. The building activity in the western town of Dur-Katlimmu, i.e. a cult centre of this deity, also attests to this (AI5). As for royal names, Ashurnasirpal actually stands for "Ashur is the guardian of the heir" (*Aššur-nāṣir-apli*), again displaying the idea of divine protection. The statement in Shamshi-Adad V's name that "Adad is my (the king's) sun" (*Šamšī-Adad*) may be grasped similarly (e.g. SA5E1:i26).

The epithet *migru*, which often is translated as "favourite", is much centred on in the context of divine support and protection to the king (CAD M II: *migru*). Ashurnasirpal II is quite often described as "favourite of Anu" (*migir Anim*) (e.g. AE1:i33), but also twice as "favourite of Enlil" (*megir Ellil*) (e.g. AE1:i11), while Shalmaneser III is called "favourite of Ishtar" (*migir Ištar*) in his prayer to Ninlil (SE154:4rev.). Ninurta, Sharrat-niphi, and Ninlil are referred to in the suffix pronouns which form parts of the royal epithet of "your favourite" (*megirka/ki*) ([AE29:4′], AE28:i11, SE154:11obv. resp.). In addition to these examples, Anu, Enlil, and Ea are described as "gods who favour me (the king)" (*ilāni migrūa*) (AE17:v99).

The words *tukultu*, *rēṣūtu*, and *nārāru* are other words which allude to divine support. Ashurnasirpal II frequently claims to be "the one who marches with the support of Ashur" (*ša ina tukulti Aššur ittanallaku*), or of the great gods, or (only twice) of Ashur, Adad, Ishtar, and Ninurta together (e.g. AE1:i12, AE1:i15–16, AE56:7 resp.). The Early Neo-Assyrian king was also "he who marches with the support of Ashur and Shamash" (*ša ina tukulti Aššur u Šamaš ittanallaku*) (e.g. AE19:7–9, SE1:7). In an elaboration of this common type of epithet Ashurnasirpal II is called "king who has always marched justly with the support of Ashur and Shamash/Ninurta" (*šarru ša ina tukulti Aššur u Šamaš/Ninurta mēšariš ittanallaku*) (e.g. AE1:i22, AE1:iii128 resp.). The claim that Ashurnasirpal II engaged in warfare "by the support/help of DN" (*ina tukulti/rēṣūti* DN) is consistently given (e.g. AE1:i42–43, AE1:iii119–20 resp). Shalmaneser III, lastly, was "the one whose support is Ninurta" (*ša tukultašu*° *Ninurta*) (e.g. SE5:iv2).

113 But Adad-narari III's governor Nergal-erish calls Shulmanu "his (the king's) lord", "great lord", and "he who dwells in Dur-Katlimmu" (*āšib Dūr-Katlimmu*) (An3E42:1′–2′).

As for divine epithets and this particular notion of divine support and protection, several deities are described as "his (the king's) helpers" (*rēṣūšu*) (e.g. AE56:7, SE1:7) as well as "his (the king's) supporters" (*tiklūšu*) (e.g. AE1:i104, SE23:6). One king of the time period, i.e. Tukulti-Ninurta II, claims in his royal name to have had Ninurta as "my (his) support" (*tukultī*) (e.g. TN2E1:16), while Shamash is, in relation to Shamshi-Adad V, "[the lord of] support" ([*bēl*] *tukulti*) (SA5E15:9). Similarly, Adad-narari II and Adad-narari III both declare through the royal name that they share that Adad is "my (their) aid" (*nārārī*) (e.g. An2E1:1obv., An3E1:1).

The verb *rabû* in the causative Š-stem is used in order to portray divine assistance in the epithets of the great gods. Ashurnasirpal II e.g. claims that the deities are "the ones who make great the kingship of Ashurnasirpal II" (*mušarbū šarrūt Aššur-nāṣir-apli*) (e.g. AE17:i11–12), some Early Neo-Assyrian kings call these deities "the ones who make my kingship great" (*mušarbū šarrūtija*) (e.g. AE17:v48, SE6:i8), and in Shalmaneser III's case they are also "the ones who made great my lordship, power, and leadership" (*ša bēlūtī kiššūtī šāpirūtī ušarbū*) (e.g. SE6:i9). Alluding also to the election process, involving e.g. naming and calling, is the great gods' epithet of "those who make my name great" (*mušarbū šumija*) (e.g. SE21:3–4).

The divine protection is even expressed in terms of "to love" (*râmu*), e.g. in the divine epithet, referring to the great gods, "they who love my kingship" (*rā'imūt šarrūtija*) (e.g. SE21:3). This notion is especially highlighted by Ashurnasirpal II who claims that Ashur and Ishtar loved his kingship (e.g. AE40:39), and also refers to "the deities" (*ilāni*) as "the ones who love me" (*ša irammūni*) (AE32:11). Additionally, Ishtar is referred to as "the mistress who loves my priesthood" (*bēlat irammu šangûtī*) (e.g. AE1:i37–38). His epithets of "beloved of Anu and Dagan" (*narām Anim u Dagan*) and "loved one of Adad" (*namad Adad*) are both quite common (e.g. AE30:1–2, AE1:i33 resp.). In the latter case, the word *namaddu*, meaning "darling" (CAD N I: *namaddu* B), is used. Tukulti-Ninurta II in his turn is called "loved one of DN" (*namad* DN) (e.g. TN2E1:33). Ashurnasirpal II is additionally "beloved of your (Ninurta's/Sharrat-niphi's) heart" (*narām libbika/ki*) (AE1:i11, AE28:i10 resp.). In his prayer to Ninlil, Shalmaneser III is described as "beloved of your divinity" (*narām ilūtiki*) (SE154: 5rev.).

Through the divine assistance in question, the deities, in this case Sharrat-niphi and the Sibitti, manifested themselves as "she/they who complies/comply with the heart (of the king)" (*mušamṣat ammar libbi*) (AE28:i5, SE95:3 resp.), while the ruler is "the king whose heart's desires Ashur/Enlil has caused him to reach" (*šarru ša biblat libbišu Aššur/Ellil ušekšidušu*) (e.g. AE40:8, AE1:i39 resp.). Adad-narari II described himself as "the select of Ashur" (*bibil libbi Aššur*) (An2E1:2), and Tukulti-Ninurta II wished to see himself as "their/your (the deities'/Ashur's) select one" (*bibil libbišunu/ka*) (e.g. TN2E4). Common to all of these royal epithets is the statement that the ruler's "heart" (*libbu*) has been filled and satisfied with the divine assistance in question. Summing up the findings of the textual evidence, the idea of the great gods as actively supporting and protecting the Early Neo-Assyrian kings is clearly present in the epigraphic sources.

As for the expressions of divine support in iconography, Albenda (1969: 47–51) argues that the emblems, hovering in mid-air or decorating the king's necklace, on the images of royal stelae convey a message of divine support. Apart from on royal stelae, these emblems are present on the Black Obelisk (SI11:A1–2), in certain scenes on cylinder seals from the period (e.g. AI37), and in the miniature reliefs of the North-West Palace (e.g. AI23:P4,49c). As for the lastly mentioned type of source, Ashurnasirpal II is portrayed standing together with his entourage holding bow and arrows while a moon crescent (Sin), a headless winged sun disk (probably Shamash), and an eight-pointed star (Ishtar) hover in mid-air above it all (AI23:P2,49a).

Divine emblems are also seen being worn by the king in the shape of minor royal jewellery. Ashurnasirpal II is e.g. represented wearing moon crescents as earrings (e.g. AI19). Furthermore, rosettes adorn much of the textiles, ornaments (e.g. bracelets), and insignia (e.g. the crown) of the king (e.g. AI4:N6, SI18) but also of royal officials (e.g. AI4:G9). This motif symbolizes the presence and support of Ishtar (Black and Green 1992: 156–57; Porter 2010: 145). The "malteser cross", arguably a symbol of Shamash (Black and Green 1992: 54–55), is worn around the necks of Ashurnasirpal II, Shamshi-Adad V, and Adad-narari III (AI19, SA5I1, An3I2). Part of an inscribed necklace of Tukulti-Ninurta II has been preserved (TN2E11). All these divine emblems (those in mid-air and in necklaces) are closely attached or linked to the royal body in apparent gestures of protection, possibly having the function similar to amulets (Black and Green 1992: 30).[114]

As for the theme of protection, J. M. Russell (1998b: 712) identifies "divine protection" as one of the most important motifs of the reliefs on the walls of the North-West Palace.[115] The human or bird-headed, winged or unwinged, horned or unhorned genii, who were stationed at entrances holding various

---

114 The royal clothing and the luxurious property of the king must have had a propagandistic value, as displayed publicly in processions, festivals, and ceremonies (Karmel Thomason 2010). These too defined the Assyrian king as the supported representative of the deities.

115 This motif is much stressed. The other motifs, identified by the scholar in question, are "military success", "service to the gods", and "Assyrian prosperity".

apotropaic instruments, had the duty to protect the palace, and therefore indirectly the king, from demons and malevolent spirits. These genii have, on the basis of cultic and ritual texts, been identified as the wise "sages" (*apkallu*) who are described in Mesopotamian myths as having lived before the Great Flood. These sages, seven in number, were believed to be in possession of extraordinary apotropaic powers (Black and Green 1992: 163–64). Some genii, behind the pollinating ones, bear apotropaic plants in their hands on the stone vessel of Bel-luballit (SA5I2). The three pairs of genii statues of the Nabu temple in Kalhu were placed at entrances, implying their protecting function (An3I8–10).[116] The goddess behind Adad-narari III in a seal scene may be protective or presenting in function (An3I13).

The same protective function can be attributed to the horned, human-headed, but with bull or lion bodies, colossi which were stationed at important palace and temple entrances. The colossi in question have variously been identified as the *lamassu*, *šēdu*, and *aladlammû* who are mentioned in the texts, but their common protective functions are undisputed (Wiggermann and Green 1993–97). The first two types of creatures are in fact labelled as protective deities (CAD L: *lamassu*, CAD Š II: *šēdu* A). Some of the colossi of the North-West Palace actually hold apotropaic plants or animals in their hands (e.g. AII8:Dd1–2). These guardians of the palace are referred to by Ashurnasirpal II as "wild beasts of the mountains and seas" (*umām šadê u tâmāti*) (e.g. AE23:19). Through their associations with Chaos and the primeval monster Tiamat (CAD U-W: *umāmu*), they were obviously regarded as suitable and potent enough to ward off the same forces. Genii and colossi were also placed at the Central Building, the Centre Palace, the Ninurta temple, and at a city gate (AI9, SI3, AI7, SI2 resp.). It may be noted that genii and colossi often are depicted in chaotic scenes and undignified poses on seals and miniature reliefs,[117] quite in contrast to the calm and majestic poses and positions which these figures occupy in the major arts.

The sacred tree is often placed in corners of rooms of the North-West Palace (e.g. AI4:B21). Besides doorways and windows, corners of rooms were believed to be common entrance points for demons and malevolent spirits (Parker-Mallowan 1983; J. M. Russell 1998b). At the same time, the date palm, most often identified as the sacred tree, was considered having apotropaic powers

---

116 The square-shaped boxes which some of these hold are probably not apotropaic in their function, but rather telling of the votive activity going on in the temple (An3I9).

117 Colossi are hunted, and bird-headed genii are pulled by their tails in the miniature reliefs (e.g. AI23:P2,49b). On a seal, the king stands shooting an arrow at a jumping *lamassu* (AI37). Such scenes naturally raise questions regarding the status of these iconographic sources.

(Parker-Mallowan 1983: 37–39). These two factors combined strongly hint to the corner trees being apotropaic, protecting the palace and the king. The frequent occurrence of images of trees in rooms S and T, often referred to as "the private suite", may speak of the high protective need for these spaces (J. M. Russell 1998b: 687–705). Adding the notion of fertility to the interpretation process, the tree of the North-West Palace may be regarded as "a protective symbol of fertility" (Collins 2010: 181).

The once attested scene from the North-West Palace where the king is "pollinated" by two bird-headed genii while he stands with one hand greeting and the other hand resting on his sword shaft (AI4:F3–4) may illustrate an act of purification, conveying royal protection (Magen 1986: 73–81). This scene is situated in room F, commonly identified as a *bīt rimki*, i.e. a ritual washing room (Læssøe 1955; J. M. Russell 1998b: 671–97). The *apkallu*, the bird-headed genii, are referred to in texts which describe apotropaic rituals (Wiggermann 1992). The theory of Gadd (1936, 1948: 91) that the genii extract purification substances from the tree onto their cones, which they then smear on the king, does not seem out of place here. Additionally, the scene may allude, through the mentioned connotations of the date palm, to the role of the king as working for the fertility and prosperity of the land.

Summing up, I have argued that there is a state ideological picture of the king as the (human) representative of the great gods in general and of Ashur in particular. The Assyrian king claims to be a link between the great gods and the foreign lands, divinely chosen, and continuously supported and protected by the Mesopotamian deities. Although the ruler associates himself with the deities in various ways, it is not tenable to talk of royal deification.

4.2 Priest and servant of the great gods

Focusing on the king's representative status and function in relation to the great gods in *practice*, the interrelated royal roles of priest[118] and servant will now be identified and discussed. I will argue that the ten kings pervadingly are presented as priests and servants both in texts and images, that religion played an important role in legitimizing Assyrian kingship, and that the priestly duty harbours aspects which do not fit with the notion of secularism.

---

118 The word "priest" is obviously anachronistic, but it may be useful if understood and employed in a looser sense. As priest, the king is involved in the cult, interacts with deities, and wears the garment (see n. 122) which is associated with the king's cultic performances.

Mesopotamian and Assyrian state ideology consistently portray the ruler as priest and servant in relation to the deities (Labat 1939; Liverani 1995: 2360–61). As concluded by Labat (1939: 361), Assyrian kingship was essentially religious in character, and the sources do not present the ruler as an autocratic despot, but he is rather portrayed as a deeply religious person who is concerned with satisfying the wishes and needs of the deities. Röllig (1981: 122), arguing primarily on the basis of the coronation texts, even refers to Assyrian kingship as a kind of theocracy. The role of Ashur as the true ruler of Aššur or Assyria is a pivotal expression of this state model (see s. 4.1). The extent of the Assyrian king's political power may have varied throughout the centuries, but his religious role and authority remained intact (Labat 1939: 25). The continuity of this role, even from Sumerian to Neo-Assyrian times, is detectable not the least in royal visual arts (Reade 1979a: 342; Winter 1989: 581–82). The active role and clear priestly status of the king distinguish – not the least when comparing the Babylonian New Year Feast with the Assyrian coronation – Assyrian state ideology from the south-Mesopotamian notion of kingship (Müller 1937; Labat 1939: 15–16).

In his capacity of heading the cult administration, the king was "the priest" (*šangû*) of the deities. The words for "priesthood" (*šangûtu*) and "kingship" (*šarrūtu*) were practically synonyms (van Driel 1969: 170–74). As already noted, the cuneiform sign 'šid' (*iššakku*) can also be read 'sanga' (*šangû*). Royal "sacred" and "profane" roles are here integrated. The Early Neo-Assyrian kings are often called 'šid' *Aššur*, and in the contexts where cultic activities are focused on the transcription should probably be *šangû Aššur*. The title *šangû* is sometimes extended with adjectives. A few kings are referred to as "exalted priest" (*šangû ṣīru*) (AE49:6, SE10:i13), and Ashurnasirpal II additionally, but only once, calls himself "holy priest" (*šangû ellu*) (AE59:3). The idea of the ritual purity of the king seems to be highlighted in the two adjectives, at least in the latter one (CAD E: *ellu*).[119] There are depictions of other priests or cultic personnel in Assyrian iconography, but the king always plays the major priestly role (Collon 1999: 24). In this regard, the king was "a kind of honorary *šangû* of all the sanctuaries of his country" (van Driel 1969: 174). The Assyrian king was *šangû* in theory *and* practice, enacting the duties of his office regularly (Menzel 1981: 3, 159–72).[120]

As for the term "priesthood" (*šangûtu*), the Early Neo-Assyrian rulers refer to the Mesopotamian deities' act of having given it to them. Ninurta and Nergal

---

119 The former epithet is probably not a profession title, since the adjective of "great" (*rabû*) is the one which is used to designate "high priest" (Menzel 1981: 194–95).

120 This priestly status appears to be very similar to the one in Egypt (Quirke 1992: 70–104).

e.g. are "the ones who love my (the king's) priesthood" (*ša šangûtī irammū*) (e.g. AE2:40, SE6:iv40), and Shamash is "the one who loves my priesthood" (*irammu šangûtī*) (An2E2:103). Ashurnasirpal II proclaims that he is "the one whose priesthood is pleasing to your (Ninurta's/Sharrat-niphi's) great divinity" (*ša šangûssu eli ilūtika/ki rabûti iṭibbu*) (e.g. AE1:i11–12, AE28:i11–13 resp.), and the same ruler prays in a blessing section that the alleged piety of this builder-king will cause Sharrat-niphi to love the king's priesthood and be pleased with his offerings (AE32:14–15). In an even more pretentious statement, this king says that "the deities" (*ilāni*) are "the ones who established for all times his (the king's) priesthood in the temples" (*šangûssu ina ekurrāti ana dāriš ukinnū*) (AE17:i22–23).

The Assyrian king had other priestly titles. The title *šaprû*, also translated as "priest" by Grayson (1996: 136), refers to a royal role of temple administrator (CAD Š I: *šabrû* A). Shalmaneser III is once called "splendid temple administrator of Ashur" (*šaprû Aššur šurruḫu*) (SE56:2).[121] Using another title but with a similar meaning, Tukulti-Ninurta II describes himself as "the exalted (temple) administrator" (*šatammu ṣīru*) (e.g. TN2E1:23). The rarely attested title of "overseer" (*parriku*) (AE173:4rev., SE1:6) may also carry allusions to royal temple activities, not the least since it is accompanied by epithets with the same meanings (CAD P: *parriku* A). Finally, the title of *išippu*, often translated as "purification priest", is attested as frequent as eleven times in the text corpus of Ashurnasirpal II (e.g. AE26:35). Due to the many apotropaic motifs and cultic scenes in the North-West Palace this is hardly surprising. While designating the king in Assyria, temple staff engaged in purification acts were referred to by this title down in Babylonia. Notably, the sage Adapa held the title of *išippi Eridu* (CAD I–J: *išippu*).

As for the iconography, the king is very often depicted as priest. The motif of "king before deity (making the gesture with pointing index-finger)" is e.g. a prominent royal visual representation in Assyrian iconography (Magen 1986: 45). Non-narrative images portray the king standing, wearing a priestly garment,[122] making the gesture with the index-finger, and having divine emblems

121 The compiler in CAD (Š I: *šabrû*) instead sees the writing pa-al, meaning *waklu*. The reading 'šapra', referring to the priest role, is more in line with the religious textual context.

122 Royal garment no. 2 in the typology of Magen (1986: 92–96). As noted by her, three different dresses are used by Ashurnasirpal II and Shalmaneser III: no. 2 (almost exclusively in cultic contexts), no. 1b (predominantly in review scenes), and the long robe (mostly in battle scenes). Shamshi-Adad V and Adad-narari III wear variants of dress no. 2. For the identifying of royal "priestly" (2) and "military" (1b, long robe) clothing, see also D. Oates 1963: 13–14.

in a necklace and/or above/in front of him (e.g. AI18, SI13).[123] These images depict the Assyrian king as a worshipper, the high priest of Ashur, and as an agent and servant of the deities (Reade 1979a: 340–44). The necklace of divine emblems conveys the idea of divine presence and support (Winter 1997: 372). As for the gesture, Reade (1963: 43, 1983: 15) regards it as a "gesture of respect and supplication" or "salutation" towards the divine emblems. Magen (1986: 94–99) among others have noted that this gesture may be a visual illustration of the ritual act of "extending the finger" (*ubāna tarāṣu*) towards the deities. The Assyrian king here reports to the deities on his pious deeds, narrated and inscribed on the relevant stele or cliff relief, and expects divine blessings in return.[124] Every stele and cliff relief of the Early Neo-Assyrian kings depict the king with the pointing finger by the right hand and a mace in his left hand, except from on the Banquet Stele where he instead holds a long staff in his right hand (AI20).

They royal priestly role is also manifested by statues of the king. The priestly garment, the necklace of divine emblems, and the sometimes bareheaded king (e.g. AI12, SI5), possibly indicating respect and humility (Madhloom 1970: 74),[125] all suggest this. Furthermore, at least one of Shalmaneser III's statues (SI5) were placed in a temple (Grayson 1996: 59). This is certainly true of the one statue (AI12) of Ashurnasirpal II (Strommenger 1970: 13). In this context, the royal statue had the attitude of a "respectful but confident anticipation of divine favour" (Reade 1983: 15). Likened to votive images they "stand in the place of the worshipper in perpetual prayer before the deity" (Bahrani 2001: 98). Making the same link, Magen (1986: 40–45) refers to these statues as *Beterstatuen*. The insignia which are held by Ashurnasirpal II on his ivory plaque as well as by Shalmaneser III on one of his Assur statues should, according to Magen (1986: 69–73), be identified as an attribute belonging to the ruler's function as *išippu* (AI25, SI6). It may also associate with the royal role of shepherd and harvester (see subs. 5.4.4).

In the statue format, the gesture aspect was naturally restrained by the material, with arms close to the body. Beside the gesture of holding insignia, the important gesture of clasped hands could also be expressed in sculpture in the round. The Assyrian king is occasionally portrayed with clasped hands

123 Adad, Ashur/Enlil, Ishtar, Marduk, Nabu, Shamash, the Sibitti, and Sin are attested as divine emblems on the monuments of the Early Neo-Assyrian kings (e.g. AI19, SI13).

124 A once attested epithet of Ashurnasirpal II calls him "he who is reached by DN's hand" (*tiriṣ qāt* [DN]) (AE154:2), indirectly alluding to the gesture and blessings in question.

125 See e.g. the scene where a bareheaded Tukulti-Ninurta I adores a cult object (see Parrot 1961: fig. 8). See also the bareheaded Adad-narari III paying his respect on a seal (An3I13).

(e.g. SI7). This gesture was supposedly "the standard pose of respect in the presence of the king or the gods" (D. Oates 1963: 15). Similarly understood, the gesture simply expresses a state of attention rather than conveying the characteristic pose of the worshipper or the ritual gesture of prayer (Kinnier-Wilson 1962: 97). Both interpretations identify the motif of royal piety.

Lastly, it should also be noted that there is a clear typological connection between type of monument and the motifs represented on it. Non-narrative iconography, which generally presents the king as priest, is found on stelae, cliff reliefs, and statues. Taking the Saba'a Stele as a case study, it indeed represents the king with the pointing gesture at divine emblems (An3I2), characteristic of what Börker Klähn (1982: 54) in her stelae typology refers to as *Standardstele*. The text is – equally characteristic for a stele – a commemorative text (An3E6). Seeing image and text as a whole, a few interesting things can be noted. The western and "international" milieu in the text corresponds to the composition of emblems, with the emblem of the west-profiled god Adad having the most prominent position, and with the Babylonian gods Marduk and Nabu present. The diminished size and crude portraying of the king are mirrored by the text's focus on the governor Nergal-erish (An3E6:23–25) and by the peripheral location of the stele respectively.

Implementing his priestly function, the Early Neo-Assyrian king presents offerings, often termed *nīqu*, to the deities in his role as their "provider" (*zāninu*). Shalmaneser III is "ceaseless provider for Ekur (Enlil temple)" (*lā mupparkû zānin Ekur*) (SE1:5), while Shamshi-Adad V and Adad-narari III each are "ceaseless provider for Esharra (Ashur temple)" (*zānin Ešarra lā mupparkû*) (e.g. SA5E2, An3E8:3). Shalmaneser III is also "provider of [your] (Ninlil's) shrine" (*zānin išrēti*[*ki*]) (SE154:11rev.). Also his father and predecessor Ashurnasirpal II boasts of his role of providing for the deities. He is five times referred to as "provider of food offerings for the great gods" (*zānin nindabê ana ilāni rabûti*) (e.g. AE1:i23–24). Although not called a *zāninu* here, Shamshi-Adad V portrays, alluding to his providing function, himself as "shepherd of shrines" (*rē'û ašrāti*) (e.g. SA5E1:i27). The grant of land for the Ashur temple, and the decrees on the organization of ceremonies and offerings of the Ashur temple, issued by Adad-narari III, also display the king's role as provider for the deities (An3E45, An3E55–56 resp.).

Regarding epithets on the providing role in practice, Shalmaneser III is "the one who gives temple shares and food offerings to the great gods" (*nādin išqī u nindabê ana ilāni rabûti*) (SE1:4). Narrative passages describe the same king as making offerings to the deities of Babylonia (e.g. SE8:27′). In his prayer to Ninlil, Shalmaneser III refers to his role as providing offerings in the epithets "holder of [your] food offerings" (*mukīl nindabê*[*ki*]) and "holder of your strewn offering" (*ṣābit serqiki*) (SE154:1obv.). Ashurnasirpal II describes himself as "the one whose deeds and food offerings the great gods of heaven and underworld love" (*ša epšēt qātišu u nadān zībišu ilāni ša šamê u erṣeti irammū*) (e.g. AE1:i24–25). Adad-narari III was "he whose ritual gesture and food offerings the great gods desired" (*ša nīš qātišu nadān zībišu iḫšuḫū ilāni rabûti*) (An3E6:7–8). In the context of consecrating the buildings of Kalhu, Ashurnasirpal II states that he "offered fruit of all sorts and wine to Ashur, my lord, and the temples of my land" (*inbē kalîšu karāni ana Aššur bēlija u ekurrāti mātija anqi*) (e.g. AE26:54–55). Similarly, after having commissioned a temple and divine statue for Ishtar-belat-Kidmuri, the same king "established for her her food and show offerings" (*nidabâša u takliša ukīnši*) (AE38:27–28), proving his providing commitment.

A special kind of fulfiling of the royal duty to provide the great gods with offerings took place in peripheral lands. At geographical extremes in the foreign lands, Shalmaneser III sacrifices to the deities, besides washing weapons and creating images, and then proceeds to arrange banquets in this clearly cultic context (e.g. SE14:70–72). As noted by Schachner (2009: 217–18), the spatial context, i.e. in or on a holy mountain, of the cliff reliefs at the Tigris source indicate their religious significance, modifying common views of them as crude expressions of state power and border establishing. Following up on this conclusion, the identifying of them as pure propaganda may be regarded as reproducing the Orientalist idea of Oriental despotism. Ashurnasirpal II does, on the other hand, never speak of offerings connected with these banquets, but he refers three times to offerings to the deities, after weapon cleansing and image creating, at the shores of "the Great Sea" (*tâmtu rabītu*), i.e. the Mediterranean (e.g. AE2:26–27). He also once tells of making sacrifices to "his deities" (*ilānišu*) after having felled trees, used for building in Assyria, on the western mountain range of Amanus (AE1:iii89).

Rituals, often termed *parṣu*, were a vital part of the priesthood role, in their complementing the actual offering of handing over material products. Shalmaneser III participated in rituals and ceremonies in Arbela and Assur at the triumphant returning from a campaign against Urartu (SE17:60–61). The narrative passages which refer to these events are unfortunately very brief and cryptic. They merely state that the king participated in "the festival" (*isinnu*) of Ishtar of Arbela, and that he took a sacred seat in Baltil, i.e. Assur. Ashurnasirpal II tells of himself as establishing and naming festivals in honour of Ninurta at the completion of the temple and cult paraphernalia dedicated to the same god (e.g. AE30:73–75). He established "strewn and incense offerings" (*sirqu, qutrīnu*) for the festival in question (AE30:75). The same king is also "the one to whom is perpetually entrusted the organization of the rites of the temples of his land" (*ša ana šutēšur parṣī ekurrāt mātišu pitqudu kajjāna*) (e.g. AE1:i24). Later kings were each "he who upholds the rites of Ekur" (*mukīl parṣī Ekur*) (e.g. SA5E2, An3E8:3). Liturgy was also a part of the cult of the Mesopotamian deities. Hymns (to Enlil) and prayers (to Ishtar, Ninlil, and Gula/Baba) are attested, and these may have once been used in the cult (AE173, AE171, SE154, An3E44 resp.).

As for iconography and the implementation of the Early Neo-Assyrian king's priestly role, he is illustrated as "maker of sacrifices" (*ēpiš nīqē*) and "king as cult participant" (*mušaklil parṣi*) – two motifs identified by Magen (1986). The cultic instrument of the cup is very much in focus here. The motif of the king holding a cup does in most cases represent the priestly act of pouring libations (Munn-Rankin 1974: 170; Brandes 1970: 151–55; J. M. Russell 1998b: 685), and is a motif identified as *pagulu ugdammir* (referring to the libation act) by Magen (1986: 65–69). The cup in itself may in its turn be regarded as a symbol of liquid offerings (Collins 2010: 184–85). Similarly understood, the motif of the king alone with his untilted cup may simply serve as a "shorthand" for libations (Porter 2010: 151). The most evident example of a libation act in the sources is when Shalmaneser III is depicted pouring libations from a cup in front of a relief (with his own image) and two divine standards (SI10:1t, see Fig. 25).[126] This scene from Lake Van/Urmia also illustrates priests, musicians, sacrifical animals, and soldiers throwing offering meat (?) into the lake. The absence of women in this scene is striking. It can be understood from a belief that cult on campaigns was a masculine domain (M. Marcus 1987). It would be too rash, or even erroneous, though to say that cult in general was restricted to men in Neo-Assyrian society (Svärd 2008).

As for other attestations of the king with the cup, he is depicted standing, holding a cup, and with an armed entourage around him, as he receives the submission act of Jehu of Israel on the Black Obelisk (SI11:A2). As for the cup and the Balawat gates, the king is also depicted sitting while holding the cup (e.g. SI10:14t.). The said ruler is also portrayed as riding bareback on a horse in approaching cultic activities dedicated to the making of a cliff relief (again portraying himself) at the Tigris source, later involving the cultic act of libation (SI10:10b.). The scene from the North-West Palace where Ashurnasirpal II sits holding a cup in his hand while human-headed genii purify him and an attendant seemingly refills his cup (AI4:G2–4) may also illustrate the king as priest. Judging from the presence of genii and the surrounding motifs, displaying cult

126 Shalmaneser III presumably performs the same ritual on a mountain in front of a stele in another, fragmentary scene which shows the stele but not the king (SI10:14t.).

acts, the interpretation of an earthly, victory banquet seems less likely.[127] On an ivory plaque from Fort Shalmaneser, the king, probably Shalmaneser III, stands with his entourage receiving tribute while holding a cup and an axe in his hands (SI23). Finally, Ashurnasirpal II is on a piece of ivory illustrated holding a cup to his mouth in his one hand and a sickle alluding to Ninurta (see s. 3.1) in his other hand (AI25).

Leaving the attribute of the cup in discussing the king's implementing of his ritual role as priest, Shamshi-Adad V is depicted as an officiating priest on the stone vessel of his field marshal Bel-luballit whose reliefs show cultic scenes in the upper register (SA5I2). The king and the crown prince or field marshal kneel on either side of what may have been a cult symbol, make the gestures of open hands and pointing fingers, while each being purified by a pair of genii. Since the relevant vessel was dedicated to Nergal, the cult symbol in question probably represented this god. As for the two adorants, it is of course also possible that the king is depicted twice. Similarly, a bareheaded king, probably Adad-narari III, gives the gestures of *ubāna tarāṣu* and open hand towards a goddess, who stands on an animal, while another goddess stands behind him and a winged sun disk hovers in mid-air over the scene (An3I13). Some sort of ritual is illustrated in these examples.

The sacred tree scene which arguably (see s. 3.1) illustrates the king venerating Ashur in the winged disk while a pair of honorary transposed genii pollinate the tree which symbolize the prosperity which is granted by the said deity is hard to avoid here (e.g. AI4:B23). The royal role of priest is here revealed by the king's garment, his gesture, and the divine emblems. The king is also depicted in tree scenes in the miniature reliefs of the North-West Palace. Depicted twice on either side of the tree, he makes the pointing gesture and holds a mace while the winged disk hovers in mid-air, the genii being absent this time (AI23:G3,29a–b). The same scene is also conveyed through seals from Kalhu and the 9th century BCE. On one of these, the king, depicted twice, makes the pointing gesture while touching a stream of water flowing from the figureless winged disk (AI32). The tree is clearly a date palm in this scene. On the seal of Mushezib-Ninurta, governor of Shadikanni, the king uses his two hands in the same way (AI33). This time though, he is purified by genii, the winged disk is antropomorph (thus being Ashur), and the tree seems to bear pomegranates. The glazed brick panel of Fort Shalmaneser which presents this king in another, genii lacking, version of the sacred tree scene, should also be mentioned

---

127 Also, banquets may be sacred (see subs. 5.4.4). According to Magen (1986), the scenes of the Assyrian king sitting with a raised cup to his mouth express the banquet motif.

(SI18). In sum, the priestly function of the ten kings is clearly illustrated in the visual sources.

The royal priestly role was not restricted to temples or outdoor sanctuaries. Also the palaces were localities in which cult directed by the king took place. The inauguration of the North-West Palace started with "Ashur, the great lord, and the deities of his (the king's) whole land" being invited in by the king (*Aššur bēlu rabû u ilāni ša māt gabbi ša ina libbi iqrâni*) (AE30:104–105). The word *qerû* in *iqrâni* can refer to inviting a deity to an offering (CAD Q: *qerû*). Through the ten day long festivities, the palace was "being consecrated" (*šurrû* Š) (e.g. AE30:102–104), a term used also to denote acts of the cult (CAD Š III: *šurrû* A). Some of the listed components of the "menu" of the associated banquet are seemingly of a cultic nature. Oxes and sheep belonging to Ishtar, as well as ducks and ghee, the latter offered to deities (CAD I–J: *iṣṣūru rabû*, CAD Ḫ: *ḫimētu*), are e.g. part of the list of the many odd and exotic menu components (AE30:106–40). Lastly, Ashurnasirpal II mentions that he arranged so that the *zāriqu* officials of his palaces took part in the inauguration (AE30:148). If the mentioned term is derived from the verb *zarāqu*, which can carry the notion of "sprinkle (liquids)" (CAD Z: *zarāqu*), these officials may then have been libation priests.

Furthermore, the adorning of palaces, e.g. the North-West Palace, is likened to that of temples, e.g. when lapis lazuli is described as decorating the doorways (e.g. AE30:32), and when exotic timber is specified as forming the core and doors of the palatial building (e.g. AE30:25–29). Temples or smaller shrines are referred to as being integrated into the palace area, e.g. at Balawat (AE50:23–24). The other way around, attributes from the palace sphere, such as royal statues, were integral parts of temple precincts (e.g. AI12, SI5). In sum, also the palace area was a locality where the royal function of priest was performed. Symbolic of the close relationship between the deities and the king is the clustering of several temples and shrines to the north and north-east of the North-West Palace (Reade 2002: 137 fig. 2), a feature (temples around palace) also found in e.g. Assur (see Fig. 2). All this of course puts further doubt into the old notion of a distinction between palace and temple in Mesopotamia, and discredits the idea of the relevance of the concept of secularism when speaking of Assyrian state ideology.

The notion of the king as "the servant" (*wardu*) of the deities is explicitly expressed by Adad-narari III and Shalmaneser IV who describe themselves with this word (An3E43:2, [S4E3:10]). The servant notion is implicitly expressed e.g. through the epithets "attentive prince" (*rubû na'du*) (e.g. AE1:i18, SE1:4), "the reverent one" (*šaḫtu*) (SE1:5, e.g. AE1:i11), "he who heeds the orders of the deities" (*ša ana ṭēmet ilāni upaqqû*) (SE1:6), "worshipper of the great gods" (*pāliḫ ilāni rabûti*) (SE16:3, e.g. AE1:i18), and "he who frequents the shrines of the deities within Esharra" (*mušte"û ašrāt ilāni ša qereb Ešarra*) (e.g. SE28:4). In other words, the king claims to have the servant-like qualities of his being attentive, respectful, and obedient.

As for the respectfulness, the word *šaḫtu* can also mean humble towards the divine (CAD Š I: *šaḫtu*), and the word *palāḫu* in *pāliḫ* also refers to fear of the deities (CAD P: *palāḫu*). The epithet "attentive prince" is standard in the titulary of some kings. In Ashurnasirpal II's case, this epithet heads a common and important cluster of royal epithets, attested e.g. in the Standard Inscription (AE23:12). The adjective "attentive" alludes to the constant readiness of the king to receive and fulfil the divine wishes. The "frequenting of shrines" referred to in the lastly mentioned epithet should carry the same connotations. The royal epithet "worshipper of the great gods" is frequently, i.e. no less than 19 times, attested in the titulary of Ashurnasirpal II, and is actually in second place in the said epithet cluster. Winter (1983: 24–28) sees these two royal epithets, along with the title "vice-regent of Ashur", as illustrated visually in the throne room of the North-West Palace. The epithet "he who heeds the orders of the deities" naturally refers to the idea that the servant-king has the duty to implement the wishes of the deities.

Regarding the narrative passages and the Early Neo-Assyrian kings as servants, Shalmaneser III is described as obeying the command of Marduk, before he "respectfully" (*palḫiš*) presents offerings to the deities of Babylon, Borsippa, and Cuthae (SE5:v4–vi5), all in the context of a Babylonian campaign. The ten kings are constantly described as obeying the "commands" (*pû, siqru, qabû, qibītu, ṭēmu, wâru* D) of the deites, most often Ashur's, e.g. concerning the commissioning of temples or cult objects, the initiating of military campaigns, and the embarking upon hunting (e.g. AE1:i104, AE2:25–26, SE6:iv42 resp.). These wishes and orders are holy and beyond questioning. Several divine epithets refer to the deities, here Ninurta, as those "whose pronouncements can not be altered" (*ša lā uttakkaru siqir šaptišu*) (AE1:i5), expressing the perfect quality of the divine orders. Also the commands of Ea and Enlil are described in these terms (e.g. AE100:2, AE46:2 resp.). The state archival material that has been preserved from Nineveh and the Late Neo-Assyrian Period gives an image of the king as constantly seeking guidance and support from the deities, e.g. through scholarly reports on omens and astrology (Starr 1990; Hunger 1992).

As for the iconography and the Early Neo-Assyrian king's status and function as servant, as already noted, his pointing finger may be understood as meaning communication with the deities, and his clasped hands may signify respect and humility. As already noted, some of the statues of Shalmaneser III exhibit the gesture of clasped hands. The unproportionally large eyes on some non-narrative royal images may, as Winter (1989: 583) has noted, express the constant attentiveness of the king regarding the wishes and needs of the deities. Unproportionally large eyes are attested through the royal image on Ashurnasirpal II's stele at the Ninurta temple as well as in a cliff relief portraying Shalmaneser III (AI19, SI16). Not only large eyes speak of the high degree of royal attentiveness, but the unproportionally large ears on some royal statues do likewise (AI12, SI8). Through his ears the king can receive the divine commands. Additionally, the king's large ears may signify the great wisdom which the ruler claims to possess (Winter 1989: 583),[128] and which was granted by the god Ea (e.g. AE38:22–24).

Summing up, I have argued that both the textual and visual sources of the Early Neo-Assyrian kings – especially the visual non-narrative ones – consistently illustrate the king in the interrelated roles of priest and servant in relation to Ashur and the great gods. This is a reflection of the notion of the non-secular and religious character of Assyrian kingship, and of the important role that religious connections played in the royal propaganda.

4.3 Master builder of the great gods

In this section, I will argue that another function of the Assyrian king was to create and care for monuments and holy objects of the deities. Based on this, I now turn to the function of the king as the master builder of the great gods. Narrative passages state that temples, cult paraphernalia, and royal "images" were created and cared for in various locations. Also in the building context, non-secularism and the intertwining of religion and politics are apparent.

Monumental building was a royal duty and prerogative in Mesopotamia, and temple building appears as a typically Mesopotamian ideological theme (Roaf 2013: 336–37, 348), although also the Egyptian kings used this theme frequently (Kuhrt 1997). Building (and fighting) for the deities are the main themes of Mesopotamian royal inscriptions (Liverani 1995: 2360–61), and in Mesopotamian state art, rulers portrayed themselves as the deities' master builder.[129] The Sumerian ruler Gudea even depicted himself as an architect (see Johansen 1978: pls. 19–22, 28–32). As for Assyria specifically, this role is e.g. reflected in the structure of many Assyrian royal inscriptions which mainly

128 To be a listener and "wide-eared" (*uznā rapšātu*) was the same as being intelligent in the terminology and belief system of ancient Mespotamia (Winter 1989: 583).
129 See e.g. Ur-Nanshe of Lagash (c. 2500), and Ur-Nammu (2112–2095) of Ur III. The latter also carries building tools on his shoulders. See Parrot 1983: figs. 158, 229 respectively.

contain a narration of military deeds followed by a building inscription. Although the narrations of warfare tend to dominate many inscriptions of the Middle and Neo-Assyrian periods, the textual component which centres on the king as producing temples and cult objects was never abandoned. As the study of Lackenbacher (1982) regarding the role of the Assyrian king as master builder shows, the phenomenon of royal building activity was a vital element of the ruler's propaganda. Some Assyrian kings like Ashurbanipal are even depicted through the age-old pose of bearing a basket on their heads, carrying the soil which were handled during the holy construction projects (see Magen 1986: figs. 5:2, 5:4). Neo-Assyrian (and Neo-Babylonian) kings liked to "boast of their humility" in this manner (Ellis 1968: 160–61).

The royal role of master builder for the deities is much highlighted by the Early Neo-Assyrian kings. However, this is expressed almost exclusively in the textual narrative. As for the exceptions, the statue of a seated Shalmaneser III, positioned at the Tabira Gate and city wall, which the relevant ruler commissioned work on, may depict the king as master builder, given the sitting pose and the text's emphasis on construction (SI4, SE25:21–47). The royal epithets referring explicitly to this master builder function are relatively few. Actually, only two epithets allude directly to Shalmaneser III's temple building role, namely "builder of the the temple of Anu and Adad" (*bāni bīt Anim bīt Adad*) and "builder of Ashur's courtyard" (*bānû kisal Aššur*) (SE54:4–5, SE103:3 resp.). Expressing the same modesty of attestation, Ashurnasirpal II is twice referred to as "the one who made and repaired the temple of Ishtar of Nineveh, my (his) mistress" (*ša bīt Ištar ša Ninua bēltī ēpušma° arṣip°*) (e.g. AE111:4). Shamshi-Adad V was "he who has dedicated heart and mind, and being at hand for, the work of Ehursagkurkurra and the temples of his land" (*ša ana šipri Eḫursagkurkurra ekurrāti mātišu gummur libbašuma bašâ uznāšu*) (e.g. SA5E1:i32–33), implying the engaging in building activities.

Proceeding to the textual narrative, Grayson (1991: 189–90) notes that Ashurnasirpal II repeatedly refers to his building projects, especially in Kalhu. Beside the North-West Palace, the king ordered "temples" or "sanctuaries" (*bīt* DN, *ekurru, māḫāzu, ešertu*) to be built in the honour of Ninurta, Sharrat-niphi, and the Sibitti. Sanctuaries for Adad, Shala, Ea-sharru, Damkina, Gula, Ishtar-belat-Kidmuri, Nabu, Enlil, and Sin are also spoken of. In Nineveh he commissioned work on a palace and the temples of Adad and Ishtar, and in Assur work was done on the temples of Sin-Shamash and Ashur. In Balawat he ordered a small palace and a temple for Mamu. As for Shalmaneser III, Grayson (1996: 5) observes that the king refers to works on the Ashur, the Anu-Adad, and Sharrat-niphi temples in Assur, and that he mentions constructions on the temple and ziggurat of Ninurta, the Nabu temple, and Fort Shalmaneser in Kalhu. The king in question also refers to works on temple (of Ishtar) and palaces in Nineveh and Balawat. The royal prerogative in monumental building was not absolute in practice. Several high officials dedicated cult paraphernalia (e.g. SE31:17–19), and the governors Nergal-erish and Bel-Harran-beli-usur (re)built cities (An3E7:13–20, S4E2:9–14 resp.), the latter seemingly independent of the king (Grayson 1996: 241).

The first step in the building process was the divine revelation to the king regarding their desires for temples.[130] Building was thus divinely inspired. In the next stage, preparations for the actual building activities were made. Planning the layouts, omen-deducted "celestial writing" could serve as model and archetype for the topographic setting of temples and royal cities (Frahm 2013: 107). As for more tangible kinds of preparations, renovations often involved the clearing away of the dilapidated building remains. Resource management was of course another preparation component. Ashurnasirpal II e.g. explicitly states that the trees which he, or in reality his soldiers or prisoners of war, felled in the west then were used in the constructing of sacred buildings in Assyria (e.g. AE1:iii88–92). The actual building, preceded by and continuously involving various rituals and purification procedures, then followed (Ellis 1968: 6–33; Lackenbacher 1982: 129–44).

The act of building is typically expressed through the following wording: "At that time ... that wall had become dilapidated, and I cleared its dilapidated (portions), reaching to its foundation in bedrock. I completely rebuilt it from its foundations to its crenellations, (and) decorated it more splendidly than before" (SE10:iv40–50).[131] The typical building inscription then proceeds to describe the luxurious material used in the construction, emphasizing the personal involvement of the king (e.g. AE30:25–32). As for the latter, the theme of royal participation in building activities for the deities is consistently conveyed in Mesopotamian state ideology (Ellis 1968: 20–33). The ultimate goals with the temple building were to "calmly settle DN in his/her cella" (*ina atmeniša nēḫiš ušēšib*) (AE40:37), and to please the relevant deity with this royal act of fulfiling his/her commands (AE40:37). In this way, the potential wrath of the gods and goddesses, so characteristic of religious thought in Mesopotamia (Bottéro 2001a: 219–23), could be avoided.

Some royal building projects are presented as new, others are renovations of earlier, decayed temples. As for the latter case, the Sharrat-niphi temple of

---

130 This revelation may e.g. come in the shape of a dream, such as in the cylinder inscriptions of Gudea regarding the Ningirsu temple (see Edzard 1998: text E3/1.1.7.CylA:i17–19).

131 Transcribed as follows: *enūma ... dūra šuātu ēnaḫma anḫūssu unakkir dannassu kiṣir šadê lū akšud ištu uššēšu adi gabadibbišu arṣip ušaklil eli maḫrê ussim ušarriḫ*.

Kalhu, reworked by the builders of Ashurnasirpal II, is even described as having "turned into a mound and ruin" (*ana tilli u karme uterra*) (AE38:21–22). In these contexts, the said king refers to temples and sanctuaries which had been built or renovated by his all distant forefathers Shamshi-Adad I (e.g. AE57:2), Shalmaneser I (e.g. AE23:15), and Ashur-uballit I (AE56:14). The pious king renovates these temples, often with a wording which expresses the concept of "heroic priority", i.e. the king outdoes his predecessors' building achievements (e.g. AE40:36). Still, adherence to the old ground plan was paradoxically a virtue (Roaf 2013: 347–48). Ideally, an Assyrian king, in this case Adad-narari III, completed the building project, here a palace in Nineveh, which was begun by his predecessor (An3E13).

The rules and regulations for renovation projects are given in the curses and blessing sections where future rulers are urged to behave in the same way as the ruling king claims to have behaved with regards to his predecessor's monuments (e.g. AE40:38–44). They shall renovate the temple (e.g. AE153) or palace (e.g. AE26:67–68, SE42:10–11) in question when it falls into decay, and if they do this they will be rewarded by the deities (e.g. SE39:13). The call to future rulers also convey instructions on what the future ruler should *not* do (e.g. AE17:v26–45). If the successor e.g. neglects, destroys, or abandons the building, the deities will punish him severely (e.g. AE17:v54–103). The duty to construct and renovate sacred buildings is thus not just related to the deities but also to the royal line (see subs. 5.4.7). A breaking of this bond between the royal generations turned the breaking party into "the Other", i.e. an hostile, enemy force (see subs. 5.4.8).

Standard narrations of (re)building often conclude with the words: "I placed my monumental and clay inscriptions therein" (*narīja u temmēnija ina libbi aškun* (SE10:l.e.2–3), alluding to the object (tablet, prism, cylinder) on which the text in question was written.[132] The inscribed objects (*narû, temmēnu, musarrû, zikir šumija*) in question could be deposited both in palaces and temples. Ashurnasirpal II explicitly states that he inscribed his *narû*, whereafter he deposited it in a temple, here to Mamu (AE50:33–34). In case of a renovation project, the inscribed object should be placed beside those of the king's predecessors. Consequently, the king mentions that he deposited his own inscription together with that of a former ruler (e.g. SE25:29–31), and he urges his successors to do likewise (e.g. AE28:v14–15). Curse sections often bring up the sacrilegious acts of changing, erasing, moving, discarding, or destroying old inscribed objects (e.g. AE17:v54–103). Especially taboo was the act

132 In the Early Neo-Assyrian Period, the former type of object probably referred to stone tablets, while the latter one seems to have refered to clay prisms (Ellis 1968: 149–50).

of replacing the predecessor's name with the ruling king's own (e.g. AE148:16–17). Blessing sections naturally urges the successor to do the opposite, thus showing loyalty towards the past.[133]

These deposited objects were seen as holy. When the king renovated a building he had the duty to respect his predecessor's inscribed objects by anointing them with oil, make sacrifices, and return them to their settings (e.g. SE13:l.e.5′–10′). Occasionally, posterity is exhorted to see, read, anoint, offer to, and return the object (e.g. AE152:17–19). The inscribed objects were clearly regarded as holy and as integral parts of the building, whether temple or palace. The act of depositing inscribed objects was part of the consecration of a building (Lackenbacher 1982).[134] Apart from being monuments for posterity and the deities, and sanctifying the constructed building, they also had an apotropaic function like other foundation deposits (Ellis 1968: 165–68). Inscribed gold and silver tablets serving as foundation deposits are preserved from the reign of Ashurnasirpal II in Apqu (AE70).

As discussed earlier (see s. 4.2), the distinction between palaces and temples is not a clearcut one, in that also palaces were seen as sacred buildings. The notion of the North-West Palace as a sacred place has already been discussed. In this context, the future ruler is urged in harsh terms to use and maintain the relevant building (e.g. AE17:v24–45). Strong curses are directed at those who neglects it, deserts it, destroys it, turns it into a storage, and the like (e.g. AE17:v54–103). The sacred status of palaces is not the least expressed by the circumstance that the Old Palace of Assur was used as a burial place for Assyrian rulers, evidenced e.g. by the sarcophagi of Ashurnasirpal II and Shamshi-Adad V (see Andrae 1938: 194–201, figs. 173–74). The other way around, royal monuments, such as the Tell al-Rimah Stele in the Adad temple of Zamahu (Börker-Klähn 1982: 196), could be a part of temples. Not only the distinction between the roles of master builder and priest was diffuse, but also the boundaries between master builder and warrior were blurred, since ambitious projects were dependent on the financial resources which military campaigns could result in (Roaf 2013: 348).

In extension, whole cities could be regarded as constructed for the sake of deities. Such is the case with Ashurnasirpal II and his Kalhu. In two texts from the Assyrian heartland the said ruler declares about Kalhu that: "I dedicated this city to Ashur, my lord" (*āla šū ana Aššur bēlija aqīssu*) (AE30:40, AE33:27′).

---

133 The name of Shalmaneser IV was substituted by that of Tiglath-pileser III on the Tell Abta Stele (Grayson 1996: 241), giving evidence that this norm was not always followed (S4E2:9).

134 Other such consecration acts were measuring, the mixing of mortar, brick moulding, basket bearing, name giving, and installation of the deity (Lackenbacher 1982: 129–44).

The same city is also called "the centre of my lordship" (*māḫāz bēlūtija*) (AE30:53). The first noun can refer to a shrine or cultic centre (CAD M I: *māḫāzu*). Thus, the whole city can be viewed as a sanctuary. In a very frequent narrative passage (e.g. AE26:46–48), Kalhu is described as having turned into a "mound and ruin" (*tillu, karmu*) since the days of Shalmaneser I who arguably founded the city. The description of the rebuilding of the city of Apqu by Adad-narari II uses the same expressions and terminology as above (e.g. An2E2:36–38). The same terminology is used to describe the rebuilding of temples and other sanctuaries (e.g. AE38:21–22). The royal creating of the capital city carried special connotations in Mesopotamia, associating with the divine sphere and cosmogony (Charpin 2011).

Ashurnasirpal II, like any other Mesopotamian ruler, presents himself as the actual builder of temples and sanctuaries. Occasionally, he acknowledges that the actual toiling was made by deported people from his military campaigns. A common expression, also found in the texts of Shalmaneser III, is that he "uprooted" (*nasāḫu*) "people" (*nišu, ṣābu, ummānu*) from unsubmissive, conquered cities and regions (e.g. AE17:ii100, SE10:ii3–6). They were brought to Kalhu to engage in various work projects of forced labour such as the building of temples, palaces, gardens, and canals.[135] Ashurnasirpal II enumerates peoples from various regions whom he used as a labour resource, giving the notion of the whole world (AE30:33–36). After conquesting, the king imposed "corvẹe" (*zābil kudurri*) (e.g. AE17:i79), "feudal duty" (*ālku*) (AE19:99), and "servitude" (*urdūtu*) (e.g. AE1:iii125) on the foreign people and elite, often consisting of forced labour in Assyria. The said king explicitly refers to these individuals, sometimes termed "state labourers" (*urāṣu*) (e.g. AE1:ii100), as performing their *kudurru* in Kalhu (e.g. AE1:ii79–80). This term can refer to earth carrying labour, i.e. building work (CAD K: *kudurru* B). Heading the hierarchy, the king was the master builder. Adding a gender perspective to this position, the king appears victoriously as "the dominant male" in this relationship (see subs. 5.4.9).

It is obvious that also architecture and its associated building rituals can express the world view of a given society, ancient or modern (Geertz 1973), in this case complementing Assyrian royal inscriptions and iconography. Temples and palaces had a political-propagandistic as well as a religious role (Winter 1993; J. M. Russell 1998b: 712), inspiring a sense of community and/or awe among the populace (Pollock 1999: 174). The architectural creations signalled that the ruler had the power and resources to control people's labour, and to

---

135 Royal gardens functioned as components of imperial propaganda in Assyria (and Persia) (Stronach 1990). For the king as "gardener/provider", see (sub)sections 5.1 and 5.4.4.

even change the landscape itself (Roaf 2013: 352). Grand architectural objects thus functioned as statements of a ruler's great power.

The Early Neo-Assyrian kings often declare that they commissioned building elements and cult paraphernalia of different kinds to various deities. Shalmaneser III refers in his inscriptions to the creation of building elements such as temple thresholds (e.g. SE93), or to cult paraphernalia such as altars (SE95) and stone maces (e.g. SE97). Thresholds and a throne base from Fort Shalmaneser are also mentioned by the king (SE30–35, SE28 resp.), as well as by his Kalhu governor who dedicated some of these objects (SE30–31, SE62). Ashurnasirpal II claims to have provided daises, thrones, and seats of the deities in his role as master builder (e.g. AE30:59–60). Moreover, a stone altar is dedicated to Enlil (AE98), stone mace heads are given to Ishtar-belat-Kidmuru and Ea (AE99, AE100 resp.), and a stone vase is dedicated to Ninurta (AE101). Not only objects of stone were given to the deities in their temples. Also smaller building elements such as bricks and "cones" (*siqqat karri*) of burned or sun-dried clay, which e.g. functioned as the facing of temples, were often inscribed with label texts (e.g. AE131, SE53:8). Even clay cones could be votive objects and dedicated to deities (An3E21).[136]

Turning to elaborate and exclusive elements made of wood or metal, Ashurnasirpal II narrates that he commissioned roofs and huge doors made of various kinds of exclusive timber for the sanctuaries of the deities. The timber made up of cedar tree (*erēnu*) is often spoken of in these contexts (e.g. AE28:10). The Banquet Stele enumerates the exotic and valuable kind of timber which were used in the building of palaces and temples in Kalhu (AE30:25–28). Cedar timber is also described as being used for gates and roofs of the Shulmanu temple in Dur-Katlimmu during Adad-narari III (An3E42). Metal door bands (*misarru*) are also referred to in building accounts (e.g. AE30:28–29). Also the creating of "colossi" (*umāmu*) are mentioned by Ashurnasirpal II (e.g. AE2:58–59). Another kind of mythical creature is referred to when the same king states that he installed "dragons" (*ušumgallu*) beside the throne of Ninurta (AE30:72–73). Tukulti-Ninurta II in his turn furnished a temple with a pair of *kurību*-genii (TN2E5:26–27).

As for the arguably most important cult paraphernalia, namely divine and royal (votive) statues, one of Shalmaneser III's royal statues is dedicated to Adad of Kurba'il and the sanctuary of this deity, and can thus be regarded as a part of the actual temple entity (SI5). The texts on his two royal statues from a city gate of Assur make it clear that also these monuments may be regarded

136 This is naturally in line with the prevalent idea in Mesopotamia of objects related to the king or deities being sacred or even divine in their own right (Selz 2008).

as sculptures for the deities in that they contain dedications and frequent references to deities in their respective narrations (SE25, SE40, SI4, SI6). As for divine statues and Shalmaneser III, he also prides himself with having commissioned a grand, luxurious statue of the Phoenician god Armada (SE55:4–6). As for Ashurnasirpal II, he e.g. refers in detail to the creating of the statues of a number of deities generally as well as specifically to that of Ishtar-belat-Kidmuri. These are described as fashioned in red gold, and as adorned with various precious stones (e.g. AE30:65–67, AE38:25–27 resp.). At the inaugurations of new or renovated temples, the divine statue was installed in its cella (e.g. AE50:24–25). This temple room was a centre point and mysteriously dimned. In a curse, the future ruler is urged not to let the divine statue be exposed to the sun (AE38:31). In another text, the temple cella of Ninurta is described as luxuriously made (AE30:69–70). His only royal statue formed an integral part of the Sharrat-niphi temple (AI12).

A characteristic feature of Shalmaneser III's text corpus is his mentioning of erecting monuments and of performing rituals when geographical extremes were reached. The theme of Shalmaneser III making the "image of my (his) kingship" (*ṣalam šarrūtija*) is frequent (e.g. SE2:ii62).[137] The word *ṣalmu* refers to an image of all kinds of material in the round or on a flat surface (CAD Ṣ: *ṣalmu*). Basically it means "image", and solely the context determines whether it alludes to reliefs, stelae, statues, or cliff reliefs. The king describes how he creates these images on his campaigns, and the divine recipients, if stated, are Ashur and Shamash (e.g. SE2:i49–50). The typical wording regarding this creating is: "I made my very great royal image (and) wrote thereon praises of Ashur, my lord, (and of) all actions of my heroism which I had done in foreign lands. I erected it therein" (SE14:71–72).[138] Ashurnsairpal II does to a much lesser degree bring up the act of erecting images in the periphery. His terminology is also much more restricted, in that he only uses the terms "image of my kingship" or "of my likeness" (*ṣalam bunnanija*) (e.g. AE1:i97–98, AE1:ii5 resp.). Also a few earlier and later kings commissioned these objects. Shamshi-Adad V e.g. claims that he erected his "image of my kingship" in a conquered city (SA5E1:ii20–27).

Most images were placed at geographical extremes, such as those at the Mediterranean, the Sea of Nairi, Mt Amanus, Mt Atalur, Mt Lallar, Cape Balira,

---

137 These monuments are alternatively and occasionally termed "(image of) my likeness" (*bunnanija*) (e.g. SE1:35), "my lordship" (*bēlūtija*) (e.g. SE2:ii8), "my strength" (*gešrūtija*) (SE40:iii3), "my power" (*kiššūtija*) (SE13:1′–2′rev.), or simply "slab" (*asumettu*) (SE3:96).

138 Transcribed in the following way: *ṣalam šarrūtija šurbâ ēpuš tanatti Aššur bēlija alkakāt qurdija mimma ša ina mātāti ētepuša° ina qerbiša ašṭur ina libbi ušezziz.*

Mt Lebanon, at an Euphrates crossing, at the sources of the Tigris and the Euphrates, on northern/eastern mountains, or on mountains named after their huge deposits of silver and alabaster (e.g. SE10:i29–30, SE10:iii27–29), while the rest were erected in a cultural landscape such as in Assur or in northern, eastern or western cities and temples (e.g. SE14:156, SE6:iii45). Image creating at the Tigris source is illustrated on the Balawat Gate (SI10:10). The Kurkh Stele and the cliff relief at Kenk Boğazı are, next to the cliff reliefs at the Tigris source, this king's archaeologically attested images outside Assyria proper (SI13, SI15, SI16–17 resp.). Ashurnasirpal II created images outside Kalhu and Assyria proper in a palace, at the source of the river Subnat, on mountains, and on a sacred feature (?) in a citadel area (AE1:i97–99, AE1:i104–105, AE33:7′, AE1:i68–69 resp.). The Kurkh Monolith and the Babil Stele are preserved from the border areas, the latter being stationed at the source of the said Subnat river (AI18, AI17 resp.).

The spatial context of the peripheral images raises questions regarding their purpose. Many of them were erected at fairly inaccessible places, namely those on cliffs and mountains, by waters, and in caves, making the propaganda dimension improbable, i.e. if focusing solely on the aspect of access to the relevant monuments. At the same time, others were situated in relatively public spaces, namely those in city squares, temples, and palaces.

These royal monuments have often been characterized as symbolic border markers (Garelli 2000: 48; Tadmor 2000: 56; Yamada 2000: 294). In this sense, Liverani (1990: 59–60) refers to them as marking "symbolic attainment of the world border" by the Assyrian king. Reade (1979a: 340–44) recognizes their religious motifs, but simultaneously talks of propaganda and describes them as "political posters and trademarks of the Assyrian empire". Morandi (1988), in his study on the topic, also emphasizes the propagating significance of these monuments. The stele here had the dual propagandistic functions of praising and intimidating. The relevant motif shows the Assyrian king as a pious and peaceful priest, while the accompanying text presents the ruler as a merciless conqueror of unsubmissive lands (Liverani 1982a: 132). These stelae (and cliff reliefs) in the periphery then had the combined function of signifying piety and triumph (Magen 1986: 52–53), and should be understood mainly as border markers, although appearing to be *Siegesdenkmal*, i.e. victory monuments (Börker-Klähn 1982: 197).

Looking again at the sources, the border marking interpretation is affirmed by the stationing of many of these stelae and cliff reliefs at borders, and by some stelae texts telling of the establishing of boundaries. Both the Pazarcik Stele (An3I5) and the Antakya Stele (An3I6) were situated at borders (the latter by the Orontes river in Syria), while their inscriptions relate border establishing

(Börker-Klähn 1982: 197; J. M. Russell 1998–2001: 251). The Para Stele (An3I7) was raised in the distant island state of Arwad, and not in its secondary setting Jebel Sinjar, thus telling of its border function (Börker-Klähn 1982: 198). The border aspect of these Assyrian monuments in the periphery thus seems clear, although the relative weight of their inherent political and religious aspects remains to be established more closely.

Stressing the religious aspect, Shafer (1998) emphasizes rituals and inaccessability, and sees "the Assyrians" as the intended recipients in her study on these royal monuments of the periphery. The references to them as political propaganda are rejected in favour of identifying them as genuine objects of cult for especially the royal line but also for the Assyrian soldiers. Similarly, Yamada (2000: 294–98) suggests, regarding the images which were created in a cultural landscape, that these functioned as worshippers and as objects by which oath swearing took place. Yet again, an interpretation which mainly sees these objects as carrying religious beliefs rather than political propaganda is put forward. The same trend is represented by Ataç (2010) in his complex understanding of the reliefs of the North-West Palace as conveying an esoteric philosophy with whom few were initiated. These stances modify the mainstream statements on Assyrian royal inscriptions and iconography as mainly or exclusively carrying political propaganda (e.g. Liverani 1979; Winter 1981; J. M. Russell 1998b; Lumsden 2004).

Obviously, the king's images must have had religious as well as political significance. As noted by Bahrani (2003: 166), reproducing notions of Oriental despotism by recognizing solely their propaganda dimension is too easily made. At the same time, there is no need to return to a naïve, old-fashioned understanding of the royal inscriptions and iconography as expressing an Assyrian *Volksseele*, and as being free from manipulation or underlying political aims (see subs. 1.4.2). That being said, the religious significance of the images is apparent e.g. through their often limited accessibility and their ritual context, and there is also the typological context which states that this kind of monument carries religious motifs, e.g. "king as venerating priest" in relation to divine emblems in mid-air. At the same time, their existence in public spaces alludes to an aim of propagating. This discussion may be an example of how misplaced and anachronistic it probably is to distinguish sacred and profane spheres in studying the cultures of the Ancient Near East. In any case, these images clearly illustrate the king's function of creating and caring for monuments and objects of the deities.

Summing up, I have argued that the king's role of master builder for the great gods is much attested in the sources, above all in the textual narrative. This role was manifested in the creating of temples, building elements, cult objects, and "images". Religious monuments also served as political propaganda. Also the creating of palaces and cities was seen as building for the deities, in line with a fundamentally non-secular type of approach.

4.4 Warrior of the great gods

In this section, I will argue that the Assyrian king was not just a priest, servant, and builder in relation to the Mesopotamian deities but also their warrior, having the mission of effectuating their theoretical world dominion. The great gods ordered the Assyrian king to engage in imperialistic warfare. This warrior role was intimately connected to the priestly role. Being engaged in an Assyrian kind of holy war, the king is described as almost superhuman.

The idea of rulers as the warrior of the deities, with the latter as the actual warriors (see s. 3.2), is not restricted to Assyria, but is a general feature of Mesopotamian state ideology (Labat 1939: 361; Liverani 1995: 2360–61). It is also found in the comparable culture of ancient Egypt (Quirke 1992: 62–66). Turning specifically to Assyria, a conquering mission is articulated e.g. in the coronation texts (see s. 2.2). In the hymn, it is e.g. said that: "May they (the great gods) give him (the king) a just sceptre to extend the land and his people!" (*ḫaṭṭa iširtu ana ruppuš māti u nišēšu liddinūniššu*) (see Livingstone 1989: text 11:17). Extending the borders of Assyria was seen as the primary duty of the Assyrian king (Tadmor 2000: 55). The act of "moving borders" was a vital part of Assyrian state ideology, and was regarded as a means of satisfying the wishes of the deities. Failure to do so on the part of the king would signal divine abandonment (Liverani 1990: 79). Tellingly, he had this imperialist role as high priest of Ashur (Reade 1983: 13). The role of "priesthood" (*šangûtu*) was intimately connected to a worldly mission of conquest (Machinist 2011: 408–409). It was solely the deities who had the legitimate authority to declare war, and the king only functioned as "the rod of wrath" in the hands of the deities (Oded 1991: 223–27). In the king's role of divinely inspired warrior, the notions of "sacralization of war" and "theologization of history" are articulated (Pongratz-Leisten 2001: 230).

The coronation message of a royal duty to extend the borders of Assyria is repeated in Early Neo-Assyrian propaganda, e.g. when Ashurnasirpal II defines himself as "he who extends the borders of his land" (*murappišu° miṣir mātišu*) (AE40:8). It is also given in the passages between the section of epithets and the start of the campaign narrations. These centrally placed passages of the text can be regarded as carrying the "abstract" or "political concept" of the whole inscription (Cancik-Kirschbaum 1997: 71). Shalmaneser III here claims that Ashur chose him in his (Ashur's) heart and with his eyes for the shepherdship of Assyria, and that the god "granted me (the king) a strong weapon which fells the insubordinate, he crowned me with an exalted crown, (and) he sternly commanded me the dominion to rule over and to make submit all the lands unsubmissive to Ashur" (SE2:i13–14).[139] The conquering theme of the coronation texts and the idea that Assyrian wars were initiated by the deities are clearly expressed in this particular abstract.

Continuing on the same theme, Ashurnasirpal II claims that Ashur called him, made his kingship supreme, and instructed and ordered warfare (AE19:25–27). In yet other abstracts, Ashur also puts a weapon in the king's hand, or makes his kingship supreme over all the rulers of the four quarters, makes his name supreme, puts a weapon in his hand, and sternly commands the king to conquer (e.g. AE1:i17–18, AE17:i54–59 resp.). Anu, Enlil, and Ea assure the king of his legitimacy, whereafter they sternly command him "to rule over and make submit all the lands unsubmissive to Ashur" (*mātāti lā māgirūt Aššur ana pêli u šuknuši*) (AE40:10–12). Additionally, the great gods are described as having "sternly commanded (the king) to rule, make submit, and govern the lands and mighty highlands" (*mātāti u ḫuršāni dannūte ana pêli šuknuše u šapāri aggiš uma"irūni*) (AE2:24–25). Interestingly enough, the verb *târu* in the D-stem is employed in some of the king's conquest narrations (e.g. AE50:19). Although this is quite speculative, its basic meaning of "to bring back" (CAD T: *târu*) may allude to the idea that the Early Neo-Assyrian kings saw themselves as restoring the borders, thereby reconquering, of the Middle Assyrian Period (Bagg 2011: 191–94).

Annals and display inscriptions are on the whole dominated by the theme of divinely ordered imperialism. The common phrase "by the command of DN" (*ina qibīt*/*pî* DN) which introduces campaign narratives is an expression of this theme (e.g. AE1:i104, SE2:ii1). With the exception of the Babylonian campaigns where sometimes solely Marduk commands warfare (SE5:v4), Ashur is always mentioned when war commanding deities are spoken of in the texts of Shalmaneser III (e.g. SE16:34–35). The texts of Ashurnasirpal II are more varied in this respect. This king marches out or engage in warfare by the command of not only Ashur alone (e.g. AE21:8′), but also by that of Ashur, Shamash, and Adad (AE1:i104), by the command of Ashur and Ishtar (e.g. AE1:i70), by that of Ashur and Ninurta (AE2:25–26), or by the command of Ashur and the divine standards (e.g. AE17:iii29–30). Ashur is however always part of the relevant phrase on commanding.

---

139 Transcribed as follows: *kakka dannu mušamqit lā māgirī ušatmeḫannima agâ ṣīra uppira bēlūti° napḫar mātāti lā māgirūt Aššur ana pêli u šuknuše aggiš uma"eranni.*

Also the subgenres of letter to and from a god tell of the military duties of the Assyrian king in relation to his divine superiors and order givers, primarily Ashur. As already noted (see s. 3.2), letters from a god present the picture of the king having conducted warfare which was divinely inspired and circumscribed. The same picture is given in letters to a god, where Ashur and all the other deities within the god's temple precinct are greeted by the king, the state of the king and his army is mentioned (S4E3, An3E43), and a note on divinely decreed warfare is made (Oppenheim 1960). Finally, a ceremonial bringing of the bodies of Assyrian soldiers, killed in battle, in front of Ashur is made under the supervision of a "lector priest" (*lišān rēšēti*) (S4E3). The king's wars were the deities' wars. Consequently, Shalmaneser III states in his letter to a god-like inscription that his military campaign to Urartu in fact was a "campaign of Ashur" (*girri Aššur*) (SE17:19).[140]

As is suggested by the above, the conquering mission is closely – although not exclusively – associated with Ashur. Also several royal epithets, in addition to the textual narrative and the winged disk, convey this idea. Shalmaneser III was e.g. "slaughterer of those [un]submissive to Ashur" (*šāgiš* [... *lā*] *kanšūt Aššur*) (SE5:i2–3). Ashurnasirpal II quite often calls himself "he who has competed with every last enemy of Ashur, above and below" (*nākirūt Aššur pāṭ gimrišunu eliš u šapliš ištananu*), and less often "conqueror of Ashur's foes" (*kāšid ajjābūt Aššur*), or "he who makes those insubordinate to Ashur submit to the borders above and below" (*mušekniš lā māgirūt Aššur ša pāṭāti eliš u šapliš*) (e.g. AE1:i27, AE1:i28, AE40:3–4 resp.). Tukulti-Ninurta II made use of Ashur's weapons to defeat their common enemies in the royal epithet of "he whose weapons Ashur has sharpened" (*ša Aššur kakkēšu ušaḫḫilu*) (e.g. TN2E2). Thus the king realized the world mastership of Ashur in particular and the great gods in general.

As for "weapons" (*kakku*), a common expression in the texts of the Early Neo-Assyrian kings is that the ruler "mustered my (his) chariots and troops" (*narkabātija ummānātija adki*) after having received the divine commands for imperialism just identified and discussed (e.g. AE1:i45, SE6:i29). On this mission, the kings needed effective weapons (beside chariots and troops), and these were then handed down to the kings from above. The great gods were "the ones who granted to his dominion their (the deities') furious weapons" (*kakkīšunu ezzūte ana širikte bēlūtišu išrukū*) and the ones who made him superior to any other king of the four quarters with respect to "the aura of his

---

140 It was however Shamshi-Adad V who started to order his annalistic accounts based on *girru* instead of according to *limmu* or *palû* (e.g. SA5E1:i53), arguably expressing military emphasis and a device to cover up campaign incontinuity (Tadmor 1981; Siddall 2013: 158).

weapons" (*šalummat kakkīšu*) (e.g. AE17:i23–24, AE17:i24–25 resp.). The theme of the deities granting weapons is, as evident from the above, often expressed in abstracts.[141] Occasionally, the king is likened to the weapons which had been provided by the deities. Adad-narari II is a "furious dagger" (*patre šalbabe*) (e.g. An2E2:19), while Ashurnasirpal II is "the weapon of the great gods" (*kašūš ilāni rabûti*) (e.g. AE1:i11). Tellingly, the word *kašūšu* denotes a divine weapon (CAD K: *kašūsu*), in this way alluding to the role of the deities of granting their weapons to the Assyrian king.

The divine weapons which the king used in his conquering mission were regarded as cult objects (Selz 2008). Several motifs on the walls of the North-West Palace speak of this. Many scenes in the eastern wing depict the king standing, as he holds a bow and two arrows in his hands, while pairs of human-headed genii seemingly purify the king with their cones and buckets (e.g. AI4:G6–7). As already mentioned, the date palm with its cluster also had an apotropaic meaning. Not only the king, but also the instruments of warfare which he holds, are being purified and sanctified. In short, this scene can be interpreted as showing the ritual cleansing of weapons (Magen 1986: 81–84), possibly in the sense of them being initiated and endowed with divine essence. The weapons in question were blessings from the deities given as rewards for the king's offerings (J. M. Russell 1998–2001: 247).

Other similar motifs may be understood in the same way. The king stands with cup and bow between attendants seemingly purified by human-headed genii (AI4:C6–8), or between greeting, bucket bearing, and double-winged, human-headed genii (e.g. AI4:H1–2). In these cases, only one weapon is being cleansed. This is also the case for the scene where the kings stands with bow and cup, or with cup and one hand on the shaft of his sword, between attendants (AI4:G9–10, AI4:G24–25 resp.). The purifying genii may here be implicit. Alternatively, these motifs illustrate the royal role as *šangû* (Magen 1986: 65–69). In any case, the king's weapons allude to a royal role of warrior. The celestial and terrestrial roles of the Assyrian king are intertwined in his use of or company of cup and genii (celestial), and bow and eunuch attendants (terrestrial), as the king manifests himself as "priest-warrior" (Brandes 1970: 151). The motifs of the king with bow and arrows and of the king libating with a hand on his sword seem to be both contrasted and complementary in room G of the North-West Palace (and on the Black Obelisk). Yet again, the military and priestly roles are intermingled. Religion and politics went hand in hand in imperial Assyria (Pongratz-Leisten 2015).

141 Visually, the Middle Assyrian "Broken Obelisk" of Ashur-bel-kala shows a divine emblem with a protruding hand give a bow and arrow to the king (see Börker-Klähn 1982: fig. 131).

As for depictions of royal or divine weaponry outside the walls of the North-West Palace, the throne base (SI14) and the obelisks (AI16, SI11–12) mostly convey scenes of tribute processions, although allusions to the king's military role are nevertheless present. On the throne base, Shalmaneser III wears the already described military dress (Magen 1986: 92–96) as he stands holding two arrows and a bow, while sword and daggers are attached to his belt (SI14:4b). On the Black Obelisk, the king has the same appearance as above as he is depicted receiving tribute and prostration from the ruler of co-operative Gilzanu. Two divine emblems, representing Ishtar and probably Shamash (in a non-anthropomorph sundisk), supervise or protect this scene (SI11:A1). The Rassam Obelisk carries tribute scenes in which Ashurnasirpal II stands greeting while having bows and sword (AI16:A1, AI16:A3).

The visual non-narrative sources also merely allude to the royal role of warrior of the deities. These allusions consist of pairs of daggers tucked down under the king's belt as well as earrings in the shape of arrows (e.g. AI19, SI18), and of the royal mace and the crooked object (the latter insignier possibly not a weapon)[142] in the ruler's hands on one of Shalmaneser III's statues (SI6). A further example of the relevant boundary blurring is seen on the Saba'a Stele where Adad-narari III has a sword in a priestly context (An3I2), by contrast to the normal royal representation in these situations. The theme/motif of the king with his weapons also tells of the idea of "the dominant male" and of warfare as a masculine sphere (see subs. 5.4.9).

As already apparent, the inscriptions of the Early Neo-Assyrian kings focus much on the royal role of warrior for the great gods (see also subs. 5.4.2). The same applies for the relevant royal iconography. As for that in the North-West Palace, the scenes of warfare are however restricted to the throne room and the western wing. On the walls of these rooms, the king is depicted on march, as actively taking part in battle, and as proceeding in triumph (see app. 13). In the said palace, the king crushes fallen enemy soldiers under his chariot (e.g. AI4:B3t.), shoots arrows at enemies from his moving chariot (AI4:WFL21t.), and is depicted on the ground while shooting arrows at besieged cities (e.g. AI4:B5b.). Moreover, a siege engine is decorated with an icon of probably the king, showing him as he shoots away an arrow (AI4:B4b.). The king is also depicted with bow and arrows on the miniature reliefs (AI23:P2,49a).[143] In light of the reputation of this king as a great and ferocious warrior (Olmstead 1918),

---

142 As already observed in section 4.2, Magen (1986: 69–70) in her turn sees these insignia as typical attributes of the Assyrian king acting as "purification priest" (*išippu*).

143 As for the warrior role and minor art, a king, probably Ashurnasirpal II, is seen crushing enemy soldiers under his chariot on a 9th century BCE cylinder seal (AI36).

the warfare scenes are relatively few in this palace. Anyway, in all of these scenes, the Assyrian king defeats "the Other", the latter defined by his making resistance (see subs. 5.4.8).

Also this king's door bands have a comparatively low proportion of warfare scenes: five in the case of the palace, four in the case of the Mamu temple.[144] There is possibly a connection between the placement of the Mamu temple and the location of Balawat. Dreams – Mamu's domain – could convey commands of warfare, and the mentioned town was situated at a marching route for the army (D. Oates 1974: 173–74; J. Oates 1983; Curtis 2008: 7–22). Barnett (1960: 14) has even likened the wide-open doors of the Mamu temple with the Roman Janus Gates which were closed only in times of peace. Regarding the motif of royal warfare and the iconography of Shalmaneser III (see app. 14), the scenes on the Balawat Gate are on the whole dominated by military motifs. Nine or ten of the 16 bands convey military scenes, i.e. "campaigns, city captures, city attacks" (Curtis 2008: 14).[145] Although D. Oates (1963: 13 n. 15) argues that Shalmaneser III is never depicted as actively taking part in battle, and that this king chose to present himself as an organizer rather than as warrior in the state art, the military context of his appearances nevertheless makes his warrior role obvious. More importantly, the king is actually depicted, on the ground or in his chariot, shooting arrows at enemy cities and forces (e.g. SI10:1b., SI10:7t. resp.), thus contrasting the motif of "king as observer" (Magen 1986: 115).

Reasons for the development of this image of Shalmaneser III as merely the commander-in-chief or only the nominal war leader are his relatively few portrayals as active warrior, and the statement in his annals that he entrusted the military campaigns of his later regnal years to his field marshal Dajjan-Ashur (e.g. SE14:141–90). This royal acknowledgement of Dajjan-Ashur's contributions was however not absolute. In the narration of his field marshal's deeds the pronoun of the 1st person singular – referring to the king – is often employed (e.g. SE16:284′), following the conventions in Assyrian royal inscriptions of the king claiming that "*I* (he) razed, *I* destroyed, *I* burned" (*appul aqqur ina išrāti ašrup*) (e.g. AE17:iv89, SE8:50′). The ruler presents himself as the actual warrior here. Similarly, Shamshi-Adad V tells us that he sent his chief eunuch Mutarris-Ashur on a military campaign (SA5E1:ii16–34). Uniquely, Shamshi-ilu relates that he embarked on warfare against Urartu without men-

---

144 Twelve of the door bands from the temple depict tribute, suggesting a more peaceful message of this monument in comparison with that of the palace. The door bands of the palace also depict hunting (4), captive processions (4), and tribute processions (3).

145 The other motifs depicted on this gate are tribute processions (4,5) and cult activities (2), thus displaying a comparatively small share of peaceful activities and roles.

tioning the king (An3E34). On the whole though, the role of the king as *the* warrior of the deities comes across clearly.

In his warfare, the king takes on divine attributes and forms, and likens himself to deities. As for metamorphic alluding royal epithets which have not already been mentioned (see s. 4.1), the king claims to be a "flood (mound)" (*abūbu*) (e.g. AE40:13, SE6:ii1), "like a storm" (*kīma anḫulli*) (e.g. An2E4:8′), "like a (catching) net" (*kīma šuškalli/sapāri*) (e.g. An2E2:21, SA5E2 resp.), and "like a flame" (*kīma nabli*) (An2E2:66). In other similes, the king likens himself to the pestilence deity Erra (SE5:iii2), the fire god Girru (SE12:20), "Adad, the flooder" *(Adad ša rāḫiṣi)* (e.g. AE1:iii120, SE5:iii3), and "Adad, the thunderer" (*Adad šāgimi*) (e.g. SA5E2). The king is here linked to mythological characters such as Ninurta avenging his father Enlil, and Marduk fighting the chaotic forces of Tiamat (Maul 1999: 210–14; Pongratz-Leisten 2001: 226–30; Annus 2002). As partly already noted, some kings also saw themselves as a raging "lion" (*labbu*) (e.g. AE1:i33), a fierce "wild bull" (*rīmu*) (SE2:ii52), or as an attacking "eagle" (*arânu*) (e.g. SA5E1:ii52) in the context of narrating military deeds. The king's warfare, here Adad-narari II's, is likened to that of the western god Dagan (An2E2:77).

Other epithets speak of the king as having battle skills and being eager to fight in terms reminiscent of how deities are described. Ashurnasirpal II e.g. portrays himself as "(the king) capable/foremost in battle" (*lē'û qabli/ašarēd tuqmāte*) (e.g. AE1:i34, AE1:i35 resp.), as "[he who requites] with battle [and] combat" ([*murīb*] *tuqumti* [*u*] *tamḫāri*) (AE19:16–17), as "martial king" (*šarru dapīnu*) (AE40:6), and as "strong one" (*gešru*) (e.g. AE17:i34), while Adad-narari II presents himself as "obdurate" (*ašṭāku*) and "martial" (*dāpinākū*) (e.g. An2E2:14), and as "very wild" (*šitmurāku*) (e.g. An2E3). The former ruler is even cosmically a "king whose commands disintegrates mountains and seas" (*šarru ša ina qibīt pîšu ušḫarmaṭu šadê u tâmāte*) (e.g. AE2:19–20). These epithets, or parts thereof, are also held by deities (Tallqvist 1938; Seux 1967), thus strengthening the bond between the human ruler and the great gods as well as between propaganda and mythology.

A clear connection between war and religion is also expressed in the mentioning of rituals following battles. Early Neo-Assyrian kings offer "sacrifices" (*nīqu*) to the deities, wash their divine "weapons" (*kakku*), and create images containing their (i.e. the deities') praises at localities in the periphery (e.g. AE1:iii84–89, SE5:ii4–5). Some kings, but especially Ashurnasirpal II, refer to an act of burning adolescent boys and girls of unsubmissive, conquered cities (e.g. AE1:ii43, SE2:i17). Sometimes this referring is added by the note that the said act served as a "burnt offering" (*maqlūtu*) (AE19:76–77, SE2:i17). Such an offering was normally based on sacrified oxen, sheep, and doves, and it was made for the appeasing of deities (CAD M I: *maqlūtu*). This atrocity then formed a part of the sacred, religiously motivated war. The statements on the presenting of war booty in Assyrian temples after military campaigns abroad may also be mentioned (e.g. SE17:62). In one instance, it is stated that 2/3 of the booty was given to the god (Ashur?), while 1/3 of it was assigned to the palace (TN2E5:28–29). Assyrian warfare was a religious act in both theory and practice.[146]

The Assyrian king was assisted by *priests* in these campaign offerings, again telling of religion as pervading war. As already noted (see s. 3.2), often two chariots with divine standards representing Adad and Nergal follow the royal chariot (e.g. AI4:B6t., SI10:1b.). Occasionally, these divine chariots are engaged in battle with their military crew shooting arrows and crushing enemies under the wheels of the chariot (e.g. AI4:B10t., SI10:9t.). Priests, wearing their conical headgears, are sometimes depicted behind these divine chariots in marching contexts (SI10:4). These likely *kalû* priests are also seen assisting Shalmaneser III at an offering at Lake Van/Urmia (SI10:1t.). Another priest is seen inspecting the entrails of a sacrified animal, performing exticipy, in the army camp of Ashurnasirpal II (AI4:B7t.). In the latter case, the priest may, as discussed, be a "diviner" (*bārû*). The notion of military campaigning as a sacred occupation is in any case there, and the same message is given by the divine emblems and birds accompanying war scenes (see s. 3.2).

Also the ceremonial use of music was connected with divinely decreed imperialism. Music functioned as an integral component of the cult (Bottéro 2001a: 22–23). Shalmaneser III sacrifices accompanied by musicians on a military campaign (SI10:1t.). Also on the Balawat gates, musicians play in front of Ashurnasirpal II and behind a procession of captives (e.g. AI13:21–22), further strengthening the association of warfare with religion. In the lastly mentioned scene, it seems plausible to regard the music as celebrating the almost ritual event of tributaries and captives lining up in relation to the king. As for ritual performances, in the North-West Palace two individuals, possibly priests, are depicted ritually wearing animal hides in the aftermath of battle (AI4:B7t.). The meaning of this scene and these persons are not immideatly clear, but it surely tells of the sacred status of war. A possible analogy is the reliefs of Sennacherib in which a procession of individuals with feather-equipped hats as well as processions of musicians with various instruments are represented, all in the context of the king displaying his great military feats (see Barnett et al. 1998: pls. 228, 320, 473, 487, 492–95).

146 As for the level of practice, oaths in treaties and the liver omens taken before embarking on campaigns are two expressions of the consistent view of wars as religious (see s. 3.2).

Nearby, in the lastly mentioned scene, Assyrian soldiers throw or hold heads of beheaded enemy soldiers in their hands, while other soldiers clap their hands and some musicians accompany (AI4:B6t.). The decapitated head of the enemy was imbued with religious symbolism (Bahrani 2008: 23–55). Once again, war and victory in battle are given a sacred meaning. Additionally, the heads of beheaded enemy rulers were publically displayed, arguably in order to invoke fear, set an example, and illustrate to the populace the adversaries' resounding defeat (see subs. 5.4.2). Ashurnasirpal II states that decapitated enemy heads were hanged up in trees in or near enemy cities (e.g. AE1:ii71). This of course brings to mind the famous "garden party scene" where Ashurbanipal and his queen are banqueting while the head of the defeated Elamite ruler Teumman hangs in a tree nearby (see Barnett 1976: pl. LXVt.). Both the severed heads and the placement of them in trees apparently had some deeper, religious meaning, beside that of inspiring horror. It should also be noted in this context that the act of building a "tower of heads" (*asītu ša qaqqadi*) outside captured enemy cities is a quite common theme in the annals of Ashurnasirpal II and Shalmaneser III (e.g. AE1:iii108, SE2:i48). In a transferred sense, also this fairly well-attested atrocity can be interpreted as a (partly) ritual act, telling of the sacred status of Assyrian warfare.

In discussing the divinely ordained warrior function, the concept of "holy war", already touched upon in section 3.2, is difficult to avoid. Several Assyriologists have referred to the warfare of the Assyrian kings as holy wars (Garelli 1979: 323; Tadmor 1997: 327; Oded 1991: 223–27). Tadmor (1983: 42) e.g. writes that every Assyrian war, led by the king as high priest of Ashur, "was on a theological as well as on a practical cult level a 'holy war' ordered by Ashur and approved by oracles, celestial and terrestial". Oded (1992: 137, 187–88) in his using of the term for ancient Assyria emphasizes that this does not mean that the Assyrian wars were "wars of religion" or that the Assyrian soldiers can be likened to "Crusaders". Oded (1992: 13–18) recognizes holy war in the Assyrian sources because wars were initiated by divine commands, religious symbols and divine insignia followed the Assyrian army on campaigns, booty was given to the temples, and religious terminology was often used in the military accounts of Assyrian royal inscriptions (all this attested in the sources of the ten kings). Holloway (2001) similarly refers to "Assyrian religious imperialism" and also stresses that it did not entail any intolerant, iconoclastic ambition of the Assyrians.

Opposing to Oded's arguments and the anachronism of the term holy war, Galter (1998: 89–94) argues that wars are not holy simply because religion is called upon. He goes on to say that the question whether to use the term holy war on Assyria may be irrelevant because of the interweaving of religion and politics in Mesopotamia. *Every* role of the king was in this sense holy. The profane and sacred elements of the king's role formed an inseparable unit (Brandes 1970: 151–54; Ataç 2010: 113–24).[147] Similarly, Pollock (1999: 186) states that a distinction between religion and politics is anachronistic for Mesopotamia in that "religion pervaded political and economic decisions" and that these in turn "affected religious beliefs and practices". Liverani (1979: 301), in his turn, argues that Assyrian state ideology was religious in character, and that a dividing into secular and sacral aspects therefore is impossible. Still, such a distinction is often made in scholarly literature, either for practical reasons or as the result of a genuine belief in the relevance of the distinction.[148] Groenewegen-Frankfort (1951: 181) e.g. refers to Assyrian narrative state art as "entirely secular". As shown above, a closer examination of the sources makes this distinction untenable. Holy wars or not, the king had the religious function of warrior of the deities. The pragmatic approach (see s. 5.3) and emphasis on violence (see subs. 5.4.2) arguably make Assyrian religious imperialism stand out in comparisons.

Summing up, the role of warrior of the great gods is amply attested. The king's warfare is tied to religious rituals, and his conquering mission is described as ordained by the deities, especially Ashur. The weapons used by the king were sanctified and given by the deities, and the king is consequently described as almost a superhuman figure in battle. The king's wars were if not regarded as "holy" then at least as religiously motivated.

4.5 Summary

The Early Neo-Assyrian kings consistently portray themselves as the link between the Mesopotamian deities and the foreign lands. In this capacity, the ruler is the representative of the great gods, chosen, supported, and protected by them. The kings are described both as "vice-regents" and "governors" of various deities, notably of Ashur. Insignia also served to demonstrate the role of the Assyrian king as the representative of the Mesopotamian deities, in this way elevating him above ordinary human beings. Narrative passages often state that the deities assist and protect the Assyrian king in the realizing of the latter's duties. As the guardians of the king, divine emblems, genii, sacred trees, and colossi convey the idea of the protected ruler visually.

---

147 The latter scholar here refers to the dual elements of *regnum* and *sacerdotium*, converging into the "mixed persona" of the Assyrian king, telling of his special status and function.

148 For the former approach, see e.g. Cifola (1995) who distinguishes "secular" and "religious" title categories. For the latter, see Frankfort 1948 and Groenewegen-Frankfort 1951.

Regarding the ever discussed topic of royal deification, in his status and function of link, the king presents himself as a human being and merely a "first among equals". The divine weapons, radiance, and personal qualities which the deities handed to the king at coronation, and which describe him as making him outstanding in relation to others, were temporary, conditional, and derived, rather than part of his essence. Concrete proofs of royal deification such as divine determinatives, cult of the king, images of the king with horns or standing on animals (i.e. how deities are portrayed) are lacking.

The king functions as "priest" and servant in relation to the great gods. This observation reflects a belief in the religious character of Assyrian kingship. The clear priestly role of the Assyrian king contrasts with the southern notion of kingship. In this role, the Early Neo-Assyrian kings sacrifice to and perform rituals in honour of the deities, thus portrayed as "libating priests". The ruler often depicts himself wearing a priestly garment, communicating with divine emblems, in these cases portrayed as "venerating priest". The cultic duties of the king were not only enacted in temples but also in for example palaces. In the related role of the servant of the great gods, the ruler portrays himself in texts and images as humble, attentive, and obeying.

Another function of the king in relation to the great gods concerned building. Both larger objects such as temples as well as various cult paraphernalia were dedicated to the deities by the Early Neo-Assyrian kings. The temples and shrines are either founded or renovated. Not only temples but also palaces and whole cities are described as dedicated to the deities. Forced labour from deportations are occasionally stated as the actual builders. A characteristic feature of Shalmaneser III's state ideology is his emphasis on creating "images" in conquered territories and/or at geographical extremes. These monuments arguably served both propagandistic and religious functions. The irrelevance of the term secularism is noted in this context.

The Early Neo-Assyrian kings also portray themselves as the warriors of the great gods. In this function, the ruler had the duty to effectuate the divine command of extending the borders of Assyria. The texts and images which describe and depict the kings as warriors, besieging enemy cities or fighting on the battlefield, are very frequent. In combat, the king is compared to deities like Adad, Erra, Girru, and Dagan, and the mythological battle of Ninurta is alluded to. The religious nature of his warfare is also expressed in the rituals connected to his military campaigns. For example, images are sanctified, divine weapons are washed, and offerings are presented. In short, the king's wars were the deities' wars, and Assyrian warfare is consequently presented as a religious act and duty. In the discussion of the term "holy war", the irrelevance in referring to secularism is once again noted.

5 The relationship between the king of Assyria and the foreign lands

This chapter centres on the relationship between the Assyrian king and the foreign lands, much focused on in the primary sources. The various elements of the foreign lands – i.e. its geography, animals, deities, and humans – which confront the Assyrian king form the basis for the dividing of the discussion into four sections. Due to its length and complexity, section 5.4 on the relationship between the king and the foreign human beings is subdivided into nine subsections. The first four of these highlight the *concrete* roles of the relevant relationship when focusing on ceremonial acts of superiority or inferiority, booty or tribute, and on royal providing and protecting, while the last five subsections highlight possible *abstract* and superimposed roles of the relevant relationship when centering on the notions ethnicity, nationalism, order/chaos, "the Self"/"the Other", and masculinity/femininity.

5.1 Overcoming the foreign landscapes

Starting off with focusing on the foreign geography, I will argue that the king here represents Order and the wild, foreign nature Chaos, and that the alterity conveyed is only functional and provisory and not essence-based. By cultivating and domesticating it, the foreign nature could become a part of the ordered world. The alterity had also the propagandistic function of focusing on the king as hero, overcoming "the difficult path" against all odds.

The images of foreign landscapes are stereotyped. This insight reflects the observation that every Mesopotamian empire had a propagandistic need of creating its own geography or mental map. The descriptions, including the toponyms themselves, of the foreign geography were manipulated to suit the ideological requirements of the day (Michalowski 1986: 144–45). Assyrian royal inscriptions contain both general and specific toponyms. The former are often pictured as semi-mythological, and were a part of an ideologically driven "mental mapping" (Parker 2011: 363). The geographical remarks in the texts of Ashurnasirpal II, as well as in those of any other Assyrian king, are consequently not free from an intention to create such a mental map (Liverani 1992b). The descriptions of the foreign nature and geography should in this regard be seen as expressions of propaganda and state ideology rather than as genuine aims towards cartology or historiography.

The Italian school, fully recognizing this, has seen the descriptions of the natural and cultural landscape of the enemy as expressing alterity according to which everything *foreign* is different, inferior, and bad. Zaccagnini (1982: 412–16) e.g. argues that the natural settings, i.e. mountains, seas, marshes, and deserts, of the enemy often are focused on, and that they are presented as divergences from the "normal" and "correct". Using the term difficult path which refers to the ruggedness and remoteness of the foreign nature, Liverani (1990: 36–37) claims that the geography and cultures of the peripheral world are described as different and inferior. The deserts are void as the underworld, the forests are places of darkness, and the mountains are hostile and desolate. The nature and resources of the foreign lands only gain meaning through the imperial power's use of them. The cultures are correspondingly seen as lacking and abnormal, and Assyrians and foreigners are juxtaposed in a natural antagonism. The natural and cultural geography of the foreign lands are here regarded as inherent national characteristics.

However, the often wild character of the foreign geography can be considered simply as chaotic, without any devaluating and essence-based meanings implied. Haas (1980: 43–44) refers to a literal demonization of "the foreign", the enemy, and the foreign landscape in various Mesopotamian and Assyrian sources. The landscape is home to an enemy likened to *gallû* demons and to creatures of Tiamat, representing Chaos and threatening the cosmic Order. Similarly, Maul (1999: 213) speaks of a view of mountains and steppes as inhabited by demons and associated with Chaos and the underworld. The king's duty was to confront these chaotic forces, and to establish order throughout the world. By the acts of creating canals, dams, aqueducts and the like, the Assyrian king tamed the chaotic nature (Cancik-Kirschbaum 2008: 78). Here it is relevant to note that also Assyrian land could be described as wild, e.g. the site where Tukulti-Ninurta I built his new capital Kar-Tukulti-Ninurta (see RIMA1: A.0.78.24:41–52).

The descriptions of wilderness in Assyrian royal inscriptions may in other words convey the idea of a functional and provisory alterity, and should thus not be understood as expressing notions of an essence-based "national" territory. The related notion of Order/Chaos seems to have been generally shared in the Ancient Near East, not the least in Egypt with its strict dichotomies (Hornung 1992). It naturally relates to the concepts of Self/Other, and identity/alterity (see subs. 5.4.8). There is also a gender aspect to this discussion. As observed by M. Marcus (1995b: 200–204), the word for "land" (*mātu*) as well as the idea of Chaos were regarded as feminine in gender. According to this idea, the confrontation between Order and Chaos then took place between masculinity and femininity. The battle between Marduk and Tiamat was thus not only a fight between Order and Chaos but also between the masculine and feminine components of creation.

Another fruitful interpretive approach connects the descriptions of the wild, foreign nature with the theme of the king as hero. The portrayal of the king as sole and supreme hero is common in Assyrian royal inscriptions (Tadmor 1997: 327; Gaspa 2007). In the narration of Sargon II confronting a snowy landscape on his way to Urartu, van Buylaere (2009: 299–303) concludes that the image of massive hindrance serves to describe the king's subsequent victory as epical. Sharing this conclusion, the descriptions of a wild, foreign nature is not so much about negative alterity or a dichotomy Assyrian/foreign as it is a propaganda device of focusing on the bravery and competence of the Assyrian king. The foreign nature is not inherently bad, but its ruggedness and remoteness serve the purpose of portraying the king as a hero who overcomes all obstacles put in his way. In line with this interpretation, there is no compelling reason to drag the idea of the foreign landscape as exhibiting genuine, national elements into this discussion.

Another rewarding dimension of this discussion deals with "real and fictive landscapes" (Ataç 2013: 385–94, 397–400). Assyrian conceptions of geography, landscape, and the physical environment drew on the idea of the potentiality to an "imaginal domain", with the borders fluid between reality and fiction. This idea was expressed through picturing the landscape, the exotic, and the foreign e.g. in their guises of trees, plants, and animals. The borders between the *oikoumene*, i.e. the known world, and the imaginal lands were fluid. Also the edges of the *oikoumene* could be portrayed as imaginal to a certain degree. According to Ataç, the ultimate goal of Assyrian imperialism was the transfiguration of the world, inaugurating a new "paradisical" dimension or a golden age through the extending of the *oikoumene* and making it into the centre of the four quarters. Similarly, Shalmaneser III's depicted and described rituals at the remote Tigris source may be understood as his transforming "a socially significant, mytho-poetic landscape into a landscape of commemoration and cult practice, illustrating Assyrian rhetorics of kingship" (Harmanşah 2007). In the same vein, the visits to the river sources were inspired by an interest for the edges of the earth (Ataç 2013: 410).[149]

Turning to the evidence of the major primary sources, the theme of difficult path is often expressed in the titulary of Shalmaneser III. In his epithets, this king is e.g. called "he who has triumphantly trodden over rivers and difficult mountains" (*nārāti šadê marṣūti ukabbisa šalṭiš*), "he who has marched on difficult ways" (*ša arḫī pašqūte ittanallaku*), "he who has marched through moun-

149 The same scholar also, although in my view much less persuasively, sees the imaginal domain present in the North-West Palace, primarily in the shape of the sacred tree in its being an embodiment of Abzu and the antediluvian cosmos (Ataç 2010, 2013: 403–11).

tains and seas" (*ištamdaḫu šadê u tâmāti*), and "he who treads upon the mountain peaks of all highlands" (*mukabbis rēšēte ša šadê kalîš ḫuršāni*) (e.g. SE23:12–13, SE2:i10, SE2:i10, SE1:9 resp.). The latter three epithets were held also by Ashurnasirpal II (AE40:5, AE40:6, AE40:3 resp.). This earlier king also referred to himself as "he who roams about on mountain paths" (*muttallik šamgāni*), and as "he who in harsh terrain scattered the forces of the rebellious" (*ša ina ašri namrāṣi uparriru kiṣir multarḫi*) (e.g. AE40:4, AE1:i40 resp.). Not only the harsh landscape but also human enemies form the difficult path in the latter royal epithet. Adad-narari II saw himself as "he who sets on fire the mountains of all lands" (*mušaḫmēṭi šadē ša mātāti*) and "he who continually crossed over mighty mountains" (*šadāni dannūtu ittatabalkitu*) (e.g. An2E2:17, An2E2:31 resp.). Finally, a mentioned statue of Ashurnasirpal II is named "he whose face is turned towards the desert" (*ana ḫuribte taruṣu pānušu*) (AE1:iii26), implying a competence to cross this kind of inhospitable terrain as well.

Proceeding to the textual narrative, the theme of difficult path is frequent. Ashurnasirpal II claims to have crossed various grand hinderances, notably mountainous areas (e.g. AE2:21). Regarding these terrestrial obstacles, the king passes through a narrow "mountain pass" (*nērebtu*) (e.g. AE1:ii19–20), he and his army manage to break through a hilly terrain which is described as unsuitable for the army's chariots and troops (e.g. AE1:i45–46), and the king chisels out way with iron axes and copper picks for himself and his army in six whole days (AE1:ii95–96). Shalmaneser III makes the same chiseling out way with his metal tools (e.g. SE2:ii41–42), and his warfare is described as heroic when "I (he) placed strong combat in the mountains" (*tāḫāza dannu ina qereb šadê aškun*) (SE1:25–26). The same king directs his troops and chariots across narrow paths and high mountains (e.g. SE6:i29, SE16:73′–74′ resp.). In a unique narrative passage, Ashurnasirpal II declares that a certain mountain was too high and steep for him to climb (e.g. AE17:i71–74). Such an acknowledgement of self-limitation on the part of the Assyrian king is seldomly expressed in Assyrian royal inscriptions. However, the following sentences reveal that he eventually, against all odds, managed to overcome this hinderance as well (e.g. AE17:i74–77).

Turning to other terrestrial hinderances, namely deserts, mountain steppes, and forests, Ashurnasirpal II also narrates that he managed to cross deserts (AE1:iii28). Tukulti-Ninurta II spent a night on march in the desert, and Adad-narari II did the same in a mountain steppe area (TN2E5:41, An2E2:111). The former king claims to have marched through and camped in a mountainous "land of thirst" (*qaqqar ṣumāmēte*), and to have pursued wells and other water sources on his army's march in the desert (TN2E5:63–64, TN2E5:42–49 resp.). A mountain steppe which the same ruler visited is described as arid and desolate (TN2E5:63–64). He also claims to have marched through a dense and great forest without any help (TN2E5:51).

As for waters, Ashurnasirpal II tells of how he ordered massive construction of boats for a river crossing (AE1:iii29), he and his army then cross various rivers such as the Euphrates, Tigris, Zab, Turnat, Lallu, Edir, Orontes, Sua, and Apre by boats in unspecified ways or by "bridges of rafts" (*raksu*) or "rafts of (inflated) goatskins" (*eleppu ša duḫšê*) (AE1:ii103–4, AE1:iii33–34 resp.). On a north-western campaign, Shalmaneser III is actually described as engaged in warfare out on the sea as he chases the cowardly enemy, heroically without waiting for his army (SE28:43–44). The same king also manages to cross broad rivers (e.g. SE8:35′). The descriptions of the aftermath of battle when Shalmaneser III brought plunder down the mountain or across a river may be similar expressions of difficult path focusing on the king as hero and the wild nature as chaotic (e.g. SE10:iii9–10, SE2:ii75 resp.). Difficult path may also be conveyed when Shamshi-Adad V and Adad-narari III claim to have conquered enemy cities in marshlands or on islands (SA5E1:iv24–27, An3E7:9–10 resp.). As for waters, Ashurnasirpal II relates that he commissioned a canal, named Patti-hegalli, from the Upper Zab to Kalhu in the shape of a water carrying tunnel which was created by drilling through a massive mountain (AE30:36–37).

Hanging on to the theme of water as a hinderance for the ruler to overcome, the Assyrian king, here Ashurnasirpal II, manages to travel by boat upstream, presumably in times of flooding, and he succeeds in crossing the moat of a besieged enemy city (AE1:iii96, AE21:9′–10′ resp.). As for Shalmaneser III and the crossing of the Euphrates, it is often pointed out that the river in question was "in flood" (*ina mīli*) (e.g. SE8:35′). The aim with this addition was presumably to emphasize the royal accomplishment in overcoming this huge obstacle. The common addition that Shalmaneser III crossed the Euphrates or went up Mt Amanus for the eleventh-or-so time may be understood similarly (e.g. SE14:99, SE31:8 resp.). Royal epithets like "he who for a fourth time went to GN" (*erbettešu ana* GN *illiku*) (e.g. An2E4:22′) may perhaps be grasped in the same way (Yamada 1998).

The Early Neo-Assyrian king also claims to have overcome long distances, e.g. when Ashurnasirpal II says that he marched to remote cities (AE1:ii48). The word "remote" (*rūqu*) is also used to describe the distance to the land which the hero of the story of the Flood, Utu-napishtim, ended up in (CAD R: *rūqu*), and which the legendary hero-king Gilgamesh managed to reach (see Parpola 1997). Similarly, the word "mountain" (*šadû*) can also refer to a distant, mythological place (CAD Š I: *šadû* A). Overcoming distances, the king conquers from a river source to the interior of a land, and he pursues the fleeing enemy (or kills and destroys to a remote land) all the way to the latter's peripheral homeland (e.g. AE33:10′, AE1:iii41–42 resp.). Tukulti-Ninurta II chases the enemy from a mountain to a tributary river (TN2E5:39). The claims of some kings that they went to "the interior" (*ša bītāni*) of lands may serve to allude to the land's remoteness and to their bravery in overcoming it (e.g. AE17:iv91–92, SE6:iii59). As for long distances and the heroic king, the idea of the unique and almost superhuman character of the king is conveyed when stating that Ashurnasirpal II "proceeded (through) the night until dawn" (*mūšu adi namāri artedi*) before he engaged – successfully of course – in warfare at sunrise (e.g. AE1:ii53–54).

As already remarked, also man-made obstacles, i.e. the *cultural* landscape, can express the theme of difficult path. The king destroys massive fortifications such as city walls of the enemy (e.g. AE17:iv57–59, SE17:39), he breaks through walls which the enemy had constructed at mountain passes (e.g. AE154:11′–18′), and he conquers mighty enemy fortresses which were often partly natural, such as those on mountain peaks (AE19:52–53, SE14:130–31). Similarly, the defence arrangements of an enemy city are described as massive (An2E2:64–66). Having made his way through the enemy's city walls, Shalmaneser III claims to have "placed fight inside his (i.e. the enemy ruler's) city" (*mitḫuṣu ina libbi ālišu aškun*) (SE20:10).

As for building – i.e. the opposite act of destroying – and difficult path, Ashurnasirpal II and his successor each announce that they reached down to water level, whereupon they sank the foundation pit of a certain building to a remarkable depth, i.e. 120 layers of brick. They go on to claim that the building in question surpassed all earlier ones after being rebuilt (e.g. AE28:v6–7, SE25:26–29). The theme of cities, fortifications, palaces, and temples "being dilapidated" (*labāru*) and having turned into "mounds and ruin hills" (*tillu u karme*) only to be splendidly rebuilt by the king conveys the same message of overcoming grand obstacles. Against all odds, the Assyrian ruler turns a ruin hill to a magnificent creation. He literally reaches rock bottom, the base of the earth, and as deep down as he could dig, in his ambition of creating outstanding buildings (e.g. AE38:21–22). The theme of building and difficult path is not only told of in Assyria proper. As occasionally mentioned by the ten kings, building activities – notably palaces and fortresses – were carried out also in the conquered regions (e.g. AE1:ii101, SE14:130–31).

Difficult path is also expressed through stressing and listing the many and varied things which the king managed to collect in the foreign lands. Various trees and plants, but also animals and people, are brought to and used (i.e. get cultivated/"domesticated") in the capital (e.g. AE30:38–52). The frequent use of the words "many" (*ma'ādu*) and "countless" (*ana lā mīni*) with regards to booty and tribute taken to Assyria (e.g. AE17:iii44–45, SE14:155) is another expression of this general idea centred on collecting (Reade 2004b). Symbolic of the centrifugal movement from a chaotic periphery to an ordered centre is the coming of foreign rulers to Assyria to deliver tribute (e.g. AE1:i100–101, SE2:ii24–27). By the act of collecting from all corners of the world, the king overcomes the difficult path in yet another way. The theme of the king as collector of exotic plants and animals and as overcomer of huge obstacles on campaigns is also common in Egyptian propaganda.[150]

In the next step of the realizing of this kind of difficult path, Ashurnasirpal II then narrates how he created orchards as well as zoological gardens in his capital (e.g. AE30:38–39, AE2:31–38 resp.). As for "orchards" (*kirû*), the king announces that he planted every kind of fruit tree in it (AE30:38–39). In other words, the Assyrian king cultivates, or uses as building elements (see s. 4.3), the wild, foreign plants and trees in the ordered world of his dominion. Assyria with the capital of Kalhu was regarded as a cosmic, ordered centre, while the foreign lands are described as extreme and abnorm (e.g. AE1:i49) and as one big chaotic periphery (Liverani 1973: 189–91). However, in a reverse and centripetal movement, the wild and chaotic foreign lands could become ordered when conquered by the Assyrian king. Expressions of this ordering, viewed as imposing civilization upon barbarism by the Italian school, are the royal (re)naming of cities and fortresses in the foreign lands (e.g. AE1:iii49–50, SE2:ii33–34), and the construction of administrative palaces in the area mentioned (e.g. AE19:35–36). As will be argued in subsection 5.4.6, ordered land was the status of land controlled by the Assyrian king, and not referring to any specific, fixed, national homeland.

As for iconography and Ashurnasirpal II, the motif of difficult path is occasionally expressed. In the North-West Palace, the king along with some soldiers are depicted crossing a river by boats while horses and other soldiers swim (AI4:B9–11b, see Fig. 13). The same ruler is also illustrated proceeding in his chariot through a mountainous region (AI4:WFL19b.), and the Assyrian army is depicted crossing hilly terrain (e.g. AI4:WFL23–24). As for Shalmaneser III and his visual sources, only the Balawat Gate conveys the motif of difficult path. The enemies are depicted on hills or mountains about to be conquered by the king's army (SI10:7t.). Assyrian chariot units drive, with the assistance of foot soldiers who drag the chariot-bound horses by the ropes, over hills or mountains (SI10:1t.). Soldiers also traverse mountains either riding or marching, and the army is depicted crossing a ford/river by means of a bridge (SI10:1t., SI10:11 resp.). As will be argued in subsection 5.4.5, there is no concentration of alterity on any particular foreign land in that alterity of every point of the compass including Babylonia is illustrated (SI10:11).

150 See e.g. "the botanical garden" in the Karnak temple and the daredevil king taking a narrow way on route to Megiddo where the enemy forces awaited (Grimal 1994: 213–17).

The royal role of "discoverer" or "explorer" is also attested. Ashurnasirpal II e.g. calls himself "opener of paths in mountains which rise perpendicularly to the sky like the edge of a sword" (*mupatti ṭūdāt šadê ša kīma šēlūt patri ana šadê ziqipta šaknū*) (e.g. AE40:15–16), and "he who opens elevated mountains of the innermost regions which not had been traversed" (*muparriru° ḫuršāni šaqūti ša durugšunu lā etiqu*) (AE56:3). The second epithet not only conveys the theme of discoverer but also of heroic priority, i.e. the king in question outdoes his royal predecessors in a certain field of action. Shalmaneser III is "the opener of path above and below" (*mupattû° ṭūdāti ša eliš u šapliš*) (e.g. SE2:i8), "he who has seen innermost and rugged (regions)" (*āmeru° durgi u šapšāqi*) (e.g. SE1:9), as well as "he who has seen the sources of the Tigris and the Euphrates" (*āmir ēnāte ša Idiqlat u Puratte*) (SE25:12–13). The lastly mentioned discoverer theme is visually expressed in the depictions of Shalmaneser III at the Tigris source (SI10:10). Not the least because of his titulary and iconography, it may be argued that Shalmaneser III in particular used the discoverer theme, visiting the outskirts of the known world, such as the river sources, Syria, Urartu, and Chaldea.

The theme of discoverer is also expressed in the textual narrative sources. Ashurnasirpal II here articulates a role of discoverer when he enumerates the multitude of trees and plants which he claims to have seen on his journeys in the foreign lands (AE30:40–48). These botanical phenomena were then apparently collected and cultivated in royal botanical gardens in Kalhu (e.g. AE30:48–52).[151] As for Shalmaneser III, he marches with his army all the way up to the river sources (SE6:ii37–38), and he ascends mountains on foot after it has been stated that "for three days the hero explored the mountain" (*ina šalāšat ūmī qarrādu šadû iḫīṭa*) (SE2:ii71–72, e.g. AE1:i50–51). In the context of the same ruler's campaign to Urartu, he states before his setting out on march that his aim was to go and see whether "it is a region with or without water" (*ša qaqqar mê lā mê*) (SE17:15). As peaceful as it sounds, these discovery themes are nevertheless framed within military narratives.

Another feature of the discoverer theme which is conveyed in the textual narrative of several Early Neo-Assyrian kings is the describing of military campaigns structured according to the itinerary style (e.g. AE1:iii1–17, SE2:i18–ii102). In these narrative sections, the theme of the king as traveller seems to be the focal point of the story. The typical phrasing here is that the king "approached" (*qerēbu*) a certain locality, received the submission and tribute

151 A Kalhu-located botanical (?) garden is depicted on the Rassam Obelisk (AI16:D3). Royal botanical gardens are often spoken of by the Sargonids (see e.g. Fuchs 1994: text 2.1:41–42). For a discussion on the archaeological evidence of royal gardens in Assyria, see Novák 2004.

of its inhabitants, whereafter he "set up camp at GN and spent the night" (GN *assakan bedāk*) there, and in the morning "moved on" (*namāšu*) from there to another locality (e.g. AE1:iii1–2). All these attestations have one thing in common: they are all given in the context of emphasizing the ruler's competence and bravery. Essence-based, derogatory remarks about foreigners and the foreign landscapes are by contrast not expressed.

Summing up, I have argued that Order stands against Chaos in the relationship between the Assyrian king and the foreign geography. The latter's alterity is functional and provisory rather than derogatory and essence-based (i.e. centering on a dichotomy Assyrian/foreign), and it primarily serves the propaganda aim of emphasizing the competence and bravery of the king. Through the act of cultivation the foreign geography could become ordered.

5.2 Pacifying the foreign animals

As for foreign nature, the Assyrian king also confronts the foreign animals, notably lions and wild bulls, triggering the role of royal hunter. I will argue that a ritual battle between Order and Chaos is pictured, not involving a dichotomy Assyrian/foreign. The king's victory over the wild beasts also expresses his manly strength and courage. In the mere collecting of these animals, domestication and inclusion into the ordered world were implied.

The motif of the king as hunter can be traced back in Mesopotamia at least to the prehistoric Uruk period (Roaf 1990: 154–55). It is also expressed among Mesopotamia's neighbours, notably in New Kingdom Egypt and imperial Persia (Kuhrt 1997). Turning to Assyria specifically, the royal role of hunter is a theme and motif which was an inherent part of the Assyrian idea of kingship (Ziegler 2011b). The hunting, here of lions, was a royal prerogative in the Neo-Assyrian Period (Herbordt 1998–2001: 269). The nature of this role needs to be identified however. The wild beasts were most often "lions" (*urmaḫḫu*, *labbu*) and "wild bulls" (*rīmu*). With regards to these and the king, Maul (1995: 395, 399) observes that a struggle between Order and Chaos is imagined here. The lions here function as the Chaos and the embodiment of the mythological danger, such as Tiamat, which threatens the Order of the world, and by slaying them the Assyrian shepherd-king saves society and his country, and defends the Order of the world from the intruding, chaotic forces. Additionally, the slaying implies the extension of the cultural landscape, thus in a sense implementing the coronation command. Similarly, J. M. Russell (2008: 182) argues that the slaying of lions and wild bulls had the effect that land was conquered for the benefit of the economic development of Assyria from the hands of the enemies, i.e. in terms of husbandry regarding lions, and agriculture regarding bulls.

Turning to the major primary sources, the motif of Ashurnasirpal II hunting wild beasts is very common. In the North-West Palace, the king is illustrated chasing and shooting at lions and wild bulls, as well as crushing them under the wheels of his chariot (e.g. AI4:B19–20t.). The hunting scenes in the throne room are situated close to the throne, hinting to the importance of this role and motif. Ashurnasirpal II is also depicted chasing and shooting at wild bulls in the miniature reliefs (e.g. AI23:S3,50a). In these reliefs, the king also hunts on foot, wearing a diadem instead of his crown (e.g. AI23:G16,36a).[152] As for Balawat and the door bands of his palace, the king is also here portrayed in the action of hunting lions and wild bulls (e.g. AI13:15–16, AI13:13–14 resp.). Hunting of ibexes may also be represented (e.g. AI13:29–30). Some of the lions on these bands look very similar to the lion on the royal seal (about to be discussed), as they stand roaring on their hindlegs (e.g. AI13:15–16). Captions and the landscapes state that the hunting took place out in the wild, i.e. lions were hunted at the river Balih, while wild bulls were hunted on the banks of the Euphrates (AE93, AE92 resp.). Once again, the hunting scenes are highlighted through their positioning, this time in the middle and supposedly most noticeable part of the gate.

The motif of "perennial hunting" is, along with "banquet scenes", the main motif of Neo-Assyrian seals (Collon 1987: 75). The earthly actions on these glyptic illustrations are often interwoven with elements from mythology. A bareheaded king, probably Ashurnasirpal II, is e.g. depicted below the emblems of Sin, the Sibitti, and Ishtar while shooting an arrow at a *lamassu* (!) which jumps over a plant (AI37). In glaring contrast, Shalmaneser III is only represented as hunter on the royal (stamp) seal, i.e. in a motif shared by several rulers (SI26).[153] Impressions from this royal seal have also been discovered from the reign of Adad-narari III (An3I11). According to Herbordt (1998–2001: 271), a variant of this hunting portrayal on the Assyrian royal seal shows the struggling lion alone. Maul (1995: 395, 399), who identifies this as the royal seal of the Neo-Assyrian Period attested by impressions at least from the reign of Shalmaneser III onwards,[154] argues that it illustrates the importance of the king's hunting role. This seal functioned both as a royal and administrative seal (Herbordt 1998–2001: 271).

---

152 Diadems could also be worn by the crown prince or field marshal (Reade 2009), but in light of the identified royal prerogative it seems clear that it is *the king* who is depicted thus.

153 As for dynastic seals and southern Mesopotamia in the first millennium BCE, the Babylonian (under Assyrian rule) royal seal where the king seizes an antilope or gazelle is identified by Collon (1987: 130, fig. 555) who labels it a counterpart to the Neo-Assyrian one.

154 Herbordt (1998–2001: 270) sees a precursor of this royal seal from the reign of Ashurnasirpal II, but the possibility for a firm dating seems not to be at hand in this case.

Also the inscriptions of Ashurnasirpal II often refer to the said role. This king e.g. claims that he killed and caught wild bulls and ostriches at the Euphrates (e.g. AE1:iii48–49), and he also announces that he killed five lions in the land Hatti with the use of his bow (AE19:33–34). The narrations of killing and capturing wild beasts generally contain precise quantifications, normally with significantly higher numbers than in the latest example (e.g. AE2:41–42). Shalmaneser III occasionally, but not very often, wrote about his hunting achievements. In an almost isolated narrative passage, the king claims that he, from his "open chariot" (*narkabtu patûtu*), killed wild bulls, calves, lions, and elephants, and that he caught elephants, bears, deer, marsh pigs, panthers, *senkurru* animals, and wild bulls, arguably in Syria (SE16:341′–47′). Safar (1951: 4) plays down the importance of this freestanding narrative passage by referring to it as a fill-in, but its separate positioning can just as well express emphasizing. Adad-narari II catches or kills e.g. elephants, Tukulti-Ninurta II chased ostriches and deer in the desert, and Shamshi-Adad V claims to have killed three lions on route to Babylonia (An2E2:125–126, TN2E5:80–82, SA5E1:iv1–3). Interestingly, there are not any royal epithets clearly referring to the king's hunting role preserved.

One kind of foreign animal stands out in the texts as being treated with great respect. The "horses" (*sisû*) of the foreign lands are by contrast never described as catched or killed, then not being part of the relevant chaotic phenomenon. Rather, they are simply pictured as being brought to Assyria in the shape of booty or tribute. This cherished status of horses can be explained by their important role in the Assyrian army (e.g. SE6:iv47–48). According to a loyalty oath, horses are not be given to enemies (TN2E5:24–25), and in another text a huge number of northern and eastern polities are said to be obliged to regularly provide Assyria with horses (SA5E1:iii44–67). Horses are not represented as maltreated in the iconographic sources either.

Royal hunting also served the purpose of displaying the king's manly strength and courage to the world. One expression of this ideal is depicted in the North-West Palace where the king is seen seizing a wild bull by its horns with his bare hands (AI4:B20t.). Ashurnasirpal II is also portrayed as stabbing and holding wild bulls in the miniature reliefs (AI23:P2,49b). These scenes clearly seek to express the propaganda image of the outstanding strength and courage of the ruler. In Balawat, the king is illustrated killing wild beasts at close distance (e.g. AI13:13–14). In a relief from Nineveh, the king is seen standing in his chariot with a lion jumping up at him, while having the edge of the arrow very close to the lion's nose (AI1:86). The diadem wearing king attacks a lion, which stands on its hindlegs, by seizing the lion's mane with his left hand and stabbing the animal's throat with his right hand in a scene of close combat from the miniature relifs (AI23:G16,36a). Sometimes the assistants in the royal hunt appear as hunters in their own right. This is especially true of some scenes on the door bands of the palace of Balawat where these e.g. are driving over lions and wild bulls (AI13:29–32). They may however have reserved the deathblow for the hands of the king whose prerogative the hunting of wild beasts was (Collon 1995: 152).[155]

The hunting of wild beasts was also a ritual-religious act. As for the lion hunt, Weissert (1997) identifies an "urban hunt", and in this way stresses the ritual aspect of the hunt by which the king acts as a saviour, liberating humans and animals from the danger of lions. In the same vein, Oded (1992: 113–17) detects a royal role of shepherd in which the king chases away the wild animals which threaten his herd. The lion hunt was a royal privilege in Mesopotamia, enacting the Ninurta myth. In this role, the king/deity acts like a faithful shepherd who protects his cattle and people from danger (Annus 2002: 102–106). C. Watanabe (1998: 444–45) also discusses the lion hunt in relation to Ninurta's mythical victory and state ritual. In this ritual, the king reinforces and reestablishes his kingship by killing the lion, just as Ninurta attained kingship and avenged his father Enlil in the divine sphere by slaying the demonic creatures of Anzu and Asag. As noted by e.g. Bohrer (2003: 202–206) and Collins (2008: 16), the interpretation of the lion hunt as a cultic act confronts the Orientalist idea of this pursuit as proof of the excesses and decadence of the cruel Oriental despot who kills out of sheer pleasure or boredom. The royal hunt can also not be reduced, as done by e.g. De Odorico (1995: 143), into simply "a sporting relaxation for the king".

The ritual dimension of the royal hunt is illustrated on the walls of the North-West Palace. In the throne room, the king is depicted pouring libations over dead lions and wild bulls, while musicians accompany this ceremonial act (AI4:B19–20b.). In a relief from Nineveh, the king is seen making libations over killed lions (AI1:214–20). Clearly then, royal hunting was a religious pursuit. The likely victory celebration in the Assyrian camp where two men wear animal hides may also be an expression of this belief in the connection between hunting and religion (AI4:B7t.). The religious nature of the hunt is also seen through the divine emblems supervising it (e.g. AI35).

As for texts and the relevant ritual-religious aspect, the function of the king as hunter is sparsely attested from the reign of Shalmaneser III, but it is brought up at least in two different passages: one integrated into the campaign

155 In a curious scene from the Rassam Obelisk, a man who seems to be a commoner is seen shooting at deers outside the city of Kalhu (AI16:A3). Possibly, this image is an early example of the vignette scenes of later relief programs, alluding to the relevant royal role.

narrative (SE10:iii41–45), and the other placed after the campaign narrative and building inscription. The latter passage which states in an idiomatic sentence that "the gods Ninurta and Nergal, who love my priesthood, granted me the wild beasts and commanded me to hunt" (*Ninurta u Nergal ša šangûtī irammū būl ṣēri ušatlimūnimma epēš ba"uri iqbûni*) emphasizes the ritual aspect of the hunting as well as the discussed association with Ninurta (e.g. SE6:iv40–44). The passage then proceeds to list the fantastic variety and amount of prey. The same idiom is expressed in the texts of Ashurnasirpal II (e.g. AE30:84–94), and has its roots in Middle Assyrian times, more precisely from the reign of Tiglath-pileser I (see RIMA2: A.0.87.1:vi55–84). The combined aspects of priesthood (libations and music) and deities (Ninurta and Nergal) make the bonds between royal hunting and the cultic sphere obvious. Moreover, the caught wild beast, here lions, are sometimes likened to "cagebirds" (*iṣṣūrī quppi*) (e.g. AE2:42). The celebrated images of the ritual hunt of Ashurbanipal in which lions are released from cages to fight the king in an arena in Nineveh naturally come to mind here (see Barnett 1976: 37, pl. VIII; Collins 2008: 117, top right).[156]

The wild beasts are not always killed, but sometimes they are just caught and collected. Royal zoological gardens are spoken of by several Assyrian kings (Cancik-Kirschbaum 2008: 77), and they were part of "universal gardens" whose function it was to present Assyria as an "artifical paradise" and manifest the king as "royal gardener and hunter" (Novák 2002: 452). The collecting of animals and plants symbolized fertility, prosperity, and the king's dominion over all the four quarters of the world (Cancik-Kirschbaum 2008: 61). According to Liverani (1979: 313–14), the collecting of plants and animals from the foreign lands to the Assyrian capital expressed the symbolic movement of goods from a savage periphery to a civilized cosmic centre. Alternatively, the movement in question may simply have signified a transition from a perceived chaotic sphere, i.e. where the king had no authority in practice, to an ordered zone in which the king effectively ruled.

Turning once again to the major primary sources, Ashurnasirpal II frequently states that he caught and collected wild animals from foreign lands. He for example claims to have caught wild bulls, ostriches, and lions on mountains and in forests (AE30:91–94), and he even manages to catch "tigers" (*mindinaš*) (AE2:35). Sometimes these animals come peacefully to the king as a part of foreign tribute. On the façade wall of the North-West Palace some tributaries bring monkeys with them (AI4:D7). In a narrative passage, we are

---

156 Additionally, a hunting hymn, attested probably from the reign of Ashurnasirpal I, similarly tells of the sacred character of royal hunting (see Frahm 2009: text 77).

informed that Ashurnasirpal II received five elephants in tribute, which he then used on the following military campaign (AE30:95–97). In captions, elephants and oxen are referred to as being part of tribute transactions (e.g. AE77). As for the sources of Shalmaneser III, a register of the Black Obelisk depicts a row of exotic and fabulous animals from Egypt (SI11:A3–D3), i.e. if the caption's toponym is interpreted correctly (Tadmor 1961: 144–45; Yamada 1998: 90 n. 17). Grayson (1996: 149–50) here identifies camels, monkeys, apes, antelopes, rhinoceroses, water buffalos, and elephants as the components of this Egyptian "tribute". Supposedly, this row of exotic animals indicates royal animal collecting of a kind.[157]

This animal catch or tribute were then domesticated and housed in zoological gardens or palaces. Ashurnasirpal II mentions that he caught, bred, and kept lions in the city area of Kalhu and in his palaces (AE2:33–35). As for the latter, the custom of having tame lions at court may also be attested in Assyrian art (van Buren 1939: 9–10). He also claims to have bred and displayed monkeys in Kalhu (AE2:31–32), and to have bred and displayed all kinds of animals, i.e. wild bulls, elephants, lions, ostriches, male and female monkeys, wild asses, deer, *aialu* deer, female bears, panthers, *senkurru* animals, and "beasts of mountains and plains", in Kalhu unspecifically or in the palaces and zoological gardens of the same city (e.g. AE2:31–38). The just enumerated "beasts (*umāmu*) of mountains and plains" are in other words both kept in zoos and placed as guardian figures in the North-West Palace (see s. 4.1). This word not only refers to creatures of Tiamat used in the service of Order, i.e. as guardian figures of palaces and temples, but also to domesticated wild beasts (CAD U-W: *umāmu*). The act of "breeding" (*walādu* Š) suggests an idea of the king as the one responsible for life and death in yet another way (CAD A I: *alādu*). Ashurnasirpal II obviously took a lot of pride in these gardens. In a uniquely personal narrative passage, this king pleads to posterity in general and to his successors in particular that the animals of his zoological gardens should be looked after (AE2:38–39).

As partly noted in sections 4.1 and 4.4, both sides of the conflict, i.e. the Assyrian king and his army on the one side and the foreign rulers and troops on the other, are quite often likened to various animals in the inscriptions of Ashurnasirpal II, more rarely in those of Shalmaneser III. Some scholars, such as Liverani (1979: 309–13), interprete these similes of the latter agents quite literally as proofs of the dehumanization and animalization of foreigners,

157 A register further down, related to the tribute of Suhu, has a portrayal of a lion which attacks a deer (SI11:A4). On account of the identified dichotomy Order/Chaos, this scene may then function as a symbolic depiction of the wild nature of the land in question.

drawing this conclusion from the collected corpus of Assyrian royal inscriptions. The reasons as to why these similes automatically should be understood figuratively, conveying praise, in the former case and literally, expressing derogation and dehumanizing, in the latter case are not immediately clear. As concluded also by D. Marcus (1977: 86–87), animal similes in Assyrian royal inscriptions largely serve to describe the human agents by associating them with the characteristic attributes and qualities of the relevant animals. Put in another way, it is not the animalization as such which is the point, but rather the choice as to *which* animals are used for the specific simile.[158] Additionally, as observed by Ataç (2010: 32–38) who discusses Assyrian hybrid creatures, the clear-cut distinction of today between human and animal elements may not have been present in ancient Assyria.

The king and his army are likened to birds (e.g. AE1:ii36, AE1:i63 resp.), the latter agent occasionally to the Anzu bird (SE5:iii5, e.g. AE1:ii107). As for the latter, another example of how an originally chaotic force can be used in the service of Order is given. As for birds and the king, Shamshi-Adad V claims to have been "like an eagle" (*kīma arâni*) in his warfare (e.g. SA5E1:ii52). The enemy is likened to the *udīnu* bird (AE17:i73), a species which, just like the cowardly enemy, dwells in and takes refugee to mountain cliffs (CAD U-W: *udīnu*), or just to birds which are described as living in nests in rugged mountains (e.g. AE1:i64–65). The king likens himself to a lion (*labbāku*), while the enemy forces can be characterized as "livestock" (*maršītu*) (e.g. AE1:i33, AE17:i75–76 resp.). The latter simile may express the idea of the multitude of the defeated enemy forces, either killed or captured. Similarly, captured Babylonian warriors are described as "locusts" (*erbû*) (SA5E1:iv34–35). The lion simile may seem paradoxical, but it is surely the powerful attributes of this regal animal which the ruler wanted to associate himself with (D. Marcus 1977: 87–88). Lastly, several details of royal buildings, furniture, weapons, jewellery, and dresses are decorated with heads, tails, paws, and hoofs of e.g. lions, wild bulls, and goats, in this manner emphasizing the importance of animals and their powerful and symbolic attributes and qualities (e.g. AI4:H16, AI4:G3, AI4:B7t. resp.).

The connection between wild beasts and human enemies is also expressed in the motif of the Assyrian king libating over enemy rulers who crawl at the

158 In Ashurbanipal's inscriptions, a defeated and captured enemy ruler is given a dog collar, and is chained up at an Assyrian city gate together with a bear and a dog (see Borger 1996: text A:viii8–14)! In this unique case, a devaluation is probably intended (due to the company), along with the equation of the enemy ruler with other forces (at least the bear) of Chaos.

feet of the king (e.g. SI11:A2),[159] as well as in the narrative passages which state that the human enemy is "caught" (*ina qāti aṣbat/akšud*) (e.g. AE1:i108–9, SE2:ii4–5), and killed or caught through the practice of "ambush" (*šubtu*) (e.g. AE17:iii82–85). The terminology used in the said narrative passages is the same for wild beasts and human enemies (CAD Ṣ: *ṣabātu*, CAD Š III: *šubtu* A). Assyrian soldiers are also depicted, in analogy with the motif of the king fighting a lion, as simultaneously grabbing the hair and stabbing the throats of enemy soldiers (e.g. AI13:25–26, SI10:9t.). Similarly, Assyrian charioteers, in addition to the ruler, drive over fallen enemy soldiers (e.g. AI13:9–10) as well as wild game (e.g. AI13:29–30, SI10:12). In the loyalty oath of Mati'-ilu of Arpad to Ashur-narari V, the former will be cursed and turned into the sacrificed lamb which was sacrificed during the solemn oath concluding if he happened to breach the oath stipulations (An5E2:10′–35′). As already argued, rather than seeing all these attestations as examples of real dehumanizing and true derogation, the enemies are simply associated with forces of Chaos. In the act of resisting the Assyrian king, both the wild beasts and the king's human enemies represent and embody Chaos.

Summing up, I have argued that there is an idea of a ritual battle between the Assyrian king and the wild animals of the foreign lands. This battle does not represent a stereotyped dichotomy of Assyrian/foreign, but it rather serves to stress the king's manly heroism as well as the necessarily chaotic nature of creatures which are not yet controlled by the Order, represented by the Assyrian king, through the acts of slaying or domesticating.

5.3 Respecting the foreign deities

Turning to the supernatural component of the foreign lands, the relationship between the Assyrian king and the foreign deities will now be discussed. I will argue that the ten kings sometimes portray themselves as the protector of foreign cults, and that an ambition of replacing these, e.g. through "godnappings", with Mesopotamian ones is not attested in the sources.[160]

In earlier Assyriology literature, the image of the Assyrian kings as destroying the cults of conquered territories and zealously imposing worship of Ashur is often given (e.g. Olmstead 1931: 452). In the 1980's, Spieckermann (1982:

159 The verbal-visual imagery of Ashurbanipal libating wine over the severed head of his Elamite enemy Teumman may also be understood in this way (Collins 2008: 133).

160 The topic of the nature of Assyrian "religious imperialism" is large, and I therefore restrict myself to contribute to the discussion on the basis of the propaganda of the ten kings.

369–72) revived this imagery. In his study on alleged Assyrian interference in the cult of Yahweh in Sargonid times, he claims that the deportations of foreign deities, which are frequently mentioned in Assyrian royal inscriptions, were followed by the replacement of these deities with Assyrian ones, whereby a cult imposing was effectuated. The general textual silence in Assyrian royal inscriptions on the matter of deity replacing does he dismiss with the idea that the imposing of Assyrian deities and their cults after these godnappings was so self-evident that the scribes did not bother to mention it. He also refers to a loyalty oath of Esarhaddon for foreign polities in which it is, according to him, stated that Ashur should be the god of the conquered lands from that time on. Spieckermann also means that the narrations of the destruction of foreign cult images and sanctuaries, although seldomly expressed, are proofs of cult destruction and deity replacing. The installing of "the weapon of Ashur" (*kakki Aššur*), and some remarks in the Old Testament regarding changes of cult in Judah, allegedly under Assyrian pressure, are also highlighted in this line of argumentation on the topic.

Another, and perhaps more subtle, version of these ideas on Assyrian cult imposing seems to be represented by the works of Parpola (1993, 1995b). This school of thought claims that an Assyrian monotheism, symbolized by the Assyrian sacred tree or "Tree of Life" and centred on the god Ashur, was propagated in the Ancient Near East by the Assyrian kings, notably by the means of peripheral monuments such as stelae and by translations of Assyrian royal inscriptions into Aramaic, the everyday language in Sargonid times (Frahm 2011b: 272–85). This approach in other words also sees an although different (i.e. more peaceful) fully deliberate religious imposing. The general lack of clear and explicit proofs of a converting mission based on discussing this Tree of Life seems this time to be explained by the nature of the message, i.e. mystical and therefore not subjected to writing.

Portrayals of the Assyrians as zealously imposing worship of Ashur on all conquered lands have been rejected by other studies. By means of a different (contextual) interpretation of "the proofs" brought up above, and by highlighting the general silence on cult imposing in the primary sources – Assyrian and foreign – it has been concluded that the Neo-Assyrian kings did *not* interfere in the cult of e.g. Yahweh (McKay 1973: 60–66; Cogan 1974), and that the god Ashur was *not* forced upon the conquered territories or on Babylonia (Postgate 1992b: 257–61; Frame 1997 resp.). Dalley (2008: 173) goes so far as to claim that "religious tolerance is a particular hallmark of Assyrian control". This attitude is not unique for the Assyrians though. Robertson (2005: 209) notes the general lack of religious difference as a source of societal tensions in Mesopotamia. He claims that "Ancient Near Eastern societies are conspicuous in the almost complete absence of such tensions".

Reacting against the obvious anachronism in the old ideas, Fales (2010: 15–19, 21–24) states that the Assyrians were not any Crusaders, but simply applied an essentially political imperialism from a theocentric world view. The examples of the Assyrian king respecting foreign deities are frequent, and express the religiously tolerant nature of Assyrian imperialism. Detecting the imagery of Oriental violence in scholarly literature, Holloway (2001) concludes that Assyrian religious imperialism was pragmatically applied and focused on political aims. In other words, Assyrian religious imperialism was not about converting subject peoples but about creating political order in the empire (Parker 2011: 367). Thus, the imperialism was religious in the sense that it was justified by referring to divine commands for border extending and to the world dominion of the Mesopotamian deities, but not in the sense that it aimed at eradicating all other cults and impose Assyrian ones. In what follows, "the proofs" for Crusader-like imperialism are discussed.

The phenomenon of godnapping is especially focused on in the debate. According to Cogan (1974: 22–41), it gave the foreign deities the status of guests, not that of captives or trophies. The local cults continued, and a returning of the divine cult statue took place in the event of political subordination. Assyrian royal inscriptions clearly express the idea that the victories of the Assyrian army were due to the support *both* of the Mesopotamian and foreign deities in which the latter had abandoned his/her worshippers and subordinated him/herself under Ashur. On the same note, Holloway (2001: xv–xix) argues that the Assyrian kings had a pragmatic view regarding the spreading of Ashur's dominion over the world and on this god's claim of world rulership. Godnapping was not thought of as iconoclastically motivated plunder, and the support of local cults is well-attested in the sources and was used as a political means to gain support from the local elites and thereby consolidate the Assyrian empire. As convincingly argued by both Holloway (2001) and Bahrani (2003: 179), the seizure of cult statues was not regarded as barbaric plunder, but rather viewed upon as psychological warfare whereby much of the enemy's source of divine support was perceived by both parties as being taken. The seized deities were in fact treated with respect, and their powers were duly recognized (Bahrani 2008: 170).

Turning to the sources of this study, the foreign deities of some polities are anonymously referred to as seized by the Assyrian king after him defeating a resisting foreign ruler (e.g. SE14:95).[161] Occasionally, the information that these deities then were brought to Assyria is added (e.g. SE6:ii7–9). These acts of

161 Godnapping is, by the way, illustrated visually e.g. in the relief program decorating the palace of Sennacherib in Nineveh (see Barnett et al. 1998: pls. 143, 380–81, 453).

godnapping are not stressed but rather mentioned in long enumerations of booty. Shalmaneser III narrates in several of his inscriptions that he deported the hostile ruler Ahuni of Bit-Adini along with his troops, court, and deities (e.g. SE6:ii7–9). He also claims to have deported the deities, along with the enemy ruler's palace women, of the Kassite, south-eastern polity of Namri (e.g. SE6:iv18–21). Ashurnasirpal II just briefly mentions that he brought away the deities of two different kings, along with women and captives, of the southern Habur area (AE1:i85, AE1:iii40). In all these examples, the mentionings of godnappings are made in unstressed and deity anonymous enumerations of booty taken on Assyrian campaigns.[162] This tendency shows that the act of godnapping was seen as undramatic, not telling of any religious fanatism. Additionally, the above discussion demonstrated that the godnapped deities had the high status of respected guests.

An alternative (or additional) action when confronted by the foreign deities and their temples could be to destroy and plunder. The former action is seldomly mentioned in Assyrian royal inscriptions,[163] while the latter one is occasionally referred to. In his analysis of eNA I-inscriptions, Schramm (1973: 13–14) discusses foreign votive gifts to Assyrian temples consisting of precious booty or divine statues, and seemingly gives the idea of e.g. godnapping as plunder. Nevertheless, interpretations of real iconoclasm should probably be avoided. As phrased by van der Spek (1993: 264), when the Assyrian kings occasionally destroyed or plundered foreign temples, they did not do this because of a religious agenda, but as giving a message of the fatal consequences of resistance, or simply out of a pragmatic urge for material resources. Similarly, Holloway (2001: 193–97) argues that the destructing and plundering of foreign sacred areas and images were meant to send political messages rather than to display statements of religious zeal. According to this interpretation, the seemingly sacrilegious acts were simply targeted at those who "chose the path of political resistance or rebellion".

Neither the smashing of foreign cult images nor the destruction of temples belonging to foreign deities are mentioned in the texts of the Early Neo-Assyrian kings. The narrations that the king plundered the temples, along with the palaces, of the defeated foreign polity are however occasionally attested. Ash-

162 Diverging from this tendency, eleven godnapped deities of Der are listed and named by Shamshi-Adad V (SA5E2:iii42′–48′). The movement of the main Der deity is also centred on in the Eponym Chronicle for the years of 831, 814, and 785 BCE (see Millard 1994).

163 Regarding destruction of foreign cult images, see Borger 1996: A v 119–20, and Luckenbill 1924: 83: 48. For the destruction of foreign sanctuaries, see e.g. Borger 1996: F v 42. See also Holloway 2001: 118–22 for a discussion on the firstly mentioned attestations.

urnasirpal II claims to have brought out the treasures, including the deities, of the temple of the rebellious ruler of Bit-Halupe (AE1:i83–89). As for Shalmaneser III, a small cylinder bearing a short text which states that the object in question is booty taken from the temple of the Syrian deity Sheru of Malaha to Assur may also be understood in this context (SE92:1–2). Possibly implying the taking and giving of temple plunder, the kings Ashur-dan II and Adad-narari II each mention that they gave foreign deities as "gifts" (*qīštu*) to Ashur (Ad2E1:58, e.g. An2E1:16–17obv.). In addition to the word's neutral meaning of "gift, present", it can signify a votive offering and a dedication to a deity (CAD Q: *qīštu*). In other words, the object presented was more than just a gift but had a recognized religious value. The interpretations of mere plunder naturally relate to the notion of Oriental violence which contains the idea of Crusader-like warfare (see subs. 5.4.8).

After the act of deporting or demolishing the relevant foreign cult image, the next step was, according to the theory of religious fanatism, to replace the destroyed foreign cult with an Assyrian one. The act of installing the so-called weapon of Ashur spoken of in the texts of Tiglath-Pileser III, Sargon II, and Sennacherib is much highlighted here (Holloway 2001: 198–200). However, administrative texts indicate that although the inner and outer core had certain religious obligations such as the installing of this weapon and the payment of fees for "temple offerings" (*ginû*) made in the Ashur temple in Assur, the vasall states were fairly free in religious matters, telling of a "liberal policy" of a kind (Cogan 1974: 9–21, 42–61). Holloway (2001: 100–177), although questioning the relevance of this distinction, argues that the weapon of Ashur was simply a holy object, a divine standard of a sort, by which the foreign rulers swore allegiance to the Assyrian king, and not an object to be worshipped as a symbol of the one true god. He draws a parallel to the apparent use of "the sword of Ashur" (*patrum ša Aššur*) in Old Assyrian times. This object witnessed the administration of oaths, legal testimonies, and the creating and sealing of vital documents in the Assyrian colony of Kanesh (Holloway 2001: 167–68). The weapon of Ashur is not referred to by the ten kings other than as in the king's hands, causing fright, flight, defeat, and submission on the part of the enemies (see subs. 5.4.2).

As for the above discussed narrative passage in the loyalty oath of Esarhaddon, used as evidence by the scholars who see an intolerant religious zeal on the part of the Assyrians, a more figurative and context-based reading of it seems more appropriate, especially in the light of the circumstance that possible proofs of cult imposing are on the whole scarce (Frahm 2011b: 282). The passage in question says that Ashur should be "your (the foreign rulers') god" (*ilukunu*) (see Parpola and K. Watanabe 1988: text 6:393–94). Still, Ashur is just “the lord of the treaty” (*bēl adê*), and (more importantly) it is the loyalty towards *Esarhaddon* and not towards Ashur which is the one highlighted in this “succession treaty”. Moreover, several foreign deities are called upon in this oath’s standard curse section (see Parpola and K. Watanabe 1988: text 6:414–93). In addition, the relevant text is from the *Late* Neo-Assyrian Period. The fragmentary loyalty oath from the time of Ashurnasirpal II does not carry a similar expression (AE175). The same figurative interpretation as above can be made in the context of Tukulti-Ninurta II forcing a defeated foreign ruler to swear an oath by Ashur (TN2E5:24–25). The treaty of Ashur-narari V with Mati’-ilu of Arpad was sworn by the latter also by several foreign deities (An5E2:vi6–26). As concluded by Dalley (1998b: 78), Assyrian vassals swore their loyalty oaths both by their own and Assyrian deities, without any substantial religious imposings attached.

Confronting a final “proof” of Assyrian Crusader-like imperialism, the allusions to Judean cultic reforms under Assyrian pressure during the reign of Manasseh have, as stated, been dissected and convincingly refuted by the biblical scholars of Cogan and McKay. As for Assyria and the other and northern Hebrew polity, Shalmaneser III does only mention and illustrate tribute and submission in his representations of his dealings with the Israelite ruler Jehu (SI11:A2, e.g. SE16:134′–35′). As for the scene on the Black Obelisk, the prostrating Jehu arguably shows his humility towards *the king* and not to the divine emblems in mid-air (SI11:A2). This can be inferred from the just identified textual focus on tribute and submission. Adad-narari III, who claims to have conquered Samaria, also tells of subordination and tribute as the only duties of Joash, its ruler (e.g. An3E8:11–14). In relation to these rulers and the cults of foreign deities in general, the Assyrian king is “the dominant male” and the new protector of the cults (see subs. 5.4.9).

The textual silence regarding alleged Assyrian cult imposing is, to my mind, a decisive argument in favour of identifying a more pragmatic and tolerant Assyrian “religious imperialism”. As noted by Frahm (2011b: 272–85), this general silence does not only characterize Assyrian sources, but also the Old Testament and the Graeco-Roman ones. He e.g. notes that the god Ashur is not even or barely mentioned in the said foreign sources. If the Assyrian kings really sought to impose the worship of Ashur on conquered lands and people, this would surely have been traumatically discussed in the sources of the defeated. The existence of a certain taboo of mentioning the names of foreign deities can of course be imagined (at least when it comes to the Old Testament), but it is difficult to see that this could have been adhered to quite so rigorously. Textual silence is of course problematic to use as evidence, but it seems much more plausible to use it here than in the arguably more speculative cases of Spieckermann (1982) and Parpola (1993).

Direct attestations of the Assyrian king as the protector and priest of foreign deities should constitute the final blow for the argumentation of those who see a zealous, Assyrian religious imperialism. As noted by Cogan (1974: 22–41), the Assyrian kings often sponsored the cults of foreign deities, presumably in the hope of gaining support from the foreign people and their deities. Similarly, Holloway (2001: 338–425) refers to the practice of Assyrian kings as protecting and promoting cultic activitites, such as temple building in honour of foreign deities, as a way of ensuring imperial stability. Exemplifying this approach, Assyrian rulers frequently provided offerings and dedicated votive objects to the crossregional and non-Assyrian cult centres of the polities Musasir and Kumme (Radner 2009: 184–85 n. 296–97).

A handful foreign deities are explicitly referred to as benificaries of royal patronage in the inscriptions of Shalmaneser III. The priesthood duties of the Assyrian king were thus not limited to the cults of Mesopotamian deities. In this priestly role, the king calls the western god Amurru "his lord" (*bēlšu*) in the text on a stone mace head dedicated to this god (SE97:1). Moreover, a text on two bricks from Assur states that Shalmaneser III commissioned a golden statue of the Phoenician god (Grayson 1996: 135) Armada of Arwad (SE55:4–6). Ashurnasirpal II also refers – although to a lesser degree – to constructive relationships with foreign deities. The western god Dagan is spoken of in his already noted royal epithet "beloved of Anu and Dagan" (e.g. AE1:i10–11). The other foreign deity who is actually named in his inscriptions is Samnuha, i.e. the god of his provincial governor Mushezib-Ninurta (AE150:3).

Moving on, Shalmaneser III also presents offerings to e.g. Adad of Aleppo and Zaban (SE2:ii87, SE5:iv2–3 resp.). Although being two manifestations of the "Mesopotamian" storm god Adad, these deities nevertheless had their bases in foreign territory, and surely displayed some divergences due to their external locations and origins. Adad-narari II claims to have made offerings to unspecified foreign deities, as well as having sacrificed to Adad of Kumme, "his lord" (An2E4:18′, An2E2:91–92 resp.). The cult of Sin of Harran – a foreign deity according to the same reasoning as on Adad above – is indirectly expressed by the divine epithet "he who dwells in Harran" (*āšib Ḫarran*), attested from Adad-narari III (e.g. An3E3:23). The Sargonid ruler Ashurbanipal mentions that Shalmaneser III ordered work on this Sin temple (see Borger 1996: 186, text "Large Egyptian Tablets":rev.37–38). Harran with its Sin temple was highly regarded by the Late Neo-Assyrian kings (Holloway 2001: 388–425), it being the last stand for Ashur-uballit II.

As for the performance of rituals to foreign deities, the site of the Tigris source has been interpreted as a natural sanctuary related to the Kumarbi myth and the cult of Hurrian deities (Schachner 2009: 218). Due to its function, the river source also had the status of "holy waters" (Yamada 2000: 299). Shalmaneser III's rituals at this same site may be seen in this light. In the text on a precious stone dedicated to the Tigris source god (Deller 1987: 56–57) Hallasua, this king calls the said god "his lord" (SE119:2). Ashurnasirpal II mentions the creating of royal images at the source of the river Subnat (AE1:i104–105), in analogy a holy site too, as well as on a sacred (?) feature (CAD E: *ēqu*) in a probably foreign city (AE1:i68–69). The acknowledging of a foreign city or temple area as holy reveals a respectful attitude on the part of the king. In conclusion, the Early Neo-Assyrian kings occasionally presented themselves as the priest of foreign deities as well.

Summing up, I have argued that the ten kings present themselves as respectful to the foreign deities. Real iconoclasm is not expressed, in that godnappings convey the theme of divine abandonment rather than disrespect or fanatism. Some kings, especially Shalmaneser III, explicitly state that they supported local foreign cults. The idea of the world dominion of Ashur and the great gods was implemented pragmatically, both in thought and deed.

5.4 Confronting the foreign elites and people

This section will focus on the interaction between the king and the foreign human beings. It is divided into nine subsections due to the prominent place which this particular relationship takes in the primary sources. The first four of these discuss the relationship in its concrete and practical aspects, while the later five address it in more abstract and theoretical terms. The foreign elites and people were confronted by the Assyrian king, the latter giving an ultimatum to the former on either peaceful or violent subordinating.

5.4.1 Status and hierarchy

Firstly, the king's relationship with the foreign elites and people in terms of status and hierarchy will be discussed.[164] I will argue that the Early Neo-Assyri-

164 This distinction between people and civilians on the one hand and elites and warriors (i.e. rulers, nobles, elders, officials, soldiers) on the other is occasionally made in the sources. In a response to a rebellion, Ashurnasirpal II e.g. distinguishes between the political leaders and the common people (e.g. AE1:i74–94). The same narrative passage also indicates that when a city or land are referred to as agents, its elites are the ones alluded to. In the treaty between Ashur-narari V and Mati'-ilu of Arpad, there is an explicit distinction between the king (and his family), the magnates, and the people (An5E2:i7′–8′). Obviously, the socio-economic understanding of ancient Assyria also makes this distinction legitimate (see subs. 1.7.2).

an kings present themselves as, both becoming and being, universal rulers in relation to these elites and people. The Assyrian king could not share his divinely ordained earthly power with any other ruler of the world.

By the Neo-Assyrian Period, the idea of the king's universal power had developed (Barjamovic 2012: 45–50). The ruler had to conquer, either by force or by voluntary submission, to realize his divinely ordered right of universal dominion over all lands, cities, elites, and people. This conquering idea is amply reflected in the titulary. The verb *kanāšu* in the Š-stem is often used in royal epithets associated with the narration of conquering. A prime example here is the epithet of Ashurnasirpal II "king who made (lands) from GN to GN submit at his feet" (*šarru ša ... ana šēpēšu ušekniša*) (e.g. AE1:iii127–28). The same ruler also calls himself "the one who has made (all lands) from sunrise to sunset submit at his feet" (*ištu ṣīt šamši adi ereb šamši ana šēpēšu ušaknišu*) (AE70:5–6), and "he who has made all lands submit [at] his feet" (*mātāti kalâšina [ana] šēpēšu ušeknišu*) (AE66:5).

The conqueror role is also told of in the frequent epithets where the king describes himself as "the conqueror" (*kāšidu*) of a certain area. Ashurnasirpal II is here "conqueror of all lands" (*kāšid mātāti kalîšina*) (AE70:4), and "conqueror of cities and the entire highlands" (*kāšid ālāni ḫuršāni pāṭ gimrišunu*) (e.g. AE1:i19). He is also "the one whose hand has conquered the entire land of Hatti" (*māt Ḫatti ana siḫirtišu qāssu ikšudu*) (e.g. AE40:21). Shalmaneser III portrays himself as the conqueror from one sea to another (e.g. SE30:12–13). The relevant seas are the Mediterranean, the Persian Gulf, and the lake of Van/Urmia. This sea-to-sea epithet was in most cases, including the present one, probably not much more than "a cliché intended to convey a general impression of world-domination" (H. F. Russell 1984: 192). Royal epithets which present the Assyrian king as conqueror from one land or region to another are frequent (e.g. AE39:4–8, SE4:l.e.10–13). The wording here is *kāšid ištu* GN *adi* GN or an attributive relative clause with *qāssu ikšudu* as its last components. Whole clusters of the titulary state Shalmaneser III as having conquered from one region to another (e.g. SE40:i6–8).

Also in the narrative passages, the king is described as the one who "make submit" (*kanāšu* Š) and "conquers" (*kašādu*) lands, cities, and mountains (to which the enemy had fled) (e.g. AE1:ii29, SE30:14–17). The claim of having conquered from one end to another is likewise attested. Ashurnasirpal II e.g. states that he conquered from the sources of the river Subnat to the interior of the lands of Nirbu or Urartu (e.g. AE1:iii122, AE2:13 resp.), or from the sources of the Subnat to that of the Tigris (AE28:iv2–3), and that he subdued all lands from sunrise to sunset (AE39:6–8). He further claims that he conquered whole lands or regions, e.g. through the statement that he managed to establish his authority over "the entire extensive" (*ana pāt gimri*) lands of Nairi (e.g. AE32:6–7). As noted by Tadmor (1973: 149), Adad-narari III centres on the conquest of two geographical extremes, Damascus and Chaldea (An3E8:15–24). The same king also claims to have conquered vast areas of the Ancient Near East, including as distant polities as Edom, Nairi, and Media (An3E8:5–14). Boundaries (*miṣru*) are frequently referred to in these narrations of conquering. Ashurnasirpal II e.g. remarks that he brought a certain land "within the boundaries of my land" (*ana miṣrī mātija*) (e.g. AE2:15), and that "[I (he) counted (the conquered territory) as within the boundaries] of my land" ([*ana miṣir*] *mātija* [*amnu*]) (AE67:8).

Not only the words *kašādu* and *kanāšu* carry the idea of the king as conqueror and subduer of all lands. The act of conquering is also described in the texts of the Early Neo-Assyrian rulers by the verb *ṣabātu* in the expression "I took GN as my own" (GN *ina ramānija aṣbat*) (e.g. AE19:103, SE16:30). Additionally, Tukulti-Ninurta II describes himself as "the king who seized from GN to GN" (*šarru ša ištu* GN *adi* GN *iṣbatu*) (TN2E6:2–5). The verb *târu* in the D-stem, meaning "to bring back", in its usage expresses the act of reconquesting (e.g. An2E2:26). Moving on through his military successes the king "puts" (*šakānu*) "victory and strength" (*lītu u danānu*) over conquered lands (e.g. AE1:iii23). In this respect, Ashurnasirpal II is commonly called "he who achieves victory over all lands" (*šākin līte eli kalîšina mātāti*) (e.g. AE1:i17). The word *lītu* is otherwise associated with the divine sphere and its extraordinary capacities (CAD L: *lītu*). The kings also conquer through "spreading" (*tabāku*) their granted radiance over lands, cities, elites, and people (e.g. AE19:100, SE28:35–36). The inhabitants of the foreign lands are supposedly pacified and conquered by this radiance.

Turning to the iconography, both Ashurnasirpal II and Shalmaneser III are depicted as conquerors in several important sources such as on the walls and door bands of the North-West Palace and the Balawat gates respectively. In this role, Shalmaneser III is majestically and characteristically (D. Oates 1963: 12 n. 11) depicted with a pair of arrows in his right hand (e.g. SI14:4b). Both kings are portrayed standing with bow and arrows (e.g. AI4:G14–15, SI10:7b.), and Shalmaneser III is also depicted sitting with this weaponry (e.g. SI10:9b.). Both kings are illustrated standing in their chariots while shooting arrows and driving over enemies (e.g. AI14:59–60, SI10:7t.), as well as standing while shooting at enemy cities with their bows (e.g. AI4:B18t., SI10:1b.). The motif in which the king holds bow and arrows in his hands arguably expresses his role as conqueror (Collins 2008: 94). The foreign side is seen conquered either in the shape of processions of tributaries and captives or through defeat in battle. In all instances, the king directs his attention to elites and people submitting or to struggling enemy soldiers. These depictions all convey the image of the Assyrian king as the universal conqueror of the submissive or unsubmissive foreign human beings. In addition, they portray him gendered as "the dominant male" (see subs. 5.4.9).

The king's universal dominion over lands, and indirectly over their elites and people, is often claimed in the sources of the ten kings. They are e.g. very commonly called "king of the universe" (*šar kiššati*) (e.g. AE1:i10, SE5:i1). This title is often regarded as Assyrian in origin and not related to authority over the city state Kish (Hallo 1957: 25–26; Garelli 1979: 319–20), but referring to universal rulership (Seux 1965b: 9). The noun *kiššatu* conveys the meaning of totality (CAD K: *kiššatu* A). According to Dalley (1998b: 76), the relevant title could be taken only after having conducted seven (connoting totality) successful military campaigns.[165] This title and the title about to be discussed, i.e. "king of the four quarters", basically convey the same meaning (Frankfort 1948: 228), but possibly the latter one had more prestige on the basis of its longer usage, cosmic connotations, and greater expressiveness (Seux 1965b: 16–20). An obvious distinction is that between notions of "compact" and "patterned" totality (Liverani 1981: 234–35). In addition to the title just discussed, in a partly reconstructed passage of the Sultan Tepe inscription (Lambert 1961), Shalmaneser III is possibly referred to as "[he who directs] the universe" ([*muštēšir*] *kiššatu*°) (SE17:4).

Quite commonly, the king is called "king of all the four quarters" (*šar kullat kibrāt erbetti*) (e.g. AE1:i10, SE2:i5). The related title "king of the four quarters" (*šar kibrāt erbetti*) is however sparsely attested in the texts of the Early Neo-Assyrian kings (e.g. AE1:i35, SE1:2). Interestingly, it is the one title associated with Shalmaneser III by his successors (e.g. An3E2:3). In any case, all the quarters are claimed to be entrusted by the deities into his royal hands (e.g. SE17:6). Tukulti-Ninurta II claims in this context to have been "he whose honoured name he (Ashur) has pronounced forever for the four quarters" (*ana mu"urūt kibrāt erbetti ana dāriš išquru*) (e.g. TN2E4). The same ruler also portrays himself as "the commander of the four quarters" (*muma"er kibrāt erbetti*) (e.g. TN2E2). Ashurnasirpal II is also twice called "king of the totality of the four quarters including all their rulers" (*šar kiššat kibrāte ša napḫar malkī kalîšunu*) (e.g. AE1:i35–36). The four quarters signify the whole known world including Assyria (Liverani 1990: 46 n. 15; Horowitz 1998: 289). This kind of authority over the four quarters implied dominion over the *oikoumene* and even beyond that (Ataç 2013: 393–94). Dalley (1998b: 76) here proposes that the title of "king

165 Such a statement relates to the general discussion on how seriously scholars should take the claims made in royal epithets, in terms of truth, distortion, and fantasy (see ss. 6.1, 6.5).

of the four quarters" had to be earned by successful royal campaigning, not seven times, but in all four points of the compass. However that may be, the two titles just discussed clearly serve to express the idea of world dominion.

Regarding other generally phrased claims of worldwide dominion over lands attested in royal epithets, some Early Neo-Assyrian kings claim to be in the position of "leading" (*redû* Gt) or "ruling" (*bêlu*) in relation to *mātāti* and *ḫuršāni*. In this role, Shalmaneser III is eleven times, but Ashurnasirpal II only once, referred to as "the leader of all lands" (*murtedû kalîš mātāte*) (AE45:7–8, e.g. SE1:2),[166] or less often as "the splendid king of all lands" (*šar mātāti šarḫu*) (AE40:5, e.g. SE2:i10), implying universal leadership. Ashurnasirpal II calls himself, twelve times, "the one who rules over the highlands in their entirety" (*ḫuršāni pāṭ gimrišunu ipellu*) (e.g. AE1:i16).

Also the textual narrative refers to the ten kings as dominating lands generally. Shalmaneser III claims control of the whole of Hatti or Chaldea (SE6:iv28, SE29:46–47 resp.), while Ashurnasirpal II brags about being in control of the whole of Laqe, Suhu, Mehru, or Hatti (e.g. AE40:22–23, AE40:23, AE40:28–29, AE42:3–4 resp.). Shamshi-Adad V portrays himself as "king of Sumer and Akkad" (*šar māt Šumerî u Akkadî*) (SA5E9:2), expressing his claim of controlling the whole of Babylonia. The related literary theme of "display of strength" in which the king marches across foreign lands, here the Mediterranean coastal area, "triumphantly" (*šalṭiš*) without encountering any resistance, is also attested (e.g. AE2:25–31, SE2:ii7–8). The word "triumph" (*šalṭu*) is intimately connected to the idea of having authority (CAD Š I: *šalṭu* B). Two other versions of this theme are Shalmaneser III's claims of marching uncontested all the way to *Muṣuruna* (Egypt or a city in Palestine) as well as to Urartu (SE16:162′, SE14:179–80 resp.). The roaming of the said ruler through Babylonia also tells of the theme in question (e.g. SE5:v3–vi5). As for this theme, the Assyrian New Year Festival (*akītu*) had the ritual demonstrating (involving processions) of the Assyrian king's control over all lands as a vital component (Pongratz-Leisten 1997a: 252).

Highlighting another theme in the textual narrative on the Assyrian king as generally dominating lands, Ashurnasirpal II claims to have placed all of the conquered land, or conquered lands and highlands from sunrise to sunset (i.e. from east to west), under one command (e.g. AE17:iii21–22, AE1:iii131–32 resp.). The expression "I placed under one command" (*pâ ištēn ušaškin*), literally "I placed under one mouth", in a clear way conveys the reluctance of the Assyrian king to share his conditionally granted power over the world of

166 It may be noted here that the verb *redû* of the Gt-participle *murtedû* also and tellingly refers to a role of herding cattle (CAD R: *redû* A), expressing the royal shepherding role.

humankind with any other ruler.[167] There could only be one real ruler at a single time. Behind this notion of the unique status of the Assyrian king is of course the coronation command which says that the king should "rule, subdue, and direct the lands and mighty highlands" (*mātāti u ḫuršāni dannūte ana pêli šuknuše u šapāri*) (AE2:24–25), eventually being the undisputed head of authority over the whole world (Liverani 1990: 79).

Also the royal iconography conveys the idea of the king's universal dominion over lands (and indirectly over its elites and people). The geographical ordering of the scenes on the Balawat Gate of Shalmaneser III according to the four quarters testifies to this (Hertel 2004). Although a positioning according to the cardinal points of the compass can not be identified on the corresponding door bands of Ashurnasirpal II, there is nevertheless a tendency of arranging the scenes geographically present (Curtis 2008: 73). A tendency of geographical grouping is also visible on the Rassam Obelisk (Reade 1980a: 20), and the same may also be the case for the historical scenes which are illustrated in the North-West Palace (Winter 1981; Lumsden 2004). The all-inclusive nature of the foreign human beings, in the sense of their variety, is conveyed also through their varying types of hair, beard, headgear, dresses, shoes, and tribute (Wäfler 1975). The Early Neo-Assyrian ruler in other words clearly depicted himself as the ruler over the whole world in the monumental visual arts preserved from this period.

The Black Obelisk can act as a case study for pointing to the notion of the world dominion of the Assyrian king and to the integration of text and image. The texts, in the shape of captions and annals, talk of Shalmaneser III as conquering everywhere (SE87–91, SE14 resp.). The images, which are laid out in five different registers, paint the picture of submission and tribute delivering from all the corners of the world, namely from the west (Israel and Patina), the north/east (Gilzanu), and the south (Egypt, Suhu) (SI11:A–D,1–5). The variety of peoples depicted on the Black Obelisk expresses the wide geographical extent of the king's campaigns (Keel and Uehlinger 1994). The four processions each represent geographical extremes, points of the compass, and Shalmaneser III is in this way portrayed as a world ruler who receives tribute from all the quarters of the world (Porada 1983: 15–16; Lieberman 1985). This ruler's generally geographical ordering of his visual arts, according to the points of the compass, is striking (M. Marcus 1987). Messagewise, text and image here reinforce each other, serving as parallels.

---

167 When this idiom (here with *ēdu* instead of *ištēn*) is associated with the behaviour of enemy rulers, the negative act of conspiracy may instead be referred to (CAD E: *ēdu*).

Turning to textual attestations which more directly and explicitly refer to the Assyrian king as the superior of foreign human beings, an important epithet of Shalmaneser III, but attested only once for Ashurnasirpal II, is "king of all people" (*šar kiššat nišē*) (AE19:22, e.g. SE1:1).[168] It also heads a common and vital cluster of epithets. Ashurnasirpal II in his turn used the epithets "commander of all people" (*šāpir kal nišē*) (AE19:21) and (above all) "he who rules all people" (*ša napḫar kiššat nišē ipellu*) (e.g. AE1:i14). As for commanding the people, Shamshi-Adad V made use of the originally divine (see s. 3.1) epithet "commander of all" (*muma"er gimrī*) (e.g. SA5E1:i28–29). The idea that the Assyrian king is the only legitimate ruler of the foreign people is expressed by the epithet "he who has placed all people under one command" (*ša napḫar kiššat nišē pâ ištēn ušaškinu*) (AE40:7). In a narrative passage from his Banquet Stele, Ashurnasirpal II states that he "by force added land to Assyria, and people to its people" (*eli māt Aššur māta eli nišīša nišī anasaḫ uraddi*) (AE30:100–101). The unifying of all people under the authority of the Assyrian king is illustrated by the deportations to, and multi-ethnic character of, the capital Kalhu (AE23:15–17).

As for the royal iconography and the motif of the Assyrian king in charge of the foreign people as well, all the processions of tributaries and captives, not only consisting of rulers, officials, nobles, and soldiers but also of civilians, which are depicted in the visual arts of a few Early Neo-Assyrian kings naturally come to mind. This motif is amply attested on obelisks, door bands, and palace walls (e.g. AI16:A1, AI15:95–97, AI4:D2–9 resp.). The gestures of the tributaries and captives, namely their clenched fists in submission and raised hand in submission and/or respectful greeting,[169] their slightly bowed backs, their sometimes being tied to ropes and neck stocks, their walking in disciplined processions, and womens' hand on their heads in mourning all display their subordination to the Assyrian king (e.g. AI13:21–24, SI10:1b.). The superiority in status of the king is illustrated by his majestic and dignified stance, but also by his foregrounded position, i.e. partly as the goal of tribute/captive processions, and partly as the centre of his entourage.

Regarding the Assyrian king and the foreign elites, there are many epithets specifically referring to the ten kings' real or fictive hegemony over foreign rulers. Several of these refer to the royal act of subordinating them. The foreign ruler is here refusing to acknowledge the king's right to overlordship and trib-

168 After collating a Tigris inscription of Shalmaneser III, Radner (2009: 190–93) suggests the minor variant "king of all great peoples", adding the logogram 'gal' to the epithet.
169 As observed by Magen (1986: 39 n. 29), this gesture may be distinguished from the similar gesture made by the Assyrian king, which she terms *karābu*, expressing a blessing greeting.

ute. In his study on the enemy ruler as presented in Assyrian royal inscriptions, Fales (1982: 428–32) notices the theme of this agent's inclination of withholding tribute and refusing submission. Since these two acts are divinely decreed, the war then becomes an unavoidable religious duty for the Assyrian king (Liverani 1990: 128). The foreign rulers who decided to challenge the Assyrian king and the Mesopotamian deities in this way were branded as enemies, rebellious, and the like. The defiant rulers would then, to use a post-colonial term, represent alterity and "the Other".

In relation to those referred to as "enemies", the Early Neo-Assyrian king is "he who treads upon the necks of his foes" (*mukabbis kišād ajjābīšu*) (e.g. AE1:i14–15, SE28:8). Ashurnasirpal II is also "slayer of his foes" (*munēr ajjābīšu*) and "conqueror of the foes of Ashur" (*kāšid ajjābūt Aššur*) (e.g. AE1:i35, AE1:i28 resp.). In the lastly mentioned epithet, the idea that the enemy ruler opposes the deities by his resistance is given again. This ruler is also once referred to as "he who destroys his enemies" (*muḫalliq zā'irīšu*) (AE56:4), while Adad-narari II is "he who has felled his foes" (*mušamqitu gērīšu*) (e.g. An2E1:4). More often, the enemy ruler is called *nakru*. The Assyrian king is "trampler of all enemies" (*dā'iš kullat nakrī*) (e.g. AE1:i15, SE28:8–9), "trampler of the lands of enemies" (*dā'iš mātāti nakrī*) (AE1:iii116), and "king who disintegrates all his enemies" (*šarru mušḫarmiṭ kullat nakrīšu*) (e.g. AE1:i35). He is also "he who has competed with every last enemy of Ashur above and below" (*nākirūt Aššur pāṭ gimrišunu eliš u šapliš ištananu*) and "he whose just hand has conquered all his enemies" (*napḫar nakrīšu ikšudu ešartu qāssu*) (e.g. AE1:i27, AE40:8–9 resp.).

Regarding rebellious and non-surrendering rulers, the Assyrian king is "he who scatters the forces of the rebellious" (*muparrir kiṣrī multarḫi*) (e.g. AE1:i15, SE28:8), "he who makes [the insubordinate] submit" (*mušeknišu°* [*lā kanšūte*]) (SE41:1), and "he who makes those unsubmissive to Ashur to the borders above and below submit" (*mušekniš lā māgirūt Aššur ša pāṭāte eliš u šapliš*) (AE40:3–4). The last epithet again expresses the idea that it is ultimately Ashur who the resisting foreign ruler opposes. Ashurnasirpal II commonly refers to himself as "king/he who makes those insubordinate to him submit" (*šarru mušakniš lā kanšūtešu*) (e.g. AE1:i14). The pronoun "him" refers either to the king or to Ashur. The Early Neo-Assyrian king is also "controller of the brazen ones" (*mula"iṭ ekṣūte*) ([SE5:i3], e.g. AE1:i19), "slayer of the obdurate" (*munēr alṭūti*) (SE5:i2), and "controller of his obdurate resistance" (*mula"iṭ ašṭūtēšu*) (e.g. An2E2:17), giving two new names for the defiant ruler. The latter is even referred to as a criminal in the epithets of "trampler of evildoers" (*mudīš targīgī*) (AE40:6) and "he who burns right up the wicked and evil" (*ḫitmuṭ raggi u ṣēni*) (e.g. An2E4:4′–5′). The underlying idea here is supposedly that it was regarded as a sin and crime against the Mesopotamian deities to oppose Assyrian imperialism.

In a less stigmatizing mode, the resisting and fought enemy is specified as "ruler" (*malku*) or less often "king" (*šarru*). Ashurnasirpal II is "he who makes all rulers bow down" (*qādid° kal malkī*), "[he who achieves] victory over the rulers of all quarters" ([*šākin*] *līte eli malkī ša kalîšina kibrāti*), and "he who smashes the weapons of the rulers of all quarters" (*mušabbir kakkī malkī ša kalîšina kibrāti*) (AE19:11, AE56:6, AE19:19–20 resp.). The same king is also "the king who forces to bow down those/rulers insubordinate to him" (*šarru mušakmiṣ° malkī lā kanšūtešu*)[170] and "he whose great hand has conquered all rulers unsubmissive to him" (*napḫar malkī lā māgirīšu ikšudu rabītu qāssu*) (e.g. AE1:i36, AE1:i39 resp.). Ashurnasirpal II is also "he who by his lordly combat has placed under one command fierce and merciless kings from sunrise to sunset" (*ša ina qitrub bēlūtišu šarrāni ekdūte lā pādûte ištu ṣīt šamši adi ereb šamši pâ ištēn ušaškin°*) (e.g. AE2:20–21). Similarly, Adad-narari III is "he who has made the rulers of the four quarters submit at his feet" (*malkī ša kibrāt erbetti ušeknišu ana šēpēšu*) (An3E8:4–5).

After defeating the enemy, the Early Neo-Assyrian king could be called "great king" (*šarru rabû*) (e.g. AE1:ii125, SE5:i1). This title is used primarily in an international context where it alludes to relations to other rulers (Cifola 1995: 81–85). The importance of it is showed by Ashurnasirpal II who has it as heading a common and vital cluster of epithets (e.g. AE31:1). The king is furthermore "he who has no rival among the rulers of the four quarters" (*ša ina malkī ša kibrāt erbetti šāninšu lā īšû*) (e.g. AE1:i12–13, SE2:i10), "he who has no antagonist" (*ša māḫira lā īšû*) (e.g. AE1:i13–14), and "king without rival" (*šar lā šanān*) (e.g. AE1:i10, SE25:2), i.e. he is someone who has eliminated all competition. Liverani (1981: 234–38) sees this as an example of an ideological, yet historically based, transition from a "heroic-competitive" stage to a "territorial" stage marked by superiority and undisputed control. Although this suggestion may certainly be problematized and questioned (see ch. 6), the royal epithets brought up for discussion here clearly convey the image of the victorious, sole, and supreme ruler.

As the eventual master of the foreign rulers, the king enjoys undisputed superiority over foreign rulers, lords, and kings. He can now call himself "[commander] of all rulers" ([*šāpir*] *malkī ša kullate*),[171] "king of all rulers" (*šar*

---

170 Tellingly, the word *kamāsu* both refer to the bowing down of enemies in front of the king and to the gesture of cult participants in front of deities (CAD K: *kamāsu* B). This imaginatively expresses the absoluteness in the surrendering of the subjugated foreign ruler.

171 The related stative of Tukulti-Ninurta II, "I am in command" (*šāpirāku*) (e.g. TN2E2), may also be noted here, indirectly telling of superiority over other rulers of the world.

kal malkī), "foremost of all rulers" (*ašarēd kalâ° malikī*), and "he who treads upon the necks of rulers insubordinate to him" (*mukabbis kišād malkī lā māgi-rūtešu*) (e.g. SE9:3, AE1:i20, AE40:12, AE19:14 resp.). Furthermore, Ashurnasirpal II is "king of lords" (*šar bēlē*) and "lord of lords" (*bēl bēlē*) (e.g. AE1:i19, AE1:i21 resp.). The last epithet is also an attribute of Nabu (An3E26:5). The said king also refers to himself in a stative form as "being lord" (*bēlāku*) (e.g. AE1:i32). The foreign rulers are also stated as subordinated in the royal epithets of "lord of kings" (*bēlum° šarrāni*) (SE17:28) and "king of kings" (*šar šarrāni*) (e.g. AE1:i21). The lastly mentioned epithet is thus not restricted to the Sargonid or Persian periods.[172] Ashurnasirpal II also refers to himself as "being royal" (*šarrāku*) in a stative form which heads a certain cluster of epithets (e.g. AE1:i32). As is apparent from the above, a hierarchy between the terms *šarru* and *bēlu* is not readily identified, but the term *malku* seems less prestigious, used only once on himself by Shalmaneser III (SE16:1), and only occasionally by Ashurnasirpal II, e.g. in his epithet of "foremost of all rulers" mentioned in this paragraph.

As for the textual narrative and the achieved status of the Assyrian king, the said status is not the least articulated by the king, concretely receiving submission from subjugated foreign polities. For example, in one narrative passage the rulers of all western lands are described as approaching the Assyrian king with humility and submission in their acts and attitudes (e.g. AE2:44–45). In a culminating and ceremonial act of subordination, the foreign ruler was expected "to seize my (the king's) feet" (*šēpīja iṣbutu*), i.e. to submit (SE14:134). Some of the above discussed royal epithets, centering on the initial phrases of *mukabbis kišād*, also convey an image of the Assyrian king as placing one of his feet on the neck of the foreign ruler. The occasional descriptions of foreign rulers as a "man loyal to me" (*dāgil pāni ša ramānija*) (Ad2E1:38, e.g. An2E2:109), literally "the one who sees my face", also allude to ceremonial eye-to-eye submission. The surrender of the defeated or pacified foreign ruler at audiences was in other words absolute.

This asymmetrical state of the relations of power is also expressed by describing the king appointing vassals or puppet kings (e.g. SE16:225′–26′). The foreign ruler was here expected to be a servant of the Assyrian king. The Urartean and Bit-Adini rulers are explicitly described as servants in the texts of Shalmaneser III (SE17:24, SE17:7 resp.), and the rulers of Damascus and Chaldea are described as doing "servitude" (*urdūtu*) in the texts of Adad-narari III (e.g. An3E8:17–18). Assyrian vassals were expected to "pull the yoke of [my

172 I point to this because Radner (2010: 30–31) in her discussion on Esarhaddon's use of this imperialistic and very prestigious royal title seems to bypass this earlier attestation.

(the king's) lordship]" (*išūṭu nīr [bēlūtija]*) (An3E4:2′). As for the nature of this servitude and yoke pulling, some western kings are mentioned as surrendering, whereafter they, or at least other high-ranking members of their courts, accompany in their capacity of "hostages" (*līṭu*) Ashurnasirpal II on his subsequent military campaign (e.g. AE1:iii69–70). The treaty of Ashur-narari V conveys these duties more elaborately. Mati'-ilu was supposed not to hide or protect deserteurs, nor to help these flee, he should assist his overlord in warfare, and generally strive for the best for his overlord whose destiny he ought to share with him (An5E2:iii21′–iv3).

The literary theme of the installing of "governors" (*šaknu*) in charge of the relevant polity tells the same story of asymmetrical power relationships (e.g. AE3:45–46, SE6:iv37–39). Especially in the texts of Ashurnasirpal II, these references to administrative measures related to the delegating and distributing of power are many. The status of *šaknu* is ambiguous however, since they too, just like the vassals, were expected to make the said servitude (and sometimes also corvée labour) in relation to their overlord (e.g. AE3:45–46). Arguably, there was a distinction between governors sent out from the core, and those who were allowed to head the administration due to their local power network (Postgate 1979, 1992a). The equivalent terms of *bēl pīḫati* and *šākin māti* are not yet used here. In the Late Neo-Assyrian imperial state, Assyrian officials with supervising duties, referred to as *qīpu*, had a strong control over the rulers they supervised (Dubovský 2012). In any case, the theme of governors also illustrates the fundamental hierarchy.

Turning to iconography, the foreign elites are portrayed variously as making resistance or surrendering. The proper attitude, according to Assyrian state ideology, is expressed e.g. on the two sides of the throne base on which two separate rows of tributaries headed by the elites of Chaldea and Patina approach the king offering tribute and submission (SI14:4–7). These tributaries with their bowed backs and clenched fists clearly express subordination (D. Oates 1963: 16–17). The extremes of the two areas – south and north – symbolically signify the wide extent of the king's dominion (D. Oates 1963: 16, Reade 1979b: 72). The throne base is through its reliefs and its epithet "he who with the support of Ashur has tread all lands under his feet as if they were footstools" (*ša ina tukulti Aššur mātāti kalîšina kīma kerṣappī ana šēpīšu ikbusu*) a concrete symbol of the other side's defeat (e.g. SE28:9–10).[173] On the Black Obelisk, foreign elites, here from Gilzanu, Israel, Suhu, and Patina, head rows

173 As for royal furniture and propaganda, Sennacherib's throne is depicted as carved to represent subject peoples supporting the king when seated (see Barnett et al. 1998: pl. 335).

of servile tributaries who in the cases of Gilzanu and Israel face the Assyrian king with his entourage (SI11:A–D1–2,4–5).

The person who heads these tributary processions, and thereby is closest to the Assyrian king, is presumably the relevant foreign ruler. Often figures in a smaller scale, most likely the ruler's son-heir (Reade 1980a: 13), accompany these leaders (e.g. SI14:6a). In their leading positions, the foreign rulers either make the gesture of clenched fists (e.g. AI4:D5, SI14:6a), bear a gift (Curtis and Tallis 2008: 66) consisting of some precious item (e.g. AI14:61–62), or are on their knees in front of the king. The emphasized scenes of the rulers of Gilzanu and Israel crawling and kissing the ground in front of the king are examples of the lastly mentioned gesture, and symbolize the extent of the king's power from the extreme east to the extreme west (Porada 1983: 15–16). On an ivory plaque from the 9th century BCE and the throne room of the North-West Palace, another ruler kisses the feet of the Assyrian king (AI26).[174] The position of the relevant ruler, i.e. Ashurnasirpal II, at the receiving end of these acts of humility and processions of tributaries naturally expresses his superior status in relation to the foreign elites.

Summing up, I have argued that the Early Neo-Assyrian kings are portrayed as the superior of the foreign lands, elites and people. The former are both in the position of *becoming* as well as in the position of *being* the superior part in relation to the latter. The Assyrian king could not share the same kind and degree of authority with any other ruler of the world. This power relationship is seen as reflecting the wishes of the Mesopotamian deities.

5.4.2 Function and reciprocity

After having identified the respective statuses of the human units of analysis, the issue of the *function* of the relevant relationship will now be discussed. In this subsection, I will identify and discuss a principle or policy of reciprocity by which the foreign elites and people were expected to give submission and tribute in exchange for life and protection from the Assyrian king. Annihilation[175] or enslavement/deportation followed in case of resistance.

---

174 The literary theme of "kissing" (*našāqu*) the feet of the Assyrian king is expressed solely in inscriptions outside the major primary sources (see e.g. RINAP3/1: text 16:iii15–26).

175 I do not mean to refer to genocide by this term. As will be argued in this subsection, the Assyrian forces' use of atrocities is not portrayed as ethno-culturally motivated, and a distinction between "guilty" and "innocent" is occasionally made. How the decisions on, and the meting out of, "punishment" were carried out in real life is of course another question.

A reciprocity principle which states that a refusal of submission and tribute payment causes annihilation or enslavement, and that a giving of the former causes royal benevolence and protection runs as a red thread in the relevant royal inscriptions. According to this logic, the chain of events in Assyrian royal inscriptions are *either* background (not always given however), marching out, battle, aftermath (i.e. plunder, destruction, killing, enslavement), and onmarch or homemarch, *or* background, marching out, tribute and submission, and onmarch or homemarch.[176] As recognized also by Fales (1982: 428–32) and Oded (1992) in their respective surveys on the topic, the violence of the Assyrian king is caused by the enemy's refusal of surrendering and paying tribute – obligations stipulated by loyalty oaths or the mere idea of Ashur's world dominion. The response or choice of the foreign land decided which of these chain of events that was realized.

The one component of this principle is that submission and tribute (here from the foreign people) bring mercy, and it is attested frequently. As for the texts of Ashurnasirpal II and the reciprocity principle, the (people of the) cities[177] in the vicinity of Mt Kirruru deliver tribute to the king on his campaign. The tribute in question is enumerated, a statement that corvée was imposed is given, and no violence is mentioned (AE1:i54–56). In the same passage, the lands of Gilzanu and Hubusku are described as having given tribute, whereafter the king's onmarch is noted without any remarks on the exercise of violence (AE1:i56–58). As for the texts of Shalmaneser III, the people of Tarsus surrender and pay tribute, and they are evidently spared (SE14:135–38). Again concluding from the absence of narrations including the mentioning of violence, the tribute paying people of Phoenician cities are likewise spared from Assyrian violence (SE16:152′–62′). In other words, foreign people could not be afflicted both by tribute and indiscriminate violence. The servile acts of paying and surrendering averted atrocities.

The other component of this principle is that resistance (again from the foreign people) brings punishment, and it too is attested frequently. In Ashurnasirpal II's reign, the people of Habhu who flee to a mountain rather than surrender or engage in battle are brutally punished (AE1:ii112–16). The notes that certain cities were fortified allude to resistance by the foreign people, in

176 Similarly, Oppenheim (1979: 121–25) identifies the standard chain of events as marching out, battle, and triumph, followed by punishing the defeated, and reporting to the deities.

177 The gentilic ending to a GN is here understood as referring to the people of a polity. In the case of a lack of this ending, the elite of the relevant polity is probably alluded to. The latter agent may be interpreted as the city/land as an institution, thus connected to its ruling elite.

that they hid behind their walls, causing the king to besiege. The (people of the) cities Kinabu and Tela of the polity Nirbu are described in this way. When the king and his army then conquer these cities they kill, destroy, plunder, and carry out various atrocities towards the besieged people (AE1:i106–10, AE1:i112–ii2 resp.). In Shalmaneser III's reign, the fleeing people of Mt Lamena is plundered of their possessions and killed by the king (SE14:135–38). Similarly, the people of Syrian cities who become frightened and flee are plundered of their possessions, have their settlements destroyed, and get killed (SE16:152′–62′). These attestations of this universally applied reciprocity principle are just a sample of the total number. The background of a certain action of the Assyrian king is not always mentioned, but when it is indeed stated, it is clear that the principle in question is in operation.

Turning to the foreign *elites* and the identified principle of reciprocity, the fate of these were yet again dependent on which response they gave towards the king's demand for submission and tribute. The reciprocity principle component of submission-gives-mercy identified above is even more apparent with regards to this agent. As for the texts of Ashurnasirpal II, the king receives tribute from the kings of the Mediterranean coast including those of Tyr, Sidon, and Byblos. This tribute is listed, and the passage is ended with the proclamation that these kings all submitted to Ashurnasirpal II. Descriptions of violence are absent (AE1:iii85–88). The same is the case when the kings of the (eastern) land Zamua submit. The said king only mentions that he imposed tribute, tax, and corvée labour (AE1:ii77–80). The kings from the western states referred to as Hatti and Hanigalbat give tribute, and the narration of this campaign is ended without further due (AE1:ii21–23). As for the texts of Shalmaneser III, the rulers of Zanziuna and Gilzanu both give up and pay tribute whereafter no acts of atrocities are mentioned (SE2:ii57–63). Furthermore, after the king of Daienu surrenders and presents tax and tribute of horses, no violence is indicated (SE8:51′). The same applies for the narration of the paying of tribute by Jehu of Israel (SE8:24″–27″). Similarly, the surrendering and tribute giving ruler of Tanakun is spared (SE14:133–35).

The royal response is of course another when the Assyrian king is confronted by hostility and resistance from the foreign elites, triggering the other component of the reciprocity principle, focusing on coercion and violence. Regarding the texts of Ashurnasirpal II, the cities of the ruler Kirteara of Larbusa are besieged and conquered, and the Assyrian army then kill, plunder, and destroy (AE1:ii39–43). The same actions are directed at a fortified (i.e. resisting) city of the ruler Ilanu of Bit-Zamani (AE1:iii105–109).[178] As for the texts of Shalmanes-

178 As for sieges and weak enemy rulers, the arch-enemy Irhulenu of Hamath is probably the one depicted lying on his sickbed (?) within the confines of his besieged city (SI10:13t.).

er III, the rulers of Hubushkia and Bit-Adini resist, and they, along with their lands,[179] are consequently described as punished heavily for this (SE2:ii63–69). Hazael of Damascus chose the path of resistance whereupon he and his army are described as vanquished (SE8:2″–21″). The unsubmissive ruler of Urartu is portrayed as defeated in the same way (SE14:141–46). Once again, these attestations of this universally applied reciprocity principle are just a sample of the total number. Quite often the background of a certain encounter is not clarified, but the principle is certainly in operation when it is indeed stated. The given samples in their great geographical spread point to a focusing on *actions* and not on ethnicity.

The reciprocity principle is often accomplished after the king's use of the ultimately divine radiance and weapons against foreign elites and people. The foreign elites and people are confronted by these, and they respond either by becoming paralyzed and surrendering or by embarking upon a panicing flight. As for the former reaction, "the radiance of Ashur" (*melammu ša Aššur*) causes elites and people to give up and pay tribute (e.g. AE17:i79–81). The same could happen after their being exposed to "the brilliance of my (the king's) weapons and awe of my lordship" (*namurrat kakkīja šurbat° bēlūtija*) or to "my mighty/furious weapons, very wild combat, and perfect strength" (*kakkīja dannūti/ezzūti tāḫāzija šitmuri gešrīja gitmālāti*) (e.g. AE19:86–90, AE1:iii46–47 resp.). As for the latter reaction, the foreign elites and people resort to panicing flight because of "the radiance of my (the king's) kingship" (*melam šarrūtija*) as well as the king's weapons and fierce warfare (e.g. AE19:80–81). In the same passage, the king also states that he "spread my (his) royal/lordly radiance/brilliance over them (foreign cities and lands)" (*melam/namurrat šarrūtija/bēlūtija elišunu atbuku*) (e.g. AE19:79). In sum, the foreign elites and people can either recognize and surrender when confronted by divine radiance and weapons and then be spared, or they can haughtily disregard them and then be punished.

As is evident from the examples given above, escaping the rebellious city was not a means of avoiding the king's punishment. Many passages refer to the slaughter of the elites and people who by fright and "to save their own lives" (*ana šūzub napištišunu*) vainly flee to the sea or more often to rugged, high mountains establishing it as a fortress (e.g. AE17:iv90–102, SE16:221′–24′). In rare cases, the enemy flees to a mountain peak whereafter the narrative intentionally breaks off (e.g. AE17:ii98–99). As observed by Weidner (1940), he then virtually "disappears" from the scene, a meaning inherent in the expres-

179 The propagandistic idea that the destiny of the ruler is unsolvably tied to that of his country and people is amply attested, notably in curses and blessing sections (e.g. AE17:v89–103).

sion of "taking to a mountain" (*šadâ emēdu*) used in other royal inscriptions (CAD E: *emēdu*). Anyway, flight and fight were regarded as equivalent evils, and only the ceremonial and symbolic acts of submission and tribute could prevent the Assyrian king from causing plundering, destruction, and killing. In iconography, the enemy soldiers are sometimes illustrated vainly fleeing to or defending themselves from mountains (e.g. AI14:59–60, SI10:2). At other times, enemy soldiers flee in panic through swimming away, usually in vain, from the approaching Assyrian army, sometimes even along with their horses (AI4:B17t., AI4:B27–28b. resp.).[180]

As for the practical nature of resistance in Assyrian royal inscriptions and the reciprocity principle, there are two other kinds of resistance (besides fight and flight) brought up in the relevant sources, namely *external* resistance from getting conquered for the first time by the Assyrian king, and centering on the word *nakāru* which means "to be hostile" and the like, and *internal* resistance in the shape of a true rebellion, and centering on the word *nabalkatu* which literally means "to cross over". It is apparent that the latter kind of resistance is described as more severely punished by the Assyrian king than the former in Assyrian royal inscriptions (Saggs 1982: 87–91).

Some Early Neo-Assyrian rulers bring up this issue of internal rebellion. Shalmaneser III faces a large Syrian-Palestinian coalition which aims at diminishing the great influence just gained by this king in the west (SE2:ii90–96), although from a historian's point of view, this rebellion was rather *external* (Grayson 1982: 260–64). Ashurnasirpal II narrates that the city Suru of the western polity of Bit-Halupe, as well as the ruler Nur-Adad of the eastern state Dagara, and all the population of Laqu, Hindanu, and Suhu rebelled against his overlordship, and that they were all gruesomely treated (AE1:i74–96, AE1:ii23–31, AE1:iii26–48 resp.). In the case of the rebellion of two kings of the eastern land Zamua, the act is qualified as withholding the tribute and corvée of Ashur (AE1:ii50). The word *nabalkatu* can tellingly enough besides its figurative meaning "to rebel" also refer to crime and black magic (CAD N I: *nabalkutu*). The end results of these kinds of rebellions were utter destruction and the exposure to various atrocities.

In addition to an internal rebellion in which the overlord seemingly faces a united front, the relevant resistance could also be more fragmentary and complex, displaying features of civil war between pro-Assyrian and anti-Assyrian factions. It could e.g. take the shape of the foreign elites putting a ruler of their own choice on the throne, often a "son of a nobody" (*mār lā mamman*)

180 As for water crossing, Assyrian soldiers come across a water course in a calm, dignified, and orderly manner, quite in contrast to the crossing of foreign troops (AI4:B9–11b.).

or a "lord of a non-throne" (*bēl lā kussî*), getting rid of the vassal or puppet king who had been appointed by the Assyrian king (see subs. 5.4.7). As the "avenger" (*mutīr gimilli*), Shalmaneser III e.g. ensures a legitimate succession to the throne of Babylon by defeating the rebel and "usurper king" (*šar ḫammā'i*) Marduk-bel-usate (e.g. SE5:iv4). The royal response in these cases is equally harsh. Also, the same ruler defeats and impales the rebellious elements of Patina who had killed the puppet king there (e.g. SE14:154).[181] Ashurnasirpal II in his turn faces a complex internal rebellion of another kind when Assyrians living in the north-west decided to oppose the king in Kalhu. The following punishments are brutal (AE1:i101–10). These kinds of rebellions were perceived of as challenges to the world order, established by the deities, and upheld by the king (Liverani 1990: 128; Fuchs 2005: 38). As already indicated, the worst kind of atrocities such as flaying and impaling are reserved for the responding to these rebellions.

In accordance with the identified reciprocity principle, the acts of cruelty of the Assyrian king were not exercised indiscriminately. Rather, these were directed at those who were regarded as sinners by withholding tribute and submission (Fuchs 2009: 112–16). Similarly, Kuhrt (1997: 518) argues that a distinction between guilty and innocent is recognized in Assyrian royal inscriptions, and that it was reflected in the varied treatment of the defeated elites and people. The same idea is identified by Saggs (1982: 87–91) who sees a policy of punishing the guilty, i.e. those opposing the king, while extending mercy and protection to those who were innocent, i.e. those acknowledging the king. In other words, guilt was measured not only on a collective but also on an individual level. There were thus a sense of "right" and "wrong" and a notion of discriminate violence in Assyrian warfare.[182]

A distinction between actual rebels (who govern) and innocent civilians (who are governed) is sometimes made in the sources, in the context of narrating royal punishing. On Shalmaneser III's Babylonian campaign, the king only killed the rebel ruler and "the guilty soldiers who were with him" (*ṣābū bēl ḫiṭṭi ša ittišu*) (SE6:ii47–48). The soldiers' epithet of *bēl ḫiṭṭi*, literally "owner of sin", alludes to sinful behaviour by being based on the word *ḫiṭṭu* meaning "sin" (CAD Ḫ: *ḫīṭu* A). Also, the sole emphasis in the campaigns against first the Syrian coalition and then the Syrian-Palestinian coalition rests on defeat-

181 Similarly, Assyrian soldiers who do not turn up in the barracks face the punishment of impaling, a threat expressed in a royal letter of Sargon II (see Parpola 1987: text 22:7–12).

182 When the Assyrian king felt that he and his army had wronged and "violated tacit and explicit international agreements and fratricide", then letters to and from a god were needed for sanctioning the (mis)deeds (Oppenheim 1960: 133–47; Pongratz-Leisten 2013: 295–96).

ing and punishing their rulers and soldiers (e.g. SE8:32′–34′). Additionally, the described internal rebellion in Patina imposes royal punishment solely to the usurper's court and his guilty soldiers (SE16:268′–86′). The terminology of guilty soldiers is applied also by Ashurnasirpal II (AE1:i82). This king also refers to a certain rebellious, foreign ruler as the "guilty man" (*bēl ḫiṭṭi*) in the context of targeted punishments (AE19:91).

Another word for "sin" (*anzillu*) is used in the context of resistance from foreign rulers, namely in Sennacherib's narration of the defiant attitude and behaviour of Hezekiah, ruler of Judah (CAD A II: *anzillu*). In the same narration, Sennacherib explicitly distinguishes between guilty and innocent inhabitants of the conquered city Ekron when discussing the relevant city seizure (see RINAP3/1: 4:43–47). In Early Neo-Assyrian sources, it is also remarked that the foreign people actively could save themselves by extraditing or killing the rebellious rulers, elders, and nobles of their own cities. Only the actual instigators, i.e the rulers, elders, and nobles, are described as being punished, and then very severely (SE14:152–54, SE2:ii79–80 resp.).

There is a distinction between approved and disapproved atrocities here. Among the latter are also the maltreatment of women of conquered polities which are not spoken of but most likely took place. This kind of violence was not considered to be heroic but sinful (Fuchs 2009).[183] The exclusion of women in violence narrations also shows that warfare was seen as a masculine domain in ancient Assyria (see subs. 5.4.9). Anyway, indiscriminate violence is thus not applied, and a clear logic in the use of royal violence is once again attested. Ignoring the logic in the royal use of violence can be seen as reproducing the Orientalism notion of Oriental violence. Admittedly, narrative passages which seemingly refer to the use of indiscriminate violence are attested, but they then most likely tell of a need for abbreviation, thus leaving out the background, rather than of the mentioned phenomenon.

The "positive" outcome of the reciprocity principle took the shapes of peace, order, tribute, and submission. Exemplified in the iconography, the foreign rulers, elites, and people are, as already noted in subsection 5.4.1, ideally represented in tribute and captive processions, as praying for mercy or making respectful greetings, while their backs are slightly bent forward in a gesture of servility (D. Oates 1963: 17). The nearby Assyrian soldiers are in contrast always majestic in their appearances, in their standing with erect and firm stances

183 With the exception of "the burning of girls (and boys)" (see below in this subsection). This general respect for women expressed in the ideological sources was hardly consistently kept in real life, with the atrocity of rape seemingly accompanying any war – ancient or modern.

next to these processions (e.g. AI13:17–18, SI10:4b.). The submission of foreign cities is sometimes represented by model cities given to the king by tributaries (e.g. SI14:5a). The scenes of tribute, like those from the Assyrian camp, are marked by order and peace, and stand in marked contrast to the chaotic and violent scenes of battle and resistance.

The "negative" outcome of the reciprocity principle took the shapes of war, chaos, killing, and enslavement. This outcome was realized when the foreign people and elites refused to acknowledge the Assyrian king, in extension Ashur and the great gods, as their overlord, and chose to deny him of his right to tribute. The prescribed response of the king was acts of annihilation, and the consequences of these acts are often mentioned in the sources, a fact which has motivated the application of an Orientalist discourse reproducing the notion of Oriental violence on the Assyrian material.[184] Far from being indiscriminate, the violence and atrocities are only inflicted upon those who have "sinned" by being unsubmissive and withholding tribute. In the following paragraphs, I will give an image of what this violence entailed, in a much more detailed way than in section 4.4 on the king as warrior.

The function of the king as "punisher" of hostile polities or of opposition in general is attested in royal titulary e.g. through the epithet of Shalmaneser III of "weapon (which smites) all quarters" (*kašūš kal kibrāte*) (SE25:3). Ashurnasirpal II is similarly "the merciless weapon which causes lands hostile to him to fall" (*kakku lā pādû mušamqit māt nakrīšu*) and "slaughterer of cities and highlands" (*šāgiš ālāni u ḫuršāni*) (e.g. AE1:i34, AE1:i34 resp.). More directly speaking of a retaliating mission, responding to resistance, are the epithets "avenger" (*mutīr gimilli*) and "he who requites with strife" (*murīb anunte*) (e.g. AE1:i21, AE23:13 resp.). In his act of punishing, the king even takes the form of a force of nature (see ss. 4.1, 4.4, 5.2), such as when Ashurnasirpal II (AE1:ii36) and his army (e.g. AE1:iii105) are "(predator) birds" (*iṣṣūru*) in their attacking enemy forces from the air.

As for the remaining types of sources and the royal punishing of resistance from the foreign *people*, the extremely common and idiomatic statement "I razed, destroyed, and burned" (*appul aqqur ina išāti ašrup*) concisely expresses the king's punishment role in this regard (e.g. AE19:79, SE2:ii46). Symbolic of the punitive destruction from the hands of the king is the expression that "he turned (enemy cities) into mounds and ruin hills" (*ana tilli u karme utēr*) (e.g. AE1:iii103), thus in a way recreating the conditions right after the mythological,

184 Just to give an example of this discourse, Mann (1994: 46–56), in his historical survey on empires, labels the Neo-Assyrian empire as purely based on coercive, military power.

devestating Great Flood.[185] The idea that people's resistance leads to terror is amply conveyed also in the iconographic sources, especially in the North-West Palace and on the Balawat gates. Their scenes mostly depict the king's army slaying enemy soldiers, but scenes of setting enemy cities ablaze clearly allude to punishing the people (AI4:WFL24, e.g. SI10:2). These images of battered enemy cities on fire visually illustrate the discussed idiom "I razed, destroyed, and burned".

Leaving the theme of razing to the ground and turning to the targeting of humans and cultivation, the people of conquered, unsubmissive cities are routinely killed and enslaved (e.g. AE1:ii20–21, SE14:129), often in suspiciously large numbers (e.g. SE10:ii4–5).[186] The idiomatic and cryptic expression, common in the texts of Ashurnasirpal II, of the king "burning boys and girls" (*batūlīšunu batulātešunu ana maqlūte aqlu*), or sometimes just boys, of the conquered cities likewise speaks of the act of punishing unsubmissive foreign people (e.g. AE1:i109), in this case possibly by targeting their youth (Fuchs 2009: 78), much in the same way as the cutting down of trees in orchards is a significant blow for coming generations (AE1:iii109, e.g. SE2:ii68). As for destroying cultivation, Shalmaneser III also mentions that he burned down the enemy land's shock of sheaves and trees (SE10:iv4, SE17:53 resp.), and that he uprooted harvests, cut down gardens, and stopped up canals (SE5:iv4–5). All these actions of course threatened the living conditions for the foreign people. The act of cutting down orchards is, by the way, also illustrated in the iconography (AI4:B3t., e.g. SI10:2t.).

As for the other victim of punitive measures, if the foreign *elites* do not give submission and tribute, the king's prescribed response is annihilation and enslavement. In the textual narrative, it is stated that Shalmaneser III cuts down soldiers with his sword like Adad himself, and several passages morbidly refer to the multitude of corpses caused by the king's warfare (e.g. SE2:ii98, SE2:ii97–101 resp.). This king also decapitates the defeated warriors and builds "towers of heads" (*asītāte ša qaqqadi*) outside the enemy cities, or he puts the heads of nobles on stakes or in heaps (e.g. SE2:ii53, SE2:ii53–54 resp.). Enemy soldiers and nobles are impaled outside the city gates, and the blood of the defeated soldiers is frequently described as colouring whole landscapes red

---

185 Similarly, the king is described as "unleashing" or "spreading" royal radiance and terror upon insubordinate lands and people (AE19:79, SE14:158–59). The relevant verb (*tabāku*) can allude to the movement of the Deluge and the expunging of sins (CAD T: *tabāku*).

186 Although Millard (1991) as well as De Odorico (1995) argue that these numbers may not necessarily be untrue but must be evaluated from case to case, they are nevertheless integral parts of an underlying propaganda purpose and thus destined to be manipulated.

(e.g. SE14:154, SE1:60′–61′ resp.). The numbers of the punished opponents are as often fantastic, presumably in order to stress the magnitude of the king's war achievements (e.g. SE10:ii24–25). Another explicitly acknowledged atrocity is the imposing of starvation caused by besieging on one of Adad-narari II's campaigns (An2E2:67–68).

The infamous Ashurnasirpal II (see below in this subsection and in section 8.1)[187] adds to the atrocities by stating that he staged massacres down to the last man standing among the enemy soldiers (e.g. AE17:iv75–83), that he caused the corpses of enemy forces to be thrown down besieged mountains (e.g. AE17:iii8–9), that he formed roads and filled mountain cracks and streets with the corpses of enemy forces (e.g. AE1:ii83, AE1:ii55 resp.), and that he basically killed and destroyed from one place to another (AE17:iii53–55). Ashurnasirpal II also claims to have burnt captives (e.g. AE1:i108), and to have made the blood of enemy soldiers flow in streams (AE21:15′). This ruler furthermore states that he blinded, flayed alive, and cut out the tongues of defeated soldier captives ([AE21:14′], AE21:13′, AE21:14′ resp.).

Regarding the fate of rebellious nobles, as well as some soldiers, under the reign of Ashurnasirpal II, they are piled up into heaps of corpses, flayed alive, impaled, their eyes are gouged out, body parts such as arms are dismembered, and they are being buried alive (e.g. AE1:i89–91, AE1:i91–92, AE1:iii108, AE1:iii112–13, AE1:ii115, AE1:ii72 resp.). Decapitated heads of nobles and soldiers are hung up in trees in palaces and outside the seized cities (e.g. AE17:iii85–86). As for rebellious officials, it is stated that the king slayed the eunuchs (and) the royal eunuchs "who were guilty" in the same manner as above (AE1:i92). The unsubmissive foreign ruler did not fare well either. He is seized, flayed alive (in Assyria or on the spot), and having his flayed skin draped over the relevant city wall (e.g. AE1:i67–68). These acts all convey, in a very gruesome way, the message of what may happen to those – regardless of ethno-cultural belonging – who dared to refuse the Assyrian king his perceived right to submission and tribute from overseas.

Moving on to the iconography, the message that elites' resistance gives terror is amply conveyed in the North-West Palace and on the Balawat gates. Scenes of mutilation (SI10:10b., e.g. AI13:9–10), decapitation (SI10:13t., e.g. AI4:B4t.), erecting of tower of heads (SI10:8b.), impalement (SI10:4b.), cutting of throats (e.g. AI13:25–26, SI10:2t.), smashing of heads (e.g. SI10:7t.), and the killing of knocked down enemies by spear (e.g. SI10:13t.) are commonly attest-

187 Against the backdrop of World War II and the expositions on violence in Ashurnasirpal II's texts, Stearns and Hansen (1953) even referred to this ruler as a "Mesopotamian Hitler".

ed.[188] The contrast between the victorious royal army and that of the enemies is made clear by number, i.e. the former is more numerous, and depiction, i.e. the latter are slouching and have bowed backs (e.g. AI4:B8t., SI10:7), they are crawling in the dust (e.g. AI4:B9t., SI10:13t.), crushed alone or in heaps under chariots (e.g. AI14:59–60, SI10:13t.), falling headlong from city walls (e.g. AI4:B5b., SI10:9t.), and they are often illustrated praying for mercy (e.g. AI14:69–70, SI10:7t.). Their corpses are seen mutilated and strewn all over the battlefield (e.g. AI4:B9t., SI10:12). The claim that it is hardly possible to detect the outcome of battles in Assyrian narrative state art is clearly not tenable on closer inspection.[189]

The harsh punishments for those guilty of rebellion were however not automatically given. There were in other words a possibility of practising the reciprocity principle less rigidly. Foreign elites and people who had behaved in a bad way could in special circumstances be forgiven. On one occasion, after an initial resistance which consisted of fortifying their city against the king, the besieged inhabitants finally surrender, whereupon it is stated that Ashurnasirpal II "saved their lives" (*ana šūzub napištišunu ušēršunu*) (e.g. AE17:iv47–48). In other but similar instances, the king "shows mercy" (*rēmūta aškun*) towards people and elites who had offered resistance but then changed their minds (e.g. AE1:iii76–77, SE2:ii58). Tellingly, the latter phrase is associated with the deities (CAD R: *rēmu*), thus once again showing the tendency to associate with the divine, but without ever going the whole way to deification, when speaking of royal attributes. In most cases however, the forgiveness on the part of the king is not absolute. Often some showing of mercy is combined with some punishments (e.g. AE19:66–67).

Returning to the rigid workings and collective level of the reciprocity principle, the unsubmissive foreign people are not always described and depicted as punished through annihilation. Descriptions of them as "captives" (*šallatu*) are also constantly attested in the narrations of the aftermath of battles. Oded (1979: 20) notes that Shalmaneser III, in comparison with his father, took masses of captives and initiated many deportations (e.g. SE16:23). Ashurnasirpal II does however talk a lot of deportations as well. The king takes elites and people as captives after the conquest of a city or land, and he further mentions that he "uprooted" (*nasāḫu*) people and troops as punishment for their resist-

188 As for the atrocity of flaying (and decapitating), this gruesome act is also and famously depicted in some reliefs of Sennacherib's palace (see Barnett et al. 1998: pls. 300–301).
189 For this claim, see Groenewegen-Frankfort 1951: 173. Scenes in which enemy soldiers are illustrated as defending themselves seemingly with dignity and valour are relatively few (e.g. AI4:B18t., and possibly SI10:16), and should be understood as exceptions to the rule.

ance (e.g. AE1:iii98–99, AE1:ii33 resp.). Foreign people and elites are described as deported from all over the world to the cosmic centre of Kalhu, where they performed corvée and made servitude (e.g. AE1:ii79–80, AE1:iii125–26 resp.). By these acts of forced labour, they became servants of the Assyrian king (Fales 2011: 229). Interestingly enough, the same word (*šallatu*) is used to name material booty as well as human captives, thus expressing their forfeited lives caused by their resistance (CAD Š I: *šallatu* A). Whether the term, in a specific attestation, refers to human beings or material booty, may be concluded from if it is accompanied by quantifications (alluding to humans) or not (De Odorico 1995: 8).

The defeated are typically deported from the conquered city to Assyrian centres as captives but sometimes also as "hostages" (*līṭu*) (e.g. SE14:174, SE14:134 resp.). Adad-narari II once refers to himself as "he who seized their (enemy polities') hostages" (*līṭīšunu aṣbat*°) (An2E2:32), while Ashurnasirpal II commonly calls himself "capturer of hostages" (*ṣābit līṭī*) (e.g. AE1:i16–17). Also, several of the latter's narrative passages refer to the seizing of hostages by him and the Assyrian army (e.g. AE2:45). The individuals of this category were supposedly mostly high-ranking members of the foreign ruler's court, notably princes and princesses (Reade 1980a: 13; Zawadzki 1995: 456). The alternative meaning of this word as "pledge" expresses the strong bond between the two rulers established in this context (CAD L: *līṭu* A). Hostages were taken to enforce obedience, free one's back (when on campaign in another corner of the empire), and to ensure a regular fulfilment of imposed obligations (Zawadzki 1995: 455). The mildest form of "self-initiated" hostage sending must have been to give an envoy, while the uttermost hostage sending self-evidently was for the foreign ruler himself to travel to the Assyrian court, along with his eldest son and designated heir.

Turning to the iconography, rows of captives are often depicted in the North-West Palace and especially on the Balawat gates. These rows consist of naked, male captives in procession, occasionally tied to their backs (AI13:17–18, e.g. SI10:12b.), or naked, male, back-tied captives in neck stocks (e.g. SI10:8b.), or of naked, male captives in procession with a rope tied between them (SI10:3). In the iconography of Ashurnasirpal II, fully dressed captives are also represented with ropes tied between them (e.g. AI13:21–22), or bearing the burden of neck stocks (AI13:23–24, SI10:4b.). In a few cases, the captured people along with their livestock are portrayed as naked and emaciated in processions (e.g. SI10:12b.). Most often, the processions of captives move *towards* the king, but in a few cases the latter person instead heads one long procession consisting of himself, his entourage, and the captives (e.g. AI13:37–38). The captives are directed and disciplined by Assyrian soldiers or eunuchs who threateningly hold short sticks or maces in their raised right hands, ready to be put to use against any disorder in the lines (e.g. AI13:37–38, SI10:9b.). In a textual imagery, a captured enemy king along with his brothers are being chained in fetters (An2E2:59).

Punishing unsubmissive, foreign elites and people could in other words mean enslavement and captivity as well as annihilation. People of all regions are illustrated as captured and annihilated, and the portrayals of naked captives also encompass the allegedly more respected west (e.g. SI10:9b.). The nakedness of the captives and enemy soldiers may be seen as associating them with death, defeat, and barbarism (Bahrani 2001: 60–64). That being said, all these portrayals of captivity and defeat tell of the status of the foreign elites and people *after* having responded defiantly to the king's requests for submission and tribute. The relationship between the king and the foreign human beings was then determined by the latter's *actions*, not by their (ethno-cultural) nature (see subss. 5.4.5–6).[190] The giving of submission and tribute saved the foreign elites and people from annihilation or captivity, and caused inclusion of a kind. In a transferred sense, references to "Assyria" and "Assyrians" in Assyrian royal inscriptions denote *political* and not ethnical terms, defining a region and people who express the requested obedience (Machinist 1993: 89). The recognition of the reciprocity principle thus undermines the ideas of anachronistic nationalism and indiscriminate Oriental violence – ideas often expressed in scholarly literature on the topic.

On a practical level, the frequent acts of annihilation on the part of the Assyrian king can be seen as him implementing a policy of determent so that people will not resist in the future. Olmstead (1918) in this sense refers to the "calculated frightfulness" (of Ashurnasirpal II) and Saggs (1984: 48–52) to "psychological warfare". In the words of Ashurnasirpal II, his violence "imposed awe of the fearful radiance of Ashur upon (in this case) the land Bit-Adini" (*pulḫi melammē Aššur eli* GN *altakan*) (AE1:iii54). The state archival material shows that the Assyrian kings in reality practised an "offensive realism", which meant that violence in practice was seen as a last resort.[191] The Assyrian empire allowed vassal states to mind their own businesses as long as they provided tribute and expressed formal allegiance (Fales 2008: 23–27, 2010). Neo-Assyrian deportations were motivated not just by the punishing, deterring dimension. Additional *political* motives were creating bonds of dependancy,

190 In a comparative approach, this character of Assyrian imperialism places it in juxtaposition to e.g. the Egyptian one, at least like the latter is often understood (Loprieno 1988: 1–13).

191 The notion of "truceless war" actually features as a curse (AE17:v100). The ideal ruler is rather "he who has governed his people in peace" (*ittabbalu nišēšu ina šulmi*) (AE40:16).

getting settlers for strategic places or deserted areas, getting workforce for royal projects, and receiving recruitment for the army (Oded 1979: 41–74). Loyalty was created by reorganization of lands and peoples. Destabilization, as a reordering of space, was regarded as a form of political organization in the Assyrian empire (Bahrani 2008: 180–81).

The identified reciprocity principle does in itself clearly tell of a pragmatic approach and of a policy centred on the *economical*. The idea that the gesture of submission must be accompanied by the delivering of tribute is consistently expressed. Taxes and tribute were centred on, and rebellion was defined by non-payment. Van der Spek (1993: 267) even claims that "the Assyrian kings did not seem to pursue some other ideal beside the economical one". Assyrian violence was not aimed at eradicating people or systems of thought, nor did it express nationalism and racism. Rather, the economic incentives were always paramount (Fuchs 2009: 74–75). This can also be seen in the care for deportees expressed in state archival sources (Bahrani 2008: 179–80) – a care given not because of humanitarianism but because of these people's economical value for example as labourers. According to Bagg (2011: 301–308), the Assyrian empire was a *Weltreich ohne Mission*, constituting a special historical case in being neither based on organized robbery nor on any civilizatory mission. Its driving force was economical and centred on maximal profit by minimal effort, in which two main strategies were used in a pragmatic way: annexation or the granting of vassalage.[192]

On a theoretical level, the reasons behind the cruel punishments are to be found in the foreign human's sinful refusal of submission and tribute paying. Similarly, the breaking of loyalty oaths was pictured as a sin towards the deities, by whom the oaths were sworn, and their cosmic order (Cancik-Kirschbaum 2008: 94–95). As has been already noted (see subs. 5.4.1), several treaties and loyalty oaths have been preserved from the Early Neo-Assyrian Period. In an inscription belonging to Adad-narari II, a vasall is described as breaking "the oath of the great gods" (*māmīt ilāni rabûti*), and thereby rebelling against the Assyrian king (An2E2:49–50). The king had a divinely ordained right to world dominion, and those who opposed him in this quest were consequently regarded as sinners. By setting themselves up against the divine order implemented by the Assyrian king, their lives were forfeited in the eyes of the deities – their creators (Bottéro 2001a: 95–105).

Turning from premises to consequences in the relevant thought construct, military campaigns of the Assyrian kings were seen as natural and unavoidable

192 The economical aspect is succinctly expressed by Adad-narari II in his claiming that the great gods had named him to seize plunder from the foreign lands (An2E2:13).

as long as the enemies insisted upon opposing divine ambitions of realizing world rule. If war broke out, the enemy was always to blame since, according to Assyrian state ideology, he by resisting did not acknowledge the superior and divine power, i.e. the great gods, which ruled the cosmos (Liverani 2005: 232–33). In line with this notion, the Assyrian king was acting out of self-defence against a threatening "cosmic rebellion" (Weippert 1972: 488).[193] This kind of "siege mentality" is expressed throughout the corpus of Assyrian royal inscriptions (Liverani 1990: 115). As noted by Liverani (1990: 150, 157–58), war was regarded as an "ordalic procedure" in which a superior power defeats an inferior one, often without battle. The enemy sins, his deities then abandon him, whereupon the attacked, innocent, provoked, and harmed Assyrian king retaliates and mercilessly inflicts the divinely decreed punishment. Summing up this idea given on the theoretical level, the great gods had decreed that the foreign elites and people should be submissive and pay tribute, or else be annihilated and enslaved, and it was the Assyrian king's duty to effectuate this cosmically charged order.

This ideological stance and world view is reflected in the Assyrian perception of war and peace. Conquest warfare was regarded as a continuous creative process, and Assyrian world rule was seen as the only way to world peace, universal harmony, and social justice (Otto 1999: 7). Similarly, Cancik-Kirschbaum (1997: 74–75) argues that peace in Assyria was not contrasted to war but to disorder, and detects a belief that it was only attainable under Assyrian rule. Outer peace was achieved by treaties, and inner peace through subjugation. Fales (2008: 18–21) discusses the phenomenon of *Pax Assyriaca* with peace on two levels: one abroad (*ṭūbu*, *sulummū*), and one at home (*šulmu*), reflecting this duality. A royal duty to protect the peace in his empire was pictured. As noted by Foster (2007: 70), peace was however ultimately possible only through the other state's eventual inclusion within Assyria. The foreign elites and people had the choice of surrendering and getting this peace through vassalage, or resisting and be subjected to the enforcement of hegemony through violence (Fales 2008: 21). The Assyrian attitude to war and peace can also be seen in the fact that both concepts were regarded as civilisatory gifts, referred to as *parṣu*, and that they in such a way functioned as integral parts of human society (Foster 2007: 78). In sum, war was seen as necessary for the creation of peace – the *Pax Assyriaca*.

A final note on the topic of Assyrian violence may focus on the circumstance that even if this phenomenon was discriminate, the emphasis on war-

---

193 This could apply also to internal, Assyrian enemies. Shamshi-Adad V emerges as a "restorer of order" in defeating an almost total rebellion in Assyria proper (Liverani 1973).

fare in the Assyrian kings' propaganda is very striking and seldom paralleled.[194] Two examples of this observation are the multitude of themes concerning warfare in the royal inscriptions of the eNA I-period (Schramm 1973: 13–14), and the Eponym Chronicle which focuses on the whereabouts of the Assyrian army (Millard 1994: 5). The deterring function can explain the relevant phenomenon partly, but possibly this emphasis also served to show the celebration of a fulfilment of divine orders, involving the ultimate sacrifices of life and death, or of the victories of the deities, i.e. the actual warriors (see s. 3.2). The Assyrian empire both integrated and exploited, and its state ideology sought to explain this friction or paradox by saying that the conquest of a polity in reality was a blessing for the conquered polity – a blessing which required compensation e.g. in the shape of sacrifices, booty, and tribute to Assyria (Parker 2011: 359–60, 365). Nevertheless, the victims of Assyrian imperialism thought otherwise. At the downfall of the Assyrian empire, the monuments of the Assyrian kings were attacked. This is e.g. true of the images of Sennacherib and of the text and image on Adad-narari III's Para Stele (Bahrani 2003: 151–52; Börker-Klähn 1982: 198 resp.).

Summing up, I have argued that there is a principle of reciprocity, by which the foreign elites and people were expected to give submission and tribute in exchange for life and protection from the Assyrian king, expressed in the sources. The violence of Assyrian forces which is often referred to in the propaganda was not indiscriminate, nor was it religiously or ethnically motivated, thus contradicting Orientalist notions of Oriental violence.

5.4.3 Realized reciprocity: tribute

In this subsection, one component of successful reciprocity will be highlighted, namely tribute. I will argue that there was a view that the foreign lands owed tribute to the great gods and that the Assyrian king enforced this obligation. The function of tribute is emphasized in the sources of Early Neo-Assyrian kings, especially in the visual and textual narrative material.

The mentioning of tribute in royal inscriptions is a standard feature, not only in Mesopotamia but also in e.g. Egypt (Liverani 1990). The Assyrian king is consistently described and depicted as receiving or imposing tribute upon the foreign lands. This is especially true for the royal inscriptions and iconogra-

194 Babylonian kings e.g. mostly bragged about their peaceful activities, although we can assume that they too carried out atrocities on their campaigns. Interestingly enough, the good-reputed Egyptian kings frequently elaborated on military (mis)deeds (Kuhrt 1997).

phy from the *Early* Neo-Assyrian Period (Porter 2003: 19–20). The relevant terminology used in the texts consists of "tribute" (*biltu*), "tax" (*maddattu*), "audience-gifts" (*nāmurtu*, *tāmartu*),[195] and "gifts" (*igisû*) (Bär 1996: 7–11). The two lastly mentioned categories arguably had a less regular and more ceremonial character than the two former ones (Bär 1996; Yamada 2000). Tribute proper (*biltu* and *maddattu*)[196] could be delivered either as annual tribute or as tribute on military campaigns (Bär 1996: 241; Yamada 2000: 236–50), and it could consist of objects, animals, and humans. Although not always explicitly stated, it was first and foremost the foreign ruler who had the responsibility of supplying it. This can be seen in the iconography where the rulers lead the tribute processions (Bär 1996: 218–22). As will be shown below, in addition to the evidence of subsections 5.4.1 and 5.4.2, tribute is portrayed as being given from the whole world to the Assyrian king.

The textual narrative – especially the commemorative texts of Early Neo-Assyrian kings – is pervaded by the theme of tribute. Occasionally, the ideological background to the giving and receiving of tribute is formulated. The burden of tribute on foreign lands is e.g. described as established by the commands of Ashur and Ninurta (AE1:i99–101). A failure of the other side to respect this command was regarded as a sacrilegious rebellion by which the tribute (and corvée) of Ashur were "withheld" (*kalû*) (e.g. AE17:iii28–29). In their role of tribute establishers, the deities Ashur, Enlil, Ishtar, and the other great gods are requested, in a pair of blessing sections, to arrange so that the righteous future ruler will receive the tribute of the four quarters (AE17:v51–52, AE40:40–41). In the middle of a commemorative text, Shamash is described as enforcing the established delivering of tribute through his own strength (An2E2:102–104). Overall though, the Mesopotamian deities had obliged the foreign lands to deliver tribute to them, and it was the task of the Assyrian king, their representative, to enforce this obligation.

Titles and epithets which refer to a royal tribute receiving role are comparatively rare, but in the textual narrative and visual sources the phenomenon of tribute is constantly focused on. As for the rare examples of epithets referring to tribute, Ashurnasirpal II calls himself "he who has received their (the enemy rulers') tribute" (*bilassunu imḫuru*) (e.g. AE1:i16), "he who has received tribute and gifts from all lands" (*māḫir bilti u igisê ša kalîšina mātāti*) (e.g. AE40:13), as well as "he who has received tribute and tax from the four quarters" (*māḫir bilta° u maddatte ša kibrāt erbetta°*) (AE56:5). The final epithet is partly attest-

---

195 Also referred to as "viewing-gifts" due to this word's deriving from the verb "to see" (*amāru*), partly explaining its audience connotation (CAD N I: *nāmurtu*, CAD T: *tāmartu*).
196 Throughout this work, I use the term tribute generically for the two terms mentioned.

ed also for Shalmaneser III (e.g. SE2:i7–8).[197] Ashurnasirpal II is also referred to as the imposer of tribute in the epithet "he who has imposed on them (the foreign rulers) tribute and tax" (*bilta u maddattu elišunu ukinnu*) (e.g. AE1:i27–28). Adad-narari II is "he who imposed upon them (the foreign rulers) tribute and audience-gifts" (*bilta u tāmarta elišunu ukinn*(*u*)) (An2E2:32). He is also "he who received the tax of GN" (*maddattu ša* GN *maḫāri*°) (An2E2:33). The above epithets clearly show the worldwide scope of the receiving of tribute. Rulers, lands, cities, and people from the whole world then deliver tribute to the relevant Assyrian kings.

As for the textual narrative and the issue *what* the tribute actually consisted of, the relevant narrative passages sometimes do not state what the tribute consists of, at other times it is specified, often in the shape of long enumerations (e.g. AE17:iii106–09, SE8:40′–41′). The tribute (and booty) is in any case often described as "countless" (*ana lā mīni*) and "many/much" (*ma'ādu*) in quantity, and as "heavy" (*kabtu*) in weight (e.g. AE1:iii2, SE14:155). The numbers are both realistic and fantastic (De Odorico 1995: 161–62). When the tribute is specified, the much sought-after horses are often mentioned as part of the tribute (e.g. AE1:i86, SE2:i28). As for animals and tribute, Ashurnasirpal II receives loads of ivory, arguably from Syrian elephants, but also from *nāḫiru*, i.e. "sea creatures" (*binût tâmdi*) in the Mediterranean (e.g. AE1:iii61–62, AE2:30 resp.). He furthermore gets monkeys (e.g. AE2:30–31), and is presented with five elephants which then follow him during his onmarch (AE30:95–97). Thirty "Bactrian camels" (*udru*) are presented to Tukulti-Ninurta II (TN2E5:78). The ten kings of course receive vast numbers of livestock consisting of oxen and sheep (e.g. AE1:iii10, SE6:iii13). Wild, but then domesticated, animals are also mentioned as forming part of tribute processions in captions (AE77, SE89).

Also humans could be given as tribute. Women are especially objectified in this way. Ashurnasirpal II e.g. receives sisters, daughters, and nieces of foreign rulers in tribute (e.g. AE19:90, AE1:i85, AE1:iii76 resp.). He also receives the daughters of nobles, female singers, and "adolescent girls" (*batultu*) as tribute from the foreign courts and lands (e.g. AE19:90, AE73, AE1:iii67 resp.). The king here emasculates his opponent by taking over his women (see subs. 5.4.9). As for actual objects, timber, metal, ivory tusks, precious stones, luxury garments, and palace furniture are commonly spoken of as parts of the tribute transactions (e.g. AE1:iii73–76, SE1:93′–95′). Also valuable products such as myrrh, purple wool, fine oil, alabaster, antimony, multi-coloured textiles, and metal utensils were handed over to the Assyrian king (TN2E5:76–79). The de-

197 For a discussion on the details of Shalmaneser III's booty and tribute, see the separate study on this historiographic and ideological topic in Yamada 2000: 225–72.

feated foreign rulers' own furniture, such as his royal bed, was also taken by his vanquisher (e.g. SA5E1:iv31–34). The great variety of the delivered tribute thus did not only correspond to the multitude of givers but also to the actual contents of the tribute. The Assyrian kings in a way collected the whole world in their capital cities (Reade 2004b).

As for the textual narrative and the issue of *where* the tribute was delivered, it could as already mentioned both be given regularly (e.g. annually) and spontaneously on military campaigns. Tribute during military campaigns are e.g. talked of in narrative passages which proclaim that Ashurnasirpal II ceremonially received tribute in various foreign cities or lands such as Tushha, Katmuhu, and Irsia (e.g. AE1:ii101–2, AE17:iv1–2, AE17:iv25–26 resp.). Adad-narari III claims to have received tribute in the conquered palace of Damascus (An3E8:21). Even provincial areas, such as Shadikanni and Bit-Halupe, are somewhat surprisingly described as having delivered tribute to the former king (e.g. AE1:iii4, AE1:iii6–7 resp.). This may be a testimony of Ashurnasirpal II's relatively loose grip on the west, while being forced to confront several rebellions in the area. Furthermore, Shalmaneser III narrates that he spectacularly received tribute, brought by boats, in Phoenician areas (e.g. SE66), or from Chaldean rulers coming to him while staying in Babylon (SE29:47–48), and Ashurnasirpal II claims to have received tribute from the whole Mediterranean coast on one campaign (e.g. AE33:15′–16′).

As for regular tribute, this tribute delivering naturally took place in Assyria proper. The foreign rulers came to the Assyrian king – not the other way around. Foreign rulers are sometimes described as annually bringing "their heavy tribute" (*bilassunu kabtu*) which the Assyrian king receives "in my (his) city Assur" (*ina Aššur ālija*) (AE67:9–10). It is interesting that Assur and not Kalhu is stated as the destination. Arguably, this can be explained by the special status of the Ashur temple, located only in Assur. As already noted, especially Ashur was associated with the establishing of tribute on the foreign polities. At other times, the foreign rulers are described as coming to Assyria carrying tribute without the passages explicitly stating a scheduled, annual delivery (AE1:i99–101). Receiving his tribute both in Assyria and on campaigns, Ashurnasirpal II could claim to have received tribute *from* and *in* "all lands" (*mātāti*) and "mountains" (*šadâni*) (AE21:6′).

As for the iconography, the throne base (SI14:4–7) and the two obelisks (AI16:A1, SI11:A1–2) are dominated by portraying the king as receiving tribute, and the foreign elites and people as giving tribute. The topic of tribute is also an important part of the motifs on the Balawat gates, and convey the scenes on the façade of the North-West Palace (e.g. SI10:5, AI4:D2–9 resp.). Ivory plaques and stone vessels also depict this motif (e.g. SI23–24, AI29 resp.). Normally, the tribute is delivered by people in a long procession, symbolizing Order, which halts at the king who stands directed at these with his entourage of personal attendants, bodyguards, officials, and courtiers. The king himself stands with insignias (bows, arrows, cups, staffs) in his hands and/or makes the greeting gesture (*karābu*) with his raised right hand (e.g. AI14:73–74, SI10:5b.). The ruler is also depicted with one of his hands resting on the shaft of his sword that hangs down from his belt (e.g. AI13:17–18). More rarely, the ruler receives his tributaries sitting, then from a throne of some kind (e.g. AI14:83–84, SI10:9b.). Often he stands (e.g. AI15:95, SI10:8) or sits (AI13:23–24, SI10:4) under a sunshade or a canopy. The central position of the Assyrian king in these scenes leaves no doubt as to who the earthly recipient of the depicted tribute is intended to be.

The tribute procession is headed by the foreign ruler and sometimes his son-heir who both normally make the gesture of clenched fists which signify submission (e.g. AI16:A1, SI14:4b). A long line of tributaries then follows, each member carrying something valuable in their hands, on their backs, or leading animals which function as gifts or tribute (e.g. AI14:81–82, SI10:5). As for animals, tribute bearers e.g. approach the king with horses on the Balawat gates (e.g. SI10:7b.), with monkeys on the façade of the North-West Palace (AI4:D7), and with various exotic animals on the Black Obelisk (SI11:A–D3).[198] Tributaries have precious objects such as ivory, metal, vessels, and furniture in their hands (e.g. AI14:81–82, SI14:5a–b). Carried on the shoulders of tributaries, their bowed backs express the heavy load of the tribute (e.g. AI14:77–78, SI14:6b).[199] Timber logs, tusks of ivory, and ingots of metal can be delivered in this way. Tribute could also be portrayed as given from boats, such as the tribute from the seafaring Phoenicians (e.g. AI14:63–66, SI10:14b.). This particular motif is centred, through its placement in the gate mid, on the door bands of the Mamu temple, of which it also can be said that twelve of its 16 bands carry scenes of tribute. To summarize the findings from the sources, the ideological image of the foreign elites and people as peacefully delivering tribute to the Assyrian king is then amply attested.

If the foreign elite chose not pay tribute, the king after defeating them seizes their goods as "booty" (*šallatu*), "plunder" (*kišittu*), or "spoils" (*ḫubtu*) instead. Early Neo-Assyrian kings repeatedly brag about their plundering of

---

198 A procession of animals from a 9th century BCE ivory plaque may also illustrate tribute animals (see Mallowan and Davies 1970: fig. 85). For identifying these animals, at least those on the Black Obelisk, as depictions of Mesopotamian deities, see Börker-Klähn 1982: 191.

199 Tribute are weighed on scales in a scene on the Rassam Obelisk (AI16:A3). The idea behind this illustration may have been to visualize the huge amount of seized metal.

foreign cities, lands, fortresses, and mountains to which the enemy had fled (e.g. AE1:ii84, SE2:ii64–65). It is e.g. very frequently claimed that "I (the king) took their (enemy cities' or rulers') booty" (*šallassunu ašlula*) (e.g. AE1:ii21, SE1:91′). Shalmaneser III additionally states that "[I (he) carried off their booty], possessions, and property" ([*šallassunu*] *būšīšunu makkūršunu* [*ūbla*]) to Assyria (e.g. SE117:7′). Assyrian soldiers are occasionally depicted carrying away spoils of war from besieged and conquered cities (e.g. AI4:WFL22b.). This booty[200] is often described as beyond counting, measuring, and weighing (e.g. AE19:83, SE8:20″–21″). As for large numbers, as well as separate positioning, the special narrative passage of Shalmaneser III which contains a summation of the spoils of war (*ḫubtu*) taken by the king in his first 20 years on the throne is quite noteworthy.

Regarding the actual forms and circumstances of royal booty seizure, booty could consist of many things (naturally displaying the same great variety as tribute) and be extracted from various situations and localities. As for forms, also humans, i.e. captives, hostages, and palace women or daughters of enemy rulers, are labelled as booty (e.g. AE1:iii22, SE6:iv19). Regarding the special narrative passage in question, a great quantity of horses, mules, oxen, donkeys, and sheep, but also of 110 610 "prisoners" (*šallatu*) (and 82 600 "killed", *dīktu*) are told of (SE10:iv34–40). As for circumstances, in a classification based on locality, Yamada (2000: 226) distinguishes between three types of booty: from conquered cities, from battlefields on the plain, and from pursuing the fleeing enemy forces. The attestations given in the preceding paragraph cover all of these types. A special case of the first type is when palaces of defeated enemy rulers are robbed of their treasures (e.g. AE2:49–51). A special case of the second type is after a naval clash when Shalmaneser III fishes up booty from the floating battlefield in question (SE28:44). Ashurnasirpal II in one passage claims that he brought booty from the whole world, or "his land" (*mātišu*), to his own palace and treasury in Kalhu (e.g. AE17:v22–23). Whether booty or tribute, the seized or delivered goods in question belonged to Ashur, and formed a part of the same flow from periphery to core (van Driel 1969: 191; Liverani 1979: 313–14).

After the conquest of a city or land, violently or peacefully, the Assyrian king "(re)establishes" (*kânu* D, *emēdu*) tribute upon the foreign polity. Ashurnasirpal II e.g. claims to have imposed "[tribute, tax, and corvée]" ([*bilta, maddatta*], *zābil* [*kudurri*]) in one situation (e.g. AE17:i88), and "duties, corvée, and state labour" (*ālku, kudurru, urāsu*) in another (AE19:99). The mentioned "duties" (*āliku/ilku*) could in Neo-Assyrian times be fulfiled both by labour and

200 In this work, and in analogy with my use of the term "tribute" (see n. 196), I use the term "booty" in the discussion as a collective name for all words connoting plundered goods.

goods (CAD I–J: *ilku* A). In cases of a background of resistance, the imposed "tribute and audience-gifts" (*biltu, tāmartu*) are specified as "being exceptionally large" (*watāru* Š) (e.g. AE1:i95–96). As observed also by Yamada (2000: 240–41), the foreign polities which had chosen the path of resistance literally paid a higher price when being imposed levels and sorts of tribute. The regularity of the imposed tribute is e.g. stated in narrative passages which convey the idea that an annual tribute was fixed after a certain peaceful conquering (e.g. AE1:iii64, SE2:ii23–24).

The installing of "governors" (*šaknu*), or literally of "governorship" (*šaknūtu*), accompanied the establishing of tribute. As already noted in subsection 5.4.1, Ashurnasirpal II frequently remarks that he appointed governors over conquered cities and lands (e.g. AE26:30–31). The theme of appointment of governors is not the least brought up and highlighted in a short but freestanding narrative passage of the annals of Shalmaneser III (SE6:iv37–39). These governors are then described as "making servitude and corvée" (*urdūti° uppušū kudurru*) (e.g. AE26:31–32), and the Assyrian ruler then announces that he received "tax" (*maddattu*) from these officials (AE53:6). This installing of governors with their obligations should not be confused with the vassal system, although also the rulers from Chaldea and Damascus are described as making servitude of a kind (An3E8:15–24).

Sometimes the king is described as extracting the resources of the foreign lands himself. As for metal and stones and the identified royal role of resource fetcher, Shalmaneser III claims to have marched to "Mt Silver" (*šad kaspi*) and "Mt Alabaster" (*šad tunni*) where he fetched the relevant resources in huge quantities (SE40:iii2–5). Although not actually given from the foreign polities to the Assyrian king, but only indirectly by them letting the Assyrian army exploit the natural resources of their territory, the said metal and stone nevertheless formed part of the flow from periphery to core. This notion of virgin territory to be freely and justly exploited by more "advanced" states and cultures is of course perfectly in line with a colonialist logic, centering on the dichotomy civilization/barbarism (Liverani 1979).

More commonly, the resource of *timber* is highlighted here. This is e.g. true of the very common theme of Shalmaneser III cutting down high-quality timber from western mountains and bringing it to Assyria (e.g. SE2:ii9). Ashurnasirpal II likewise narrates that he felled such trees in the Mediterranean area (e.g. AE50:25–27). Scenes in which Assyrian soldiers cut down trees for timber are found on the walls of the North-West Palace (AI4:WFL15t.), and other army members are depicted on the Balawat gates carrying timber (AI14:71–72, SI10:14t.). Possibly, the king himself is seen using an axe on a tree in a scene on an ivory plaque (AI27:5a). Supposedly, the king, in analogy with his role as builder, here makes the symbolically significant first strike against the tree. The same tool is illustrated on another ivory plaque which portrays Shalmaneser III holding his axe and a cup while receiving tributaries (SI23). The attribute of axe in the king's hands may then express the king's role as timber provider.[201] Sometimes the king explicitly states that the gained timber was put to use in his palaces and temples in Assyria (e.g. AE50:28–32). As for Kalhu, descriptions on how Ashurnasirpal II adorned the North-West Palace with exotic timber are elaborate (e.g. AE23:18–19). In procuring and handling timber for the deities, the king associates himself with heroic and legendary tree fellers such as the Sargonic kings and the brother-in-arms Gilgamesh and Enkidu (Weissert 2011: 305).

As for the practical dimension of tribute, the importance of tribute in the mechanics of the Assyrian empire has often been noted and stressed. The dependency theory developed by Wallerstein (1974) according to which a core unidirectionally extracts resources from a dependent periphery has frequently been applied on the Neo-Assyrian empire (e.g. Ekholm and Friedman 1979; Larsen 1979b: 92–102; Robertson 2005: 207). Similarly, Tadmor (1975: 37–38) has recognized the economical, rather than ideological, forces and motives behind Assyrian expansion. Sharing this view on things, Grayson (1995a: 968) detects wealth gaining as a vital incitament for Assyrian imperialism, and regards it as a sign of a pragmatic and practical mentality of the Assyrians. There was a constant need of tribute (or booty for that matter), for strengthening the power of the Assyrian king, for extolling his glory, and for "paying off" those who assisted him (Elat 1982: 244).

As for the theoretical dimension of tribute, at least ever since the inscriptions of Ashur-dan II, the foreign lands were supposed to pay tribute to Ashur (van Driel 1969: 191). The Assyrian king, i.e. the link in this transaction, is portrayed as the only receiver in annals and on reliefs (Bär 1996: 11–15). The phenomenon of tribute here expresses a ceremonial, hierachical system which should be separated from the concepts of booty and trophies (Bär 1996: 240). Gifts have in the state ideology a tendency to be portrayed as tribute, implying the superiority of the receiver (Liverani 1990: 267, 192–93). The Egyptian "tribute" on the Black Obelisk (SI11:A–D3) should e.g. be understood as mere trading gifts for the Egyptians but signifying submission for the Assyrians (Elat 1975: 32).[202] Historical events are in this way seen through an ideological lens.

---

201 Additionally or alternatively, it may allude to the king's role as overcomer of the difficult path, clearing out way in harsh, rocky terrain (see s. 5.1). The axe may of course also symbolize warfare and the role of the Assyrian king as the warrior of the deities (see s. 4.4).

202 Recognizing this, Reade (1979a: 333–34) suggests that this particular scene is either an "idle boast" or a representation of tribute from the Egyptianized city state of Byblos.

In the symbolic notion of tribute, and in the transactions between centre (Order) and periphery (Chaos), an accumulation of surplus in the Assyrian "cosmic capital" is realized in exchange of ideological values such as life and protection (Liverani 1990: 191). According to the principle of "diversification of goods", the resources receive meaning only in Assyria, and these are therefore directed to the capital and the palace which symbolize microcosm and the completion of creation (Liverani 1979: 313–14). Tribute was in other words not just explained by practical (i.e. economical) but also by theoretical (function of the divine world order) reasons.

Summing up, tribute transactions formed a vital part of the successful reciprocity identified in the previous subsection. Tribute had a theoretical as well as an underlying practical motivation. The foreign lands were obliged to pay tribute to the great gods, notably Ashur, and this delivery was administered by the king, the deities' representative. The function of tribute is much stressed in the sources of the ten kings, both visually and textually.

5.4.4 Realized reciprocity: paternalism

In this subsection, another expression of successful reciprocity between the Assyrian king and the foreign elites and people is identified and discussed, namely paternalism. This time, the Assyrian king is the giver and the foreign elites and people are the takers. The former portrays himself as the benevolent sun and as the protective and providing shepherd in relation to his foreign subordinates. The topics of royal farming and banquets are also used.

Both the images of the ruler as "sun" (*šamšu*) and "shepherd" (*rē'û*) have a long history in Mesopotamian state ideology, starting from the 3rd millennium BCE (Seux 1967: 25–26). These epithets are often regarded as part of the southern Mesopotamian tradition of kingship which were imported to the Assyrian court during the Middle Assyrian Period (Seux 1980–83: 162–63; Machinist 1983a: 525, 1993). The royal sun imagery had related expressions in the whole of Ancient Near East, particularly in Egypt and the Hittite state (Charpin 2013: 99–100).[203] The simile to the sun(god) most probably refers to Shamash's universal dominion and legal authority over all in connection with the king's ambitious territorial claims (see s. 3.1). In his role of implementing Order worldwide, the Assyrian king functioned as the sun of all lands (Maul 1999: 206). This sun imagery also expresses a Mesopotamian "ideology of protection", de-

203 As the Amarna archive shows, Assyria was in close contact with "the great kings" of both of these states (Liverani 1990: 41–43), making ideological borrowing much plausible.

rived in analogy from various social relations (Liverani 1990: 187). The role of sun was paternalistic, since it was interchangeable with the image of the king as father. The just (an attribute of Shamash) ruler in this regard functioned as a father to his people (Charpin 2013: 71–78) in a relationship typical of patrimonial states (see s. 1.6).

As a shepherd, the Assyrian king tends the foreign people who then are likened to cattle. The former's responsibilities in this context were to provide and protect. As noted by Oded (1992: 103, 113), the Assyrian king regarded himself as a "universal shepherd". The king's role to "sustain peace and security and provide abundance was not limited to Assyria proper but had a global dimension". In this benevolent role, he functioned as the shepherd of the whole world and of humankind.[204] According to Scurlock (2013: 171–75), Mesopotamian kings presented themselves as "good shepherds", with "ethical responsibility" highlighted. Mesopotamian kingship was not about power but about responsibility, and the self-sacrifice of Dumuzi in the story of Inanna's descent is called upon to exemplify this. The imagery of the king as sun and shepherd were thus paternalistic, signifying royal benevolence and the distribution of resources to the people under his care. The foreign lands gave tribute, while these received the ideological goods of order, justice, and protection (Liverani 1979: 313–14). By taking on the role of shepherd also over foreigners, the Assyrian king also manifested himself as "the dominant male", while emasculating his defeated opponents (see subs. 5.4.9).

Turning firstly to the sun imagery in the sources, an important epithet of Shalmaneser III is "sun of all people" (*šamšu kiššat nišē*) (e.g. SE1:2, AE1:i10). Along e.g. with the related epithet "king of all people" (see subs. 5.4.1), it forms a very common and prominent cluster of royal epithets (e.g. SE1:1–2). The epithet focused on here is attested as prominent as in second place in one context (SE5:ii2). Ashurnasirpal II is once referred to, also and simply, as "the sun" (*šamšu*) (AE19:22). The translation "sun(god)", preferred e.g. by Grayson (1991: 258), is caused by the divine determinative which normally preceeds the actual spelling out of the word for sun, and should probably not be understood literally. As argued already in section 4.1, a *simile* to the sungod Shamash and his attributes is more likely expressed.[205] The king as the likeness of the sungod may be alluded to in the writing of the word for king. It is interesting to note

204 This image of shepherding and peace confronts the proposed different understanding of the king's shepherd role in Assyria which stresses its coercive aspect (Magen 1986: 18).

205 The Early Neo-Assyrian king e.g. never – in contrast to Shamash – wears horns on his head, stands on animals, or holds ring and rod in his hands – all of them divine attributes.

that the relevant cuneiform sign 'man' can also be read 20, which is a number associated with Shamash.[206]

In his capacity of sun, the king directs his protective rays over his people and land. Ashurnasirpal II here once calls himself "he whose protection spreads like the rays of the sun over his land" (*ša kīma šarūr šamši andullušu eli mātišu šuparrurū*), and also once "[he whose protection] is spread out [over his land]" ([*ša*] *šuparruru* [*andillašu*° *eli mātišu*]) (AE40:16, AE153:6 resp.). The protective aspect is expressed by the word *andullu* which literally means "shelter, canopy" and more figuratively "(divine or royal) protection/aegis" (CAD A II: *andullu*). Ashurnasirpal II is also three times referred to as "the aegis of the (four) quarters" (*ṣalūl kibrāti*) (e.g. AE2:19). The related D-stem verb *ṣullulu* carries the notion of "to roof over, cover", and in a transferred sense "to give protection" by deity to man, by an official to his king (CAD Ṣ: *ṣullulu* A).[207] The noun (*ṣalūlu*) in the cited epithet also refers to a protective shade and shelter (CAD Ṣ: *ṣulūlu* A). The Late Neo-Assyrian portrayal of the king as mankind's "shadow, protection" (*ṣillu*) in analogy with the divine protection of the king, their mediator, arguably expresses the same kind of idea (Machinist 2011: 417–19).

As for the imagery of the king as shepherd in the sources, Ashurnasirpal II refers four times to himself as "shepherd" (*rē'û*) (e.g. AE2:19). He also describes himself twice as "shepherd of the four quarters" (*rē'û kibrāt erbetta*°) (e.g. AE40:7), and in an insecurely dated text a king bears the epithet "shepherd of Assyria" (*rē'û māt Aššur*) (see RIMA1: A.0.0.1019). Adjectives can accompany the title of shepherd. Shalmaneser III is here described as a protector and provider of the foreign people in his epithet "righteous shepherd" (*rē'û kīnu*) (e.g. SE1:5).[208] This pastoral epithet is attested in first position of a sequence once (SE5:i5). Tukulti-Ninurta II is peacefully "the beloved shepherd" (*rē'û narām*) (e.g. TN2E1:16–17). Ashurnasirpal II in his turn often calls himself "amazing shepherd" (*rē'û tabrâte*°) (e.g. AE1:i13). The translation "shepherd of mankind" is equally possible when interpreting the relevant word as a noun (CAD T: *tabrātu*). The same king also, six times, refers to himself as "chief herdsman" (*utullu*) (e.g. AE1:i21). Such a herdsman was in charge of cows and sheep, and the epithet is also used to describe deities and the king (CAD U-W: *utullu* A).

206 As revealed in MZL (sign 708, page 404). The normal sign for king, i.e. the sign 'lugal', is rarely used, the attestations of AE17:i13 and SE2:i10 forming two exceptions to this rule.
207 The latter meaning may be expressed in the well-attested scenes where the king's personal (eunuch) attendants hold a sunshade above his head (e.g. AI14:73–74, SI10:8).
208 "Righteous" presumably in the sense of the king being a legal authority. The relevant adjective can alternatively be translated "legitimate" or "faithful" (CAD K: *kīnu*).

The people under the king's care are once again metaphorically described as cattle to be herded.

The king is also called "[he whose] hand you (Ashur) have granted the sceptre which herds the people" ([*ša*] *ḫaṭṭa murte'ât nišē tušatmeḫu qāta*) (AE154:3). The shepherd's staff (*šibirru*) or sceptre (*ḫaṭṭu*) are referred to as royal and divine insignia in Mesopotamian texts (CAD Š II: *šibirru*, CAD Ḫ: *ḫaṭṭu*).[209] In the epithet just cited, Ashur is the one handing the shepherd insignier to the king. This is also the case in a narrative passage which declares that Shalmaneser III is responsible for "[the shepherding] of people" ([*rē'ūt*] *nišē*) (SE5:i6). In the sections of "call to future rulers", it is similarly and commonly expressed that Ashur will name the successor "for the shepherdship of Assyria" (*rē'ūt nišē māt Aššur*) (e.g. AE28:13–14). Tukulti-Ninurta II presents himself as "he to whom by order of Shamash the holy sceptre was given" (*ša ina zikri Šamaš ḫaṭṭu ellutu nadnataššum*) (e.g. TN2E2). Interestingly enough, Shamshi-Adad V is – just like the god Nusku (e.g. An2E2:3) – "bearer of the just sceptre" (*nāši ḫaṭṭi ešrete*) (e.g. SA5E1:i27–28).

Various motifs depict the king as shepherd, i.e. as him holding a staff (a long straight stick) or a sceptre (a short crooked stick) in his hands. In Ashurnasirpal II's statue e.g., the king holds a sceptre in his one hand, thus alluding to his pastoral duties (AI12). Shalmaneser III holds a sceptre-like insignier in one of his statues (SI6). The image of the former king having a staff on the Banquet Stele fits well with the text of the same monument which stresses the themes of banquet, creating of canals and gardens, and the resettling and rebuilding of people and cities respectively (AI20, AE30). This king is seen in the same gesture beside one of the sacred tree scenes in the North-West Palace (AI4:B12, AI4:B14). This proximity provides evidence in the interpretation of this scene which is, in another form, attested also on the brick panel of Fort Shalmaneser (SI18).[210] Ashurnasirpal II is often depicted on the Balawat gates holding a staff when receiving tributaries and captives (e.g. AI13:35–36, AI13:17–18 resp.). This king here arguably functions as the shepherd of the foreign people. The shepherding and paternal role of the Assyrian king over the foreign people may also be indirectly expressed by the "images" set up in the foreign lands, conveying notions of peaceful, pious, and righteous rule (Reade

---

209 Scurlock (2013: 173) however argues that *šibirru* means "ring", related to the Babylonian form *šewerru*, and that *ḫaṭṭu* then complementary means "rod, stick". This interpretation is naturally complicated by the fact that the Assyrian king never holds a ring in his hands.

210 As noted in section 3.1, this tree is probably pollinated, symbolically bringing fertility and prosperity to Assyria by the hands of the king through the aid of the winged disk.

1979a: 340–44). The idea of the rulers as benevolent kings of the foreign people is clearly illustrated.

Possible implementations of the king's paternalistic roles as sun, shepherd, and herdsman are the projects concerning agriculture, rebuilding of deserted and decayed cities, and resettling of exiled people which are referred to in integrated and separate narrative passages of the inscriptions of the Early Neo-Assyrian kings. In the words of Schramm (1973: 102–103), these projects express the theme of "royal providing for his land". The king here creates food and shelter for his people, and by these pastoral actions, the king provides for his herd. The spending of wealth by kings, e.g. through building projects, agriculture, and festivals served to create order and legitimacy in the developed state (Baines and Yoffee 1998). This picture painted of the Assyrian ruler as allocating resources for the welfare of his people contradicts the idea of Oriental decadence with the Oriental ruler living in extravagance and isolation in his harem-equipped palace (see subs. 5.4.8).

Beginning with a discussion on the firstly mentioned implementation aspect, i.e. that which centres on agricultural measures and on the theme of king as farmer, Ashurnasirpal II sometimes claim to have stored "barley and straw" (*še'u u tibnu*) in foreign cities and local palaces, i.e. administrative centres (e.g. AE17:ii26–28). The local population (at least in times of bad harvests) as well as the bureaucracy and army could have benefited from this storing. Shalmaneser III speaks of the frequent use of plows "in the districts of my (his) land" (*ina šiddi mātija*) and of the great harvests of barley and straw which this activity resulted in (SE6:iv45–46). Within the same narrative framework, Tukulti-Ninurta II states that he focused on agriculture "for the needs of my (his) land" (*ana erišti mātija*) (TN2E5:132–33). Siddall (2013: 160), in his identifying of the Early Neo-Assyrian rulers' roles, brings up the theme of "king as farmer" in this context.[211] The Early Neo-Assyrian king thus presented himself both as gardener (see s. 5.1) and farmer.

Another and related expression of the implementation of the king's sun and shepherding duties is his rebuilding of cities and his resettling of people. Early Neo-Assyrian kings e.g. declare that they have rebuilt cities and local palaces in the Jezirah which had been abandoned due to population pressures from the migrating Arameans (SE2:ii38, e.g. AE30:78–84). Resettling of refugees, and the initial misery of these, are themes in the inscriptions of Ashurdan II, Adad-narari II, and Ashurnasirpal II (Schramm 1973: 15). Ashurnasirpal II in this context boasts about having brought back and resettled the refu-

---

211 A theme which, according to him, conveys the role of administrator in Early Neo-Assyrian state ideology. The two other roles which Siddall (2013: 160) identifies are priest and warrior.

geeing Assyrians in a "peaceful dwelling" (*šubtu nēḫtu*) (AE19:94–95). The given positive value of calm and peace, expressed by *nēḫtu* (CAD N II: *nēḫtu*), contrasts with the surrounding laudations of royal warfare. Ashurnasirpal II furthermore claims to have resettled foreign people who had fled or initially defended their settlements, but then changed their minds and had submitted to the king (e.g. AE17:ii28–31). Also the foreign people and elites were then herded and shepherded by the Assyrian king.

Another imagery of implementation presents the king as harvester, thus obtaining sustenance for the people under his care. Ashurnasirpal II e.g. announces that he "reaped the harvest" (*eṣāda eṣēdu*) of the land just conquered (e.g. AE17:iv107). [212] Possibly, this act had a symbolic meaning similar to that conveyed by the image of the basket bearing king, carrying away the first soil from the building site, as well as laying the first brick, in times of temple constructing (see s. 4.3), or of the king making the first cut with his axe in his role as timber provider (see subs. 5.4.3). In another narrative passage, the same king states that he reaped and stored the harvest in four cities of the land Nairi "for the bodily strength of my land" (*ana emūqi mātija*) (AE19:96–97). Again, it is not immediatly clear who was to benefit from this harvesting, but alongside the army on march and local administration, a provisioning for the local people in times of failure of the crop seems not out of the question. In any case, the king as sun and shepherd had the duty to prepare for lean years through storing of grain and the like, as expressed in royal inscriptions of the eNA I and II-periods (Schramm 1973: 15). Lastly, on an ivory plaque found next to the Banquet Stele, Ashurnasirpal II is represented with a sickle in one of his hands (AI25). This tool, along with its bird-headed shaft which alludes to the agricultural god Ninurta (Mallowan and Davies 1970: 1), may both refer to the royal role of harvester.

Occasionally, the sun and shepherding roles of the king imply superhuman and divine-like capabilities. The canal which Ashurnasirpal II commissioned in order to provide his new capital with freshwater for people and for irrigation purposes was called "Canal of Abundance" (*Patti-ḫegalli*), and it was constructed partly by drilling through solid rock (e.g. AE30:37). In this context, the said ruler portrays himself as irrigating the meadows and banks of the Tigris (AE30:38). According to Charpin (2013: 82), the Mesopotamian king presented himself as having cosmic and divine kinds of power within him. The identified dimensions of divinity, namely cosmology, mythology, and politics, were here transposed to the image of royal authority on the earthly level (Frahm 2013:

212 Harvesting could in a transferred sense refer to the mowing down of enemies (CAD E: *eṣēdu*), but the contexts of the attestations in this paragraph all tell of a literal interpretation.

97–99). Ultimately though, the blessing of abundance derived from the deities, and the kings (if pious) merely channelled these bestowings. In blessing sections, the deities are asked to convey "plenty, wealth, and abundance" (*nuḫšu, ṭuḫdu, ḫegallu*) on the land of the future, righteous ruler (e.g. AE40:41). In curse sections on the other hand, they are requested to cause "famine, hunger, and need" (*bubūtu, nibrītu, ḫušaḫḫu*) upon the country of the misbehaving, future ruler (AE17:v94–96).

Royal banquets also serve to express the king's role as provider and protector, and these deserve special attention in the discussion. Several Akkadian words can be translated "(royal) banquet", first and foremost *naptanu, qarētu*, and *tašīltu*.[213] The latter two seem to have had a less cultic connotation than the firstly mentioned (CAD N I: *naptanu*, CAD Q: *qerītu*, CAD T: *tašīltu*). The word *naptanu* is attested in the texts of Shalmaneser III where it serves to name the cultic meals taken at the Tigris source (see ss. 4.2–3). Staying with typology issues, royal banquets could be both open and closed in relation to the general public (Glassner 1987–90), and they could both be held at home and abroad. As for the latter locality, Shalmaneser III held a banquet, here referred to as a *qarētu*, in Babylon (e.g. SE5:vi4), while Ashurnasirpal II in his turn relates of a *tašīltu* which he arranged and held in the conquered palace of a subjugated foreign ruler (AE1:iii82).

The grand banquet which Ashurnasirpal II held in order to inaugurate the North-West Palace and his new capital city should be especially noted. 47 000 "men and women ... from every part of my (his) land" (*ṣābī sinnišāti ... ša pirik mātija gabbi*), 5 000 foreign "dignitaries" (*ṣīru*) and "envoys" (*šapru*), 16 000 "people" (*napištu*)[214] of Kalhu, and 1 500 *zāriqu* officials of his palaces, were "invited" (*qariūte*) to attend this event (AE30:141–51).[215] The king claims that for ten whole days these guests were provided with food and drink (which were taken from the grand "menu"), bathed, and anointed with oil (AE30:151–52). The narration of this event ends with Ashurnasirpal II proclaiming that "I (he) thus honoured them and returned them to their lands in peace and joy" (*ukabbissunūti ina šulme u ḫadê ana mātātišunu uterrašunu*) (AE30:153–54). The word *kabātu* in the D-stem, given by the first cited word, not only means "to honour someone", but also to "make heavy", plausibly with food and drink.

---

213 Turning to the English-Akkadian dictionaries, EAC also enumerates *šūkultu* and *tākultu*, while AEAD in its turn only brings up *qarētu* (EAC: banquet, feast, AEAD: banquet).

214 The word for "people" (*napištu*) means "soul, living being, person (of menial status)", and it refers to the forced, deported labour (Wiseman 1952: 39 n. 147, CAD N I: *napištu*).

215 The word translated as "invited" by Grayson is in one case (AE30:150) the verb *šasû* which has the connotation of a herald's shouting or calling out a proclaimation or order (CAD Š II: *šasû*). The participation by free will can, on the whole, be questioned.

Additionally, it refers to the act of extinguishing fire (CAD K: *kabātu*). By providing for the people, the act of rebellion (i.e. fire) is prevented.[216] The name of the celebration is not given, but possibly it had the status of *qarētu*, since the worldly aspect of it is highlighted, and a (verbal adjective) form of the verb *qerû* is used (AE30:142).

A few scenes depict the king sitting with a cup in his hand, seemingly banqueting (Magen 1986: 119). In the North-West Palace, this scene is complemented by a pair of human-headed genii and two eunuch attendants, one of whom refills the king's cup (AI4:G2–4).[217] On an ivory plaque, a king, probably Ashurnasirpal II, stands receiving officials and courtiers while an attendant pours his cup (AI28). The standing king with a cup (AI22), a motif painted on glazed bricks, may also illustrate a banqueting king (Reade 1983: 44). In another scene in ivory, the king, probably Shalmaneser III, sits with a cup at a table opposite a sitting, refilling eunuch, and with six guests who sit drinking at other tables (SI21). Obviously, the widely including banquet described above is not explicitly illustrated here, but rather some sort of social gathering within the ruling class. This of course brings up the issue that the "shepherding" of the elite and the people must have been differentiated. The motif of banqueting scenes is a very important one on Neo-Assyrian seals (Collon 1987: 75). In one example, a bareheaded man, probably Shalmaneser III, sits with a cup in front of a pot stand and a fan flagging eunuch (SI25). The nature of these depicted banquets, in terms of public or private, ritual or "worldly" (whatever these distinctions are worth) is hard to establish, but it is not far-fetched that they at least indirectly refer to the public, worldly feasts which expressed the royal role of shepherding the people.

Trying to understand these royal banquets from a general sociological and anthropological viewpoint, a reciprocity principle by which the king provides and protects while the guests – in this case foreign – acknowledge their subordinate statuses through participating is realized at these banquets, like the one at Kalhu just described (Dietler 2001: 76–89). Furthermore, the two sides are joined symbolically in the sharing of meals, carrying mutual commitments of protection and loyalty respectively (Cook and Glowacki 2003: 196–97). The phenomenon of feasts held by a building leader to reward those who have worked on the accomplished building is, by the way, a well-attested custom in space and time (Hayden 2001: 31–37).

---

216 It is interesting to note here that this equating of rebellion with heat, flames, and fire was expressed also in ancient Egyptian propaganda sources (Lichtheim 2006 I: 107 n. 1).

217 In addition, the cup can be understood as a ritual vessel, raised in the gesture of ackowledging the deities (Collins 2008: 52), thus associated with the priestly role (see s. 4.2).

Regarding banquets as political propaganda, the Assyrian kings wanted to make manifest their intent to provide and protect their new subordinates by these feasts. The great banquet in Kalhu, which was luxurious judging from the "menu", here served to express an ideology of imperial domination (Herrmann 1992). The "grand imperial spectacles", such as the said banquet, were important components of imperial propaganda (Barjamovic 2012: 55–59). Similarly understood, Collins (2008: 31) claims that this banquet was intended to impress and overwhelm its participants, and to convey the notion of the king as granting an almost divine benevolence. The event may also be regarded as carrying the dual aim "to bring the empire and its ideology to the local as well as the foreign dignitaries" (Barjamovic 2011: 61), i.e. it served to maximize the diffusion of Early Neo-Assyrian state ideology. In any case, royal banquets were not simply innocent picnics, but they rather functioned as crucial components of the enacting of imperial propaganda.

Summing up, another manifestation of successful reciprocity between the Assyrian king and the foreign human beings has been identified and discussed, namely paternalism, displayed by the former. The Assyrian king had the role as a protective and providing sun and shepherd in relation to the foreign elites and people. Agricultural and demographic measures as well as royal banquets here functioned as implementations of this role.

5.4.5 Differentiation of the foreign people and lands

In this subsection, the foreign people and lands are differentiated in the sense that the uniformity of this unit of analysis is examined. The supposed special status and function of Babylonia, and the allegedly greater Assyrian respect for the west than for the north or the east are the main focal points. I will argue for a relative uniformity – at least in the political-ideological domain.

Scholars have often detected a differentiation of the foreign lands in the sources of the Assyrian kings. Liverani (1979: 304) e.g. claims that the geographic and ethnographic landscape of Assyrian royal inscriptions "is stereotyped but differentiated". Reade (1979a: 333–34) argues that "foreign states were grouped in categories and treated accordingly", and then distinguishes between independent states regarded as equals, independent states but not equals, independent but uncivilized "states", and tributary states. Babylonia, belonging to the first category, clearly held a special place, judging e.g. from its position in Assyrian historical writing.[218] In this context, a distinction be-

---

218 The histories of Assyria and Babylonia are intertwined in the Synchronistic History (An3E59) and the Synchronistic King List (see Grayson 1980–83: 116–25, texts 3.12–17).

tween the traditional southern centres and "the Sealand" (*māt tâmti*) situated in the southernmost part of Mesopotamia and inhabited by Chaldean tribes is made both by the Babylonians and the Assyrian kings (Brinkman 1968: 181–219, 260–64). As for the divide along west-east/north, Winter (2010: 548) stresses the relations between Assyria and the west, and claims that Assyria was open for influences from the west but not from the east. Alleged cultural influences from the west such as architecture, annals, reliefs, *adû* oaths, and Aramaic are refererred to in this context (Tadmor 1982; Winter 2010). In other words, the foreign lands were not uniform, and the enemy was not automatically an "abhorrant other" (Siddall 2013: 165–66).

Beginning with the status and function of Babylonia, there are several indications of a favoured status of this country, especially in the texts and images of Shalmaneser III. This king describes how he helps his Babylonian counterpart Marduk-zakir-shumi I to quell a rebellion instigated by the latter's brother Marduk-bel-usate (e.g. SE5:iv1–v3). Shalmaneser III does this for the sake of "vengeance" (*ana tūr gimilli*) (e.g. SE6:ii43). This phrase alludes to Ninurta's motivations for avenging his father Enlil (Annus 2002: 97). The literal translation "to return a favour" may refer to past events in the history of the agreement which Assyrian and Babylonian rulers had with each other at this time (CAD G: *gimillu*). This agreement e.g. stipulated that if the line of succession in one country was threatened, the other party should intervene and assist the legitimate heir (Brinkman 1968: 181).

The Synchronistic History refers to the two parties in this way: "Together they (Shalmaneser III and Nabu-apla-iddina) made a peace treaty. [The peoples of Assyria and Karduniash (Babylonia) were joined together. They established a boundary line.]"[219] (An3E59:iii24–25, An3E59:iii3′–5′). In the same text, Adad-narari II is said to have defeated two Babylonian rulers, whereafter the same acts as above are said to have taken place, with the difference that "Akkad" and not Karduniash is talked of, and that the two rulers "gave their daughters to one another (in marriage)" (*mārātīšunu ana aḫāmeš iddinū*) (An3E59:iii17). Shamshi-Adad V in his turn is described as having defeated two Babylonian rulers, making offerings in Babylonian cities, receiving tribute and tax, and after that establishing a new boundary (An3E59:iii6′–iv14). Adad-narari III is pictured as someone who initiated peace efforts, achieving the joining together of the two peoples, and as fixing a new boundary line by "mutual consent" (*ištēniš*) (An3E59:iv15–22). In addition to saying something of the closeness in

219 Transcription runs as follows: *ṭūbta sulummâ gamra itti aḫāmeš iškunu* [*nišē māt Aššur u māt Karduniaš itti aḫāmeš ib*]*balū* [*miṣru taḫūmu ištēniš u*]*kinnū.*

the relationship between the two by its content, the Synchronistic History in itself tells of a special status of Babylonia.

Moving on, another indication of the recognized strength of the Babylonian king is Ashurnasirpal II's mentioning of Babylonia as having the power to send support troops (whom he however defeats) to another land, in this case Suhu (AE1:iii17). Similarly, this king's general silence on the subject of lasting power over Babylonia is telling. In the fragmentarily preserved treaty between Shamshi-Adad V and Marduk-zakir-shumi I (SA5E15), the latter ruler emerges as the stronger party (Brinkman 1968). Solely the former ruler bears obligations, the latter ruler is the one called king, and Marduk is listed first of all in the curse section.[220] Regarding iconography and the suggested strength of Babylonia in relation to Assyria in the latter's propaganda, the emphasized scene on the front of the throne base of Fort Shalmanser where Shalmaneser III and Marduk-zakir-shumi I meet each other clasping hands on seemingly equal terms may also indicate a favoured position (SI14:7c). Shalmaneser III here arguably "admits another as his equal", while the scene as a whole then "suggests international harmony" (Reade 1979b: 70–74).

In intervening in Babylonian affairs, Shalmaneser III claims to obey the command of Marduk, and "the rebel king" (*šar ḫammā'i*) Marduk-bel-usate is then portrayed as overwhelmed by the radiance of this same Babylonian god (SE5:iv4–v4, SE14:78 resp.). Shalmaneser III's support from this non-Assyrian deity is exceptional. Also Shamshi-Adad V refers to Marduk as giving guiding "words" (*amātu*) (SA5E15:16′).[221] Marduk is also listed in some invocation of gods sections of commemorative texts (see app. 4). In Ashur's absence, Marduk can appear as the first god in deity lists, with Nabu coming on second place (SA5E15:16′–2rev., S4E2:1–4). Nabu can also be placed before Marduk (An3E9:27rev.). The emblems of Marduk and Nabu are depicted on the Saba'a, Tell al-Rimah, and Tell Abta stelae (An3I2, An3I3, S4I1 resp.). Furthermore, on the two lastly mentioned monuments the Babylonian gods in question are emphasized by their closeness (to the nearby ruler and his pointed finger) and size respectively. Adad-narari III also pays his respects to Babylonian deities on an official's seal (An3I12).

The elaborate narration of Shalmaneser III honouring the Babylonian deities Marduk, Sarpanitu, Nabu, Nana, and Nergal is another point in the case

---

220 In a later stage of the historical development, Shamshi-Adad V calls himself "king of Sumer and Akkad" (SA5E9:2). This usage of the age-old toponyms of Sumer and Akkad may be seen as a recognition and revering of the history of Babylonia.

221 In another attestation from the royal inscriptions of Shamshi-Adad V, solely Ashur is described as overwhelming the hostile Babylonian ruler (SA5E2:27′–29′).

(SE5:v4–vi5). Moreover, the priests (?) of Babylon offer Adad-narari III a cultic meal – an offer which normally is given only to the Babylonian king (Tadmor 1973: 150). More specifically, he is invited to consume "the remnant offerings" (*rēḫtu*) of Marduk, Nabu, and Nergal in Babylon, Borsippa, and Cuthae, and he furthermore makes some "pure offerings" (*nīqu ellu*) at these localities (An3E8:23–24). Similarly, Shamshi-Adad is said, in the Synchronistic History, to have made offerings in the same cities (An3E59:iv9–10). As for cult activity and the revered Babylonia, the circumstance that Shalmaneser III seemingly (at least judging from his texts) did not erect a "royal image" in Babylonian temples and cities has also been taken in support of the idea of the privileged status of Babylonia (Yamada 2000: 294).

Regarding the Assyrian king and the Babylonian people, Shalmaneser III's narration which tells of him establishing "freedom and protection" (*kidinnu, šubarrû*) at a "banquet" (*qerētu*) in Babylonia indicates a favoured Babylonian status (SE5:vi4). The "temple cities" of Babylonia were granted special protection and privileges throughout the Neo-Assyrian Period. The relevant establishing of freedom and protection, notably from taxes and labour duties, is otherwise only associated with the granted status of the old Assyrian city of Assur (Tadmor 2011: 105).[222] The Assyrian king's intervention in Babylonian affairs for the sake of his patronage over temple cities against pressures from Chaldean tribes is a topic of special significance in Assyrian royal inscriptions from the second half of the ninth century BCE (Tadmor 1973: 149–50). In the Synchronistic History, Adad-narari III is initiating peaceful relations by setting abducted Babylonians free, and then providing for these. The Assyrians and Babylonians are then said to have been joined together (An3E59:iv19–21). In fact, on the basis of continuity of the archaeological remains between the Late Neo-Assyrian Period and the following Neo-Babylonian Period, Reade (1981a: 167) even questions if the Assyrians and Babylonians really were regarded as two separate peoples.

This image of Babylonia as favoured by the Early Neo-Assyrian kings is not unambiguous. The scene on the throne base may not after all express equal status. The Assyrian side, i.e. the king with his entourage, is more heavily armed than the Babylonian side, and the staff of the Assyrian king is somewhat longer. The latter circumstance may of course be an error of the artisan or simply a reflection of reality, but it may also along with the weapons serve to express the superiority and seniority of Shalmaneser III. Parallels to depictions of high officials standing opposite the king in a similar manner naturally come

222 The privileged positions of temple cities are contrasted to those of "royal cities", e.g. Dur-Sharrukin and Nineveh, which had the obligation to provide labour and resources.

to mind (e.g. An3I6). Possibly the Babylonian king then had the status and function of a high royal official in the eyes of the Assyrians. Similarly, D. Oates (1963: 21–22) sees a depiction of Babylonia as a subordinate client state on the throne base. Even if the event seems to occur on terms of equality, the scene's handclasping "is not a mere gesture of greeting between equals" since the accompanying caption makes it clear that subordination and hierarchy are implied. The caption in question has a triumphal tone, referring to "display of strength" and to Shalmaneser III as taking over roles and authority from the Babylonian king (SE59). Taking text and image together, the Assyrian king is clearly the dominant figure.[223]

Offering somewhat of a compromise, Schneider (1991: 135–46) sees a development from a portrayal of Marduk-zakir-shumi I as equal to weak in Shalmaneser III's annals. However, the Babylonian king is described as calling for "aid" (*nārāru*) and derogatory as "king of Karduniash" (see below in this subsection) already in the earliest narration of the event inscribed on the Balawat Gate (SE5:iv1). Moreover, the image of Babylonia and Assyria as two equally powerful states in the time of especially Shalmaneser III has often been challenged (e.g. Chamaza 2002: 81; Fuchs 2011: 264–69). The narration and the ending of the Synchronistic History arguably tell of the notion of the military and moral superiority of Assyria over Babylonia (An3E59). Consequently, it would be odd if the Assyrian king gave his Babylonian counterpart equal status even in an initial stage of his reign.

Having recognized this, it is far from unique to describe the Assyrian king as helping or avenging an ousted vassal or puppet king in Assyrian royal inscriptions (e.g. AE17:iv109–20, SE16:268′–86′). The description of the two rivalling Babylonian royal brothers and throne pretendents as having "divided [the land] equally (between them)" ([*māta*] *malmališ izūzū*) alludes to a common theme of disruption of the political world order – an order established and supervised by the Assyrian king and ultimately by the great gods (e.g. SE14:75). According to this logic, it was not up to these two individuals to delegate authority between themselves. On the ideological level, the Babylonian king was regarded as an inferior in relation to the Assyrian king, and his status can here be likened to that of a puppet king.

Moreover, Marduk-bel-usate and his troops are not spared because they are Babylonians. This usurper is on the contrary, like any other "rebel", "felled with weapons" (*ina kakkī ušamqit*) (e.g. SE14:80–81). Massacres on Babylonian

223 Magen (1986: 125) even sees, in her classifying of this royal visual representation, the meeting as part of a tribute scene. However, the epigraph in question does not focus on tribute, and the relevant tribute procession is not from Babylonia proper but from Chaldea.

rebel troops are elaborately described in the annals of Shalmaneser III (e.g. SE5:v2–3). His father in his turn relates how he massacred the Babylonian support troops who had been sent to assist the south-western ruler of Suhu (AE1:iii21). Similarly, in analogy with descriptions of any other land, the same king states that "I (he) made fear of my (his) lordship reach as far as Karduniash" (*pulḫat bēlūtija adi māt Karduniaš akšud*) (AE1:iii23). In the epithet of Adad-narari II of "he who caused the defeat of Shamash-mudammiq, king of Karduniash, from GN to GN" (*dabdâšu ša Šamaš-mudammiq šar māt Karduniaš ištu* GN *adi* GN *iškunu*), Assyrian violence against Babylonia is extolled (An2E2:26–27). The relationship between Assyria and Babylonia, which was often hostile as shown by his two southern military campaigns, is also emphasized by Shamshi-Adad V (Weidner 1933–34; Reade 1978). This ruler evidently resorted to much killing, plundering, and godnapping in dealing with his Babylonian foes (An3E59:iii6′–iv9). Some of these foes were then flayed alive in Nineveh (SA5E2:iv5′–10′). If Babylonia was so respected and esteemed, these expressions, which carry connotations to the use of brute violence, would hardly be made.

Shalmaneser III, as well as Ashurnasirpal II, in all this refers to his southern counterpart as "king of Karduniash" (*šar māt Karduniaš*) (e.g. SE5:iv1, AE1:iii19 resp.). As observed by Brinkman (1968: 259), Assyrian allusions to the Kassite past of the Babylonians may carry derogatory meaning, associating the land and its inhabitants with "mountain peoples". Ashurnasirpal II uses the apellative of Kassite in other contexts as well, e.g. when he narrates that the ruler of Suhu attacks him with the support of "extensive" Kassite troops (AE1:iii17–18). The adjective in question (*rapšu*) is also and tellingly used when referring to the about-to-be-discussed mountain peoples of Guti and Lullumu. A further associating of Babylonians with mountain peoples may also be expressed when the Babylonian king is said to flee from Shamshi-Adad V to a city not far away from the borders of Elam, i.e. to a polity at least bordering to the Iranian mountains (SA5E4:2′–4′). Unstated enemies, probably of Babylonia or Der, are explicitly spoken of as fleeing to Elam (SA5E4:21′–34′). A derogatory ambition is likely given in this king's description of Babylonian troops as "hordes" (*gunnu*) (SA5E1:iv43).

From a historian's point of view, diverging ideological, political, and theological traditions likewise speak against ignoring the socio-cultural border between Assyria and Babylonia altogether. For example, the variations between Assyrian and Babylonian state ideology, and the varying role of the king in the justice system serve to illustrate the differences between the two countries in yet other ways (Garelli 1981; Postgate 1974 resp.). Among the ideological diverging points are the Assyrian king's much profiled roles as warrior and priest, set against the corresponding Babylonian ideological discourse (Garelli 1981: 4–5). In contrast, the Babylonian king's legal role was much more developed (Postgate 1974: 421–25). As for diverging points and theology, although Marduk and Nabu are clearly venerated by the Early Neo-Assyrian kings, Ashur keeps his status as the patron deity of Assyria, and he is yet to absorb the god and cult of Marduk (Chamaza 2002).

As already noted, "the Sealand" of the Chaldeans was in Neo-Assyrian times distinguished from Babylonia proper. Babylonia was in this sense differentiated. Shalmaneser III declares that he received tribute from Chaldean kings coming to him in Babylon (e.g. SE29:47–48). The same ruler may also have claimed that he gave libation offerings during his stay in Chaldea, as suggested by Radner (2009: 190–93) in her collation of a Tigris text. Adad-narari III claims to have received tribute from Chaldean kings (An3E59:iv11–12). Military confrontation, due to resistance, is spoken of in other contexts (e.g. AE1:iii24, SE5:vi5–6). Ashurnasirpal II proudly proclaims that "awe of my weapons overwhelmed Chaldea" (*šuribat kakkīja māt Kaldi ussaḫḫip*) (AE1:iii24). The Chaldean tribe of Bit-Jakin is depicted being defeated on the Balawat gates (AI13:27–28). The other important Chaldean tribes, Bit-Dakkuri and Bit-Amukani, are seen carrying tribute to Shalmaneser III on one side of his throne base (SI14:4–5). Also in this case, *actions* and not essence determined the nature of the relationship between the Assyrian king and the foreign lands – at least in the propaganda.

A peculiar feature of some of the sources is the occasional highlighting by Shamshi-Adad V (e.g. SA5E4:6′–20′), the Synchronistic History (An3E59:iv7–9), and the Eponym Chronicle (see Millard 1994) of the city state of Der (close to Babylonia, the Zagros, and the Diyala tributary), or more precisely of the godnapped deities of that polity. Der is also described as a "cosmic city" reminiscent of how Babylon can be described. Der is here "the great city whose foundations are as firm as bedrock" (*māḫāzu rabâ ša kīma kiṣir šadê šuršudā išdāšu* (SA5E2:iii38′–39′). This polity is still pictured as being under the obligations of submission and tribute paying. Warfare against Der is highlighted in the preserved letter from a god (SA5E4).

To summarize, the status and function of Babylonia proper in the propaganda of the Early Neo-Assyrian kings is ambiguous. It had a culturally based privileged position, but it was politically still regarded as subordinate and part of a world which the Assyrian king had to control and protect from "rebellion". Such a conclusion may reflect the ambivalent feelings towards Babylonia that the Assyrian kings often displayed. Deference to cultural superiority was here combined with a paternalistic attitude in the Assyrian, imperial, self-proclaimed role as the guardian of Babylonian culture (Beaulieu 2005: 54). Assyria's troubled and ambivalent relations to Babylonia are even described in terms of a *Kulturkampf* in the context of the Tukulti-Ninurta I Epic where the Assyrian forces e.g. plunder Babylonian libraries (Machinist 1983a: 519). That being said, the ten kings present themselves as the superior party of the political relationship in question. The Chaldeans are described as subordinate both on the political and cultural levels, while the city state of Der is culturally elevated but still politically subordinated.

As for the alleged differentiation between west and north/east, the evidence is not conclusive, although a certain higher respect for the Phoenician states, especially in Ashurnasirpal II's case, and a certain lower respect for the about-to-be-discussed Urartu region occasionally shine through. The visual historical narrative of Ashurnasirpal II almost entirely depicts scenes from the west. This is true for his two gates at Balawat, the Rassam Obelisk, and the throne room of the North-West Palace (AI13–14, AI16, AI4:B resp.). Both in text and image, the theme of the subordination and tribute payment of the Phoenician city states of Arwad, Sidon, Tyr, and Byblos is highlighted. Phoenician tribute (AI14:63–66, AI14:79–80) is the centre of attention in terms of placement on the gate of the Mamu temple (Curtis and Tallis 2008: 72–74). The king's texts similarly put emphasis on his dealings with this area and people (e.g. AE1:iii84–92).[224] The western preference of Ashurnasirpal II and the broader one of Shalmaneser III in terms of scene locations in their iconography naturally correspond to the respective orientations of their military campaigns. It is however difficult to avoid the impression that the former king was especially proud of his encounters with Phoenicia. Ultimately though, the reciprocity principle, which states tribute and submission or annihilation and deportation, overarched any other considerations.

Turning from the issue of differentiating through highlighting to that of examining possible variations in the treatment of foreign elites and people, it is worth noticing that there tends to be a predominance of scenes with peaceful subordination in western milieus on Shalmaneser III's Balawat Gate, while the scenes in the north or east most often depict warfare (e.g. SI10:5, SI10:3b. resp.). On the other hand, peaceful tribute scenes are also attested from the north or east, and massacres are illustrated from the west as well (e.g. SI10:7b., SI10:9t. resp.). Among the many scenes from the west in the iconography of Ashurnasirpal II, it is striking that his captives and deportees are sometimes depicted stripped of their clothes (AI13:17–18), tied to one another by a rope (e.g. AI13:21–22), and bearing the yoke of neck stocks (AI13:23–24). Both west-

224 Also Adad-narari III focused much on the west in his royal inscriptions (Tadmor 1973: 147), such as in the text on the Pazarcik Stele, centering on western polities (An3E3).

erners and people from the east or north are depicted in this way in the corresponding iconography of Shalmaneser III, again expressing the lack of differentiation (e.g. SI10:9b., SI10:1b. resp.).

As for the differentiating of foreign *rulers*, not only western rulers are specifically named and thus regarded as actual persons, but many northern and eastern rulers, e.g. the rulers of Zamua, Shubru, and Urartu, are individualized in this manner (e.g. AE1:ii61, SE10:ii11, SE10:iii30–31 resp.). Moreover, both Ashurnasirpal II and Shalmaneser III indiscriminately refers to "the fierce and merciless kings from sunrise to sunset" (*šarrāni ekdūti u lā pādûti ultu ṣīt šamše adi ereb šamši*) (e.g. AE2:20–21, SE5:i4–5). The royal title of "king", i.e. *šarru*, allegedly more prestigious than *malku* (see subs. 5.4.1), is also used of northern and eastern rulers (e.g. AE17:iii19, SE6:i34). Similarly, the possibly belittling epithet of *nasīku*, meaning "sheikh, tribal leader", is used for leaders of the west (Laqu), north (Bit-Zamani), and east (Dagara) (AE1:iii45, AE19:91, AE17: ii78–79 resp.). As for iconography, a distinction in treatment between west and east or north is probably not made on the Black Obelisk either, although seemingly so. As noted by Porada (1983: 16), the different contexts – ceremonial or military – of the receiving of the rulers of Israel and Gilzanu respectively may be explained by their different, initial reactions to the Assyrian king's demand for tribute and submission rather than by any real differentiation in value (SI11:A1–2).

The frequent idiom which states that the Early Neo-Assyrian kings "counted (conquered) people as Assyrians" (*ana nišē māt Aššur amnušunūti*) covers not only the west but also the north and east. Ashurnasirpal II uses this idiom when stating the destinies of people from the city or mountain pass of Babitu to the mountain of Hashmar or Namru (e.g. AE3:44–45), the whole land of Zamua (AE33:13′), and the area from Mt Kirruru to Gilzanu (e.g. AE40:24–25). In other words, many people from the east or north were counted as Assyrians. Shalmaneser III mainly refers to the elite of Bit-Adini being viewed in this way, but in one other passage he sweepingly declares that people from west to north and east also were regarded in this manner (SE2:ii75, SE5:ii3 resp.). This expression has generally been interpreted as a sign of an inclusive, non-ethnical, and integration-focused foreign policy of the Assyrian kings (e.g. Oded 1979: 84–86), and also as a testimony of the flexibility of the concept of "Assyrians" (Machinist 1993: 89). The relevant verb *manû* clearly conveys the meaning of "count as, change into" (CAD M I: *manû*), expressing the noted flexibility in question (see subs. 5.4.6).

The phenomenon of acculturation – whatever that entailed – is applied to the commenting on the idiom discussed above as well as to the understanding of the Assyrian king's custom of renaming conquered, foreign cities by giving these Akkadian names. The policy in question has sometimes been suggested as expressing cultural imperialism (Pongratz-Leisten 1997b: 339). Irrespective of the worth of this claim, it is interesting to note that several cities in the west, e.g. Til-Barsip which is turned into Kar-Shalmaneser, are also renamed (e.g. SE2:ii34–35). As for religion and acculturation, the Early Neo-Assyrian rulers announce that they honoured – at least in their own view on things – various sanctuaries in western and northern or eastern temples or palaces by placing their royal images in these localities (e.g. SE16:284′–86′, AE1:ii91 resp.), and Shalmaneser III furthermore claims to have sacrificed to northern or eastern deities as well as to western ones (SE119, SE6:ii25–26 resp.). Moreover, godnapping was evidently a policy used against both western and northern or eastern regions (e.g. SE5:iii5–6, SE14:125–26 resp.).

As indicated above, the northern polity of Urartu are differentiated – although not consistently. The story of Shalmaneser III initiating warfare on Urartu (SE17) contrasts with that centred on Babylonia (e.g. SE5:iv1–vi7) in terms of emphasis on violence. The different genres of the two texts can explain this in part. More importantly though, the Urartean soldiers are in contrast to those of the west portrayed as naked and only wearing helmets on the palace gate of the same ruler (SI10:2). Soldiers of the Urartean battlefield of Mt Urina are depicted in the same manner on the Balawat gates of Ashurnasirpal II (AI14:59–60). Nakedness may be perceived of as barbaric, but it could symbolize masculine strength when portraying warriors, such as in the case of the displayed, well-trained body of Naram-Sin (Winter 1996: 22; Bahrani 2001: 57–60). Nevertheless, Shalmaneser III's statement on his slaughtering of the soon-discussed mountain people Gutians is embedded in a description of a campaign against Urartu (SE5:iii2).[225] Shamshi-ilu explicitly seems to equate Urartu with Gutium (An3E34:11–13). All these observations, together with the depictions of a hilly Urartean landscape, may allude to a Urartean status of being mountain people and fierce warriors. As shown above, this differentiation is however not given consistently. Urartu may have been regarded as culturally inferior, but the peace and well-being which the reciprocity principle could give them were open also to them.

As for the west, the Arameans have a special status and function in the primary sources, in the sense that they are referred to as having seized land from Assyria and Assyrians in the migrating times of the 12th to 10th centuries BCE. The Early Neo-Assyrian kings then claim to reconquer this lost land. The idiomatic narrative passage which tells of this historical phase is once attested

225 Understanding this apparent associating, Gutians had become synonymous for people in the Zagros area, among them the Urarteans, in Neo-Assyrian times (Larsen 1999: 140–41).

in the inscriptions of Shalmaneser III (SE2:ii37–38). Before him, Ashur-dan II claimed that Assyrians had been enslaved by Arameans (e.g. Ad2E1:17–18). Ashurnasirpal II in his turn declares that he reclaimed cities and lands which the Arameans had seized by force from Assyrians, and that he defeated and deported *aḫlamû* Arameans to Assyria (AE19:93–96). Due to their hostile and non-sedentary ways these *aḫlamû* Arameans were regarded as "the enemies of Ashur" by Middle Assyrian kings (Cancik-Kirschbaum 2008: 58). Echoing this imagery, Arameans are described as being used as auxiliary troops by an enemy of Adad-narari II (An2E2:53).

The idiomatic narrative passage in question is obviously a literary topos, independent from the attitude towards the western Aramean states of the later Early Neo-Assyrian kings' own days.[226] For example, already in Early Neo-Assyrian times, the Akkadian language was influenced by Aramaic (Tadmor 1982). The governor of Guzana wrote his commemorative inscriptions both in Akkadian and Aramaic (AE148). Also Aramaic art influences can be detected, e.g. in the shape of the Nabu Stele (SA5I1) (Börker-Klähn 1982: 196). Evidently, a distinction between *topos* and *mimesis* needs to be made here. In the *topos* the foreigner is stereotyped in the propaganda, while in the *mimesis* the foreigner is stereotyped in more mundane sources, with the latter stereotype being far more realistic and much less ideologically coloured (Loprieno 1988). To summarize, the Arameans were differentiated ideologically, having a special function, but not in the sense that their worth was belittled. When spoken of negatively, it was because of their *actions*, i.e. their hostility and resistance (Cancik-Kirschbaum 2008: 56) An underlying disregard for their cultural ways, i.e. their nomadic, non-urban life style, does not come across clearly in the propaganda of the ten kings.

The eastern people Gutians are described by Shalmaneser III as "troops of the mountain" (*ṣāb šadî*), and their land is "extensive" (*rapaštu*) (SE118:5′, SE28:41 resp.). The same king then claims to have "slaughtered the extensive Guti like the god Erra" (*māt Qutie rapaštu° kī Erra ašgiš*) (SE5:iii2). Similarly, Ashurnasirpal II mentions that "he, by (his) weapons, felled the extensive troops of the Lullumu in battle" (*ummānāt Lullume rapšāti ina qereb tamḫāri ina kakkī lū ušamqit*) (e.g. AE28:iii11–13), another archaic mountain people from the east and Zamua.[227] Lullu, a short form for Lullumu, are along with the Arameans described as seizing lands in the texts of Tukulti-Ninurta II

226 Giving an example of the same kind, Ashurnasirpal II's refers to some Habur rulers as kings of "Hanigalbat", i.e. as rulers over the long-gone state of Mitanni (e.g. AE17:ii73–74).

227 This ethnic group is depicted on the Naram-Sin victory stele from the Sargonic Period (Winter 1996). For the equating of Lullumu with the Zamua region, see Fuchs 2011: 247.

(TN2E5:34–35). It is clear that these supposedly derogatory descriptions merely reflect literary topos and intertextuality, since it was anachronistic to refer to Gutium and Lullumu in this period, being distant from the Sumerians and the 3rd millennium BCE (Prechel 1992: 173).[228]

The apparent dehumanization of these kinds of peoples which is attested in Sumerian literature like "the Curse of Agade" is in any case not found in the propaganda of the Early Neo-Assyrian rulers (see Cooper 1983: lines 154–55). Prejudice against other peoples, whenever expressed, rather centred on way of living (urban or non-urban) than on essential *ethnos* in the Mesopotamian world view (Limet 2005: 370–71). Illustrative of this attitude is the circumstance that the phenomenon of "domestication" (CAD T: *tarbītu* A) can be conveyed by the word "town-bred" (*tarbīt āli*) (AE77). The relevant peoples are negatively differentiated due to their *actions*, namely resistance. A certain disregard for their culture, due to their non-urban way of life, may be detected, but the Assyrian reciprocity principle applied also to these peoples. Additionally, these descriptions merely reflect literary topoi.

To summarize, any consistent variation with regards to emphasis or treatment, other than that determined by the reciprocity principle, in line with the alleged divide between west and north or east, is not clearly detectable in the propaganda of the ten kings. In a few cases however, certain derogatory views, but still with the reciprocity principle in operation, tend to shine through. These views express devaluating images of the relevant peoples as nomads (*aḫlamû* Arameans) or mountain dwellers (Urarteans, Gutians, Lullumu). The highlighting of Phoenicia may be seen as a recognition of this land's culture. All this shows that the cultural but not the political sphere, determined by reciprocity, can express ideological differentiation.

Although infrequently mentioned or illustrated, Egypt is given a special status in the sources. This land is not explicitly referred to as under the dominion of any Early Neo-Assyrian king, and the register on the Black Obelisk which centres on this country only depicts the delivery of a row of exotic animals (SI11:A–D3). However, the delivery of this "tribute" conveys a propagandistic image of its subordination (Elat 1982: 72; Liverani 1990: 267). An alternative image of confrontation, due to resistance, is given by the narration that Egypt took part in the great Syrian-Palestine coalition against Shalmaneser III at Qarqar in 853 BCE (SE2:ii90–96). The wished-for, subordinate status on the Black Obelisk, dated to around 827 BCE, may express Egypt's final status, developing from "rebellion" to submission.

---

228 The appearance and usage of the third millennium BCE people known as *Umman-manda* in the much later Sargonid Period may be another example of this type (Adalı 2011).

Respect for the Egyptian culture may be expressed by the proposed borrowing of ideological goods such as the obelisk by the Assyrian kings during the Middle Assyrian Period, a borrowing in *form* and not in function (Frahm 2011a: 73–75), or by the idea of having stone orthostats with large-scaled reliefs in the North-West Palace (Reade 2002: 189). The respected status of Egyptians may also be seen in the statement of Sargon II that "I (he) caused Assyrians and Egyptians to join [with] one another" ([*nišē*] *māt Aššur u māt Muṣur* [*itti*] *aḫāmeš ablul*) (see Tadmor 2011: 264, text Nimrud Prism D:iv47–48). Although this statement focuses on reopening trading activities, the parallelism of the two ethnonyms speak of a certain recognition of equality. As already observed, the theme of the joining of Assyrians with another people is otherwise spoken of in relation to Babylonians, implying a high regard for the two ancient cultures and peoples of Egypt and Babylonia.

A problem in the discussion on Egypt in the Akkadian sources is the circumstance that the toponym of *Muṣur*/*Muṣri* can denote not only Egypt but also a few polities on the eastern side of the Tigris, in south-eastern Anatolia, and possibly also in Syria-Palestine (Röllig and Kessler 1993–97: 264–69). The context of the relevant attestation consequently determines the given interpretation. Following this logic, the Black Obelisk illustrates *Egyptian* "tribute". The relevant caption refers to *māt Muṣri* and its delivering of various exotic animals, such as several "female elephants" (*pīrtu*), a "river ox" (*alap nāri*), and a "rhinoceros" (*sadēja*), arguably tells of this toponym's African localization (SE89). Also, the *Muṣrajja* who take part in the Syrian-Palestinian coalition against Shalmaneser III need to refer to Egyptians. As noted by Yamada (1998: 90 n. 17), the textual context makes it clear that the country in question had to be a great land in the south-west, i.e. Egypt.[229]

As for iconography and the toponym confusion, in light of the African animals portrayed in the relevant register, combined with the presence of a pair of sphinx-like creatures, it seems safe to recognize *Egyptian* gifts or tribute (SI11:A–D3). Collon (1995: 161) seems to state conclusively (apparently on the looks alone) that the depicted elephant is Indian, and that the tribute in question then is eastern. However, identifying this grand tribute as part of that of the obscure trans-Tigris state of Musri is not very convincing. Besides, making statements solely on the basis of how Assyrian artists chose to depict a certain animal or people is risky, especially since these had a tendency to give distorted and coloured portrayals (Schwyn 2006: 328–29). The beards which the persons leading the animals carry could be an argument against an Egypt inter-

229 See also Tadmor 1961 for this African identification. For an identification of *Muṣrajja* as a people from a locality in the northern part of present-day Syria, see Garelli 1971: 38–40.

pretation since Egyptians are normally depicted clean-shaven in their own art, but at least northern Egypt was dominated by rulers of Libyan origins at this time, and Libyans are portrayed with beards in the art of the New Kingdom (1552–1069) (Loprieno 1988: 22–34). The described and depicted animal delivery on the obelisk is then Egyptian.

Summing up, in this discussion on the differentiation of the foreign lands and people, I have argued for a relative uniformity in terms of status. Although certain lands were culturally regarded (Babylonia, Phoenicia, Egypt) and culturally disregarded (Urarteans, Arameans, Lullumu, Gutians), all lands were regarded the same way politically, i.e. as subordinates of the Assyrian king. Literary topoi and intertextuality influenced the portrayals.

5.4.6 Alleged roles of ethnicity and nationalism

In this subsection, the claims of a crucial Assyrian/foreign dichotomy in Assyrian state ideology is examined more closely. I will argue that an application of the concepts of nationalism and essence-based ethnicity on the Assyrian material is anachronistic and weakly supported respectively. The Early Neo-Assyrian kings, on the contrary, presented themselves as universal, non-nationalistic rulers, and with ethnicity much in the background.

The issue of ethnicity in Mesopotamia has of course been discussed earlier in Assyriology. This is especially true of the discussion on the distinction between Sumerians and Akkadians (e.g. Westenholz 1979). In the earliest Assyriology literature, a belief in the relevance of races, nations, and essence-based *ethnos* for understanding ancient Mesopotamia is often expressed. Nowadays, the scholarly mainstream seems to focus on constructed *ethnos*, emphasizing *language* as a dividing line (e.g. Roux 1992: 147–51). Ideas on essence-based *ethnos*, forming various ancient nations, are however far from abandoned. Bottéro (2001a) e.g. detects a certain Sumerian mentality, at least regarding religious thought, which contrasts to that of the Akkadians who arguably were a part of a larger Semitic *ethnos*. The identifying of a Semitic nation may be regarded as an important component of many literary productions inspired by Orientalism and its discourses (Said 1978).

Related to this discussion on the role of ethnicity and the existence of nationalism in ancient Mesopotamia are the issues of xenophobia and racism.[230]

230 Nationalism is here understood, using the definition of Limet (2005: 377), as "a kind of ethnocentrism expressed in radical ethnic feelings that sometimes slip towards xenophobia and reject other peoples who are held to be of lower rank, edging towards racism".

Bottéro (2001a: 96) here argues that racism or "true alterity" did not exist in Mesopotamia, and that "the idea of 'foreigners' (*aḫû*) mattered only on the linguistic, economic, and political level". In other words, it was not because of their foreignness that Mesopotamian kings went to war against the foreign lands. Robertson (2005: 208) notes that societal tensions produced by ethnic differences rarely are detected in the sources, and that the relational norms rather were coexistence and assimilation. The "stranger/foreigner" (*nakru*/*aḫû*) was not stigmatized and did not form a separate social class in Mesopotamia (Machinist 1986; Prechel 1992: 181). This circumstance is also reflected in political discourse. Yoffee (1993: 305) here talks of the "non-national character of Mesopotamian political authority". Limet (2005: 370–71) even claims that people in Mesopotamia hardly knew ethnic prejudice, and that the general attitude towards foreigners was tolerance. The xenophobia which did exist rather targeted pastoralists and "mountain peoples".

The topic of ancient Assyria as a "nation" has been discussed frequently. One line of thought identifies a fixed, essence-based Assyrian *ethnos* expressed in the primary sources. Especially in older literature this identifying is accompanied by referring to Assyrians as a distinct race. However, some scholarly literature of today likewise refers to an idea of "the Assyrian race and nation", identifying notions of essence-based ethnicity. According to these interpretations, the wars of the Assyrian kings were nationalistic wars, and the relevant relations of power revolved around the concept of nations. This line of thought represents the belief in primordial ethnicity (see s. 1.6).

Another line of thought regarding this nation issue is represented by the Italian school who detects an idea of an ethnic identity of a perennial or constructed sense of the Assyrians (see s. 1.6). This idea then functioned as a vital part of Assyrian imperialism. Zaccagnini (1982: 409–13) claims that the foreign enemy is portrayed as a "necessary dialectic term for the Assyrian reality", and he refers to an "ethno-centrism" which conveys "an extremely rigid dualistic vision". Pongratz-Leisten (2001: 224) and Limet (2005: 381–85) similarly, but more cautiously, detect some kind of constructed Assyrian nationalism. The latter scholar vaguely defines its expression as reverence for ancient times, i.e. for the religious beliefs and cultural traditions of the past (Limet 2005: 382–83). In the context of discussing the state ideology of Ashurnasirpal II, Cifarelli (1995) refers to "cultural identity and differentiation" in the inscriptions of this king, and identifies a "visual discourse of alterity". Although she prefers to use the terms identity and alterity, nationalism and constructed *ethnos* are clearly imagined. Similarly, in the context of Assyrian colonization of the Hurrite state Hanigalbat, Harrak (1987: 274) talks of nationalities and a policy of non-integration. Tadmor (1975: 43, 2011: 285) occasionally ranks the degree of expressed "nationalism" exhibited by individual Assyrian kings. Sennacherib is here "the most nationalistic king", while Ashurnasirpal II is "the outstanding Assyrian nationalist".

Liverani (1990: 290–94), who of course is a prime representative of the Italian school, identifies a self-image of the Assyrians which defines them as unique and chosen. Although acknowledging the modernity of the concept of nationalism, he goes on to claim that the Assyrians nevertheless had "some kind of 'nationalistic' feeling" (Liverani 1992a: 1033). The foreigners were, according to Liverani (1979: 306–307, 309–313), considered sub-humans, animal-like, strange, abnormal, unorganized, and chaotic. According to this understanding, the foreign lands were a chaotic periphery in need of Assyrian civilization. Their otherness had to be eradicated by the king, either by death or by "Assyrianization". This term implied the creation of imperial provinces, a unified administration, imperial officials, destruction of temples and palaces, and cross-deportations. Liverani takes the treatment of Til-Barsip as an example of implemented Assyrianization. After its eventual conquest by Shalmaneser III, this city was renamed, its people were deported, and an Assyrian-styled palace was built (Liverani 1992a: 1033).

A more radical view on the issue of Assyrian *ethnos* and nationalism is articulated by Bahrani (2008: 179) who argues that ethnicity was an unknown concept to people in Assyria/Mesopotamia. Machinist (1993: 89) similarly argues that "Assyria" and "Assyrian" in Assyrian royal inscriptions[231] "are not ethnical but political terms, defining a region and people who express the requested obedience". Before him, Pečirková (1987: 169, 188) referred to the Assyrian empire by its disinterest in the race and faiths of the conquered territories, and stated that the crucial factor instead was the degree of loyalty towards the king. The empire was not based on racial or nationalistic concepts. Saggs (1982: 92), who identifies a logic in the treatment of Assyrian prisoners of war, sees a complete lack of Assyrian racialism, and argues that punishments were not based on ethno-cultural belonging. The king's universal domain implied no distinction between peoples on ethno-religious grounds. Instead, it was everything beyond the control of the Assyrian kings that was considered antithetical. The independent countries were in this way thought of as the *Gegenwelt* (Pongratz-Leisten 2001: 202). Thus, a dichotomy of homeland/foreign land was not centred on by the Assyrian kings, but rather the goal of world domination

231 This remark expresses an important distinction, namely between how the issue is dealt with in the ideological sources, and the role ethnicity played in real life. Possibly, the downplaying of constructed ethnicities in the ideological sources may be connected to the common imperialist tactics of co-opting through rhetorics of inclusion (Lamprichs 1995: 31, 381).

implying a conflict in which the king and his enemies stand in a juxtaposed relation of polarity and opposition in which ethnicity was irrelevant (Steiner 1982: 646–47).

Elaborating on the topic of Assyrian imperial identities, as Postgate (2007: 59, 351) observes, it is difficult do detect in the primary sources a definition of what it meant to be an Assyrian. The evasiveness of this concept may not be a coincidence (Postgate 1992b: 252). Assyrian imperialism and imperial identity were inclusive in character in which assimilation was sought, promoting the ideal of a universal empire (Barjamovic 2011: 41–42, 2012: 47, 2013: 137–50). Bagg (2011: 281–95, 301) emphatically dismisses the idea that Assyrianization – at least not in the west – meant any cultural or religious impositions. The distinction between Assyrians and non-Assyrians centred on whether the individual in question lived in an area of Assyrian administration or not, thus expressing an imperial identity of a political kind. Following up on this conclusion on identity, there were no real *Abgrenzungen* or *Ausgrenzungen* in terms of ethnicity and culture in the Neo-Assyrian state (Röllig 1996: 111–12). All these apparent stances of social constructivism (see s. 1.6) seem to argue that nationalism is a modern idea (deriving from the European colonialism and nationalism of the 19th century CE), and that an applying of it onto ancient Assyria is anachronistic and thus unsuitable.

The relevant discussion is often confused because of the circumstance that the different time periods of Assyrian history often are blended into one. The fundamentally political identity identified above may have been more culturally-based in earlier periods. Barjamovic (2013: 137–50, 153) e.g. claims that there is a marked difference between the Middle and Neo-Assyrian periods in terms of views on integration and internal social structure. With the latter period, a change towards universalism, ethnic pluralism, and a centering on the patrimonialism of the absolute ruler replaced the earlier less inclusive views. In other words, when discussing earlier periods (Harrak 1987), the notion of constructed ethnicity may not be out of place.

Turning finally to the major primary sources, if nationalism was – as argued by the scholars who detect an essence-based or perennial/constructed Assyrian *ethnos* – an inherent feature and even driving force of Assyrian imperialism, one would expect to find the terms "Assyria", "Assyrian", and the like occurring everywhere in the sources. The title "king of Assyria" (*šar māt Aššur*) both contains a relevant term and is amply attested (e.g. AE1:i28, SE1:1). The supposed essence-based, static, and fixed character of the concept of *māt Aššur*, as expressed in the state ideology, can however be questioned. Ashurnasirpal II e.g. states, when referring to conquered areas, that "I (he) brought GN within the boundaries of my land" (GN *ana miṣrī mātija utēr*) (e.g. AE50:10–

19). This expression is also in use as a royal epithet (An2E2:26).[232] Similarly, the coronation command exhorts the crowned king "to extend" (*ruppušu*) the boundaries of Assyria (see Livingstone 1989: text 11:17; Müller 1937: text 1:ii34–35). Ashurnasirpal II here called himself "he who extends the borders of his land" (*murappišu° miṣir mātišu*) (AE40:8).

The term *māt Aššur* denoted the land under the king's direct dominion at any given time, and was an administrative rather than cultural concept (Bagg 2011: 301). In other words, not only the concept of Assyrians was fluid and flexible but also the idea of Assyria and its boundaries. Apart from this circumstance, "king of Assyria" is not the most common of Ashurnasirpal II's nor Shalmaneser III's titles, and the title of "king of the universe" (*šar kiššati*) is almost as frequently attested. Furthermore, it is rarely attested in a primary position, not even in Assur. In fact, the relevant title is absent from most titulary sections of the annals of the latter king. As revealed by appendix 12, the evidence of the eNA I and III-phases taken together gives some priority to this title, but the total number of attestations from these phases are relatively few, which naturally affects the potential to generalize. In any case, the land of Assyria and its boundaries were not static but dynamic.

Just a few other royal epithets refer to the alleged "homeland" as the source of authority in a geographical sense, e.g. "he who leads in peace the population of Assyria" (*ša ina šulme ittanarrû ba'ūlāt māt Aššur*) (SE1:5–6). Also, in relation to Adad-narari III, the great gods are "those who made his shepherdship as pleasing as a healthy plant to the Assyrians" (*rē'ūssu kīma šamme balṭi eli nišē māt Aššur uṭibbū*) (e.g. An3E8:2). In Ashurnasirpal II's case, the king is also "the avenger" (*mutīr gimilli*) (e.g. AE40:7) and possibly "the shepherd" (*rē'û*) of Assyria – the latter epithet attested in an unsecurely dated text (see RIMA2: A.0.0.1019). However, with the unclear implications of the toponym in question, these epithets do not prove much. Additionally, they are rarely attested in the text corpora of the ten rulers.

Seldom is it stated that something is "Assyrian" or belonging to Assyria. The epithet "Assyrian Ishtar" (*Ištar Aššurītu*) may simply refer to a need of distinguishing between different cults rather than signifying a national goddess (SE43:10). Similarly, Ashurnasirpal II twice refers to Ashur as the "Assyrian Enlil" (*Ellil Aššurû*) (e.g. AE154:1), and his father Tukulti-Ninurta II talks of it once (TN2E23:1). The former also once calls the same deity "the Assyrian god" (*ilu Aššurû*) (AE17:v89). In the texts of Adad-narari III, Enlil, Ninlil, and Ishtar are all called "Assyrian" (*Aššurû*), and the notion of "the great gods of

232 The Early Neo-Assyrian kings often define their borders. Shamshi-Adad V e.g. claims that the border of Assyria revolved e.g. around Nairi, Til-Barsip, and Enzi (SA5E1:ii7–13).

Assyria" (*ilāni rabûti ša māt Aššur*) is articulated (e.g. An3E2:11–12, An3E2:17 resp.). However, in light of the demonstrated fluid concept of Assyrianness in the ideological sources (at least), these divine epithets do not provide any hard evidence in their meanings.

Another kind of attestation which is often called upon in order to claim the presence of an Assyrian nation state in Assyrian royal inscriptions is the mentioning of foreign tributaries coming to Assur, and of the king carrying his tribute and booty (including felled timber), captives, and hostages to the same city. The king here receives or brings tribute and booty "to my city Assur" (*ana Aššur ālija*) (e.g. AE67:9–10, SE5:iii6). Also, defeated enemy rulers are brought to Assyria to be flayed and having their skin draped over the walls of Assyrian cities (e.g. AE17:i88–89). All these narrative passages and expressions may however reflect an understanding of Assur and Assyria as the cosmic centre, without any ideas of "diversification of men" according to ethnicity implied – a diversification seen by Liverani (1979: 309–13).

In Ashurnasirpal II's time, mostly Kalhu had this status of a cosmic centre, in terms of cities. The king repeatedly mentions that he embarked upon military campaigns by marching out from his new capital (e.g. AE1:iii1), and he similarly hears of rebellions from reports coming to him "while I was in Kalhu" (*ina Kalḫi usbāku*) (e.g. AE1:iii26–27), defined as "the centre of my (his) lordship" (*māḫāz bēlūtija*) (AE30:53). In the reign of the Middle Assyrian ruler Tukulti-Ninurta I, this king's new capital Kar-Tukulti-Ninurta functioned ideologically as the centre and microcosm in question (Dolce 1997). Similarly, the Late Neo-Assyrian ruler Sargon II refers to his new capital Dur-Sharrukin as a representation of cosmos (Cancik-Kirschbaum 2008: 74). Without doubt, Assyrian rulers mainly talk of building activity in what historians define as Assyria proper. Once again though, the notion of Assyria in general and of Assur or Kalhu in particular as the cosmic centre may be expressed, just as well as some sort of constructed ethnicity.[233]

Proceeding from the terms Assyria, Assyrian, and Assur to that of "Assyrians", the commonly used and partly discussed (see subs. 5.4.5) idiom in the texts of Ashurnasirpal II as well as in those of Shalmaneser III in which the

---

233 This idea of the capital as a microcosm and cosmic centre is not uniquely Assyrian. Babylon and Persepolis were regarded in the same way by their rulers (van de Mieroop 2005; Ehrenberg 2008: 109–110 resp). As for Achaemenidian state ideology, the dichotomy of unity/diversity is highlighted. The diversity of the world caused by sin and fragmentation expressed e.g. by differences in geography, material resources, and peoples is brought to an harmonious unity by the Persian king. This unification is e.g. visualized through the depictions of tributaries of foreign lands approaching the benevolent king in his cosmic centre (Lincoln 2008).

king declares that "I (the king) counted them (foreign elites and people) as Assyrians" (*ana nišē māt Aššur amnušunūti)* (e.g. AE26:29–30, SE20:18–19) indicates the flexibility of the concept of Assyrians, and simultaneously expresses a recognition of the foreigner's equal status (Oded 1979: 84–88; Snell 1993: 222; Kuhrt 1997: 533; Beaulieu 2005: 51). The notion of a fixed, essence-based nation state is not given here, but the idiom rather points to a political identity of some sort. The elites and people who were turned into Assyrians in this way were deportees and former inhabitants of conquered cities or lands, and may thus be regarded as subjected to a policy of Assyrianization. The exact implications of this policy is hard to follow, but the relevant idiom seems to express a goal of inclusion and integration.

As for the nature of this inclusion and integration, every individual regardless of ethnicity or social standing was regarded as a "servant" (*wardu*) of the king (Garelli 1979: 323). This includes even the crown prince. Sennacherib e.g. introduces himself as "your servant" (*uradka*) in letters to his father Sargon II (see Parpola 1987: text 31:2). In accordance with this conclusion, also Assyrians are depicted throwing themselves to the king's feet. As interpreted by Schachner (2007: 59), a delegation of Assyrians are illustrated in this way on the Balawat Gate of Shalmaneser III, and what seems to be Assyrian soldiers (one in each scene) are portrayed in the same manner on the walls of the throne room of the North-West Palace and on the embossed bronze helmet (SI10:10t., AI4:B18b., AI24:22b. resp.). Shamshi-Adad V claims that Assyria, after the great rebellion against him, bowed down at his feet, using the footstool metaphor (SA5E1:i53, SA5E1:ii15–16 resp.). In relation to this story of rebellion, it is made clear that also Assyrians were obliged to swear "oaths of loyalty" (*tamētu*) to their superior (SA5E1:i43). This swearing is amply attested in the Late Neo-Assyrian state archives, e.g. in the so-called Zakutu Treaty (see Parpola and K. Watanabe 1988: text 8).

Moreover, as shown in subsection 5.4.4 on the Assyrian king as the paternalistic shepherd and sun of all people and lands, there is no clear distinction – at least not in the state ideology – made between people due to ethnicity.[234] Similarly talking of relative ethnical neutrality, Assyrian "royal cities" were not excempted from taxes and labour duties (with the occasional exception of Assur) in the granting of privileges to cities (Tadmor 2011: 129), in contrast to the statuses of several Babylonian ones (see subs. 5.4.5). In line with the reciprocity principle, all that really mattered was how the "foreign" elites and people chose to respond to the territorial and material claims of the Assyri-

234 The ninth century BCE ruler Kilamuwa of Sam'alla actually presents his Assyrian superior as a benefactor (Fales 1979), naturally telling of this ruler's inclusion and integration.

an king. The relationship was in other words not defined based on essence such as ethnicity, but on *actions*. Whether ethnically foreign or Assyrian, all were servants and cattle of the Assyrian king. According to this view, the concept of Assyrians basically expressed a *political* identity.

A prominent case for those who see a crucial Assyrian/foreign dichotomy expressed in Assyrian state ideology is the theme of Assyrian settlers and officials located outside the core area. These are referred to as "Assyrians" (*amēlē Aššurajja/Aššurû*), arguably alluding to a constructed ethnicity.[235] This settling of Assyrians is one part of a series of administrative measures which the Italian school refers to as Assyrianization, implying cultural imperialism. Archaeologists also tend to talk of Assyrianization, pointing to the imposition of uniformity and standardization with regards e.g. to household wares such as ceramics, to architectural features such as building types, settlement layouts, and urban planning, to Assyrian-styled luxury items such as ivories, cylinder seals, and sculpture, and to the occurrence of clay tablets with cuneiform in Assyrian paleography and with a language conveying the Assyrian dialect.[236] The distribution of Assyrian pottery in light of Assyrian imperialism has been especially centered on in this debate on the reach of Assyria (Anastasio 2010; Hausleiter 2010).

Turning more firmly to the major primary sources, Shalmaneser III only once uses the idiom "I settled therein Assyrians" (*amēlē Aššurajja ina libbi ušēšib*) in the context of his defeating of Arameans in the west (SE2:ii34). The same idiom is expressed in the texts of his father in which north-western settlements are described as being reconquered from the hands of the Arameans. Ashurnasirpal II in this context refers to Shalmaneser I or II as the original settler of "Assyrians" (*amēlē Aššurajja*) in the relevant fortress cities by and in the Nairi lands. After driving away the occupying Arameans, the Assyrians are here resettled in a peaceful environment (AE19:92–95). In one other passage, the same king refers to a colonization of a western city with "Assyrians" (*amēlē Aššurajja*) without giving any background of earlier possession and settlement (AE1:iii82–83). In yet another passage, the hardships of "the weakened Assyrians" (*nišē māt Aššur anšāte*), who had been driven into exile by hunger and famine and had gone up to the lands of Shubru, are relieved and this people are resettled by the king (e.g. AE1:ii7–8).[237]

235 The already demonstrated flexibility and fluidity of the concept of Assyria arguably rules out the interpretation of a fixed, essence-based Assyrian ethnicity.

236 Such as Bernbeck (2010) who in his discussion on the Assyrian empire even draws a parallel to the USA and the spreading of its material culture across the globe in today's world.

237 In the Synchronistic History, the lands of Babylonia (here termed Sumer and Akkad) and Assyria are actual agents (An3E59:iv28–30), hinting to constructed ethnicities of some kind.

However, these seemingly solid proofs of the relevance of nationality and ethnicity in Assyrian state ideology can be questioned. The resettling of foreign people in the north-west, who had regretted their original flight or resistance, is told of by Ashurnasirpal II (e.g. AE17:ii28–31). The other way around, Assyrians living in the north-west are brutally punished for their rebellion towards his overlordship in another of his narrative passages (e.g. AE1:i101–110). On fairly the same note, from Shamshi-Adad V's version of the internal rebellion in 826–820 BCE, it is apparent that also Assyrians could be "evil" (*lemuttu*), do "rebellious and hostile acts" (*nabalkatu*, *nakāru*), and be subjected to forced submission, as conveyed through the idiomatic phrase "I (the king) made NN submit at my feet" (*ana šēpīja ušakniš*) (SA5E1:i39–53). Expressed yet again, the political dimension overarchs any other considerations, whether religious, cultural, or ethnic, in Assyrian state ideology. Loyalty and rebellion were met with paternalism and military force respectively – regardless of the agent in question. Moreover, the just discussed references to Assyrian settlers are relatively few.

The uniformity of Assyrianization can be interpreted more cautiously as "administrative policies" (Schramm 1973: 103) which responded to the need for creating a firm and effective royal grip over the conquered region. Furthermore, the colonies of Assyrian settlers should probably be understood in the light of economic policies (Tadmor 1975: 37–38), not as part of a conscious program to implement cultural imperialism. As noted recently also by Fales (2008: 20–21), Assyrianization seems not to have carried with it any deliberate cultural imperialism or true expressions of nationalism and constructed or essence-based *ethnos*. He concludes that "Assyrianness" was not a pivotal element of Assyrian imperialism, and that submission and "money" instead were focused on by the Assyrian rulers, both in theory and practice.

Leaving discussions based on the word Assyria and its derivatives, one of the strongest cases for recognizing a constructed ethnicity as a force in Assyrian state ideology is the frequent use of ethnonyms attached to the mentioning of foreign rulers, elites, and people through use of the gentilic suffixes *-ajja* or *-û* to a toponym. Western rulers can e.g. (quite anachronistic) be referred to as "Hittites" (*Ḫattajja*) (e.g. AE1:ii22). Admittedly, this phenomenon may speak of the belief in a constructed ethnicity, being expressed also in ideological sources. However, when the gentilic suffix is attached to the name of a city, it is arguably more justified to see an urban rather than ethnic identity expressed in the sources (e.g. AE1:i78, [SE1:67′]). In any case, the reciprocity principle (see subs. 5.4.2) by which *actions* and not essence is highlighted is fully and consistently in operation.

Moving on to a phenomenon related to that of ethnonyms, actual ethnographic remarks are practically absent in the sources of the Early Neo-Assyrian rulers. As Zaccagnini (1982: 412) admits, there are just a few examples of ethnographic observations in the pre-Sargonid, Assyrian royal inscriptions. A renamed city "which the people of Hatti call Pitru" (*ša amēlū Ḫattajja ša Pitru iqabbūšuni*) is spoken of in the texts of Shalmaneser III (SE10:i42–43), and Ashurnasirpal II uses the same expression on toponyms named by the people called Lullu (e.g. AE1:ii34). These poor attestations can be compared to the frequent ones in the famous narration of Sargon II's eighth campaign (Zaccagnini 1982), even though quantity is not really the issue here, but rather how to understand these attestations qualitatively.

Another argument in favour of the interpretation of a political identity is the lack in Akkadian of a clear word for "foreign". The word *nakru* seems to be used in its meaning of "enemy" and as a way of varying other words which share its meaning such as *ajjābu*, *zā'iru*, and *gērû* (CAD N I: *nakru*). The words of *wabru* and *ubāru*, referring to "foreign" residents living in Mesopotamia (CAD U-W: *wabru*, CAD U-W: *ubāru*), is not attested in the relevant sources. The word which is commonly translated as "foreign" (*aḫû*) is not attested in the sources of Shalmaneser III, and only once in those of Ashurnasirpal II. In the curse section of the Ninurta Stele, a future Assyrian king who, as a way of avoiding the curses, lets an "enemy, foreigner, (or) evil foe" (*nakra aḫâ ajjāba lemna*) erase and change the relevant inscription or building is cursed (AE17:v67–70). Even here, the focal point is not on the foreign element and its supposed negative connotations. Also, the word *aḫû* may simply mean "alien, odd, outsider, and hostile" (CAD A I: *aḫû*). Instead of "the foreigner" (essence-defined), the real opponent is then "the rebel" or "the enemy" (actions-defined). All said and done, the issue of "foreignness" is simply not focused on in the source base proper of this study.[238]

Summing up, I have argued that ethnicity does *not* play a vital role in the propaganda of the ten kings. Occasionally, a notion of a constructed *ethnos* shines through, but the concept of political identity was always supreme. The terms "Assyria" and "Assyrians" are fluid and dynamic, and do not refer to any anachronistic Assyrian nation state. It was the political dimension and the idea of the Assyrian king as representing Order which were centred on.

5.4.7 Emphasis on the king and the ruling class

As argued above, a dichotomy of Assyrian/foreign is not useful in the pursuit of grasping the nature of the (often antagonistic) relationship between the As-

238 A similar conclusion is reached by Assmann (1996) with regards to the Egyptians, often seen as chauvinistic. Instead of ethnicity and nationalism, it was family, village, and town

syrian king and the foreign lands. Below, I will argue that the real dichotomy simply centres around the king alone or with his magnates, together forming the core of an Assyrian ruling class, and his/their enemies.

Kingship was a central institution in ancient Mesopotamia, both in theory and in practice. According to the Sumerian King List (see Jacobsen 1939), kingship was lowered from heaven by the deities in their act of installing a political system in the society of the newly created mankind (Ziegler 2011a). As for Assyria, at the time of the Middle Assyrian Period the title of king and the institution of kingship were firmly established as focal points of the political order. In the Neo-Assyrian Period, the king maintained his function as the central component of the relevant state ideology (Kuhrt 1997: 362). Kingship was the reference point for the cosmic order, and everyone was fixed to a human hierarchy centred around the Assyrian king (Liverani 1979: 312). Seux (1980–83: 172–73) even detects a gradual transition from theocracy to autocracy with regards to Assyrian state ideology. The relationship between kings and foreign rulers is put to the fore in state official sources (Radner 2010), showing that kingship was also an international norm. This is most clearly shown in the Amarna correspondence from Middle Assyrian times in which the kings of the Ancient Near East interact, such as the Egyptian king whose polity is paradigmatic of strong kingship (Assmann 1990).

There are many ways through which the Early Neo-Assyrian king is emphasized in the epigraphic sources. The person of the king is e.g. much stressed through the royal titulary (see apps. 8–12) which makes up a great share of inscriptions. The king also functions as the narrator in the annalistic component of Assyrian royal inscriptions. The credit for defeating enemies, building sanctuaries, and enforcing tribute is here taken by the king alone in his expressions of *I* conquered, *I* built, and so on (e.g. AE2:53, SE28:32). The king as sole and supreme hero is a characteristic theme in Assyrian royal inscriptions, and it illustrates the one-sided angle of these sources (Tadmor 1997: 326–27). The first person perspective which the king has in the preserved propaganda in itself tells of the relevant emphasis on the ruler. Thus, not only the things that he *did* elevated the Assyrian king's position, but also the things he *was*, namely the holder of the divinely decreed kingship and hence the primary viewpoint of the Assyrian state. The king could here, with some credibility, say that he in fact *was* the state, following the governing principles of patrimonial states which focus on one supreme (male) ruler.

---

which were the main identity sources. The outsider was simply the *Fremde*. The chauvinistic label is much dependent on the foreigner *topos* in the propaganda (Loprieno 1988: 22–34).

The claimed outstanding personal qualities of the ruler similarly tells, in their variety and number, of the emphasis on the king in the inscriptions.[239] Several outstanding personal qualities such as "celebrated, exalted, and important" (*nâdāku, ṣīrāku, kabtāku*) are claimed by Ashurnasirpal II in a certain cluster of descriptive stative formations (AE1:i32–33). Tellingly, ahead of this cluster is the identification "I am king" (*šarrāku*) (AE1:i32). Sometimes the king, here Adad-narari III, simply states that he was "the king" (*šarru*) (e.g. An3E6:28). This term was symbolically loaded in Assyrian history, at first reserved for Ashur (see s. 1.1). Moving on, Adad-narari II claims that "I am (he is) the greatest" (*šurbâku*) (e.g. An2E2:15). The extraordinary personal qualities of "heroic" (*qarrādāku/qarrādu*) (e.g. AE1:i32, SE2:ii71), "strong" (*dannu*) (e.g. AE1:i9, SE16:1), and "competent/wise" (*itpēšu/eršu*) (SE16:1, e.g. AE2:23 resp.) likewise aim to highlight the Assyrian ruler. The epithet *eršu* heads a cluster of epithets (AE2:23). Ashurnasirpal II claims to have created temples, palaces, cities, and statues with a cunning which the wisdom god Ea had given him (e.g. AE32:8–9).[240]

This tendency of focusing on the king is striking also in Assyrian state art. Reade consequently refers to the North-West Palace as conveying "a massive corpus of *personal* propaganda" (Reade 1979a: 331). Winter (1983: 21) notes that all action emanates from the king, and that the visitor of the North-West Palace must have been confronted by the king in every situation and position. Shalmaneser III is constantly in focus on the Balawat Gate, e.g. receiving tribute or facing cities under siege (e.g. SI10:7b., SI10:8t. resp.). The said rulers are also highlighted on the Rassam and Black obelisks where they are portrayed receiving tribute and submission (AI16:A1,3, SI11:A1–2). The centering on the king is achieved in various ways. He is both focused on by means of his royal entourage whose members are lined up so as to centre him (e.g. AI30, SI10:4), and through the directions and compositions of processions of tributaries and captives, i.e. these move towards him, and their leader is closest to the Assyrian king (e.g. AI4:B5–6b., SI10:5). The king is also centred on by his standing (e.g. AI13:17–18, SI10:8b.) or sitting (AI4:B7b., SI10:4) under a canopy, or by his sitting on a fixed (e.g. AI4:G3, SI10:9b.) or mobile throne (AI14:83–84). Thus, even without the help of the king's characteristic attributes of crown and other bodily-worn insignia, it is uncomplicated to recognize and isolate the Assyrian king in a given scene.

---

239 Another centering is seen in royal letters with their stress on the king's person, as given e.g. in the passage which focuses on the king's health (see e.g. Parpola 1987: text 1:1–2).

240 It therefore comes as no surprise to find out that the North-West Palace is referred to as "Palace-Full-Of-Wisdom" (*ekal kullat nēmeqi*) by the king in question (AE30:103).

Disregarding the mentioned observation on the sole, supreme, royal hero, the impression of an "Assyrian side" fighting against a "foreign side" in the iconography is easily arrived at. The uniform appearance of Assyrian soldiers, e.g. wearing a certain type of pointed, monochromed helmet, is contrasted with the colourful and diverse appearances of the juxtaposed foreign soldiers and elites. A visualization of national armies fighting each other is therefore sometimes identified (e.g. Cifarelli 1995: 229–324). However, Assyrian royal inscriptions clearly state that it is *the king* and not "the Assyrians" who conducts the warfare. The Assyrian soldiers, by their compact and victorious presence, merely serve to convey a visual illustration of the power and efficiency of the king. In this role, they are simply the extended arm of the king. The king's army then symbolizes the power and efficiency of the king and his warfare, rather than conducting any "war between civilizations" (Huntington 1996). By way of repitition, the soldiers emerge as a unit and as an indicator of the central point of the scenes, namely the Assyrian king. The Assyrian army thus embodies the power of the king (Bahrani 2008: 108–109, 213).

The strength of this extended arm is e.g. seen on the three Balawat gates and in the North-West Palace where the king's soldiers are standing erect and not crouching (e.g. AI4:B3–4t., SI10:4), vigorously and not in panic swimming over waters (AI4:B9–11b., SI10:15b.), storming cities through ladders (e.g. AI4:B5b., SI10:13t.), undermining and breaching walls of besieged cities (e.g. AI4:B4–5b., SI10:4b.), as well as killing enemy soldiers (e.g. AI4:B3–4t., SI10:3b.). They are impersonally represented in symmetrical rows (thus representing Order) as marching (e.g. SI10:1t.), riding (e.g. SI10:9t.), driving chariots (e.g. AI13:25–28, SI10:4t.), or shooting arrows on enemy cities (e.g. AI13:11–12, SI10:4). The king's soldiers are strong and muscular (e.g. AI13:15–16, SI10:4), and they are occasionally represented in social perspective (SI10:7t.), expressing a narrative device which centred on the need that the viewer had to be able to separate the two groups of soldiers from each other.[241] As noted also by Collins (2008: 98), the neat rows of depicted Assyrian soldiers served to convey the impression of Order fighting against Chaos. Accordingly, it was the king and his enemies who faced each other in these scenes. The same interpretation can be made of the scenes which depict the king and his assistants hunting wild game (e.g. AI13:29–32). The king with his men (Order) defeat wild lions and bulls (Chaos).

241 It must be said though that this separation primarily was achieved by other means. The enemy soldiers are depicted as "the Other", being unorganized, crouching, mercy seeking, panicing, fleeing, killed, and with their corpses strewn around (e.g. AI4:B8–11t., SI10:13).

This emphasis on the king and kingship is also seen in the frequent theme of royal genealogy. Royal descent was along with divine choice a king's major legitimacy grounds (Tadmor 1981: 26–30), and royal lineage was an integral part of the ideology of the Assyrian state (Postgate 2008: 178). The "seed of kingship" (*zēr šarrūti*) was a part of Mesopotamian royal ideology (Lambert 1974b). Shamshi-Adad V is here "the eternal royal offspring" (*zēr šarrūti dārû*) (e.g. SA5E2). The two patronyms of "son of Tukulti-Ninurta (II)" (*mār/apal Tukultī-Ninurta*) and "son of Ashurnasirpal (II)" (*mār/apal Aššur-nāṣir-apli*) are the most common "titles" in the texts of Ashurnasirpal II and Shalmaneser III respectively (e.g. AE23:1, SE1:10). Tellingly, the word *aplu* has the dual meaning of "son" and "heir" (CAD A II: *aplu*). Especially Shalmaneser III is also commonly referred to as "prince" (*rubû*) (e.g. SE1:1), i.e. a title traditionally associated with descent (Larsen 1974: 295–99). Ashurnasirpal II's title "legitimate prince" (*rubû kēnu*) puts further emphasis on this notion of a royal line (e.g. AE1:i24). The contempt towards other rulers who were not of royal descent or not the intended heir is expressed e.g. by the epithets of "son of a nobody" (*mār lā mamman*) and "lord of a non-throne" (*bēl lā kussî*) (Yamada 2000: 189, 222).[242] Royal genealogy is also a *motif*, namely on the reverse of the Terqa Stele (TN2I1) which probably shows the king's father (J. M. Russell 1998–2001: 245).

Moving away from the immediate father-son aspect of genealogy, the ancestry of the king is often referred to, e.g. by the epithets "my fathers" (*abbūa*) (e.g. AE30:79, SE56:4), and less often by "former kings" (*šarrāni maḫrûti*) (SE13:l.e.6′–7′). The ruling king is "the grandson" (*mār māri*) in relation to these (e.g. AE40:18). The predecessor is specifically named in the epithets (referring to current rulers) of "offspring of Ashur-dan (II)" (*liblibbi ša Aššur-dān*) (e.g. AE1:i30),[243] and "offspring of Tukulti-Ninurta (II)" (*ṣīt libbi ša Tukultī-Ninurta*) (SE154). Adad-narari III talks much of his ancestry, not the least in a text which gives a long list of royal ancestors. The king is here "the offspring of Ilu-kapkapi" (*liblib ša Ilu-kapkapi*), "the offspring of Tukulti-Ninurta I" (*liblibbi Tukultī-Ninurta*), "the offspring of Shalmaneser I" (*liblibbi ša Šulmānu-ašarēd*), "grandson of Ashurnasirpal II" (*mār māri ša Aššur-nāṣir-apli*), and "the descendant of Adad-narari II" (*pir'i Adad-nārārī*) (An3E1:14–24).[244] A king's titulary

242 In external sources, the Neo-Babylonian king Nabopolassar does in fact brag about being "the son of a nobody" in his inscriptions, perhaps with the intention to present himself as a "self-made man" or as singled out by the Mesopotamian deities (see Langdon 1912: text 4:4).

243 The word *liblibbu* is also associated with the god Shamash, son of Sin, once again testifying to the close ideological relationship between the king and the sun (CAD L: *liblibbu*).

244 In other texts, Adad-narari III also stresses that he was the son of king Shamshi-Adad V but also, quite noteworthy, of queen Sammuramat (e.g. An3E5:1, An3E3:2–3 resp.).

normally names and characterizes the two-three closest royal predecessors. In the texts of Ashurnasirpal II, epithets list and remember Ashur-dan II as a re-settler of the west, Adad-narari II as a powerful ruler, and Tukulti-Ninurta II as a ferocious warrior (e.g. AE1:i28–31). Successors are, in their turn, called upon as "later princes" (*rubû arkû*) in the concluding formulae (e.g. AE40:38, SE43:9).

A concrete manifestation of this belief in the sacredness of the royal line and ancestors is the royal burial site under the Old Palace of Assur, from where e.g. the sarcophagi of Ashurnasirpal II and Shamshi-Adad V have been excavated (Andrae 1938). Adad-narari II tells of his own stele in the Row of Stelae in Assur, raised beside those of his ancestors (An2E9). Also the Assyrian King List may be seen as a concrete expression of the importance attributed to the royal line. It may have played a part in the royal burial (Cancik-Kirschbaum 2008: 115), and it may also have been worn, inscribed on a tablet, around the king's neck at coronation (Renger 2011b: 3). Royal succession, and the related phenomenon of dynastic marriages, were not only crucial on an ideological level, but also in the concrete maintenance of the Neo-Assyrian empire (Radner 2010).[245] The importance of dynastic marriages (here between Assyria and Babylonia) is told of e.g. in the Synchronistic History (e.g. An3E59:iii17). Focusing on the royal line, the enemy ruler was a *personal* enemy of the Assyrian king, and not an abstract enemy to the Assyrian state or alleged nation (Fuchs 2009: 88). The often attested antagonism thus revolved around the concept of king versus foreign ruler.

The Assyrian king not only passively had to belong to the royal line, he was also obliged to *actively* work for his predecessors and successors. The king had to respect the monuments and inscriptions of his predecessors, and instruct his successors to do likewise. This two-fold duty clearly comes across in the sections of blessings and curses, containing addresses to future rulers. These addresses both convey instructions on what the future ruler should do as well as what he should *not* do. As for the former, he should respect and rebuild (when needed) the building or monument in question (e.g. AE17:v24, SE25:34–35), and he should respect, by reading, anointing, make an offering to, and return the predecessor's inscription to its place after renovation (e.g. AE50:44–46, SE13:l.e.1′–10′). Ashur will, alone or less often in the company of other deities,[246] then listen to the prayers of the pious successor (e.g. SE25:36).

---

245 Radner (2010: 31) even sees political failures in these areas, especially that of dynastic marriages, as contributing greatly to the subsequent downfall of the Neo-Assyrian empire.

246 Uniquely only Adad or Ishtar (SE41:5, AE56:17 resp.). The remaining, alternative attestations put Ashur in pair with Adad or Nergal (SE42:12–13, SE47:12–13 resp.).

In more elaborate passages Ashur will, along with Enlil and the great gods, bring prosperity to this king's land, and grant this ruler domination over the world (e.g. AE17:v45–54).[247] The impious successor will, in his turn, evoke divine anger, inflict famine upon his land, as well as causing himself to sit in chains before his enemies. He will moreover have to witness the destruction of his (name and) seed (e.g. AE32:18–21). The ruler who follows the instructions given is in contrast described as one who works "for the well-being of his seed" (*ana šulum zērišu*) (e.g. SE93:3).[248]

The Early Neo-Assyrian kings also express their roles of working for, if not alongside, their royal ancestors in their "building inscriptions". In his act of actively working for the royal line through rebuilding, and in extension through the related acts of reconquering and resettling, the king sometimes refers to the royal master builders who had commissioned work on the relevant building or city before him. In this way, Ashurnasirpal II repeatedly refers to Shalmaneser I, notably in the context of his rebuilding of Kalhu (e.g. AE23:14–15). Similarly, Tukulti-Ninurta II refers to Tukulti-Ninurta I concerning his reorganizing of an unmentioned city in the Balih area (?) (TN2E5:119–20). Regarding temple renovations, the former king refers to Shamshi-Adad I and Ashur-uballit I as earlier master builders (e.g. AE40:31–32, AE56:14 resp.). Also Shalmaneser III lists famous predecessors such as Adad-narari I, Tukulti-Ninurta I, and Tiglath-pileser I as earlier master builders of the city wall of Assur (e.g. SE10:iv41–45). Also these attestations bear witness to the importance attributed to kingship and the royal line.

Another kind of work in honour of the royal line is the phenomenon of erecting monuments and creating inscriptions adjacent to those of earlier Assyrian kings. Narrations of these acts are occasionally attested. Ashurnasirpal II e.g. claims to have created an image beside those of Tiglath-pileser I and Tukulti-Ninurta I or II at the source of the Subnat river (e.g. AE1:i104–105). Shalmaneser III raised an image on a mountain beside that of Anum-hirbe (e.g. SE29:24–26). The supreme value of kingship and the irrelevance of nationality are expressed by the referring even to "non-Assyrian" kings like Anum-hirbe.[249] Shalmaneser III also commissioned a stele beside that of Ashurnasirpal

---

247 A concrete and possible example of the duty fulfilment in question is the noted repair by Tukulti-Ninurta II of a libation vessel in silver dedicated to Ashur, previously worked on by the Middle Assyrian rulers of Ashur-uballit I (?) and Tukulti-Ninurta I (TN2E23).

248 In a wider sense of his working for his royal predecessors, Ashurnasirpal II also describes himself as "the avenger of his fathers" (*mutīr gimilli abbīšu*) (AE1:i21).

249 This man was apparently a legendary eastern Anatolian ruler from the Old Assyrian Period, remembered well into Neo-Assyrian times (Yamada 2000: 104 n. 99).

II in Kurkh (AI18, SI13), and at the Tigris source his artisans carved images beside that of Tiglath-pileser I (SI16–17). In an extreme form of this associating with previous Assyrian rulers, Shalmaneser IV commissioned an inscription on a monument of Adad-narari III (S4E1, An3I5).

A king's modelling of his royal inscriptions closely on one/those of his predecessors is a similar phenomenon. The royal inscriptions of Tiglath-pileser I e.g. are echoed, especially concerning warfare narration, in those of eNA I-kings (Schramm 1973: 14–17). Earlier royal iconography could also be a source of inspiration for later rulers. The Nabu Stele of Shamshi-Adad V can be used as an example of this as well as of the integration approach between text and image (SA5I1). The stele depicts the king making the pointing gesture near divine emblems, while its text gives an annalistic inscription (SA5E1). The archaic-shaped beard of the king and the archaic cuneiform palaeography here served to associate the ruling king with his distant and powerful predecessor Shamshi-Adad I (Reade 1979a: 341–42; Grayson 1996: 180–81). The description in the annals of the king facing a grand rebellion (SA5E1:i39–53) is reminiscent of the similar royal narrations from the Sargonic and Old Akkadian Period (Franke 1995). The combined message of text and image is that Shamshi-Adad V was a heroic, traditional ruler.

The theme of "heroic priority" also stresses the predominance of the king as well as the vital role of the royal line. It was the duty of every king to surpass his predecessors either in war or in building (Garelli 1982: 24). Also in the texts of the Early Neo-Assyrian kings "heroic priority" is frequently expressed. In Shalmaneser III's case, it can refer to him entering regions unknown to his predecessors (e.g. SE1:20–21), as producing unprecedented harvests (SE6:iv45–46), or as creating comparatively outstanding monuments (e.g. SE27:9–11). As for Ashurnasirpal II, he claims to have entered mountains and cities which none of his predecessors had ever visited (e.g. AE1:i50, AE1:ii73 resp.), he builds temples and decorates palaces and temples in a grander way than previous rulers had managed (e.g. AE40:36, AE56:16 resp.), and he imposes levels of tribute higher than ever before (AE1:ii78–79). He also fashions a divine statue and builds temples which had not existed before (AE1:ii133, AE30:53–55 resp.), and he triumphantly states that the ruler of Suhu had not delivered tribute formerly (AE1:i100).

In yet other, and perhaps more special, ways of expressing heroic priority, the enemy army is sometimes described as massive or beyond counting (e.g. AE1:iii52, SE2:i32), presumably in order to stress the major achievement of the king in defeating it. When the Assyrian army by contrast is described as innumerable, the aim is probably to express the great power of the king (e.g. SE16:88′). In a related imagery, Adad-narari III claims that he managed to defeat the whole of Hatti and Amurru (basically the entire Syrian-Palestine coastal area) "in (just) one year" (*ina ištēt šatti*) (e.g. An3E7:4–5), in this way articulating a comparison with his predecessors who supposedly needed more time to defeat their formidable opponents (Tadmor 1973: 143). Expressing another very special way of enacting heroic priority, Adad-narari II claims to have used a military technique not used before by any of his predecessors on the throne (An2E2:53–54). In sum, it was the *king* and not "the Assyrians" who were the main protagonist of the often antagonistic power relations. *Kingship* was the primary identity of the ten rulers.

Although the king mostly describes himself as acting heroically alone, the primary sources do occasionally – especially in iconography and the state documents – present him as the head of an Assyrian ruling class. As noted in subsection 1.7.2, this class consisted of the king, his higher officials and courtiers, and their respective social affiliations. Identifying such an institutionalized Assyrian ruling class, Parpola (1995a) has even suggested that the highest Neo-Assyrian officials,[250] together with the king, formed a royal cabinet or council in analogy with the divine council. Similarly, Roaf (2008: 209) has suggested that the genii in the North-West Palace allude to the vital role of human sages (i.e. the king's scholars) in the palace. In the same vein, Ataç (2010: 201) highlights the role and influence of the king's scholars. Pongratz-Leisten (2013: 292–93) centres on the role of scholars in shaping power relations by (re)creating the authority of kingship. According to these interpretations – at least that of Parpola – the relevant socio-economic class functioned also as an *ideological* entity in addition to an underlying practical one. As will be shown below, this understanding is valid even if not embracing the elaborate and controversial idea on an analogous human council.

Both Ashurnasirpal II and Shalmaneser III are depicted accompanied by an entourage which typically consists of bodyguards, attendants (sunshade, napkin, and fly wisk bearers), and various officials (e.g. AI13:23–24, SI14:6a). The high official standing in front of the king wears a diadem which may indicate his status of son and crown prince (Reade 2009: 262), or possibly he was brother to the king (Reade 1967: 46). High officials were sometimes of royal descent in the Neo-Assyrian empire (Grayson 1993: 30). Alternatively, the king's "field marshal" (*turtānu*) may be the one illustrated, reporting to the king on the successes of the campaign. The individuals, both eunuchs (*ša rēši*)

250 Namely the field marshal (*turtānu*), the chief eunuch (*rab ša rēši*), the chief cup-bearer (*rab šaqê*), the vizier (*šukkallu*), the treasurer (*masennu*), the chief judge (*sartennu*), the palace herald (*nāgir ekalli*), the chief scholar (*ummânu*), and the governors (*bēl pīḫati* or *šakin māti*). For a discussion on the statuses and functions of these officials, see Mattila 2000.

and bearded ones (*ša ziqni*), who are depicted with greeting or clasped hands in these scenes may possibly portray other high members of the ruling class in question, such as the chief eunuch (*rab ša rēši*) who was another official with extensive military duties (Mattila 2000: 70–76).[251] The man who introduces processions to the king by waving (?) may be "the palace herald" (*nāgir ekalli*). The king along with the described entourage form a special cluster in these scenes. In this way, the artisans managed to focus on the elite as well as on just the king. The said cluster can also be expressed, as on an ivory plaque probably belonging to Shalmaneser III (SI21), in the shape of a banquet scene. The king here evidently hosts a banquet which has six seated guests, supposedly high officials and courtiers.[252]

If the iconography of the Early Neo-Assyrian kings on the whole seems to support the idea of a ruling class, inscriptions largely portray them as sole heroes. However, there are examples of officials having prominent roles also in the textual source base proper of this study. Beginning with the earliest phase of the Early Neo-Assyrian Period, a field marshal of Adad-narari II is honoured by being named (other than as a *limmu*) in the context of a campaign narration of the said ruler (An2E2:64). Two high officials are also named in their roles as leaders of a certain building project of Adad-narari II (An2E1:20′–21′rev.). Cities are described as handed over to the Assyrian magnates in the royal inscriptions of Adad-narari II and Tukulti-Ninurta II, forming a special theme in the texts from this period (Schramm 1973: 14). All in all, officials are not often highlighted in the sources of this phase.

Continuing with the evidence from Ashurnasirpal II's reign, the strength of the high, royal officials is especially conveyed in ideological sources from the loosely controlled outer core. Mushezib-Ninurta, the governor of Shadikanni, refers to himself as a "vice-regent" (*iššakku*) who has his own "palace" (*ekallu*) (AE151:1). This palace is archaeologically attested through the remains of colossi and lions at the doorways, and through reliefs on orthostats and stelae (AI6, AI10). In the iconographic sources from Kalhu, a few depictions in relief form illustrate officials in leading positions, possibly representing the king in his absence (e.g. AI4:B7t.). Moreover, decorated cylinder seals from the 9th century BCE show eunuchs taking the king's role in the sacred tree scene (see Collon 1987: figs. 812, 866), although it is probably wrong to see a real usurpation of the king's priestly role. Considering the ample sources from this reign, the emphasis on officials is modest.

---

251 This official may also be seen standing under a canopy, receiving captives or standing alone, in the iconography of Early Neo-Assyrian kings (AI4:B7t., SI10:13b. resp.).

252 Such royal banquets are spoken of in Middle Assyrian texts (Glassner 1987–90: 263).

As for the reign of Shalmaneser III, there are more examples of the emphasis on officials. His later field marshal Dajjan-Ashur conducted campaigns in the king's name (e.g. SE14:175–76). This stress on an official in Assyrian royal inscriptions is very rare. Consequently, Reade (1981a: 159) and Yamada (2000: 325–32) have both referred to the Black Obelisk as a monument of Dajjan-Ashur. Schneider (1991: 242–49) argues, inspired by Olmstead's theory of Dajjan-Ashur as the actual ruler, that this official was much and "unduly" emphasized in the final edition of Shalmaneser III's annals. In the same vein, Fuchs (2008: 65–66) claims that references to the *second* eponymat of NN (normally reserved for the king) in fact refers to that of Dajjan-Ashur and not to that of the king, and he even suggests that Shalmaneser III was out of play in the 820's, with Dajjan-Ashur completely in charge. I should add here that also Shalmaneser III's earlier field marshal, Ashur-bel-ka"in, plays a prominent role in a royal inscription dated to 856 BCE (SE17:10–30). Last but not least, the mayor of Kalhu, Shamash-bela-usur, in his turn actually dedicated a throne base and several door sills to the king's review palace of Fort Shalmaneser (e.g. SE57:7, SE30:32–34 resp.).

Regarding influential officials in the reign of Shamshi-Adad V, a man named Mutarris-Ashur, who was the chief eunuch of the relevant ruler, is similarly and positively highlighted in the royal annals. This official is described as having excellent personal qualities, and as conducting warfare by the orders of the king in question (SA5E1:ii17–18). The field marshal Bel-luballit and the treasurer (and later field marshal) Jahalu commissioned monuments in their own right. The former's stone vessel is described as dedicated for his life, not mentioning the king, to the Nergal temple of Tarbisu (SA5I2, SA5E12), and the latter's clay cube has a text focusing on his own eponymate (SE130). These sources also tell of relative emphasis.

It is however with the first half of the 8th century BCE that the emphasis on officials in state-sponsored sources reaches its peak (Grayson 1996: 200–201). The mayor Bel-tarsi-ilumma dedicates a pair of statues representing the god Nabu to the Nabu temple of Kalhu, while stating that Adad-narari III and Sammuramat were his superiors (An3I8, An3E26:8–9). The provincial governor Nergal-erish, who was given much authority in a preserved decree (An3E9), dedicates a stele to the god Shulmanu on behalf of Adad-narari III (An3E42). Royal grants and decrees from this period show that the high officials aquired great wealth in the service of the king, e.g. through land protected from taxation (An3E48–54). Telling of this quite noteworthy internal power relationship, officials refer to deities (and not the king) as their "lords" (*bēlu*) (e.g. An3E37), and the king and an official jointly greet various deities on a seal (An3I12). A dedication of a cylinder seal is stated as being made for the lives of the governor of Assur and the king (An3E40).

Two high officials of this period deserve special attention for their great influence in relation to the authority of the Assyrian king, namely the provincial governor Bel-Harran-beli-usur and the field marshal Shamshi-ilu. Integrating text and image, the Tell Abta Stele shows the former in royal poses (S4I1), while the text states that Bel-Harran-beli-usur created a city in the desert, that he named it after himself, and that he protected it from taxes and other impositions. Moreover, he claims to have received building orders from above (from the deities), he created the stele and placed it in a temple, and he provided for the deities of his new city. Furthermore, his name is actually mentioned before that of the king's (S4E2). All this tell of his relative independence *vis-à-vis* the king in Kalhu (Grayson 1996: 241). Text and image here work together in conveying the message of this official's status.

Shamshi-ilu claims, in a text which has the same structure as a royal inscription (Grayson 1996: 231), a number of (royal) epithets for himself. He is "temple administrator" (*šatammu*), "conqueror" (*kāšidu*), "the one who fells (enemies)" (*mušamqitu*), "overwhelmer (of enemies)" (*sāpinu*), and (like) the Anzu bird (An3E34:8–16). Elsewhere, he is also "fearless in battle" (*lā ādiru tuqumte*) (An3E35:3′). He also gives a campaign narration and talks of a dedication of two gateway lions without mentioning the king, and moreover calls his provincial city "my lordly city" (*āl bēlūtija*) (An3E34:19–24). He establishes "(city) privileges" (*kidinnu*) in another place (An3E35:12′). Shamshi-ilu (?) also claims to have built a city next to Baltil (inner Assur), and depositing a *narû* there upon the completion of it (An3E36). Moreover, Adad-narari III and Shamshi-ilu are establishing a border together (An3E2:4–8), and the latter also claims that he defeated Damascus and established another border by himself (Grayson 1996: 240), even if the name and titles of the relevant ruler in this case is included in the text (S4E1:4–13). Shamshi-ilu may also be seen on the Antakya Stele (An3I6).

The royal propaganda can not hide the existence of another but symbiotic power faction in Neo-Assyrian society.[253] The thesis of Siddall (2013) that the emergence of very powerful officials in the 8th century BCE merely is a result of a controlled administrative reform seems much forced in light of the obvious usurpations. Still, both Bel-Harran-beli-usur and Shamshi-ilu refer to their

253 This power was institutionalized to some degree. High officials erected stelae in the Row of Stelae between the city walls of Assur (Reade 2004a), and the eponyms defined the most powerful people of the day, namely the king and his high officials (Larsen 1976: 192–217). The eponym lists and chronicles also naturally highlight these officials (see Millard 1994). Also, "the chief scholars" (*ummânu*) of Assyrian kings are mentioned along with the king in Assyrian or synchronistic king lists (see Grayson 1980–83: 116–25, texts 3.11–12, 14, 17).

kings, telling of an idea of a single body. The general confusion and arbitraryness in the use of the pronouns *I* and *he* in the narration of Dajjan-Ashur's deeds may also express the idea of a single unit, i.e. the Assyrian ruling class, carrying out the feats (e.g. SE14:185). Similarly, the Assyrian army fly, as a single body, like the Anzu bird against the enemy army (SE5:iii5, e.g. AE19:74). Within the ruling class, there were both centripetal (working for decentralization) and centrifugal (working for centralization) forces at play. Sometimes the kings were relatively powerful, while at other times the nobility and the high officials were relatively powerful. In other words, it was a zero-sum game. Although seemingly in conflict, the king and his officials lived in symbiosis, and thus formed the Assyrian ruling class.

Arguably, the socio-economic factor rather than any identity based on ethnicity then defined the king's side. As noted by Lamprichs (1995: 381) in his work on the structure of the Neo-Assyrian empire, the population of the empire was divided, both in core and periphery, according to the lines of elite and people. The elites frequently interacted with each other, having the supposed ethnical boundaries systematically crossed. The elite and people of both core and periphery of a certain polity were on the other hand alienated from each other.[254] Authority was given to the Neo-Assyrian king by the elites of which the former was a member. Internal and external elites functioned as pillars in the spreading of imperial ideology, and they were "the essential ingredient in the institution of kingship" (Parker 2011: 358–59, 364, 376). The idea of a nation state fighting another is further complicated by the population structure of these alleged nations. The issue if for example slaves counted as part of these national communities arises. Taken together, the socio-economic dividing line seems far more relevant, isolating the Assyrian king and the ruling class as the righteous "unit of analysis" on earth.

Summing up, the often attested antagonistic relations in Assyrian state ideology are not described in terms of a dichtomy Assyrian/foreign, but rather in terms of the king, alone or as part of a ruling class, against "the enemy". Assisted by his magnates, the king had the duty to realize the theoretical world dominion of the Mesopotamian deities. Kingship and class-belonging manifest the primary identities of the Early Neo-Assyrian kings.

5.4.8 Self versus Other: identity and alterity

In this subsection, I will more firmly centre on the applying of post-colonial theory. The Orientalist notions of Oriental despotism, violence, and decadence

254 For this perception of the Mesopotamian society as binary divided into rulers and the ruled, see also the recent anthology edited by Charvát and Maříková Vlčková (2010).

in literature will be identified and discussed, and the polarization according to which the foreign lands and people in their exposure to alterity are "Chaos", "the Other", and "the subaltern" in the sources is then focused on.

As for the images of the Neo-Assyrian Period and kings in non-scholarly literature, the judgement on the character of the Neo-Assyrian empire has been harsh. Already the Babylonians commented negatively on its nature. Their priests explained the fall of Assyria as the result of divine retribution for the alleged sins committed by its kings (Beaulieu 2005: 57). In the Hebrew Bible, the Assyrians are seen as merciless conquerors and as the agents as well as the ultimate victims of the divine wrath which Yahweh inflicted upon the Hebrews. Prophets like Isaiah, Hoshea, and Nahum condemn the alleged decadence, sins, and hybris of the Assyrian state and kings.

Also classical Graeco-Roman sources sometimes focus on ancient Assyria (Rollinger 2011; Weissert 2011). The sources in question combine a picture of Assyria containing admiration for its imperial achievements and statements about the brutality and decadence of its rulers (Frahm 2006: 74–78). As for the aspect of decadence, the excesses and depravity, but also femininity, of the Assyrian king Sardanapalos (probably alluding to Ashurbanipal) are identified and highlighted, and the Assyrian-Babylonian queen Semiramis (probably referring to Sammuramat) is described as a she-devil, in her cruel and despotic ways (McCall 1998: 184–85; Asher-Greve 2006).

Progressing from ancient times, the image of ancient Assyria in Europe has often been negatively stereotyped and long dependent on the Bible and the classical authors (Frahm 2006: 74–78). As noted by Cancik-Kirschbaum (2011: 368 n. 49), the identification of the Assyrians as part of a Semitic nation has also been made and emphasized, within the historical frames of anti-Semitism and Nazism. Also scholars are, as well as have been, much influenced by the Bible and Graeco-Roman sources. As noted by Holloway (2006b: i–xviii) in his anthology on Assyriology and Orientalism, this has often resulted in an Orientalist discourse. Ancient Assyria is here pictured as "the Other" and as the archetypal Orient (Fales 2010: 13–17). Oriental violence, despotism, and decadence are three important elements of Orientalism (Said 1978), and the Neo-Assyrian empire is, as well as has been, seen as a typical representative of these cultural characteristics (Bahrani 2003; Fales 2009: 28 n. 3; Richardson 2010: xix). In marked contrast to the above, the ancient Assyrians are seen, by laymen and some scholars alike (e.g. Parpola 2004), as the ancestors, in a positive light, to the ethnic group of present-day Assyrians. Ideas about ancient Assyria as a true nation state, bearing a direct link to modern times, are commonly expressed in these contexts.

Expressions of the said Orientalist notions of Oriental despotism, violence and decadence have been noted throughout this study, but in order to get an overview, a brief and concise summary will be given here. The notion of Oriental despotism was confronted by pointing to the sources which tell of a pious priest-king and not of a worldly-centred tyrant, whatever that image was worth in real life. More importantly, the identifying of a ruling class speaks against the idea of the sole and remote Oriental ruler who gets juxtaposed with the (positively) stereotyped "Occidental" ruler. The notion of Oriental violence was focused on when I identified a logic in the Assyrian use of violence, telling of discriminate violence along the lines of a reciprocity principle which says that violence is only used against those who had done something bad in the eyes of the Assyrian king. The notion of Oriental decadence, lastly, was confronted by looking at the priestly role of the king, and I also noted that royal hunting is often religiously motivated and not an occupation of a bored, sporting, and reckless Oriental ruler. Moreover, the decadence of debauchery is nowhere to be seen in the sources. These rather tell of restraint on the part of the king and of the low exposure of women. The atrocity of rape is e.g. neither talked of nor visualized in the sources.

The constantly expressed *polarization* between the Assyrian king and the enemy ruler tells of the need for post-colonial theory to be used. The enemy is stereotypically portrayed as the direct opposite of the king, thus expressing his chaotic nature. In more theoretical terms, and clearly telling of alterity, he is also "the Other" and "the subaltern". The enemy is "the rebel" who dares to be unsubmissive towards the king and therefore towards Ashur. He is here e.g. presented as "the obstinate enemy" (*nakru šapṣu*) (SE40:iii6). In terms of personal qualities, the enemy ruler is treacherous, i.e. breaks oaths and treaties, he is ungrateful, arrogant, hostile, or even mad (Fales 1982: 427–31).[255] As succinctly expressed by Fales (1982: 427), the enemy in Assyrian royal inscriptions "either does what he is not supposed to do, or does not do what he is supposed to do". In the enemy ruler's status of subaltern, he is both different and subordinate. The Assyrian king on the other hand stands as the good example, representing Order in a cosmic struggle (Maul 1999). In terms of identity, he represents "the Self" in the sources.[256]

The enemy ruler goes against the divinely sanctioned Order when he resists the Assyrian king. Instead of "trusting" (*takālu*) in the Mesopotamian dei-

255 The other way around, the Neo-Babylonian king Nabonidus in his texts contemptuously (Tadmor 2011: 674 n. 42) calls Sennacherib king of Subartu, one who planned evil, desecrated holy sites, had no mercy, and the like (see Langdon 1912: 270–72, col. i, lines 7–40).

256 The following paragraphs will mainly focus on "the Other" (the enemy side) and those aspects which belong to him that have not been treated so far in this study. The aspects belonging to "the Self" (the Assyrian ruling class) have been considerably explored already.

ties and their Order, the enemy ruler trusts "in himself" (*ana ramānišu*) (Fales 1982: 427–31), or as in the texts of Shalmaneser III "in each others (a coalition's) help" (*ana rēṣūti aḫāmiš*), "in the massiveness of his troops" (*ana gipiš ummānātišu*), or "[in] remote [highlands]" ([*ina ḫuršāni*] *birūti*) used as a place of refuge (SE2:i43, SE2:i32, SE17:37 resp.). The resisting enemy of Ashurnasirpal II additionally trusts "in his might" (*ana emūqīšu*) and "in his extensive Kassite troops" (*ana ummānāt māt Kašši rapši*) (AE1:iii39, AE1:iii17 resp.). The resisting enemy forces also trusted "in their numerous troops" (*ana ummānātišunu madāte*) (e.g. AE1:iii52), "in their strong walls" (*ana dūrīšunu dannūte*) (AE1:i114), and in "their fortified city and a rugged mountain" (*āl dannūtišunu u šadû marṣu*) (AE17:ii52–53). Basically, the enemy trusted in everything else than in the deities, and by doing so he was godless and presumptuous (Kuhrt 1997: 516). The Assyrian side put their trust in the divine, while the enemy trusted in the human-profane (Liverani 1995: 2361). The former side, i.e. the Assyrian king, in this regard presented himself as a pious, humble, and God-fearing priest and servant of the deities (see s. 4.2). The polarity of piety versus impiety is thus clearly expressed.

A related polarization, which also can signify the dichotomy of Self/Other, focuses on the theme of the fleeing enemy ruler. As proved already in subsection 5.4.2, the theme of the fright and flight of the enemy ruler is extremely common. In the said subsection, it was also shown that the fright and flight of the subaltern enemy often was caused by the royal (but ultimately divine) radiance which was directed at the foreign elites and people, in this way related to the just discussed theme of not trusting in the deities. Anyway, while the corageous Assyrian king without hesitation marches out to engage in battle, the enemy ruler either makes an initial futile attempt to resist and then flees, or he flees without ever trying to resist. Most often he takes refugee to a mountain peak (e.g. AE17:iii59–61, SE6:i68–69). This kind of juxtaposition also highlights the non-national character of the antagonism. More relevantly, it conveys the said dichotomy of Self/Other.[257]

As for his or theirs chaotic nature in terms of violence, the subaltern enemy side is sometimes considered to be wild. The epithet which tells of "the fierce and merciless kings from sunrise to sunset" has already been mentioned (e.g. AE2:20–21, SE5:i4–5). More specifically, the ruler Ahuni of Til-Barsip is e.g. said to "start hostilities" (*igranni*), and to be arrogantly and violently "roaming about with force and strength" (*šipṣu u danānu iltakanu*) (SE2:i32, SE20:7–8 resp.). The same action, i.e. fierce warfare, is positive and "ordered" if conduct-

257 The theme of the fleeing enemy will be explored further in subsection 5.4.9.

ed by the Assyrian king, but negative and "chaotic" if exercised by the enemy, devaluatingly called "the man of GN" (*amēl* GN).[258] Certain words in the Akkadian vocabulary concerning warfare, such as *kitru* and *katāru*, were actually restricted to describe the behaviour of foreign troops (Liverani 1982b). In this view on things, a polarity between ordered and chaotic violence is expressed. The discriminate violence of the Early Neo-Assyrian kings relates only to the former type of violence.

In his act of exercising chaotic violence, the enemy is thus seen as wild. The subaltern enemy is even likened to a chaotic, wild beast when he is described as being subjected to the Assyrian king's act of "capturing" (*ṣabātu*, *kašādu*). Hostile foreign elites and people are in several passages explicitly described as being captured (e.g. AE1:i82, SE2:ii46). The claims that the Assyrian king "took (cities or the enemy ruler with his goods and people) for myself (himself)" (*ana ramānija aṣbat*), or that "he brought (humans and things) for myself" (*ana pānija uterra*) may be similarly understood (e.g. AE1:iii101, SE5:iii5–6 resp.). The Early Neo-Assyrian kings also claim to have "confined" (*esēru*) enemy rulers to their cities by the act of besieging (e.g. AE1:iii46, SE40:iii6–7). The verb *esēru* is also used to describe the predicament of birds in a cage (CAD E: *esēru* B), a simile famously used to describe Hezekiah in the annals of Sennacherib (see RINAP3/1: text 4:52). The wild nature and mentality of the enemy is conveyed by these portrayals. The Assyrian king naturally stands at the opposite pole of this imagery, not the least in his role of hunter in which he slays and captures wild beasts (see s. 5.2). He is here "the Self", and represents the only valid perspective.

As a further testimony of the chaotic character of the obstinate foreign ruler, this agent is also described as suffering mentally. The Babylonian usurper Marduk-bel-usate is e.g. "the one who did not know what he was doing" (*lā mūdê alakte ramānišu*), literally "he who did not know his own behaviour" (SE5:iv4). As already shown in subsection 5.4.7, the Early Neo-Assyrian rulers are by contrast presented as wise. Although from a text of the later Sargonid period, Sennacherib refers to the king of Elam as someone "who has neither reason nor intelligence", with the failing qualities being *ṭēmu* and *milku* (see RINAP3/1: text 22:v33–34). Similarly, the arch-enemy of Sargon II, i.e. Rusa of Urartu, is described as getting mentally (?) ill in the observation that "he threw himself onto his bed like a woman in labour" (*kīma ḫarišti ina erši innadi*) after having fled from Sargon II and his army (see Mayer 1983: 83, line 151). Additionally, an outright feminization (see subs. 5.4.9) of the enemy ruler takes

---

258 This occasionally attested expression arguably carries the notion of disrespect or even contempt, and may express some kind of *damnatio memoriae* (Fales 2011: 221).

place through the cited simile (Chapman 2004: 37).[259] Anyway, the described "Other" is regarded as insain.

Summing up, I centred, more firmly, on the use of post-colonial theory in this subsection. The Orientalist notions of Oriental despotism, decadence, and violence in literature were identified and discussed, and the dichotomy according to which the foreign lands and people in their exposure to alterity are "Chaos", "the Other", and "the subaltern" in the primary sources was then focused on. The relevant juxtaposition was achived by polarizations.

5.4.9 Gendered roles and relations

Gender also played a role in the world view of the Assyrian kings, and this will now be discussed. Focusing especially on the role of warfare, I will argue that the Assyrian king is presented as "the dominant male" and that the other side is portrayed as emasculated or even feminized. Firstly, after a very brief introduction, gender construction in ancient Assyria is discussed, and after that the gendered dimension of Assyrian propaganda is centred on.

Gender studies have become an important part of research within the humanities. Still, as noted by Pollock and Bernbeck (2000: 150), analyses based on gender theory have comparatively rarely been made in the discipline of Assyriology. For example, Liverani (1979: 305–14), i.e. a major authority on the topic, ignores the gender aspect of Mesopotamian, or more precisely Assyrian, state ideology altogether in his overview of underpinning polarities. Moreover, most of the gender analyses which have been conducted rather subscribe to an atomistic, first wave approach in which the pursuit of "finding women in the sources" without taking overarching patriarchal structures into account seems to be the overall aim. In the following paragraphs, I will focus on the social role of gender by discussing the connotations masculinity and femininity may have had in ancient Assyria.

In the much attested topic of warfare, there is a clear divide between men and women. Warfare is a male domain in royal inscriptions and iconography. Violence and dominance feature as vital components of a Mesopotamian king's ideal masculinity (Bahrani 2008: 107). Winter (1996: 11–15), in her discussion on the symbolism of the image of Naram-Sin on his victory stele, centres on masculinity while arguing that the king represents himself rhetorically as "the dominant male". His sexuality, expressed through his bare skin and muscles,

---

259 Roaf (2012) suggests that the passage on Rusa's flight tells of suicide. However, in light of the imagery of child bearing, the feminization aspect seems more relevant to focus on here.

is linked to potency, which is linked to male vigor, which in its turn is linked to authority and dominance. Ashurnasirpal II, who represented himself in much the same way, therefore also comes across as "the dominant male" (Winter 1997: 370–71). On the basis of the androcentrism of Assyrian society, Assyrian imperial ideology was a nuanced interplay between sex, gender, and power in which a masculinized dominant class stood against a feminized Other, with coercion forming the basis (Assante 2007: 384).[260] Violence was a male domain in ancient Mesopotamia/Assyria.[261]

Chapman (2004: 1, 3–7, 20) argues that the battleground was regarded as the site of a masculinity contest, and that Assyrian royal inscriptions consistently convey a gendered language through their emphasis on military matters. The Assyrian king in this context represented ideal masculinity, while the foreign enemy who was fused into a single Other stood for failed masculinity or even feminization.[262] The polarity in question served to divide the male sex into legitimate and illegitimate members,[263] and had the aim of justifying unequal relations of power. Outright feminization is above all attested in the curse sections of Neo-Assyrian treaties which sometimes contain threats to turn the opposing enemy or enemies into women if he or they should break the relevant oath (Chapman 2004: 40–58). Warfare was clearly tied to masculinity in ancient Assyria. The related pursuit of royal hunting may be understood similarly, in that it was used to display the king's manly strength and courage (Pollock and Bernbeck 2000: 162; Chapman 2004: 13, 23–34). Women are not part of hunting scenes, neither in texts nor in images, and the relevant patron deities are the male ones of Nergal and Ninurta.

---

260 Somewhat ironically, Assyrian kings and soldiers are, in the late Egyptian story-cycle of king Petubastis, themselves portrayed as cowardly and effeminate, arguably carrying the same degrading meaning (see e.g. Lichtheim 2006 III: 155/iii 40–41). Furthermore, Assyria, or "Khor" (Lichtheim 2006 III: 156 n. 5), is also described as made into (?) a "widow" by Egypt, here explicitly expressing feminization (see Lichtheim 2006 II: 77/line 32 of the page).
261 The idea that the conclusion that warfare was a male domain in Assyria is "banal" is valid only if accepting that warfare everywhere and in all times has been a male prerogative.
262 As for the gendered nature of Assyrian royal inscriptions, the Hittite annals are called *pišnadar* in Hittite, a word which can be translated "manliness" or "manly deeds" (Güterbock 1983: 30–31). Since Hittite historiography by many is regarded as inspiring the genre of Assyrian royal inscriptions (e.g. Goetze 1957: 174–75; Güterbock 1957), this is highly noteworthy. Discussing mainly from the curse sections of Hittite texts, Hoffner (1966) shows that masculinity in the Ancient Near East was tied to war, weapons, and sexual virility, while femininity was connected to symbols such as mirrors, distaffs, and specific clothing.
263 The "chief eunuch" (*rab ša rēši*), who was an important military officer, clearly represented the male side in this confrontation, if not seeing him as representing a "third gender".

There are examples of female elements "encroaching" upon the masculine sphere of warfare. Concluding from more mundane sources, border crossing women of Assyrian society – here women exercising black magic – were seen as an anomaly, and as a threat to dominant, male norms (Rollin 1983: 44). Not only female practicians of black magic but also the goddess Ishtar, who is much associated with warfare, were regarded as expressions of this chaotic "liminal femininity". Ishtar conveys in her not androgynous duality a "derailed normative femininity" and "radical alterity" which symbolizes a Chaos gendered female. Her sexuality, i.e. she is also connected to love and sexuality (Black and Green 1992: 108–109), is here identified as the source of her dangerous nature, having the potential to wreak havoc upon the dominant norms (Bahrani 2001: 141–60). In the treaty of Ashur-narari V with Mati'-ilu, Ishtar is tellingly and in a liminal sense called both "mistress of femininity and masculinity" (*bēlat sinnišūti bēlit° zikarūti*) (An5E2:v12). Liminal femininity may also be expressed in the epithet of Kutushar of "lady who is the like of Anu and Dagan" (*bēltu šinnat Anum° u Dagan*) (e.g. SA5E1:i18–19). It must be said though that normally male deities were the ones associated with violence and military activities. Nergal, Ninurta, and the Sibitti were all patrons of war (Black and Green 1992: 136, 143, 162).

Arguably, these border crossing examples weigh lightly in the context of the almost complete absence of any women acting through warfare in royal inscriptions and iconography. A notable exception is Sammuramat who seemingly is portrayed as engaged in warfare activities, border establishing, and stele erecting in Syria at the side of her son Adad-narari III (An3E3:1–18). These two are also on the same hierarchical level in the text on a pair of statues from the Nabu temple (An3E26:8–9). Sammuramat also had a stele of her own in the Row of Stelae in Assur, told of in the accompanying text (An3E25). However, this queen may be understood as acting simply as a widow working for her deceased husband (Shamshi-Adad V) in taking care of his child, and not being formally powerful in her own right (Siddall 2013: 99–100). As concluded by Siddall (2013: 100), "Assyrian royal ideology could not accommodate the presence of an authoritative female figure".

As concluded already in subsection 1.7.2, it is clear both from texts and images that political positions in Assyria more or less were reserved for men. At least in this sense, Assyrian women were subordinated, living in a patriarchal society and state. Also the coloured descriptions of foreign courts only highlight male figures in political contexts. In one passage, the king, his brother, and his sons are enumerated as if only they mattered, expressing the ideal of patrilinearity and hence the political system of patrimonialism which centred on the male line (AE1:i100–101). Relations between political leaders revolved, not the least in the Amarna correspondence and age, around the concept of "brotherhood" (*aḫḫūtu*), while vassals, i.e. subordinates, were referred to as "sons" (*māru*) (Liverani 1990; Tadmor 2011: 619). In the human sphere, political power was intimately connected to masculinity.

Also in the divine sphere, there was an intertwining of power and gender, in that goddesses generally play a peripheral role among the group of great gods (see apps. 4–7).[264] Moreover, they are often defined either as mothers, wives, or sisters or daughters to a male deity, thus expressing their subordination through dependency. For example, Ninlil is a mother (e.g. SA5E15:5, An3E34:13), Gula is a wife (e.g. An3E34:8), and Sharrat-niphi is a sister (e.g. AE28:i3) of male deities. In a long deity list of a treaty, a number of gods are mentioned, *followed* by their respective, less-known goddess-spouses (An5E2:vi7–24). Stol (2012: 403–404) and Bottéro (2001a) here refer to "the decline of the goddesses" in the history of religion in Mesopotamia. Thus, the male domain was associated with political power in the sources, while the female one was connected to the *lack* of political power.

As noted already in subsection 1.7.2, the relative invisibility of Assyrian women – or of any woman acting in her own right – in the ideological sources is another point in the case. M. Marcus (1995a: 2498) interprets the absence of women on the throne base and Black Obelisk as serving to support the legitimacy of the patriarchal power structure by making women invisible. Not even Assyrian queens are highlighted in the state art (Ornan 2002: 461–65).[265] A glazed brick from Nineveh and the time of Ashurnasirpal II seems however to represent the queen, sitting on a throne, holding what seems to be an egg in her raised right hand, and wearing her typical mural crown. An attendant stands behind her, and the whole scene is decorated with rosettes, symbolizing Ishtar (AI21). The textual evidence is equally poor. Also, as already observed in subsection 1.7.2, the proper word for "queen" (*šarratu*) refers only to goddesses or foreign (ruling) queens (Melville 2004: 43, 51).[266] The Assyrian queen is simply referred to as "she of the palace" (*sēgallu*). Consequently, Melville (2004: 37) talks of a "male-oriented society" and of a view of the Assyrian

---

264 The goddesses Ishtar and Sharrat-niphi form exceptions to this rule. For Ishtar as having moved into a masculine sphere of violence and dominance, see Bahrani 2001: 141–60. The epithet of Ninlil, "foremost of the deities" (*ašaretti ilāni*), is also noteworthy (An3E34:13).

265 Assyrian queens may however be represented by the motif of scorpions, connected to the names and images of queens. As scorpions they arguably served as the complementary counterpart to the royal lion, expressing their role of "mother of the land" (Galter 2007).

266 Turning to the primary sources of this study, Ishtar and Sharrat-niphi are described by the epithet of *šarratu* in some of Ashurnasirpal II's inscriptions (AE99:1, AE28:i1 resp.).

political sphere as a "male sphere of influence". The structurally strong positions of queens in Egypt and the Hittite state are certainly not attested in Assyria (Kuhrt 1997).

In fact, only a pair of Assyrian queens, namely Sammuramat and Naqi'a/Zaqutu, are described as politically important (Macgregor 2012: 82–85, 95–122), forming exceptions to the rule.[267] The strong role which the queen-mother Naqi'a/Zaqutu seems to have had in the reign of Esarhaddon should not be seen as telling of a structurally based strong position of power for women (Melville 1999). More often, we do not even know the names of the king's wives (Barberon 2011). The matronym (adding to the patronym) of Adad-narari III of "son of Sammuramat" (*mār Sammurāmat*) is a prominent exception to the rule of almost invisible Assyrian queens (An3E3:2–3). This queen is merely called "the palace woman" (*sēgallu*) of Shamshi-Adad V, "the mother" (*ummu*) of Adad-narari III, and "the daughter-in-law" (*kallatu*) of Shalmaneser III (An3E25:2–6), and she is not called *šarratu*. Moreover, as tentatively concluded by Svärd (2012: 232), the Neo-Assyrian queens tend to take on a male-gendered role in the primary sources. To summarize the discussion in this and the preceding paragraph, the "invisibility" of Assyrian women in the ideological sources also indicates their subordinate status.

Assyrian palace reliefs convey a male world of sport and war, with women present only as weak and passive agents (Collins 2008: 25). When (foreign) women are indeed depicted in Assyrian state art, they tend to be represented as passive, anonymous deportees (Albenda 1987: 17–21). Women are here wailing with a hand on their heads (e.g. AI13:25–26, SI10:13b.), or making gestures of submission by one or two raised open hands in deportation rows or from the crenellations of city walls (e.g. AI4:B8b., SI10:3b.). Women are not molested or otherwise ill-treated neither in inscriptions nor in iconography, supposedly in recognition of their status of civilians and as belonging to the private, family sphere. The reliefs of Sennacherib are informative concerning this issue. Here, a woman captive seems to turn to her Assyrian soldier-guard as if he were her protector (see Barnett et al. 1998: pl. 393). Another Assyrian guard is even depicted providing female captives with water, thus caring for their needs, on an ivory plaque from Kalhu (see Mallowan and Davies 1970: fig. 94).[268] Anyway, women are clearly associated with weakness, anynomity, and passivity.

---

267 For another view, based on another definition of power and set of sources, see Svärd 2012: 90–135 (on queens) and 140–57 (on female administrators referred to as *šakintu*).

268 However, another guard seems to be threatening his women and children captives (by his stick), and in another scene Assyrian soldiers shoot their arrows at locations where also women are situated (see Barnett et al. 1998: pls. 84, 240–41, 454). It may be too rash to see these as exceptions to the rule, since the art narrative logic is not always easy to determine.

In several of these depictions women are portrayed as mothers, restricted to the family sphere. This may not so much reflect the artist's impression of foreign gender structures than conveying Assyrian values and norms (Schwyn 2006: 328–29). Processions of captives are frequently segregated according to sex. Women are here depicted with children or babies in their care (e.g. AI4:B5b., SI9). On a Neo-Assyrian seal from Nineveh, a veiled woman is seen holding a baby in her arms next to a soldier (see Collon 1987: fig. 752). The role of women as mothers or "begetters" (*ālittu*) is highlighted also in sections of curses (AE148:34). On an ivory plaque from the 9th century BCE, four veiled women are depicted at the crest of a city wall in their greeting, through music, a soldier who either arrives or departs (see Mallowan and Davies 1970: fig. 6). The dichotomy of private and female versus public and male may here be symbolized by the city wall. In conclusion, foreign and, in extension, Assyrian women seem thus not to have been associated with the public, political sphere in the major primary sources.[269]

To summarize this discussion on gender construction in Assyria, femininity was associated with weakness through its exclusion from warfare (liminal femininity excepted), as well as with (political) subordination and alienation. Masculinity had the connotations of military strength, as well as of (political) superiority and non-alienation. The Assyrian woman was the Other within the Self in Assyrian political discourse. The low status of women in the Assyrian patriarchal society is reflected in the passivity, subordination, and roles as outsiders which women display in Assyrian ideological sources. This status is then used in a gendered portrayal of the juxtaposed foreign ruler. The Assyrian king, representing ideal masculinity, here stands against an opponent characterized by failed masculinity or even feminization.

It is now time to focus on the gendered imagery of the Assyrian king. As noted above, ideal masculinity much emphasizes the quality of physical strength. Expressions of the dichotomy of male/female concerning the antagonism between the Assyrian king and the resisting foreign ruler, elites, and people thus often focus on this theme. Several epithets, such as the relatively common ones of "strong male" (*zikru dannu*) (e.g. AE1:i14, SE2:i9) and "heroic man" (*eṭlu qardu*) (e.g. AE1:i12, SE5:i1), here allude to the king as the paradigmatic male. Both nouns (*zikru*, *eṭlu*) convey notions of masculinity (CAD Z: *zikaru*, CAD E: *eṭlu*), and serve as "metaphors for successful masculine performance" (Chapman 2004: 23). The adjectives (*dannu*, *qardu*) both refer to strength, a primary trait of the ideal man engaged in the masculinity contest,

269 This image of Assyrian women being restricted to the private sphere may be, at least partly, revised by looking at other sources, as shown by the study of Macgregor (2012).

and show that royal masculinity first and foremost was associated with strength, heroism, and courage (Chapman 2004: 23–24).[270]

Beyond those two royal epithets specifically, Ashurnasirpal II once describes himself as solely *eṭlu* (AE66:4), and in six cases he identifies himself explicitly in a stative form as "manly" (*zikarāku*) (e.g. AE1:i33). Adad-narari II is additionally "the man of Ashur" (*eṭlu ša Aššur*) (An2E2:77). Stressing his physique, Tukulti-Ninurta II is "swift" (*munnarbāku*) (e.g. TN2E1:30). The very common title "strong king" (*šarru dannu*) (e.g. AE1:i9, SE1:1) can be regarded as a military title (Cifola 1995: 80). Since masculinity was enacted on the battlefield, this title is then part of the evidence of a gendered royal status. Similarly, Ashurnasirpal II refers to himself as "king whose strength is worthy of praise" (*šarru ša tanattašu° danānu*) and as "strong clamp" (*gišginû dannu*) (AE30:22, AE19:13 resp.).[271]

Consequently, the king's warfare is characterized by "manliness" (*zikrūtu, meṭlūtu*). He claims to have conducted warfare "with concentrated manliness (*ina kiṣir zikrūti*) like a wild bull", and he chases wild game with "the close combat of my (his) manliness" (*ina qitrub meṭlūtija*) (SE2:ii52, SE6:iv43–44 resp.). Both phrases, through their use of the dual keywords in question (*eṭlu, zikaru*), relate to notions of masculinity. As argued by Pollock and Bernbeck (2000: 162), the mastering of weapons and wild animals was associated with manliness and important males in Mesopotamia. The relevant manly warfare of the king is divine-like (see s. 3.2) and thus typically "merciless" (*lā pādû*) (SE5:i2, e.g. AE1:iii127), "fierce" (*ekdu*) (SE40:i2, e.g. AE1:i19), "furious" (*ezzu*) (e.g. AE40:13–15), and "very wild" (*šitmurru*) (e.g. AE19:72–73). The Assyrian king's knowledge on warfare was superior to that of his opponents (Fuchs 2012: 35). Occasionally, the king's opponents are also described as strong, but then solely in the ambition of emphasizing the king's achievement in defeating them. Foreign rulers are in this context portrayed as "fierce and merciless" (*ekdūte u lā pādûte*) (e.g. AE2:20–21, SE5:i4–5), and wild beasts are "strong" (*dannūtu*) (e.g. AE1:iii48). These were then exposed to the Assyrian king's manly warfare.

Courage is, as observed, a trait considered characteristic of ideal masculinity. There are many royal epithets which in different ways speak of the heroism of Assyrian kings (Gaspa 2007: 236–57). The common (in the case of Ashurnasirpal II) epithet of "fearless in battle" (*lā ādiru tuqumti*) refers to this personal

---

270 Also gods are referred to by these epithets. For *eṭlu*, see e.g. Adad (SE131:3), and for *zikaru* (attested in other time periods), see Ninurta, Nabu, and Girru (Tallqvist 1938: 95).

271 Tellingly, the cuneiform sign 'kal' in its logographic usage both expresses the words for "strong" and "man", the latter termed 'guruš' (MZL: guruš/sign 496/pages 352–53).

quality (SE5:i4, e.g. AE1:i13). It is actually, counting by exemplars, the fifth most common of his royal epithets. The Early Neo-Assyrian king is also "the heroic male" (*zikru qardu*) (AE153:5, SE2:i9), and Ashurnasirpal II quite often calls himself only "hero/heroic" (*uršānu/uršānāku*) (e.g. AE1:i32), and sometimes he refers to himself by the epithet "prominent and merciless hero" (*uršānu tizqāru lā pādû*) (e.g. AE1:i20). The heroism of the ruler is a prime theme of the picture of the courageous king.

As for narrative passages and the relevant theme, it is stated that "his (the king's) proud heart was set for battle" (*gapšu libbušu tuqumta ūbla*) (AE1:i51, SE2:ii71), and the Assyrian kings bravely pursue the fleeing enemy without waiting for their respective armies to catch up (SE28:43–44, e.g. AE17:iii31–32). By contrast to the cowardly enemy who flees, the Assyrian king bravely advances. Similarly, Ashurnasirpal II claims to have conducted warfare with "my (his) thickness of heart and rage of weapons" (*gipiš libbija u šušmur kakkīja*) (AE1:i82). Interestingly enough, the here attested expression "thickening of heart" (*gipiš libbi*) apparently denotes courage when applied to the Assyrian king, but arrogance when applied to the foreign ruler (CAD G: *gipšu*). Moving on, in the initiation of his military campaign to Urartu, Shalmaneser III urges his army to be brave and disciplined (SE17:17–25). Bravery is also associated with manliness in the Tukulti-Ninurta I Epic where the Assyrian soldiers, facing war, exclaim: "Let us act manly!" (*mutūta nillik*) (see Machinist 1983a: 114, v A-rev. 14′). Courage and bravery were clearly parts of ideal masculinity in Assyria.[272]

According to the just identified concept of a paradigmatic and dominant male, there can only exist one ideal ruler, namely the Assyrian king, at a single time. The titulary expression which presents the king as "he who has no rival" (*šāninišu° lā īšû*) (AE18:II2), and more importantly the epithet of "he who has no rival among the rulers of the four quarters" (*ša ina malkī ša kibrāt erbetti šāninšu lā īšû*) (e.g. AE2:3, SE1:8) may here allude to the outcome of the identified masculinity contest (Chapman 2004: 24–28). The standard title of "king without rival" (*šar lā šanān*) (e.g. AE1:i10, SE25:2) heads a certain cluster of epithets in one of Ashurnasirpal II's inscriptions (AE29:2′), thus attesting to its importance. Tukulti-Ninurta II and Shamshi-Adad V each presented themselves as "king of the universe without rival/equal" (*šar kiššati lā šanān/maḫri*) (e.g. TN2E3, SA5E2). Additionally, the fixed expression "there was no rival"

---

272 A belief similar to the Greek idea of *andreia* ("male courage") or the Roman idea of *virtus* ("male virtue/valor") may be at hand. For a discussion on these concepts, see e.g. Sidebottom 2004: 28. The notion of warfare as a masculine domain, and the idea of inferior war performances as expressing feminization were held also in ancient Greece (Bassi 1998).

(*šānin*° *ul ibši*) is employed in some narrative passages which convey the theme of "display of strength" (AE1:i43, AE17:i61), again attesting to the theme of the unrivalled ruler.

As for iconography and ideal masculinity, the king is portrayed as the dominant male through his weapons, beard, and emphasized muscles (Winter 1997: 370). The first and third features naturally allude to his manly strength and to the battlefield as the venue of the masculinity contest. As observed by Chapman (2004: 50–58), pointing to the threat of broken bows in curses, especially the bow seems to have been symbolic of the manly strength of the king. Telling of the link between the bow and manliness, the words "valour" (*qardūtu*) and "bow" (*qaštu*) are symbolically connected to each other in inscriptions (An3E35:16′). Many depictions show the Assyrian king with a bow in his one hand, both used as an insignier (e.g. AI13:23–24, SI14:6a), and as an actual weapon (e.g. AI4:B18t., SI10:9t.). Also the emphasized muscular arms and legs of the Assyrian king on statues, stelae, and reliefs arguably speak of his status of the dominant male (e.g. AI12, SI6). Musculature, as well as bow, beard, and firm and solid postures were all considered metaphors for masculine power in Assyria (Chapman 2004: 47).

The beards of the Assyrian kings relate to the image of a "manly, mature, noble, and powerful (man), like the lion with his mane" (Winter 1997: 370–71). Beard length clearly indicated rank in Assyria (Madhloom 1970: 87). Thus, the beard was regarded as a source of manly pride. Seen in this light, it is easy to comprehend the symbolism imbued in the descriptions of foreign rulers sweeping (in the act of cleaning) the palace floor or the king's sandals with their beards at their Assyrian superior's feet, expressed in texts from the Sargonid period (see e.g. Parpola 1987: texts 1:28–30, 6:26–30; Streck 1916 II: text 34:28–29), conveying emasculation and humiliation (Chapman 2004: 39; Larsen 1999: 148 resp.). Moreover, an Assyrian soldier-guard is depicted pulling one of his captives by his beard in the reliefs of Sennacherib (see Barnett et al. 1998: pl. 388). It is also possible that the images of Assyrian soldiers grasping the hair of their opponents and holding a dagger at their throats do not represent the cutting of throats but rather that of the cutting of beards (e.g. AI4:B8t., SI10:3b.). The reliefs of Sennacherib clearly shows this act (see Barnett et al. 1998: pls. 174–75). Similarly, Sennacherib removes the moustaches of Elamites, qualified as their "pride" (see RINAP3/1: text 22:vi10–11), the relevant masculinity term being *bāštu* (Winter 1996).

The time has now come to centre on the gendered imagery of the foreign side. A very common theme which tells of failed masculinity, namely the enemy lacking courage, tells of the enemy ruler fleeing the scene of battle instead of facing the Assyrian king "man to man". The enemy ruler either flees at the coming of the Assyrian army, abandons his property and settlement, and saves his life rather than engage in futile fighting, or he resists whereafter he flees, most often in vain, to a remote and fortified place, most often a mountain site (Liverani 1992b: 149). In a certain sense, the enemy flees to a "liminal zone" and "sphere of unreality" (Rivaroli and Verderame 2005: 303), or infamously perishes out of existence, as conveyed by the expression of *šadâšu emēdu* (Weidner 1940). Since the relevant theme has been discussed earlier (see subs. 5.4.2), I will discuss it only briefly here.

Most often the king's enemies take to a mountain peak (e.g. AE17:iii6, SE6:ii5–6),[273] but sometimes they flee to forests (SE17:44), across the river (SE2:ii32), to the sea (SE6:ii12–13), or to another city (e.g. SE6:ii46). As for fleeing in iconography, enemy soldiers are depicted, on the Balawat gates, as escaping by taking to the mountains (AI14:59–60, SI10:2). On palace reliefs, citizens of enemy cities are portrayed swimming in the waters of their moat as they try to get away from the assaults of the Assyrian soldiers (AI4:B17t.). Similarly, foreign troops, along with their horses, are seen crossing in panic over waters (AI4:B27–28b.). The enemy gives a flagrant display of his cowardice. The enemy's fear and cowardice are here juxtaposed with the Assyrian king's strength and courage (Chapman 2004: 35).

In his act of fleeing, the enemy ruler is often "overwhelmed" (*saḫāpu*) by fear of the radiance or weapons which the king directs at him (e.g. SE28:42–43). A usurper, Surri of Patina, is even said to die as a result of this overwhelming (SE14:151–52). The masculine strength and courage of the Assyrian king are presumably expressed in his exuding of terror and radiance (Chapman 2004: 33). The foreign ruler and his people are pictured as being afraid to do battle (e.g. AE1:i62, SE2:ii68), and he/they flee cowardly "in order to save his/their life/lives" (*ana šūzub napištīšu/šunu*) (e.g. AE19:80–81, SE40:i32–33). The international coalition forces who challenge Shalmaneser III are e.g. commonly described as running away to save their lives after having suffered what seems to have been initial but decisive defeats (e.g. SE8:19′), thus expressing emasculation and failed masculinity.

Another common phrase similarly refers to the cowardly nature of the enemy, but also to his inability to protect and provide for his own people. He is here said to disgracefully and impiously "abandon the city of his kingship" (*āl šarrūtišu umdaššir*) (e.g. SE6:i58). The rebellious Babylonian usurper e.g. is described as fleeing "like a fox through a hole" (*kīma šēlubi ina pilše*) when he

273 In an attempt to avoid fighting "man to man", the enemy ruler is often described as hiding behind the walls of his fortified mountains and cities (e.g. AE1:i114, SE16:167′–68′).

manages to escape from a siege (SE5:v1).[274] The cowardly enemy could also flee through riding. Rusa flees from the approaching Sargon II by riding on a "mare" (*atānu*) (see Mayer 1983: 83, line 140). As noted by Chapman (2004: 36–37), the special mentioning of Rusa as riding on a *female* horse, i.e. a mare, adds to the latter's humiliation and feminization.[275] Women are riding on donkeys in the iconography (see Barnett et al. 1998: pls. 371, 464–65), perhaps making up a distant parallel which conveyed disgrace. Anyway, an Urartu ruler flees like "a thief" (*šarrāqu*) in the night, and a Babylonian king is similarly said to have fled out of his besieged city in the middle of the night (An3E34:17, SA5E2:iii27′–29′ resp.). All the attestations of this paragraph tell of the enemy ruler failing and fooling his own people.

Quite paradoxically, not only the theme of the fleeing ruler but also that of the surrendering ruler expressed failed masculinity, although the latter role was officially recommended and encouraged (Chapman 2004: 33–41). The above discussed overwhelming by means of weapons and radiance could also (actually more often) inspire obedience upon the targeted recipient (e.g. AE1:i80–81, SE1:27–28). Numerous passages additionally relate, in general terms, how the enemy elites and people become afraid and therefore surrender (e.g. AE1:iii103–104). Tributaries are represented with bowed backs, clenched fists, and their leaders as prostrating in front of the king's feet (e.g. AI13:33–36, SI11:A1). Attacked enemy soldiers pitifully raise one hand in gestures of seeking for mercy (e.g. AI4:B4t., SI10:9t.). Mountain-based, northern soldiers raise both of their arms in the air in an apparent gesture of submission (AI14:59–60, SI10:2t.). According to the world view of the Assyrian king, by surrendering without a fight to him, the enemy forces save their lives, but in the process lose an important part of their masculinity.

Another act which tells of the cowardly nature of the enemy is his tendency of "ganging up". The theme of "one against many" identified by Liverani (1990: 115) is here in operation in that the assemblies of coalition forces are told of in relation to the sole, heroic king (e.g. AE1:iii27, SE14:91–92). In this context, the enemy army is sometimes described as massive or beyond counting (e.g. AE1:iii52, SE2:i32), presumably in order to stress the major achievement of the king in defeating it. This idea of being surrounded by pressing and hostile for-

274 Although D. Marcus (1977: 88) seems to regard this simile as flattering by referring to foxes as "wily and cunning", this animal may have been associated otherwise in ancient Assyria. Moreover, it is hard to believe in a positive imagery being given in this context.

275 A positive imagery seems, based on the narrative context and aims of royal inscriptions, out of the question. Moreover, as noted by Larsen (1999: 136), also non-royal Urarteans are likened to women, them being in the state of shivering fright, facing Assyrian might.

ces which are arrogant, wicked, and dangerous is characteristic of Assyrian state ideology (Liverani 1990: 115). Ganging up, combined with the admitting of weakness, can also be seen as expressions of cowardice. Regarding this theme, the Babylonian ruler is forced to ask Shalmaneser III for help in quelling the rebellion in his country (SE5:iv1–2), and the Syrian-Palestinian rulers are obliged to form coalitions instead of fighting man to man against Shalmaneser III (e.g. SE2:ii90–96).[276] Similarly, Ashurnasirpal II narrates how various hostile polities "took hold of one another" (*aḫā'iš iṣbutū*), i.e. formed alliances, against him (e.g. AE1:i112–13). In sum, the foreign enemy was cowardly and treacherous, while the Assyrian king was brave and righteous (Fales 1991: 135–39).

As for failed masculinity and the aftermath of surrender or battles, the declarations that the Assyrian king seizes, plunders (e.g. AE1:iii21–23, SE2:ii81), and/or destroys (e.g. SE2:ii89) the enemy ruler's palace, i.e. the symbol of the latter's power, convey the idea of failed masculinity in that the masculinity of the enemy is at the same time destroyed (Chapman 2004: 38). Depictions of tributaries and Assyrian soldiers carrying away furniture and other precious goods, arguably from palaces, are standard (e.g. AI16:C2, SI14:6b), and the same kind of tribute or booty is often enumerated and listed among the outcomes of conducted campaigns (e.g. AE1:iii74–75, SE88). Early Neo-Assyrian kings arranged banquets in the defeated or surrendering enemy ruler's own palace, thus taking over the latter's royal role of provider and protector (AE1:iii82, SE5:vi4). The royal role of harvester is also usurped by the conquering Assyrian king (e.g. AE17:iv107–108). Similarly, the mentioning of the king as seizing or destroying the enemy ruler's "royal city" (*āl šarrūti*) (e.g. SE20:9–10, AE17:iii79–82 resp.) is another example of the latter's humiliation. This city was supposedly central for the relevant ruler's sovereignty (Fales 2011: 221). The acts of sanctuary takeover and godnapping may also attest to the emasculated status of the enemy ruler. In this case, he failed to protect the temples of his dominion.[277]

The handing over of weapons to the Assyrian king may also signify failed masculinity given the military connotations of masculinity. This act of submission is amply attested also in the iconography, e.g. on the throne base, Balawat gates, and the two Kalhu obelisks. The handing over of e.g. bows, spears, royal horses, and helmets are illustrated here (e.g. SI14:4–7, SI11:A1–2,D5). The Assyrian king can also seize the horses or destroy the weapons and chariots of the

---

276 An exception to this tendency of ganging up is Hazael of Damascus who alone faced Shalmaneser III after the breaking up of the Syrian-Palestinian coalition (e.g. SE16:122′–130′).
277 In one obscure passage, the king's own nobles are brought into the temples and palaces of the foreign ruler, supposedly marking some sort of transition of authority (AE1:i83).

enemy (e.g. AE1:iii36, SE10:ii3–6). Also an impious Assyrian (successor) king could experience failed masculinity in this way. In one of Ashurnasirpal II's curses, the oath breaking ruler will have his bow broken (AE175:3). In curses from the Neo-Assyrian Period, Ishtar is called upon to seize the weapons of the disloyal (An5E2:v12–13), and to break the bow of the impious ruler in the midst of battle (see Parpola and K. Watanabe 1988: 48, text 6:453–54). A ruler's weapons functioned not only as insignia or weapons but also as vital signs of masculinity (Chapman 2004: 50–58).

Returning to representations of foreign women in text and image but staying with the polarized, gendered imagery of the king and his opponents, women as surrendering and grieving captives are both described and depicted in the relevant sources. The Assyrian king is here arguably portrayed as their new paternal shepherd and as the head of an enlarged patriarchy. As noted by Chapman (2004: 29–33), shepherding imageries are tied metaphorically to the role of a husband as protector and provider of his wife. Examining firstly the visual evidence, this role may be illustrated in scenes where the king stands holding his pastoral staff while receiving e.g. female captives. The propaganda motif of "father figure" may be conveyed in relation to the depicted children captives (e.g. AI13:17–18). This motif is naturally in line with the spirit of the patrimonialism. The failed masculinity and poor shepherdship of the foreign ruler is also illustrated in the scenes of women and children surrendering and praying for mercy on the door band from the Anu-Adad temple (SI9). Assyrian women are absent from all these images. This fact may in its turn signify the successful masculinity of the Assyrian king in providing and protecting his own women (Chapman 2004: 32).

Turning to the textual evidence, the enemy ruler's failed masculinity, i.e. his inability to take care of his own people, especially his family, is shown in the passages (e.g. AE1:iii22–23, SE14:48–50) which refer to his women and children being taken as booty (Chapman 2004: 41–45). This scenario "validates his own (the king's) masculinity, but also essentially cuckolds his enemy, whose manhood and reputation are thereby dealt a terrible blow" (Melville 2004: 56). The foreign women are specified, as well as objectified, as booty or tribute (e.g. AE1:i85, SE6:iv19), hostages (SE40:iii7–8), and "marriage" partners (e.g. AE19:90, SE2:ii28). As for the first fate, Ashurnasirpal II states that he seized the palace women and daughters of the defeated foreign ruler as booty or tribute (e.g. AE1:i85). Regarding the last fate, the same king proclaims that he took the foreign ruler's sister, his brother's daughter, and the daughters of the ruler's nobles "along with their rich dowry" (*adi nadunnîša ma'adî*) in some sort of marriage (e.g. AE19:90, AE1:iii76, AE19:90 resp.). Tukulti-Ninurta II relates that he received two sisters with their respective dowries as tribute from the western polity Laqu (TN2E5:101–102). In all of these examples, the Assyrian king supposedly acts as the new paternal shepherd of an enlarged, international patriarchy.

In some depictions, women captives have their dresses folded up so that part of their legs are shown (e.g. AI13:23–24, SI10:4b.). Cifarelli (1995: 308–12), using Biblical analogies, has interpreted this as a form of shaming and sexual molestation, thus deviating from the depictional norms of clothed and unmolested women. The exposure may also express the incapability of the defeated foreign ruler to protect and provide for his women (Chapman 2004: 46–47). Possibly, the modest exposure in question simply served to visually express the transference of exploited women under the authority of the defeated foreign ruler to that of the Assyrian king. Such a transference is seemingly conveyed in the narrative passages which e.g. state that Ashurnasirpal II received 200 "adolescent girls" (*batultu*) and female singers and musicians as booty or tribute (AE1:iii67, AE73 resp.).[278] The interpretation of Cifarelli of shaming and molestation seems less likely in light of the norms of respecting women in the sources and of the anachronistic aspect (Bahrani 2001: 129–30). Women and children are only portrayed as ill-treated if politically active, like the Arab queens were (Albenda 1987: 21). Also in relation to these "exposed" women, the Assyrian king thus takes on the role of the new paternal shepherd of an enlarged, international patriarchy.

Admittedly, outright feminization is quite rare in royal inscriptions from the Early Neo-Assyrian Period. However, in one passage which tells of tribute delivered from the eastern polity of Sipirmena, its tributaries are described as effeminately "arranging (their hair) like women" (*ša kīma sinnišāti ṣaprūni*) (AE1:ii75–76, AE17:iii97). Its keyword *ṣapāru* may also carry the meaning of "to squint or wink (with eyes)" (CAD Ṣ: *ṣapāru* A), possibly alluding to flirtation and the seducing ways of Ishtar.[279] In any case, a feminization is attested in the discussed passage.[280] In some iconography, what seems to be men are depicted making the same gesture as women from the crenellations of city walls, indicating their feminization (e.g. AI4:B17t.). In the curse section of the treaty between Ashur-narari V and Mati'-ilu of Arpad, it is stated that the latter should be a "(female) prostitute" (*ḫarimtu*), that his (sex)life should be that of a mule,

278 The latter group of people is otherwise clearly illustrated in the depictions of female musicians being part of tributary processions (see Orlamünde 2011a: pls. II.21a–d).

279 Note e.g. the much noted episode in the Gilgamesh Epic where Ishtar vainly tries to seduce the reluctant and even deliberately insulting hero (see Parpola 1997: tablet vi).

280 In a related imagery, enemies in Hanigalbat are described as screaming (out of fear) like "children" (*šerru*) due to the assaults of the approaching Assyrian army (An2E2:66–67).

that his wives should be extremely old, his soldiers should turn into women, and their bows should be taken away from them, to their great "shame" (*bāštu*), in case of his breaking the treaty (An5E2:v8–15). Feminization is also attested in the curse sections of the Late Neo-Assyrian Period (see e.g. Leichty 2011: text 98:rev.55–56).

Although the theme of feminization is concentrated to the curse sections of royal inscriptions and treaties, it is not restricted to these kind of sources. Also omen literature has the theme of people changing from men to women, portraying it as a bad fate (see Guinan 1997). As for legends, the Old Assyrian text on Sargon of Akkad which portrays the enemy as dressed in women's clothing may constitute a distant parallel (see Günbattı 1997: lines 20–25 rev.). In yet other sources, the hero Gilgamesh is described as cutting off the genitals of the Bull of Heaven in the Gilgamesh Epic (see Parpola 1997: tablet vi), and a reference to the treatment of Elamite captives in Sennacherib's royal inscriptions may speak of the same act (see RINAP3/1: text 22:vi11–12). The idea of feminization as degrading, or as in the latter cases, equivalent to losing virility, is arguably expressed in these examples. Although rarely expressed in the major primary sources, feminization of enemies is nevertheless firmly attested in Assyrian inscriptions as a whole.

Summing up, I have argued that gender plays an important part in Assyrian propaganda. In the Assyrian patriarchal society and state, the female sex and gender were linked to weakness and subordination. These associations were then used to describe the Assyrian king's opponents in a devaluating sense, giving emasculation and feminization. The Assyrian king presents himself as the paradigmatic male, linked to strength and superiority.

5.5 Summary

This chapter has focused on the Assyrian king's interaction with various aspects of the foreign lands. Firstly, the king meeting the foreign landscape and animals was centred on. It was found that the ruggedness and remoteness, i.e. "difficult path", of the foreign geography are often portrayed. Its wildness serves to symbolize a chaos which is provisory and not essence-based. Through conquering and cultivation the geography can become ordered. The overcoming acts also serve to portray the king as hero. The wild beasts of the foreign lands also confront the king. Symbolizing chaos, they are hunted and slayed. As hunter, the king enacts the role of Ninurta. The ritual-religious character of the royal hunt is also expressed by the narrative passage which states that gods have commanded the king to hunt. Alternatively, he could catch and collect these animals in zoos. The collecting of them symbolize domestication and a transference to the ordered world.

The king's relationship with the foreign deities is described as characterized by mutual respect. At least Shalmaneser III occasionally presents himself in a priestly role in relation to them. The theme of "godnapping" conveys the ideas of divine abandonment and fulfilment of divine orders, i.e. the foreign deities had abandoned their worshippers and locality, and had ordered the Assyrian king to conquer. Tenable evidence of true iconoclasm and a fanatic imposition of Mesopotamian deities is not attested. The general lack of references to these alleged impositions is especially noted here.

Turning to the king and the human component of the foreign lands, a distinction between "elites" and "people" is made in the sources. Early Neo-Assyrian kings present themselves as the masters of all lands, often "the universe" or "the four quarters", as well as over all foreign elites and people. The mission of conquering could be achieved either peacefully or by force, depending on the responses of the foreign elites and people. According to the "reciprocity principle" identified in this book, they are spared and included if they give submission and tribute, but annihilated and enslaved if they resist. As for the latter choice on the part of the foreign side, by refusing to submit to the Assyrian king, who is presented as the deities' representative on earth, and by withholding the tribute which they owe the king and ultimately the great gods, their lives were forfeited in the eyes of the king and the deities.

Descriptions and depictions of the flaying, impaling, dismembering, and burning of the king's captured enemies are numerous. Especially symbolically loaded was the severing of the killed enemies' heads, hanged up in trees, used in cultic games, and turned into "tower of heads". Depicted rows of war prisoners, sometimes tied up and given neck stocks, illustrate another kind of fate. Guilt seems to be established on two levels: collectively and sometimes individually. As for the latter, innocent individuals, notably civilians, within a rebellious polity could be spared. Occasionally, the Assyrian king extends mercy to those who have initially resisted. Disapproved atrocities, e.g. the not mentioned maltreatment of women, are distinguished. The emphasis on violence may relate to deterrent and celebrative purposes.

In the event of delivered tribute and displayed submission, the king reciprocates by taking on the roles of sun and shepherd. In these roles, he had the paternalistic duty to provide and protect. Banquets, demographic and agricultural reforms are described as some of the ways of implementing this royal obligation. Being a part of successful reciprocity, tribute (as well as the booty in the failed reciprocity) had an ideological as well as a practical dimension. As for the former, tribute was due to Ashur and the great gods as world rulers. As for the latter, tribute was vital for the imperial economy.

At least concerning ideology and relations of power, the unit of analysis of foreign people and lands is quite uniform. Even Babylonia and Egypt are portrayed as subordinate to Shalmaneser III. A certain disregard for pastoralists (Arameans) and "mountain peoples" (e.g. Urarteans) can be detected, but still with the reciprocity principle firmly in operation. Regarding the issue of nationalism, racism, and ethnicity as possible components of Assyrian state ideology, the first two terms are obviously anachronistic and non-applicable. The component of *ethnos* is however relevant to discuss. The terms Assyria and Assyrians are mostly described as flexible and dynamic, referring to *political* identities. Similarly, so-called Assyrianization centred on political measures rather than on any agenda of cultural imperialism. In other words, in the often antagonistic relations between the king and the foreign lands, a dichotomy of Assyrian/foreign is not a focal point. Tendencies towards a constructed *ethnos* are present but suppressed. A belief in a fixed and static Assyrian *ethnos* is definitively not expressed in the sources. Ethnicity was *not* an important component of Assyrian state ideology.

The main dichotomy in question instead revolves around the king, representing Order, and "the enemy", representing Chaos. As for the former, the king along with his high officials can be said to form the Assyrian ruling class, functioning as the superior part in an open (theoretical-ideological) as well as underlying (practical-economical) dichotomy of rulers versus ruled. The primary identity of the kings was obviously *kingship*, expressed e.g. through their constant references to the royal line. Confrontations between the Assyrian king and foreign polities then occurred between royal/ruler houses – not between nations. Patrimonialism, focusing on the mighty ruler and on inequalities based on class and sex, was found to be relevant here.

Post-colonial theory was e.g. used in identifying images of negative stereotyping in the primary sources. While the Assyrian king had the identity of "the Self", the foreign side functioned as "the Other" in a status of alterity. The theory was also used in identifying and discussing Orientalist features in the scholarly debate regarding ancient Assyria and Assyrian state ideology. These features include Orientalist ideas of Oriental violence, despotism, and decadence applied to the Assyrian sources. As for the first feature, the identified logic in the royal use of violence exposes the images of the Assyrians as conducting indiscriminate violence as an offspring of Orientalism. Similarly, the Orientalist view on the Mesopotamian ruler as despotic and decadent is contradicted by the primary sources which present the propagandistic image of the Assyrian king as pious, humble, restrained, and as part of a ruling class. In relation to theory, anachronisms with regards to "nationalism", iconoclastic religious imperialism, and "secularism" were also noted.

The antagonism between the Assyrian king and his enemies is not only illustrated by the simple dichotomies of king/enemy and ruling class/ruled, or by the abstract one of Order/Chaos, but also through polarities based on gender. Ideal and failed masculinities stand juxtaposed in this relationship. It follows that an ideological and hierarchical dichotomy of masculinity versus femininity is at play. Warfare was a masculine sphere in ancient Assyria, liminal femininity aside, and it was enacted on the battlefield. The Early Neo-Assyrian kings present themselves as embodying ideal masculinity (displaying strength and courage), while the foreign elites and people (displaying weakness and cowardice) are represented as one sort of emasculated or feminized Other. This feminization of his opponents is a reflection of the low status of women in the Assyrian patriarchal society. The enemy ruler's failed masculinity is conveyed also by his inability to protect his own authority and possessions, i.e. his palace, temples, capital city, royal duties, weapons, and palace women. The Assyrian king here takes over his enemy's authority and possessions, thereby manifesting himself as the dominant male.

6 Ideological development within the reigns

In this chapter, the issue regarding the presence or absence of ideological variation and development within the respective reigns of Ashurnasirpal II, Shalmaneser III, and of some other Early Neo-Assyrian kings (where meaningful) is highlighted. Its first section gives an introductory and general overview of the relevant discussion in scholarly literature, the following three sections present conclusions on the subject based on general and/or strategic comparisons while focusing on the primary sources of the relevant rulers, and the final section lastly provides a summary with reflections.

6.1 Introduction

Generally speaking, ideological development can be innovative both within and beyond the existing ideological framework. Thus, innovation can either reformulate tradition or break with it. In the defence of *status quo*, ideological development inititated by the king and his immediate circle was not always considered positively in the higher echelons of Mesopotamian and Assyrian societies (Garelli 1979: 320–25; Pečírková 1993). According to Pečírková (1993: 244), initiated political-ideological reform was actually the downfall of several Assyrian kings, such as Tukulti-Ninurta I, Shalmaneser III, and Sennacherib. As a result, change therefore had to be masked and presented as being in line with tradition and its age-old legitimacy grounds.

Nevertheless, ideological change within reigns has been noted by a few modern scholars, although the phenomenon largely has been neglected in Assyriological research. Often the royal titulary e.g. is analysed without taking much consideration on change and variation. However, a pioneering study on ideological development within reigns was made by Liverani (1981) who highlights the change, in time and place, of a certain section of Sennacherib's annals. His underlying stance is that variations in ideological sources are not due to e.g. scribal errors or artistic elaborations. On the contrary, these are meaningful and reflect adaptions to historical and ideological changes. Consequently, these deserve to be observed and taken seriously.

A part of such an understanding is the notion that the ruler must "earn" his titles and claims. Liverani (1981: 234–36) here sees a tendency of Assyrian royal titulary, within individual reigns, developing from a "heroic-competitive stage" to a "territorial stage", the latter marked by unquestioned control and superiority. In the latter stage, the king has firm control over the inner core, the compact totality (*kiššatu*), and the patterned totality (*kibrāt erbetti*). A similar idea is identified by Dalley (1998b: 76) who argues that the Assyrian king could not claim the titles of “king of the universe”[281] and “king of the four quarters” before having conducted vital, numerous, and successful military campaigns in various directions. Cifola (1995: 146) presents another picture, although fully subscribing to the idea that titles had to be earned. She argues that Assyrian titulary developed gradually, within reigns, from religiously orientated epithets to more secular, heroic, and military ones.[282] However, in Ashurnasirpal II's case, this process is claimed to be reversed (Cifola 1995: 147). Referring to the extension of the king's domains, Cifola (1995: 147) also argues that there is a tendency of a gradual abandonment of the allegedly local title “king of Assyria”. Adding to these observations, Tadmor (1981: 14–21) notes a literary convention in Assyrian annals which states that the king had to describe a great military campaign or all his military victories as taking place in the king's first regnal year.

Not only the presenting of the role of the Assyrian king as warrior may have varied according to regnal phase. While identifying “pietistic-pastoral” epithets, relating to deities and the people respectively as the receiving ends, Liverani (1981: 244–45) argues that these royal epithets developed from expressing a state of fear and insecurity to a state of divine confirmation and royal expertise. In relation to the great gods, the king initially stressed his piety and priestly role, but later on focused on divine support and on a unity of the king and the deities. The people turned from being the object of conquests to the object of peaceful government. Regarding the royal role of temple builder, another literary convention presents the Assyrian king as a pious master builder and restorer of temples right after accession (Tadmor 1981: 21–25). Logically, the themes of royal descent and divine choice, i.e. the two major legitimacy grounds (Tadmor 1981: 25), ought to have been emphasized in a king's first regnal phase as he had not yet earned his position through actions.[283] The theme of difficult path may also belong to an earlier regnal phase, since the role of discoverer fits nicely into the imagery of a ruler exploring the regions to be conquered early on in his reign.

Concrete historical developments may have inspired ideological change too. It is however often difficult to say whether ideology was revised to explain

281 In chapters 6–9, in order to save space and avoid repetitions, epithets and narrative idioms which have been transcribed in chapters 3–5 are as a rule not given in transcription again.
282 The scholar in question even sees an intentional ordering of royal epithets in sequences according to which religious epithets preceed those of war and triumph, and according to which epithets signifying heroism proceed those of military triumph (Cifola 1995: 146).
283 Even though such an ordering (at least regarding the theme of divine choice) seems to contradict the identified development pattern in Liverani 1981 presented above.

a historical event, or if it was the change in ideology that brought about the historical event (van de Mieroop 1999). Obviously, content and context must be brought together in the analysis, in order to establish the likely causal chain from case to case. That being said, Liverani (1981: 252–57) observes how the varying editions of Sennacherib's annals focusing on events in Babylon may be explained by historical change, e.g. reflected in the description of the said ruler's puppet king Bel-ibni. Similarly, Schneider (1991: 135–46) detects a development in the description of Marduk-zakir-shumi I, from equal to weak, in the annals of Shalmaneser III. According to her, the annalistic text as such was changed because of the encounter with Babylon. The narration changed from being structured on eponyms (*limmu*) to regnal years (*palû*) – a move inspired by Babylonian traditions (Schneider 1991: 80–87).

Continuing with other possible examples of the influence of historical events on propaganda (or the other way around), the powerful position of the field marshal Dajjan-Ashur has also been seen reflected in ideological change. The excluding of a narration from regnal year five in the annals on the Kurkh Stele (SE2) arguably glosses over a proposed "palace revolution" in which the said official was deeply involved (Olmstead 1921; Schneider 1991: 127–35, 242–44). The later Black Obelisk (SI11) is here regarded as a monument both of the king and Dajjan-Ashur (Reade 1981a: 159; Yamada 2000: 325–32; Fuchs 2008: 65). Important historical events such as Ashurnasirpal II's move from Assur to Kalhu, his reaching of the Mediterranean and Phoenicia, the reaching of various river sources, the encounters with great coalitions in the reign of Shalmaneser III, and the creation of the two main palaces of the two rulers, namely the North-West Palace and Fort Shalmaneser, should hypothetically also be reflected through ideological change.

6.2 Ideology and regnal phases of Ashurnasirpal II

In this section, ideological change and continuity in the reign of Ashurnasirpal II is investigated. Firstly, a general comparison is made, then a strategic comparison focusing on two texts from the Ninurta temple is conducted. I will argue that the overall impression is one of continuity, although certain ideological themes may tentatively be tied to specific regnal phases. There is not any real evidence for the grand ideological schemes mentioned above.

The thesis of Liverani which says that ideological development within a reign moves linearly from a heroic-competitive stage to a territorial stage is hard to substantiate in the propaganda of Ashurnasirpal II. The narrative in his commemorative texts rather portrays the strive towards control and submission as continuous and as a cyclical process (e.g. AE1). Moreover, epithets such as "king without rival", "great king" (in its competitive sense), "hero" (*uršānu*, *qarrādu*), and "(dominant) male" (*eṭlu*, *zikaru*) which should belong to the early phase only are attested also in the later phase (e.g. AE56:1, AE31:1, AE1:i32, AE23:2 resp.). The circumstance that epithets concerning tribute are found mostly in the later phase gives some credit to his argument, but in light of the overall lack of a clear pattern this does not prove much (e.g. AE3:28). In the textual narrative, the theme of tribute is naturally not restricted to any phase (e.g. AE17:iv53–57, AE2:49–51).

Continuing with exploring the potential for an application of Liverani's thesis here, the theme of heroic priority is only attested late (e.g. AE30:53–55). The related heroic theme of difficult path is, both in narrative passages and royal epithets, clearly expressed in both regnal halves (e.g. AE1:i45–54, AE40:4). Furthermore, the observation of Tadmor on the ideological theme of a king conducting a great, or *all* of his, campaign(s) at the beginning of his reign is hard to apply here, since this theme is simply not present in the texts of Ashurnasirpal II. Great military campaigns are rather conducted continuously throughout his reign. The visual, warrior-related motif of the ritual cleansing of the ruler's weapons is attested only in the first phase (e.g. AI4:G6), but in light of the difficulty of dating the art in the North-West Palace outside the throne room, this should not be so conclusive.

Staying with the theme of the Assyrian king and the dimension of coercion, the thesis of Liverani, Cifola, and Dalley regarding a king's earning of certain important titles is likewise difficult to substantiate. The title "king of the four quarters" is used by Ashurnasirpal II in an early inscription in which there are not any claims of a southern dominion (AE17:i40). Similarly, the title "king of the universe" is claimed right from the start of his reign (e.g. AE19:6). It may be noted in this context that much less powerful rulers are attested bearing this title, thus making the claim of earning problematic (see Seux 1967: 308–12). Moreover, in contradiction to the idea of Cifola, there is not any gradual abandonment due to imperial expansion of the title "king of Assyria", as proved by frequent late attestations (e.g. AE1:iii113). The local character of this title should also be questioned (see subs. 5.4.6).

Turning to more peaceful royal roles and internal ideological development, Cifola's identified pattern of state ideology changing from an emphasis on the religious to focusing on secular, heroic, and military aspects does not stand the test here. As for royal epithets, the king calls himself "purification priest" (AE26:35, AE1:i21), "provider of offerings for the great gods" (AE17:i19, AE8), and "he whose deeds and offerings the great gods of heaven and underworld love" (AE17:i21–22, AE1:i24–25) in both regnal phases. Narrative passages centering on offerings and weapon cleansing at the felling of trees or the reaching of large bodies of water e.g. are only attested in the later half of his reign (AE1:iii89, e.g. AE2:26–27 resp.). An argument in favour of Cifola's thesis is that the motif of "king as venerating priest" is attested only in the first phase (e.g. AI17). Also, the motifs of "king as libating priest" and "king being ritually purified" are also restricted to this phase (e.g. AI4:G8, AI4:G3 resp.), i.e. if accepting the dating of the reliefs in rooms G–H of his North-West Palace. The insecure dating and the textual evidence make this argument inconclusive. Her idea of a special, reversed case for Ashurnasirpal II does not stand the test either, in light of the above and the lack of a clear phase profile of the priestly theme/motif.

Liverani's idea that there is a change from fear and insecurity to one of confirmation in relation to the deities, also seems unapplicable here. The theme of divine choice and royal epithets concerning divine favour are brought up early as well as late in the reign (e.g. AE17:i33–34, AE154:3 resp.). In addition, narrative passages and royal epithets regarding divine support are amply found also in inscriptions from the first half of his reign (e.g. AE17:iv60, AE17:i37 resp.). Moreover, priestly epithets including the keywords of *palāḫu*, *šaḫtu*, and *na'adu*, denoting fear of the divine, are attested also in the later regnal half (e.g. AE2:17, AE28:i9, AE15 resp.). Thus, this move from fear and insecurity to divine confirmation is not expressed.

Turning to the idea of Tadmor of the literary convention to present the Assyrian king as a great master builder at the start of his reign, there seems not to be any such convention articulated in the texts of Ashurnasirpal II. In commemorative texts, the main focal point is warfare and conquering, as expressed right after the invocation of deities and the royal titulary (e.g. AE19). If anything, the trend seems to be royal building in the later half. Divine statues are created only late, and the creating of "royal images" is similarly restricted to the relevant regnal phase (e.g. AE30:64–68, AE1:i105 resp.). These attestations are too numerous to be dismissed right away, but it is of course possible that this phase profile merely is a result of the predominance of late texts in the text corpus of Ashurnasirpal II (see app. 1). More importantly, I would say that typology is arguably a more important aspect than internal chronology as far as variations and changes in the royal role of master builder is concerned. Texts which commemorate buildings or cult objects, such as dedicatory texts, naturally carry a lot of building themes.

Not even the proposed development of pastoral epithets according to which the people first are regarded as objects to be conquered and then as objects to be peacefully governed is evidenced. Royal epithets such as "amazing shepherd", "he who rules all people", "sun (of all people)", and "chief herdsman", are all attested from the first regnal phase as well (e.g. AE19:21, AE19:18, AE19:22, AE17:i15 resp.). Finally, the hypothesis that lineage and royal genealogy ought to be stressed in earlier texts is not found. The ruler is frequently called "son", "grandson", and the like, also in later inscriptions (e.g. AE9:1, AE40:18 resp.), and narrative passages which centre on the royal line are also notorious in later sources (e.g. AE1:i104–5).

There are however some tendencies expressed in the sources. Tree felling and image creating have already been identified as late. Possibly, the acts of felling trees and creating images in the foreign lands should be seen as two ways for the Assyrian king to demonstrate his extended authority. The theme of zoological gardens is only attested late (e.g. AE2:31–38), and it too may convey the idea of extended authority (here in the animal kingdom). The role of royal hunter is almost exclusively attested late in the textual narrative (e.g. AE1:iii48–49). The lastly mentioned tendency is however disturbed by the hunting reliefs in the North-West Palace which may be dated to the early-middle part of the reign (AI4:B19–20), in analogy with those giving a historical narrative. Another interesting tendency is the theme of royal wisdom as a late phenomenon. The Assyrian king is here referred to as "wise", "intelligent", "he who knows" (*mūdû*), and "open to understanding and wisdom" (*pēt uzni nēmeqi*) only in late texts (e.g. AE29:8′, AE2:23, AE2:23, AE2:23 resp.). Possibly, the idea of Liverani that royal expertise characterizes a later development stage of a king's propaganda is expressed here.[284]

Another tendency which may carry some meaning concerns the descriptions of some enemy peoples. References to Arameans having seized land are only made in early texts, while the mentioning of the mountain people of the Lullumu is largely restricted to later texts (e.g. AE19:92–96, AE1:iii119 resp.). This tendency may express the leaving of a historical phase of reconquering just accomplished by the king, confronted by a new kind of threat. Also in line with historical developments, the river Subnat is brought up as a border in both regnal halves (e.g. AE3:37–38, AE23:9), and the conquering of and control over the west and the land Hatti is concentrated to the later half of the reign (e.g. AE3:34–37). Historically "correct", the theme of "display of strength" is attested only in late inscriptions, referring to triumphant marches in the west along the Mediterranean coast (e.g. AE1:iii84–88). Also in line with historical developments, Babylon is only referred to in the later half when Babylonian troops in Suhu are fought against (e.g. AE1:iii15–26), while the cultural influ-

284 The study of Pongratz-Leisten (1999) regarding the increased development of the theme of the king as wise and a scholar refers to change *between* rather than within reigns.

ence is noticeable already in the first regnal half by the presence of Babylonian deities in early deity sequences (see app. 4).

Continuing with the likely link between historical developments and ideological change, the move from Assur to Kalhu may be highlighted. A consistent pattern of "before/after" is difficult to detect. Kalhu is very much centred on already in the early texts of Ashurnasirpal II, and Assur is not spoken of so much in early texts either (e.g. AE17). Moreover, the god Ashur (the patron deity of Assur) is much focused on also in the textual narrative and epithets of the later half of this ruler's reign. As for the latter, the title of "vice-regent of Ashur" runs throughout the reign (e.g. AE23:1, AE30:1). As for the former, Ashurnasirpal II conducts warfare by the command and in support of Ashur (e.g. AE21:8′–9′, AE17:ii83–100 resp.), he is given authority by him (e.g. AE30:20–21), and he makes offerings to Ashur in later texts (e.g. AE1:iii135). Lands are unsubmissive and obliged to give tribute to Ashur also in later texts (e.g. AE40:11, AE1:ii50 resp.). Moreover, Ashur is consistently listed in first place in deity sequences throughout the reign (see app. 4), and Kalhu is actually stated as being dedicated to Ashur (AE30:40). There is of course not any official abandonment of devotion to Ashur.

Nevertheless, Reade (2002: 191, 199) argues that Ashurnasirpal II "promoted" Ninurta as the patron deity of Kalhu in the later stages of his reign, e.g. by commissioning this god's temple around 865 BCE. Ninurta is however highlighted also in early inscriptions, both in the textual narrative and epithets (e.g. AE26:70, AE17:i6 resp.). There is in other words not any sudden official switch of devotion from Ashur to Ninurta in analogy with the replacing of capital city from Assur to Kalhu. In fact, the relevant gods are often mentioned together, e.g. as tribute commanding, curse implementing, listening to prayers, and war commanding (AE1:i99–101, AE36:4′–8′, AE36:1′–4′, AE2:25–26 resp.). Additionally, several royal epithets, such as "king who marches justly with the support of Ashur and Ninurta", have both deities, acting together, as components (e.g. AE1:iii128). The discussion of these two paragraphs shows that there is not any consistent ideological change dependent on before/after the move of capital from Assur to Kalhu.

Turning finally to the strategic comparison, a look at the early inscription on the Ninurta Stele (AE17) and at the late one in the Ninurta temple (AE1) may be the most rewarding and fair comparison available. These texts are both substantial, they are of the same genre (annals), and they have the same provenance (Kalhu and the Ninurta temple). The only setbacks are their different placement (outside/inside) and iconographic or typological context (stele/wall reliefs). A perfect comparison is however hardly attainable.

Both texts start with an invocation of deities. In AE17 (i1–12) no less than 13 deities are enumerated, with Ashur at the head and Ninurta in seventh place. In AE1 (i1–9) only Ninurta is invoked. AE1 (i9–17) then has a section of royal epithets which starts with "strong king". Also heroic-competitive, fearfulness expressing, and priestly epithets are found in this section. A short statement that Ashur has chosen and handed over weapons to the king follows in AE1 (i17–18). Both texts then have a cluster of epithets which begins with "attentive prince", followed by a genealogy (AE1:i18–31, AE17:i12–32). Heroic-competitive, fearfulness expressing, and priestly epithets are included in the cluster. The only territorial title is "king of Assyria".

After a brief statement that the great gods have given the king power (AE1:i31, AE17:i33–34), another section of royal epithets starting with "I am king" follows (AE1:32–36, AE17:i34–44). These are mostly heroic and military, but also include the title "king of the four quarters". Interestingly, the epithet "vice-regent of Ashur and Ninurta" of AE17 is replaced by "king of Assyria" in AE1. After a short statement that the deities have fixed the king's destinies (AE1:36–37, AE17:i44–46), it is narrated that Ishtar has commanded the king to embark on military campaigns (AE1:i37–38, AE17:i46–49). After a small epithet section starting with "attentive prince" and referring both to priesthood and warfare (AE1:i38–40, AE17:i49–54), an "abstract" which tells of how Ashur has chosen the king and commanded royal warfare, is likewise given in both texts (AE1:i40–43, AE17:i54–59).

Thereafter, a long and detailed narrative of the king's military campaigns takes place (AE1:i43–ii125, AE17:i59–iv120). The narrative of AE17 was copied into AE1. In AE17 (v1–24), a description of building activities in Kalhu, focusing on the building of the palace (not the temple), then follows. Later princes are called upon to respect the king's monument (AE17:v24–25). A list of what the successor should *not* do to it is expressed, and a long list of blessings and curses is given (AE17:v25–45, AE17:v45–103 resp.). The text of AE17 ends at this point. Instead of a description of building in Kalhu, AE1 (ii125–26) has a short cluster of epithets which begins with "great king", followed by a genealogy. Both heroic and territorial titles are attested here. Another and longer section of royal epithets follows, focusing on geographical extremes (AE1:ii126–31). Both heroic and territorial titles are given, and the emphasis is on conquest. Then a description of the building of sacred buildings and cult objects in Kalhu is given (AE1:ii131–35).

The narrative of military campaigns then returns, interluded once by a narration of royal hunting (AE1:iii1–113, AE1:iii48–50 resp.). A short cluster of epithets which starts with "great king" and another genealogy is presented (AE1:iii113–14), followed by another and longer section of royal epithets which includes aspects of royal heroism, warfare, and shepherding (AE1:iii114–18). The brief statement that Ashur has given the king power and weapons then returns, whereafter a narration focusing on conquest and geographical extremes follows (AE1:iii118–19, AE1:iii119–26 resp.). A long section of royal epithets which starts with "attentive prince" is then conveyed (AE1:iii126–32). It includes heroic (to a great extent), fearfulness expressing, and priestly epithets. The title of "king of the four quarters" is used. The annals end with a note on various building activities in Kalhu (AE1:iii132–36), similar to that of AE17. A variation is found through the existence of the issue of deportation of foreign peoples to Kalhu.

Drawing conclusions from this comparison, although certain tendencies may be expressed, there is not any consistent development from a heroic-competitive to a territorial, from a state of fearfulness to one of confirmation, or from a priestly to a military-heroic state being attested in the relevant sources. Pretentious territorial titles are used in the titulary right from the start, and the title of "king of Assyria" is in fact more popular in the later text. The narrative on military campaigns was merely copied from AE17 to AE1. It is of course possible that the noted variation in the section of invocation of deities reflects a switched emphasis from Ashur to Ninurta, but variations (here and generally) may be explained by the varying typological and situational contexts and considerations rather than by any change in ideology. As already noted, the Ninurta temple was a *secondary* location for the relevant stele, and this may explain the absent stress on Ninurta in AE17.

Summing up the findings of this section, the general impression is one of ideological continuity between the two regnal phases. Some ideological features may however be temporally biased, such as those of royal hunting and wisdom, tree felling, image creating, and Arameans as land seizers. There is inadequate evidence to confirm any grand ideological development scheme or the idea that royal titles and epithets had to be earned before taken.

6.3 Ideology and regnal phases of Shalmaneser III

In this section, ideological change and continuity in the reign of Shalmaneser III is investigated. Firstly, a general comparison is made, then a strategic comparison focusing on three texts from each of his three regnal phases is conducted. I will argue that the overall impression is one of continuity, indicating the existence of an ideological program right from the start. Some ideological themes are preliminary identified as restricted in time, but there is not any conclusive evidence for grand ideological development schemes.

As appendices 8–9 indicate, there are stronger grounds of claiming a development from a heroic-competitive to a territorial stage in the texts of this ruler than in those of the former. The common expressions which present the king as having conquered or subdued from one locality to another e.g. are largely absent from the last regnal phase (e.g. SE24:5–8). Regarding warfare and the ruler's roles, themes restricted to early texts are the deities commanding warfare upon coronation (SE1:11–13), the simile to "Adad the flooder" (e.g. SE2:ii98), and atrocities such as the building of "tower of heads" (e.g. SE2:i25). This may however be a result of the less abbreviated nature of his earlier annals. In the annals from the final third phase, there seems to be less emphasis on the exercise of violence. In analogy with the above, this may however be explained by the abbreviated nature of the annals in question rather than conveying some kind of changed view on the role of royal violence. Problematic for an adoption of the thesis of Liverani is the circumstance that epithets such as "king without rival", "hero" (*ālilu*), "(dominant) male", and "great king" are not restricted to the first phase (e.g. SE25:2, SE5:iv2, SE6:i20, SE24:1 resp.). Moreover, the epithet "rival of the great rulers of the universe, and of kings" is only attested late (SE40:i3–4), i.e. when Shalmaneser III should have been in complete territorial control.

Continuing with discussing the role of violence and the relevant ideological scheme, the heroic theme of difficult path is expressed throughout the reign (e.g. SE16:273′–74′, SE2:ii41–42), although epithets expressing this theme are concentrated to the first two phases. In line with Tadmor's argument, the epithet "he whose hands at the beginning of his reign conquered the upper and lower sea" (*ina šurrât šarrūtišu tâmtum elītum u tâmtum šupālītum qāssu ikšudu*) is expressed in the first regnal third (SE1:7–8). However, military campaigns are not restricted or concentrated to the beginning of the king's reign. As in the case of Ashurnasipal II, the king describes his conquesting as a continuous, cyclical process, not as a fixed, linear development (e.g. SE10). As for the iconography, the motifs of "king in battle", "observing battle", "on march", and "receiving captives" are all restricted to the first phase (e.g. SI10:1b., SI10:4b., SI10:11b., SI10:3b. resp.), and the motif of "king receiving tribute/booty" is concentrated to the said regnal phase (e.g. SI14:6a, SI10:9b. resp.). This may however be due to the fact that these attestations almost exclusively derive from the same source, i.e. the Balawat Gate, thus revealing this tendency as typologically biased.

Regarding conquesting and the idea of the required earning of titles and epithets such as "king of (all) the four quarters", this title is taken right from the start, and in a narration which does not bring up the south (e.g. SE1:2). Similarly, the title "king of the universe" is expressed already in the first regnal phase (e.g. SE20:1), i.e. when it is highly unlikely that Shalmaneser III had conducted seven major, successful military campaigns, following the criteria of Dalley (1998b: 76). Moreover, once again in contradiction to the idea of Cifola, the supposedly local title of "king of Assyria" is not restricted to early inscriptions, as proved by frequent and clearly late attestations (e.g. SE27:1). The titulary tells of universal dominion right from the beginning.

As for the role of royal priest and ideological change, there are some arguments in favour of Cifola's thesis on a development from religious to heroic-military titles. Most importantly, the priestly epithets of the king seem to be concentrated to the first two regnal phases (e.g. SE1:5). Also, the motif of "king as venerating priest" is again expressed almost exclusively in earlier iconography (e.g. SI10:10b.). However, the statues representing the king as priest are attested from all regnal phases (SI4–8), and the theme of royal heroism and militancy is, as shown in the paragraphs above, much present also in early texts. Liverani's idea of a change of mood from fearfulness to divine confirmation is difficult to substantiate. Royal epithets containing the words *palāḫu* and *na'adu* are found in the last and middle phases respectively (e.g. SE16:3, SE8:10–11 resp.), and the narrative theme of divine choice is present throughout the king's reign, e.g. in the shape of abstracts (e.g. SE1:11–13, SE5:i6–ii2). Additionally, epithets focusing on divine favour such as *nišītu*, *šaknu*, and *šakkanakku* of DN are attested completely or largely from the first two regnal phases (e.g. SE6:i14, SE26:2, SE1:3 resp.).

The literary convention of concentrating royal building activities to the start of the reign, present in texts of Sargonid kings according to Tadmor, is not found in the major primary sources. Again, annals focus on military campaigning right from the king ascending the throne, and typological factors such as dedications seem to trigger building themes much more effectively. Royal epithets concerning the king's role as master builder (*bānû*) are distributed throughout the reign (e.g. SE103:3, SE54:4–5), and many texts centering on building from Fort Shalmaneser are dated to the middle phase (e.g. SE28–37). The building theme is not restricted to the early regnal phase.

The idea of Liverani on the development of the Assyrian ruler's role in relation to the people, from exercising discipline to displaying benevolence, can definitively be discarded here. Shalmaneser III calls himself "shepherd" and "sun of all people" also in the first phase (e.g. SE1:5, SE2:i5 resp.), and the once attested epithet "he who leads in peace the population of Assyria" derives from the first phase (SE1:5–6). Additionally, the references to the king being granted the shepherdship of Assyria by the deities is only found in early inscriptions (e.g. SE1:11). The title of "king of all people" heads a certain cluster of epithets which dominates nearly every edition of Shalmaneser III's annals (e.g. SE6:i11). Lastly, the common theme of royal descent is focused on throughout the reign, i.e. also in later regnal phases, both in narrative passages and in royal epithets (e.g. SE27:6–8, SE8:20 resp.).

Turning to actual tendencies of ideological development within the reign, the narrative theme of royal hunting is restricted to the last two phases (e.g. SE16:341′–47′). Its attestations are too numerous to be dismissed right away. The same trend is seen in the texts of Ashurnasirpal II. Possibly, hunting largely took place in conquered territory, symbolizing the king's extended authority.[285] Another tendency which is repeated in the sources of Shalmaneser III is that of royal wisdom as a late phenomenon. Royal epithets claiming this status, i.e. "he who knows" and "competent/wise ruler", is only attested from the final regnal third. The attestations are few however, being restricted to one single text (SE16:1–2). As already observed, the notion of gradual gaining of royal wisdom fits well with the image of Liverani regarding this topic. Also the theme of the king as tree feller seems to be a late phenomenon – again in line with the sources of his predecessor (e.g. SE14:140–41).

A temporal bias with regards to image creating is by contrast clearly absent (e.g. SE3:87–89, SE14:30–31). A fourth tendency which may be meaningful is the theme of godnapping, almost being restricted to the later two phases (e.g. SE16:22–23). It is reasonable to assume that this act was made also in the earliest phase, but that the king for some reason preferred not to narrate it at the time. The theme of honouring the foreign deities, by respecting their wishes of abductions, is thus emphasized in later propaganda. Perhaps the extended dominion and polity of the Assyrian conqueror-king called for a more universalist approach. It must be said though that Shalmaneser III makes offerings to foreign forms of Adad and the Babylonian deities also in early texts (e.g. SE5:iv2–3, SE5:v3–vi5 resp.). The relevant tendency may thus be seen as gradual rather than abrupt. Finally, some themes are only attested in the earliest phase, having the character of inherited goods from his father, namely the burning of boys and girls, the resettling of Assyrians and creating of palaces abroad, and the image of Arameans as having seizing lands (SE2:i17, SE2:ii33–38, SE2:ii38 resp.).

Regarding ideological change and specific historical events, the themes of display of strength in Babylonia and on the Mediterranean coast, and control over the land Hatti, are quite logically used already in the first phase (e.g. SE2:ii7–8, SE6:iv28 resp.). Similarly, authority over Chaldea is expressed only from the middle phase onwards (e.g. SE29:46–48). The focusing on the king's encounter with various coalitions is reflected in the ideological development

285 A similar argument is found in Winter 2000: 68. The practice of an urban hunt within Assyria identified by Weissert (1997) naturally complicates this interpretation.

(e.g. SE40:i14–24). In other words, historical events are duly incorporated and remoulded into the existing ideological fabric. That being said, there is always a danger of circular reasoning, since the history of ancient Assyria is to a considerable extent reconstructed from propaganda sources.

The decline of authority at the end of the king's reign, eventually leading to a rebellion, may also be expressed through ideological change. The theme of appointing puppet kings, which may express weakness and a less tight control (than direct rule), is expressed almost exclusively in the last regnal third (e.g. SE14:95), and the theme of officials and governors as donors and dedicators of objects is restricted to the last two regnal phases (e.g. SE31:17–19). More importantly, the field marshal Dajjan-Ashur is an important character in the final edition of the king's annals (SE14, SE16). Arguably, this is a reflection of the deteriorating authority of Shalmaneser III, of the ascendancy of the new bureaucracy, and of the overshadowing of the traditional elite (Reade 1981a: 156–60; Schneider 1991: 244–46). This may very well be true, although the perceived status of this official seems somewhat exaggerated. Shalmaneser III's inclusion of Dajjan-Ashur may also be seen as an extraordinary bestowing of honour, due to friendship and long service, and the ruler as the ultimate source of authority is made apparent in the annals, not the least because the narration of the field marshal's campaigns often uses the pronoun "I", thus referring to the king, when speaking of this official's deeds (e.g. SE16:328′). Shalmaneser III is in other words still the main focal point. All in all, a tendency pointing to the increasing power of officials may however be identified also in the propaganda of the king in question.

Continuing on the topic of ideological change, Dajjan-Ashur, and royal power, a military campaign from the fifth regnal year is lacking in the annals on the Kurkh Stele (SE2). In later annals, a brief narration of a campaign to Mount Kashiari is given (e.g. SE6:ii16–18). Olmstead (1921: 380–82) and Schneider (1991: 242–44) believe that this exclusion serves to gloss over a regnal year in which Dajjan-Ashur arguably rose to power in a palace revolution which successfully targeted the old establishment. This idea seems overly imaginative. The relevant exclusion may rather be explained by the need for abbreviations or the probable circumstance that the king did not conduct a significant military campaign in this year. The eponym-based way of structuring the narration made it possible to cover the latter circumstance up. In later annals, which used regnal years, this was not possible any more. Moreover, Dajjan-Ashur is mentioned as the eponym of the following sixth year on the Kurkh Stele (SE2:ii78). There was consequently not any specific taboo regarding this official at the time. As for the shift from eponyms to regnal years, the idea of Schneider (1991: 68–96) that it reflects a royal program to focus even more on the king himself is persuasive.[286] In sum, the idea of a palace revolution does not add to the tendency identified above.

As for Babylonia and ideological development, Shalmaneser III entered this land in 851–50 BCE. Babylonian deities are mentioned and have epithets in texts from the early phase (e.g. SE5:vi2), and Marduk is described as overwhelming enemies early on (SE5:v4). The southern deities are however listed only in texts from the middle phase onwards (see app. 4). As noted in the introduction, the switch from eponyms to regnal years has also been seen as a development inspired by the Babylonian custom of dating (Schneider 1991: 80–87). This argument is attractive, but the question remains why the shift from eponyms to regnal years does not occur already in the annals edition which firstly relates the king's campaigns in Babylonia (SE5). This objection may be met by the argument that the change simply evolved in court circles a few years after the king's southern missions. As observed, an increased stress on the person of the Assyrian king was, in addition, expressed by the shift in question. The identified late emphasis on both the king and his high officials may seem like a paradox, but it can equally well express a stress on the new elite (see subs. 1.7.2). In any case, it is obvious that Babylonia with its age-old religion and culture influenced Assyrian propaganda.

As noted in the introduction, a historically determined change in the description of Marduk-zakir-shumi I in the annals of Shalmaneser III has been seen (Schneider 1991: 135–46). A shift of the image of the said king from him being active to passive and helpless, starting from the handclasping scene on the throne base of the second phase is here seen (SI14:7c). However, this king's name is always mentioned (indicating the same degree of respect), slaughtering of Babylonians is claimed in the earliest version, the king in question was arguably powerful at the end of his reign (see s. 6.3), the earliest (SE5) and latest (SE16) annals editions describing the events are similar (e.g. with regards to Marduk-zakir-shumi I seeking assistance), and the need for abbreviations in the later narrations must have played a part. Also, the scene on the throne base may, as noted in subsection 5.4.5, not express equality. Marduk-zakir-shumi I is thus consistently portrayed as a subordinate to Shalmaneser III throughout the latter's reign. The image of Babylonia's weakness throughout the reign thus displays continuity.

Turning to the method of strategic comparison, the most rewarding option is probably to focus on the varying annals editions attested from Kalhu, not the least since there are not any annals preserved from the first regnal phase in

286 However, as shown by various features in e.g. SE1 such as royal epithets and the ruler narrating in first person, there was an overwhelming focusing on the king right from the start.

Assur. Texts SE1 (from Fort Shalmaneser) and SE3 (from the local Nabu temple) represent the first phase, while text SE8 (on a citadel colossi) represents the middle phase, and the texts SE14 (on the Black Obelisk) and SE16 (on a citadel statue) represent the final regnal phase. The texts in question have the same provenance (Kalhu), are of the same literary subgenre (annals), and they together cover all the three regnal phases of Shalmaneser III.

By contrast to SE1, the inscription SE3 (1–85) begins with an invocation of deities. Seven gods and goddesses are listed. Ashur is heading the list, and there are not any Babylonian deities included. Text SE8 does not have an invocation of deities. Text SE14 (1–14) does, in contrast to SE16, on the other hand have such a feature. In the case of this inscription, 13 deities are listed, with Ashur firstly enumerated, and Marduk among those listed. It is interesting to note that Ashur is consistently placed at the top of these lists, expressing a facet of divine hierarchy which is fairly standard (see app. 4).

A cluster of royal epithets is then attested in all texts mentioned (SE1:1–9, SE3:1–85, SE8:1–19, SE14:15–17, SE16:1–3). The cluster always, with the exception of SE16, starts with "king of all people", and in SE3 epithets connoting heroism, territorial rule, fearfulness, confirmation, and especially warfare are attested. In SE1, the priestly aspect is emphasized. The territorial titles are "king of Assyria" and "king of all four quarters". The said cluster of royal epithets is almost identic in SE8, with the notable exception of "king of Assyria" being absent. In SE14, the cluster in question is much shortened, but still with "king of all people" firstly enumerated and "king of Assyria" excluded. Royal epithets which clearly express militarism, fearfulness, and priesthood are here lacking, but this condition may be due to the abbreviated state of the cluster rather than signifying any ideological change. In the likewise late SE16, there is a short cluster of epithets beginning with "strong and wise/competent ruler". All relevant aspects, with the exception of titles of militarism, are expressed in this cluster. In all inscriptions, a short genealogy is then given. SE1 (10–11) and SE3 (1–85) present slightly different versions, and SE8 (20–24) comes up with yet another version which subsequently is used also in the later inscriptions of SE14 (17–21) and SE16 (4–5).

After these clusters of divine and royal names and epithets, an abstract which presents Ashur as the one who has given Shalmaneser III authority and weapons, and has ordered royal imperialism is conveyed in SE1 (11–13) and SE3 (1–85). It may also have been expressed in SE8 in the unfortunate lacuna of this text. Right after the genealogy, SE8 (24–40) instead has an elaborate narration regarding the king's conquesting from GN to GN. In SE14 and SE16, both the relevant abstract and the relevant conquesting narration are absent. Returning to SE1 (14–15) and SE3 (1–85), a brief statement that Shalmaneser III, after having "greatly taken a seat upon his throne", mobilized his chariots and troops is given. This statement was probably a part also of SE8, and most evidently is a part of SE14 (22–24) and SE16 (6–7).

Thereafter, a chronologically ordered narration of military campaigns begins. In SE1 (15–95′) and SE3 (1–85, 85–99), the narration is structured around eponyms and the itinerary expression "moving on" (*namāšu*), and the military campaigns are described in relative detail. In SE8 (1′–27″), the narration is structured around regnal years, and the military campaigns are narrated in an abbreviated way. Texts SE14 (24–190) and SE16 (7–341′) are also structured around regnal years, and display an even greater degree of abbreviation. The text SE16 (341′–48′) adds two narrative passages to the description of the last military campaign in regnal year 31. The first one states that the gods Ninurta and Nergal have ordered the king to hunt, whereafter a detailed list of felled prey follows. The last one briefly states that the king strengthened his army by aquiring chariots and by equipping their horses.

Drawing conclusions from this comparison, the overall impression is one of continuity. The discussed cluster of royal epithets as well as the ordering of deities remain stable throughout the reign. The various aspects regarding royal epithets of heroism-competition, territorial rule, fearfulness, divine confirmation, priesthood, and royal warfare are not restricted to any particular regnal phase. Interesting variations are the title "king of Assyria" as an early phenomenon, and the emergence of Marduk in list of deities in the later phases. As for the former, I have however shown already that this standard title is attested also in the king's final regnal phase. The move from eponyms to regnal years seems to be the one major, significant change, possibly implying an intention to focus even stronger on the ruler. It may also speak of Assyria's special relationship with Babylonia. Speaking generally, abbreviations may explain much variation. As noted by Grayson (1981: 36–47), variations in the narration of military campaigns seem to a large extent depend on banal editorial considerations, most importantly abbreviations.

Summing up the findings of this section, the general impression is, once again, continuity in terms of the king's ideology and his three regnal phases. Some ideological features such as royal wisdom, royal hunting, godnapping, and tree felling may however be noted, all occurring as late phenomena. An increased emphasis on the king and his officials has also been observed. Neither the idea of grand ideological development schemes nor the idea of the king earning titles can be convincingly substantiated in the sources.

6.4 Ideology and regnal phases of the other kings

In this section, ideological change and continuity in the reigns of some of the other Early Neo-Assyrian kings (where meaningful) are investigated. I will once again argue that there are not any grand ideological scheme detectable, and that the thesis of earning titles is questionable. A few features, such as royal hunting, the power of high officials, and the relative strength *vis-à-vis* Babylonia are tentatively identified as restricted in terms of regnal phases.

Because of the relative small number and non-varied nature of the preserved primary sources, it is only meaningful to make strategic comparisons here (see apps. 1–2). Only Adad-narari II and III have texts which are dated so as to make such comparison possible, and only Adad-narari III has iconography for a fair strategic comparison. In other cases, the relevant texts or images are either undated (Ashur-dan II and III), represent only one regnal phase (Tukulti-Ninurta II), or represent two phases but do not share a common provenance or typology (Shamshi-Adad V, Shalmaneser IV, Ashur-narari V). Still, after the said strategic comparisons, some broad notes on tendencies (linked to historical events) in the other reigns will be made.

Beginning chronologically with the reign of Adad-narari II (911–891), two annals editions on clay tablets from Assur, one dated to 909 BCE (An2E1) and the other to 893 BCE (An2E2), will be compared. These texts are both quite substantial, of the same genre (annals), and they have the same origin (Assur). In other words, this comparison can be considered quite fair.

Text An2E1 (1–7) starts with the royal name, a section of royal epithets beginning with "great king", and a genealogy. By contrast, An2E2 (1–12) begins with an invocation of deities headed by Ashur, the royal name, the royal epithet of "attentive prince", a note on the various blessings which the deities gave the king, a brief section of royal epithets beginning with "strong king", and a genealogy. In An2E1 (8–9′rev.), the king states that he went on a military campaign right in his accession year and in his first regnal year, and some lines, interrupted by a lacuna, focusing on military encounters and related events follow. The warfare narrations are structured around "months" (*warḫu*). In the same text, a building inscription concerning the facing of the quay wall at a city entrance and below the Ashur temple then follows, and it goes on with a call to future rulers regarding the king's work, and a blessing (An2E1:10′–18′ rev.). A dating and the naming of two high officials who were in charge of the project conclude this text (An2E1:19′–21′rev.).

After the introductory sections and passages referred to above, the inscription of An2E2 (13–35) instead continues with a short note on the great gods giving the king authority and orders, and goes on with a very long section of royal epithets or epithet-like utterances beginning with "I am king". Then a claim of having rebuilt, and providing it with a palace, the city of Apqu is made (An2E2:36–38). Thereafter the long warfare narration, structured around eponyms and covering the years 901–894 BCE, follows (An2E2:39–119). Text

An2E2 (120–121) then gives a note on the constructing of palaces, agricultural activities, and the strengthening of the cavallery, before it provides another note on hunting ordered by Ninurta and Nergal (An2E2:122–27). A building inscription centering on the rebuilding of the Gula temple of Ashur, a brief call to future rulers, a section of blessings and curses, and a dating conclude this clearly later dated text (An2E2:128–34).

Following up on this comparison, there is not any grand ideological development scheme detectable. As for the thesis of development from heroic-competetive to territorial rule, An2E2 (15) describes the king as hero, and it focuses much on conquering. The idea of a development from religious to military royal titles is not present. The arguably most religious title, "attentive prince", is attested in both texts (An2E1:3, An2E2:5). Also, the later text is the one focusing on divine names and epithets. The idea of earning titles can also be rejected. Adad-narari II refers to himself as "king of the universe" and "king of all four quarters" already in An2E1 (1–2), in which campaigning in all directions is not conveyed. Furthermore, the king actually drops the former title in An2E2. Similarly, the title "king of Assyria" is actually stronger in An2E2, attested as much as three times (An2E2:10,16,134).

The ideas on massive building and campaigning early on in the reign can not be detected – at least not clearly. The narration of building projects are largely concentrated to the building inscriptions, and the narration of the military campaigning is evenly spread out, appearing as a cyclical feature. It should be said though that the mentioning of six continuous campaigns against Hanigalbat in An2E2 (39–90) may speak of a relevant highlighting. Fearfulness, royal descent, and divine choice are substantially expressed both in An2E1 (1–7) and An2E2 (5–12). The notion of a development from conquest to peaceful governing of the foreign peoples can find some support in the circumstance that the title "sungod of all people" is found only in An2E2 (10), but the referring to violent conquest is still pervading An2E2.

Turning to ideological themes possibly restricted in time, the two notes at the end of An2E2 concerning palace building, agricultural activities, strengthening of the army, and hunting occur only in this later text. It is difficult to evaluate the importance of these tendencies, especially since these are solely tied to this strategic comparison, but it is interesting to observe that, once again, royal hunting is a late phenomenon. The switch from structuring the war narrations around months to eponyms may have practical reasons. Possibly, the wars narrated in An2E1 occurred in the same year. All in all, continuity rather than change should be stressed in the comparison.

Moving on to ideological development in the reign of Adad-narari III, it is unfortunate that there is not any annalistic text from this king preserved. In light of the circumstances, the best (if not the only) option is to focus on the texts and images on the Pazarcik (An3E3, An3I5) and Antakya (An3E2, An3I6) stelae. They are similar in terms of content, both are so-called border monuments, they are both situated in the border areas or foreign lands, and the former monument probably belongs to an earlier regnal phase than the latter one. The strategic comparison should thus be seen as fair and valid.

Beginning with the texts, the early Pazarcik Stele starts with stating that the stele commemorates a certain border, and continues with the name of the king, the title "king of Assyria", and a genealogy which brings up his parents, Shamshi-Adad V and Sammuramat, with their titles (An3E3:1–7). A brief historical narrative then follows which says that the king of Kummuh caused the king and the queen-mother to cross the Euphrates and fight against a coalition headed by the ruler of Arpad (An3E3:7–15). The king and his mother of course won, and it is then stated that a border between the rulers of Kummuh and Gurgum was established by the two previously mentioned (An3E3:15–18). A number of deities are then said to protect, e.g. with a curse, the border for the sake of the Kummuh ruler (An3E3:19–23).

The text on the later Antakya Stele starts with the royal name, a few epithets beginning with "great king", and a genealogy (An3E2:1–3). The text then states that the stele marks the border, established jointly by Adad-narari III and the field marshal Shamshi-ilu, between two Syrian rulers of Hamath and Arpad, to the benefit in terms of urban and agricultural areas of the latter (An3E2:4–11). Atarshumki, the Arpad ruler, may actually be the same person focused on in An3E3. The text concludes with naming the deities who protect the border establishing, and who punish those who intend to disregard it (An3E2:11–19). Turning to the iconographical evidence, both stelae (An3I5–6) each contains a moon standard, but the Antakya Stele stands out by complementing the crescent with the unclear traces of two individuals in relief, possibly representing Adad-narari III and Shamshi-ilu (see s. 2.1).

Commenting on this comparison, the relative brevity of the two inscriptions hinder any evaluation of the issue of ideological development schemes, but there are still some interesting points to draw. Sammuramat is centered on in An3E3, while Shamshi-ilu is focused on in An3E2 as well as in the iconography of An3I6. This is of course in line with the standard perception of the reign, namely as Adad-narari III first being influenced (as being merely a minor) by his mother, and then by his field marshal (see s. 8.1).

Moving on to making some broad notes concerning the issue of historical events and ideological development within eNA I and eNA III-reigns, the different view on Babylonia in the late text of Adad-narari II where the king is said to have defeated his Babylonian counterpart, and the eventual friendly speaking of Babylonia in the Synchronistic History edited during Adad-narari III is noticeable (An2E2:26–29, An3E59:iii17–21 resp.). This may reflect the historical situation of Adad-narari II's times where Assyria and Babylonia first were enemies and then allies, rather than the difference in genre between royal annals and chronicles. As for Babylonia, it is also interesting to observe the change in tone between Marduk-zakir-shumi I and Shamshi-Adad V in their treaty and in the latter's annals (SA5E15, SA5E1 resp.). In the former and early text, the Babylonian king has the upperhand, while the situation is reversed in the latter and later text (see subs. 5.4.5). Again, this ideological development is historically conditioned. Lastly, many texts belonging to high officials, notably those of Shamshi-ilu and Nergal-erish (e.g. An3E34, An3E6 resp.), in the reign of Adad-narari III are late, perhaps telling of a background of a gradual decline of royal authority.

Summing up the modest findings of this section, grand ideological development schemes and the idea of earning titles were not detected in the strategic comparisons, nor any other of the theses referred to in section 6.1. Royal hunting as a late phenomenon under Adad-narari II, the switch of emphasis from Sammuramat to high officials under Adad-narari III, and the historically conditioned changes in viewing Babylonia under Adad-narari II and Shamshi-Adad V may be a few examples of ideological change.

6.5 Summary and reflections

From the discussion above, a number of points can be made. Firstly, it is difficult to substantiate any fixed, grand scheme of ideological development according to which the state ideology of a particular ruler gradually changes from heroism-militarism to territorial rule (Liverani), from priesthood to military leadership (Cifola), and the like. Although tendencies may occasionally exist – sometimes in the opposite direction – the exceptions to the rule are simply too many to ignore. Liverani's analysis of Sennacherib's annals editions and Cifola's analysis of the royal titles and epithets of some of the Assyrian kings thus seem to have limited general application.

Secondly, certain individual themes may on the other hand be chronologically dependent. Royal hunt, royal wisdom, tree felling, references to Arameans as land seizers, and the creating of royal images (the final one only in Ashurnasirpal II's case) may have that character, although further studies need to be made in order to confirm these examples as temporally biased. Because of the inadequate temporal distribution of the motifs, it is hardly possible to make firm conclusions on the basis of the iconography.

Thirdly, the general impression of ideological continuity within the studied reigns indicates that the rulers in question each had an established ideological program right from their seizing of the throne, which they then kept throughout their reigns. This may especially be said of Shalmaneser III with his remarkable continuity, spanning nearly three decades, regarding deity hierarchy and a specific cluster of royal epithets. The Assyrian rulers then formulated their world view full-fledgedly and not in a bit by bit-manner.

Fourthly and more generally, the idea of several scholars, notably Liverani, that the Assyrian king's titles had to be "earned" and can be explained by historical events should be modified. Although this idea is certainly valid in a wider sense (historical events and ideological development went hand in hand and influenced each other), it should be recognized that royal epithets are, at least to some extent, to use the wording of Cifola (1995: 148), "bombastic and rhetorical", and not always earned. This is also indicated by the circumstance that also fairly anonymous rulers claim worldwide dominion.

Fifthly, it is clear that other factors such as typology, i.e. literary genre and type of monument, and to some degree also archaeological context, e.g. type of site, building, or room, are more important to focus on as far as variations in the ideological sources are concerned. As for the former, annals centre on the king as warrior, stelae portray the king as venerating priest, obelisks convey scenes of tribute, and so on. As for the archaeological context, the issue of ideological variation and change depending on provenance in terms of cities or regions will be the focal point of the following chapter.

7 Local propaganda and regional politics

In this chapter, the issue regarding the existence or lack of ideological variation and trends due to the provenances of the major primary sources is highlighted. Its first section gives an introductory and general overview of the relevant discussion in scholarly literature, and the following two sections present conclusions on the subject based on general and strategic comparisons while focusing on the primary sources of Ashurnasirpal II and Shalmaneser III. The next section deals with the stated issue and the primary sources of the other Early Neo-Assyrian kings, and the final section lastly provides a summary with reflections. As made clear below, the discussion on local propaganda is closely connected to the aspect of regional politics.

7.1 Introduction

It almost goes without saying that there is potential to find variations in propaganda depending on provenance. A uniformity in ideological expression from the foreign lands to the Assyrian heartland can not be taken for granted. This is not the least evident from the circumstance that even within the said heartland there were clear historical and archaeologically based differences, such as between the cities of Assur and Nineveh (Radner 2011). The question is what the relation between local ideas on rule (which must have existed) and standardizing tendencies was in the Early Neo-Assyrian state.

Also the issue of ideological variation caused by provenance has been relatively neglected in Assyriological research (Liverani 1981: 231 n. 12; Cifola 1995: 2–3). The study of Liverani (1981: 248–51) centering on variations in Sennacherib's titulary in this context stands out as a groundbreaking study once again. The scholar in question observes varying annals editions in Assur and Nineveh, and concludes that the edition from Assur does *not* focus on military-territorial superiority by which Ashur has commanded warfare, but rather on peaceful roles where the Assyrian ruler had the defensive function of protecting the people from external threats. By contrast, the edition from Nineveh highlights warfare and divinely ordained imperialism.

Proceeding from this study, the special profile of propaganda from Assur is much about, in an Old Assyrian fashion, seeing the ruler strictly as a "first among equals". Arguably, there was a resistance in Assur against the idea of a strong kingdom of a Babylonian character (Oppenheim 1979: 133–35). The special role of Assur is also seen in the privileges granted to its inhabitants (Tadmor 2011: 126–34), in the temple of Ashur, and in the proposed tradition of a public recital of letters to Ashur (Oppenheim 1960). A special ideological profile of Kalhu, and later also of Dur-Sharrukin/Khorsabad and Nineveh, are the monumental reliefs which lined the walls of palaces and temples. A standard inscription (AE53) was inscribed everywhere in the Old Palace of Assur, like the standard inscription of Kalhu (AE23) in relation to the North-West Palace (Orlamünde 2011b: 447–50), but without the grand reliefs celebrating the might of the imperialist and increasingly autocratic king (Seux 1980–83: 172–73). Although not exclusively attested in Balawat, the impressive embossings on door bands from this town may tell of a local tradition.[287] The locally diverging patron deities Ashur (Assur), Ishtar (Nineveh, Arbela), Ninurta (Kalhu), and Mamu (Balawat) of the named great Assyrian centres must also be reckoned with as for ideological variation. In short, there are good grounds to investigate the issue of local propaganda.

The topic of local propaganda is intimately connected with regional politics. During the reign of Ashurnasirpal II, Assur was given less prominence, and Kalhu and Nineveh were highlighted instead (Schramm 1973: 18). Nineveh had grown in importance already before the mentioned king,[288] and at the beginning of his reign he conducted his military campaigns from this city, arguably a sign of Nineveh being a vital administrative centre, i.e. as a (if not *the*) seat of residence during his first few years on the throne (Börker-Klähn 1982: 184 n. 1). Later on, Kalhu usurped the role of departure point for the army. Assur is not mentioned as a destination for booty and tribute. All this tells of moves directed by geopolitical concerns (Schneider 1991: 234–39). Also regarding the inscriptions of Shalmaneser III, this shift of departure point for the army from Nineveh to Kalhu is articulated,[289] even though the former city is by contrast not described as a seat of residence. As opposed to in the inscriptions of his father, Assur is frequently stated as being the destination for booty and tribute (Schneider 1991: 234–39). This coming and going of the Assyrian army thus tells of regional politics.

The change of capital city from Assur to Kalhu seems pivotal to focus on in this discussion. Radner (2011: 323–25) has suggested that the move aimed at counterbalancing the regional dominance of Arbela and Nineveh which had gradually evolved. According to a related analysis, the move served to establish a new social order, alienating the traditional elite and fostering an elite

---

287 The special status of this town as a "new town" and as a way station and supply base for the Assyrian army (D. Oates 1974: 173–75) makes local traditions even more likely.
288 Note e.g. the expression of Tukulti-Ninurta II, indicating which seat of residence he had in his stating that "While I was residing in Nineveh ..." (*ina Ninua usbākūni* ...) (TN2E5:9).
289 Also Arbela is occasionally stated as a departure point for the army (e.g. SE6:iii58).

directly dependent on the king (Larsen 1979b: 85–86; Reade 1981a: 156–60; Barjamovic 2011: 61). This is of course a development which follows the model of the patrimonial state. Anyway, according to Postgate and Reade (1976–80: 320), the move was made because of the central location of Kalhu, its good communications, the pristine character of the land (with lots of potential for ambitious building projects), and because the move was a way to avoid taking sides between Assur and Nineveh. The central location of Kalhu could also have implied the realization of the idea of the Assyrian capital city as "the city at the center of the world" (Liverani 1973: 189–90).

Regional politics are by its very nature a source of controversy. Localities and people stand against each other in a fight over power and resources. Opposition is created, and rebellions and civil wars may eventually erupt. The traditional and privileged centre Assur is often spoken of as a notorious centre of opposition in Neo-Assyrian times, whose establishment had to be appeased or pacified by the elsewhere residing ruler (Garelli 1973: 209–10; Oppenheim 1979: 133–35; Frahm 2010: 89–90). Frahm (2010: 89–90) presumes a tension between the elite of Assur and the absent Neo-Assyrian ruler, and provides several examples of opposition with Assur as its origin. The move of capital by Ashurnasirpal II away from Assur was triggered by a desire to strengthen the position of the king at the expense of "the old urban elites" (Schneider 1991: 244–46; Radner 2011: 323 n. 4). At the same time, the king with his scholars continued to define Assur "as the nexus of authority and cultural identity" of Assyria (Pongratz-Leisten 2013: 287).

There was a constant struggle for power between the king and the nobility in the Early Neo-Assyrian Period (Larsen 1979b: 85–86). As two results of this, the civil war at the end of Shalmaneser III's reign as well as the increased decentralization of authority in the first half of the 8th millennium BCE were the consequences of a deep rift between the old establishments of the old urban centres and the new imperial administration or bureaucracy, represented mostly by eunuchs, in the new urban centres (Reade 1981a: 156–60; Schneider 1991: 244–46). As for the former phenomenon, the conflict between the arguably sidestepped crown prince Ashur-da"in-apli and Dajjan-Ashur at the end of the king's reign was a conflict between old and new establishments (Schneider 1991: 244–46).[290] The crown prince here reacted to the proposed great and

290 Fuchs (2008: 65–68) claims that Dajjan-Ashur (855–826) died in the same year that the rebellion broke out, and also states that Ashur-da"in-apli indeed was the designated heir to the throne. The Dajjan-Ashur clique who backed Shamshi-Adad V, and who also comprised the following field marshal Jahalu (826–816), eventually emerged as the victorious faction.

usurped power of the field marshal (Olmstead 1921: 381–82).[291] As for the latter phenomenon, the identified voluntarily (Siddall 2013) or forced (e.g. Grayson 1996: 200–201) decentralization of political authority in the first half of the eighth century BCE during which the outer provinces and the border areas – and the high officials in charge of these areas – greatly benefited may also carry some meaning in the present discussion revolving around local propaganda and regional politics.

7.2 Ashurnasirpal II and local propaganda

In this section, the issue of local propaganda and regional politics in the reign of Ashurnasirpal II is investigated. Firstly, a general comparison is made, then a strategic comparison, focusing on two texts from Assur and Nineveh, is conducted. I will e.g. argue that the scarcity of propaganda from Assur and the lack of clear local propaganda in the heartland point to a conscious move towards autocracy and ideological standardization respectively.

The statistics on the spatial distribution of the major primary sources (see app. 3) may be presented and discussed initially. Ashurnasirpal II invested a lot of effort and prestige in the elevation of Kalhu. This is not the least reflected in the large share of the major primary sources deriving from this city. As much as 65 % of his iconographic entities come from Kalhu, and no less than 41 % of his inscriptions have this city as their provenance. By contrast, Assur seems neglected as far as proportions are concerned. There are not any securely dated iconography that comes from this city, and only 12 % of his inscriptions derive from the old city in question. Nineveh was considerably better treated when it comes to shares of primary sources. 8 % of Ashurnasirpal II's iconography and 24 % of this ruler's texts have this age-old city as their origins. Balawat was highlighted by the ruler in question. 5 % of the king's iconography and 18 % of his inscriptions derive from this elevated inner core town. As for iconography and the outer core or the border areas/foreign lands, the relevant numbers are 11 % and 5 % respectively. The corresponding figures regarding the inscriptions are 2 % and 1 % respectively.

Turning to a qualitative evaluation and the city Assur, the royal epithets of Ashurnasirpal II from this urban centre are much varied, and display a great representativity of the whole epithet collection. The king as hero and

291 Providing another picture, Lambert (1974a: 109) suggests that Dajjan-Ashur, and not crown prince Ashur-da"in-apli, led the army simply for safety reasons, because of a strong opposition within the armed forces who might have tried to assasinate the latter on campaign.

warrior is much highlighted (e.g. AE153:12–13, AE153:6–11 resp.). In other words, not just roles of a peaceful character are expressed in inscriptions from Assur. Interestingly, the epithet of "shepherd" is absent, possibly implying a resistance towards this south Mesopotamian notion of leadership (see subs. 5.4.4).[292] On the other hand, the imagery of "sun", also a south Mesopotamian import (see subs. 5.4.4), is present (e.g. AE153:2). Epithets which of age are associated with Assur such as "vice-regent of Ashur", "prince", "king of Assyria", and "lord" are all attested also outside Assur (e.g. AE41:1, AE29:4′, AE1:i28, AE20:42 resp.). The secondly and fourthly mentioned epithets are even given to foreign rulers (e.g. AE35:8, AE1:i19 resp.). Both violent and peaceful activities of the ruler are expressed in the textual narrative from Assur (e.g. AE154:11–20′, AE52:3′–10′ resp.).

Regarding texts with Assur provenances and the divine sphere, not only Ashur is included in these texts. Ishtar is centred on in a royal prayer (AE171), Sin and Shamash are highlighted in building inscriptions (e.g. AE52:3′–9′rev.), and Ninurta is focused on in commemorative texts (e.g. [AE153:1]). Enlil is a frequent component of royal epithets (e.g. AE154:2), although perhaps in this god's role as merging with Ashur. As for divine epithets, Ashur is "lord of all lands" not in Assur but in Nineveh (AE40:9), and he is called "king of all the great gods" also in Kalhu (AE17:i1). The god in question is heading sequences also in Kalhu and the border areas (see app. 4). The primacy of Ashur is thus not just connected to Assur. On the whole, the propaganda from Assur lacks a clearly defined local character.

Moving on to Kalhu, the royal epithets are of all possible kinds, displaying a great representativity in relation to the whole collection of epithets. It is noticeable that the theme of the wise king is expressed only in royal epithets from this city (AE2:23). The epithet of "purification priest" is amply attested in Kalhu (e.g. AE1:i21).[293] A local stamp on the sources is given by the frequent inclusion of Ninurta in the king's epithets, such as in "vice-regent of Ashur and Ninurta" and in "chosen of Enlil and Ninurta" (e.g. AE17:i37, AE23:1 resp.). Just as Ashur and Enlil are linked in Assur is Ninurta and Enlil linked in Kalhu (Reade 2002: 191). Ninurta, and not only Marduk, is referred to as "sage", and he is also "foremost among the deities" (*ašarēd ilāni*) (e.g. AE3:9, AE169:2 resp.). Ashurnasirpal II arguably had a program to establish Ninurta as the

---

292 The inscribed stele belonging to the Row of Stelae, and the inscribed royal sarcophagus from the Old Palace from this city may speak of a local stamp on the ideological sources (AE108, AE115 resp.). They arguably hark back to a more traditional notion of rulership.

293 This priestly role seems to be much alluded to on the walls of the North-West Palace, not the least through the nearly omnipresent apotropaic motifs (J. M. Russell 1998b).

patron deity of Kalhu, replacing Ishtar-mistress-of-Kidmuru (Reade 2002: 191, 198–99). Despite this primacy, neither Ashur (from Assur) nor Ishtar (from Nineveh) are neglected in the divine titulary from Kalhu (e.g. AE28:v15, AE1:i37–38 resp.). The neglecting of building a shrine for Ashur in Kalhu (Reade 2002: 199) may paradoxically be seen as a sign of respect. Ninurta does not dominate deity sequences in Kalhu or anywhere else (see app. 4). As already noted, Kalhu was cherished by Ashurnasirpal II as "the centre of my (his) lordship" (AE30:53). Nevertheless, the city was explicitly dedicated to Ashur and not to Ninurta (e.g. AE30:40).

As for the textual narrative, the range of themes is great, not giving a clear and consistent local profile. The texts from Kalhu, and those from the border areas, may be slightly more focused on violence than those from other localities, but at least in the former case this may be due to typological factors, such as the fact that AE1, which speaks much of atrocities, was inscribed in the temple of the warring god Ninurta (Porter 2003: 84–85), and to the many annals deriving from Kalhu. The themes of the ruler holding banquets, or hunting and collecting wild animals, or creating gardens and orchards are however typical features of the inscriptions from Kalhu (e.g. AE30:102–54, AE1:iii48–49, AE30:36–52 resp.). Furthermore, building activities and deportations are also much highlighted (e.g. AE23:14–22, AE30:33–36 resp.).

Turning finally to the iconography of Kalhu, neither wall reliefs nor colossi are restricted, although concentrated, to Kalhu (see also AI1, AI5–6, AI10).[294] It may be noted though that minor arts (AI23–37) largely derive from Kalhu, although this probably is a result of the history of excavations rather than symptomatic of any ideological trend. The motifs attested from Kalhu are wide-ranging. The motifs of "king in battle", "on march", "receiving captives/booty/ tribute" are all attested from the new capital city (e.g. AI4:B18t., AI4:WFL19b., AI4:B18b., AI4:WFL24b., AI4:D2 resp.). The motif of "king as hunter" and the priestly ones of "king as venerating/libating priest" are also attested from the relevant city (e.g. AI23:G8,31a, AI19, AI22 resp.). Some motifs, such as "king being ritually purified", weapon cleansing, "king as shepherd", and "king at banquet" are attested only from Kalhu (e.g. AI4:F4, AI4:G6, AI4:B14, AI4:G3 resp.).[295] Ashurnasirpal II is represented both as warrior and violent and as priestly and benevolent in Kalhu. In sum, although some local marks on the visual and textual propaganda from Kalhu can tentatively be identified, it is

294 I should add here that Orlamünde (2011b: 453) also suggests a dating to Ashurnasirpal II of some of the fragmentary colossi excavated from the Old Palace in Assur.

295 Note however that the king in question appears as shepherd on the door bands from Balawat, holding a staff while receiving processions of various kinds (e.g. AI14:67–68).

nevertheless hardly justified to talk of a certain clearly distinguished local propaganda of Kalhu.

Continuing to Nineveh, also in the case of royal epithets from this city there is a great variety and range. Nevertheless, some features stand out, possibly indicating a local propaganda of a sort. The theme of difficult path is much highlighted, and the role of the king as conqueror and extender of borders is a recurring theme (e.g. AE56:3, AE40:8 resp.). The notion of the king as "progeny" (*nabnītu*) is also unique to Nineveh (AE40:6). The presence of the title "priest" (*šangû*) obviously alludes to a priestly function also in this urban centre (e.g. AE59:3). Ishtar is highlighted e.g. in the royal epithets of "he who made and repaired the Ishtar temple" or "he who marches with the support of (e.g.) Ishtar" (AE111:4, AE56:7 resp.). Neither Ashur nor Ninurta are however neglected. Ashur, Adad, Ishtar, and Ninurta are e.g. "his (the king's) lords" (e.g. AE66:4–5), and Ashur and Ishtar are "those who love my (the king's) kingship" (AE:40:38–39). The patron deity of Nineveh is consistently placed at or towards the end of deity sequences (see app. 4). The textual narrative from Nineveh involves both violent and peaceful roles of the king. The theme of royal hunting is absent, but the theme of royal wisdom is expressed (AE40:33–34). There are not many motifs preserved from Nineveh. The few which exist show the king as hunter, bow shooting and libating (AI1:86, AI1:214–20 resp). Thus, a clearly defined local propaganda is hard to pinpoint also in the case of the sources from Nineveh.

Turning to Balawat and its attested royal epithets, the corpus include "basic titles"[296] and additionally echoes many of the peaceful epithets attested in AE23, i.e. the Standard Inscription of Kalhu (e.g. AE51:1, AE51:5–6 resp.), but otherwise the relevant epithets are almost completely stressing royal heroism and militarism (e.g. AE51:3–11). Clear priestly epithets are lacking. The textual narrative has a partly different character. It conveys both an image of the king as violent and benevolent-peaceful. The role of the king as master builder of temples, palaces, and the town is unproportionally high (e.g. AE50:21–34), although in a smaller extent to the texts from Kalhu. The ideological theme of royal hunt is attested more than once (e.g. AE94).

As for the royal iconography of Balawat, the door bands are naturally highlighted (AI13–14). The Balawat gates display a tendency of focusing on the king being engaged in warfare and receiving tribute. The motifs of "king in battle" and "receiving captives" are only attested in Balawat (e.g. AI13:9–10, AE13:21–22 resp.) and Kalhu, something which almost also can be said of the motif

296 A term used by Liverani (1981: 233) to denote titles such as "great/strong king".

"king receiving tribute" (e.g. AI14:73–74). Similarly, the motif of "the king as hunter" is predominantly found in Balawat (e.g. AI13:29–30) and Kalhu. Priestly motifs, attested in Kalhu, are lacking. The motif of "the king as shepherd" is attested insofar as the king is frequently depicted holding a staff while receiving processions (e.g. AI13:35–36). Taken together, there seems to be a clear emphasis on military matters in the texts and images from Balawat, justifying a cautious identifying of local propaganda in relation to this locality. This particular profile of Ashurnasirpal II's propaganda in Balawat may be explained by the function of this town as lying on a marching route and being a way station of the Assyrian army.

Moving on to the outer core and possible local propaganda in the time of Ashurnasirpal II, there are several things to note. Adad is e.g. highlighted in the western areas, e.g. through the many divine epithets which are given to this god in the text of Adad-it'i, the governor of Guzana (AE148). In the said inscription there is an almost complete focus on this god who was honoured with many cult centres in the west. Furthermore, the governor of Shadikanni, Mushezib-Ninurta, calls himelf "vice-regent", and additionally highlights his local deity (AE149–51). The palace of the latter royal official was decorated with reliefed orthostats, colossi, and lions (AI6, AI10), all fashioned in an Assyrianized, Syrian-Hittite style (J. M. Russell 1998–2001: 250). By contrast, the palace of the governor of Dur-Katlimmu was decorated (AI5) in the style of the North-West Palace (J. M. Russell 1998–2001: 248), indicating centralization and homogenization. Taken together though, local propaganda is highly relevant to talk of regarding the sources from the distant provinces.

As for the issue of local propaganda and the border areas or foreign lands, the royal epithets attested from these peripheral regions share the characteristics of those from Balawat. Many epithets focus on royal violence, heroism, and territorial dominion (e.g. AE19:11–15, AE20:43, AE19:22 resp.), although basic titles and epithets centering on peace, tending, and benevolence also are attested (e.g. AE19:5, AE19:21 resp.). Overall though, the epithets stress coercion. As for the textual narrative, there is a dominance of descriptions of military campaigns and atrocities, although this may be due to typology represented by the annals of the Kurkh Monolith (AE19). The theme of royal hunting is also given (e.g. AE19:33–34). As for the iconography, the image is completely different. The Assyrian ruler is only peacefully depicted as a venerating priest, making the pointing gesture (e.g. AI18). The proposed dual function of stelae in the periphery may be expressed here. The messages of royal stelae, attested both in the core and periphery, are here interpreted as simultaneously conveying intimidation and speaking of peacefulness and priesthood (Börker-Klähn 1982: 54–60; Liverani 1992b: 132). All things combined, a clearly defined local propaganda is not conveyed.

Turning to the methodological component of strategic comparison, the standard inscriptions of Kalhu (AE23) and Nineveh (AE40) may be compared. They are both summary inscriptions, similarly dated, having the same status, and having a similar type of closer provenance, i.e. palace/temple.

Both standard inscriptions start with a cluster of royal epithets with genealogy, the former beginning with "vice-regent of Ashur", and the latter with "great king" (AE23:1–5, AE40:1–10). AE23 (5–6) goes on to state that Ashur had chosen and armed Ashurnasirpal II, and briefly informs that the king had engaged in warfare against opponents in the eastern mountains (AE23:6–8). Text AE40 instead states that Anu, Enlil, and Ea had chosen and invested Ashurnasirpal II, and that these had ordered the king "to make lands unsubmissive to Ashur submit" (AE40:10–12). Another cluster of royal epithets, beginning with "heroic man", and a genealogy then follow (AE40:12–19).

Both texts then have a long note on the geographical extent of the king's conquests (AE23:8–11, AE40:19–27), and they both state that the king has counted conquered people as Assyrians (AE23:11, AE40:24–25). AE23 (11–12) adds a statement of the installing of governors, and another cluster of royal epithets, starting with "attentive prince", comes next (AE23:12–14). The same text finishes with a note on the building of Kalhu, mentioning the deportations of people to this city, and giving a longer description of the constructing of the North-West Palace (AE23:14–22). By contrast, AE40 (28–30) finishes with a brief statement that Ashurnasirpal II went to Mehru to fetch timber for the rebuilding of the temple of Ishtar in Nineveh. The process of rebuilding is described, involving the themes of previous builders, wise king, and heroic priority (AE40:30–37), a call to future rulers with blessings given by Ashur and Ishtar follows (AE40:38–41), and a curse to be implemented by Adad subsequently ends this inscription (AE40:42–44).

To evaluate this strategic comparison, the texts differ structurally quite a lot. Possibly, this has to do with the varying archaeological contexts (temples or palaces) of the two texts, although tendencies of local propaganda also may have played a part. The royal epithets are much varied in both cities, although a few ideological tendencies may be discerned. AE23 seems to be slightly more focused on priesthood than AE40, and the latter definitively stands out by the frequent use of the theme difficult path. Nineveh's status of a departure point for the army may explain the latter theme. As for the former theme and war/peace, the genealogy with royal epithets in AE40 is more focused on violence than that of AE23. Possibly, the slightly more violent AE40 may be due to the fact that this text is connected with the war goddess Ishtar, not the least through it being inscribed in her local temple.

Moving on with the evaluation, the function of Anu, Enlil, and Ea, but not Ashur, as the crowning and commanding gods in AE40 is noticeable. This should not be overdramatized though, since the following sentence clearly states Ashur as a principal god. Overall, Ashur plays a substantial role in both inscriptions. Unsurprisingly, Ishtar is highlighted in AE40, and Ninurta is often mentioned in AE23. The special note on governors in AE23 may allude to the administrative focusing present in texts from Kalhu. The major role of city building and deportations in AE23 may be explained in the same way. On the whole, there are not any striking differences in content between the two standard inscriptions from Kalhu and Nineveh, although certain tentatively identified, individual ideological trends are discernable.

Summing up the findings of this section, the propaganda expressed in Assur, Kalhu, and Nineveh appears fairly uniform, arguably pointing to a move towards ideological standardization. By contrast, Balawat and the distant provinces (especially the latter) display clearer traces of local propaganda – the former with an emphasis on warfare. In terms of spatial distribution of the sources, Assur is neglected, at the advantage of Kalhu, Nineveh, and Balawat, arguably as a result of carefully planned regional politics.

7.3 Shalmaneser III and local propaganda

In this section, local propaganda and regional politics in the reign of Shalmaneser III is investigated. Firstly a general comparison is made, then a strategic comparison focusing on two texts from Kalhu and Assur is conducted. I will e.g. argue that the relatively plentyful ideological sources from Assur tell of a strategy to appease the old nobility, and that the absence of clear, delimited local ideologies in the Assyrian core is a reflection of an ongoing program to centralize and standardize propaganda in Assyria.

Beginning once again with the issue of the spatial distribution of the major primary sources (see app. 3) in terms of provenance, also in the case of this king Kalhu dominates when it comes to iconographical entities.[297] Over half of them, i.e. 58 %, have such an origin. The share of texts from Kalhu is however not quite so significant, namely 24 %. By contrast to his father, Shalmaneser III seems to have favoured Assur, the old capital city. As much as 19 % of his iconography and 41 % of his texts derive from Assur. Nineveh is, by contrast, not so much centred on as far as proportions of the king's sources are concerned. Just 4 % of his iconography and inscriptions may come from this city. Balawat was highlighted also by Shalmaneser III. The sources include the Bala-

297 Here it may be worth noting that as much as 6,5 % of this ruler's text corpus can not be assigned to any particular locality – this in contrast to Ashurnasirpal II's statistics.

wat Gate, making up 4 % of his image corpus, and 17 % of his text corpus. While iconography from the outer core is lacking, iconography from the border areas/foreign lands amounts to 15 %. The corresponding figures for the share of texts are 1 % and 5 % respectively.

Turning more clearly to the issue of local propaganda, the king's epithets in Assur are wide-ranging, displaying a great representativity of the whole corpus. The king presents himself as a warrior just as well as a priest and master builder (e.g. SE10:ii51–iii5, SE6:ii49–50, SE25:21–34 resp.). The only attestation of the epithet "priest" (*šangû*) and all the references to him as "builder" (*bānû*) are however from Assur (SE10:i13, e.g. SE101:5 resp.). Also noteworthy is the treatment of the two southern Mesopotamian epithets of "sun" and "shepherd". The former is attested (e.g. SE6:i12), while the latter is absent. As with the texts of his father, the epithets of "vice-regent of Ashur", "king of Assyria", "prince", and "lord" are not just attested in Assur but also in other cities and regions (e.g. SE2:i5, SE3, SE8:3, SE17:28 resp.).

Also the textual narrative deriving from Assur is wide-ranging and all-inclusive. Again, there is not any special focus on priesthood and peaceful roles generally. The frequent references to earlier master builders in texts from this city may allude to the importance of royal ancestry held in Assur (e.g. SE10:iv40–50). The emphasis on booty, e.g. through the booty summation, may be explained by the use of Assur as the homecoming venue of the army (SE10:iv34–40). However, the phrase, implying army movement, "to my city Assur" is not only given in texts from Assur (e.g. SE10:ii5–6) but also from Kalhu and Kurkh (e.g. SE14:141, SE2:ii75 resp.). Somewhat surprisingly, the theme of royal hunting is amply given in Assur provenanced texts (e.g. SE6:iv40–44). As for the king and the few examples of iconography, an obelisk centering on tribute and some statues depicting the ruler as priest remain from Assur and Shalmaneser III's reign (e.g. SI12, SI8 resp.).

Regarding the deities, Assur, and the issue of local propaganda, Ashur is listed in first place consistently also in texts from Kalhu and the border areas (see app. 4). Similarly, Ashur's epithet "king of all the great gods" is not restricted to Assur (SE2:i1). Marduk is mentioned as "sage of the deities" (SE10:i8), and Ninurta is referred to as "foremost among the deities" in texts from Assur (e.g. SE10:i4). There is thus not any blind favouring of Ashur present. Moreover, the antagonistic, i.e. in relation to Assur, city of Babylon is certainly mentioned and clearly not taboo (e.g. SE10:ii41), but the narration of the king treating the people of Babylonia in a favoured way, or the capacity of Marduk as overwhelming the enemy, are not found in Assur texts. All in all though, although certain trends may exist, the overall impression is one of ideological diversity and representativity in the city Assur.

Moving on to Kalhu, the royal epithets of Shalmaneser III represent every possible ideological nuance attested in the propaganda of this ruler. He is variously described as a warrior, hero, priest, shepherd, engaged in overcoming the difficult path, and so on (e.g. SE28:8, SE30:10, SE57:4, SE1:5–6, SE8:11 resp.). Some trends may however be possible to discern. The theme of royal wisdom is e.g. restricted to epithets from Kalhu (SE16:1–2). The lack of the epithet *šangû* is made up for by the use of other priestly titles such as *perriku* and *šaprû* (SE1:6, SE56:2 resp.). Ninurta is unproportionally present in the titulary of the said king, such as in "chosen of Enlil and Ninurta" and "he whose support is Ninurta" (e.g. [SE16:1], [SE16:48–49] resp.). This may be a local stamp on the state ideology. Ninurta is however not dominating deity sequences in texts from Kalhu (see app. 4), and Ashur and Ishtar are frequently referred to (e.g. SE14:1–2, SE14:13 resp.).

Also the textual narrative is characterized by its wide-ranging and representative character. Some trends are however visible. Shalmaneser III is presented as an architect, fitting to the role of him commissioning numerous buildings in the new capital city (e.g. SE56:3–7). The theme of appointing puppet kings is only attested in inscriptions from Kalhu, possibly as an expression of the administrative focusing of this city project (e.g. SE16:281′–82′). Kalhu is also the place, alongside Assur, for narrations on the divine ordering of royal hunt and the enumeration of its end results (e.g. SE16:341′–47′). The person of Dajjan-Ashur is highlighted only in inscriptions deriving from Kalhu, indicating in yet another way that this city was the centre of the new, powerful establishment (e.g. SE14:141–90). Similarly, the idiom "when I was in Kalhu", emphasizing this city's status of the primary royal residence, is only found in texts from Kalhu (e.g. SE16:268′).

Turning to the royal iconography of Kalhu, both major and minor arts have been excavated from the urban centre in question. The king's few and fragmentary wall reliefs and colossi are restricted to Kalhu, pointing to the grand scale and status of this city (SI1, SI2–3 resp.). The motifs are on the whole primarily peaceful and priestly. A few attestations of the king as receiving booty or tribute exist (e.g. SI14:4b.), but the image of the king as warrior is not illustrated. Instead, he is represented as a venerating or libating priest (e.g. SI18, SI19–20 resp.), or in a priestly dress and pose on statues (SI5, SI7). He is also depicted at banquets (SI21, SI25), and as meeting his Babylonian counterpart Marduk-zakir-shumi I (SI14:7c). Typological considerations may explain the variations between the two media text and image. Summing up the whole discussion on Kalhu, although certain ideological trends exist, a clear local propaganda is hard to discern.

Moving on to the rest of the inner core, the sources from Nineveh are too few and fragmentary for a fair evaluation. That being said, as for the royal epithets, basic titles dominate (e.g. SE107:1–2), but it is noticeable that "vice-regent of Ashur" is used (SE95:4), and that the epithet of "conqueror" recurs ([SE38:4′]). As for the textual narrative, the short texts (no long text is preserved) naturally shape and limit the ideological content. Noteworthy is the circumstance that Nineveh is referred to as "my city" ([SE95:4]). Also noteworthy is the fact that a prayer to Ninlil (linked to the Ninivite Mullissu/Ishtar) has been found in Assur, and not in Nineveh (SE154). Ishtar consistently features at or towards the end of deity sequences, regardless of provenance (see app. 4). As already discussed (see s. 2.1), the royal seal which depicts the king slaying a lion may come from Nineveh (SI26). This motif is however not brought up in the relevant textual narrative.

As for Balawat, there are many royal epithets which refer to violence, territorial control, and heroism (e.g. SE5:i2, SE5:i3, SE5:i4 resp.), although quite a few centre on divine choice and on the peaceful and benevolent nature of the king's rule (e.g. SE5:i5, SE5:ii2 resp.). Priesthood is not directly spoken of. The textual narrative from this town is much dominated by the theme of royal militarism and imperialism (e.g. SE5). Also the iconography, i.e. the door bands (SI10), has a strong focus on military matters. The warfare connected motifs of "king in battle", "observing battle", "on march", and "receiving captives" are in fact restricted to Balawat (e.g. SI10:16b., SI10:15t., SI10:11b., SI10:13b. resp.). The king often receives different kinds of processions, characteristically holding a bow and two arrows in his hands (e.g. SI10:9b.). His priesthood is however visualized through the royal illustrations of "venerating" and "libating priest" (e.g. SI10:1t.). A royal banquet may be alluded to in the depicted offering scenes at the Tigris source (SI10:10), while "banquets" (*naptanu*) are spoken of in such contexts in the texts (e.g. SE14:70–71). On the whole, Balawat may be said to contain a local propaganda in the sense that militarism is highlighted in it. The military profile of this town may explain this particular ideological feature.

Regarding the distant provincial areas, the ideological sources are extremely sparse. The atypical Sultan Tepe text (SE17) was copied or created in an Assyrian scribal school in the Balih town of Sultan Tepe (Lambert 1961: 156). This may be indicative of the strive towards centralization and uniformity which was present in this period (see s. 7.2). The border areas have more material to discuss. The royal epithets from the cliffs and stelae of the periphery centre on royal violence, control, and heroism (e.g. SE23:9–10, SE2:i6, SE23:12–13 resp.), although expressions of divine choice and royal benevolence occasionally occur (e.g. SE2:i6, SE2:i5 resp.). Noticeable is the high degree of the theme difficult path – a feature quite logical when considering the geographical contexts (harsh and distant) of these monuments (e.g. SE2:i10). The textual narrative shares the characteristics identified above, in that much emphasis is on warfare and conquering (e.g. SE2:ii45–47). Turning finally to the royal iconography, the only preserved motif is that of the ruler as venerating priest (e.g. SI13, SI15–17). Again, this mixed message given by texts and images may be telling of a dual strategy of intimidation and promises of benevolence. Typology may be regarded as more important than provenance here, in that commemorative texts and the image of the king as venerating priest are typically found on Assyrian, royal stelae.

Turning lastly to the strategic comparison, the best comparison available may be that between SE8 (from Kalhu) and SE10 (from Assur). They are both annals, they both come from citadel areas, and they are dated similarly, to 841 and 839 BCE respectively. This is a basis for a fair comparison.

SE10 (i1–9) starts with an invocation of deities. Ashur of course heads the list, but it is noticeable that the deities Ninurta (Kalhu), Ishtar (Nineveh, Arbela), and Marduk (Babylon) are included and thus not censored because of the Assur provenance. SE8 lacks a corresponding section. Both texts then have the same cluster of royal epithets which begins with "king of all people" (SE8:1–19, SE10:i10–13). SE10 has a much abbreviated version of it though. Identical genealogies, i.e. in relation to each others, then follow in the texts (SE8:20–24, SE10:i13–18). While SE8 (24–40) has a section on the geographical extent of the king's conquests, SE10 (i19–21) instead notes that the king mobilized his army directly after his ascending the throne.

After a lacuna, the descriptions of military campaigns (of regnal years 3–15, and 18 after a new lacuna) structured around regnal years follow in SE8 (1′–27″). The military campaigns of the king's first 20 regnal years are narrated without a break in SE10 (i21–iv34). The latter narrations are more abbreviated. It may also be noted here that offerings in Babylonia are mentioned in the Assur text, thus not taboo, but that Nineveh is not mentioned as a departure point in the relevant text, this in contrast to SE8. This exclusion may be explained either by editorial concerns, as an effect of abbreviations, or as a sign of a local ideology in which the rival city of Nineveh should not be spoken of. After the campaign narrations, SE8 suddenly breaks off, either due to a lacuna or because the inscription actually ended at this point.

SE10 (iv34–40) continues with a list of the total amount of booty taken by the king during his first 20 years on the throne. This focusing on booty may be explained by the role of Assur as a traditional destination for booty and tribute. A building inscription follows, including references to earlier master builders (SE10:iv40–b.e.3). This focusing on the royal line may also be a typical expression of a local Assur ideology. Also the call to future rulers with the connected blessings given by Ashur and Adad centres on genealogy (SE10:b.e.3–l.e.1). A dating, followed by a brief note on the strengthening of the army, conclude the text (SE10:l.e.1–2, SE10:l.e.2 resp.). The latter feature is just another example of the conclusion that militarism and heroism is a part of propaganda also from Assur. On the whole, although certain ideological variations are detectable, the overall impression is one of relative uniformity. Editorial considerations, notably involving abbreviations, may account for some of the variations between the compared two inscriptions.

Summing up the findings of this section, the propaganda expressed in Assur, Kalhu, and Nineveh is fairly uniform, arguably pointing to a move towards ideological standardization. The few sources from the outer core, produced by Assyrian scribal schools, tell the same story. By contrast, the propaganda from Balawat displays local ideological imprints, having an emphasis on warfare. In terms of spatial distribution of the sources, both Assur and Kalhu are highlighted, in contrast to his predecessor's reign.

7.4 The other kings and local propaganda

In this section, local propaganda of the other Early Neo-Assyrian kings are searched for. Two different kinds of evidence, the statistics on spatial distribution, and some strategic comparisons will be used. I will e.g. argue that there is a change from focusing on Assur in eNA I-times to centering on the outer core in eNA III-times, telling of a probably forced decentralization. There is also an emphasis on local deities and officials in eNA III-times.

Regarding the evidence to be used in the relevant strategic comparisons, only the reigns of Shamshi-Adad V and (barely also) that of Adad-narari III can provide meaningful material for these comparisons. In other reigns, the text or image corpora have only one identified provenance, or the comparison is hindered by great differences regarding literary genre and/or type of monument. Although promising at first sight, Adad-narari II's annals from Nineveh (An2E5) are simply too fragmentarily preserved to be meaningfully compared with the much better preserved ones from Assur (e.g. An2E2).

Turning firstly to the evidence of spatial distribution of the major primary sources (see app. 3), it is noticeable although not surprising that Assur dominates (62 %) and that Kalhu is non-existent in terms of text distribution in the eNA I-phase. The dominance becomes even stronger if counting by exemplars (69 %). Nineveh and the rest of the inner core are fairly well-represented with theirs 19 % and 10 % respectively. As for the eNA III-phase, the situation is quite different. Assur heads the list by its 36 %, but Kalhu has now a share of 30 %. Nineveh contributes with 12 %, while the distant provinces are represented by as much as 9 % of the text corpus.

Evaluating the first two tables of appendix 3, the spatial distribution in eNA I-times is hardly surprising. The relative strength of Nineveh is only to be expected since it was a royal residence (TN2E5:9), and a point of departure and arrival for military movements (e.g. TN2E5:8,13). The nearby (?) Nemed-Tukulti-Ninurta was "made into a special centre" by Tukulti-Ninurta II (Grayson 1991: 179). Turning to the spatial distribution of eNA III-times, there are however a few interesting things to pick up on. Firstly, it is noticeable that Assur is stronger than Kalhu, actually much stronger too if counting by exemplars. The trend which Shalmaneser III set seems to have continued. Secondly, Nineveh regains much of its proportion from the time of Ashurnasirpal II. If counting by exemplars, Nineveh actually has a greater share of the sources than Kalhu. Thirdly, Balawat loses its importance and has no such provenanced texts. Fourthly, the distant provinces share of the sources is considerably stronger, in both ways of counting, in the eNA III-phase.

Turning to the third table of appendix 3, illustrating the spatial distribution of the iconographic entities, the eNA III-phase, plus the Terqa Stele of Tukulti-Ninurta II, has almost 50 % of its sources in either the outer core or in the border areas/foreign lands. Kalhu stands for only 24 %, while Nineveh represents a share of 12 %, and Balawat is again without sources. Somewhat surprisingly, also Assur does not contribute at all to the corpus. Thus, points 2–4 in the paragraph above still stands, while the first point on Assur's strength can not be substantiated when it comes to the visual arts.

Moving on to the strategic comparisons, as illustrated by appendix 1, the annals of Shamshi-Adad V have been preserved from Assur, Kalhu, and (barely) Nineveh. SA5E1 and SA5E2 derive from Kalhu and Assur respectively, they are both substantial in length, they were composed in the same regnal phase (814–812 BCE), and they both derive from royal stelae. All in all, the conditions for conducting a strategic comparison are quite good.

SA5E1 (i1–38) begins with a long invocation of or dedication to Ninurta, and goes on with a smaller section of royal epithets headed by "strong king", and a genealogy. Thereafter a relating of how the king put down the internal rebellion is made (SA5E1i39–53), followed by the narrating of his military campaigns year after year (SA5E1i53–iv45). The text abruptly but intentionally ends in the middle of a certain campaign narrating. As for the fragmentary SA5E2, large portions of the text are identical to that on SA5E1. Grayson (1996: 180–91) partly edits the two texts together. The beginning has not been preserved but it probably included a dedication to Anu or Adad, or both, since the stele was found in the Anu-Adad temple of Assur (Grayson 1996: 181, 189). After some narrations of rebellion and campaigning there is a considerable lacuna, and the returning campaign narration deals with the fourth campaign

(SA5E2iii1′–16′). The text ends abruptly after having narrated two further campaigns of the king (SA5E2iii17′–iv29).

Evaluating this comparison, the obvious imprint of local propaganda is the difference in gods (Ninurta and Anu-Adad respectively) to whom the stelae were dedicated. Otherwise, the great duplicate portions indicate homogeneity. The themes of image raising and hunting, present in SA5E1 (iii20–22, iv2–3) but absent in SA5E2, are probably not locality restricted, since SA5E2 may have brought these up too if not being in a fragmentary state. The continuation of campaign narration in SA5E2 (iii1′–iv29′) does not express any clear local imprint. Niniveh is actually referred to as a favourite city of the king in the Assur text (SA5E2:iv7′–8′)! The Assur text is also far from free from violence, in that enemies are e.g. flayed (SA5E2:iv10′). In sum, similarity and not difference should be stressed.

Turning to Shamshi-Adad V's son and successor, Adad-narari III, a strategic comparison is meaningful by looking at the texts An3E7 and An3E8. These come from Tell al-Rimah (i.e. the outer core) and Kalhu respectively, they are annalistic-like, and they are dated to the same regnal phase. Two setbacks are the texts' relative brevity and their different type of monument (stele and slab respectively). Still, a comparison seems defendable.

Text An3E7 (1–3) starts with an invocation of or dedication to Adad, followed by the king's name, a few of his titles headed by "strong king", and a genealogy. An3E8 (1–14) begins with the marker "palace of Adad-narari III" (*ekal Adad-nārārī*), a number of royal epithets, here headed by "great king", and a further section of royal epithets centering on the theme "conqueror from GN to GN". It is noticeable that a genealogy is missing. An3E7 (4–20) continues with some brief notes on the king making heroic feats in the west, followed by a statement, which concludes the text, that the king decreed authority of various kinds to his provincial governor Nergal-erish. An3E8 (15–24) instead concludes with a brief narrating that the king subjected the rulers of Damascus and Chaldea, and that he acted as priest in Babylonia.

Evaluating this comparison, the Kalhu text e.g. conveys the aspects of shepherd, divine choice, priest, and warrior in its titulary section (An3E8:1–5). A reference to building is made in the introducing words of "palace of Adad-narari III" (An3E8:1). Put differently, the Kalhu text is wide-ranging and anything but niched in terms of attested themes. The absence of a genealogy is probably not so telling, since another slab from Kalhu carries an extremely long one (An3E1). The inclusion in An3E7 (9–12) of the themes of image creating and tree felling may speak of a local imprint or of just a coincidence. The two texts are not at all long – an argument for the latter alternative. Also An3E7 (4–5) tells of warfare. Two likely local imprints are the focusing in An3E7 on

Adad and on a decree to Nergal-erish. These imprints may tell of a westerly dimension and a likely weakening of royal authority respectively. In sum, both similarities and differences may be noted.

Iconography is also relevant to include as the objects of strategic comparisons. The option here is to compare the imagery on the Saba'a and Tell el-Rimah stelae (An3I2–3) with that on the Antakya Stele (An3I6). They represent the outer core and the border areas/foreign lands respectively, come from the same regnal phase, and are all found on royal stelae.

The two provincial stelae in question both depict the king making the pointing gesture towards deity emblems hovering in mid-air. There are however some differences. The Saba'a Stele (An3I2) is much cruder and less skillfully executed, the royal dress is unorthodox, and the deity emblems are proportionally much larger, all in relation to the Tell al-Rimah Stele (An3I3). The divine emblems are eight to ten in number, and both stelae have the emblems of Marduk and Nabu closest to the king. Turning to the actual focus of comparison, the Antakya Stele (An3I6) merely represents a moon crescent on a standard, with two individuals discernable on either side of it.

Evaluating this comparison in a few words, it seems only logical that the stelae closest to the Assyrian heartland or inner core illustrate the standard imagery of the venerating king addressing divine emblems, while the more distant, Syrian stele is adapted to local tastes, here centering on the emblem of the moon god Sin of Harran (Börker-Klähn 1982: 197). Stelae with moon crescents seem to have been commonly made and raised in the west (J. M. Russell 1998–2001: 251), and they can here tell of locally adapted propaganda. In other words, an expression of local propaganda is present here.

Summing up the findings of this section, the three strategic comparisons revealed little traces of local propaganda. The centering on patron deities, and the highlighting of high officials and locally adapted propaganda away from the core have however been detected. The statistics on spatial distribution of the sources tell of a shift from Assur in eNA I-times to the distant provinces in eNA III-times, perhaps telling of a decline of royal authority.

7.5 Summary and reflections

To begin with, when examining the major primary sources for potential local propaganda, the issue of regional politics must be addressed. A second point to make is that a distinction between quantitative and qualitative ideological variations should be made. In other words, both the spatial distribution of the ideological sources, in terms of cities and regions, as well as ideological variations within the preserved propaganda according to locality matter.

As for ideological variations in terms of *quantity* (spatial distribution), clear patterns exist. In eNA I-times, Assur but also, although to a lesser extent, Nineveh have a great share. As for Nineveh, the nearby (?) city Nemed-Tukulti-Ninurta has a vital but diffuse role in the reign of Tukulti-Ninurta II. Ashurnasirpal II mainly favoured Kalhu, and to some extent Nineveh, while Shalmaneser III favoured both Ashur and Kalhu. The role of Assur as the traditional centre, and therefore conservative by nature, and thus a potential source of opposition to be fought or appeased when various royal reforms occurred, and the divide between an old elite, primarily residing in Assur, and a new establishment, headed by eunuchs residing in Kalhu, can be used to explain the significant shift of favour in terms of spatial distribution about to be discussed. In eNA III-times, the distant provincial and border areas' shares of the sources raise significantly, perhaps telling of a political decentralization of a sort.

Discussing on the basis of the picture presented in section 7.1, Ashurnasirpal II's move from Assur to Kalhu may be seen as an attempt to get away from the traditions, restraints, and resistance which marked Assur, and by establishing a new centre he could create his own power base, including a new bureaucracy. This process may have begun already in the reign of his father who stayed in Nineveh and made Nemed-Tukulti-Ninurta into a special centre. Also, the Kalhu move brought with it a more central position of the capital in Assyria, presumably needed in order to administrate the expanding state more effectively. It is likely that this move created or sustained opposition among the elite of Assur and possibly also that of Nineveh. As for Nineveh, although many sources come from this city, in light of the great emphasis on it by the king's direct predecessors, this may be greatly relativized. Shalmaneser III's many sources and projects in Assur may be regarded as a way of responding to, by appeasing and "buying off", this opposition.

In the long run this did not work, since a rebellion including Assur, Nineveh, and Balawat broke out at the end of his reign. The participation of urban centres with a military character such as Nineveh and Balawat may speak of a divide also within the Assyrian army, i.e. not only within the civilian sector of society, whatever that distinction is worth (Fuchs 2005: 55–56; Assante 2007). His successor Shamshi-Adad V finally managed to put down this wide-ranging rebellion, hereby achieving a victory for the king, Kalhu, and the new establishment. This establishment, headed by royal eunuchs, then emerges as very powerful in eNA III-times. As a respons to this, a revolt erupted in Assur during this period (see Millard 1994). The first ruler of the Late Neo-Assyrian Period, Tiglath-pileser III, may then have achieved in restoring the strong kingship in Assyria from his Kalhu base.

Admittedly, the reconstruction of events above is somewhat speculative because of the lack of explicit sources on the topic. Having said that, in state ideological terms, the relevant move from Assur to Kalhu conveys a royal intention to focus more on the person of the king, being the centre point of a steadily changing political formation. This observation in its turn tell of the relevance of the concept of patrimonialism when talking of the Neo-Assyrian state. The Assyrian king exercise paternalism, and creates a power base of officials who are directly dependent on the ruler for the well-developing of their careers. The latter feature is often associated with the Late Neo-Assyrian Period (Larsen 1999: 367–77), but it may thus have been in existence already in the ninth century BCE. This development is temporarily halted in eNA III-times when the sources of high officials almost take over.

Focusing on variations in terms of *quality* and the potential expressions of local propaganda, the results are fairly similar with respect to Ashurnasirpal II and Shalmaneser III, although not much can be said about state art from Assur in the former case, or about propaganda from Nineveh in the latter case. The conclusions below are thus valid for the propaganda of both rulers. Although certain ideological trends exist (see ss. 7.2–3), the impression of uniformity is dominant. There is e.g. no special ideology in Assur which only focuses on priesthood and building, or any Kalhu and Nineveh ideologies which solely centre on warfare and conquests. The ideological expressions from the named three centres are wide-ranging and with a high degree of representativity of the whole corpus. Probably, the absence of clear local propaganda in Assur, Kalhu, and Nineveh should not be seen as a proof of the lack of local ideas and traditions, but rather as an indication of a royal program to standardize and homogenize perceptions of rule in Assyria. Thus, the relative uniformity then speaks of a movement towards ideological centralization in correspondence with related urges in the geopolitical field.

Moving on, although peaceful royal roles are included, the propaganda from Balawat seems to emphasize military matters, perhaps as a reflection of this town's status of support point for the army. The few state ideological expressions from the western provinces which have been preserved often tell of clearly defined local ideologies. This finding is not surprising because the region in question is situated outside the Assyrian heartland. Dur-Katlimmu and Sultan Tepe seem here to function as Assyrian enclaves, presenting art and texts in an Assyrian fashion. The ideological sources from the border areas, i.e. stelae or cliff reliefs and their texts, consistently convey images which depict the ruler as a venerating priest, and texts which describe the king as a conqueror and fierce warrior. Possibly, this dual, mixed message reflects a combined message of intimidation and promising benevolence. Alternatively, the inscriptions may have been regarded as symbolical, simply carrying the notion of great royal power.[298] Generally speaking, typology (literary genre, type of monument, type of media) and editorial considerations (notably abbreviations) may account for some of the ideological variations.

In sum, three major ideological trends have been identified. On the one hand, the move to Kalhu served to highlight the role of the king at the expense of the old nobility residing primarily in Assur. On the other, the general lack of local propaganda, at least in the core, is a testimony of the king's intent to standardize and to gain control over all ideological expressions of his country. A move towards royal autocracy is common to both trends. The third trend, which takes place in eNA III-times, diminishes the role of the king and the capital city in favour of the high officials and the distant provinces. It seems like the Early Neo-Assyrian kings in the end were consumed by their own creation, i.e. the new elite consisting of royal eunuchs who were given vast areas to govern relatively freely, a price paid in connection with their aid in putting down the internal rebellion in the early years of Shamshi-Adad V. Tiglath-pileser III then restored a strong kingship.

298 See J. M. Russell 1999: 229–30 for a similar argumentation. The named scholar talks of the "imbuing of an aura of royalty" as one of the reasons behind the inscriptional program in the North-West Palace, the others being "marking ownership" and "decoration".

8 Ideological comparison between the reigns

In this chapter, a comparison between mainly the propaganda of Ashurnasirpal II and Shalmaneser III is conducted. In its first section, a brief overview centering mainly on the topic of differences between the two kings as treated in scholarly literature is given. The two following sections turn to the major primary sources, and conduct both general and strategic comparisons. In a fourth section, strategic comparisons focusing on the other Early Neo-Assyrian kings and drawing from the royal epithets and royal visual representations are conducted. A final section gives a summary with reflections.

8.1 Introduction

Textbooks on Mesopotamian history tend to focus on Ashurnasirpal II rather than on Shalmaneser III (e.g. Roux 1992: 288–99), arguably because of the spectacular character of this king's palace and because of his radical decision of changing capital city. In less inclusive scholarly literature, the importance of Ashurnasirpal II is relativized, and the successor Shalmaneser III is emphasized. Liverani (2004: 213–15) e.g. claims that the former king was the last ruler of a historical period of reclaiming lost territory, and that the latter king was the first ruler of a truly imperialist phase. The military campaigns of the earlier king took place *within* the borders established in Middle Assyrian times, while those of the later king often occurred *beyond* those borders. Ashurnasirpal II was an imperialist only in the propaganda, while Shamaneser III was an imperialist also in deeds (Liverani 2004: 220).

This understanding of Shalmaneser III as an expansionist in comparison with his more known father is not unique to Liverani's works (Baker 2006–2008: 581; Bagg 2011: 191–205). Only with Shalmaneser III did Assyria start to leave real marks in Syria (Winter 2010: 542), and the said ruler was the first Assyrian king to put a lot of strength in western campaigns, thus opening the grounds for later military advances in the area (Grayson 2007: 52, 58). Not the least in respect to his western campaigns, the reign of Shalmaneser III was a "transitional stage" (Schneider 1991: 252–53), breaking through a historical-military watershed of a kind (Yamada 2000: 1, 308). While Ashurnasirpal II's advances in the west were of a surveying kind, those of his successor were of a conquering sort (Bagg 2011: 191–205). In the context of the latter's foreign policy, it is even claimed that "the novelty in the policy of Shalmaneser III is absolute" (Liverani 1988: 91 n. 38).

In other scholarly literature, the two rulers are spoken of more as equals. Here it is commonly stated that, just like his father, Shalmaneser III was a powerful and significant king (Schramm 1973: 70), and that there was a great continuity between the two reigns (Kuhrt 1997: 487; Beaulieu 2005: 50). It is sometimes stated that the two kings simply chose to realize the "state ethos" differently. According to Lambert (1974a: 107–109), Ashurnasirpal II was pragmatic and conducted more targeted campaigns, geographically and chronologically, while his successor campaigned fanatically all over the place. Hallo (1964: 156) in his turn gives a reversed picture of this. For sure, Ashurnasirpal II had a conscious and methodical strategy for reconquering, whose implementing laid the foundations for future conquests (Liverani 1992b: 96–99, 115). It is also claimed that *both* kings conducted carefully planned military campaigns, on which Ashurnasirpal II marched everywhere except to Babylonia, while Shalmaneser III went in all directions but focused mainly on the north and the west (Grayson 1976: 136–37).

There are of course also viewpoints which put Shalmaneser III in an inferior position in relation to his predecessor. An older view concerning the two kings and their respective historical importances is given by Olmstead (1921: 380–81) who presents Shalmaneser III as a weak ruler, cowardly and imitating, who had Dajjan-Ashur as the actual man in charge. In line with this understanding, Ashurnasirpal II was successful in his military campaigns, while the military plans of Shalmaneser III largely failed. The apparent failure to defeat the Syrian-Palestinian coalition is often spoken of in the context of arriving at this evaluation (Grayson 1976; Yamada 2000).

Given their alleged, varying historical contributions, differences in state ideologies between the two kings are only to be expected. A feature often highlighted in this context is the identified phenomenon of "calculated frightfulness" of Assyrian kings, arguably present and especially greatly visible in the texts of Ashurnasirpal II (Olmstead 1918: 225). This king is presented as more savage than others, which very well may have corresponded to reality (Lambert 1974a: 107). Siddall (2013: 158, 168) also juxtaposes the two kings and refers to Ashurnasirpal II and his deeds as "sadist(ic)", quite in contrast to those of Shalmaneser III. Ashurnasirpal II is here characterized as ferocious, spontaneously campaigning, using calculated frightfulness, and as a "nationalist" (because of using the Neo-Assyrian dialect), while Shalmaneser III is understood as conducting well-planned, annual campaigns, focusing on material gains, refraining from describing atrocities, and consistently using Standard Babylonian (Tadmor 1975: 36).

Following this line of thought, Cifola (1995: 93–96) states that Ashurnasirpal II was a ferocious king who did not care much for justice and shepherding, and who saw his greatness in his military power. Shalmaneser III, by contrast, did not celebrate war, but he rather emphasized the constructive view of the steady flow towards Assur of goods from the periphery and of the expanding of the area delivering tribute, thus focusing on effective reign (Cifola 1995: 115). Ataç (2013: 405) argues that the art of Shalmaneser III stresses tributaries, submission, and reconciliation. M. Marcus (1995a: 2490–91) also sees a tendency in the sources of Shalmaneser III of a stress on tribute and of an avoidance of narrating war, at least not in great detail, arguing that for him it was more about collecting than about dominating. All this is contrasted with the sources of Ashurnasirpal II, both with regards to texts and images. These proposed ideological differences have been explained in different ways. M. Marcus (1995a: 2491) speculates that "emerging nations", here under Ashurnasirpal II, have a stronger need for "arrogant display of power" than already established ones, here under Shalmaneser III.

The relevant differences have also been dismissed, e.g. by Grayson (1976: 137–38) who refers to editorial needs for abbreviating, and by Porter (2003: 84–85) who notices that the very brutal AE1 is inscribed upon the walls of the temple of the warrior god Ninurta. According to this view, also Shalmaneser III was a ruler executing terror and operating calculated frightfulness (Olmstead 1921: 347). According to Pettinato (1988: 99, 109), the said king continued with terror and warfare conveying religious fanatism, but with a new and underlying idea of inclusion and universalism. Shalmaneser III here counts to those visionary kings who vainly tried to reform Assyrian political life (Pečírková 1993: 244). Minor ideological features which this ruler did introduce were the focus on the erecting of monuments in the periphery and on the performing of rituals at large bodies of water (Grayson 1976: 138). Shalmaneser III, allegedly yet another ruthless imperialist ruler, also arguably stands out a little by his stress on tree felling, boat building, and (once again) image making (Cameron 1950: 7–8).

The other reigns have received far less attention in research, understandably so in light of the ample sources from the two reigns in question. Still, some words concerning the historical context of eNA I and III-propaganda should be said. The eNA I-phase is often seen as a period of revival, with its kings fighting against intruding Arameans, and striving to reattain the borders of the stronger MA II-phase (e.g. Grayson 1991: 131). The eNA III-phase is commonly regarded as a period of decline, at least in terms of royal authority and imperialist ambitions (e.g. Grayson 1996: 200–201), although the recent study by Siddall (2013) has challenged this view (see s. 1.1). It remains to be seen whether the relevant strategic comparisons will discover any clear *ideological* variations between the reigns and phases. The recent sketch by Siddall (2013: 167) of Early Neo-Assyrian state ideology between 934–811 BCE stresses the continuity part at the expense of innovation.

8.2 General comparison Ashurnasirpal II–Shalmaneser III

This section conducts a general comparison of the propaganda of Ashurnasirpal II and Shalmaneser III, structured according to type of source. I will argue that, although there are fundamental ideological similarities, the differences are many. Also, the images of Ashurnasirpal II as a fierce warrior and of Shalmaneser III as a tribute receiver need to be problematized.

Starting with the royal iconography, many features are shared but clear variations are still present. As for the visual representations (see apps. 13–14),[299] the list of Ashurnasirpal II (see app. 15) is headed in order of frequency by "libating priest", "receiving tribute", and "having his weapons ritually cleansed", while the list of Shalmaneser III (see app. 15) is headed by "receiving tribute", "in battle", and "venerating priest". As for motifs involving the execution of violence, these are a little bit more frequent in the case of Ashurnasirpal II but surprisingly modest in the context of the discussion above. Proportionally, the motif of "king in battle" is even stronger in the case of his successor. This motif comes on fifth place in the list of Ashurnasirpal II. Shalmaneser III also figures in the motif "observing battle", while Ashurnasirpal II often is depicted "having his weapons ritually cleansed". The former motif may speak of this ruler as an active organizer of his warfare (D. Oates 1963: 13 n. 15). The latter motif is restricted to the North-West Palace. Royal hunting is almost restricted to the earlier ruler who is seen 16 times pursuing this activity, while Shalmaneser III's only such image is on the royal seal. If not counting the pursuit of hunting among the theme of violence, Shalmaneser III may actually be labelled as the ferocious one of the two, executing the calculated frightfulness in question.

Turning to more peaceful royal roles and motifs, the illustrating of "the king receiving tribute" is more often attested (20 versus 12 attestations) in the propaganda of Ashurnasirpal, but proportionally the motif in question is stronger for Shalmaneser III while also "leading" the list of royal visual representations. Considering the much identifying of this royal role as typical for the latter ruler, the relative strength of this motif in the propaganda of Shalmaneser III is modest. The motifs of "receiving captives/booty" do not alter this impression. Another peaceful role and motif is "the king as shepherd". It characterizes the iconography of Ashurnasirpal II (4 versus 0 attestations), especially if including the many representations of this king receiving processions

299 In this section, to save space and avoid repetitions, source references to divine or royal epithets and royal motifs are not given when simply discussing their attestations in either reigns. See instead the columns on source attestations in appendices 5–10 and 13–14.

holding a long staff, while Shalmaneser III instead stands holding bow and arrows in his hands (e.g. AI13:33–34, SI10:5t. resp.).

Moving on to the king's role as priest, the motif of "libating priest" is characterizing the propaganda of Ashurnasirpal (23 versus 4 attestations), while the motifs of "venerating priest" and "priest (statue)" are stronger in the case of Shalmaneser III. The motif in the North-West Palace of "the king being ritually purified" may be considered as a part of the motifs illustrating the king as priest, given the ritual dimension. Considering the circumstance that the total number of motif attestations are greatly uneven, i.e. 130 attestations for Ashurnasirpal II, and 59 for Shalmaneser III (see apps. 13–15), the overarching motif of "king as priest" is fairly proportionally distributed, but with a slight inclination towards the representing of Shalmaneser III.

Ashurnasirpal II is the only king of the two being attested as "felling tree" and as "being crowned", while Shalmaneser III alone has the motifs of "meeting another ruler", "receiving timber", and "enthroned (statue)". As for the latter king, the first motif may speak of his special relationship with Babylonia, and the last one may tell of his role as a master builder, here in Assur. As for trees and the crowning scene with its accompanying bird-headed genii, the notion of Ashurnasirpal II being protected is amply given through the frequent illustrations of apotropaic colossi, genii, and trees. The sacred tree, also symbolizing prosperity, is a typical motif of Ashurnasirpal II. The idea of prosperity also links the king to his role as shepherd.

Proceeding to the source of royal titulary, both the alphabetically and the quantitatively ordered lists of royal epithets (see apps. 8–9 and app. 11 resp.) show that the titulary of Ashurnasirpal II alludes much more to violence. The latter kind of list e.g. gives nine epithets alluding to or clearly expressing violence, warfare heroism, and physical strength, while the corresponding figure for Shalmaneser III is five only. A continuation of that frequency list only strengthens that conclusion. Ashurnasirpal II has many violent and heroic epithets which are common in his own titulary but either uncommon or absent in the titulary of his successor. Among these count "great king" (alluding to rivalry), "heroic man",[300] "he who has no rival among the rulers of the four quarters", "fearless in battle", "(destructive) weapon", "merciless weapon", "fierce dragon", "he who scatters the forces of the rebellious", "hero/warrior", "king capable in battle", "avenger", and "controller of the brazen ones". The frequent stating of this king as being in charge of kings/rulers/lords everywhere, and the sporadic ones of him having established one single authority add to

300 The related royal epithet of "strong male", similarly telling of a notion of ideal masculinity and the dominant male, is however equally distributed between the two.

this list. The relatively common epithet of "seizer of hostages" is unique to Ashurnasirpal II, and is indicative of this ruler's inclination of referring to taking hostages (see subs. 5.4.2 and below).

Moving on to more peaceful aspects of the titulary, the theme of the king receiving tribute is more common in the titulary of Shalmaneser III than in that of his predecessor. His frequent epithet "receiver of booty and tax from all the four quarters" accounts for much of that impression. In light of the discussion above, one would expect a stronger dominance than this though. Moving on, the relevant ruler stands out as the only one who uses the epithet of "builder", here in relation to his Assur. The priestly role however comes out more clearly in the epithet collection of Ashurnasirpal II, at least if looking at the more commonly attested royal epithets. The said ruler is here called "worshipper of the great gods" and "purification priest". Also, the expressions of the king as "he who marches with the support of DN" are more frequent and varied in the case of this ruler, even if they also tell of the king's military role, here intertwined with the priestly. This result seemingly stands in sharp contrast to the notion of the king being merely a ferocious and ruthless warrior. The idea and theme of the king as "shepherd", with or without adjectives, and "chief herdsman" is much stronger in the propaganda of Ashurnasirpal II, affirming the conclusion on this topic with regards to royal iconography. The latter epithet is not even held by Shalmaneser III.

One may also note that the standard, although not "nationalist" (see subs. 5.4.6), title of "king of Assyria" is relatively stronger in the case of Ashurnasirpal II. Even if not seeing the alleged local character of this title, the idea of the Assyrian king as a universal ruler of all lands and people(s) is much centred on in the propaganda of Shalmaneser III. This ruler is e.g. commonly called in the same cluster of epithets "king of all people",[301] "king of all the four quarters", "leader of all lands", and "sun of all people". This ideological phenomenon may be connected to the broader geographical horizons of this ruler (see s. 8.1), reaching further and further away in terms of military campaigns. This king's tendency of having the theme of difficult path in common royal epithets may be explained similarly. Shalmaneser III is e.g. "he who has seen innermost and rugged regions", "he who has trodden upon the mountain peaks of all highlands", and "opener of paths above and below".

Another observation on differences in the royal titulary may focus on the varying strength of the patronym "son/heir of RN". The patronym heads both lists, but it is relatively stronger in the sources of Shalmaneser III (see app. 11).

301 Ashurnasirpal II has the not so infrequent variant "he who rules all people", likewise telling of royal paternalism in relation to his conquered, foreign subjects.

This may be explained by the circumstance that since Ashurnasirpal II was presumably seen as a greater Assyrian king than the short-reigned Tukulti-Ninurta II, the patronym was a more potent source of legitimacy for Shalmaneser III. The emphasis on patronyms, and not on matronyms, naturally tells of the existence of a male-centred political discourse in Assyria.

Also the issue of local propaganda and regional politics is relevant when comparing the titulary of the two rulers. Ninurta, the patron god of Kalhu, comes across in a fair number of Ashurnasirpal II's epithets, such as in "chosen of Enlil and Ninurta", "designate" or "favourite" of Ninurta, "vice-regent of Ashur and Ninurta", and in "he who marches with the support of Ashur and Ninurta". Other gods than Ashur are referred to in the king's frequent epithets of "beloved of Anu and Dagan", "designate of Sin", "favourite of Anu", and "beloved of Adad", all epithets non-existent in the propaganda of Shalmaneser III. As noted in subsection 7.2 however, Ashur was occasionally highlighted also by Ashurnasirpal II. By contrast, Assur and Ashur are centred on in the sources of Shalmaneser III. The standard title of "vice-regent of Ashur" is strikingly strong in the relevant propaganda, he is "the prudent appointee of Ashur", and the focus on Enlil (=Ashur?) is strong by the dual epithets of "chosen of/appointed by Enlil". At least the former epithet, i.e. "chosen of Enlil", is seldomly attested in the texts of Ashurnasirpal II. Shalmaneser III is also described as "he who frequents the Esharra", i.e. the temple area of Ashur. As noted in subsection 7.3, Ninurta and the other deities are far from forgotten however. The unusual prominence of the epithet "prince", typical for the Old Assyrian Period when Assur dominated, may also be a testimony of Shalmaneser III's dedication to this city.

Turning lastly to the textual narrative, the similarities are many but clear differences exist in the two text corpora. Ashurnasirpal II has several themes which are lacking or are very weak in the texts of his successor. The former king e.g. talks of bringing lands and people within the boundaries of his land, placing all under one single authority (e.g. AE50:10–19, AE17:iii21–22 resp.). This tells of the reconquering phase of this king (see s. 8.1). Similarly understood, Ashurnasirpal II often refers to the imposition of tribute and labour duties, and of the installing of governors in reconquered territories (e.g. AE17:iv48–49, AE1:iii104 resp.). The statement that this ruler took hostages is also typical of this earlier king's inscriptions (e.g. AE1:iii104). In other words, the aspect of coercion is stressed by Ashurnasirpal II.

The descriptions of atrocities, involving the killing of subjects and destructing of objects, directed against enemy polities are more frequent and varied in the texts of Ashurnasirpal II than in the texts of Shalmaneser III. Ashurnasirpal II e.g. stands out as having flayed and burnt hostile opponents and captives respectively (e.g. AE17:i88–89, AE1:i108 resp.). He also profiles himself by the cutting of limbs, the gouging out of eyes, the cutting out of tongues of enemies, and by the hanging of severed heads in trees (e.g. AE17:iv99–100, AE1:iii113, AE21:14′, AE1:ii71 resp.). These themes are all absent in the texts of Shalmaneser III. Although expressed in both reigns, the theme of burning boys and girls is a theme of Ashurnasirpal II, judging from quantity and priority (e.g. AE17:ii62–63). Even though Shalmaneser III certainly does not present himself as a dove of peace, the theme of royal violence and atrocities is clearly stronger in the texts of Ashurnasirpal II.

Moving on to more peaceful themes, Ashurnasirpal II stands out as a master builder in several respects. Unique to this ruler is the claim that Ashurnasirpal II acted as a master builder with the wisdom which Ea had given him (e.g. AE40:33–36). He creates "wild beasts" and "dragons" for his palaces and temples (e.g. AE35:9–10, AE30:72–73 resp.), he stresses the creating of divine statues (e.g. AE1:ii132–33), and he brags about the luxurious building of palaces and temples (e.g. AE23:17–22). Ashurnasirpal II builds or rebuilds cities, notably Kalhu and Balawat, after these having turned into "ruin hills" (e.g. AE26:46–48). Ashurnasirpal II not only builds or rebuilds palaces in Kalhu, Nineveh, and Balawat, but also in the distant provinces, saying that he "inaugurated" (*šarrû* D) these palaces in various cities (e.g. AE1:ii101). The king in question also talks more of naming or renaming conquered sites of various kinds (e.g. AE1:i69). Also typical of the inscriptions of this king is the statement that he deported people to Kalhu to be used as forced labour in building projects there (e.g. AE30:33–36).

Another theme which makes Ashurnasirpal II stand out in relation to Shalmaneser III is of course the great banquet in the North-West Palace (AE30:102–54). Also, his emphasis on breeding and displaying wild animals in zoos and palaces is characteristic (e.g. AE2:31–38). The king in question even calls out to future rulers with a request to keep these animals alive (AE2:38–39). Wild animals are also occasionally listed among the received tribute (e.g. AE77). Animal similes are more common in the texts of Ashurnasirpal II, both with regards to himself and his own army and to his enemies (e.g. AE17:i85, AE1:i49–52 resp.). In a related notion of benevolence, Ashurnasirpal II profiles himself as creating gardens and orchards, as irrigating fields by creating a canal, and as reaping and storing harvests (e.g. AE26:54, AE30:36–38, AE1:iii82 resp.). An idiom states that he stored barley and straw in provincial cities and palaces (e.g. AE30:78–84). Also the theme of Ashurnasirpal II as a resettler of people, both of "Assyrians" and "foreigners", is a characteristic ideological feature (e.g. AE17:ii30–31).

Ashurnasirpal II talks more of (constructed) ethnicity than his successor. The opposition between "Assyrians" and "Arameans" in the context of reconquest is more often spoken of (e.g. AE19:91–96), and the Lullumu and Hanigalbat are frequently highlighted (e.g. AE23:6–7, AE19:102 resp.).[302] The rebellion of Assyrians in the west is centred on (e.g. AE1:i101–10). The related feature of royal genealogy is stressed differently by this ruler. The elaborate instructions, causing either curses or blessings, directed at future rulers on the Ninurta Stele are unique (AE17:v24–103). Shalmaneser I is highlighted among his predecessors, arguably because of this king's role as the original founder of Kalhu (e.g. AE32:7). The king's stele in the Row of Stelae and his sarcophagus in the Old Palace, spoken of in texts, tell of a wish to connect to Assur and the long royal line (AE108, AE115 resp.).

Also Shalmaneser III has narrative themes which are modest or non-existent in the propaganda of his predecessor. The theme of facing grand, international coalitions including Egypt and some Arab tribes (e.g. SE2:ii89–102), in the end receiving tribute from as distant countries as Israel and Egypt is characteristic (e.g. SE88, SE89 resp.). His ambitious military plans (see s. 8.1) are expressed e.g. in the common statements that "he ruled over the whole of Chaldea or Hatti" (e.g. SE59:47, SE28:24 resp.), and by his separate note on the strengthening of the Assyrian army (e.g. SE11:l.e.ii1–2). These features may be explained by the allegedly wider geographic horizon of this king. This may also be the case for the frequently attested idiom that the king crossed rivers, traversed mountains, or entered regions for the eleventh-or-so number of time (e.g. SE14:100–101). The theme of avenging or saving and (re)installing puppet kings may also be explained by him campaigning wide and far (e.g. SE14:146–56). Common and typical statements tell that the ruler "claimed conquered cities as my (his) own", that he "confined enemy rulers to their (besieged) cities", and that the enemy ruler cowardly abandoned his own attacked city (e.g. SE6:ii22, SE8:16″, SE6:i58 resp.). Shalmaneser III is in other words not at all presented as an all peaceful ruler, but he on the contrary appears as a forceful imperialist ruler.

Although the narrative theme of the king receiving tribute or taking booty is very much attested also in the texts of Ashurnasirpal II, the proportions between the themes of booty and tribute on the one hand and on royal violence and atrocities on the other are different. On the basis of this perspective, it may thus be argued that tribute is more centred on in the inscriptions of Shalmaneser III, and that the degree of violence is less. The frequent idiom which states that the king in question brought his tribute or booty to "my (his) city Assur" is telling of this emphasis as well as of the central position of Assur (e.g.

---

302 Shalmaneser III centres on the defeating of Urartu and Gutium, portraying them both as distant, wild, and exotic, inhabited by "mountain peoples" (e.g. SE17:41–57, SE28:41 resp.).

SE40:iii1–2). The special theme of booty summation in a text from Assur adds to this impression (SE10:iv34–40). Also the theme of the ruler procuring timber, metal, and stone by himself in the foreign lands, i.e. directly from the sources, is associated with Shalmaneser III. He fetches alabaster and silver from Anatolian mountains (SE40:iii2–5), and he narrates much more often of tree felling in Syria-Palestine (e.g. SE3:89–90).

A narrative theme which is clearly highlighted in comparison with Ashurnasirpal II is the theme of the creating and erecting of "images" such as stelae, statues, or cliff reliefs in the periphery, at the shores of rivers, river sources, lakes, and seas, on mountains and cliffs, and in various parts of urban centres (e.g. SE3:87–89, SE3:91–92, SE6:iii45 resp.). This theme is insignificant in the texts of his predecessor. The ruler in question gave his and the deities' praises on the monuments erected at these sites (e.g. SE16:42–43). Also the closely related theme of making sacrifices and arranging banquets at the reaching of geographical extremes is characteristic of Shalmaneser III's textual narrative (e.g. SE16:40–42). Moreover, the old, Sargonic ideological theme of the triumphant, imperialist king washing weapons in the far-flung sea or lake is also much more common in the texts of Shalmaneser III than in those of Ashurnasirpal II (e.g. SE1:34).[303]

The special role of Babylonia, its cities, people, and deities in the time of Shalmaneser III comes across e.g. in the unique narrations of Marduk overwhelming the king's enemies, and of this god ordering him to turn to warfare (SE14:188, SE5:v4 resp.). Ashur alone normally features in these roles. After his allegedly victorious intervention, Shalmaneser III claims to have visited temples in Babylon, Borsippa, and Cuthae, making sacrifices and displaying pious humility (e.g. SE5:v3–vi5). The ruler in question also claims to have affirmed the traditional privileges of the mentioned temple cities, arranging a grand banquet (SE5:vi4–5), arguably signifying royal protection (see subs. 5.4.4). The "display of strength" in Babylonia, thus not only in the west, also shows his geographical emphases and preferences (SE5:v3–vi5).

However, not only Babylonian deities are honoured by Shalmaneser III. He offers also to two local forms of Adad (e.g. SE5:iv2–3, SE2:ii87), gives a votive object to the Tigris source god Hallasua (SE119), and commissions a divine statue of a Phoenician god (SE55:4–6). Additionally, the theme of godnapping is also more common in the propaganda of Shalmaneser III (e.g. SE10:ii3–5). There is not any indication that Ashurnasirpal II disrespected foreign deities (see s. 5.3), but he obviously did not express his honouring just as much as his

303 For Sargonic influences on Assyrian royal inscriptions, see notably Liverani 1993 and Kienast 1997. For Sargonic state ideology in general, see Frayne 1993 and Franke 1995.

son and successor did. Possibly, the wider geographical horizon of Shalmaneser III may explain also this ideological tendency.

An emphasis on royal officials in the textual narrative of Shalmaneser III may tentatively be identified. These officials are not seldomly spoken of as alone dedicators of gifts to a deity or to the king. The mayor of Kalhu, Shamash-bela-usur, e.g. provides Fort Shalmaneser with a throne base and several door sills (e.g. SE30:32–34), and the likely Shalmaneser III official, later serving Shamshi-Adad V, Bel-luballit dedicates cult objects in his own right (SA5E12–13, SA5I2). The emphasis on Dajjan-Ashur is of course another point in the case (e.g. SE14:141–90). His earliest field marshal, Ashur-bel-ka"in, is also mentioned separately (e.g. SE17:10). The switch from narrating after eponyms, naming royal officials, to narrating after regnal years, may be understood as a reaction against this internal, gradual, political development which highlights the role of high officials (see ss. 6.3, 7.4–5).

Summing up, although the propaganda of Ashurnasirpal II and Shalmaneser III are fundamentally shared, there are certain ideological motifs and themes, identified and discussed above, which give the respective propaganda of the two rulers their own individual character. Shalmaneser III was not blindly following, neither politically nor ideologically, in the footsteps of his reconquering father, but actually presents himself as more of an imperialist than Ashurnasirpal II does. Furthermore, the images of Ashurnasirpal II as only a fierce warrior and of Shalmaneser III as only a peaceful ruler who focused on imposing and receiving tribute need to be revised.

8.3 Strategic comparison Ashurnasirpal II–Shalmaneser III

In the following, comparisons between selected propaganda pieces of the two rulers are conducted. I will argue that individual ideological traits such as hunting, shepherding, and image making shine through, although the two kings express fundamentally the same state ideology. Again, their respective repute of being warrior and tribute receiver should be problematized.

It is now meaningful to take both epigraphic and iconographic evidence into account when comparing. The best sources for comparisons are, in my view, the Kurkh monoliths with texts and images, and the two palace gates in Balawat with texts and images. As for the former, these monuments stood next to each other, and their texts are both annals and written early on in the two respective reigns. As for the latter, these monuments come from the same town and type of building, are embossed on the same material, i.e. bronze bands, and the texts are commemorative in both cases.[304] The two comparisons should, by any reasonable standards, be considered as fair.

Beginning with the Kurkh monoliths, the images on the Kurkh Monolith (AI18) and the Kurkh Stele (SI13) are basically the same. They both illustrate the king wearing his crown, priestly garment, armed with mace and daggers, and making the pointing gesture in the presence of deity emblems hovering in mid-air. Adad, Ishtar, Shamash, Ashur/Enlil, and Sin are illustrated on both stelae, but at least on the Kurkh Stele the emblem of the Sibitti of seven dots is added. Ashurnasirpal II may also have had the necklace of divine emblems which Shalmaneser III certainly has. The emblems of Adad, Shamash, Sin, and Ashur/Enlil are possible to discern, although also the Kurkh stele is poorly preserved. The earlier king is depicted more slender than the later one, arguably a case for the thesis that the two rulers belong to two separate art historical phases.[305] Except for concerning one circumstance, the Kurkh monoliths, in terms of iconography, may be regarded as examples of the *lack* of ideological differences, namely that of the varying size of the two stelae. The 220 cm high Kurkh Stele is 45 cm higher than the Kurkh Monolith (Börker-Klähn 1982: 182, 187), thus displaying heroic priority visually, and in a more general sense, the increased ambitions of Shalmaneser III.

Turning to the inscriptions on these twin monuments, both AE19 (1–4) and SE2 (i1–4) start with an invocation of deities which in both cases is headed by Ashur. Within these two invocations SE2 enumerates Anu, Enlil, Ea, Sin, Shamash, and Ishtar as great gods who give power, while AE19 lists Adad, Sin, Shamash, and Ishtar as great gods who go ahead of the king's troops. AE19 (5–22) then gives a long cluster of royal epithets which begins with "great king, strong king", while SE2 (i5–10) instead goes on with a long cluster beginning with "king of all people, prince, vice-regent of Ashur". The latter cluster also involves several expressions of difficult path. A genealogy follows in both texts (AE19:23–25, SE2:i11–12). The closest predecessors of Ashurnasirpal II are described as slayers and city founders, while Shalmaneser III describes these as priest-conquerors and slayers, with Tukulti-Ninurta II as the ferocious one and Ashurnasirpal II as a priest.

The narrative part of the two inscriptions are introduced by short and slightly varying notes on the circumstance that Ashur has chosen, crowned,

304 The only significant downside of this latter selection of comparison is the circumstance that AE51 is a display inscription while SE5 is an annalistic inscription.

305 Strommenger (1970: 32–33), Madhloom (1970: 118–22), and Winter (1997: 369) all argue for the two rulers belonging to the same art phase, while Czichon (1992: 191) by contrast identifies an art historical break with the reign of Shalmaneser III.

armed, and ordered the two rulers to engage in warfare (AE19:25–27, SE2:i12–14). In Shalmaneser III's case, Ashur grants "the shepherdship" of people and Assyria in the ruler's hands. Both inscriptions then add, in slightly varying ways, a brief note on the circumstance that the relevant rulers mobilized their armies (AE19:28–29, SE2:i14–15). After those initial textual elements, the narrations of military campaigns follow in both inscriptions. The campaign narratives of AE19 (29–103) and SE2 (i15–ii102) express many different ideological themes, although the exercise of royal violence features prominently, in accordance with the genre. Both narrations abruptly but intentionally ends, and they are both structured around eponyms.

To evaluate, the ideological similarities of the royal iconography are striking, alluding to the usefulness of royal lineage, through imitating a work of a predecessor, as a source of legitimacy in Shalmaneser III's case. The varying size of the two monuments may speak of heroic priority and of the greater ambitions of the said ruler. Also the texts underline similarities. They are structured in the same way in terms of content components, both use numerous themes but with an emphasis on royal violence, and they both partly narrate in an itinerary style (e.g. AE19:52–60, SE2:ii40–66) and according to eponyms. Some differences exist however. The royal epithets are less violent but more ambitious in SE2, and the mentioned section of epithets also contains several expressions of difficult path. The narrative themes of image creating and facing large coalitions further profile SE2 (e.g. ii44, ii89–102 resp.). The ideological themes in SE2, typical of Ashurnasirpal II, such as the burning of boys and girls (i17), the juxtaposition of Assyrians and Arameans (ii37–38), the use of eponyms, and of the itinerary style conveying the royal discoverer theme (see s. 5.1), the notion of shepherdship, and of the king chiseling out way in mountainous regions (e.g. ii41–42) tell of the great influence of AE19 upon SE2. Once again, connecting with royal predecessors was a potent source of authority. All in all, also in the case of the inscriptions, the overall impression is ideological continuity in Kurkh.

Moving on to the bronze bands of the palace gates in Balawat, those of Ashurnasirpal (AI13) illustrate in five cases warfare, in four hunting, in four captive processions, and in three tribute. Drawing from this, the visual representations of the king (see app. 13) are "king in battle" (four), "receiving captives" (four) "receiving tribute" (three), and "king as hunter" (three). The scenes are mostly from the west, i.e. Hatti and the Aramean polities, but also from the south-west, i.e. Suhu. Tendencies of grouping according to geography and themes exist (Reade 1979b). The height of the doors which made up the gate is estimated to just over four meters (Curtis and Tallis 2008: 72). As for the bronze bands of Shalmaneser III (SI10), they are dominated by warfare (including captive processions) on 9,5 bands, on 4,5 of them the scenes convey tribute processions, and on two of them the motif is cult, i.e. expedition to the holy river sources, image carving, and stele dedicating. Drawing from this, the king's visual representations (see app. 14) are "king in battle" (twelve), "observing battle" (six), "on march" (one), "receiving captives" (two), "receiving booty or timber" (two), "receiving tribute" (seven), "venerating priest" (three), "libating priest" (two), and "receiving submissive Assyrians" (one). In terms of geography, the scenes are fetched from all cardinal points of the compass.[306] The height of this palace gate was probably around seven and a half meters (Unger 1920: 102; Schachner 2007: 23).

In comparing the visual sources of the two gates, it is striking that the military aspect comes across much in the iconography of Shalmaneser III. Atrocities of various kinds are much more often depicted on the gate of this ruler (e.g. SI10:4). The royal hunt as a feature of Ashurnasirpal II is less surprising (e.g. AI13:15–16). Tribute is highlighted on both gates.[307] While Ashurnasirpal II often holds a long shepherd's staff in his hand (e.g. AI13:33–34), Shalmaneser III is often depicted holding bow and arrows while receiving processions of various kinds (e.g. SI10:5t.). The priestly role is expressed more clearly on the gate of Shalmaneser III. The representations of priests and of divine chariots engaged in warfare may be seen as strengthening this impression (e.g. SI10:4, SI10:9t. resp.). Moving on, the motif of difficult path is also more frequent on the bands of this king (e.g. SI10:1t.). The more diverse geography of SI10, and its arrangement according to the four quarters, are also indicative of the greater horizon of Shalmaneser III. The motif of the king as observer and of the highlighted role of officials may also be seen as expressions of ideological differences and profiling (e.g. SI10:4, SI10:11b. resp.). Also noteworthy is the substantial difference in height between the two gates, again visually displaying the ideas of heroic priority and of a strengthening of royal ambitions. In sum, the two gates convey basically the same propaganda but with varying emphasis.

Turning to the dual commmorative texts which were inscribed twice, i.e. on each lining of the two doors, both texts, AE51 (1) and SE5 (i1), begin with the same short cluster of royal epithets which starts with "great king". Repetitive genealogies are then given (AE51:1–3, SE5:i1). Another block of royal epithets follows in both texts (AE51:3–11, SE5:i1–6). Both starts with "heroic man" but

306 As already noted in subsection 5.4.2, it has even been suggested that the geographical ordering of the scenes reflects the notion of the four quarters (Hertel 2004).

307 As for Balawat gates and tribute, no less than twelve of Ashurnasirpal II's bands from the Mamu temple illustrate such scenes while only four of them depict warfare (AI14).

then differ considerably. AE51 (11–13) then claims that Ashur had chosen and armed the king, while SE5 (i6–ii2) adds the aspect of investiture and the notion of shepherdship. The latter text also includes the claim that the gods Ashur and Ninurta had given the king world dominion, and gives the royal epithets of "strong king, sun of all people" (SE2:ii1–2).

Moving on to the more narrative aspects of the two texts, SE5 (ii2–5) then goes on by arguing that the king swept across the foreign lands as a "flood" and like Erra and Adad. AE51 (13–26) instead argues that the king violently subdued or even massacred various mountain peoples with the aid of the deities, presents the king as a conqueror from GN to GN, declares that he counted conquered people as people of his land, and briefly notes that he appointed governors and imposed corvée. A third set of royal epithets then follows, beginning with "attentive prince, worshipper of the great gods" (AE51:26–28). Instead of a narrative of military campaigns, AE51 (28–30) mentions that the king rebuilt and named the town, and then concludes by referring to the palace and its gate. The annals of SE5 (ii2–vi7), by contrast, provides a narrative of military campaigns, arranged around eponyms, emphasizing the king's encounters with Urartu, Bit-Adini, Chaldea, and especially Babylonia. The text in question abruptly but intentionally ends.

The comparison is obviously hampered by the varying subgenres of the two texts, display inscription (AE51) versus annals (SE5). The building theme thus comes across clearer in AE51, while the military aspect is emphasized in SE5. Still, image making thus building is centred on in SE5 (e.g. ii3), and the king's role as warrior is highlighted also in AE51. The themes of warfare, conquering, and imperialism permeate the narrative and non-narrative parts of both texts. The geographical range of SE5 serves to differentiate this text from AE51, e.g. by their focusing on GNN which basically only Shalmaneser III had to do with. It is clear that this king drew inspiration from the works of Ashurnasirpal II, not only in the sense that he followed his father's example of furnishing Balawat. The first cluster of royal epithets is identical, and the second one is headed by the same epithet. Furthermore, the SE5 epithets of "controller of the brazen ones, decked with radiance, fearless in battle" which are common in the titulary of Ashurnasirpal II but infrequent in that of Shalmaneser III bear clear traces of his father's ideological influence here (SE5:i3, SE5:i3–4, SE5:i4 resp.). In sum, the same may be said of the texts as with the images above, namely that there is a fundamentally shared propaganda expressed in the sources, but that clear differences, expressing emphasis on different ideological aspects, nevertheless exist.

The strategic comparisons of the Kurkh monoliths and the bronze bands of the palaces in Balawat have shown that, although the two kings' propaganda basically convey the same message, individual ideological traits often shine through. The themes and motifs of heroic priority, difficult path, royal genealogy, image making, and the broad range of toponyms are some of the ideological elements which distinguish the propaganda of Shalmaneser III, while hunting, building, and shepherding are themes and motifs typical of Ashurnasirpal II. The comparisons have also made clear that the kings' respective repute of tribute receiver and warrior should be problematized.

8.4 The other kings and strategic comparisons

This section contains strategic comparisons, based on the relevant royal epithets and visual representations, concerning the propaganda of the other Early Neo-Assyrian kings in relation to one another and to the just treated two kings.[308] I will argue that the evidence mainly talks of continuity, although especially the reign of Adad-narari III stands out with various nuances of change, such as increased stress on Babylonia and high officials.

Beginning with the royal epithets and their frequency in the respective reigns (see apps. 11–12), the three kings of the eNA I-phase have the same epithets as Ashurnasirpal II on their top four positions. Ashur-dan II even has the same ordering of these four in relation to Ashurnasirpal II. The former's meagerly preserved epithets also tend to focus much on Ashur. Adad-narari II has "king of Assyria" on top, but an international horizon is confirmed by the title of "king of the four quarters". The relative strength within Tukulti-Ninurta II's titles mirrors that of Ashurnasirpal II to a close degree.

Turning to the royal epithets and their frequency in the eNA III-phase, the attestations from the reign of Shamshi-Adad V are quite meagre, but the top epithets are quite normal, e.g. with his patronym and "king of Assyria" as heading the list. The amount of attestations from Adad-narari III is however promising of a fair evaluation. It is noticeable that "king of Assyria" heads the list, while his patronym comes on second place. His international focus is conveyed through the title of "king of the universe" on third place. The title of "overseer" comes on fourth place, setting this list apart. The frequency of this and the most common title may be regarded as an expression of the influences of genre, here decrees. The final three rulers of the eNA III-phase have two things in common: few attestations and modest authority claims. Ashur-dan III e.g. has only epithets which tell of divine choice and royal descent, while

308 The said sources are highly ideologically charged (see s. 2.1) and enough well-attested so as to make at least a comparison based on the preserved royal epithets meaningful.

his predecessor Shalmaneser IV has "strong king" as the only indication of an expanding state. Ashur-narari V lastly has only "king of Assyria", but this may be seen as determined by the genre, i.e. loyalty oaths.

As for the royal visual representations, the frequency of the sources are perhaps too meagre for a fair evaluation. Nevertheless, there are ten examples from the eNA III-phase, nine of them depicting "king as venerating priest", and the tenth of them representing "king as hunter". The latter motif, attested from the royal seal and Adad-narari III's times, tells of continuity and conformity in terms of ideological program developing. The former motif has seven attestations from Adad-narari III and two from Shamshi-Adad V. It is difficult to say what this scarcity of sources and uniformity of motifs depend on, whether reflecting unfortunate preservation circumstances or a relative royal weakness in the relevant time phase, with its rulers not having the strength of financing and carrying out ambitious building and monument making projects. Possibly, the truth lies somewhere in between. The motif of "venerating priest" is determined by the type of monument, i.e. stelae.

Concluding with an evaluation of the above made strategic comparisons, it is obvious that the force of continuity is stronger than that of change. The circumstance in eNA I-times of its three kings sharing their top four-titles with Ashurnasirpal II indicates this as well as that the latter was not a great reformer – at least not in terms of royal titulary. The slight emphasis on Ashur presumably tells of the capital status which Assur had at the time.

Moving on to the eNA III-titularies and Shamshi-Adad V, it is likely that this king sought to reconstruct an authority which had been affected through his possible usurper status and through his engaging in a civil war. Expressions of this reconstructing are his use of an archaic script and beard on the Nabu Stele (SA5I1), thus linking him with the great Shamshi-Adad I (Reade 1979a: 341–42; Grayson 1996: 181), his justifying of the civil war in a narrative section of his annals (SA5E1:i39–53), his "letter from a god" (SA5E4), and his use of several divine epithets as royal ones (see apps. 5–7, 10), perhaps telling of him needing an extraordinary kind of legitimacy to rule.

Adad-narari III focused much on his genre-determined title "overseer", and this may tell of a focusing on defensiveness and internal affairs. The peaceful and traditional motif of "venerating priest" may also tell of this. According to Siddall (2013: 171–87), the royal ideology of Adad-narari III mainly signified continuity, but it nevertheless had a few features denoting change, such as a promotion of Nabu, a change in royal attire, a focus on dynastic past and antiquity worship, and modesty in the military field of action. While Ashurnasirpal II promoted Ninurta, Adad-narari III focused on Nabu. The latter ruler also commissioned work on a new royal palace in Kalhu. Adad-narari III thus comes across as an initiator of some change.

The modest claims by the last three kings of the period strengthen the mentioned trend of inward looking and relative weakness in the international arena. By contrast, the sources of high officials, such as those of Shamshi-ilu and Bel-Harran-beli-usur, carry wide-ranging authority claims, telling of a shift of power balance in the Assyrian imperial state. The archive from the Governor's Palace in Kalhu begins at this point in time (Postgate 1973), perhaps telling of a strenghtened role of this office and official. Also indicative of the decline of royal authority is the Saba'a Stele with its divine emblems almost outsizing the figure of the king (An3I2). The Babylonian gods Marduk and Nabu are here seen closest to the king, telling of a "Babylonization" of a sort – a development which of course reached a climax in the time of Tiglath-pileser III. Moreover, it is only in the primary sources of the eNA III-phase where Babylonian deities are depicted (as divine emblems).

Summing up, I have argued that the textual and visual evidence for the here focused eNA I and eNA III-phases largely speaks of continuity, although especially the reign of Adad-narari III stands out with some indications of change, such as increased emphasis on high officials and Babylonia. Additionally, internal affairs and non-military roles were highlighted.

8.5 Summary and reflections

This chapter has first and foremost demonstrated that, although the propaganda of Ashurnasirpal II and Shalmaneser III are fundamentally the same, hence their common treatment in chapters 3–5, clear ideological differences, mostly by varying emphasis, between the two exist, making both rulers stand out as leaving their own individual marks upon the basic tenets of Assyrian state ideology. In other words, there is diversity within the unity.

I noted in the introductory section that Ashurnasirpal II is often focused on of the two relevant rulers in textbooks on Mesopotamian history, implying that his "contribution" historically and ideologically was greater as well as closely determining that of his son and successor Shalmaneser III. According to this arisen picture, the propaganda of the latter was both more modest and very closely following that of his father and predecessor.

For sure, Shalmaneser III emphasized his connection with this king, e.g. through the use of his patronym, the reuse of ideological goods, and the erection of monuments beside those of Ashurnasirpal II, e.g. in Kurkh and Balawat. This does not mean however that he simply imitated the propaganda of his father. The themes and/or motifs of image making and other rituals in the periphery, his acting as priest (on the Balawat Gate), the king as observer of battle, the emphasis on his royal officials, and of him facing large coalitions, highlighting difficult path and the campaigning in all four quarters, e.g. in Babylonia, the Levant, Urartu, and Media, serve to profile the propaganda of Shalmaneser III. The themes and/or motifs of the king as shepherd and as hunter, his building of cities, palaces and temples, the juxtapositioning of Assyrians and Arameans, the emphasis on the west, the use of eponyms, and the theme of discoverer through the itinerary style of narration in their turn all serve to profile the propaganda of Ashurnasirpal II.

The contribution of Shalmaneser III may in fact, both in terms of history (see s. 8.1) and ideology, be regarded as greater than that of Ashurnasirpal II. His royal epithets talk more of universal dominion, his military campaigns, emphasized in the propaganda, reached more widely and included even the Levant and Babylonia, and his monuments of the strategic comparison, i.e. among the Kurkh monoliths and the palace gates of Balawat, are substantially larger in size, displaying heroic priority and greater claims. Thus, Shalmaneser III was in his propaganda not a copycat, yet influenced by his father, but an innovator, inaugurating a new imperial phase. From an archaeologial viewpoint, he built a new palace (Fort Shalmaneser) to have aside of the North-West Palace, and the Balawat Gate must have been nearly as imposing as the reliefed stone slabs which decorated his father's palace.[309]

The slentrian image of Ashurnasirpal II as a ferocious warrior, implementing calculated frightfulness, and of Shalmaneser III as a peaceful tribute receiver needs to be modified. Although trends in that direction exist, the roles are reversed on some of the monuments such as the Balawat gates. The point to make here is that the reciprocity principle (see subs. 5.4.2) overarched any other considerations. Supposedly, Shalmaneser III did not have to resort to violence as much as the reconquering Ashurnasirpal II had to do.

The above conclusion on diversity within the unity can also be made in relation to the propaganda of the other Early Neo-Assyrian kings. Continuity between eNA I-times and Ashurnasirpal II was especially noted. While stressing continuity, Shamshi-Adad V also embraced change in his aim of reasserting authority after a civil war, e.g. through his use of the literary genre letter from a god. Adad-narari III and his three son-successors similarly stressed continuity, but focused much on internal affairs and non-military roles. Together with the high profile of high officials in the propaganda, this may be indicative of a change due to a decline of royal authority. The upsurge in the illustrating of

309 To say that the kings of the North-West Palace after Ashurnasirpal II had an identical ideological program to this king just because they resided there would be to go too far.

the Babylonian gods Marduk and Nabu in the eNA III-phase is also noteworthy, telling of a Babylonization of a kind.

Typological considerations may also add to the explaining of the varying ideological emphasis. In the eNA III-phase e.g., most of the iconography are stelae images, and they tend to convey the motif of "king as venerating priest". The aspects of addressee, especially relevant for the discussion on AE1, editorial considerations involving the use of abbreviations, as well as the apparent separation between text and image seen e.g. in the cases of the Kurkh monoliths here and AE23 before must also be taken into account.

9 The development of Assyrian state ideology

In this final discussion chapter of the study, the identified Early Neo-Assyrian (eNA I–III) state ideology is placed in a wider historical-ideological context, focusing on the Old (OA I–II), Middle (MA I–II), and Late Neo-Assyrian (lNA I–II)[310] propaganda in relation to the one presented and discussed in chapters 3–8. Firstly, the topic is introduced in section 9.1 by some references from the scholarly debate, then the royal iconography and titulary of older and younger times are looked upon in comparison in section 9.2, and in section 9.3 the older and younger textual narrative themes are looked upon in the same way. The chapter ends by a summary with reflections.

9.1 Introduction

Early Neo-Assyrian state ideology has to be placed within the larger structure of Assyrian state ideology to be fully understood. The development of Assyrian state ideology is closely linked to the historic developments of the Assyrian state, not the least because historians' outlining of ancient history is to a considerable extent based on the claims made by kings and rulers in various propagandistic sources. Anyway, in the outline of Assyrian history, the story begins with the semi-independent "governors" of Assur in the later half of the third millennium BCE, and continues with the Assur-based, mercantile city state of the Old Assyrian Period. A historical-ideological break then occurs, represented by Assyrian empire building. Postgate (1992b: 247–51) identifies four different phases in the development of the Assyrian empire, namely the time between c. 1450–1208 BCE (a high point ended with the death of Tukulti-Ninurta I), that between 1207–935 (largely a period of decline), the time between 934–745, i.e. the Early Neo-Assyrian Period, and that between 744–609, i.e. the Late Neo-Assyrian or Sargonid Period.

The ideology of the semi-independent Assur rulers of the third millennium BCE escapes us, but the ideology of the Old Assyrian state comes across in comparatively many sources. Larsen (1974, 1976: 149) focuses on four different ruler titles whose attestations are dependent on type of inscription, and which express different roles in relation to the people and the deities. The title "vice-regent of Ashur" refers to the ruler's priestly duties, the epithet "prince" alludes to the ruler's genealogy, the epithet "overseer" tells of the ruler's judicial-

310 For a fuller explanation of these numeral-provided terms, see below and appendix 16.

administrative authority, and the epithet "lord" refers to the status of the ruler as the head of political authority. The title of "king" was not yet used, and the political power of the ruler was quite limited, with "the city assembly", and possibly also the eponyms, figuring as sharing political power in the Old Assyrian city state (Larsen 1976: 109–223). The Amorite king Shamshi-Adad I who had his base in the Habur area conquered Assur and integrated it as one component of his regional state. The ideology of this ruler bears influences from the Old Akkadian and Babylonian periods and regions respectively, e.g. through his references to Ashur-Enlil, and his inclusion of the themes of warfare, booty seizing, and tribute receiving in Assyrian royal inscriptions (Grayson 1987: 47; Galter 1997: 55; Kienast 1997). This king heralds and represents the delimited OA II-phase.

In his treatise on political and ideological history in the Amarna age, Liverani (1990: 53, 56–57) describes the ideological character of the Middle Assyrian state, having moved away from the city state format to that of a larger, territorial state. This process was started primarily with the MA I-reign of Ashur-uballit I, attested as writer of letters in the Amarna correspondence. The new state ethos was to, by the command of Ashur and the great gods, extend the borders of Assyria. The Assyrian ruler, now known as "king", functioned as Ashur's representative on earth in this mission. With the reign of Adad-narari I, the role of the king as warrior is also expressed in royal inscriptions (Grayson 1987: 128; Galter 1997: 57). According to Machinist (2011: 413–24), the reign of Tukulti-Ninurta I[311] presented further elements of this revised ideology, namely the idea of the king as divinely connected or created, the notion of royal radiance, and the idea of the king as an "image" of the deities. Despite especially the firstly and lastly mentioned points, there remained a decisive hesitation on the part of the Assyrian king to formulate royal deification. Another important time period was the reign of Tiglath-pileser I in which the first true royal annals were composed (Tadmor 1981: 14–19; Grayson 1991: 6). The White Obelisk of Ashurnasirpal I (see s. 2.2) also tells of the changed character of Middle Assyrian propaganda through its images of the ruler conducting warfare and hunting.

Turning to the Neo-Assyrian Period, the developed state ideology focusing on divinely ordered imperialism continued, but royal iconography was greatly developed, with the North-West Palace serving as a model for the architectural program of later kings (Barjamovic 2011: 27). Variations within the period are detectable. Some scholars centre on the differences between the two phases of

311 Following the above historical outline of Postgate, this king ended the MA I-phase.

the period. Winter (1983: 28) explains the dominance of historical narrative in royal art after Ashurnasirpal II as a testimony of a successive secularization of the state and/or as an adaptation to the more heterogeneous viewers of the Sargonid Period, requiring a less esoteric visual language. The development of Assyrian propaganda from Ashurnasirpal II to Ashurbanipal shows that visual propaganda was preferred more and more (J. M. Russell 1999: 217) – a phenomenon which may be explained by the argument on adaptation. Staying with iconography, the gradual decline of the Early Neo-Assyrian sacred tree scene,[312] arguably illustrating prosperity, has been explained by the shift of the state economy, from one based on agriculture to one based on warfare (Porter 2003: 19–20). Similarly, the decline of tribute scenes in the 7th century BCE has been understood as a reflection of a shift in the political organization of the state, from centering on vasall states giving tribute to provinces paying taxes (Bär 1996: 230).[313]

Another focal point has been the increased emphasis on the king. Seux (1980–83: 172–73) here refers to a gradual development from theocracy to autocracy. Pongratz-Leisten (2009: 426–27) identifies a historical shift from the temple to the king and the latter's role as builder and caretaker of the cult in Mesopotamia. In her words: "The agency of the king replaces the temple as the key-metaphor for the social and cosmic order". In the time period 745–612 BCE, the Assyrian king "is presented in a more grandiose and sometimes even magnanimous light" (Beaulieu 2005: 52). The king is occasionally represented in social perspective, displaying his greater status (Barnett 1960: 16; Reade 1979a: 331–32).[314] Some scholars even identify an idea of the semi-divine nature of the Assyrian king (Parpola 1995b, 1999). A perceived change in the 7th century BCE from "a visible" to "an inaccessible" Assyrian king also relates to this discussion (Marti 2011). Lanfranchi (2003: 106) discerns a development towards "tyranny" in Neo-Assyrian times.[315]

The focal point of the overview above is on change. Continuity is however commonly identified, often in the same paper or book which pinpoints change.[316] Lambert (1998: 68) e.g. claims, regarding Assyrian state ideology,

312 The motif of pollinating genii was not completely abandoned in the state art of Late Neo-Assyrian kings, as proved e.g. by the reliefs of Sennacherib (see Barnett et al. 1998: pl. 204).
313 This change of emphasis on tribute that is visible at least in the preserved royal iconography justifies the separating of the period into the two phases INA I and II (Magen 1986).
314 These scholars identify Tiglath-pileser III and Esarhaddon respectively as the king in social perspective. Also Sennacherib can be seen like this (see Barnett et al. 1998: pl. 205).
315 Also noteworthy is the development of the theology of Ashur-Anshar under Sennacherib according to which this Assyrian god took Marduk's place (Chamaza 2002: 71–167).
316 As discussed in section 6.1, change could either reformulate or break with tradition.

that "the continuity of tradition is remarkable". Similarly, Frankfort (1948: 223–30) states that there is "an unbroken tradition" from Old to Neo-Assyrian times in terms of the rulers' epithets. The political-ideological structure of the Old Assyrian state never disappeared completely, and the overall impression of the development of Assyrian royal inscriptions is one of continuity (Renger 1997: 171, 175). Also Cancik-Kirschbaum (2008: 103–104) stresses the aspect of continuity, e.g. by referring to the idea of a royal/ruler dynasty as running through all Assyrian, historical phases. The image of the Assyrian king in later times preserved elements of the idea of the traditional Mesopotamian/Sumerian city state ruler (Reade 1979a: 342).

Stressing continuity between the Middle and Neo-Assyrian periods is even more common. Focusing on the texts, Kuhrt (1997: 478) states that it in historical-ideological terms was "a relative continuity" between the two periods. Focusing on the art, Collon (1995: 129) argues that there is "a strong continuity" between these periods, and that the monuments of the Middle Assyrian state served as a model for the Neo-Assyrian period and state, expressing "a conscious revival of style". All evidence taken together, the characterization by Postgate (1995: 405–10) of Assyrian state ideology as a special case in relation to Mesopotamian state ideology generally and as a "hybrid" of old and new ideological elements, captures the observation that change and continuity existed alongside in Assyrian ideology history.

9.2 Early Neo-Assyrian propaganda in history: royal iconography and titulary

In this section, the 21 visual representations of the Early Neo-Assyrian kings and the 20 most common royal titles and epithets of these rulers are examined according to if they were used before and/or after the time period in question. The discussion thus centres on ideological change and continuity. The data provided by Magen on motifs and Seux on titulary are consulted. I will e.g. argue that Early Neo-Assyrian state ideology was groundbreaking in iconography, but that it was following the paths of Middle Assyrian state ideology, although containing elaborations, regarding the royal titulary.

As for royal visual representations, there are not any preserved ones from the Old Assyrian Period, and only a few of them from the Middle Assyrian Period, then belonging to Tukulti-Ninurta I (e.g. on a cult socle), Tiglath-pileser I (e.g. on a cliff relief), Ashur-bel-kala (on the Broken Obelisk), and Ashurnasirpal I (on the White Obelisk) (Magen 1986: 9–19). The greater proportion of royal iconography and motifs derives from the Neo-Assyrian Period, from the capital cities Kalhu, Dur Sharrukin, and Nineveh.

Beginning with the visual representations and the combined most common one in the time of the ten kings (see app. 16), the motif of "receiving tribute" is attested from Ashurnasirpal I, Tiglath-pileser III, and Sargon II (Magen 1986: 115–16, motif IX). The motif of "venerating priest" runs through the Middle and Neo-Assyrian periods. It was expressed also in the reigns of e.g. Tukulti-Ninurta I, Tiglath-pileser I, Ashurnasirpal I, and in the reigns of all the Late Neo-Assyrian kings except Esarhaddon (Magen 1986: 45–55, motif IIIb). The third most common motif of "libating priest" is also attested from Ashurnasirpal I, Ashurbanipal, and possibly Tiglath-pileser III (Magen 1986: 65–69, motif IVa). Next, "king in battle" additionally comes from the reigns of Ashurnasirpal I, Tiglath-pileser III, and Sargon II (Magen 1986: 114, motif VII). Weapon cleansing is in another form attested also from the time of Tiglath-pileser III (Magen 1986: 81–84, motif IVd).

Moving further down the list, the motif of "royal hunter" is attested also from the sources of Ashurnasirpal I, Sargon II, Ashurbanipal, and possibly also from those of Esarhaddon (Magen 1986: 29–36, motif I). Assyrian kings are depicted receiving captives and booty also in the reigns of Tiglath-pileser III, Sargon II, Sennacherib, and Ashurbanipal (Magen 1986: 117, motif X). The motif of "the king being ritually purified" is also expressed in the time of Sargon II and possibly also in that of Sennacherib (Magen 1986: 73–81, motif IVc). Assyrian rulers "observe battle" also in the time of Sargon II (Magen 1986: 115, motif VIII). The motif of "priest (statue)" is restriced to Ashurnasirpal II and Shalmaneser III, but Magen instead identifies the motifs of "king in front of god with clasped hands" for Sargon II (Magen 1986: 40–45, motif IIIa), and "king as purification priest" for a Middle Assyrian king (Magen 1986: 69–73, motif IVb). The latter motif is also identified by Strommenger (1970: 11–13) in her study on Assyrian sculpture in the round.

Turning to those royal visual representations which have less than five attestations in the Early Neo-Assyrian Period, the motif of "banqueting" is also given in the propaganda of Ashurnasirpal I, Sargon II, Ashurbanipal, and possibly also in that of Tukulti-Ninurta I (Magen 1986: 119, motif XIII). The king is "on march" also in the sources of Ashurnasirpal I, Sargon II, Sennacherib, and possibly also in those of Ashurbanipal (Magen 1986: 113, motif VI), and the motif of "triumphant entry" is attested for the same kings with the possible addition of Tukulti-Ninurta I (Magen 1986: 118, motif XII). Moving on, the motif of "shepherd" is also seen in the propaganda of Ashur-bel-kala, Tiglath-pileser III, Sargon II, and Esarhaddon (Magen 1986: 113, motif V), and the motif of "master builder" is conveyed in the iconography of Sennacherib and Ashurbanipal (Magen 1986: 36–40, motif II).

The rare motifs of "receiving submissive Assyrians", "felling tree", "receiving timber", "being crowned", and "meeting another ruler" are apparently unique to the ten rulers. Reversely, only a few motifs can not be covered by the royal iconography of the Early Neo-Assyrian Period, namely "king in front of god making the *appa labānu*-gesture", i.e. nose stroking (Magen 1986: 55–65, motif IIIc), army cleansing by means of plants in the king's hands (Magen 1986: 84–91, motif IVe), and "king as triumphator" treading on or blinding defeated enemies (Magen 1986: 118, motif XI). The firstly mentioned of these is attested from the reigns of Sennacherib, Esarhaddon, and Ashurbanipal, and may be seen as a late version of the *ubāna tarāṣu*-gesture (Magen 1986: 94–108), the second of these, attested from Tiglath-pileser III, Sargon II, Sennacherib, and Ashurbanipal, may be regarded as a variation of the weapon cleansing motif, while the last of these motifs, used by Tiglath-pileser III, Sargon II, and possibly also by Tukulti-Ninurta I, is well-attested in the texts of the ten kings (see subss. 5.4.1–2).

Commenting on this data, it is striking that royal iconography is completely lacking from the Old Assyrian Period. The contributions of the following Middle Assyrian Period are also quite modest. The phase of MA I gives little and non-narrative art, while that of MA II provides more and give some variety, thanks largely to the White Obelisk. It was with the time of Ashurnasirpal II that monumental art through the use of reliefed stone orthostats covering palace and temple walls was initated. Almost every single royal motif which were used in the following Late Neo-Assyrian Period are expressed already in the art of the Early Neo-Assyrian Period. There are not any motifs from the Middle Assyrian Period that were abandoned. The Early Neo-Assyrian Period also stands out by the use of royal statues. Perhaps somewhat surprisingly, the lNA I-phase appears to be ideologically closer to the Early Neo-Assyrian Period than to the lNA II-phase. The motifs of the king receiving tribute and being engaged in battle are e.g. abandoned in the lNA II-phase, telling of another view on kingship. This revising of motifs was accompanied with developments in the way narrative art was depicted on the palace walls of Nineveh.[317] Nevertheless, it ought to be recognized that the Early Neo-Assyrian royal iconography formed the beginning of monumental art as well as of a wide-ranged visual propaganda in Assyria.

Moving on to the royal titulary, the titles and epithets belonging to Assyrian rulers have been preserved from all the identified periods and phases. Although the quantity of these of course varies greatly from the Old Assyrian Period (with comparatively few attestations) to the Late Neo-Assyrian Period

317 For example, the different use of registers, the more frequent use of epigraphs/captions, and the greatly increased focus on historical narrative (Reade 1979b, 1983).

(with comparatively many attestations), this kind of material is nevertheless an excellent source for examining ideological development.

The most common epithet combined in the Early Neo-Assyrian Period (see app. 16) is "son/heir of RN". It is attested through all phases,[318] showing that royal genealogy, e.g. by patronyms, was a constant source of legitimacy. On second place comes "king of Assyria". It is attested from the reign of Ashur-uballit I all the way to the end (Seux 1967: 301), showing that the abandoning of the city state format took place in the MA I-phase. The title of "king" was used only from the Middle Assyrian Period onwards. On third place, the title "king of the universe" is attested from Shamshi-Adad I of the OA II-phase onwards, right down to the last kings of Assyria (Seux 1967: 308–10). On fourth place, the title "strong king" is likewise attested from the reign of Shamshi-Adad I onwards (Seux 1967: 295–96, see RIMA1: A.0.39.6:6). The title on place number five is "vice-regent of Ashur" – a title which by contrast is attested in all phases of Assyrian ideology history, starting with the Old Assyrian I-rulers Silulu and Erishum I. It is however noteworthy that neither Sennacherib nor Esarhaddon seem to have taken this title (Seux 1967: 112–15). On sixth place, the title "great king" was taken by kings from Shamshi-Adad I onwards, by Ashur-uballit I, Ashur-bel-kala, and all the Late Neo-Assyrian rulers (Seux 1967: 300). The epithet "attentive prince" on seventh place is also widely distributed (Seux 1967: 254).

Moving further down the list, the epithet "appointee of Enlil" was a standard feature of Assyrian titulary ever since the days of Shamshi-Adad I (Seux 1967: 280, 112–15). The epithet "conqueror (*kāšidu*) of/from GN (to GN)" was used also by e.g. Shalmaneser I, Tiglath-pileser I, Sargon II, and Esarhaddon, displaying it as a Middle and Neo-Assyrian phenomenon (Seux 1967: 139). The notion of "heroic man" was embraced e.g. by Tiglath-pileser I and Sargon II.[319] With another adjective attached, the noun is also used to describe Sennacherib and Esarhaddon (Seux 1967: 92–93). Shalmaneser III's common epithet "king of all people" is attested also for the MA I-kings Enlil-narari, Shalmaneser I, and Ashur-nadin-apli, and in a way also for Tukulti-Ninurta I (Seux 1967: 313). The epithet "prince" is used in all phases of Assyrian ideology history, mostly

318 See RIMA1: A.0.27.1:5 (OA I), A.0.39.9:4 (OA II), A.0.73.1:2 (MA I), RIMA2: A.0.87.3:5 (MA II), RINAP1: 58:2 (lNA I), and RINAP4: 20:5 (lNA II). It should be noted though that the attestations of patronyms are weak in the lNA I-phase. For some reason, Tiglath-pileser III did not consider the patronym as an effective source of legitimacy.

319 The related epithet "strong male", attested 20 times, was used also by kings such as Tukulti-Ninurta I and Tiglath-pileser III. With another adjective, or without one, this epithet is attested also in the reigns of Sennacherib and Esarhaddon (Seux 1967: 377–78).

when referring to successors. Also Tukulti-Ninurta I and Sargon II are called this as ruling kings, and with an added adjective the noun is attested for many different rulers (Seux 1967: 251–56). The epithet "he who has no rival among the rulers of the four quarters" seems to be restricted to the eNA II-phase (Seux 1967: 120).[320]

As for the last of the 20 listed epithets, "fearless in battle" was used only by the two eNA II-kings and Sargon II, even though a slightly modified version of this epithet was used by Esarhaddon (Seux 1967: 34–35). As far as I can see, the epithet "he who marches with the support of Ashur" was used just by some Early Neo-Assyrian rulers starting with Adad-narari II (Seux 1967: 38–40, 130). The epithet "sun of all people" is attested also for Tukulti-Ninurta I and Esarhaddon (Seux 1967: 284). Next, the epithet "king of the four quarters" was used from the Middle Assyrian Period all the way through Sargonid times (Seux 1967: 305–308). The related epithet "king of *all* the four quarters" was used also by Tiglath-pileser I and Ashur-bel-kala (Seux 1967: 313–14). As already noted (see s. 9.1), the title of (just) "king" is attested from the MA I-phase onwards. Lastly, the simile "like Adad" was put to use at least also by Tiglath-pileser I and III, and by Sennacherib.[321]

Concluding from all this data, it is obvious that there is a striking difference between the two Old Assyrian phases. Shamshi-Adad I introduced new concepts of rule. The Middle Assyrian rulers were much influenced by the ideological developments in OA II. The Early Neo-Assyrian kings were in their turn much influenced by the Middle Assyrian rulers of both the MA I and MA II-phases. There is a fundamental continuity between the Middle and Neo-Assyrian periods. Also, the ideological connection between the Early and Late Neo-Assyrian periods is obvious. Regarding continuity, the ideology expressed in the early city state polity of the OA I-phase was not completely without a trace in the much later imperial polity of the lNA II-phase. The refraining from royal deification, and the two frequent titles of "vice-regent of Ashur" and "prince" are three clear testimonies of this.

9.3 Early Neo-Assyrian propaganda in history: textual narrative

This section will investigate whether the most characteristic narrative themes of each section of chapters 3–5 also are found in earlier and later royal inscrip-

320 Note however that the Urartean king Sardur I also used this epithet, as well as the epithet "fearless in battle" (Seux 1967: 120, 34–35). Assyrian propaganda thus had some effect.

321 This simile is not listed in the epithet collection of Seux. For the relevant attestations, see RIMA2: A.0.87.1:iv90 (MA I), RINAP1: 16:8 (lNA I), and RINAP3/1: 18:v22′ (lNA II).

tions. The data gathering in question was made through surveying the relevant royal inscriptions, and it could not use any works comparable to those of Magen and Seux, thus the separate position of this discussion in relation to that of section 9.2. In common with the distribution of the royal titulary over time, the textual narrative themes are attested from all of the relevant phases. I will argue that the textual narrative themes of the Early Neo-Assyrian Period are telling of a continuity in relation to Middle Assyrian state ideology, that there is a firm link with the Late Assyrian sources, and that there is a discontinuity with the Old Assyrian sources.

Having the textual narrative themes (see app. 16) and the Old Assyrian sources as the first focal points, the idea of divine choice is attested in both phases. Ilu-shumma is the favourite of Ashur and Ishtar (see RIMA1: A.0.32.2:4–6), and Anu and Enlil call the name of Shamshi-Adad I (see RIMA1: A.0.39.1:12–17). The king is a priest in both phases, at least indirectly expressed. Erishum I dedicates a mace to Adad (see RIMA1: A.0.33.16:1′–3′), and another cultic instrument is provided by Shamshi-Adad I (see RIMA1: A.0.39.6). In both phases, the ruler claims to be a master builder. Shalim-ahum e.g. refers to his ordered constructions on the Ashur temple (see RIMA1: A.0.31.1:7–11), while Shamshi-Adad I commissions a brand new temple for Ashur-Enlil (see RIMA1: A.0.39.1:18–58).

Only the OA I-phase presents the ruler with paternalistic duties. Erishum I talks of his mission of ensuring justice (see RIMA1: A.0.33.1:26–74), and Ilu-shumma claims that he facilitated streams of water (see RIMA1: A.0.32.2:30–48), probably for irrigation. References to the royal line are extremely common in both phases. Royal genealogy, call to future rulers, and previous builders are the main themes here. Shamshi-Adad I refers to his ancestor Ila-kabkabu as well as to Manishtusu, the latter of the Sargonic dynasty, as previous master builders (see RIMA1: A.0.39.9:5–7, A.0.39.2:10–13 resp.), while his successor Puzur-Sin in a famous text totally rejects Shamshi-Adad I as "a foreign plague, not of the flesh of the city Ashur" (*šibiṭ aḫtim lā šīr āl Aššur*) (see RIMA1: A.0.40.1001:24–25). Heroic priority is expressed in both phases. Puzur-Sin commissions the construction of a wall which none before him had built (see RIMA1: A.0.40.1001:30–36), and a sanctuary, not renovated since Sargonic times, is rebuilt by Shamshi-Adad I within the Ishtar temple in Nineveh (see RIMA1: A.0.39.2:i7–ii20).

Babylonia is emphasized in both phases. Ilu-shumma refers to the giving of "freedom" (*andurārum*) to the Akkadians, i.e. people of south Mesopotamia (see RIMA1: A.0.32.2:49–65), and Shamshi-Adad I e.g. calls himself "king of Akkad" (see RIMA1: A.0.39.6:7). As already remarked in section 9.1, the latter ruler was greatly influenced by south Mesopotamian culture. Only to be expected, the notion of an Assyria is not conveyed in the Old Assyrian sources. The city state ideal may be highlighted by Puzur-Sin's criticism of Shamshi-Adad I who had a large territorial state, centred in the Habur, in which Assur only was a minor part. The latter king nevertheless refers to Assur as "my city" (see e.g. RIMA1: A.0.39.1:56–57). Gendered imagery is expressed insofar as the Old Assyrian ruler is pictured as the self-evident head of political authority (see RIMA1: A.0.33.2:1–44), and as the one in charge of conducting warfare (see RIMA1: A.0.39.2001:3–8).

As shown by appendix 16, many narrative themes which are expressed in the Early Neo-Assyrian Period are lacking in the OA I-phase. There are several gaps regarding the OA II-phase as well, although a few more themes are present here. The deities are e.g. presented as conquerors when Shamshi-Adad I claims that he conducted warfare and won "by the command of Ishtar" (see RIMA1: A.0.39.2001:6–7). The notion of the ruler as warrior is introducted in the OA II-phase (see e.g. RIMA1: A.0.39.1001). A related theme is also a newcomer, that of the ruler receiving tribute (see RIMA1: A.0.39.1:73–80). Telling of the wider horizon of Shamshi-Adad I is also the theme of respecting foreign deities. The ruler in question e.g. dedicates cult objects to Itur-mer, a deity of Mari, as well as to Dagan of the Habur city Terqa (see RIMA1: A.0.39.4–5, A.0.39.7–8 resp.). This of course reflects this ruler's wider cultic obligations, in his running of a transregional polity.

Moving on to the Middle Assyrian Period, it is striking to note that virtually all the narrative themes conveyed by the Early Neo-Assyrian kings are expressed in the royal inscriptions of this time period. The only exceptions in the case of the MA I-phase are the themes of "hunter" and "respecting foreign deities", while the MA II-phase in a way presents a complete match.

As for chapter three, the great gods have the power to allot regions to Tukulti-Ninurta I (see RIMA1: A.0.78.1:iv24–35), and Tiglath-pileser I refers to Enlil as "lord of all lands" (see RIMA2: A.0.87.1:i3–4). The Mesopotamian deities are also presented as actual conquerors in both phases. Tukulti-Ninurta I conquers by the support of Ashur, Enlil, Shamash, and Ishtar, of which the last deity also is said to go in front of the army (see RIMA1: A.0.78.5:48–56), and the gods Ashur, Ninurta, and Adad are said to march alongside the MA II-ruler Ashur-bel-kala (see RIMA2: A.0.89.2:i 9′–10′).

Turning to characteristic themes from chapter four, Ashur is claimed to have chosen and invested Shalmaneser I (see RIMA1: A.0.77.1:22–26), and the great gods grant authority and insignia to Tiglath-pileser I in a long passage (see RIMA2: A.0.87.1:i15–27). As for the role of priest, Shalmaneser I is responsible for "providership" (*zāninūtu*) in relation to temples (see RIMA1: A.0.77.1008:v6′), and Tiglath-pileser I makes offerings to Adad, implementing the duty of priesthood (see RIMA2: A.0.87.1:viii9–10). The theme of the king as master builder is frequently expressed. Tukulti-Ninurta I e.g. refers to the creating of his temple-provided new capital city Kar-Tukulti-Ninurta (see RIMA1: A.0.78.22:39–54), and Tiglath-pileser I e.g. talks of rebuilding the Anu-Adad temple in Assur (see RIMA2: A.0.87.1:vii60–114). The role of the king as warrior is very often expressed, especially in the MA II-phase. Adad-narari I e.g. narrates of his warfare against Hanigalbat/Mitanni (see RIMA1: A.0.76.3:4–51), and the annals of Tiglath-pileser I is permeated with this theme (see e.g. RIMA2: A.0.87:1).

Regarding characteristic narrative themes of chapter five and the royal inscriptions of the Middle Assyrian Period, difficult path is commonly expressed in both phases. Tukulti-Ninurta I e.g. breaks through mountainous areas by cutting out way with metal tools (see RIMA1: A.0.78.23:40–45), and Ashur-bel-kala arguably manages to traverse mountains (see RIMA2: A.0.89.2:i12′–18′). The statement by Shalmaneser I that he took wild beasts as booty from conquered areas may not refer to a royal role of hunter (see RIMA1: A.0.77.1:105–106), but so does for sure that of Tiglath-pileser I when he claims to have hunted wild bulls, elephants, and lions – all by the command of Ninurta (see RIMA2: A.0.87.1:vi55–84). Foreign deities are not spoken of in MA I-sources, but in MA II-times foreign deities are brought to Assyria and apparently used, thus recognizing their powers, as gate keepers of several important temples in Assyria (see RIMA2: A.0.87.1:iv32–39).

Tukulti-Ninurta I is presented as having authority over all, or at least vast, lands in the enumeration of conquered GNN (see RIMA1: A.0.78.2:17–35, A.0.78.1:iv24–35), and Tiglath-pileser I states that he conquered land after land, city after city, mountain after mountain, and subdued ruler after ruler (see RIMA2: A.0.87.1:i51–61). The seizing of booty is a frequent topic in both phases. Adad-narari I seizes booty after his victory against Hanigalbat (see RIMA1: A.0.76.3:31–34), and Tiglath-pileser I does the same after defeating a large coalition (see RIMA2: A.0.87.1:iv71–v8). As for deportations, Tukulti-Ninurta I claims to have brought 28 800 "Hittites" to Assyria (see RIMA1: A.0.78.23:27–30), and Tiglath-pileser I arguably seized 6 000 enemy soldiers and regarded them as subjects of his land (see RIMA2: A.0.87.1:i84–88). Also the Middle Assyrian king claimed world dominion.

Regarding the key themes of subsections 5.4.3–4, Adad-narari I also, in another stage, receives a considerable amount of tribute from Hanigalbat (see RIMA1: A.0.76.3:12–14), and Tiglath-pileser I likewise receives tribute, e.g. through the shape of horses (see RIMA2: A.0.87.3:13–14). As for fetching resources, Tukulti-Ninurta I takes and uses timber felled in Mehru (see RIMA1: A.0.78.1:iii12–20), while Tiglath-pileser I seizes valuable stone sorts in the lands of Nairi (see RIMA2: A.0.87.1:viii11–16). Royal paternalism is expressed clearly in both phases. Ashur chose Tukulti-Ninurta I to be royal shepherd and herdsman (see RIMA1: A.0.78.1:i21–24), and Tiglath-pileser I claims to have brought contentment to his people, and to have placed them in a "peaceful dwelling" (see RIMA2: A.0.87.1:vii33–35).

Babylonia is emphasized in both phases. Tukulti-Ninurta I claims to have defeated and captured the king of Babylonia, and then calls himself "king of Sumer and Akkad" (see RIMA1: A.0.78.5:53–69),[322] while Tiglath-pileser I conquers lands and cities from Babylonia, defeating its king several times (see RIMA2: A.0.87.4:37–51). The notion of Assyria is established by Ashur-uballit I at the latest. This king refers to his work in the Ishtar temple in Nineveh (see RIMA1: 115, A.0.73.1001), now turned into an Assyrian urban centre. Similarly, Tiglath-pileser I narrates of the commissioning of various works in the mentioned city (see e.g. RIMA2: A.0.87.10:54–62).

References to the royal line are frequent, notably through royal genealogy, call to future rulers, and previous builders. The firstly mentioned ideological theme is e.g. highlighted in a building inscription of Adad-narari I (see RIMA1: A.0.76.1:18–32). Tiglath-pileser I e.g. provides extensive genealogies with several, long epithets for each listed predecessor (see RIMA2: A.0.87.1:vii42–59). Also heroic priority is consistently expressed in the two phases. Shalmaneser I e.g. claims to have rebuilt the Ashur temple in a more skillful way than before (see RIMA1: A.0.77.1:135–36), and Tiglath-pileser I traverses a mountain which no other king had visited (see RIMA2: A.0.87.1:iii37–39). The enemy is routinely portrayed as a subaltern "Other" (see RIMA1: A.0.77:56–87, RIMA2: A.0.87.1: v82–98). As for gendered imagery, a curse section asks Ishtar to turn the misbehaving ruler into a woman and to cause his male genitals to dwindle away (see RIMA1: A.0.78.1:vi9–15), while the MA II-ruler is the natural head of political authority and the paradigmatic warrior (see RIMA2: A.0.87.1:i46–61).

As shown by appendix 16, almost all the characteristic themes of chapters 3–5 are expressed in the two historical phases (lNA I–II) of the Late Neo-Assyrian Period. The only exception is that of the theme of king as hunter, which is not attested in the lNA I-phase. The following paragraphs will give examples of how an ideological continuity between the Early and Late Neo-Assyrian periods can be detected. The sources of Tiglath-pileser III, i.e. the first ruler of the lNA I-phase, and Sennacherib, i.e. the first ruler of the lNA II-phase, will be highlighted in this discussion on Sargonid propaganda.

---

322 See also the Tukulti-Ninurta I Epic where the king in question in a more elaborate way presents himself as the rightful ruler over Babylonia (see Machinist 1983a).

Regarding the themes of chapter three, the great gods of Mesopotamia are described as being in charge of earth, heaven, and underworld in a text of Tiglath-pileser III (see RINAP1: 35:i1–20), and Sennacherib claims that Ashur had a world dominion which this god could entrust the governance of to him (see RINAP3/1: 16:i15–22). Divine warfare is referred to when Tiglath-pileser III announces that he conducted warfare in Ashur's name (see RINAP1: 6:4–5), and when Sennacherib claims that he defeated an international coalition by the support of Ashur (see RINAP3/1: 4:44).

Turning to the themes of chapter four, several great gods pick out Tiglath-pileser III to conquer and lead the foreign lands (see RINAP1: 35:i21–35), and Ashur is talked of as giving a kingship without rival to Sennacherib (see RINAP3/1: 1:4), similarly expressing the king's status of the deities' representative. As for the priestly role, the great gods are said to establish the priesthood of Tiglath-pileser III (see RINAP1: 37:11), and Sennacherib gives offerings and gifts to the deities upon entering his newly built palace (see RINAP3/1: 1:92). A role of master builder is referred to in a label text which alludes to work on the platform of the Ashur temple (see RINAP1: 58), and through the words of Sennacherib that he built his new palace, and invited the deities inside (see RINAP3/1: 1:63–92). Regarding warfare, Tiglath-pileser III e.g. claims to have destroyed and burnt a conquered enemy city (see RINAP1: 8:8–9), and the annals of Sennacherib naturally tell of several military campaigns by this ruler (see RINAP3/1: 1:16–62).

Moving on to the characteristic themes of chapter five, Tiglath-pileser III narrates that he pursued the fleeing enemy by climbing up a high mountain (see RINAP1: 15:10–11), and Sennacherib similarly traverses wild mountain terrain on his campaign marching onwards (see RINAP3/1: 3:21), likewise speaking of difficult path. Captions to the famous scenes where Ashurbanipal hunts lions (see Gerardi 1988: 14–15), as well as the royal seal which shows the ruler stabbing a lion, tell of the Late Neo-Assyrian king's role as hunter. As for respecting foreign deities, Tiglath-pileser III claims to have adorned and returned statues of foreign deities (see RINAP1: 5:1), and Sennacherib speaks of godnapping in Philistine Ashkelon without mentioning any violence motivated by iconoclasm (see RINAP3/1: 4:39).

As for the Late Neo-Assyrian king and his foreign, human subjects, Tiglath-pileser III claims to have exercised authority from one distant GN to another, and he also claims to have gathered and included (as Assyrians) foreign peoples (see RINAP1: 5:5–8,11–12). Sennacherib e.g. narrates that he was the overlord or ruler of several distant western rulers and lands, and he also claims to have taken care of the innocent civilians of Ekron whom he spared (see RINAP3/1: 4:36–38,46–47). Tiglath-pileser III seizes booty in the shape of animals after having defeated and punished a certain polity (see RINAP1: 7:6–8), and Sennacherib seizes booty from a coalition after a successful battle against it (see RINAP3/1: 1:27–29). Regarding deportations, Tiglath-pileser III settles the people of foreign lands in a newly built city (see RINAP1: 5:2–3), and Sennacherib arguably deported as many as 208 000 people on one of his southern campaigns (see RINAP3/1: 1:60).

Tribute in the shape of talents of gold and silver is given by a foreign ruler to Tiglath-pileser III (see RINAP1: 6:5–7), and Sennacherib claims to have received tribute from the distant land of Media (see RINAP3/1: 3:33). Concerning the fetching of resources, Tiglath-pileser III speaks of offering the great gods lapis lazuli which had been hewn directly from the mountain (see RINAP1: 8:3–4), and Sennacherib tells of the limestone and timber fetching directly related to his providing his temples and palaces in his new capital Nineveh with gateway colossi (see RINAP3/1: 16:v79–vi10). As for paternalism, Tiglath-pileser III claims to have shepherded conquered peoples in safe pastures (see RINAP1: 35:15′–17′), while Sennacherib tells of how he provided the citizens of the multicultural metropolis Nineveh with land and water for growing crops and plants there (see RINAP3/1: 1:88–90).

Regarding the highlighting of Babylonia, Tiglath-pileser III e.g. brags about having sacrificed to Marduk (see RINAP1: 16:12), and Sennacherib talks much of his encounter with Marduk-apla-iddina II and of his attempts to govern Babylonia (see RINAP3/1: 1:5–54). The notion of Assyria is expressed e.g. when foreign people are described as inhabitants of Assyria (see RINAP1: 14:8–10), or when the king is said to exercise dominion over it (see RINAP3/1: 1:66), in this way speaking of a polity beyond the city state.

Royal line references are expressed e.g. when Tiglath-pileser III instructs a future ruler on how to treat his inscription (see RINAP1: 35:iii6′–10′), and when Sennacherib refers to his ancestors and the time immemorial earlier kings (see RINAP3/1: 1:66). The notion of heroic priority is conveyed when Tiglath-pileser III claims to have encountered a western land which none of his predecessors had ever heard of (see RINAP1: [42:27′–30′]), and when Sennacherib narrates that he conquered a southern, foreign polity which no Assyrian king had ruled since time immemorial (see RINAP3/1: 1:58). The enemy is routinely portrayed as a subaltern "Other" in relation to the Assyrian king (see RINAP1: 35:i21′–37′, RINAP3/2: 46:42–47). Turning lastly to the gendered imagery, the picture of Rusa as lying on his sickbed "like a woman in labour" has already been noted (see Mayer 1983: 83, line 151). In a curse section of a text of Esarhaddon, Ishtar is urged to turn the misbehaving ruler from a man to a woman (see RINAP4: 98:53–57rev.).

Concluding from all the textual narrative themes and the data just provided, it is easy to see that there is a great continuity between the Middle and

Neo-Assyrian periods in terms of textual narrative themes and royal inscriptions. The same is true of the relationship between the textual narrative themes of the Early and Late Neo-Assyrian periods. The Old Assyrian period again stands out, and again there is a clear ideological division of that period into before and after Shamshi-Adad I (OA I–II). Still, it is worth pointing out that the ideological themes of divine choice, emphasis on Babylonia, references to the royal line, heroic priority, gendered imagery, and the king as master builder and priest run through the whole of Assyrian ideology history. With the Middle Assyrian Period, the added roles of the ruler, now termed king, as warrior, booty seizer, and tribute receiver were firmly established, while the polity was enlarged from a city state to a territorial state.

9.4 Summary and reflections

This chapter aimed at placing the identified Early Neo-Assyrian state ideology into a wider historical-ideological context by noting the presence or absence of the most common royal visual representations and royal epithets of the Early Neo-Assyrian Period in the propaganda of earlier and later Assyrian periods, and by noting the absence or presence of key textual narrative themes of the chapters 3–5 in the royal inscriptions of earlier and later periods. The relevant contextualization had to, out of necessity, be quite rough, in the sense of my leaving out the aspects of quantitative and qualitative differences,[323] but all the same it should be able to give a fairly well-founded indication on how to situate the propaganda of the Early Neo-Assyrian kings in the overall development of Assyrian state ideology.

The Early Neo-Assyrian Period, especially the ninth century BCE, stands out when it comes to royal iconography, both in terms of scale and range of motifs, heralding the grand developments of the lNA I and II-phases. Although grand visual arrangements surely existed also in earlier periods,[324] these have not been satisfactory preserved because of the use of different and more perishable media such as wall textiles, paintings in *stucco* or on glazed tiles. Even so, the innovative way of Ashurnasirpal II, who probably was inspired by Syri-

323 Such as the increasingly more "political" notions of *iššak Aššur* over time, as it is integrated into epithet clusters which focus on more worldly, notably military, matters. See Larsen 1976: 149 for an image of the title as basically "religious" in Old Assyrian times.

324 Tukulti-Ninurta I's palace in Kar-Tukulti-Ninurta e.g. bore wall decorations (Eickhoff 1976–80), and it has been suggested that the scenes on the White Obelisk reflect the visual program on the palace walls which has not been preserved (Pittman 1997).

an-Hittite art which he encountered on his campaigns (e.g. Winter 2010: 539, *contra* Orlamünde 2011b: 466–67), of expressing his state ideology visually through stone orthostats, covering much of his palaces and temples, and which were decorated with various narrative scenes and royal motifs, makes the Early Neo-Assyrian state ideology stand out. In terms of royal visual representations the relevant period was truly groundbreaking.

Regarding the royal titulary and the textual narrative themes, the situation is much different. Firstly, a striking feature is the remarkable continuity between the Middle Assyrian (both the MA I and II-phases) and the Neo-Assyrian ideological sources. In this context, Early Neo-Assyrian state ideology appears as a continuation, although with elaborations, of Middle Assyrian state ideology. Secondly, there is also a strong link with the Late Neo-Assyrian Period in terms of propaganda. Thirdly, another important point to make here is that the Old Assyrian Period expresses two separate phases, i.e. OA I and II, with their own ideological character. The Amorite and Babylonian-influenced ruler Shamshi-Adad I introduced several royal epithets and narrative themes which were to be standard in later royal inscriptions. In this way, the OA II-phase is closely tied to the later ideological developments which took place in Middle and Neo-Assyrian times. The noted, increased emphasis on the ruler is in line with the development of a patrimonial state, in which independent power factions are eliminated.

Fourthly and lastly, the ideology of rule expressed in the first Old Assyrian phase may seem to be remote from the imperial ideology of the first millennium BCE because of the lack of ideological themes and motifs which were to be vital later, such as the ruler as warrior and hunter. Still, several ideological features of the eldest times were kept all through Sargonid times, such as the title "vice-regent of Ashur", the structure of building inscriptions, the constant references to the ruler line, the statement that "Ashur is king", and the related lack of royal deification. Although called "king" from the Middle Assyrian Period onwards, the Assyrian ruler was modestly "the vice-regent" as well as "the overseer" right down to the end of Assyrian history.[325] It is in this strange and fascinating mix of change and continuity which Early Neo-Assyrian state ideology ought to be placed.

325 However, although the notion of "first among *equals*" remained until the end, it of course "became increasingly hypocritical in practice" (Barjamovic 2013: 148), with the Assyrian polity having evolved into the likeness of a patrimonial state (see subs. 5.4.7).

10 Conclusion of the study

10.1 Final conclusions and reflections

In this section of the last chapter of this book, I will make some final conclusions and reflections based on the findings of this study on Early Neo-Assyrian state ideology.[326] In the process, I take the opportunity to confront some of the (I dare to say) misguided criticism that I have received in the course of the six years during which I have worked with this project.

A first point that I would like to make, in a reiterating mode, focuses on the nature of the major primary sources. In contrast to recent trends, I have argued that these sources indeed express ideology and propaganda. This is evident from their content which conveys a systematically biased perspective. The issue of availability does not hinder this interpretation, not the least because many Assyrian monuments (with their royal inscriptions and iconography) were placed in comparatively public spaces. Regarding these dual aspects of content and availability in the evaluating of the primary sources, it is unfair to put so much emphasis on the latter and to almost completely ignore the former. Also, and as already stated, the aspect of availability does not univocally speak against the propaganda interpretation. The utterly biased perspective which the aspect of content gives is however hard to come by. Also, the content aspect is arguably the fundamental one, since the other aspect can always be disputed, not the least seen from a preservation angle.

To my mind, it is naïve to believe that these sources were made only for the deities and the cult, and that the claims made in them are representative for the whole Assyrian society. This perspective from above, which seems to argue that an Assyrian *Volksseele* is conveyed by the major primary sources, is clearly untenable. This perspective aside, it seems to me that the said view on the sources is based on a presumption that the ancient world and its inhabitants were fundamentally different from our own/ourselves, and that people in those days lived together in harmony and unison in a somewhat otherworldly universe which harboured social laws unknown to us in the modern world. Perhaps this presumption is inspired by the scarcity of expressions of dissent and opposition in the preserved sources. In any case, I believe that the displayed relativism in question is quite misleading. Rulers and elites have always had a need to create and diffuse a picture of themselves as legitimate and irreplaceable. The Assyrian rulers and elites should not be seen as exceptions to the rule in this respect.

326 For actual summaries, see the concluding (sub)section of each discussion chapter.

A second point to make here relates to the issue of selecting primary sources for a specific study. It is often claimed that the choice of studying royal inscriptions and iconography is telling of a perspective from above. This is of course very unfair. Although there is undoubtedly a tendency of scholars with a perspective from below tending to chose more mundane sources to study, while the scholars with the opposite outlook tend to centre on highflown propagandistic sources, it all comes down to which *perspective* the study has – not to which sources are selected. In this study, I have followed the stance of Liverani (2005) who makes a similar case, saying that for him it is all about revealing and exposing the mechanisms by which a ruling class naturalized their privileges in ancient societies. Thus, focusing on royal sources does not necessarily tell of a perspective from above.

A third point focuses on the issue of Assyrian state violence. Naturally, I do not in any way gloss over the frequent expressions of cruel violence attested in the sources. This should be clear e.g. by my detailed accounts of the depicted and described violence. What I do is to identify a certain *logic* (the reciprocity priniciple) in the use of Assyrian state violence, exposing the long-held Orientalist notion of a special Oriental violence characterized by indiscrimination. The logic in question of course does not make the violence any "better", and the principle clearly tells of a certain intolerant ideology. Still, Assyria was probably not worse than any other ancient power conducting warfare, but for some reason, they chose to tell about it, and this is of course quite thought provoking.[327] Perhaps its violence had a deterring function as well as expressing a celebrating of the fulfilment of divine orders. It must be said though that Assyrian culture was not only about destruction, but the propaganda also tells a lot of construction (of temples, settlements, and so on). Also, the contemporary violence, not the least in *today's* Iraq, puts Assyrian violence in a favourable light, given Assyria's religious tolerance and its taboo on maltreating women in the context of its military campaigns. But of course, the ideological sources convey an "ideal" version of reality.

The application of theory and the recognition of ideological change and variation in time and space are elements represented by the present study. As for the former element, theory is in some circles believed to give a biased perspective and to stand in juxtaposition to non-theoretical scholars purported

---

327 Comparisons with other cultures of the Ancient Near East were made throughout this study. It was e.g. noted that Egyptian propaganda often tells of various atrocities, thus questioning the established image of Egyptian culture as altogether peaceful and sophisticated. Also, although Babylonian rulers focused on cult rather than on warfare in their inscriptions, we can safely assume that they, with their armies, carried out the same kind of atrocities.

objectivity. I would instead say that it is unavoidable that scholars are influenced by their backgrounds, and that a complete objectivity is unattainable. Instead of haughtily pretend that you are unbiased, the ambition should be to humbly ackowledge this bias but make sure that the study is designed and conducted in a fair way, following all scientific rules. In a related way, similarly haughty, positivistic stances which e.g. proclaim that "the texts should speak for themselves" are obviously futile. The sources do not come to us unfiltered, and hermeneutic difficulties should be humbly acknowledged. In the interpretative process, theories are very helpful tools.

Turning to the results of the said two elements of this work, and beginning with the former one, post-colonial theory was e.g. used to discuss features of Orientalism in popular and scholarly literature on ancient Assyria, centering on the terms Orientalist despotism, violence, and decadence which were refuted. A king's power can grow and wane, thus being dynamic and not fixed, but Oriental despotism connotes something static and essence-based. The dichotomy of "Self"/"Other" represents the juxtaposition of the Assyrian king with the foreign lands in the sources. Also gender theory turned out to be fruitful. Focusing on gender, it was e.g. demonstrated that while the Assyrian king presents himself as having ideal masculinity (being strong, courageous, active), the enemy is portrayed with failed masculinity, or even with feminization. Gendered imagery was yet another way to belittle the enemy side. The related concept of patrimonialism, distinguished from the concept of Oriental despotism, was found to be applicable to the sources under study. I also exposed the references to nationalism and Assyria as an ancient nation state as being anachronistic. Furthermore, I have concluded that ethnicity does not play a great role in the said sources.

As for the latter element, I have hopefully also demonstrated the fruitful role of focusing on ideological variation (in place) and change (in time). Although the propaganda from the Early Neo-Assyrian Period is coherent and cohesive enough to justify the term Early Neo-Assyrian state ideology, some features telling of variation and change have been discovered, such as the roles of deities, high officials, and Babylonia in different regnal phases, localities, and reigns. The idea of an ideological program right from the start was noted on ideological development within reigns, and the notion of ideological standardization in the Assyrian heartland was noted on local propaganda. In the ideological comparison between Ashurnasirpal II and Shalmaneser III, commonly held views were questioned, and the latter's role as having greater claims and as being more than just a tribute receiver was identified. When situating Early Neo-Assyrian state ideology in the overall development of Assyrian propaganda, especially the novelty of the former king's iconographical program and the textual link to Middle and Late Neo-Assyrian sources were observed. Early Neo-Assyrian state ideology also has links to the remote OA I-phase when the polity was insignificant in size.

A final point that I would like to make centres on the concepts of cultural relativism and universalism. Although it is certainly misleading to say that we can never really understand people in antiquity because of our position as outsiders in time and place, it is equally misleading to believe that we some day can fully understand the people living in ancient times. Many aspects in the Assyrian sources are still very unclear, and we will probably never understand the full significances of these. The phenomenon of hanging severed heads of enemies in trees outside conquered enemy cities e.g. is hard to grasp for us. As noted in the discussion, it can not simply be seen as a way of deterring, but it had religious overtones too. Also the image of people wearing animal hides in the Assyrian camp is distant to us. There will always be aspects in need of being clarified, and it is of course the modern scholar's task to come as close to the truth (whatever that is) as is possible. It is my hope that the present study contributes in this everlasting ambition.

10.2 Further research

An obvious way of conducting further research on the topic of this book is to include the sources of more kings and time periods. Furthermore, my centering on inscriptions and iconography can be complemented by including analyses based on basic archaeological remains such as household wares and settlement layouts. Similarly, highlighting the development of architecture, such as palace and temple building, can also be a way forward. The role of ritual in Assyrian propaganda as well as in the political life of the Assyrian imperial state may also be rewarding to take a closer look upon. Finally – and in a more general sense – a more common use of post-colonial theory and gender theory would benefit the discipline of Assyriology.

Bibliography

Adalı, S. F. 2011. *The Scourge of God: The Umman-manda and Its Significance in the First Millennium BC*. State Archives of Assyria Studies 20. Helsinki: Neo-Assyrian Text Corpus Project.

Albenda, P. 1969. Expressions of Kingship in Assyrian Art. *Journal of the Ancient Near Eastern Society* 2: 41–53.

Albenda, P. 1986. *The Palace of Sargon, King of Assyria*. Synthèse 22. Paris: Éditions recherche sur les civilisations.

Albenda, P. 1987. Woman, Child and Family: Their Imagery in Assyrian Art. Pp. 17–21 in *La femme dans le Proche-Orient antique*, ed. J. M. Durand. Comptes rendu de la rencontre assyriologique internationale 33. Paris: Éditions recherche sur les civilisations.

Albenda, P. 1994. Assyrian Sacred Trees in the Brooklyn Museum. *Iraq* 56: 123–33.

Albrektsson, B. 1967. *History and the Gods: An Essay on the Idea of Historical Events as Divine Manifestations in the Ancient Near East and in Israel*. Coniectanea Biblica – Old Testament Series 1. Lund: CWK Gleerup.

Althusser, L. 1971. Ideology and Ideological State Apparatuses. Pp. 127–86 in *Lenin and Philosophy and Other Essays by Louis Althusser*, edited and translated by B. Brewster. New York and London: Monthly Review Press.

Anastasio, S. 2010. *Atlas of the Assyrian Pottery of the Iron Age*. Subartu 24. Turnhout: Brepols.

Andrae, W. 1923. *Die farbige Keramik aus Assur und ihre Vorstufen in altassyrischen Wandmalereien*. Berlin: Scarabaeus.

Andrae, W. 1938. *Das wiedererstandene Assur*. Sendschriften der Deutsche Orient-Gesellschaft 9. Leipzig: J. C. Hinrichs.

Annus, A. 2002. *The God Ninurta in the Mythology and Royal Ideology of Ancient Mesopotamia*. State Archives of Assyria Studies 14. Helsinki: Neo-Assyrian Text Corpus Project.

Asher-Greve, J. 2006. From 'Semiramis of Babylon' to 'Semiramis of Hammersmith'. Pp. 322–73 in Holloway 2006a.

Assante, J. 2007. The Lead Inlays of Tukulti-Ninurta I: Pornography as Imperial Strategy. Pp. 369–407 in *Ancient Near Eastern Art in Context*, eds. J. Cheng and M. H. Feldman. Culture and History of the Ancient Near East 26. Leiden and Boston: Brill.

Assmann, J. 1990. *Ma'at. Gerechtigkeit und Unsterblichkeit im Alten Ägypten*. Munich: C. H. Beck.

Assmann, J. 1996. Zum Konzept der Fremdheit im alten Ägypten. Pp. 77–99 in Schuster 1996.

Ataç, M.-A. 2010. *The Mythology of Kingship in Neo-Assyrian Art*. Cambridge: Cambridge University Press.

Ataç, M.-A. 2013. 'Imaginal' Landscapes in Assyrian Imperial Monuments. Pp. 383–423 in Hill et al. 2013a.

Bachelot, L. 1991. La fonction politique des reliefs néo-assyriens. Pp. 109–28 in *Marchands, diplomates et empereurs*, eds. D. Charpin and F. Joannès. Paris: Éditions recherche sur les civilisations.

Bagg, A. M. 2011. *Die Assyrer und das Westland. Studien zur historischen Geographie und Herrschaftspraxis in der Levante im 1 Jt. v. u. Z.* Orientalia Lovaniensia Analecta 216. Leuven, Paris, and Walpole: Peeters.

Bahrani, Z. 2001. *Women of Babylon: Gender and Representation in Mesopotamia*. London and New York: Routledge.

Bahrani, Z. 2003. *The Graven Image: Representation in Babylonia and Assyria*. Archaeology, Culture, and Society. Philadelphia: University of Pennsylvania Press.
Bahrani, Z. 2008. *Rituals of War: The Body and Violence in Mesopotamia*. New York: Zone Books.
Baines, J. and N. Yoffee. 1998. Order, Legitimacy, and Wealth in Ancient Egypt and Mesopotamia. Pp. 199–260 in *Archaic States*, eds. G. M. Feinan and J. Marcus. Advanced Seminar Series. Santa Fe: School of American Research Press.
Baker, H. D. 2006–08. Salmanassar III. *Reallexikon der Assyriologie und vorderasiatischen Archäologie* 11: 581–85.
Bär, J. 1996. *Der assyrische Tribut und seine Darstellung. Eine Untersuchung zur imperialen Ideologie im neuassyrischen Reich*. Alter Orient und Altes Testament 243. Neukirchen-Vluyn and Kevelaer: Neukirchener Verlag and Butzon & Bercker.
Barberon, L. 2011. La reine: Cette femme trop peu connue. *Dossiers d'Archéologie* 348: 74–77.
Barjamovic, G. 2011. Pride, Pomp and Circumstance: Palace, Court and Household in Assyria 879–612 BCE. Pp. 27–61 in *Royal Courts in Dynastic States and Empires*, ed. J. Duindam et al. Rulers & Elites 1. Leiden: Brill.
Barjamovic, G. 2012. Propaganda and Practice in Assyrian and Persian Imperial Culture. Pp. 43–59 in *Universal Empire*, eds. P. F. Bang and D. Kolodziejczyk. Cambridge: Cambridge University Press.
Barjamovic, G. 2013. Mesopotamian Empires. Pp. 120–60 in *The Oxford Handbook of the State in the Ancient Near East and Mediterranean*, eds. P. F. Bang and W. Scheidel. Oxford: Oxford University Press.
Barnett, R. D. 1960. *Assyrian Palace Reliefs and Their Influence on the Sculptures of Babylonia and Persia*. London: Batchworth Press.
Barnett, R. D. 1976. *Sculptures from the North Palace of Ashurbanipal at Nineveh*. London: Trustees of the British Museum.
Barnett, R. D. and M. Faulkner. 1962. *The Sculptures of Ashurnasirpal II (883–859 B.C.), Tiglath-Pileser III (745–727 B.C.), and Esarhaddon (681–669 B.C.) from the Central and Southwest Palaces of Nimrud*. London: British Museum Press.
Barnett, R. D., E. Bleibtreu, and G. Turner. 1998. *Sculptures from the Southwest Palace of Sennacherib at Nineveh*. London: British Museum Press.
Barthes, R. 1967. *Elements of Semiology*, translated by A. Lavers and C. Smith. Cape Editions 4. London: Jonathan Cape.
Bartl, P. V. 1999–2001. Zum Felsrelief von Eğil. *State Archives of Assyria Bulletin* 13: 27–37.
Bassi, K. 1998. *Acting Like Men: Gender, Drama, and Nostalgia in Ancient Greece*. Ann Arbor: University of Michigan Press.
Beaulieu, P.-A. 2005. World Hegemony, 900–300 BCE. Pp. 48–61 in Snell 2005.
de Beauvoir, S. 1997 [1949]. *The Second Sex*, translated and edited by H. M. Parshley. Vintage Classics. London: Vintage Books.
Berlejung, A. 1996. Die Macht der Insignien: Überlegungen zu einem Ritual der Investitur des Königs und dessen königsideologischen Implikationen. *Ugarit-Forschungen* 28: 1–35.
Bernbeck, R. 2010. Imperialist Networks: Ancient Assyria and the United States. *Present Pasts* 2/1: 142–68.
Black, J. and A. Green. 1992. *Gods, Demons, and Symbols of Ancient Mesopotamia: An Illustrated Dictionary*, with illustrations by T. Rickards. London: British Museum Press.
Bohrer, F. N. 2003. *Orientalism and Visual Culture: Imagining Mesopotamia in Nineteenth-Century Europe*. Cambridge: Cambridge University Press.

Borger, R. 1961. *Einleitung in die assyrischen Königsinschriften. Erster Teil: 721–612 v. Chr.* Handbuch der Orientalistik 5/1:1. Leiden: Brill.

Borger, R. 1996. *Beiträge zum Inschriftenwerk Assurbanipals. Die Prismenklassen A, B, C, K, D, E, F, G, H, J und T sowie andere Inschriften, mit einem Beitrag von Andreas Fuchs.* Wiesbaden: Harrassowitz.

Borger, R. 2003. *Mesopotamisches Zeichenlexikon.* Alter Orient und Altes Testament 305. Münster: Ugarit-Verlag.

Börker-Klähn, J. 1982. *Altvorderasiatische Bildstelen und Vergleichbare Felsreliefs I–II.* Baghdader Forschungen 4. Mainz am Rhein: Philipp von Zabern.

Born, H. and U. Seidl. 1995. *Schutzwaffen aus Assyrien und Urartu.* Sammlung Axel Guttmann 4. Mainz am Rhein: Philipp von Zabern.

Bottéro, J. 2001a. *Religion in Ancient Mesopotamia*, translated by T. Lavender Fagan. Chicago: University Press of Chicago.

Bottéro, J. 2001b. Women's Rights. Pp. 112–26 in *Everyday Life in Ancient Mesopotamia*, ed. J. Bottéro, translated by A. Nevill. Edinburgh: Edinburgh University Press.

Brandes, M. A. 1970. La salle dite 'G' du palais d'Assurnasirpal II à Kalakh: Lieu de cérémonielle rituelle. Pp. 147–54 in *Actes de la Rencontre Assyriologique Internationale*, ed. A. Finet. Comptes rendu de la rencontre assyriologique internationale 17. Brussels: Comité Belge de recherches en Mésopotamie.

Brentjes, B. 1994. Selbstverherrlichung oder Legitimitätsanspruch? Gedanken zu dem Thronrelief von Nimrud-Kalah. *Altorientalische Forschungen* 21: 50–64.

Brinkman, J. A. 1968. *A Political History of Post-Kassite Babylonia 1158–722 B.C.* Analecta Orientalia 43. Rome: Pontificio istituto biblico.

Brinkman, J. A. 1977. Mesopotamian Chronology of the Historical Period. Pp. 335–48 in A. L. Oppenheim, *Ancient Mesopotamia.* 2nd revised (by E. Reiner) ed. Chicago: University Press of Chicago.

Brisch, N. (ed.). 2008. *Religion and Power: Divine Kingship in the Ancient World and Beyond.* Oriental Institute Seminars 4. Chicago: Oriental Institute.

van Buren, E. D. 1939. *The Fauna of Ancient Mesopotamia as Represented in Art.* Analecta Orientalia 18. Rome: Pontificio istituto biblico.

Butler, J. 1990. *Gender Trouble: Feminism and the Subversion of Identity.* Thinking Gender. New York: Routledge.

van Buylaere, G. 2009. I Feared the Snow and Turned Back. Pp. 295–306 in Luukko et al. 2009.

Cameron, G. 1950. The Annals of Shalmaneser III, King of Assyria: A New Text. *Sumer* 6/1: 6–27.

Campbell Thompson, R. and R. W. Hutchinson. 1931. The Site of the Palace of Ashurnasirpal at Nineveh, Excavated in 1929/30 on Behalf of the British Museum. *Annals of Archaeology and Anthropology* 18: 79–112.

Canby, J. V. 1971. Decorated Garments in Ashurnasirpal's Sculpture. *Iraq* 33: 31–53.

Cancik-Kirschbaum, E. 1995. Konzeption und Legitimation von Herrschaft in neuassyrischer Zeit. Mythos und Ritual in VS 24, 92. *Welt des Orients* 26: 5–20.

Cancik-Kirschbaum, E. 1997. Rechtfertigung von politischem Handeln in Assyrien im 13./12. Jh.v. Chr. Pp. 69–77 in Pongratz-Leisten et al. 1997.

Cancik-Kirschbaum, E. 2008. *Die Assyrer. Geschichte, Gesellschaft und Kultur.* 2nd ed. C. H. Beck Wissen. Munich: C. H. Beck.

Cancik-Kirschbaum, E. 2011. Assyrien und die Universalgeschichtsschreibung des 19. Jahrhunderts n. Chr. Pp. 347–69 in Renger 2011a.

Cassin, E. 1968. *La splendeur divine: Introduction à l'étude de la mentalité mésopotamienne.* Civilisations et sociétés 8. Paris: Mouton & Co.

Cavigneaux, A. and B. K. Ismail. 1990. Die Statthalter von Suḫu und Mari im 8. Jh. v. Chr. anhand neuer Texte aus den irakischen Grabungen im Stadtgebiet des Qadisija-Damms. *Baghdader Mitteilungen* 21: 321–456.

Chamaza, G. W. V. 2002. *Die Omnipotenz Aššurs. Entwicklungen in der Aššur-Theologie unter den Sargoniden Sargon II., Sanherib und Asarhaddon.* Alter Orient und Altes Testament 295. Münster: Ugarit-Verlag.

Chapman, C. R. 2004. *The Gendered Language of Warfare in the Israelite-Assyrian Encounter.* Harvard Semitic Monographs 62. Winona Lake: Eisenbrauns.

Charpin, D. 2011. Les rois créateurs de capitales. *Dossiers d'Archéologie* 348: 8–13.

Charpin, D. 2013. 'I am the Sun of Babylon': Solar Aspects of Royal Power in Old Babylonian Mesopotamia. Pp. 65–96 in Hill et al. 2013a.

Charvát, P. and P. Maříková Vlčková (eds.). 2010. *Who was King? Who was Not King? The Rulers and the Ruled in the Ancient Near East.* Prague: Institute of Archaeology of the Academy of Sciences of the Czech Republic.

Cifarelli, M. 1995. *Enmity, Alienation, and Assyrianization: the Role of Cultural Difference in the Visual and Verbal Expression of Assyrian Ideology in the Reign of Aššurnasirpal II (883–859 B.C.).* Ph.D.-thesis, Columbia University.

Cifola, B. 1995. *Analysis of Variants in the Assyrian Royal Titulary from the Origins to Tiglath-Pileser III.* Istituto universitario orientale 47. Naples: Istituto universitario orientale.

Cifola, B. 2004. The Titles of Tukulti-Ninurta I after the Babylonian Campaign: A Re-Evaluation. Pp. 7–15 in Frame 2004.

Cixous, H. 1976. The Laugh of the Medusa. *Signs* 1/4: 875–93.

Cogan, M. 1974. *Imperialism and Religion: Assyria, Judah and Israel in the Eighth and Seventh Centuries B.C.E.* Society of Biblical Literature Dissertation Series 19. Missoula: Society of Biblical Literature.

Cogan, M. and I. Eph'al (eds.). 1991. *Ah, Assyria ... Studies in Assyrian History and Ancient Near Eastern Historiography, Presented to Hayim Tadmor.* Scripta Hierosolymitana 33. Jerusalem: Hebrew University Press.

Cohen, A. and S. E. Kangas (eds.). 2010. *Assyrian Reliefs from the Palace of Ashurnasirpal II: A Cultural Biography.* Hanover and London: University Press of New England.

Cohen, M. E. 2011. *An English to Akkadian Companion to the Assyrian Dictionaries, with an introduction by Erle V. Leichty.* Philadelphia: CDL Press.

Collins, P. 2008. *Assyrian Palace Sculptures.* London: British Museum Press.

Collins, P. 2010. Attending the King in the Assyrian Reliefs. Pp. 181–97 in Cohen and Kangas 2010.

Collon, D. 1987. *First Impressions: Cylinder Seals in the Ancient Near East.* London: British Museum Press.

Collon, D. 1995. *Ancient Near Eastern Art.* London: British Museum Press.

Collon, D. 1999. Depictions of Priests and Priestesses in the Ancient Near East. Pp. 17–46 in K. Watanabe 1999.

Collon, D. 2001. *Catalogue of the Western Asiatic Seals in the British Museum. Cylinder Seals V. Neo-Assyrian and Neo-Babylonian Periods.* London: British Museum Press.

Cook, A. G. and M. Glowacki. 2003. Pots, Politics, and Power: Huari Ceramic Assemblages and Imperial Administration. Pp. 173–202 in *The Archaeology and Politics of Food and Feasting in Early States and Empires*, ed. T. L. Bray. New York: Kluwer Academic.

Cooper, J. 1983. *The Curse of Agade*. Johns Hopkins Near Eastern Studies. Baltimore: Johns Hopkins University Press.

Cooper, J. 2000. Assyrian Prophecies, the Assyrian Tree, and the Mesopotamian Origin of Jewish Monotheism, Greek Philosophy, Christian Theology, Gnosticism, and Much More. *Journal of the American Oriental Society* 120/3: 430–44.

Cooper, J. 2008. Divine Kingship in Ancient Mesopotamia: A Fleeting Phenomenon. Pp. 261–65 in Brisch 2008.

Curtis, J. E. 2008. The Evidence for Bronze Gate Overlay in Mesopotamia. Pp. 75–83 in Curtis and Tallis 2008.

Curtis, J. E. and N. Tallis (eds.). 2008. *The Balawat Gates of Ashurnasirpal II*. London: British Museum Press.

Curtis, J. E., H. McCall, D. Collon, and L. al-Gailani Werr (eds.). 2008. *New Light on Nimrud: Proceedings of the Nimrud Conference 11th–13th March 2002*. London: British Institute for the Study of Iraq and British Museum Press.

Czichon, R. M. 1992. *Die Gestaltungsprinzipien der neuassyrischen Flachbildskunst und ihre Entwicklung vom 9. zum 7. Jahrhundert v. Chr.* Münchner vorderasiatische Studien 13. Munich and Vienna: Profil Verlag.

Dalley, S. (ed.). 1998a. *The Legacy of Mesopotamia*. Legacy Series. Oxford: Oxford University Press.

Dalley, S. 1998b. The Influence of Mesopotamia Upon Israel and the Bible. Pp. 57–80 in Dalley 1998a.

Dalley, S. 2008. The Identity of the Princesses in Tomb II and a New Analysis of Events in 701 B.C. Pp. 171–75 in Curtis et al. 2008.

Dalley, S. and J. N. Postgate. 1984. *The Tablets from Fort Shalmaneser*. Cuneiform Texts from Nimrud 3. London: British School of Archaeology in Iraq.

Damerji, M. S. B. 1999. *Gräber assyrischer Königinnen aus Nimrud*. Mainz am Rhein: Verlag des Römisch-Germanischen Zentralmuseums Mainz.

Davies, L. G., C. B. F. Walker, J. E. Curtis, and N. Tallis. 2008. Description of the Mamu Temple Gates. Pp. 54–69 in Curtis and Tallis 2008.

De Filippi, W. 1977. The Royal Inscriptions of Assur-naṣir-apli II. *Assur* 1/7: 123–69.

Deller, Kh. 1957. Zur sprachlichen Einordnung der Inschriften Aššurnaṣirpals II. 883–859. *Orientalia Nova Series* 26: 144–56.

Deller, Kh. 1987. Assyrische Königsinschriften auf 'Perlen'. *Nouvelles assyriologiques brèves et utilitaires* 1987/1: 56–57.

Deller, Kh. 1992. Neuassyrische Rituale für den Einsatz der Götter-Streitwagen. *Baghdader Mitteilungen* 23: 341–46.

Deller, Kh. 1993. Die Bestallungsurkunde des Nergal-apil-kumuja von Kalhu. *Baghdader Mitteilungen* 24: 219–42.

Démare-Lafont, S. 2011. Aspekte der Stellung der assyrischen Frauen. Pp. 239–49 in Renger 2011a.

De Odorico, M. 1995. *The Use of Numbers and Quantifications in the Assyrian Royal Inscriptions*. State Archives of Assyria Studies 3. Helsinki: Neo-Assyrian Text Corpus Project.

Dercksen, J. G. (ed.). 2004. *Assyria and Beyond: Studies Presented to Mogens Trolle Larsen*. Uitgaven van het Nederlands historisch-archaeologisch instituut te Istanbul 100. Leiden: Nederlands instituut voor het Nabije Oosten.

Dietler, M. 2001. Theorizing the Feast: Rituals of Consumption, Commensal Politics, and Power in African Contexts. Pp. 65–114 in Dietler and Hayden 2001.

Dietler, M. and B. Hayden (eds.). 2001. *Feasts: Archaeological and Ethnographic Perspectives on Food, Politics, and Power*. Smithsonian Series in Archaeological Inquiry. Washington D.C. and London: Smithsonian Institute Press.

Dietrich, M. and O. Loretz (eds.). 1995. *Vom Alten Orient zum Alten Testament. Festschrift Wolfram von Soden*. Alter Orient und Altes Testament 240. Neukirchen-Vluyn and Kevelaer: Neukirchener Verlag and Butzon & Bercker.

Dolce, R. 1997. The City of Kar-Tukulti-Ninurta: Cosmic Characteristics and Topographical Aspects. Pp. 251–58 in Hauptmann and Waetzoldt 1997.

van Driel, G. 1969. *The Cult of Aššur*. Studia Semitica Neerlandica 13. Assen: van Gorcum.

Driver, G. and J. Miles. 1935. *The Assyrian Laws*. Ancient Codes and Laws of the Near East 2. Oxford: Clarendon Press.

Dubovský, P. 2012. King's Direct Control: Neo-Assyrian *Qēpu* Officials. Pp. 449–60 in Wilhelm 2012.

Ebeling, E. 1919. *Keilschrifttexte aus Assur religiösen Inhalts I*. Wissenschaftliche Veröffentlichungen der Deutschen Orient-Gesellschaft 28. Berlin: Deutsche Orient-Gesellschaft.

Ebeling, E. 1923. *Keilschrifttexte aus Assur religiösen Inhalts II*. Wissenschaftliche Veröffentlichungen der Deutschen Orient-Gesellschaft 34. Berlin: Deutsche Orient-Gesellschaft.

Ebeling, E. 1953. *Literarische Keilschrifttexte aus Assur*. Berlin: Akademie Verlag.

Edzard, D. O. 1998. *Gudea and His Dynasty*. Royal Inscriptions of Mesopotamia, Early Periods 3/1. Toronto: University of Toronto Press.

Ehrenberg, E. 2008. Dieu et mon droit: Kingship in Late Babylonian and Early Persian Times. Pp. 103–31 in Brisch 2008.

Eickhoff, T. 1976–80. Kār-Tukulti-Ninurta. B. Archäologisch. *Reallexikon der Assyriologie und vorderasiatischen Archäologie* 5: 456–59.

Ekholm, K. and J. Friedman. 1979. 'Capital' Imperialism and Exploitation in Ancient World Systems. Pp. 41–58 in Larsen 1979a.

Elat, M. 1975. The Campaigns of Shalmaneser III Against Aram and Israel. *Israel Exploration Journal* 25: 25–35.

Elat, M. 1982. The Impact of Tribute and Booty on Countries and People within the Assyrian Empire. Pp. 244–51 in Hirsch and Hunger 1982.

Ellis, R. S. 1968. *Foundation Deposits in Ancient Mesopotamia*. Yale Near Eastern Researches 2. New York and London: Yale University Press.

Ellul, J. 1965. *Propaganda: The Formation of Men's Attitudes*, translated by K. Kellen and J. Lerner, and introduced by K. Kellen. New York: Vintage Books.

Engnell, I. 1943. *Studies in Divine Kingship in the Ancient Near East*. Uppsala: Almqvist & Wiksell.

Eph'al, I. and N. Na'aman (eds.). 2009. *Royal Assyrian Inscriptions: History, Historiography, and Ideology*. Jerusalem: Israel Academy of Sciences.

Eriksen, T. H. 1993. *Ethnicity and Nationalism: Anthropological Perspectives*. Anthropology, Culture, and Society. London: Pluto Press.

Fadhil, A. 1990. Die Grabinschrift der Mullissu-mukannišat-Ninua aus Nimrud/Kalḫu und andere in ihrem Grab gefundene Schriftträgern. *Baghdader Mitteilungen* 20: 471–82.

Faist, B. 2010. Kingship and Institutional Development in the Middle Assyrian Period. Pp. 15–24 in Lanfranchi and Rollinger 2010.

Fales, F. M. 1979. Kilamuwa and the Foreign Kings: Propaganda vs. Power. *Welt des Orients* 10: 6–22.

Fales, F. M. (ed.). 1981a. *Assyrian Royal Inscriptions: New Horizons in Literary, Ideological, and Historical Analysis*. Oriens Antiqui Collectio 17. Rome: Istituto per l'Oriente.

Fales, F. M. 1981b. A Literary Code in Assyrian Royal Inscriptions: The Case of Ashurbanipal's Egyptian Campaigns. Pp. 169–202 in Fales 1981a.

Fales, F. M. 1982. The Enemy in Assyrian Royal Inscriptions: 'The Moral Judgment'. Pp. 425–35 in Nissen and Renger 1982.

Fales, F. M. 1991. Narrative and Ideological Variations in the Account of Sargon's Eighth Campaign. Pp. 129–47 in Cogan and Eph'al 1991.

Fales, F. M. 1999–2001. Assyrian Royal Inscriptions: Newer Horizons. *State Archives of Assyria Bulletin* 13: 115–44.

Fales, F. M. 2007. Multilingualism on Multiple Media in the Neo-Assyrian Period: A Review of the Evidence. *State Archives of Assyria Bulletin* 16: 95–122.

Fales, F. M. 2008. On Pax Assyriaca in the Eighth-Seventh Centuries BCE and Its Implications. Pp. 17–35 in *Isaiah's Vision of Peace in Biblical and Modern International Relations*, eds. R. Cohen and R. Westbrook. Culture & Religion in International Relations. New York and London: Palgrave & Macmillan.

Fales, F. M. 2009. 'To Speak Kindly to Him/Them' as Item of Assyrian Political Discourse. Pp. 27–40 in Luukko et al. 2009.

Fales, F. M. 2010. *Guerre et paix en Assyrie: Religion et impérialisme*. Les conférences de l'école pratique des hautes études 2. Paris: Cerf.

Fales, F. M. 2011. Die Ausbreitung Assyriens gegen Westen und seine fortschreitende Verwurzelung. Der Fall der Nordwestlichen Jezira. Pp. 211–37 in Renger 2011a.

Fales, F. M. and J. N. Postgate. 1992. *Imperial Administrative Records, Part 1: Palace and Temple Administration*. State Archives of Assyria 7. Helsinki: Helsinki University Press.

Fales, F. M., G. B. Lanfranchi, S. de Martino, and L. Milano (eds.). 2000. *Landscapes, Territories, Frontiers, and Horizons in the Ancient Near East*. History of the Ancient Near East Monographs 3/2 (= Comptes rendu de la rencontre assyriologique internationale 44). Padua: Sargon srl.

Finkel, I. L. 2008a. The Inscribed Edging Strips of the Mamu Temple Gates. Pp. 70–71 in Curtis and Tallis 2008.

Finkel, I. L. 2008b. Ashurnasirpal's Stone Inscriptions from Balawat. Pp. 94–96 in Curtis and Tallis 2008.

Finkelstein, J. J. 1953. Cuneiform Texts from Tell Billa. *Journal of Cuneiform Studies* 7: 111–76.

Foster, B. R. 2007. Water under the Straw: Peace in Mesopotamia. Pp. 66–80 in *War and Peace in the Ancient World*, ed. K. A. Raaflaub. The Ancient World – Comparative Histories. Oxford: Blackwell.

Foucault, M. 1982 [1969]. *The Archaeology of Knowledge and the Discourse on Language*, translated by A. M. Sheridan Smith. Pantheon Paperback Edition. New York: Pantheon Books.

Frahm, E. 2006. Images of Assyria in Nineteenth- and Twentieth-Century Western Scholarship. Pp. 74–94 in Holloway 2006a.

Frahm, E. 2009. *Historische und historisch-literarische Texte*. Keilschrifttexte aus Assur literarischen Inhalts 3 (= Wissenschaftliche Veröffentlichungen der Deutschen Orient-Gesellschaft 121). Wiesbaden: Harrassowitz.

Frahm, E. 2010. Hochverrat in Assur. Pp. 89–137 in *Assur-Forschungen*, eds. S. M. Maul and N. P. Heeßel. Academy Publication. Wiesbaden: Harrassowitz.

Frahm, E. 2011a. Die Inschriftenreste auf den Obeliskenfragmenten aus Assur. Pp. 59–75 in Orlamünde 2011a.

Frahm, E. 2011b. Mensch, Land und Volk: Aššur im Alten Testament. Pp. 267–85 in Renger 2011a.

Frahm, E. 2013. Rising Suns and Falling Stars: Assyrian Kings and the Cosmos. Pp. 97–120 in Hill et al. 2013a.

Frame, G. 1997. The God Aššur in Babylonia. Pp. 55–64 in Parpola and Whiting 1997.

Frame, G. (ed.). 2004. *From the Upper Sea to the Lower Sea: Studies on the History of Assyria and Babylonia in Honour of A. K. Grayson*. Uitgaven van het Nederlands historisch-archaeologisch instituut te Istanbul 101. Leuven: Nederlands instituut voor het Nabije Oosten.

Franke, S. 1995. *Königsinschriften und Königsideologie. Die Könige von Akkade zwischen Tradition und Neuerung*. Altorientalistik 1. Münster and Hamburg: Lit.

Frankfort, H. 1948. *Kingship and the Gods: A Study of Ancient Near Eastern Religion as the Integration of Society and Nature*. An Oriental Institute Essay. Chicago: University of Chicago Press.

Frayne, D. 1993. *Sargonic and Gutian Periods (2234–2113)*. Royal Inscriptions of Mesopotamia Early Periods 2. Toronto: Toronto University Press.

Frazer, J. G. 1894. *The Golden Bough: A Study in Comparative Religion I–II*. London: Macmillan.

Fuchs, A. 1994. *Die Inschriften Sargons II. aus Khorsabad*. Göttingen: Cuvillier.

Fuchs, A. 1998. *Die Annalen des Jahres 711 v. Chr.* State Archives of Assyria Studies 8. Helsinki: Neo-Assyrian Text Corpus Project.

Fuchs, A. 2005. War das Neuassyrische Reich ein Militärstaat? Pp. 35–60 in *Krieg – Gesellschaft – Institutionen*, ed. B. Meißner et al. Berlin: Akademie Verlag.

Fuchs, A. 2008. Der Turtān Šamšī-ilu und die große Zeit der assyrischen Großen. *Welt des Orients* 38: 61–145.

Fuchs, A. 2009. Waren die Assyrer grausam? Pp. 65–119 in *Extreme Formen von Gewalt in Bild und Text des Altertums*, ed. M. Zimmermann. Münchner Studien zur alten Welt 5. Munich: Herbert Utz.

Fuchs, A. 2011. Das Osttigrisgebiet von Agum II. bis zu Darius I. (ca. 1500 bis 500 v. Chr.). Pp. 229–320 in Miglus and Muehl 2011.

Fuchs, A. 2012. Wissenstransfer und -anwendung im Bereich des Heerwesens und der Militärtechnik des neuassyrischen Reiches. Pp. 31–60 in *Wissenskultur im Alten Orient*, ed. H. Neumann. Colloquien der Deutschen Orient-Gesellschaft 4. Wiesbaden: Harrassowitz.

Gadd, C. J. 1936. *The Stones of Assyria: The Surviving Remains of Assyrian Sculpture, Their Recovery and Their Original Positions*. London: Chatoo.

Gadd, C. J. 1948. *Ideas of Divine Rule in the Ancient East*. The Schweich Lectures of the British Academy, 1945. London: Oxford University Press.

Galter, H. D. 1997. Assyrische Königsinschriften des 2. Jts. v. Chr. Die Entwicklung einer Textgattung. Pp. 53–59 in Hauptmann and Waetzoldt 1997.

Galter, H. D. 1998. Book review of B. Oded, *War, Peace, and Empire: Justifications for War in Assyrian Royal Inscriptions*. *Journal of the American Oriental Society* 118/1: 89–91.

Galter, H. D. 2007. Der Skorpion und die Königin. Zur Tiersymbolik bei den Assyrern. *Journal for Semitics* 16/3: 646–71.

Garelli, P. 1971. Nouveau coup d'oeil sur Muṣur. Pp. 37–48 in *Hommages à André Dupont-Sommer*, eds. A. Caquout and M. Philonenko. Paris: Libraire d'Amerique et d'Orient Adrien.

Garelli, P. 1972. Problèmes de stratification sociale dans l'empire Assyrien. Pp. 73–79 in *Gesellschaftsklassen im Alten Zweistromland und in den angrenzenden Gebieten*, ed. D. O. Edzard. Abhandlungen philosophisch-historische Klasse 75 (= Comptes rendu de la rencontre assyriologique internationale 18). Munich: Verlag der bayerischen Akademie der Wissenschaften.

Garelli, P. 1973. Les sujets du roi d'Assyrie. Pp. 189–213 in *La voix de l'opposition en Mesopotamie*, ed. A. Finet. Brussels: Institut des hautes études de Belgique.

Garelli, P. 1974a. Remarques sur l'administration de l'empire Assyrien. *Revue d'assyriologie et d'archéologie orientale* 68: 129–40.

Garelli, P. (ed.). 1974b. *Le palais et la royauté: Proceedings of the 19th Rencontre Assyriologique Internationale*. Comptes rendu de la rencontre assyriologique internationale 19. Paris: Geuthner.

Garelli, P. 1979. L'Etat et la légitimité royale sous l'empire Assyrien. Pp. 319–28 in Larsen 1979a.

Garelli, P. 1981. La conception de la royauté en Assyrie. Pp. 1–11 in Fales 1981a.

Garelli, P. 1982. La propagande royale Assyrienne. *Akkadica* 27: 16–29.

Garelli, P. 2000. Territoires et frontières dans le inscriptions royales médio-assyrienne. Pp. 45–48 in Fales et al. 2000.

Gaspa, S. 2007. *Qarrādūtu*: il motivo dell'eroismo del re assiro nella titulatura regia sargonide tra rievocazioni letterarie, concezioni religiose ed aspirazioni. Pp. 233–68 in *Eroi, eroismi, eroizzazioni*, ed. A. Coppola. Padua: Sargon srl.

Gaspa, S. and M. Luukko. 2008. A Bibliography of Neo-Assyrian Studies: 1998–2006. *State Archives of Assyria Bulletin* 17: 189–257.

Geertz, C. 1973. *The Interpretation of Cultures: Selected Essays by Clifford Geertz*. Basic Books Classics. New York: Basic Books.

Gelb, I. J. et al. (eds.). 1956–2011. *The Assyrian Dictionary of the Oriental Institute of the University of Chicago*. Chicago: Oriental Institute.

Gelio, R. 1981. La délégation envoyée par Gygès, roi de Lydie: Un cas de propagande idéologique. Pp. 203–24 in Fales 1981a.

George, A. 2011. *Cuneiform Royal Inscriptions and Related Texts in the Schøyen Collection*, with contributions by M. Civil et al. Cornell University Studies in Assyriology and Sumerology 17. Bethesda: CDL Press.

Gerardi, P. 1988. Epigraphs and Assyrian Palace Reliefs. *Journal of Cuneiform Studies* 40/1: 1–35.

Giovino, M. 2007. *The Assyrian Sacred Tree: A History of Interpretations*. Orbis Biblicus et Orientalis 230. Fribourg and Göttingen: Academic Press and Vandenhoeck & Ruprecht.

Glassner, J.-J. 1987–90. Mahlzeit. *Reallexikon der Assyriologie und vorderasiatischen Archäologie* 7: 259–67.

Goetze, A. 1957. *Kulturgeschichte Kleinasiens*. Handbuch der Altertumwissenschaft 2. Munich: C. H. Beck.

Gramsci, A. 1971 [1926–37]. *Selections from the Prison Notebooks of Antonio Gramsci*, edited and translated by Q. Hoare and G. Nowell Smith. London: International Publishers Co.

Grayson, A. K. 1975. *Assyrian and Babylonian Chronicles*. Texts from Cuneiform Sources 5. Locust Valley: J. J. Augustin Publisher.

Grayson, A. K. 1976. Studies in Neo-Assyrian History: The Ninth Century B.C. *Bibliotheca Orientalis* 33: 134–45.

Grayson, A. K. 1980–83. Königslisten und Chroniken. B. Akkadisch. *Reallexikon der Assyriologie und vorderasiatischen Archäologie* 6: 89–101.

Grayson, A. K. 1981. Assyrian Royal Inscriptions: Literary Characteristics. Pp. 35–47 in Fales 1981a.

Grayson, A. K. 1982. Assyria: Ashur-Dan II to Ashur-Nirari V (934–745 B.C.). Pp. 238–81 in *Cambridge Ancient History II* 3/1, ed. J. Boardman et al. Cambridge: Cambridge University Press.

Grayson, A. K. 1987. *Assyrian Rulers of the Third and Second Millennia BC (to 1115 BC)*. Royal Inscriptions of Mesopotamia, Assyrian Periods 1. Toronto, Buffalo, and London: University of Toronto Press.

Grayson, A. K. 1991. *Assyrian Rulers of the Early First Millennium BC I (1114–859 BC)*. Royal Inscriptions of Mesopotamia, Assyrian Periods 2. Toronto, Buffalo, and London: University of Toronto Press.

Grayson, A. K. 1993. Assyrian Officials and Power in the Ninth and Eighth Centuries. *State Archives of Assyria Bulletin* 7/1: 19–52.

Grayson, A. K. 1995a. Assyrian Rule of Conquered Territory in Ancient Western Asia. Pp. 959–68 in Sasson 1995.

Grayson, A. K. 1995b. Eunuchs in Power: Their Role in the Assyrian Bureaucracy. Pp. 85–98 in Dietrich and Loretz 1995.

Grayson, A. K. 1996. *Assyrian Rulers of the Early First Millennium BC II (858–745 BC)*. Royal Inscriptions of Mesopotamia, Assyrian Periods 3. Toronto, Buffalo, and London: University of Toronto Press.

Grayson, A. K. 2007. Shalmaneser III and the Levantine States: The Damascus Coalition Rebellion. Pp. 51–58 in *Perspectives on Hebrew Scriptures* 2/5, ed. E. Ben Zvi. New Jersey: Gorgias Press.

Grayson, A. K. and J. Novotny. 2012. *The Royal Inscriptions of Sennacherib, King of Assyria (704–681 BC), Part 1*. Royal Inscriptions of the Neo-Assyrian Period 3/1. Winona Lake: Eisenbrauns.

Grayson, A. K. and J. Novotny. 2014. *The Royal Inscriptions of Sennacherib, King of Assyria (704–681 BC), Part 2*. Royal Inscriptions of the Neo-Assyrian Period 3/2. Winona Lake: Eisenbrauns.

Grimal, N. 1994. *A History of Ancient Egypt*, translated by I. Shaw. Oxford and Cambridge: Blackwell.

Groenewegen-Frankfort, H. A. 1951. *Arrest and Movement: An Essay on Space and Time in the Representational Art of the Ancient Near East*. London: Faber and Faber.

Guinan, A. K. 1997. Auguries of Hegemony: The Sex Omens of Mesopotamia. *Gender and History* 9/3: 462–79.

Günbattı, C. 1997. Kültepe'den Akadlı Sargon'a Ait Bir Tablet. *Archivum Anatolicum* 3: 131–55.

Güterbock, H. G. 1957. Narration in Anatolian, Syrian, and Assyrian Art. *American Journal of Archaeology* 61: 62–71.

Güterbock, H. G. 1983. Hittite Historiography: A Survey. Pp. 21–35 in Tadmor and Weinfeld 1983.

Haas, V. 1980. Die Dämonisierung des Fremden und des Feindes im Alten Orient. *Rocznik Orientalistyczny* 41/2: 37–44.

Hallo, W. W. 1957. *Early Mesopotamian Royal Titles: A Philologic and Historical Analysis*. American Oriental Series 43. New Haven: American Oriental Society.

Hallo, W. W. 1964. From Qarqar to Carchemish: Assyria and Israel in the Light of New Discoveries. Pp. 152–88 in *The Biblical Archaeologist Reader II*, eds. D. N. Freedman and E. F. Campbell. New York: Anchor.

Hämeen-Anttila, J. 2000. *A Sketch of Neo-Assyrian Grammar*. State Archives of Assyria Studies 13. Helsinki: Neo-Assyrian Text Corpus Project.

Harmanşah, Ö. 2007. Source of the Tigris: Event, Place and Performance in the Assyrian Landscapes of the Early Iron Age. *Archaeological Dialogues* 14/2: 179–204.

Harper, P. O. and H. Pittman (eds.). 1983. *Essays on Near Eastern Art and Archaeology in Honor of Charles Kyrle Wilkinson*. New York: Metropolitan Museum of Art.

Harrak, A. 1987. *Assyria and Hanigalbat*. Texte und Studien zur Orientalistik 4. Hildesheim, Zurich, and New York: Georg Olms Verlag.

Hauptmann, H. and H. Waetzoldt (eds.). 1997. *Assyrien im Wandel der Zeiten*. Comptes rendu de la rencontre assyriologique internationale 39. Heidelberg: Heidelberger Orientverlag.

Hausleiter, A. 2010. *Neuassyrische Keramik im Kerngebiet Assyriens. Chronologie und Formen*. Abhandlungen der Deutschen Orient-Gesellschaft 27. Wiesbaden: Harrassowitz.

Hayden, B. 2001. Fabulous Feast: A Prolegomenon to the Importance of Feasting. Pp. 23–64 in Dietler and Hayden 2001.

Herbordt, S. 1996. Ein Königssiegel Assurnasirpals II. (?) aus Assur. *Baghdader Mitteilungen* 27: 411–17.

Herbordt, S. 1998–2001. Neuassyrische Kunstperiode IV. Glyptik. *Reallexikon der Assyriologie und vorderasiatischen Archäologie* 9: 279–83.

Herrmann, G. 1992. *The Small Collections from Fort Shalmaneser*. Ivories from Nimrud 5. London: British School of Archaeology in Iraq.

Herrmann, G., S. Laidlaw, and H. Coffey. 2009. *Ivories from the North West Palace (1845–1992)*. Ivories from Nimrud 6. London: British Institute for the Study of Iraq.

Hertel, T. 2004. The Balawat Gate Narratives of Shalmaneser III. Pp. 299–315 in Dercksen 2004.

Hill, J. A., P. Jones, and A. J. Morales (eds.). 2013a. *Experiencing Power, Generating Authority: Cosmos, Politics, and the Ideology of Kingship in Ancient Egypt and Mesopotamia*. Philadelphia: University of Pennsylvania Museum.

Hill, J. A., P. Jones, and A. J. Morales. 2013b. Comparing Kingship in Ancient Egypt and Mesopotamia: Cosmos, Politics, and Landscape. Pp. 3–29 in Hill et al. 2013a.

Hirsch, H. and H. Hunger (eds.). 1982. *Vorträge gehalten auf der 28. Rencontre Assyriologique Internationale in Wien 6.–10. Juli 1981*. Archiv für Orientforschung Beiheft 19 (= Comptes rendu de la rencontre assyriologique internationale 28). Vienna: Horn Verlag Ferdinand Berger.

Hoffner, H. A. Jr. 1966. Symbols for Masculinity and Femininity: Their Use in Ancient Near Eastern Sympathetic Magic Rituals. *Journal of Biblical Literature* 85: 329–32.

Holloway, S. W. 2001. *Aššur is king! Aššur is King!: Religion in the Exercise of Power in the Neo-Assyrian Empire*. Culture and History of the Ancient Near East 10. Leiden: Brill.

Holloway, S. W. (ed.). 2006a. *Orientalism, Assyriology, and the Bible*. Hebrew Bible Monographs 10. Sheffield: Sheffield Phoenix Press.

Holloway, S. W. 2006b. Introduction: Orientalism, Assyriology, and the Bible. Pp. i–xviii in Holloway 2006a.

Hornung, E. 1992. *Idea into Image: Essays on Ancient Egyptian Thought*, translated by E. Bredeck. New York: Timken.

Horowitz, W. 1998. *Mesopotamian Cosmic Geography*. Mesopotamian Civilizations 8. Winona Lake: Eisenbrauns.

Hrouda, B. 1965. *Die Kulturgeschichte des assyrischen Flachbildes*. Saarbrücker Beiträge zur Altertumskunde 2. Bonn: Rudolf Habelt Verlag.

Hunger, H. 1992. *Astrological Reports to Assyrian Kings*. State Archives of Assyria 8. Helsinki: Helsinki University Press.

Huntington, S. P. 1996. *The Clash of Civilizations and The Remaking of World Order*. A Touchstone Book. New York: Simon & Schuster.

Jacobsen, T. 1939. *The Sumerian King List*. Assyriological Studies 11. Chicago: University of Chicago Press.

Jacobsen, T. 1976. *The Treasures of Darkness: A History of Mesopotamian Religion*. Yale Paperbounds 326. New Haven and London: Yale University Press.

Johansen, F. 1978. *Statues of Gudea Ancient and Modern*. Mesopotamia 6. Copenhagen: Akademisk Forlag.

Jones, L. (ed.). 2005. *Encyclopedia of Religion I–XV*. 2nd ed. Detroit: Thomson Gale.

Jursa, M. 2007. Rasappa. *Reallexikon der Assyriologie und vorderasiatischen Archäologie* 11: 254.

Kantorowicz, E. H. 1957. *The King's Two Bodies: A Study in Medieval Political Theology*. Princeton: Princeton University Press.

Karlsson, M. 2013. *Early Neo-Assyrian State Ideology: Relations of Power in the Inscriptions and Iconography of Ashurnasirpal II (883–859) and Shalmaneser III (858–824)*. Ph.D.-thesis, Uppsala University.

Karmel Thomason, A. 2010. Banquets, Baubles, and Bronzes: Material Comforts in the Neo-Assyrian Palaces. Pp. 198–214 in Cohen and Kangas 2010.

Kataja, L. and R. Whiting. 1995. *Grants, Decrees, and Gifts of the Neo-Assyrian Period*. State Archives of Assyria 12. Helsinki: Helsinki University Press.

Keel, O. and C. Uehlinger. 1994. Der Assyrerkönig Salmanassar III. und Jehu von Israel auf dem Schwarzen Obelisken aus Nimrud. *Zeitschrift für katholische Theologie* 116: 391–420.

Kienast, B. 1997. Altakkadische und assyrische Königsinschriften. Pp. 67–69 in Hauptmann and Waetzoldt 1997.

King, L. W. 1915. *Bronze Reliefs from the Gates of Shalmaneser, King of Assyria B.C. 860–825*. London: Trustees of the British Museum.

Kinnier-Wilson, J. V. 1962. The Kurba'il Statue of Shalmaneser III. *Iraq* 24: 90–115.

Kinnier-Wilson, J. V. 1972. *The Nimrud Wine Lists: A Study of Men and Administration in the Eighth Century B.C.* Cuneiform Texts from Nimrud 1. London: British School of Archaeology in Iraq.

Kühne, H. 1987–88. Report on the Excavation at Tall Šah Hamad/Dūr-Katlimmu 1988. *Annales archéologiques arabes syriennes* 37/38: 142–57.

Kuhrt, A. 1997. *The Ancient Near East c. 3000–330 BC I–II*. Routledge History of the Ancient World. London and New York: Routledge.

Kwasman, T. and S. Parpola. 1991. *Legal Transactions of the Royal Court of Nineveh, Part 1: Tiglath-pileser III through Esarhaddon*. State Archives of Assyria 6. Helsinki: Helsinki University Press.

Labat, R. 1939. *Le caractère religieux de la royauté assyro-babylonienne*. Paris: Librairie d'Amerique et d'Orient Adrien.

Lackenbacher, S. 1982. *Le roi bâtisseur: Les récits de construction assyriens des origines à Teglathphalasar III*. Études assyriologiques 11. Paris: Centre national de la recherche scientifique.

Lambert, W. G. 1961. The Sultantepe Tablets. VIII. Shalmaneser in Ararat. *Anatolian Studies* 11: 143–58.

Lambert, W. G. 1974a. The Reigns of Aššurnaṣirpal II and Shalmaneser III: An Interpretation. *Iraq* 36: 103–109.

Lambert, W. G. 1974b. The Seed of Kingship. Pp. 427–44 in Garelli 1974b.

Lambert, W. G. 1983. The God Aššur. *Iraq* 45: 82–86.
Lambert, W. G. 1998. Kingship in Ancient Mesopotamia. Pp. 54–70 in *King and Messiah in Israel and the Ancient Near East*, ed. J. Day. Jsot Suppl. Series 270. Sheffield: Sheffield Academic Press.
Lambert, W. G. 2002. The Background of the Neo-Assyrian Sacred Tree. Pp. 321–26 in Parpola and Whiting 2002.
Lamprichs, R. 1995. *Die Westexpansion des neuassyrischen Reiches. Eine Strukturanalyse.* Alter Orient und Altes Testament 239. Neukirchen-Vluyn and Kevelaer: Neukirchener Verlag and Butzon & Bercker.
Lanfranchi, G. B. 2003. Ideological Implications of the Problem of Royal Responsibility in the Neo-Assyrian Period. *Eretz-Israel* 27: 100–10.
Lanfranchi, G. B. and R. Rollinger (eds.). 2010. *Concepts of Kingship in Antiquity: Proceedings of the European Science Foundation Exploratory Workshop, Held in Padova, November 28th–December 1st 2007.* History of the Ancient Near East Monographs 11. Padua: Sargon srl.
Langdon, S. 1912. *Neubabylonische Königsinschriften.* Vorderasiatische Bibliothek 4. Leipzig: J. C. Hinrichs.
Larsen, M. T. 1974. The City and Its King: On the Old Assyrian Notion of Kingship. Pp. 285–300 in Garelli 1974b.
Larsen, M. T. 1976. *The Old Assyrian City-State and Its Colonies.* Mesopotamia 4. Copenhagen: Akademisk Forlag.
Larsen, M. T. (ed.). 1979a. *Power and Propaganda: A Symposium on Ancient Empires.* Mesopotamia 7. Copenhagen: Akademisk Forlag.
Larsen, M. T. 1979b. The Tradition of Empire in Mesopotamia. Pp. 75–103 in Larsen 1979a.
Larsen, M. T. 1999. *Gudens skugga: det assyriska imperiets historia*, translated by L. Eberhard Nyman. Stockholm and Stehag: Brutus Östlings Bokförlag Symposion.
Læssøe, J. 1955. *Studies on the Assyrian Ritual and Series bît rimki.* Copenhagen: Munksgaard.
Layard, A. H. 1849. *The Monuments of Nineveh from Drawings Made on the Spot.* London: John Murray.
Layard, A. H. 1853a. *A Second Series of the Monuments of Nineveh.* London: John Murray.
Layard, A. H. 1853b. *Discoveries in the Ruins of Nineveh and Babylon.* New York: G. P. Putnam and Co.
Leichty, E. 2011. *The Royal Inscriptions of Esarhaddon, King of Assyria (680–669 BC).* Royal Inscriptions of the Neo-Assyrian Period 4. Winona Lake: Eisenbrauns.
Lewy, J. 1956. On Some Institutions of the Old Assyrian Empire. *Hebrew Union College Annual* 27: 1–79.
Lichtheim, M. 2006 [1973–80]. *Ancient Egyptian Literature: A Book of Readings I–III.* Berkeley, Los Angeles, and London: University of California Press.
Lieberman, S. J. 1985. Giving Directions on the Black Obelisk of Shalmaneser III. *Revue d'assyriologie et d'archéologie orientale* 79: 88.
Limet, H. 2005. Ethnicity. Pp. 370–83 in Snell 2005.
Lincoln, B. 2008. The Role of Religion in Achaemenian Imperialism. Pp. 221–41 in Brisch 2008.
Liverani, M. 1973. Memorandum on the Approach to Historiographic Texts. *Orientalia Nova Series* 42: 178–94.
Liverani, M. 1979. The Ideology of the Neo-Assyrian Empire. Pp. 297–317 in Larsen 1979a.

Liverani, M. 1981. Critique of Variants and the Titulary of Sennacherib. Pp. 225–57 in Fales 1981a.

Liverani, M. 1982a. *Studies on the Annals of Assurnasirpal II: Morphological Analysis*. Vicino oriente 5. Rome: Università di Roma "La Sapienza".

Liverani, M. 1982b. *Kitru, katāru. Mesopotamia* 17: 43–66.

Liverani, M. 1988. The Growth of the Assyrian Empire in the Habur/Middle Euphrates Area: A New Paradigm. *State Archives of Assyria Bulletin* 2: 81–98.

Liverani, M. 1990. *Prestige and Interest: International Relations in the Near East ca. 1600–1100 BC*. History of the Ancient Near East Monographs 1. Padua: Sargon srl.

Liverani, M. 1992a. Nationality and Political Identity. Pp. 1031–37 in *The Anchor Bible Dictionary IV*, ed. D. N. Freedman. New York: Doubleday.

Liverani, M. 1992b. *Studies on the Annals of Assurnasirpal II: Topographical Analysis*. Quademi di geografica storica 4. Rome: Università di Roma "La Sapienza".

Liverani, M. 1993. Model and Actualization: The Kings of Akkad in the Historical Tradition. Pp. 41–67 in *Akkad, the First World Empire: Structure, Ideology, Traditions*, ed. M. Liverani. Padua: Sargon srl.

Liverani, M. 1995. The Deeds of Ancient Mesopotamian Kings. Pp. 2353–66 in Sasson 1995.

Liverani, M. 2004. Assyria in the Ninth Century: Continuity or Change? Pp. 213–26 in Frame 2004.

Liverani, M. 2005. Imperialism. Pp. 223–43 in Pollock and Bernbeck 2005.

Liverani, M. 2014 [1988]. *The Ancient Near East: History, Society and Economy*, translated by S. Tabatabai. London and New York: Routledge.

Livingstone, A. 1989. *Court Poetry and Literary Miscellanea*. State Archives of Assyria 3. Helsinki: Helsinki University Press.

Loprieno, A. 1988. *Topos und Mimesis. Zum Ausländer in der ägyptischen Literatur*. Ägyptologische Abhandlungen 48. Wiesbaden: Harrassowitz.

Luckenbill, D. D. 1924. *The Annals of Sennacherib*. Oriental Institute Publications 2. Chicago: University of Chicago Press.

Lumsden, S. 2004. Narrative Art and Empire: The Throneroom of Aššurnasirpal II. Pp. 359–85 in Dercksen 2004.

Luukko, M., S. Svärd, and R. Mattila (eds.). 2009. *Of God(s), Trees, Kings, and Scholars: Neo-Assyrian and Related Studies in Honour of Simo Parpola*. Studia Orientalia 106. Helsinki: Finnish Oriental Society.

Macgregor, S. L. 2012. *Beyond Hearth and Home: Women in the Public Sphere in Neo-Assyrian Society*. State Archives of Assyria Studies 21. Helsinki: Neo-Assyrian Text Corpus Project.

Machinist, P. 1983a. *The Epic of Tukulti-Ninurta I: A Study in Middle Assyrian Literature*. Ann Arbor: University Microfilms International.

Machinist, P. 1983b. Assyria and Its Image in First Isaiah. *Journal of the American Oriental Society* 103: 719–37.

Machinist, P. 1986. On Self-Consciousness in Mesopotamia. Pp. 183–202 in *The Origins and Diversity of Axial Age Civilizations*, ed. S. N. Eisenstadt. SUNY Series in Near Eastern Studies. New York: State University of New York Press.

Machinist, P. 1993. Assyrians on Assyria in the First Millennium B.C. Pp. 77–104 in *Anfänge politischen Denkens in der Antike*, ed. K. Raaflaub. Schriften des historischen Kollegs. Kolloquien 24. Munich: Oldenbourg Verlag.

Machinist, P. 2011. Kingship and Divinity in Imperial Assyria. Pp. 405–30 in Renger 2011a.

Madhloom, T. A. 1970. *The Chronology of Neo-Assyrian Art*. London: Athlone Press.

Magen, U. 1986. *Assyrische Königsdarstellungen – Aspekte der Herrschaft, eine Typologie*. Baghdader Forschungen 9. Mainz am Rhein: Philipp von Zabern.
Mahmoud, A. and H. Kühne. 1993–94. Tall Agaga/Šadikanni 1984–90. *Archiv für Orientforschung* 40/41: 215–21.
Mallowan, M. E. L. 1957. *Twenty-Five Years of Mesopotamian Discovery 1932–1956*. 1st ed. London: British School of Archaeology in Iraq.
Mallowan, M. E. L. 1966. *Nimrud and its Remains I–II*. London: Collins.
Mallowan, M. E. L. and L. G. Davies. 1970. *Ivories in Assyrian Style (1949–1963)*. Ivories from Nimrud 2. London: British School of Archaeology in Iraq.
Mann, M. 1994. *Geschichte der Macht, Band 1. Von den Anfängen bis zur griechischen Antike*. Theorie und Gesellschaft. Frankfurt am Main and New York: Campus Verlag.
Marcus, D. 1977. Animal Similes in Assyrian Royal Inscriptions. *Orientalia Nova Series* 46: 86–106.
Marcus, M. 1987. Geography as an Organizing Principle in the Imperial Art of Shalmaneser III. *Iraq* 49: 77–90.
Marcus, M. 1995a. Art and Ideology in Ancient Western Asia. Pp. 2487–2505 in Sasson 1995.
Marcus, M. 1995b. Geography as Visual Ideology: Landscape, Knowledge, and Power in Neo-Assyrian Art. Pp. 193–202 in *Neo-Assyrian Geography*, ed. M. Liverani. Quaderni di geografia storica 5. Rome: Università di Roma "La Sapienza".
Marti, L. 2011. Rois visibles, rois inaccessibles: Le changement dans l'idéologie royale assyrienne. *Dossiers d'Archéologie* 348: 60–61.
Marx, K. (and F. Engels). 1970 [1845–46]. *The German Ideology*, edited and introduced by C. J. Arthur. London: Lawrence & Wishart.
Masetti-Rouault, M. G. 2010. Rural Economy and Steppe Management in an Assyrian Colony. Pp. 129–49 in *Dūr-Katlimmu 2008 and Beyond*, ed. H. Kühne. Studia Chaburensia 1. Wiesbaden: Harrassowitz.
Mattila, R. 2000. *The King's Magnates: A Study of the Highest Officials of the Neo-Assyrian Empire*. State Archives of Assyria Studies 11. Helsinki: Neo-Assyrian Text Corpus Project.
Mattila, R. and K. Radner. 1997. A Bibliography of Neo-Assyrian Studies: 1988–1997. *State Archives of Assyria Bulletin* 11: 115–37.
Maul, S. M. 1995. Das 'dreifache Königtum'. Überlegungen zu einer Sonderform des neuassyrischen Königssiegels. Pp. 395–402 in *Beiträge zur Kulturgeschichte Vorderasiens*, ed. U. Finkbeiner et al. Mainz am Rhein: Philipp von Zabern.
Maul, S. M. 1999. Der assyrische König – Hüter der Weltordnung. Pp. 210–14 in K. Watanabe 1999.
Mayer, W. 1983. Sargons Feldzug gegen Urartu – 714 v. Chr. Text und Übersetzung. *Mitteilungen der Deutschen Orient-Gesellschaft* 115: 65–131.
Mayer, W. 1987. Ein Mythos von der Erschaffung des Menschen und des Königs. *Orientalia Nova Series* 56: 55–68.
McCall, H. 1998. Rediscovery and Aftermath. Pp. 183–213 in Dalley 1998a.
McKay, J. W. 1973. *Religion in Judah under the Assyrians 732–609 BC*. Studies in Biblical Theology 2/26. London: SCM Press.
Melville, S. C. 1999. *The Role of Naqia/Zakutu in Sargonid Politics*. State Archives of Assyria Studies 9. Helsinki: Neo-Assyrian Text Corpus Project.
Melville, S. C. 2004. Neo-Assyrian Royal Women and Male Identity: Status as a Social Tool. *Journal of the American Oriental Society* 124/1: 37–57.
Menzel, B. 1981. *Assyrische Tempel. Untersuchungen zu Kult, Administration und Personal I–II*. Studia Pohl 10. Rome: Biblical Institute Press.

Meuszyński, J. 1972. The Representations of the Four-Winged Genies on the Bas-Reliefs from Assurnasir-apli II Times. *Études et Travaux* 6: 27–70.
Meuszyński, J. 1976. Neo-Assyrian Reliefs from the Central Area of Nimrud Citadel. *Iraq* 38: 37–43.
Meuszyński, J. 1981. *Die Rekonstruktion der Relief-darstellungen und ihrer Anordnung im Nordwestpalast von Kalhu (Nimrud). Räume: B.C.D.E.F.G.H.L.N.P.* Baghdader Forschungen 2. Mainz am Rhein: Philipp von Zabern.
Michalowski, P. 1986. Mental Maps and Ideology: Reflections on Subartu. Pp. 129–56 in *The Origins of Cities in Dry-Farming Syria and Mesopotamia in the Third Millennium B.C.*, ed. H. Weiss. Guilford: Four Quarters Publishing.
Michalowski, P. 2008. The Mortal Kings of Ur: A Short Century of Divine Rule in Ancient Mesopotamia. Pp. 33–45 in Brisch 2008.
Michalowski, P. 2009. Aššur during the Ur III Period. Pp. 149–56 in *Here & There Across the Ancient Near East*, ed. O. Drewnowska-Rymarz. Warszaw: Agade.
Michel, E. 1947–52. Die Assur-Texte Salmanassars III. (858–824). *Welt des Orients* 1: 5–20, 57–71, 205–22, 255–71, 385–96.
van de Mieroop, M. 1999. *Cuneiform Texts and the Writing of History*. Approaching the Ancient World. London: Routledge.
van de Mieroop, M. 2005. *King Hammurabi of Babylon: A Biography*. Blackwell Ancient Lives. Oxford: Blackwell.
Miglus, P. A. and S. Muehl (eds.). 2011. *Between the Cultures: The Central Tigris Region From the 3rd to the 1st Millennium BC*. Heidelberger Studien zum Alten Orient 14. Heidelberg: Heidelberg Orientverlag.
Millard, A. R. 1991. Large Numbers in the Assyrian Royal Inscriptions. Pp. 213–22 in Cogan and Eph'al 1991.
Millard, A. R. 1994. *The Eponyms of the Assyrian Empire 910–612 B.C.* State Archives of Assyria Studies 2. Helsinki: Neo-Assyrian Text Corpus Project.
Morandi, D. 1988. Stele e statue reali assire: Localazione, diffusione e implicazione ideologiche. *Mesopotamia* 23: 105–55.
Müller, K. Fr. 1937. Das assyrische Ritual. Teil 1: Texte zum assyrischen Königsritual. *Mitteilungen der Vorderasiatisch-Ägyptischen Gesellschaft* 41/3: 1–89.
Munn-Rankin, J. M. 1974. Two Reliefs of an Assyrian King with Bowl. *Iraq* 36: 169–71.
Nissen, H. J. and J. Renger (eds.). 1982. *Mesopotamien und seine Nachbarn. Politische und kulturelle Wechselbeziehungen im alten Vorderasien vom 4. bis 1. Jahrtausend v. Chr.* Berliner Beiträge zum Vorderen Orient 1 (= Comptes rendu de la rencontre assyriologique internationale 25). Berlin: Dietrich Reimer Verlag.
Novák, M. 2002. The Artificial Paradise: Programme and Ideology of Royal Gardens. Pp. 443–60 in Parpola and Whiting 2002.
Novák, M. 2004. From Ashur to Nineveh: The Assyrian Town-Planning Programme. *Iraq* 66: 177–85.
Nunn, A. 2006. *Knaufplatten und Knäufe aus Assur*. Wissenschaftliche Veröffentlichungen der Deutschen Orient-Gesellschaft 112. Saarwellingen: Saarländische Druckerei und Verlag.
Oates, D. 1957. Ezida: The Temple of Nabu. *Iraq* 19: 26–39.
Oates, D. 1959. Fort Shalmaneser – An Interim Report. *Iraq* 21: 98–129.
Oates, D. 1962. The Excavations at Nimrud (Kalhu), 1961. *Iraq* 24: 1–25.
Oates, D. 1963. The Excavations at Nimrud (Kalhu), 1962. *Iraq* 25: 6–37.
Oates, D. 1974. Balawat (Imgur-Enlil): The Site and Its Buildings. *Iraq* 36: 173–78.

Oates, J. 1983. Balawat: Recent Excavations and a New Gate. Pp. 40–47 in Harper and Pittman 1983.

Oded, B. 1979. *Mass Deportations and Deportees in the Neo-Assyrian Empire*. Wiesbaden: Reichert Verlag.

Oded, B. 1991. 'The Command of the God' as a Reason for Going to War in the Assyrian Royal Inscriptions. Pp. 223–30 in Cogan and Eph'al 1991.

Oded, B. 1992. *War, Peace, and Empire: Justifications for War in Assyrian Royal Inscriptions*. Wiesbaden: Reichert Verlag.

Olmstead, A. T. 1916. *Assyrian Historiography: A Source Study*. University of Missouri Studies, Social Sciences Series 3/1. Columbia: University of Missouri Press.

Olmstead, A. T. 1918. The Calculated Frightfulness of Ashur naṣir apal. *Journal of the American Oriental Society* 38: 209–63.

Olmstead, A. T. 1921. Shalmaneser III and the Establishment of the Assyrian Power. *Journal of the American Oriental Society* 41: 345–82.

Olmstead, A. T. 1931. *History of Palestine and Syria to the Macedonian Conquest*. New York: Scribner.

Oppenheim, A. L. 1943. Akkadian *pul(u)h(t)u and melammu*. *Journal of the American Oriental Society* 63: 31–34.

Oppenheim, A. L. 1960. The City of Assur in 714 B.C. *Journal of the Ancient Near Eastern Society* 19: 133–47.

Oppenheim, A. L. 1979. Neo-Assyrian and Neo-Babylonian Empires. Pp. 111–44 in *Propaganda and Communication in World History I*, ed. H. Lasswell et al. Honolulu: University Press of Hawaii.

Orlamünde, J. 2011a. *Die Obeliskenfragmente aus Assur, mit einem Beitrag zu den Inschriften von Eckart Frahm*. Wissenschaftliche Veröffentlichungen der Deutschen Orient-Gesellschaft 135. Wiesbaden: Harrassowitz.

Orlamünde, J. 2011b. Zu den Orthostaten aus Assur. Pp. 441–70 in Renger 2011a.

Ornan, T. 2002. The Queen in Public: Royal Women in Neo-Assyrian Art. Pp. 461–77 in Parpola and Whiting 2002.

Orthmann, W. 1971. *Untersuchungen zur späthethitischen Kunst*. Saarbrücker Beiträge zur Altertumskunde 8. Bonn: Rudolf Habelt Verlag.

Otto, E. 1999. Human Rights: The Influence of the Hebrew Bible. *Journal of Northwest Semitic Languages* 25: 1–20.

Paley, S. M. 1976. *King of the World: Ashur-nasir-pal II of Assyria, 883–859 B.C.* New York: Brooklyn Museum.

Paley, S. M. and R. P. Sobolewski. 1987. *The Reconstruction of the Relief Presentations and Their Positions in the Northwest Palace at Kalhu (Nimrud): Rooms I.S.T.Z, West-Wing*. Baghdader Forschungen 10. Mainz am Rhein: Philipp von Zabern.

Paley, S. M. and R. P. Sobolewski. 1992. *The Reconstruction of the Relief Presentations and Their Positions in the Northwest Palace at Kalhu (Nimrud): The Principal Entrances and Courtyards*. Baghdader Forschungen 14. Mainz am Rhein: Philipp von Zabern.

Panofsky, E. 1972 [1939]. *Studies in Iconology: Humanistic Themes in the Art of the Renaissance*. Icon Editions. New York, Evanston, San Francisco, and London: Harper & Row Publishers.

Parker, B. J. 2011. The Construction and Performance of Kingship in the Neo-Assyrian Empire. *Journal of Anthropological Research* 67/3: 357–86.

Parker-Mallowan, B. 1983. Magic and Ritual in the North West Palace Reliefs. Pp. 32–39 in Harper and Pittman 1983.

Parpola, S. 1981. Assyrian Royal Inscriptions and Neo-Assyrian Letters. Pp. 117–42 in Fales 1981a.

Parpola, S. 1987. *The Correspondence of Sargon II, Part I: Letters from Assyria and the West.* State Archives of Assyria 1. Helsinki: Helsinki University Press.

Parpola, S. 1993. The Assyrian Tree of Life: Tracing the Origins of Jewish Monotheism and Greek Philosophy. *Journal of Near Eastern Studies* 52: 161–208.

Parpola, S. 1995a. The Assyrian Cabinet. Pp. 379–401 in Dietrich and Loretz 1995.

Parpola, S. 1995b. *Assyrian Prophecies*. State Archives of Assyria 9. Helsinki: Helsinki University Press.

Parpola, S. 1997. *The Standard Babylonian Epic of Gilgamesh*. State Archives of Assyria Cuneiform Texts 1. Helsinki: Neo-Assyrian Text Corpus Project.

Parpola, S. 1999. Sons of God: The Ideology of Assyrian Kingship. *Archaeology Oddysey* 2/5: 16–27.

Parpola, S. 2004. National and Ethnic Identity in the Neo-Assyrian Empire and Assyrian Identity in Post-Empire Times. *Journal of Assyrian Academic Studies* 18/2: 5–22.

Parpola, S. 2007a. The Neo-Assyrian Ruling Class. Pp. 257–74 in *Studien zu Ritual und Sozialgeschichte im Alten Orient*, ed. T. R. Kämmerer. Beiheft zur Zeitschrift für die alttestamentliche Wissenschaft 374. Berlin and New York: Walter de Gruyter.

Parpola, S. et al. (eds.). 2007b. *Assyrian-English-Assyrian Dictionary*. Helsinki: Neo-Assyrian Text Corpus Project.

Parpola, S. and M. Porter. 2001. *The Helsinki Atlas of the Near East in the Neo-Assyrian Period*. Helsinki: Neo-Assyrian Text Corpus Project and Casco Bay Assyriological Institute.

Parpola, S. and K. Watanabe. 1988. *Neo-Assyrian Treaties and Loyalty Oaths*. State Archives of Assyria 3. Helsinki: Helsinki University Press.

Parpola, S. and R. M. Whiting (eds.). 1997. *Assyria 1995: Proceedings of the 10th Anniversary Symposium of the Neo-Assyrian Text Corpus Project, Helsinki, September 7–11, 1995*. Helsinki: Neo-Assyrian Text Corpus Project.

Parpola, S. and R. M. Whiting (eds.). 2002. *Sex and Gender in the Ancient Near East.* Comptes rendu de la rencontre assyriologique internationale 47. Helsinki: Neo-Assyrian Text Corpus Project.

Parrot, A. 1961. *Nineveh and Babylon*. 1st ed. Arts of Mankind Series. London: Thames and Hudson.

Parrot, A. 1983 [1960]. *Sumer und Akkad*. 4th ed. Universum der Kunst. Munich: C. H. Beck.

Pečírková, J. 1987. The Administrative Methods of Assyrian Imperialism. *Archív Orientální* 55: 162–75.

Pečírková, J. 1993. Politics and Tradition in the Assyrian Empire. Pp. 243–48 in *Every Day Life in Ancient Near East*, eds. J. Zablocka and S. Zawadzki. Šulmu 4 (= Seria historia 182). Poznan: U.A.M.

Pedersén, O. 1985–86. *Archives and Libraries in the City of Assur: A Survey of the Material from the German Excavations I–II*. Studia Semitica Upsaliensia 6 and 8. Uppsala and Stockholm: Uppsala University and Almqvist & Wiksell.

Pettinato, G. 1988. *Semiramis, Herrin über Assur und Babylon. Biographie*. Zurich and Munich: Artemis Verlag.

Pittman, H. 1997. Unwinding the White Obelisk. Pp. 347–51 in Hauptmann and Waetzoldt 1997.

Pollock, S. 1999. *Ancient Mesopotamia: The Eden That Never Was*. Case Studies in Early Societies 1. Cambridge: Cambridge University Press.

Pollock, S. and R. Bernbeck. 2000. And they said, 'Let us make Gods in our Image': Gendered Ideologies in Ancient Mesopotamia. Pp. 150–64 in *Reading the Body*, ed. A. E. Rautman. Regendering the Past. Philadelphia: University of Pennsylvania Press.

Pollock, S. and R. Bernbeck (eds.). 2005. *Archaeologies of the Middle East: Critical Perspectives*. Blackwell Studies in Global Archaeology 4. Oxford: Blackwell.

Ponchia, S. 2012. Administrators and Administrated in Neo-Assyrian Times. Pp. 213–24 in Wilhelm 2012.

Pongratz-Leisten, B. 1997a. The Interplay of Military Strategy and Cultic Practice in Assyrian Politics. Pp. 245–52 in Parpola and Whiting 1997.

Pongratz-Leisten, B. 1997b. Toponyme als Ausdruck assyrischen Herrschaftsanspruchs. Pp. 325–43 in Pongratz-Leisten et al. 1997.

Pongratz-Leisten, B. 1999. *Herrschaftswissen in Mesopotamien. Formen der Kommunikation zwischen Gott und König im 2. und 1. Jahrtausend v. Chr.* State Archives of Assyria Studies 10. Helsinki: Neo-Assyrian Text Corpus Project.

Pongratz-Leisten, B. 2001. The Other and the Enemy in the Mesopotamian Conception of the World. Pp. 195–231 in *Mythology and Mythologies*, ed. R. M. Whiting. Melammu Symposia 2. Helsinki: Neo-Assyrian Text Corpus Project.

Pongratz-Leisten, B. 2009. Reflections on the Translatability of the Notion of Holiness. Pp. 409–28 in Luukko et al. 2009.

Pongratz-Leisten, B. 2013. All the King's Men: Authority, Kingship, and the Rise of the Elites in Assyria. Pp. 285–309 in Hill et al. 2013a.

Pongratz-Leisten, B. 2015. *Religion and Ideology in Assyria*. Studies in Ancient Near Eastern Records 6. Boston and Berlin: Walter de Gruyter.

Pongratz-Leisten, B., H. Kühne, and P. Xella (eds.). 1997. *Ana šadî Labnāni lū allik. Beiträge zu altorientalischen und mittelmeerischen Kulturen. Festschrift W. Röllig*. Alter Orient und Altes Testament 247. Münster: Ugarit-Verlag.

Porada, E. 1983. Remarks About Some Assyrian Reliefs. *Anatolian Studies* 33: 15–18.

Porter, B. N. 2003. *Trees, Kings, and Politics: Studies in Assyrian Iconography*. Orbis Biblicus et Orientalis 197. Fribourg and Göttingen: Academic Press and Vandenhoeck und Ruprecht.

Porter, B. N. 2010. Decorations, Political Posters, Time Capsules, and Living Gods: The Meaning and Function of the Assyrian Palace Carvings in the Hood Museum of Art. Pp. 143–58 in Cohen and Kangas 2010.

Postgate, J. N. 1973. *The Governor's Palace Archive*. Cuneiform Texts from Nimrud 2. London: British School of Archaeology in Iraq.

Postgate, J. N. 1974. Royal Exercise of Justice under the Assyrian Empire. Pp. 417–26 in Garelli 1974b.

Postgate, J. N. 1979. The Economic Structure of the Assyrian Empire. Pp. 193–222 in Larsen 1979a.

Postgate, J. N. 1992a. *Early Mesopotamia: Society and Economy at the Dawn of History*. 1st ed. London: Routledge.

Postgate, J. N. 1992b. The Land of Ashur and the Yoke of Ashur. *Journal of World Archaeology* 23: 247–63.

Postgate, J. N. 1995. Royal Ideology and State Administration in Sumer and Akkad. Pp. 395–411 in Sasson 1995.

Postgate, J. N. 2007. *The Land of Assur & the Yoke of Assur: Studies on Assyria 1971–2005*. Oxford: Oxbow Books.

Postgate, J. N. 2008. The Tombs in the Light of Mesopotamian Funerary Traditions. Pp. 177–80 in Curtis et al. 2008.

Postgate, J. N. and J. E. Reade. 1976–80. Kalḫu. *Reallexikon der Assyriologie und vorderasiatischen Archäologie* 5: 303–23.

Prechel, D. 1992. Fremde in Mesopotamien. Pp. 173–85 in *Aussenseiter und Randgruppen*, ed. V. Haas. Xenia 32. Konstanz: Universitätsverlag Konstanz.

Pritchard, J. 1969. *The Ancient Near East in Pictures, Relating to the Old Testament.* 2nd ed. Princeton: Princeton University Press.

Quirke, S. 1992. *Ancient Egyptian Religion*. London: British Museum Press.

Radner, K. 1998. Der Gott Salmanu ("Shulmanu") und seine Beziehung zur Stadt Dur-Katlimmu. *Welt des Orients* 29: 33–51.

Radner, K. 2006–08. Provinz. C. Assyrien. *Reallexikon der Assyriologie und vorderasiatischen Archäologie* 11: 42–68.

Radner, K. 2009. Die assyrischen Königsinschriften an der Tigrisgrotte. Pp. 172–202 in Schachner 2009.

Radner, K. 2010. Assyrian and Non-Assyrian Kingship in the First Millennium BC. Pp. 25–34 in Lanfranchi and Rollinger 2010.

Radner, K. 2011. The Assur-Nineveh-Arbela Triangle: Central Assyria in the Neo-Assyrian Period. Pp. 321–29 in Miglus and Muehl 2011.

Rassam, H. 1897. *Asshur and the Land of Nimrod*. Cincinatti and New York: Curts & Jennings and Eaton & Mains.

Reade, J. E. 1963. A Glazed Brick Panel from Nimrud. *Iraq* 25: 38–47.

Reade, J. E. 1967. Two Slabs from Sennacherib's Palace. *Iraq* 29: 42–48.

Reade, J. E. 1978. Assyrian Campaigns 840–811 B.C. and the Babylonian Frontier. *Zeitschrift für Assyriologie und vorderasiatische Archäologie* 68: 251–60.

Reade, J. E. 1979a. Ideology and Propaganda in Assyrian Art. Pp. 329–43 in Larsen 1979a.

Reade, J. E. 1979b. Narrative Composition in Assyrian Sculpture. *Baghdader Mitteilungen* 10: 52–110.

Reade, J. E. 1980a. The Rassam Obelisk. *Iraq* 42: 1–22.

Reade, J. E. 1980b. Space, Scale, and Significance in Assyrian Art. *Baghdader Mitteilungen* 11: 71–74.

Reade, J. E. 1981a. Neo-Assyrian Monuments in Their Historical Context. Pp. 143–67 in Fales 1981a.

Reade, J. E. 1981b. Fragments of Assyrian Monuments. *Iraq* 43: 145–56.

Reade, J. E. 1983. *Assyrian Sculpture.* 1st ed. London: British Museum Press.

Reade, J. E. 1985. Text and Sculptures from the North-West Palace, Nimrud. *Iraq* 47: 203–14.

Reade, J. E. 1986. Not Shalmaneser but Kidudu. *Baghdader Mitteilungen* 17: 299–300.

Reade, J. E. 1989. Shalmaneser or Ashurnasirpal in Ararat? *State Archives of Assyria Bulletin* 3: 93–97.

Reade, J. E. 2002. The Ziggurat and Temples of Nimrud. *Iraq* 64: 135–216.

Reade, J. E. 2004a. The Historical Status of the Assur Stelas. Pp. 455–73 in Dercksen 2004.

Reade, J. E. 2004b. The Assyrians as Collectors: From Accumulation to Synthesis. Pp. 255–68 in Frame 2004.

Reade, J. E. 2005. Religious Ritual in Assyrian Sculpture. Pp. 7–61 in *Ritual and Politics in Ancient Mesopotamia*, ed. B. N. Porter. American Oriental Series 88. New Haven: American Oriental Society.

Reade, J. E. 2009. Fez, Diadem, Turban, Chaplet: Power-Dressing at the Assyrian Court. Pp. 239–64 in Luukko et al. 2009.

Reade, J. E. and I. L. Finkel. 2002. Appendix 2. Pp. 204–10 in Reade 2002.
Reade, J. E. and I. L. Finkel. 2008. Catalogue. Pp. 9–105 in Searight et al. 2008.
Renger, J. 1980–83. Königsinschriften. B. Akkadisch. *Reallexikon der Assyriologie und vorderasiatischen Archäologie* 6: 65–77.
Renger, J. 1997. Aspekte von Kontinuität und Diskontinuität in den assyrischen Königsinschriften. Pp. 169–75 in Hauptmann and Waetzoldt 1997.
Renger, J. (ed.). 2011a. *Assur – Gott, Stadt und Land.* Colloquien der Deutschen Orient-Gesellschaft 5. Wiesbaden: Harrassowitz.
Renger, J. 2011b. Die Erforschung der Stadt durch die Deutsche Orient-Gesellschaft eingebettet in die Wechselfälle deutscher Geschichte im 20. Jh. Pp. 1–13 in Renger 2011a.
Richardson, S. 1999–2001. An Assyrian Garden of Ancestors: Room I, Northwest Palace, Kalḫu. *State Archives of Assyria Bulletin* 13: 145–216.
Richardson, S. 2010. Introduction. Pp. i–xxxi in *Rebellions and Peripheries in the Cuneiform World*, ed. S. Richardson. American Oriental Series 91. New Haven: American Oriental Society.
Rivaroli, M. and L. Verderame. 2005. To be a Non-Assyrian. Pp. 290–305 in *Ethnicity in Ancient Mesopotamia*, ed. W. H. van Soldt. Comptes rendu de la rencontre assyriologique internationale 48. Leiden: Nederlands instituut voor het Nabije Oosten.
Roaf, M. 1990. *Cultural Atlas of Mesopotamia and the Ancient Near East.* Equinox Books. New York and Oxford: Facts on File.
Roaf, M. 1995 The Chief Cupbearer, His Daughter, the King, and the Eponym Official for 860 B.C. *Nouvelles assyriologiques brèves et utilitaires* 1995/4: 84–85.
Roaf, M. 2008. The Decor of the Throne Room of the Palace of Ashurnasirpal. Pp. 209–13 in Curtis et al. 2008.
Roaf, M. 2012. Did Rusa Commit Suicide? Pp. 771–80 in Wilhelm 2012.
Roaf, M. 2013. Mesopotamian Kings and the Built Environment. Pp. 331–59 in Hill et al. 2013a.
Robertson, J. F. 2005. Social Tensions in the Ancient Near East. Pp. 196–210 in Snell 2005.
Röllig, W. 1981. Zum 'Sakralen Königtum' im Alten Orient. Pp. 114–25 in *Staat und Religion*, ed. B. Gladigow. Patmos Paperbacks. Düsseldorf: Patmos Verlag.
Röllig, W. 1996. Deportation und Integration. Das Schicksal von Fremden im assyrischen und babylonischen Staat. Pp. 100–114 in Schuster 1996.
Röllig, W. and Kh. Kessler. 1993–97. Mişir, Mizru, Muşur, Muşri III, Muzir. *Reallexikon der Assyriologie und vorderasiatischen Archäologie* 8: 264–69.
Rollin, S. 1983. Women and Witchcraft in Ancient Assyria (c. 900–600 BC). Pp. 34–45 in *Images of Women in Antiquity*, eds. A. Cameron and A. Kuhrt. London and Sydney: Croom Helm.
Rollinger, R. 2011. Assur, Assyrien und die klassische Überlieferung. Nachwirken, Deutungsmuster und historische Reflexion. Pp. 311–45 in Renger 2011a.
Ross, J. C. 2005. Representations, Reality, and Ideology. Pp. 327–50 in Pollock and Bernbeck 2005.
Roux, G. 1992. *Ancient Iraq.* 3rd ed. London: Penguin Books.
Russell, H. F. 1984. Shalmaneser III's Campaign to Urartu in 856 B.C. and the Historical Geography of Eastern Anatolia According to the Assyrian Sources. *Anatolian Studies* 34: 171–201.
Russell, J. M. 1991. *Sennacherib's Palace Without Rival at Nineveh.* London and Chicago: University of Chicago Press.

Russell, J. M. 1998a. *The Final Sack of Nineveh: The Discovery, Documentation, and Destruction of King Sennacherib's Throne Room at Nineveh, Iraq*. New Haven and London: Yale University Press.

Russell, J. M. 1998b. The Program of the Palace of Assurnasirpal II at Nimrud: Issues in the Research and Presentation of Assyrian Art. *American Journal of Archaeology* 102/4: 655–715.

Russell, J. M. 1998–2001. Neuassyrische Kunstperiode III. *Reallexikon der Assyriologie und vorderasiatischen Archäologie* 9: 244–65.

Russell, J. M. 1999. *The Writing on the Wall: Studies in the Archaeological Context of Late Assyrian Palace Inscriptions*. Mesopotamian Civilizations 9. Winona Lake: Eisenbrauns.

Russell, J. M. 2008. Thoughts on Room Function in the North-West Palace. Pp. 181–93 in Curtis et al. 2008.

Sachs, A. J. 1953. The Late Assyrian Royal-Seal Type. *Iraq* 15: 167–70.

Safar, F. 1951. A Further Text of Shalmaneser III from Assur. *Sumer* 7: 3–21.

Saggs, H. W. F. 1982. Assyrian Prisoners of War and the Right to Live. Pp. 85–93 in Hirsch and Hunger 1982.

Saggs, H. W. F. 1984. *The Might That Was Assyria*. Great Civilization Series. London: Sidgwick & Jackson.

Saggs, H. W. F. 2001. *The Nimrud Letters, 1952*. Cuneiform Texts from Nimrud 5. London: British Institute for the Study of Iraq.

Said, E. 1978. *Orientalism*. London: Routledge and Kegan Paul.

Saporetti, C. 1984. *The Middle Assyrian Laws*. Graphemic Categorization 2. Malibu: Undena Publications.

Sasson, J. M. (ed.). 1995. *Civilizations of the Ancient Near East I–IV*. New York: Scribner.

Schachner, A. 2007. *Bilder eines Weltreichs. Kunst- und Kulturgeschichtliche Untersuchungen zu den Verzierungen eines Tores aus Balawat (Imgur-Enlil) aus der Zeit von Salmanassar III, König von Assyrien*. Subartu 20. Turnhout: Brepols.

Schachner, A. 2009. *Assyriens Könige an einer der Quellen des Tigris. Archäologische Forschungen im Höhlensystem von Birkleyn und am sogenannten Tigris-Tunnel*. Istanbuler Forschungen 51. Tübingen: Ernst Wasmuth Verlag.

Schloen, J. D. 2001. *The House of the Father as Fact and Symbol: Patrimonialism in Ugarit and the Ancient Near East*. Studies in the Archaeology and History of the Levant 2. Winona Lake: Eisenbrauns.

Schneider, T. J. 1991. *A New Analysis of the Royal Annals of Shalmaneser III*. Ph.D.-thesis, University of Pennsylvania.

Schneider, T. J. 2011. *Introdution to Ancient Mesopotamian Religion*. Grand Rapids: W. B. Eerdmans Pub. Co.

Schramm, W. 1973. *Einleitung in die assyrischen Königsinschriften. Zweiter Teil: 934–722 v. Chr.* Handbuch der Orientalistik 5/1:2. Leiden: Brill.

Schroer, S. (ed.). 2006a. *Images and Gender: Contributions to the Hermeneutics of Reading Ancient Art*. Orbis Biblicus et Orientalis 220. Fribourg and Göttingen: Academic Press and Vandenhoeck & Ruprecht.

Schroer, S. 2006b. Einleitung. Pp. 1–22 in Schroer 2006a.

Schuster, M. (ed.). 1996. *Die Begegnung mit der Fremden. Wertungen und Wirkungen in Hochkulturen vom Altertum bis zur Gegenwart*. Colloquium Rauricum 4. Stuttgart and Leipzig: B. G. Teubner.

Schwyn, I. 2006. Kinder und ihre Betreuungspersonen auf den neuassyrischen Palastreliefs. Pp. 323–30 in Schroer 2006a.

Scurlock, J. 2013. Images of Tammuz: The Intersection of Death, Divinity, and Royal Authority in Ancient Mesopotamia. Pp. 151–82 in Hill et al. 2013a.

Searight, A., J. E. Reade, and I. Finkel. 2008. *Assyrian Stone Vessels and Related Material in the British Museum*, with contributions by K. Kitchen et al. Oxford: Oxbow Books.

Selz, G. 2008. The Divine Prototypes. Pp. 13–31 in Brisch 2008.

Seux, J.-M. 1965a. Remarques sur le titre royal assyrien *'iššakki Aššur'*. *Revue d'assyriologie et d'archéologie orientale* 59: 101–109.

Seux, J.-M. 1965b. Les titres royaux *'šar kiššati'* et *'šar kibrāt arba'i'*. *Revue d'assyriologie et d'archéologie orientale* 59: 1–18.

Seux, J.-M. 1967. *Épithètes royales akkadiennes et sumériennes*. Paris: Centre national de la recherche scientifique.

Seux, J.-M. 1980–83. Königtum. *Reallexikon der Assyriologie und vorderasiatischen Archäologie* 6: 140–73.

Shafer, A. T. 1998. *The Carving of an Empire: Neo-Assyrian Monuments on the Periphery*. Ph.D.-thesis, Harvard University.

Siddall, L. R. 2013. *The Reign of Adad-nīrārī III: An Historical and Ideological Analysis of an Assyrian King and His Times*. Cuneiform Monographs 45. Leiden: Brill.

Sidebottom, H. 2004. *Ancient Warfare: A Very Short Introduction*. Very Short Introductions. Oxford: Oxford University Press.

Sinha, M. 1995. *Colonial Masculinity: The "Manly Englishman" and the "Effeminate Bengali" in the Late Nineteenth Century*. Studies in Imperialism. Manchester: Manchester University Press.

Snell, D. C. 1993. Ancient Israelite and Neo-Assyrian Societies and Economies: A Comparative Approach. Pp. 221–24 in Snell et al. 1993.

Snell, D. C. (ed.). 2005. *A Companion to the Ancient Near East*. Blackwell Companions to the Ancient World. Oxford: Blackwell.

Snell, D. C., M. E. Cohen, and D. B. Weisberg (eds.). 1993. *The Tablet and the Scroll: Near Eastern Studies in Honor of William W. Hallo*. Bethesda: CDL Press.

Sobolewski, R. P. 1982a. The Shalmaneser III Building in the Central Area of the Nimrud Citadel. Pp. 329–40 in Hirsch and Hunger 1982.

Sobolewski, R. P. 1982b. The Polish Work at Nimrud: Ten Years of Excavation and Study. *Zeitschrift für Assyriologie und vorderasiatische Archäologie* 71: 248–73.

von Soden, W. 1959–81. *Akkadisches Handwörterbuch I–III*. Wiesbaden: Harrassowitz.

von Soden, W. 1963. Die Assyrer und der Krieg. *Iraq* 25: 131–44.

von Soden, W. 1995. *Grundriß der akkadischen Grammatik*. 3rd ed. Analecta Orientalia 33. Rome: Biblical Institute Press.

Sollors, W. 1989. Introduction. Pp. xiii–xiv in *The Invention of Ethnicity*, ed. W. Sollors. New York: Oxford University Press.

Solvang, E. K. 2006. Another Look 'Inside': Harems and the Interpretation of Women. Pp. 374–98 in Holloway 2006a.

van der Spek, R. J. 1993. Assyriology and History: A Comparative Study of War and Empire in Assyria, Athens, and Rome. Pp. 262–76 in Snell et al. 1993.

Spieckermann, H. 1982. *Juda unter Assur in der Sargonidenzeit*. Forschungen zur Religion und Literatur des Alten und Neuen Testaments 129. Göttingen: Vandenhoeck & Ruprecht.

Spivak, G. C. 1988. Can the Subaltern speak? Pp. 271–313 in *Marxism and the Interpretation of Culture*, eds. C. Nelson and L. Grossberg. Urbana: University of Illinois Press.

Starr, I. 1990. *Queries to the Sungod: Divination and Politics in Sargonid Assyria*. State Archives of Assyria 4. Helsinki: Helsinki University Press.

Stearns, J. B. and D. P. Hansen. 1953. *The Assyrian Reliefs at Dartmouth*. Hanover: Dartmouth College Museum.

Steiner, G. 1982. Der Gegensatz 'Eigenes Land' – 'Ausland, Fremdland, Feindland' in den Vorstellungen des alten Orients. Pp. 633–64 in Nissen and Renger 1982.

Stol, M. 2012. *Vrouwen van Babylon: Prinsessen, Priesteressen, Prostituees, in die Bakermat van de Cultuur*. Utrecht: Uitgeverij Kok.

Streck, M. 1916. *Assurbanipal und die letzten assyrischen Könige bis zum Untergang Niniveh's I–III*. Vorderasiatische Bibliothek 7. Leipzig: J. C. Hinrichs.

Strommenger, E. 1970. *Die neuassyrische Rundskulptur*. Abhandlungen der Deutschen Orient-Gesellschaft 15. Berlin: Gebr. Mann Verlag.

Stronach, D. 1990. The Garden as a Political Statement: Some Case Studies from the Near East in the First Millennium B.C. *Bulletin of the Asia Institute Nova Series* 4: 171–80.

Svärd, S. 2008. *Women's Roles in the Neo-Assyrian Era: Female Agency in the Empire*. Saarbrücken: VDM Verlag Dr. Müller.

Svärd, S. 2012. *Power and Women in the Neo-Assyrian Palaces*. Ph.D-thesis, University of Helsinki.

Tadmor, H. 1961. Que and Musri. *Israel Exploration Journal* 11: 143–50.

Tadmor, H. 1973. The Historical Inscriptions of Adad-Nirari III. *Iraq* 35: 141–50.

Tadmor, H. 1975. Assyria and the West: The Ninth Century and Its Aftermath. Pp. 36–48 in *Unity and Diversity*, eds. H. Goedicke and J. J. M. Roberts. Johns Hopkins Near Eastern Studies. Baltimore and London: Johns Hopkins University Press.

Tadmor, H. 1981. History and Ideology in the Assyrian Royal Inscriptions. Pp. 13–33 in Fales 1981a.

Tadmor, H. 1982. The Aramaization of Assyria. Pp. 449–70 in Nissen and Renger 1982.

Tadmor, H. 1983. Autobiographical Apology in the Royal Assyrian Literature. Pp. 36–57 in Tadmor and Weinfeld 1983.

Tadmor, H. 1997. Propaganda, Literature, Historiography: Cracking the Code of the Assyrian Royal Inscriptions. Pp. 325–38 in Parpola and Whiting 1997.

Tadmor, H. 2000. World Dominion: The Expanding Horizon of the Assyrian Empire. Pp. 55–62 in Fales et al. 2000.

Tadmor, H. 2002. The Role of the Chief Eunuch and the Place of Eunuchs in the Assyrian Empire. Pp. 603–11 in Parpola and Whiting 2002.

Tadmor, H. 2011. *With My Many Chariots I Have Gone Up the Heights of the Mountains: Historical and Literary Studies on Ancient Mesopotamia and Israel*, edited by M. Cogan. Jerusalem: Israel Exploration Society.

Tadmor, H. and S. Yamada. 2011. *The Royal Inscriptions of Tiglath-Pileser III (744–727 BC) and Shalmaneser V (726–722 BC), Kings of Assyria*. Royal Inscriptions of the Neo-Assyrian Period 1. Winona Lake: Eisenbrauns.

Tadmor, H. and M. Weinfeld (eds.). 1983. *History, Historiography, and Interpretation: Studies in Biblical and Cuneiform Literatures*. Jerusalem: Magnes Press and Hebrew University.

Tallqvist, K. 1938. *Akkadische Götterepitheta*. Studia Orientalia 7. Helsinki: Societas Orientalis Fennica.

Taşyürek, O. A. 1975. Some New Assyrian Rock-Reliefs in Turkey. *Anatolian Studies* 25: 169–81.

Taşyürek, O. A. 1979. A Rock Relief of Shalmaneser III on the Euphrates. *Iraq* 41: 47–53.

Thureau-Dangin, F. 1931. *Arslan Tash*. Bibliothèque archéologique et historique 16. Paris: Geuthner.

Thureau-Dangin, F. and M. Dunand. 1936. *Til-Barsip*. Bibliothèque archéologique et historique 23. Paris: Geuthner.

van der Toorn, K. 2000. Prophecy between Immanence and Transcendence. Pp. 71–87 in *Prophecy in Its Ancient Near Eastern Context: Mesopotamian, Biblical, and Arabian Perspectives*, ed. M. Nissinen. Society of Biblical Literature Symposium Series. Atlanta: Society of Biblical Literature.

Turner, G. 1970. The State Apartments of Late Assyrian Palaces. *Iraq* 39: 177–213.

Unger, E. 1920. Die Wiederherstellung des Bronzetores von Balawat. *Mitteilungen des Deutschen Archäologischen Instituts Athen* 45: 1–105.

Wäfler, M. 1975. *Nicht-Assyrer neuassyrischer Darstellungen*. Alter Orient und Altes Testament 26. Kevelaer and Neukirchen-Vluyn: Butzon & Bercker and Neukirchener Verlag.

Wäfler, M. 1976. Das neuassyrische Felsreliefs von Eğil. *Archäologischer Anzeiger* 1976/3: 290–305.

Wallerstein, I. 1974. *The Modern World-System: Capitalist Agriculture and the Origins of the European World-Economy in the Sixteenth Century*. Studies in Social Discontinuity. New York: Academic Press.

Watanabe, C. E. 1998. Symbolism of the Royal Lion Hunt in Assyria. Pp. 439–50 in *Intellectual Life in the Ancient Near East*, ed. J. Prosecky. Comptes rendu de la rencontre assyriologique internationale 43. Prague: Academy of Sciences of the Czech Republic.

Watanabe, K. (ed.). 1999. *Priests and Officials in the Ancient Near East*. Colloquium on the Ancient Near East 2. Heidelberg: Universitätsverlag C. Winter.

Weber, M. 1978 [1922]. *Economy and Society: An Outline of Interpretive Sociology I–II*, edited by G. Roth and C. Wittich. Berkeley: University of California Press.

Weeks, N. K. 1983. Causality in the Assyrian Royal Inscriptions. *Orientalia Lovaniensia Periodica* 14: 115–27.

Weidner, E. F. 1933–34. Die Feldzüge Šamši-Adads V. gegen Babylonien. *Archiv für Orientforschung* 9: 89–104.

Weidner, E. F. 1939. *Die Reliefs der assyrischen Könige*. Archiv für Orientforschung Beiheft 4. Berlin: Im Selbstverlage des Herausgebers.

Weidner, E. F. 1940. Texte, Wörter, Sachen. *Archiv für Orientforschung* 13: 230–37.

Weidner, E. F. 1956. Hof- und Harems-Erlasse assyrischer Könige aus dem 2. Jahrtausende v. Chr. *Archiv für Orientforschung* 17: 257–93.

Weinfeld, M. 1983. Divine Intervention in War in Ancient Israel and in the Ancient Near East. Pp. 121–47 in Tadmor and Weinfeld 1983.

Weippert, M. 1972. 'Heiliger Krieg' in Israel und Assyrien. *Zeitschrift für die alttestamentliche Wissenschaft* 84: 460–93.

Weissert, E. 1997. Royal Hunt and Royal Triumph in a Prism Fragment of Ashurbanipal (82-5-22,2). Pp. 339–58 in Parpola and Whiting 1997.

Weissert, E. 2011. Jesajas Beschreibung der Hybris des assyrischen Königs und seine Auseinandersetzung mit ihr. Pp. 287–309 in Renger 2011a.

Westenholz, A. 1979. The Old Akkadian Empire in Contemporary Opinion. Pp. 107–24 in Larsen 1979a.

Wiggermann, F. A. M. 1992. *Mesopotamian Protective Spirits: The Ritual Texts*. Cuneiform Monographs 1. Groningen: Styx.

Wiggermann, F. A. M. and A. Green. 1993–97. Mischwesen. *Reallexikon der Assyriologie und vorderasiatischen Archäologie* 8: 222–64.

Wilhelm, G. (ed.). 2012. *Organization, Representation, and Symbols of Power in the Ancient Near East: Proceedings of the 5th RAI at Würzburg 20–25 July 2008*. Comptes rendu de la rencontre assyriologique internationale 54. Winona Lake: Eisenbrauns.

Winter, I. 1981. Royal Rhetoric and the Development of Historical Narrative in Neo-Assyrian Reliefs. *Studies in Visual Communication* 7: 2–38.

Winter, I. 1983. The Program of the Throneroom of Assurnasirpal II. Pp. 15–31 in Harper and Pittman 1983.

Winter, I. 1989. The Body of the Able Ruler: Toward an Understanding of the Statues of Gudea. Pp. 573–84 in *Studies in Honour of Åke W. Sjöberg*, ed. H. Behrens et al. Occasional Publications of the Samuel Noah Kramer Fund 11. Philadelphia: University of Philadelphia Press.

Winter, I. 1993. 'Seat of Kingship'/'A Wonder to Behold': The Palace as Construct in the Ancient Near East. *Ars orientalis* 23: 27–55.

Winter, I. 1996. Sex, Rhetoric, and the Public Monument: The Alluring Body of Naram-Sîn of Agade. Pp. 11–26 in *Sexuality in Ancient Art*, ed. N. B. Kampen. Cambridge Studies in New Art History and Criticism. Cambridge: Cambridge University Press.

Winter, I. 1997. Art in Empire: The Royal Image and the Visual Dimensions of Assyrian Ideology. Pp. 359–81 in Parpola and Whiting 1997.

Winter, I. 2000. Tree(s) on the Mountain: Landscape and Territory on the Victory Stele of Naram-Sîn of Agade. Pp. 63–76 in Fales et al. 2000.

Winter, I. 2008. Touched by the Gods: Visual Evidence for the Divine Status of Rulers in the Ancient Near East. Pp. 75–101 in Brisch 2008.

Winter, I. 2010. *On Art in the Ancient Near East, vol. 1: Of the First Millennium B.C.E.* Culture and History of the Ancient Near East 34. Leiden and Boston: Brill.

Wiseman, D. J. 1952. A New Stela of Aššur-nāṣir-pal II. *Iraq* 14: 24–44.

Wiseman, D. J. and J. A. Black. 1996. *Literary Texts from the Temple of Nabû*. Cuneiform Texts from Nimrud 4. London: British School of Archaeology in Iraq.

Wittfogel, K. 1977 [1957]. *Die orientalische Despotien. Eine vergleichende Untersuchung totaler Macht*. Ullstein Buch 3309. Frankfurt am Main: Ullstein.

Yamada, S. 1998. The Manipulative Counting of the Euphrates Crossings in the Later Inscriptions of Shalmaneser III. *Journal of Cuneiform Studies* 50: 87–94.

Yamada, S. 2000. *The Construction of the Assyrian Empire: A Historical Study of the Inscriptions of Shalmaneser III (859–824 BC) Relating to His Campaigns to the West*. Culture and History of the Ancient Near East 3. Leiden: Brill.

Yoffee, N. 1993. The Late Great Tradition in Ancient Mesopotamia. Pp. 300–308 in Snell et al. 1993.

Zaccagnini, C. 1982. The Enemy in the Neo-Assyrian Royal Inscriptions: The 'Ethnographic' Description. Pp. 409–24 in Nissen and Renger 1982.

Zawadzki, S. 1995. Hostages in Assyrian Royal Inscriptions. Pp. 449–58 in *Immigration and Emigration within the Ancient Near East*, eds. K. van Leberghe and A. Schoors. Orientalia Lovaniensia Analecta 65. Leuven: Peeters.

Zettler, R. L. 1996. Written Documents as Excavated Artifacts and the Holistic Interpretation of the Mesopotamian Archaeological Record. Pp. 81–101 in *The Study of the Ancient Near East in the 21st Century*, eds. J. Cooper and G. M. Schwartz. William Foxwell Albright Centennial Conference. Winona Lake: Eisenbrauns.

Zettler, R. L. 2006. Tišatal and Nineveh at the End of the 3rd Millennium BCE. Pp. 503–14 in *If a Man Builds a Joyful House*, ed. A. K. Guinan et al. Cuneiform Monographs 31. Leiden and Boston: Brill.

Ziegler, N. 2011a. Après le déluge: La royauté descend des cieux. *Dossiers d'Archéologie* 348: 2–5.

Ziegler, N. 2011b. Les rois chasseurs. *Dossiers d'Archéologie* 348: 68–69.

Figures

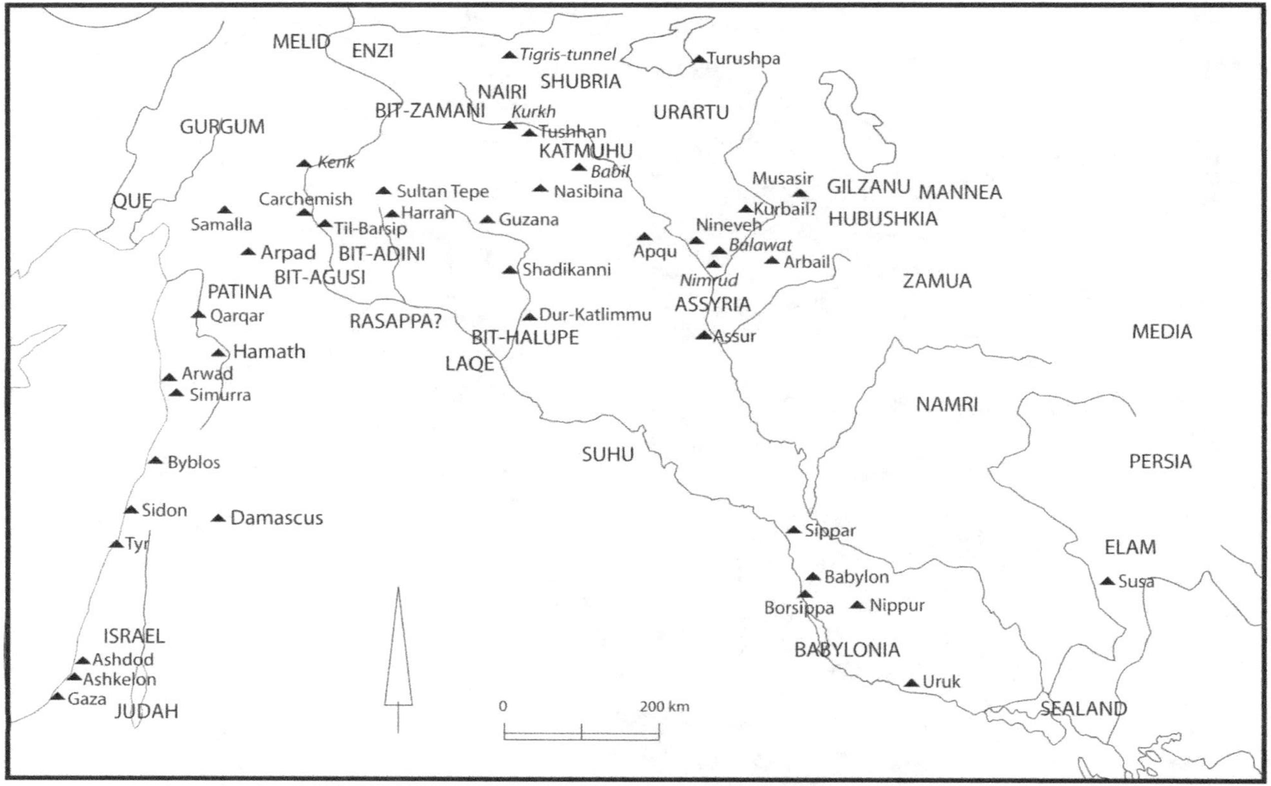

Fig. 1: Map of the Near East in the Early Neo-Assyrian Period. Toponyms written with large letters refer to regions or countries, those with small letters to cities. Italics indicate modern place names. Placement of toponyms follows Parpola and M. Porter 2001.

Fig. 2: Map of the city Assur. The city's temples and palaces are situated at the northern part of the city. The Old Palace, i.e. the initial residence of Ashurnasirpal II, is to the west of the ziggurat of the Ashur temple (the black square). To the (south-)west of the Old Palace are temples to Ishtar, Sin-Shamash, and Anu-Adad, while the Ashur temple is situated to the north-east of the ziggurat. The Tabira Gate is at the western end, and the Row of Stelae is to be found in the south, between the doubly fortified city walls. Map after Nunn 2006: pl. 1.

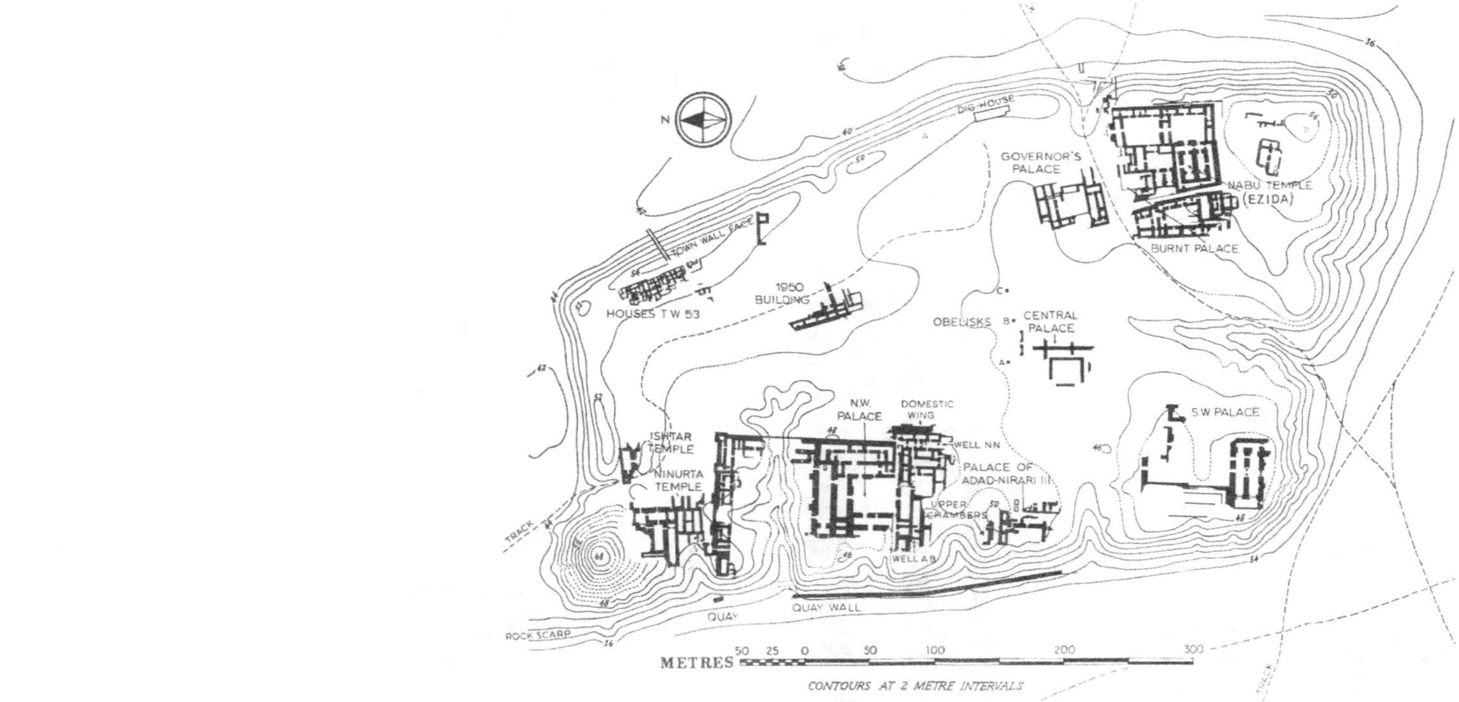

Fig. 3: Map of the citadel of Kalhu. The North-West Palace and the temples to Ninurta and Sharrat-niphi (called Ishtar on the map) in the lower left, and the area of the Central and Shalmaneser III's Buildings in the mid, close to the "obelisks" and "Central Palace" of the map. Note also the palace of Adad-narari III in the lower mid, and the Nabu temple and administrative "palaces" in the upper right. Fort Shalmaneser was in the outer city, to the south-east. Map after Mallowan 1966: pl. 1.

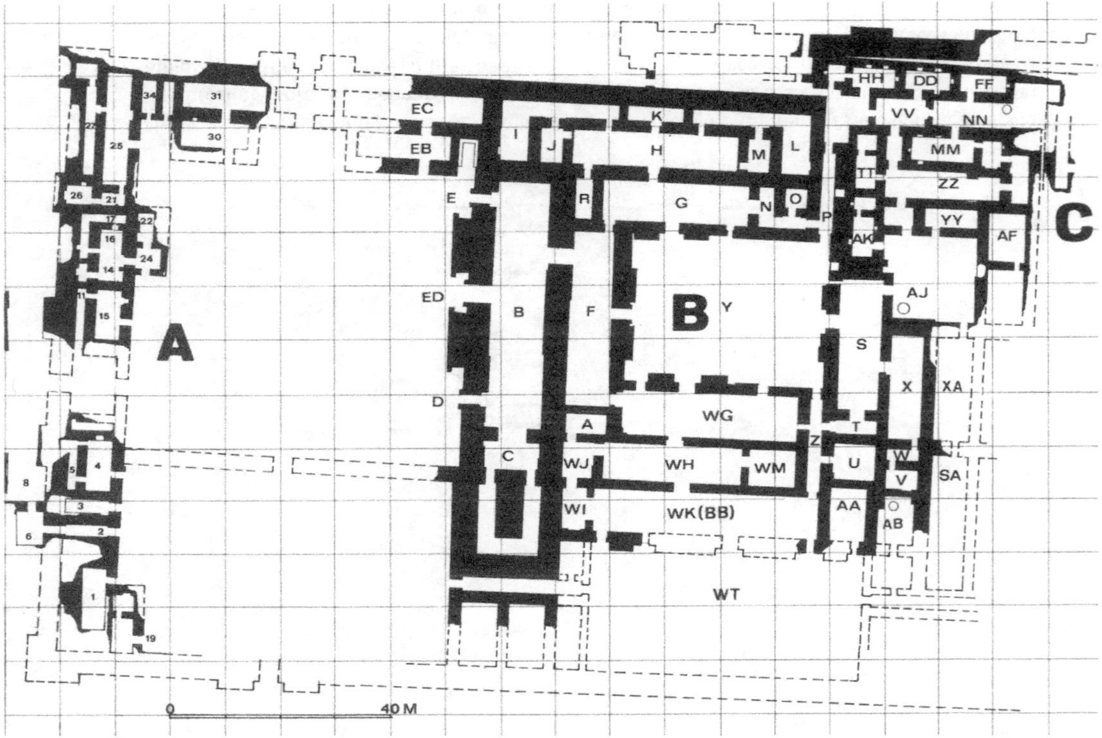

Fig. 4: Plan of the North-West Palace. Large A stands for the outer palace, large B for the inner palace, large C for the domestic wing, ED for the main entrance, small B for the throne room. The Banquet Stele stood east of E. Rooms with W as first letter comprise the western wing, S and T (e.g.) the southern wing, while G and H (e.g.) form the eastern wing. Plan after Paley and Sobolewski 1987: pl. 1.

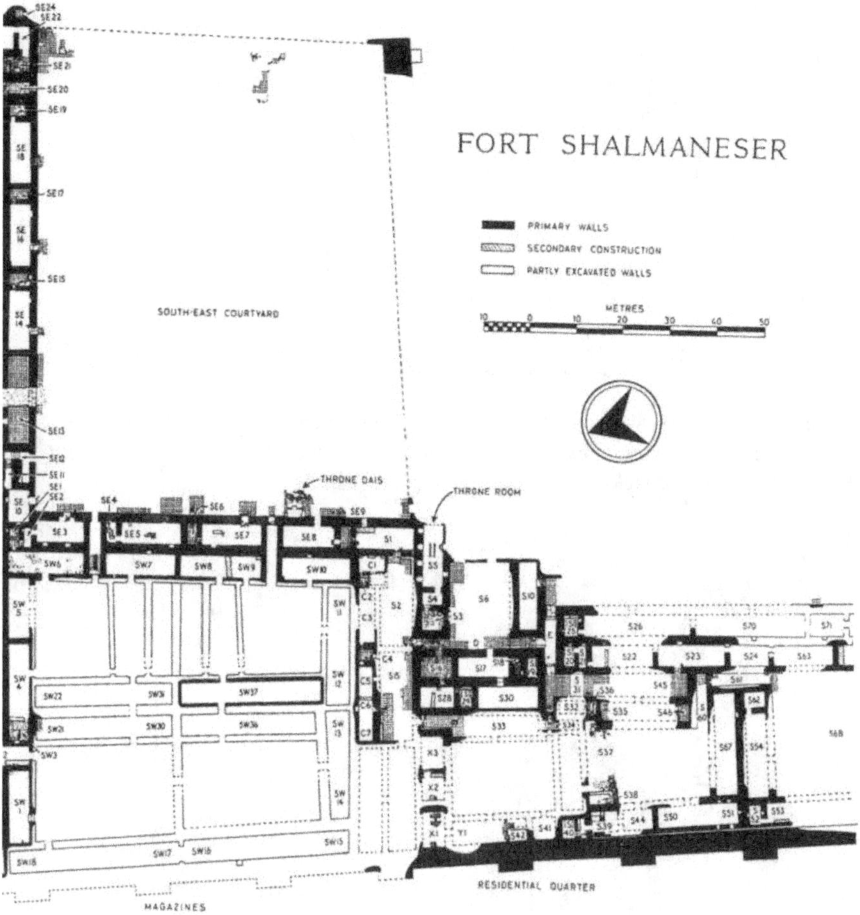

Fig. 5: Plan of Fort Shalmaneser. Central part of Shalmaneser III's "review palace" in Kalhu. For the king's throne room and dais, see the arrows. Outside the map, to the left or north, are the remains of military barracks, as well as more courtyards and storage spaces. The black areas mark the primary walls of the palace, while the grey areas signify secondary constructions. Plan after Herrmann 1992: 6.

Fig. 6: King in battle 1. Ashurnasirpal II fighting enemies from his chariot. Carved stone panel in the British Museum taken from the North-West Palace. Reproduced from Layard 1849: pl. 13 (cf. Meuszyński 1981: fig. B3). Brought up e.g. in s. 4.4.

Fig. 7: King in battle 2. Ashurnasirpal II fighting enemies on foot. Carved stone panel in the British Museum taken from the North-West Palace. Reproduced from Layard 1849: pl. 17 (cf. Meuszyński 1981: fig. B18). Brought up e.g. in s. 4.4.

Fig. 8: King as hunter. Ashurnasirpal II hunting lions. Carved stone panel in the British Museum taken from the North-West Palace. Reproduced from Layard 1849: pl. 10 (cf. Meuszyński 1981: fig. B19). Brought up e.g. in s. 5.2.

Fig. 9: King as libating priest. Ashurnasirpal II libating after a hunt. Carved stone panel in the British Museum taken from the North-West Palace. Reproduced from Layard 1849: pl. 12 (cf. Meuszyński 1981: fig. B20). Brought up e.g. in s. 5.2.

Fig. 10: Deities as warriors 1. Divine chariots taking part in battle. Carved stone panel in the British Museum taken from the North-West Palace. Reproduced from Layard 1849: pl. 11 (cf. Meuszyński 1981: fig. B4). Brought up e.g. in s. 3.2.

Fig. 11: Deities as warriors 2. God fighting a demon. Carved stone panel in the British Museum taken from the Ninurta temple. Reproduced from Layard 1853a: pl. 5 (cf. Meuszyński 1972). Brought up e.g. in s. 3.2.

Fig. 12: "Display of strength". Ashurnasirpal II proceeding in triumph. Carved stone panel in the British Museum taken from the North-West Palace. Reproduced from Layard 1849: pl. 21 (cf. Meuszyński 1981: fig. B5). Brought up e.g. in subs. 5.4.1.

Fig. 13: "Difficult path". Ashurnasirpal II crossing a river. Carved stone panel in the British Museum taken from the North-West Palace. Reproduced from Layard 1849: pl. 15 (cf. Meuszyński 1981: fig. B9). Brought up e.g. in s. 5.1.

Fig. 14: King banqueting. Ashurnasirpal II at a banquet. Carved stone panel in the British Museum taken from the North-West Palace. Reproduced from Layard 1849: pl. 5 (cf. Meuszyński 1981: fig. G2–4). Brought up e.g. in subs. 5.4.4.

Fig. 15: The sacred tree scene (king as venerating priest). Carved stone panel in the British Museum taken from the North-West Palace. Reproduced from Layard 1849: pl. 25 (cf. Meuszyński 1981: fig. B23). Brought up e.g. in s. 4.2.

Fig. 16: Human and bird-headed genii. Carved stone panels in the British Museum taken from the North-West Palace. Reproduced from Layard 1849: pl. 36 (cf. Meuszyński 1981 or Paley and Sobolewski 1992). Brought up e.g. in s. 4.1.

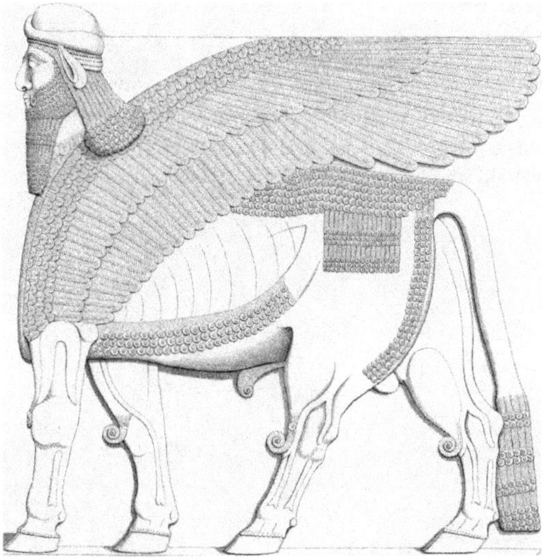

Fig. 17: Human-headed bull colossus. Statuary in the British Museum taken from the North-West Palace. Reproduced from Layard 1849: pl. 4 (cf. Meuszyński 1981 or Paley and Sobolewski 1992). Brought up e.g. in s. 4.1.

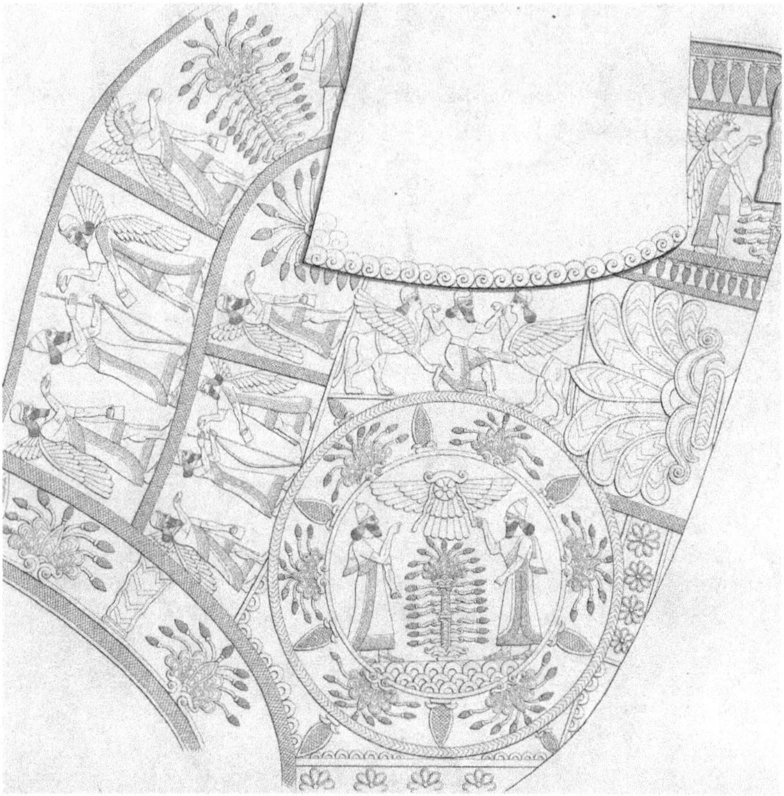

Fig. 18: King having his weapons ritually purified. Ashurnasirpal II and various mythical creatures interacting on the embroidery of the king's garment. Detail on a carved stone panel in the British Museum taken from the North-West Palace. Reproduced from Layard 1849: pl. 6 (cf. Canby 1971: fig. 19a). Brought up e.g. in s. 4.4.

Fig. 19: (left) The statue of Ashurnasirpal II (king as priest (statue)). Statue in the British Museum taken from the Sharrat-niphi temple. Reproduced from Layard 1853b: 361 (cf. Strommenger 1970: Abb. 2d). Brought up e.g. in s. 4.2.

Fig. 20: (right) The Ninurta Stele (king as venerating priest). Ashurnasirpal II in cult. Stele in the British Museum taken from the Ninurta temple. Reproduced from Layard 1853a: pl. 4 (cf. Börker-Klähn 1982: fig. 136). Brought up e.g. in s. 4.2.

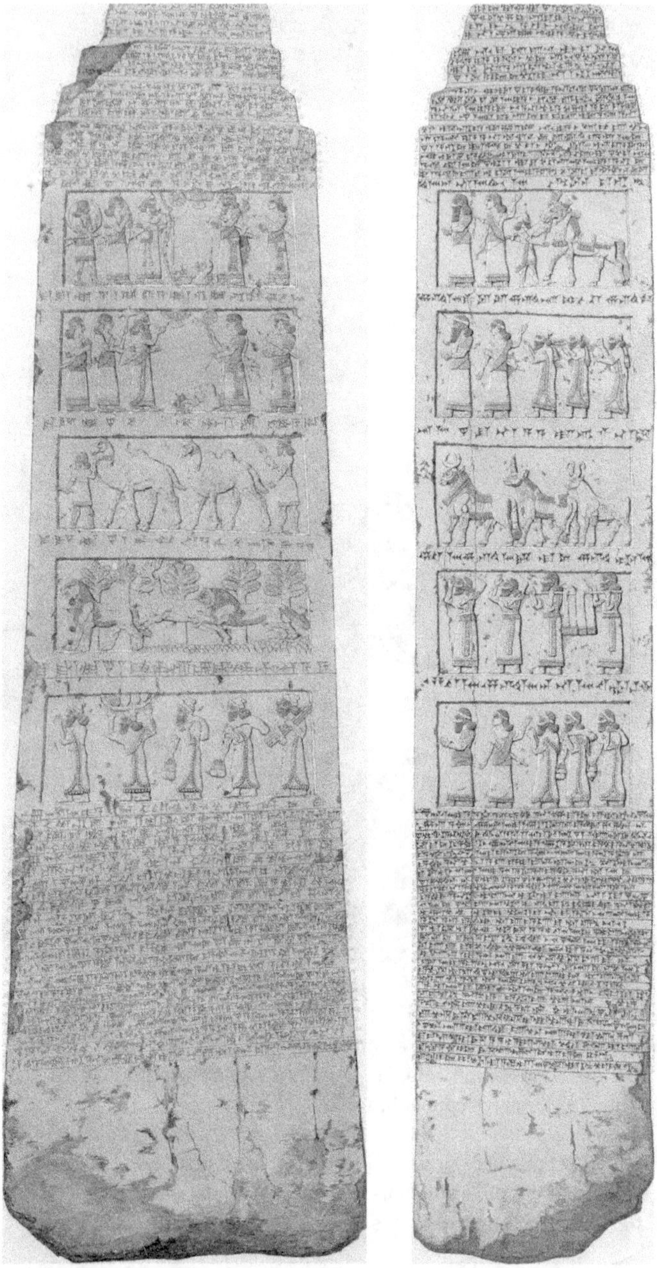

Fig. 21–22: King receiving tribute 1–2 (The Black Obelisk). Two sides of the monument showing the king receiving tribute processions. Obelisk in the British Museum taken from Shalmaneser's Building. Reproduced from Layard 1849: pls. 53–54 (cf. Börker-Klähn 1982: fig. 152). Brought up e.g. in subs. 5.4.3.

Fig. 23–24: King receiving tribute 3–4 (The Black Obelisk). Two sides of the monument showing tribute processions. Obelisk in the British Museum taken from Shalmaneser's Building. Reproduced from Layard 1849: pls. 55–56 (cf. Börker-Klähn 1982: fig. 152). Brought up e.g. in subs. 5.4.3.

Fig. 25–26: King as priest 1–2. Shalmaneser III making sacrifices at Lake Van (upper register) and attacking Sugunia (lower register). Bronze bands in the British Museum taken from the local palace in Balawat. Reproduced from King 1915: pls. 1–2 (cf. Schachner 2007: pl. 17). Brought up e.g. in ss. 4.2 and 5.3.

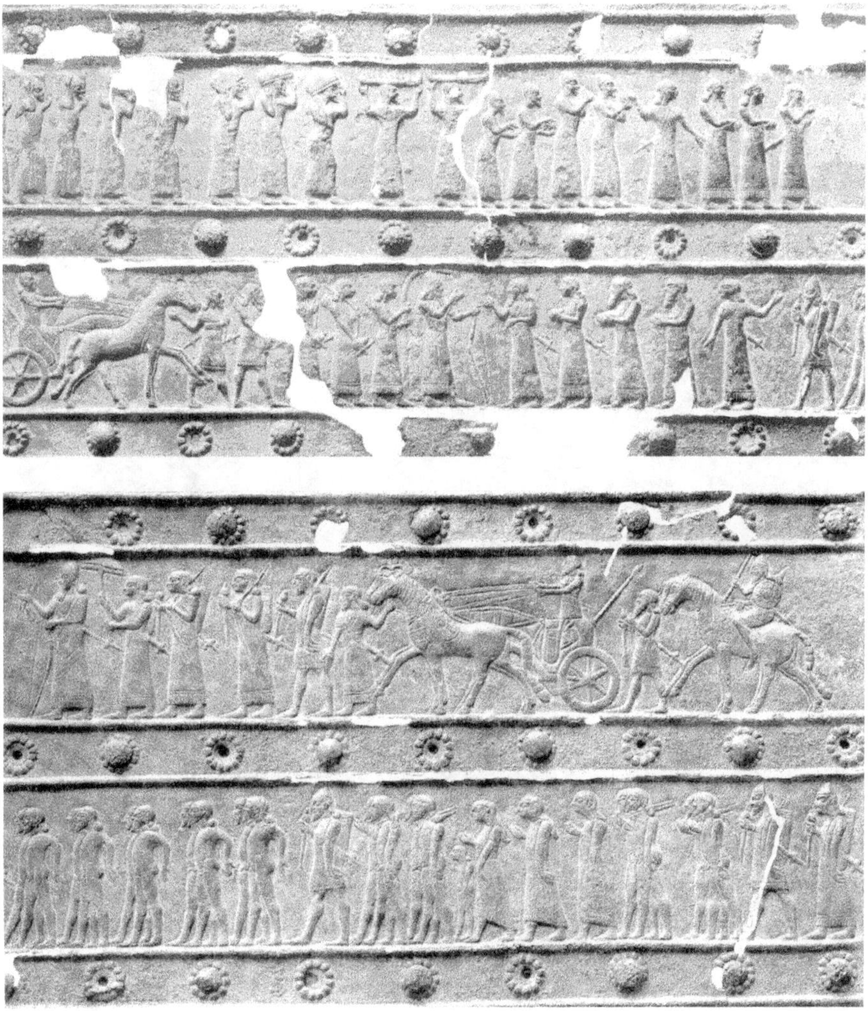

Fig. 27–28: King receiving captives 1–2. Shalmaneser III receiving tribute from Phoenicia (upper register) and captives from Hazazu (lower). Bronze bands in the British Museum taken from the local palace in Balawat. Reproduced from King 1915: pls. 14–15 (cf. Schachner 2007: pls. 24–25). Brought up e.g. in subs. 5.4.2.

Fig. 29: (left) The Nabu Stele (king as venerating priest). Shamshi-Adad V with divine emblems. Stele in the British Museum taken from the Nabu temple. Reproduced from Rassam 1897 (cf. Börker-Klähn 1982: fig. 161). Brought up e.g. in s. 4.2.

Fig. 30: (right) Statue of a deity/genie. A god – Nabu or a genie – standing with clasped hands. Statue in the British Museum taken from the Nabu temple. Reproduced from Rassam 1897 (cf. Strommenger 1970: pl. 8). Brought up e.g. in s. 3.1.

Appendices and indices

1 List of the inscriptions

This appendix lists and classifies all the texts belonging to the major primary sources of Ashurnasirpal II (175 texts/1123 exs.), Shalmaneser III (154 texts/515 exs.), and of the other kings (123 texts/251 exs.). The abbreviations in the first row stand for: **b ref** reference in book, **p ref** reference in publication, **gn** (suggested) genre, **A** Assur, **K** Kalhu (Nimrud), **N** Nineveh, **ic** the rest of the inner core (including Balawat), **oc** the outer core, **bf** the border areas/foreign lands, **of** the two latest mentioned areas combined, **1/2/3** first/second/third regnal phase. Abbreviations in the genre column stand for: commemorative text (co), caption (ca), dedicatory text (de), label text (lt), royal prayer (rp), royal hymn (rh), royal decree (rd), loyalty oath (lo), letter to/from a god (ltg/lfg), royal chronicle (rc). For the abbreviations in the first column, see "Abbreviations". All the texts which are named according to the standard pattern of "A.0." refer to the publications of RIMA2/3. All numbers following author/publisher and publishing year (see second col.) refer to texts and not to pages. Crosses indicate attestation, empty cell lack of attestation. If a text has several exemplars, this is indicated by numbers in parantheses (see second col.) and crosses in italic (see cols. 4–8/9). New exemplars have been added from the publications of Frahm 2009 and George 2011. The final column provides an index. The numbers in the index column refer to (sub)sections. The epigraphic sources listed here are described in section 2.1.

b ref	p ref	gn	A	K	N	ic	oc	bf	1	2	index
AE1	A.0.101.1 (4)	co		x						x	1.5, 1.7.1, 2.1, 3.1/2, 4.1/2/3/4, 5.1/2/3, 5.4.1/2/3/4/5/6/7/8/9, 6.2, 7.2, 8.2
AE2	A.0.101.2 (8)	co		x						x	2.1, 4.1/2/3/4, 5.1/2, 5.4.1/2/3/4/7/8/9, 6.2, 8.2
AE3	A.0.101.3	co		x						x	2.1, 4.1, 5.4.1/5, 6.2, 7.2
AE4	A.0.101.4	co		x							2.1, 4.1
AE5	A.0.101.5	co		x						x	2.1
AE6	A.0.101.6	co		x						x	2.1, 4.1
AE7	A.0.101.7	co		x						x	2.1
AE8	A.0.101.8	co		x						x?	2.1, 3.1
AE9	A.0.101.9	co		x						x?	2.1, 6.2
AE10	A.0.101.10	co		x						x?	2.1
AE11	A.0.101.11	co		x						x?	2.1
AE12	A.0.101.12	co		x						x?	2.1
AE13	A.0.101.13	co		x						x?	2.1
AE14	A.0.101.14	co		x						x?	2.1
AE15	A.0.101.15 (4)	co			x					x	2.1
AE16	A.0.101.16	co	x								2.1
AE17	A.0.101.17	co		x					x		1.4.2, 1.5, 1.7.1, 2.1, 3.1/2, 4.1/2/3/4, 5.4.1/2/3/4/5/6/7/8/9, 6.2, 7.2, 8.2
AE18	Finkel 2008a: temple door leaf text (2)	co				x				x?	2.1
AE19	A.0.101.19	co						x	x		2.1, 3.2, 4.1/3/4, 5.1/2, 5.4.1/2/3/4/5/6/7/9, 6.2, 7.2, 8.2/3
AE20	A.0.101.20	co						x			2.1, 3.1, 4.1, 6.2, 7.2
AE21	A.0.101.21 (2)	co	x								2.1, 4.4, 5.1, 5.4.2/3, 6.2, 8.2
AE22	A.0.101.22	co	x								2.1
AE23	A.0.101.23 (406)	co		x					x	x	2.1, 4.1/2/3, 5.4.1/2/3/7/9, 6.2, 7.1/2, 8.2/4

AE24	A.0.101.24	co	x				x	2.1
AE25	A.0.101.25	co	x					2.1
AE26	A.0.101.26 (16)	co	x		x	x		2.1, 3.2, 4.2/3, 5.4.3/6, 6.2, 8.2
AE27	A.0.101.27	co	x					2.1
AE28	A.0.101.28 (2)	co	x				x	1.5, 2.1, 3.1/2, 4.1/2/3, 5.1, 5.4.1/4/5/9, 6.2, 7.2
AE29	A.0.101.29	co	x					2.1, 3.2, 4.1, 6.2, 7.2
AE30	A.0.101.30	co	x				x	1.4.2, 1.5, 2.1, 4.1/2/3, 5.1/2, 5.4.1/3/4/6/7/9, 6.2, 7.2, 8.2
AE31	A.0.101.31 (3)	co	x				x?	2.1, 4.1, 5.4.1/9
AE32	A.0.101.32	co	x				x?	1.4, 2.1, 4.2, 5.4.1/7, 6.2, 8.2
AE33	A.0.101.33	co		x?			x?	2.1, 4.3, 5.1, 5.4.3/5
AE34	A.0.101.34 (6)	co	x				x?	2.1
AE35	A.0.101.35 (11)	co	x	x			x?	1.4, 2.1, 7.2, 8.2
AE36	A.0.101.36 (2)	co	x					2.1, 6.2
AE37	A.0.101.37	co?	x					2.1
AE38	A.0.101.38 (25?)	co	x				x?	2.1, 4.2/3, 5.1, 6.2
AE39	A.0.101.39	co	x				x?	2.1, 5.4.1
AE40	A.0.101.40 (31)	co		x			x?	2.1, 3.1, 4.1/3/4, 5.1, 5.4.1/2/3/4/5/6/7/9, 6.2, 7.2, 8.2
AE41	A.0.101.41 (5)	co		x			x?	2.1, 7.2
AE42	A.0.101.42 (2)	co		x			x?	2.1, 5.4.1
AE43	A.0.101.43	co		x			x?	2.1
AE44	A.0.101.44	co		x			x?	2.1
AE45	A.0.101.45 (5)	co		x				2.1, 5.4.1
AE46	A.0.101.46	co		x				2.1, 4.1/2
AE47	A.0.101.47 (2)	co		x				2.1, 3.1, 4.1
AE48	A.0.101.48	co		x				2.1
AE49	A.0.101.49	co		x?				2.1, 3.1, 4.2
AE50	A.0.101.50 (4)	co			x		x?	2.1, 3.1, 4.2/3/4, 5.4.3/6/7, 7.2, 8.2

(continued)

b ref	p ref	gn	A	K	N	ic	oc	bf	1	2	index
AE51	A.0.101.51 (2)	co				x				x?	2.1, 5.4.1, 7.2, 8.3
AE52	A.0.101.52	co	x						x?		2.1, 7.2
AE53	A.0.101.53 (40)	co	x		x				x?		2.1, 5.4.3, 7.1
AE54	A.0.101.54	co				x					2.1
AE55	A.0.101.55	co		x							2.1
AE56	A.0.101.56 (25)	co			x					x?	2.1, 3.1, 4.1/3, 5.1, 5.4.1/3/7, 7.2
AE57	A.0.101.57 (19)	co			x						2.1, 4.1/3
AE58	A.0.101.58	co			x						2.1
AE59	A.0.101.59	co			x						2.1, 4.2, 7.2
AE60	A.0.101.60	co?			x						2.1
AE61	A.0.101.61	co			x						2.1
AE62	A.0.101.62	co			x						2.1
AE63	A.0.101.63	co			x						2.1
AE64	A.0.101.64	co			x						2.1
AE65	A.0.101.65	co			x						2.1
AE66	A.0.101.66 (17)	co			x					x?	2.1, 5.4.9, 7.2
AE67	A.0.101.67 (12)	co	x							x?	2.1, 5.4.1/3/6
AE68	A.0.101.68	co	x								2.1
AE69	A.0.101.69	co	x								2.1
AE70	A.0.101.70 (2)	co				x					2.1, 4.3, 5.4.1
AE71	A.0.101.71	ca		x						x	2.1
AE72	A.0.101.72	ca		x						x	2.1
AE73	A.0.101.73	ca		x						x	2.1, 5.4.9
AE74	A.0.101.74	ca		x						x	2.1
AE75	A.0.101.75	ca		x						x	2.1
AE76	A.0.101.76	ca		x						x	2.1
AE77	A.0.101.77	ca		x						x	2.1, 5.2, 5.4.3/5, 8.2

AE78	A.0.101.78	ca	x			x	2.1
AE79	A.0.101.79	ca		x			2.1
AE80	A.0.101.80	ca			x	x?	2.1, 8.3
AE81	A.0.101.81	ca			x	x?	2.1, 8.3
AE82	A.0.101.82	ca			x	x?	2.1, 8.3
AE83	A.0.101.83	ca			x	x?	2.1, 8.3
AE84	A.0.101.84	ca			x	x?	2.1, 8.3
AE85	A.0.101.85	ca			x	x?	2.1, 8.3
AE86	A.0.101.86	ca			x	x?	2.1, 8.3
AE87	A.0.101.87	ca			x	x?	2.1, 8.3
AE88	A.0.101.88	ca			x	x?	2.1, 8.3
AE89	A.0.101.89	ca			x	x?	2.1, 8.3
AE90	A.0.101.90	ca			x	x?	2.1, 8.3
AE91	A.0.101.91	ca			x	x?	2.1, 8.3
AE92	A.0.101.92	ca			x	x?	2.1, 5.2, 8.3
AE93	A.0.101.93	ca			x	x?	2.1, 5.2, 8.3
AE94	A.0.101.94	ca			x	x?	2.1, 8.3
AE95	A.0.101.95	ca			x	x?	2.1, 8.3
AE96	A.0.101.96	ca			x	x?	2.1, 8.3
AE97	A.0.101.97	ca			x	x?	2.1, 8.3
AE98	A.0.101.98	de	x				2.1, 3.1/2, 4.3
AE99	A.0.101.99 (2)	de	x				2.1, 4.3, 5.4.9
AE100	A.0.101.100	de	x				2.1, 4.2/3
AE101	A.0.101.101 (2)	de	x				2.1, 4.3
AE102	A.0.101.102 (6)	lt	x				2.1
AE103	A.0.101.103	lt	x				2.1
AE104	A.0.101.104	lt	x				2.1
AE105	A.0.101.105	lt	x				2.1
AE106	A.0.101.106	lt	x				2.1
AE107	A.0.101.107	lt	x				2.1

(continued)

b ref	p ref	gn	A	K	N	ic	oc	bf	1	2	index
AE108	A.0.101.108	lt	x								2.1, 7.2, 8.2
AE109	A.0.101.109 (7)	lt		x							2.1
AE110	A.0.101.110	lt?		x							2.1
AE111	A.0.101.111 (43)	lt			x						2.1, 4.3, 7.2
AE112	A.0.101.112 (5)	lt			x						2.1
AE113	A.0.101.113 (66)	lt		*x*	x						2.1
AE114	A.0.101.114 (4)	lt	x								2.1
AE115	A.0.101.115 (50)	lt	*x*	*x*	*x*	*x*					2.1, 7.2, 8.2
AE116	A.0.101.116 (9)	lt	*x*		x						2.1
AE117	A.0.101.117 (3)	lt	*x*		x?						2.1
AE118	A.0.101.118 (27)	lt	*x*		x						2.1
AE119	A.0.101.119	lt	x								2.1
AE120	A.0.101.120 (4)	lt		x							2.1
AE121	A.0.101.121 (3)	lt		x							2.1
AE122	A.0.101.122	lt		x							2.1
AE123	A.0.101.123 (14)	lt		x							2.1
AE124	A.0.101.124 (4)	lt		x							2.1
AE125	A.0.101.125 (11)	lt		x							2.1
AE126	A.0.101.126 (7)	lt			x						2.1
AE127	A.0.101.127 (14)	lt			x						2.1
AE128	A.0.101.128	lt			x						2.1
AE129	A.0.101.129 (16)	lt	x								2.1
AE130	A.0.101.130 (5)	lt		x							2.1
AE131	A.0.101.131	lt		x							2.1, 4.3
AE132	A.0.101.132	lt		x							2.1
AE133	A.0.101.133 (3)	co			x						2.1
AE134	A.0.101.134 (3)	co			x						2.1

AE135	A.0.101.135 (20)	lt			x					2.1
AE136	A.0.101.136	co			x					2.1
AE137	A.0.101.137 (8)	lt			x					2.1
AE138	A.0.101.138 (4)	lt?	x							2.1
AE139	A.0.101.1001	co			x					2.1
AE140	A.0.101.1002	co			x					2.1
AE141	A.0.101.1003	co			x					2.1
AE142	A.0.101.1004	ca	x							2.1
AE143	A.0.101.1005	co?	x							2.1
AE144	A.0.101.1006	co		x						2.1
AE145	A.0.101.2001	de		x						2.1
AE146	A.0.101.2002	de		x						2.1
AE147	A.0.101.2003	de		x						2.1
AE148	A.0.101.2004	de					x			2.1, 3.1/2, 4.1/2/3, 5.4.5/9, 7.2
AE149	A.0.101.2005	lt					x		x	2.1, 7.2
AE150	A.0.101.2006	de					x		x	1.5, 2.1, 5.3
AE151	A.0.101.2007 (2)	lt					x		x	2.1, 5.4.7
AE152	Finkel 2008b: "stone text 3"	co				x			x?	2.1, 4.3
AE153	Frahm 2009: 23	co	x						x?	1.5, 2.1, 4.1/3, 5.4.4/9, 7.2
AE154	Frahm 2009: 24	co	x					x?		2.1, 3.2, 4.1/2/4, 5.1, 5.4.4/6, 6.2, 7.2
AE155	Davies et al. 2008: MM L1	ca				x			x?	2.1
AE156	Davies et al. 2008: MM L2	ca				x			x?	2.1
AE157	Davies et al. 2008: MM L6	ca				x			x?	2.1
AE158	Davies et al. 2008: MM L8	ca				x			x?	2.1
AE159	Davies et al. 2008: MM R2	ca				x			x?	2.1
AE160	Davies et al. 2008: MM R3	ca				x			x?	2.1
AE161	Davies et al. 2008: MM R5	ca				x			x?	2.1
AE162	Davies et al. 2008: MM R7	ca				x			x?	2.1
AE163	Davies et al. 2008: MM R8	ca				x			x?	2.1
AE164	Curtis & Tallis 2008: NIM 1	ca		x				x?		2.1

(continued)

b ref	p ref	gn	A	K	N	ic	oc	bf	1	2	index
AE165	Curtis & Tallis 2008: NIM 2	ca		x					x?		2.1
AE166	Curtis & Tallis 2008: NIM 3	ca		x					x?		2.1
AE167	Reade & Finkel 2008: 601	de		x							2.1
AE168	Reade & Finkel 2008: 603	de			x						2.1
AE169	Reade & Finkel 2008: 607	de		x							2.1, 7.2
AE170	Reade & Finkel 2008: 615	de		x?							2.1
AE171	Ebeling 1923: 334	rp	x								2.1, 4.1/2, 7.2
AE172	Ebeling 1923: 342	rh	x								2.1
AE173	Ebeling 1953: 64	rh	x								2.1, 4.1/2
AE174	Kataja & Whiting 1995: 82/83/84 (3)	rd		x					x?		2.1, 4.1
AE175	Frahm 2009: 66	lo	x								2.1, 3.1, 5.3, 5.4.9

b ref	p ref	gn	A	K	N	ic	of	1	2	3	index
SE1	A.0.102.1	co		x				x			1.7.1, 2.1, 3.1, 4.1/2/3, 5.1, 5.4.1/2/3/4/6/7/9, 6.3, 7.3
SE2	A.0.102.1 (3)	co		x	x		x	x			1.5, 1.7.1, 2.1, 3.1/2, 4.1/2/3/4, 5.1/2/3, 5.4.1/2/3/4/5/6/7/8/9, 6.3, 7.3, 8.2/3
SE3	A.0.102.3	co		x				x			2.1, 4.3, 6.3, 8.2
SE4	A.0.102.4	co					x				2.1, 5.4.1
SE5	A.0.102.5 (2)	co				x		x			1.5, 2.1, 3.1/2, 4.1/4, 5.1/2/3, 5.4.1/2/4/5/6/7/8/9, 6.3, 7.3, 8.2/3
SE6	A.0.102.6 (14)	co	x	x					x		1.5, 1.7.1, 2.1, 3.1/2, 4.1/2/3/4, 5.1/2/3, 5.4.1/2/3/4/5/7/8/9, 6.3, 7.1/3, 8.2
SE7	A.0.102.7	co		x				x?			2.1
SE8	A.0.102.8 (4)	co		x					x		2.1, 4.2/4, 5.1, 5.4.2/3/9, 6.3, 7.3, 8.2
SE9	A.0.102.9	co	x?						x?		2.1, 4.1, 5.4.1
SE10	A.0.102.10	co	x						x		1.5, 2.1, 3.1/2, 4.2/3, 5.1/2, 5.4.2/3/5/6/7/9, 6.3, 7.3, 8.2
SE11	A.0.102.11	co	x						x		1.5, 2.1, 3.1/2, 8.2
SE12	A.0.102.12	co		x?					x		2.1, 3.2, 4.1/2/4, 5.4.2
SE13	A.0.102.13	co	x						x		2.1, 4.3, 5.4.7
SE14	A.0.102.14	co		x						x	1.5, 1.7.1, 2.1, 3.1/2, 4.2/3/4, 5.1, 5.4.1/2/3/5/7/9, 6.3, 7.3, 8.2
SE15	A.0.102.15	co	x							x?	2.1, 3.1
SE16	A.0.102.16	co		x						x	1.7.1, 2.1, 4.1/2/4, 5.1/2/3, 5.4.1/2/5/7/9, 6.3, 7.3, 8.2
SE17	A.0.102.17	co					x	x			2.1, 3.1/2, 4.2/4, 5.1, 5.4.1/2/5/7/8/9, 7.3, 8.2
SE18	A.0.102.18 (4)	co	x					x			2.1
SE19	A.0.102.19	co		x							2.1, 3.1/2

(continued)

b ref	p ref	gn	A	K	N	ic	of	1	2	3	index
SE20	A.0.102.20	co					x	x			2.1, 3.1, 5.1, 5.4.6/8/9, 6.3
SE21	A.0.102.21	co					x	x			1.5, 2.1, 4.1/3
SE22	A.0.102.22	co					x	x			2.1
SE23	A.0.102.23	co					x		x		2.1, 4.1, 5.1, 7.3
SE24	A.0.102.24	co					x		x		2.1, 6.3
SE25	A.0.102.25	co	x					x			1.5, 2.1, 3.2, 4.1/3/4, 5.1, 5.4.1/2/7/9, 6.3, 7.3
SE26	A.0.102.26	co	x					x			2.1, 4.1, 6.2
SE27	A.0.102.27	co	x							x?	2.1, 5.4.7, 6.3
SE28	A.0.102.28	co		x					x		2.1, 4.2/3, 5.1, 5.4.1/2/3/7/9, 6.3, 7.3, 8.2
SE29	A.0.102.29	co		x					x		2.1, 5.4.1/3/5/7, 6.3
SE30	A.0.102.30	co		x					x		2.1, 4.3, 5.4.1/7, 7.3, 8.2
SE31	A.0.102.31 (3)	co		x					x		2.1, 4.3, 5.1, 6.3
SE32	A.0.102.32	co		x					x		2.1, 4.3
SE33	A.0.102.33	co		x					x		2.1, 4.3
SE34	A.0.102.34	co		x					x		2.1, 4.3
SE35	A.0.102.35	co		x					x		2.1, 4.3
SE36	A.0.102.36 (2)	co		x					x		2.1, 4.3
SE37	A.0.102.37	co		x					x		2.1, 4.3
SE38	A.0.102.38	co			x				x?		2.1, 7.3
SE39	A.0.102.39 (7)	co	x						x		2.1
SE40	A.0.102.40	co	x							x	2.1, 4.3, 5.4.1/3/8/9, 6.3, 8.2
SE41	A.0.102.41 (11)	co				x					2.1, 3.2, 5.4.1/7
SE42	A.0.102.42 (4)	co	x							x	1.5, 2.1, 4.3, 5.4.7
SE43	A.0.102.43 (12)	co	x							x	2.1, 5.4.6/7
SE44	A.0.102.44 (109?)	co	x						x?		2.1

SE45	A.0.102.45 (3)	co	x				x?	2.1
SE46	A.0.102.46 (4)	co	x				x	1.5, 2.1
SE47	A.0.102.47 (4)	co	x				x?	2.1, 5.4.7
SE48	A.0.102.48 (2)	co	x				x?	2.1
SE49	A.0.102.49 (2)	co	x					2.1, 3.1, 4.1
SE50	A.0.102.50	co	x					2.1
SE51	A.0.102.51 (4)	co	x					2.1
SE52	A.0.102.52	co?	x					2.1
SE53	A.0.102.53 (2)	co	x			x?		2.1, 4.3
SE54	A.0.102.54 (4)	lt	x				x?	2.1, 4.3, 6.2
SE55	A.0.102.55 (2)	co	x					1.5, 2.1, 4.3, 5.3, 8.2
SE56	A.0.102.56 (2)	co		x				2.1, 4.1/2, 5.4.7, 7.3
SE57	A.0.102.57	co		x			x	2.1, 5.4.7, 7.3
SE58	A.0.102.58	co			x			2.1
SE59	A.0.102.59	ca?		x			x	2.1, 5.4.5, 8.2
SE60	A.0.102.60	ca		x			x	2.1
SE61	A.0.102.61	ca		x			x	2.1
SE62	A.0.102.62	ca		x			x	2.1, 4.3
SE63	A.0.102.63	ca			x	x		2.1, 8.3
SE64	A.0.102.64	ca			x	x		2.1, 8.3
SE65	A.0.102.65	ca			x	x		2.1, 8.3
SE66	A.0.102.66	ca			x	x		2.1, 5.4.3, 8.3
SE67	A.0.102.67	ca			x	x		2.1, 8.3
SE68	A.0.102.68	ca			x	x		2.1, 8.3
SE69	A.0.102.69	ca			x	x		2.1, 8.3
SE70	A.0.102.70	ca			x	x		2.1, 8.3
SE71	A.0.102.71	ca			x	x		2.1, 8.3
SE72	A.0.102.72	ca			x	x		2.1, 8.3
SE73	A.0.102.73	ca			x	x		2.1, 8.3
SE74	A.0.102.74	ca			x	x		2.1, 8.3

(continued)

b ref	p ref	gn	A	K	N	ic	of	1	2	3	index
SE75	A.0.102.75	ca				x		x			2.1, 8.3
SE76	A.0.102.76	ca				x		x			2.1, 5.4.2, 8.3
SE77	A.0.102.77	ca				x		x			2.1, 8.3
SE78	A.0.102.78	ca				x		x			2.1, 8.3
SE79	A.0.102.79	ca				x		x			2.1, 8.3
SE80	A.0.102.80	ca				x		x			2.1, 8.3
SE81	A.0.102.81	ca				x		x			2.1, 8.3
SE82	A.0.102.82	ca				x		x			2.1, 8.3
SE83	A.0.102.83	ca				x		x			2.1, 8.3
SE84	A.0.102.84	ca				x		x			2.1, 8.3
SE85	A.0.102.85	ca				x		x			2.1, 8.3
SE86	A.0.102.86	ca				x		x			2.1, 8.3
SE87	A.0.102.87	ca		x						x	2.1
SE88	A.0.102.88	ca		x						x	2.1, 5.3, 5.4.9, 8.2
SE89	A.0.102.89	ca		x						x	2.1, 5.4.3, 8.2
SE90	A.0.102.90	ca		x						x	2.1
SE91	A.0.102.91	ca		x						x	2.1
SE92	A.0.102.92	lt	x?								1.5, 2.1, 5.3
SE93	A.0.102.93 (2)	de	x						x?		2.1, 4.3, 5.4.7
SE94	A.0.102.94	de	x						x?		2.1
SE95	A.0.102.95	de			x						1.5, 2.1, 3.1/2, 4.1/3, 7.3
SE96	A.0.102.96 (2)	de				x					2.1
SE97	A.0.102.97	de									1.5, 2.1, 4.3, 5.3
SE98	Fadhil 1990: A/B (2)	co		x							2.1
SE99	A.0.102.99 (14)	lt	x							x?	2.1
SE100	A.0.102.100 (12)	lt	x							x?	2.1
SE101	A.0.102.101	lt	x						x?		2.1, 7.3

SE102	A.0.102.102 (6)	lt	x						x?		2.1
SE103	A.0.102.103 (2)	lt	x					x?			2.1, 4.3, 6.3
SE104	A.0.102.104 (13)	lt	x			x					2.1
SE105	A.0.102.105 (3)	lt									2.1
SE106	A.0.102.106 (43)	lt	x		x						2.1
SE107	A.0.102.107 (5)	lt			x						2.1, 7.3
SE108	A.0.102.108 (7)	lt	x								2.1
SE109	A.0.102.109 (5)	lt	x								2.1
SE110	A.0.102.110 (2)	lt	x								2.1
SE111	A.0.102.111 (77)	lt		x							2.1
SE112	A.0.102.112	co?		x							2.1
SE113	A.0.102.113	lt		x							2.1
SE114	A.0.102.114	lt		x							2.1
SE115	A.0.102.115	lt		x							2.1
SE116	A.0.102.116	lt			x						2.1
SE117	A.0.102.1001	co									2.1, 5.4.3
SE118	A.0.102.1002	co		x					x?		2.1, 5.4.5
SE119	A.0.102.1003	de									2.1, 3.1, 5.3, 5.4.5, 8.2
SE120	A.0.102.1004	lt									2.1
SE121	A.0.102.1005	de				x					2.1
SE122	A.0.102.1006	?				x					2.1
SE123	A.0.102.1007	?	x								2.1
SE124	A.0.102.1008	co			x						2.1
SE125	A.0.102.1009	co?				x					2.1
SE126	A.0.102.1010	co?			x						2.1
SE127	A.0.102.1011	de?									2.1
SE128	A.0.102.1012	?									2.1
SE129	A.0.102.1013	?									2.1
SE130	A.0.102.1003	de?								x?	2.1
SE131	Frahm 2009: 28	co	x						x?		2.1, 3.1

(continued)

b ref	p ref	gn	A	K	N	ic	of	1	2	3	index
SE132	Frahm 2011a: K.1	co?	x								2.1
SE133	Frahm 2011a: K.2	co?	x								2.1
SE134	Frahm 2011a: III:1	ca	x								2.1
SE135	Frahm 2011a: III:2	ca	x								2.1
SE136	Frahm 2011a: III:3	ca	x								2.1
SE137	Frahm 2011a: III:4	ca	x								2.1
SE138	Frahm 2011a: III:5	ca	x								2.1
SE139	Frahm 2011a: III:6	ca	x								2.1
SE140	Frahm 2011a: III:9	ca	x								2.1
SE141	Frahm 2011a: III:10	ca	x								2.1
SE142	Frahm 2011a: III:12	ca	x								2.1
SE143	Frahm 2011a: III:13	ca	x								2.1
SE144	Frahm 2011a: III:17	ca	x								2.1
SE145	Frahm 2011a: III:20	ca	x								2.1
SE146	Frahm 2011a: III:22	ca	x								2.1
SE147	Frahm 2011a: III:49	ca	x								2.1
SE148	Frahm 2011a: III:61	ca	x								2.1
SE149	Frahm 2011a: III:63	ca	x								2.1
SE150	Frahm 2011a: III:65	ca	x								2.1
SE151	Frahm 2011a: III:67	ca	x								2.1
SE152	Frahm 2011a: III:68	ca	x								2.1
SE153	Reade & Finkel 2008: 608	de		x?							2.1
SE154	Ebeling 1919: 98	rp	x								1.7.2, 2.1, 4.1/2, 5.4.7

b ref	p ref	gn	A	K	N	ic	oc	bf	1	2	index
Ad2E1	A.0.98.1 (3)	co	x								2.1, 3.2, 4.1, 5.3, 5.4.1/5
Ad2E2	A.0.98.2	co	x								2.1
Ad2E3	A.0.98.3 (12)	co	x								2.1
Ad2E4	A.0.98.4 (2)	de	x								2.1, 4.1
Ad2E5	A.0.98.5 (4)	lt	x								2.1
Ad2E6	A.0.98.6	lt				x					2.1
Ad2E7	A.0.98.1001	lt	x								2.1
An2E1	A.0.99.1 (3)	co	x						x		2.1, 4.1, 5.3, 5.4.2/7, 6.4
An2E2	A.0.99.2 (3)	co	x							x	2.1, 3.1, 4.1/2/3/4, 5.1/2/3, 5.4.1/2/3/4/5/6/7/9, 6.4, 7.2/4
An2E3	A.0.99.3	co	x							x	2.1, 4.4
An2E4	A.0.99.4 (3)	co	x							x	2.1, 4.1/4, 5.1/3, 5.4.2
An2E5	A.0.99.5	co			x					x	2.1, 7.4
An2E6	A.0.99.6	lt	x								2.1
An2E7	A.0.99.7 (10)	lt			x						2.1
An2E8	A.0.99.8	lt				x					2.1
An2E9	A.0.99.1002	lt	x								2.1, 5.4.7
An2E10	A.0.99.1003	?	x								2.1
An2E11	Frahm 2009: 18	co	x?								2.1
An2E12	Fadhil 1990: p. 481t.	lt	x?								2.1
TN2E1	A.0.100.1	co	x								2.1, 3.1/2, 4.1/2, 5.4.1/4/7, 7.2
TN2E2	A.0.100.2	co	x								2.1, 4.1/4, 5.4.1/4
TN2E3	A.0.100.3	co	x								2.1, 4.3, 5.4.6/9
TN2E4	A.0.100.4	co	x								2.1, 4.1, 5.4.1
TN2E5	A.0.100.5 (4)	co	x							x	1.5, 2.1, 4.4, 5.1/2/3, 5.4.3/4/5/7/9, 7.1/4
TN2E6	A.0.100.6	lt				x?					2.1, 5.4.1
TN2E7	A.0.100.7	co	x?								2.1

(continued)

b ref	p ref	gn	A	K	N	ic	oc	bf	1	2	index
TN2E8	A.0.100.8	de?									2.1
TN2E9	A.0.100.9	lt					x				2.1
TN2E10	A.0.100.10	lt									2.1
TN2E11	A.0.100.11	lt				x?					2.1, 4.1
TN2E12	A.0.100.12	lt			x						2.1
TN2E13	A.0.100.13 (2)	lt			x						2.1
TN2E14	A.0.100.14 (2)	co	x								2.1
TN2E15	A.0.100.15 (3)	lt	x								2.1
TN2E16	A.0.100.16 (5)	lt	x								2.1
TN2E17	A.0.100.17	lt			x						2.1
TN2E18	A.0.100.1001	lt?			x						2.1
TN2E19	A.0.100.1002	lt?			x						2.1
TN2E20	A.0.100.1003	lt?			x?						2.1
TN2E21	A.0.100.1004	co?						x			2.1
TN2E22	Frahm 2009: 21	co	x?							x	2.1
TN2E23	Frahm 2009: 22	co	x?								2.1, 4.1, 5.4.6/7
SA5E1	A.0.103.1 (2)	co		x	*x*					x	1.5, 1.7.1, 2.1, 3.1/2, 4.1/2/3/4, 5.1/2, 5.4.1/3/4/5/6/7/9, 6.4, 7.4
SA5E2	A.0.103.2	co	x							x	1.5, 2.1, 3.1/2, 4.1/2/4, 5.3, 5.4.5/7/9, 7.4
SA5E3	A.0.103.3	co	x								2.1
SA5E4	A.0.103.4	lfg	x?							x	2.1, 3.2, 4.4, 5.4.5, 7.4
SA5E5	A.0.103.5 (9)	de	x								1.5, 2.1, 4.1
SA5E6	A.0.103.6 (3)	de	x								2.1
SA5E7	A.0.103.7 (4)	de	x								2.1
SA5E8	A.0.103.8	de	x								2.1
SA5E9	A.0.103.9 (15)	lt	*x*		x					x	2.1, 5.4.1/5

SA5E10	A.0.103.10	lt		x							2.1
SA5E11	A.0.103.2001	lt	x?								2.1
SA5E12	A.0.102.1001	de				x				x	2.1, 3.1, 7.4
SA5E13	A.0.102.1002	lt				x				x	2.1, 7.4
SA5E14	Kataja & Whiting 1995: 76t.	rd			x?						2.1
SA5E15	Parpola & Watanabe 1988: 1	lo		x?					x?		1.5, 2.1, 3.1/2, 4.1, 5.4.5/7/9, 6.4
An3E1	A.0.104.1 (3)	co		x							2.1, 4.1, 5.4.7
An3E2	A.0.104.2	co						x		x?	1.5, 2.1, 5.4.6/7, 6.4
An3E3	A.0.104.3	co						x	x?		2.1, 5.3, 5.4.5/7/9, 6.4
An3E4	A.0.104.4	co									2.1, 5.4.1
An3E5	A.0.104.5, Siddall 2013: A1	co					x				2.1, 3.1, 4.1/3, 5.4.7
An3E6	A.0.104.6	co					x			x?	2.1, 3.1/2, 4.1/2, 5.4.5/7, 6.4
An3E7	A.0.104.7	co					x			x?	2.1, 3.1, 4.3, 5.1, 5.4.7, 8.4
An3E8	A.0.104.8	co		x						x	2.1, 4.1/2, 5.3, 5.4.1/3/5/6, 8.4
An3E9	A.0.104.9	rd			x						2.1, 4.1, 5.4.5/7
An3E10	A.0.104.10 (15)	de	x								2.1
An3E11	A.0.104.11 (2)	de	x								2.1
An3E12	A.0.104.12 (4)	lt	x								2.1
An3E13	A.0.104.13 (4)	co			x				x?		2.1, 4.3
An3E14	A.0.104.14 (13)	co			x						2.1
An3E15	A.0.104.15 (11)	lt			x						2.1
An3E16	A.0.104.16 (2)	lt		x							2.1
An3E17	A.0.104.17	lt?		x							2.1
An3E18	A.0.104.18	lt?		x							2.1
An3E19	A.0.104.19 (2)	lt?		x							2.1
An3E20	A.0.104.20	lt		x							2.1
An3E21	A.0.104.21 (2)	de	x								2.1, 4.3
An3E22	A.0.104.1001	co						x			2.1
An3E23	A.0.104.1002	lt?			x						2.1
An3E24	A.0.104.1003	ca			x						2.1

(continued)

b ref	p ref	gn	A	K	N	ic	oc	bf	1	2	index
An3E25	A.0.104.2001	lt	x								2.1, 5.4.9
An3E26	A.0.104.2002 (2)	de		x					x?		2.1, 3.1/2, 5.4.1/7/9
An3E27	A.0.104.2003	lt		x?							2.1
An3E28	A.0.104.2004	lt		x?							2.1
An3E29	A.0.104.2005	lt		x?							2.1
An3E30	A.0.104.2006	lt					x?		x?		2.1
An3E31	A.0.104.2007	de?	x						x?		2.1
An3E32	A.0.104.2008	lt					x?		x?		2.1
An3E33	A.0.104.2009	de									2.1
An3E34	A.0.104.2010 (2)	co						x		x	2.1, 3.1/2, 4.4, 5.4.5/7/9, 6.4
An3E35	A.0.104.2011	co				x?				x	2.1, 5.4.7/9
An3E36	A.0.104.2012	co	x								2.1, 5.4.7
An3E37	A.0.104.2013	de	x?								2.1, 5.4.7
An3E38	A.0.104.2014	lt		x							2.1
An3E39	A.0.104.2015	lt									2.1
An3E40	A.0.104.2016	de	x?								2.1, 5.4.7
An3E41	A.0.104.2017	lt									2.1
An3E42	Siddall 2013: B1	de					x				2.1, 3.1, 4.1, 5.4.7
An3E43	Frahm 2009: 29	ltg	x?								2.1, 3.2, 4.1/2/4
An3E44	Frahm 2009: 79	rp	x?								2.1, 3.1, 4.2
An3E45	Kataja & Whiting 1995: 1/2/3 (3)	rd	x							x	2.1, 3.1, 4.1/2
An3E46	Kataja & Whiting 1995: 4	rd	x								2.1
An3E47	Kataja & Whiting 1995: 5	rd	x								2.1
An3E48	Kataja & Whiting 1995: 6	rd		x?							2.1, 5.4.7
An3E49	Kataja & Whiting 1995: 7	rd		x?							2.1, 5.4.7
An3E50	Kataja & Whiting 1995: 8	rd		x?							2.1, 5.4.7
An3E51	Kataja & Whiting 1995: 9	rd		x?							1.7.2, 2.1, 5.4.7

An3E52	Kataja & Whiting 1995: 10	rd		x?						x	2.1, 5.4.7
An3E53	Kataja & Whiting 1995: 11	rd		x?						x	2.1, 5.4.7
An3E54	Kataja & Whiting 1995: 12	rd		x?							2.1, 5.4.7
An3E55	Kataja & Whiting 1995: 69/70 (2)	rd	x						x		2.1, 3.1, 4.2
An3E56	Kataja & Whiting 1995: 71/72/73 (3)	rd	x							x	2.1, 3.1, 4.2
An3E57	Kataja & Whiting 1995: 74	rd	x								2.1
An3E58	Kataja & Whiting 1995: 76b.	rd			x?					x	2.1
An3E59	Grayson 1975: 21 (3)	rc		x?						x	2.1, 5.4.3/5/7, 6.4
S4E1	A.0.105.1	co						x		x	2.1, 4.1, 5.4.7
S4E2	A.0.105.2	co					x?				1.5, 2.1, 3.1/2, 4.1/3, 5.4.5/7
S4E3	A.0.105.3	ltg	x?						x		2.1, 3.2, 4.1/2/4
S4E4	A.0.105.1001	lt?	x								2.1
Ad3E1	A.0.106.1	co?	x								2.1, 3.2
An5E1	A.0.107.1	rd									2.1
An5E2	Parpola & Watanabe 1988: 2	lo		x?					x?		1.5, 2.1, 3.1/2, 4.1, 5.2/3, 5.4.1/9

2 List of the iconography

This appendix lists and classifies all the iconographic entities of Ashurnasirpal II (37), Shalmaneser III (26), and the other kings (17), totalling 80. The abbreviations in the first row stand for: **b ref** reference in book, **A** Assur, **K** Kalhu (Nimrud), **N** Nineveh, **ic** the rest of the inner core (including Balawat), **oc** the outer core, **bf** the border areas/foreign lands, **of** the two latest mentioned areas combined, **1/2/3** first/second/third regnal phase. For the abbreviations in the first column, see "Abbreviations". All numbers following author/publisher and publishing year (see publication column) refer to figures/plates and not to pages. Crosses indicate attestation, empty cell lack of attestation. The final column provides an index. The numbers in the index column refer to (sub)sections. The entities are primarily listed according to their respective types and size, and secondarily, whenever relevant, also to order in/date of relevant publication. The iconographic sources listed here belong to the foundations of this study, and are described in section 2.1.

b ref	publication(s)	iconographic entity	A	K	N	ic	oc	bf	1	2	index
AI1	Weidner 1939: 86; J. M. Russell 1998a: 214–220	wall reliefs, Nabu or Ishtar temple			x					x?	2.1, 5.2, 7.2
AI2	Meuszyński 1972	wall reliefs, Ninurta temple		x						x	2.1, 3.2
AI3	Meuszyński 1976: 8–10	wall reliefs, Central Building		x							2.1, 3.2
AI4	Meuszyński 1981; Paley & Sobolewski 1987, 1992	(monumental) wall reliefs, North-West Palace		x					x		1.7.2, 2.1, 3.1/2, 4.1/4, 5.4.1/2/3/4/5/6/7/9, 6.2, 7.2
AI5	Kühne 1987–88: 17	wall relief, local palace					x				2.1, 4.1, 7.2
AI6	Mahmoud & Kühne 1993–94: 23–29	wall reliefs, local palace					x			x	2.1, 5.4.7, 7.2
AI7	Meuszyński 1972	colossi, Ninurta temple		x						x	2.1, 4.1
AI8	Meuszyński 1981; Paley & Sobolewski 1992	colossi, North-West Palace		x							2.1, 4.1
AI9	Meuszyński 1976: 8–10	colossi, Central Building		x							2.1, 4.1
AI10	Mahmoud & Kühne 1993–94: 23–29	colossi and sculpture, local palace					x			x	2.1, 5.4.7
AI11	Madhloom 1970: LXXVI, 2	sculptures, Sharrat-niphi temple		x						x?	2.1, 3.2
AI12	Strommenger 1970: 1	statue, Sharrat-niphi temple		x						x?	2.1, 3.1, 4.1/2/3, 5.4.4
AI13	Curtis & Tallis 2008: 5–38	embossings on door bands, local palace				x				x?	2.1, 4.4, 5.2, 5.4.1/2/3/4/5/7/9, 7.2, 8.2/3
AI14	Curtis & Tallis 2008: 55–88	embossings on door bands, Mamu temple				x				x?	2.1, 3.1/2, 4.1, 5.4.1/2/3/4/5/7/9, 7.2, 8.3
AI15	Curtis & Tallis 2008: 95–97	embossings on door bands, North-West Palace		x					x		2.1, 5.4.1/3

AI16	Börker-Klähn 1982: 138	reliefs on Rassam Obelisk	x						x	2.1, 4.4, 5.1/2, 5.4.1/3/5/7/9
AI17	Börker-Klähn 1982: 134	relief on Babil Stele					x	x		2.1, 4.1, 6.2, 7.2
AI18	Börker-Klähn 1982: 135	relief on Kurkh Monolith					x	x		2.1, 4.2, 8.3
AI19	Börker-Klähn 1982: 136	relief on Ninurta temple stele	x					x		2.1, 4.1/2/4, 7.2
AI20	Börker-Klähn 1982: 137	relief on Banquet Stele	x						x	2.1, 4.2, 5.4.4
AI21	Campbell Thompson & Hutchinson 1931: 31:2	painting on glazed brick, local palace?		x					x?	2.1, 5.4.9
AI22	Reade 1983: 41	painting on glazed brick	x							2.1, 5.4.4, 7.2
AI23	Layard 1853a; Canby 1971; Paley 1976	(miniature) wall reliefs, North-West Palace	x					x		2.1, 4.1/2/4, 5.2, 7.2
AI24	Born & Seidl 1995: 22	embossings on metal helmet								2.1, 4.1, 5.4.1/6
AI25	Mallowan & Davies 1970: I:1	carving on ivory	x							2.1, 3.1, 4.2, 5.4.4
AI26	Mallowan & Davies 1970: IV:4	carving on ivory	x							2.1, 5.4.1/2
AI27	Mallowan & Davies 1970: IV:5	carving on ivory	x							2.1, 5.4.3
AI28	Mallowan & Davies 1970: V:8	carving on ivory	x							2.1, 5.4.4
AI29	Searight et al. 2008: 600	reliefs on stone vessel, Ninurta temple	x							2.1, 5.4.3
AI30	Searight et al. 2008: 603	reliefs on stone vessel, Nabu temple		x						2.1, 5.4.7
AI31	Collon 1987: 339	engraving on seal	x							2.1, 4.2
AI32	Collon 1987: 340	engraving on seal	x?							2.1, 3.1, 4.2
AI33	Collon 1987: 341	engraving on seal				x?				2.1, 3.1, 4.2
AI34	Collon 1987: 447	engraving on seal								2.1
AI35	Collon 1987: 693	engraving on seal	x?							2.1, 5.2
AI36	Collon 1987: 733	engraving on seal	x							2.1, 4.1/4
AI37	Collon 1987: 880	engraving on seal	x?							2.1, 4.1, 5.2

b ref	publication	iconographic entity	A	K	N	ic	of	1	2	3	index
SI1	Meuszyński 1976: 11	wall relief, Centre Palace		x					x		2.1, 7.3
SI2	Mallowan 1966: 6	colossus, city gate		x							2.1, 4.1
SI3	Sobolewski 1982a: 6	colossi, Centre Palace		x					x		2.1, 4.1
SI4	Strommenger 1970: 2–3	seated statue, city gate	x					x			2.1, 4.3
SI5	Strommenger 1970: 4–5	Kurba'il Statue, Fort Shalmaneser		x?					x		2.1, 4.1/2/3, 7.3
SI6	Strommenger 1970: 6a	statue, city gate	x							x	2.1, 4.2/4, 5.4.4/8, 7.3
SI7	Strommenger 1970: 6b, 7	statue, Kalhu citadel		x						x	2.1, 4.2, 7.3
SI8	Strommenger 1970: 15c–d	statue AX2, temple	x								2.1, 4.2, 7.3
SI9	Curtis & Tallis 2008: 100b	embossings on a door band, Anu-Adad temple	x						x?		2.1, 3.1, 4.2, 5.4.9
SI10	Schachner 2007: 1–16, 17–62	embossings on door bands, local palace				x		x			2.1, 3.2, 4.1/2/3/4, 5.1/2, 5.4.1/2/3/4/5/6/7/9, 6.3, 7.3, 8.2/3
SI11	Börker-Klähn 1982: 152	reliefs on Black Obelisk		x						x	2.1, 4.1/2/4, 5.2/3, 5.4.1/2/3/5/7/9
SI12	Orlamünde 2011a: III	reliefs on Assur Obelisk	x								2.1, 7.3
SI13	Börker-Klähn 1982: 148	relief on Kurkh Stele					x	x			2.1, 4.2, 7.3, 8.3
SI14	D. Oates 1963: 3–7	reliefs on throne base, Fort Shalmaneser		x				x?			2.1, 4.1/4, 5.4.1/2/3/5/7/8, 6.3, 7.3
SI15	Taşyürek 1979: 15–16	relief on a cliff at Kenk					x	x			2.1, 4.3
SI16	Schachner 2009: 225–227	relief on a cliff at the Tigris source					x	x			2.1, 4.1/2/3, 5.4.7
SI17	Schachner 2009: 228–233	relief on a cliff at the Tigris source					x		x		2.1, 4.1/3, 5.4.7
SI18	Reade 1963: 9	painting on a glazed brick panel		x							2.1, 3.2, 4.1/2/4, 5.4.4, 7.3

SI19	Mallowan & Davies 1970: II:2	carving on ivory	x		2.1, 4.2
SI20	Mallowan & Davies 1970: III:3	carving on ivory	x		2.1, 4.2
SI21	Mallowan & Davies 1970: V:7	carving on ivory	x		2.1, 5.4.4/7, 7.3
SI22	Mallowan & Davies 1970: XIII:41	carving on ivory	x		2.1
SI23	Mallowan & Davies 1970: XX–XXI:67	carving on ivory	x		2.1, 4.2, 5.4.3
SI24	Mallowan & Davies 1970: XX–XXI:69	carving on ivory	x		2.1, 5.4.3
SI25	Collon 1987: 338	engraving on seal	x?		2.1, 5.4.4
SI26	Sachs 1953: 18:1	engraving on the royal seal		x?	2.1, 5.2, 7.3

b ref	publication(s)	iconographic entity	A	K	N	ic	oc	bf	1	2	index
TN2I1	Orthmann 1971: 5a	relief on Terqa Stele						x			2.1, 3.2, 5.4.7
SA5I1	Börker-Klähn 1982: 161	relief on Nabu Stele		x						x	2.1, 3.1, 4.1/2, 5.4.6/7, 8.4
SA5I2	Searight et al. 2008: 602	reliefs on a stone vessel, Nergal temple				x				x	2.1, 4.1/2, 5.4.7, 8.3
An3I1	Reade 1981b: 20c	obelisk fragment			x						2.1
An3I2	Börker-Klähn 1982: 163	relief on Saba'a Stele					x			x?	2.1, 4.1/2/4, 5.4.5, 7.4, 8.4
An3I3	Börker-Klähn 1982: 164	relief on Tell al-Rimah Stele					x			x?	2.1, 5.4.5, 7.4
An3I4	Börker-Klähn 1982: 165	relief on Dur-Katlimmu Stele					x				2.1
An3I5	Börker-Klähn 1982: 166	relief on Pazarcik Stele						x	x?		2.1, 4.3, 5.4.7, 6.4
An3I6	Börker-Klähn 1982: 167	relief on Antakya Stele						x		x?	2.1, 4.3, 5.4.5/7, 6.4, 7.4
An3I7	Börker-Klähn 1982: 168	relief on Para Stele						x			2.1, 4.3
An3I8	Strommenger 1970: 8–9	pair of statues, Nabu temple		x					x?		2.1, 3.1, 4.1, 5.4.7
An3I9	Strommenger 1970: Abb. 8	pair of statues, Nabu temple		x					x?		2.1, 4.1
An3I10	Strommenger 1970: 10	pair of statues, Nabu temple		x					x?		2.1, 3.1, 4.1
An3I11	Sachs 1953: 19:7	engraving on the royal seal			x?						2.1, 5.2
An3I12	Collon 1987: 554	engraving on seal									2.1, 3.1, 5.4.5/7
An3I13	Collon 1987: 573	engraving on seal									2.1, 3.1, 4.1/2
S4I1	Pritchard 1969: 453	relief on Tell Abta Stele					x?				2.1, 4.1, 5.4.5/7

3 Spatial distribution of the major primary sources

This appendix gives the spatial distribution of the totally 452 “texts”, 1889 “exemplars”, and 80 “iconographic entities” of the kings of the Early Neo-Assyrian Period (see apps. 1–2). The abbreviations stand for: **A** Assur, **K** Kalhu (Nimrud), **N** Nineveh, **B** Balawat, **ic** the rest of the inner core, **oc** the outer core, **bf** the border areas or foreign lands, **unpr** unprovenanced. Numbers within parantheses indicate quantity of texts/exemplars or iconographic entities. This appendix is centred on in section 2.1 and chapter 7.

texts	A	K	N	B	ic	oc	bf	unpr
eNA I (42)	61,9 % (26)	0 % (0)	19,0 % (8)	0 % (0)	9,5 % (4)	2,4 % (1)	2,4 % (1)	4,8 % (2)
Ashurnasirpal II (175)	12,0 % (21)	41,1 % (72)	24,0 % (42)	17,7 % (31)	1,1 % (2)	2,3 % (4)	1,1 % (2)	0,6 % (1)
Shalmaneser III (154)	40,9 % (63)	24,0 % (37)	3,9 % (6)	16,9 % (26)	2,6 % (4)	0,6 % (1)	4,5 % (7)	6,5 % (10)
eNA III (81)	35,8 % (29)	29,6 % (24)	12,3 % (10)	0 % (0)	3,7 % (3)	8,6 % (7)	3,7 % (3)	6,2 % (5)
Total in %	**30,8**	**29,4**	**14,6**	**12,6**	**2,9**	**2,9**	**2,9**	**4,0**

exemplars	A	K	N	B	ic	oc	bf	unpr
eNA I (85)	69,4 % (59)	0 % (0)	21,2 % (18)	0 % (0)	4,7 % (4)	1,2 % (1)	1,2 % (1)	2,4 % (2)
Ashurnasirpal II (1123)	10,2 % (114)	53,8 % (605)	31,3 % (352)	3,5 % (39)	0,3 % (3)	0,4 % (5)	0,2 % (2)	0,3 % (3)
Shalmaneser III (515)	58,6 % (302)	23,9 % (123)	4,1 % (21)	5,2 % (27)	3,1 % (16)	0,2 % (1)	1,4 % (7)	3,5 % (18)
eNA III (166)	41,6 % (69)	18,7 % (31)	28,3 % (47)	0 % (0)	1,8 % (3)	4,2 % (7)	2,4 % (4)	3,0 % (5)
Total in %	**28,8**	**40,2**	**23,2**	**3,5**	**1,4**	**0,7**	**0,7**	**1,5**

iconographic entities	A	K	N	B	ic	oc	bf	unpr
Ashurnasirpal II (37)	0 % (0)	64,9 % (24)	8,1 % (3)	5,4 % (2)	0 % (0)	10,8 % (4)	5,4 % (2)	5,4 % (2)
Shalmaneser III (26)	19,2 % (5)	57,7 % (15)	3,8 % (1)	3,8 % (1)	0 % (0)	0 % (0)	15,4 % (4)	0 % (0)
eNA I & III (17)	0 % (0)	23,5 % (4)	11,8 % (2)	0 % (0)	5,9 % (1)	23,5 % (4)	23,5 % (4)	11,8 % (2)
Total in %	**6,3**	**53,8**	**7,5**	**3,8**	**1,3**	**10,0**	**12,5**	**5,0**

4 Deity hierarchy in the texts

This appendix, used e.g. in chapter 3, illustrates internal hierarchy among the great gods based on the longest deity sequences (three units or more for eNA II, five or more for eNA I, III) in the sections of "invocation of deities" and "concluding formulae" found in the texts of the Early Neo-Assyrian kings. Numbers indicate position in sequence. Empty cell denotes absence in sequence. Crosses stand for unknown order in alternative version of the same edition. The text abbreviations in bold refer to the text codes in appendix 1, and the king abbreviations in bold to those in "Abbreviations". In the second table, letters refer to the six editions of Shalmaneser III's annals, identified and termed A–F in Schramm 1973: 70–81. Elsewhere, A and B refer to sections of invocations of deities and concluding formulae respectively.

Deity hierarchy in the inscriptions of Ashurnasirpal II

	17A	17B	19	20	32	38B1	38B2	47	49
Aššur	1		1	1	1	1	1	1	1
Anu	2	1		2				2	
Enlil	11	2		3				3	
Ea/Nudimmud	3	3		4				4	
Sîn	4		3	5					
Adad	6		2	6			2	5	2
Marduk	5			8					
Šamaš	12		4	7		2		6	
Ninurta/Utulu	7			9	2				
Nusku	8			11					
Nergal	10			10					
Ninlil/Mullissu	9			12					
Erra							3		
Ištar	13		5	13	3	3			3

Deity hierarchy in the inscriptions of Shalmaneser III

	1	A	B	C	D	E	F	21	22	39	43	46
Aššur		1		1		1	1	1	1	1	1	1
Anu		2		2		2	2			2		
Enlil/Bēl		3		3		3	3					
Ea		4		4		7	4					
Adad						4	6	4	2	3	2	2
Sîn		5		5		8	5	2	3			3
Šamaš		6		6		-/x	7	3	4			4
Ninurta/Utulu				7		5	9					
Ištar		7		8		6	13	5	5		3	5
Marduk/Bēl						9	8					
Nergal						-/x	10					6
Nusku						-/x	11					
Ninlil/Mullissu						-/x	12					

Deity hierarchy in the inscriptions of the other kings

	Ad2E3B	An2E2A	TN2E1A	SA5E15B	An3E2B	An3E3B	An3E9B	An3E34A	An3E52B	S4E1B	S4E2A	An5E2B
Aššur	1	1	1		1	1	1	1	1	1		1
Anu			2	3				2				2
Enlil/Bēl	1*	2	3		4		5	3	3			4
Ea			4	5				4				6
Adad	2		6	8	2	3			5	3		12
Sîn	3	3	5	7	6	4					4	8
Šamaš	4	4	7	6		5	2		2	5	3	10
Ninurta/Utulu		6	9		5		6		7			18
Ištar	5	10	13				8	8	4		5	
Marduk/Bēl		5	8	1		2	4	5		2	1	14
Nergal		7	10				7		6			
Nusku		8	11									
Ninlil/Mullissu		9	12	4								5
Nabû				2			3	6			2	16
Sibitti								7	8	4		
Zababa				9								
Bēr					3							
Gula								9				19
Antu												3
Damkina												7
Nūr												11
Nikkal												9
Šala												13
Ṣarpanītu												15
Tašmētu												17
Uraš												20

5 Divine titles and epithets in the texts of Ashurnasirpal II

Listing in alphabetical order of all the divine titles and epithets attested in the text corpus of Ashurnasirpal II. Quantifications (abbr. **quant**) indicate total number of attestations in "texts" and "exemplars" with the latter numbers within parantheses. If an epithet is shared by several deities, numbers first refer to those valid for an individual deity mirroring the order of the third column, and then to the total number of attestations, all deities combined. The final column (abbr. **at/in**, attestations/index) gives information on place of attestation in the primary sources and provides a complete index referring to the relevant (sub)sections in the book. The data concerning attestations and index are separated graphically by "/". If an epithet is attested more than five times, a selection of the first, i.e. in their order in the AE-list, and "best", i.e. fully assigned and largely unreconstructed, attestations is given. When an epithet is shared by several deities, at least one attestation for each deity is provided, the respective data separated graphically by ";". The prefix AE is implicit. This appendix is referred to mainly in chapter 3.

title/epithet	translation	deity	quant	at/in
abi ilāni	father of the deities	Enlil	4 (5)	8, 17:i8, 20:3, [47:2]
aḫḫūšu/ša	his/her brothers	“the gods”	2 (3)	28:i3; 148:5/4.2
ālik pānija	he who marches ahead of me	Nergal	1 (1)	154:14′/3.2
ālikat maḫri	she who marches in the front	Sharrat-niphi	1 (2)	28:i3
ālikūt maḫri ummānātija	they who march in the front of my troops	Ashur, Adad, Ishtar, Shamash, Sin	1 x 5 = 5 (5)	19:4/3.2, 8.3
ālilu	heroic one	Ninurta	3 (6)	1:i6, 3:11, 4
apkal ilāni	sage of the deities	Marduk, Ninurta	3, 3 (3, 6) = 6 (9)	8, 17:i5, 20:8; 1:i5, 3:9/3.1
aplu rēštu	first son	Ninurta	3 (6)	1:i1–2, 3:3, 4/3.1
ašarēd ilāni	foremost among the deities	Ninurta	4 (7)	1:i1, 3:1, 4, 169:2/7.2
ašarēd kibrāti	foremost in the quarters	Ninurta	3 (6)	1:i4, 3:7, 4/3.1
āšib bīt Kidmuri	who dwells in the Kidmuri temple	Enlil	1 (1)	98:2
āšib ekurri šī	who dwells in this temple	Mamu	1 (4)	50:39
āšib Guzāni	who dwells in the city Guzana	Adad	1 (1)	148:7
āšib Kalḫi	who dwells in Kalhu	Ninurta	4 (7)	1:i9, 3:16–17, 4, [169:5]
āšib Sikānu	who dwells in the city Sikanu	Adad	1 (1)	148:25
āšibat ekurri šuātu	who dwells in that temple	Ishtar	1 (1)	32:17
āšibat Kalḫi	who dwells in Kalhu	Ishtar	1 (2)	28:i7
āšibūt Eḫursag-kurkura	who dwell in Ehursagkurkura	Ashur, the great gods	1 x 2 = 2 (2)	153:4′
[āšibūt] parakkī	[who dwell] in the sanctuaries	“the deities”	1 (1)	175:8′
bānû kullati	creator of all	Enlil	3 (3)	8, 17:i9, [20:3]/3.1
bēlagê	lord of the lunar disc	Sin	2 (2)	8, 17:i4
bēl bēlē	lord of lords	Ninurta/Utulu	4 (8)	1:i5, 3:10, 4, 101:3
bēl dīnišu	lord of his legal case	Adad	1 (1)	148:18/4.1
bēl Ḫabur	lord of the Habur river	Adad	1 (1)	148:25
bēl ḫegalli	lord of abundance	Adad	2 (3)	[20:6], 47:4/3.1
bēlī/šu	my/his lord(s)	Adad, Ashur, Enlil,	2, 49, 1, 10, 1, 1, 10, 4,	66:5; 1:ii25; 98:2; 30:60;

		"the deities", the great gods, Mamu, Ninurta, Shamash, Sin	3 (34, 577, 1, 10, 410, 4, 23, 15, 14) = 81 (1088)	1:i15; 50:24; 1:i9; 67:12; 67:12/3.1, 4.1/2/3
bēl mātāti	lord of all lands	Anu, Ashur	2, 1 (3, 31) = 3 (34)	[20:2], 47:2; 40:9/3.1, 6.2, 7.2
bēl mehî u šagašte	lord of storm and destruction	Ninurta	1 (4)	32:19
bēl nagbē u tâmāti	lord of springs and seas	Ninurta	3 (6)	1:i6, 3:11–12, 4
bēl nēmeqi ḫasīsi	lord of wisdom and intelligence	Ea	5 (6)	8, 17:i4, [20:4], 47:3, [100:1–2]/3.1
bēl šīmāti	lord of destinies	Ashur	2 (3)	17:v90, 152:20
bēl šipṭi u šagašte	lord of judgement and destruction	Erra, Ninurta	1, 1 (25, 2) = 2 (27)	38:45; 36:6′
bēl tîrāte	lord of omens	Marduk	3 (3)	8, 17:i5, [20:8]
bēlat irammu šangûtī	mistress who loves my priesthood	Ishtar	4 (7)	1:i37–38, 4, 8, 17:i47/4.2
bēlat Kidmuri	mistress of Kidmuru	Ishtar	3 (75)	38:19, 38:26, 38:35/1.7.2, 4.3, 7.2
bēlat Ninua	mistress of Nineveh	Ishtar	2 (29)	1:iii92, 56:17
bēlat qabli u tāḫāzi	mistress of battle and combat	Ishtar, Sharrat-niphi	5, 1 (21, 2) = 6 (23)	26:69, 28:v15, 29:25′, 32:19; 28:i4/3.2
bēltī/šu	my/his mistress	Ishtar, Shala, Sharrat-niphi	18, 1, 1 (210, 1, 2) = 20 (213)	1:iii92, 30:108, 30:109; 148:29; 28:i7/3.1, 4.1
bēltu rabītu	great mistress	Ishtar, Sharrat-niphi	1, 2 (25, 3) = 3 (28)	56:19; 28:i1, 32:14/3.1, 4.1
bēlu	lord	Ashur, Ninurta	4, 1 (11, 3) = 5 (14)	1:ii26, 17:ii85, 28:v15, 50:38; 31:17
(*bēlu*) *nābû šumī*	(lord) who called my name	Ashur	11 (491)	1:i17, 1:i40, 1:iii118, 2:7–8, 3:29/4.1
bēlu rabû	great lord(s)	Adad, Ashur, Enlil, Mamu, Ninurta	2, 28, 2, 1, 3 (2, 125, 32, 4, 11) = 36 (174)	49:6′; 1:i40; 98:2; 50:32; 1:i9/3.1, 4.3
bukur Nudimmud	child of Nudimmud	Ninurta	4 (7)	1:i2, 3:3, 4, 169:4/4.1
bukurti Anim	child of Anu	Sharrat-niphi	1 (2)	28:i3/4.1, 5.4.9

(continued)

title/epithet	translation	deity	quant	at/in
dajjān kibrāti	judge of the quarters	Shamash	5 (8)	1:i44, 4, 8, 17: i62, 154:11/3.1
dajjān šamê u erṣeti	judge of heaven and underworld	Shamash	5 (30)	8, 17:i9, 20:7, 38:34–35, 47:5
dāliḫat tâmāte	who stirs up the seas	Sharrat-niphi	1 (2)	28:i3
dandannu	all-powerful	Ninurta	4 (7)	1:i1, 3:1, 4, [169:1]/3.1
ekdu	fierce	Ninurta	3 (6)	1:i4, 3:7, 4/3.2
Ellil Aššurû	Assyrian Enlil	Ashur	2 (3)	152:20, 154:1/5.4.6
eršu	wise	Sin	3 (3)	8, 17:i4, 20:5/3.1
ezzu lā pādû	furious and merciless	Ninurta	3 (6)	1:i7, 3:12, 4/3.2
gešertu	strong	Sharrat-niphi	1 (2)	28:i1/3.2
gešru	strong	Adad, Ninurta	1, 5 (1, 9) = 6 (10)	17:i6; 1:i1, 3:1, 101:1, [169:1]]/3.2
gešru rēštu	first in strength	Anu	2 (2)	8, 17:i2
gešru šūturu	strongest	Adad	2 (3)	20:6, 47:4/3.1/2
gitmāltu	perfect	Ishtar	1 (2)	28:i6/3.1
gitmālu	perfect	Nergal, Ninurta	3, 3 (3, 6) = 6 (9)	8, 17:i8, 20:10; 1:i6, 3:11/3.1
gugal nārāti	canal inspector of water courses	Adad	1 (1)	148:5/3.1
gugal šamê u erṣeti	canal inspector of heaven and underworld	Adad	4 (61)	1:ii135, 38:44, 40:42–43, 148:1
gugallu šamru	impetuous canal inspector	Ninurta	3 (6)	1:i4, 3:8, 4
hāmim tuqmāte	who concentrates on battles	Ninurta	3 (6)	1:i2, 3:3, 4/3.2
ḫīrti Ellil	spouse of Enlil	Ninlil	3 (3)	8, 17:i7, [20:11]
[*ilāni*] *ammar* [*ina ṭuppi*] *annê* [*šum-šunu zakrū*]	all [deities who are named on] this [tablet]	"the deities"	1 (1)	175:9′

ilāni ellūtu	holy gods	Shamash, Sin	1, 1 (4, 4) = 2 (8)	1:iii90
ilānī	my deities	"the deities"	2 (12)	1:iii89, 2:27/4.1
ilāni migrīja	gods who favour me	Anu, Ea, Enlil	1 x 3 = 3 (3)	17:v99/4.1
ilāni rabûti	great gods	Adad, Anu, Ashur, Damkina, Ea, Ea-sharru, Enlil, Gula, Ishtar, Belat-Kidmuri, Marduk, Nabu, Nergal, Ninlil, Ninurta, Nusku, Shala, Shamash, Sharrat-niphi, Sibitti, Sin	11, 2, 12, 2, 4, 1, 6, 3, 7, 1, 2, 1, 3, 2, 6, 2, 2, 8, 3, 1, 9 (35, 5, 37, 3, 9, 1, 11, 4, 27, 1, 5, 1, 6, 5, 26, 5, 5, 23, 4, 1, 24) = 88 (238)	e.g. 17:i11, 28:v9, 30:58/1.5, 3.1, 4.1
ilāni rabûti ša šamê erṣeti	great gods of heaven and underworld	"the deities"	5 (15)	1:i25, 2:24, 4, 8, 17:i22/4.1
ilāni rēṣīšu	deities, his helpers	Adad, Ashur, Ishtar, Ninurta	1, 1, 1, 1 (25, 25, 25, 25) = 4 (100)	56:7/4.1, 7.2
ilāni tiklīšu	gods, his supporters	Adad, Ashur, Ninurta, Shamash	9, 8, 2, 14 (445, 41,24, 458) = 33 (968)	1:i22, 1:i104, 1:iii120, 1:iii128, 2:10/4.1
ilitti Ekur	offspring of Ekur	Ninurta	3 (6)	1:i2, 3:4, 4/4.1
iltu rēmēnītu	compassionate goddess	Ishtar	1 (2)	28:i7/3.2
ilu Aššurû	Assyrian god	Ashur	1 (1)	17:v89/5.4.6
ilu multālu	circumspect god	Nusku	3 (3)	8, 17:i7, 20:11/3.1
ilu rēmēnû	compassionate god	Adad, Ninurta	1, 3 (1, 6) = 4 (7)	148:6; 1:i9, 3:16, 4/3.2
ilu ša ina balušu purussû šamê ū erṣeti lā ipparrisu	god without whom no decisions are taken in heaven or underworld	Ninurta	3 (6)	1:i3, 3:6, 4
ilu šarḫu	splendid god	Ninurta	3 (6)	1:i7, 3:13, 4/3.1
ina ilāti šūturat nabnīssa	whose form is outstanding among the goddesses	Sharrat-niphi	1 (2)	28:i2/3.1
ina kibrāt mātāti kalīšina nabû šumuša	whose name is called in the corners of all lands	Ishtar	1 (2)	28:i6–7/3.1

(continued)

title/epithet	translation	deity	quant	at/in
Ištar ša Ninua	Ishtar of Nineveh	Ishtar	11 (230)	40:29, 40:31, 56:14, 57:2, 111:4/4.3
kābisi erṣeti rapašti	who treads the wide underworld	Ninurta	3 (6)	1:i3, 3:5, 4
kakkīšunu ezzūte ana širikte bēlūt-išu išrukū	who granted to his dominion their furious weapons	"the deities"	3 (6)	1:i26, 17:i23–24, 20:30–31/4.4
kaškaš ilāni	who is all-powerful among the deities	Adad	9 (13)	1:iii130, 17:i6, 17:i38, [20:45], 152:4
kullat mātātišunu ana šēpēšu uše-knišā	who made all their lands submit at his feet	Ashur, Shamash	3, 3 (6, 6) = 6 (12)	1:i23, 17:i18–19, 20:24/3.2
lē'ât Anunnakī	capable of the Anunnakis	Sharrat-niphi	1 (2)	28:i3
lē'û	capable one	Ninurta	3 (6)	1:i2, 3:4, 4
lē'û rapšu	widely capable	Ninurta	3 (6)	1:i5, 3:9, 4
lēqât unnīnī	who takes petitions	Sharrat-niphi	1 (2)	28:i5
māḫirat tešlītē	who receives supplications	Sharrat-niphi	1 (2)	28:i6
malik ilāni	ruler of the deities	Ninurta	3 (6)	1:i2, 3:4, 4
mālikat aḫḫīša	counsellor of her brothers	Sharrat-niphi	1 (2)	28:i3
mu'abbit lemnūte	destroyer of the evil ones	Ninurta	3 (6)	1:i8, 3:14, 4/3.2
muḫalliq zā'irī	destroyer of enemies	Ninurta	3 (6)	1:i8, 3:15, 4/3.2
mukīl markas šamê erṣeti	who holds the bond of heaven and underworld	Ninurta	4 (8)	1:i2–3, 3:4–5, 4, [101:2]
multālu	circumspect	Ninurta	3 (6)	1:i5, 3:9, 4
muma"ir gimrī	commander of all	Shamash	4 (5)	8, 17:i9, [20:7], 47:5/3.1
munarriṭ ḫuršāni	who shakes the highlands	Enlil	1 (1)	98:1–2/3.2
munarriṭat ḫuršāni	who shakes the highlands	Sharrat-niphi	1 (2)	28:i4/3.2
munnarbu	swift	Ninurta	3 (6)	1:i4, 3:6, 4

mušakniš lā māgirī	who makes the insubordinate submit	Ninurta	3 (6)	1:i8, 3:15, 4/3.2
mušalqat līti	who takes hold of victory	Sharrat-niphi	1 (2)	28:i5
mušamqit lemnūte	who causes the evil ones to fall	Ninurta	2 (2)	8, 17:i6/3.2
mušamqit targīgī	who causes the evildoers to fall	Ninurta	3 (6)	1:i7, 3:13, 4/3.2
mušamṣat ammar libbi	who complies with the heart	Sharrat-niphi	1 (2)	28:i5/4.1
mušarbū šarrūt Aššur-nāṣir-apli	who make the kingship of Ashur-nasirpal II great	"the deities"	3 (4)	17:i11–12, 20:14, 47:6–7/4.1
mušarbū šarrūtija	who make my kingship great	"the deities", Ashur, Adad, Enlil	1, 11, 1, 1 (1, 465, 6, 1) =14 (473)	1:i77; 1:i17, 1:iii118; 1:i77; 17:v48/4.1
mušarbû šarrūtija eli šarrāni ša kibrāt erbetti	who makes my kingship surpass the kings of the four quarters	Ashur	2 (5)	1:i41, 17:i55–56/3.1
mušaznin ḫenuni	who rains down plenty	Adad	1 (1)	148:1–2
mušīm šīmāt mātāti	who decrees the destinies of all lands	Ea	1 (1)	100:1/3.1
mušīm šīmāti	who decree(s) destinies	Anu, the great gods	2, 2 (2, 3) = 4 (5)	8, 17:i2–3; [20:13], 47:6/3.1
mušimmū šīmāt māti	who decree the destinies of the land	the great gods	2 (2)	8, 17:i11/3.1
mušpardu qereb Apzî	who illuminates the interior of Abzu	Ninurta	3 (6)	1:i8, 3:14, 4
muṭaḫḫidu° kibrāti	who makes the (four) quarters flourish	Adad	1 (1)	148:6/3.1
nādin ḫaṭṭi u purussê ana napḫar kal ālāni	who gives sceptre and (powers of) decisions to the totality of cities	Ninurta	3 (6)	1:i4, 3:7–8, 4/3.1
nādin išqū° u nindabê ana ilāni	who provides temple shares and food offerings for the gods	Adad	1 (1)	148:3–5/4.2

(continued)

title/epithet	translation	deity	quant	at/in
nādin rîti u mašqīte ana nišē kal ālāni	who provides pasturage and watering for the people of all cities	Adad	1 (1)	148:2–3/3.1
nāṣir apli	guardian of the heir	Ashur	RN	e.g. 1:i9/4.1
nāši ḫaṭṭi ellate	bearer of the holy sceptre	Nusku	3 (3)	8, 17:i7, [20:10]
nebûtu	radiant	Ishtar	1 (2)	28:i6/3.1
nūr šamê u erṣeti	light of heaven and underworld	Ninurta	3 (6)	1:i8, 3:14, 4
pēti uzuni^{o} *ḫasīsi*	opener of understanding and intelligence	Ea	1 (25)	38:23
pētû nagbē	opener of springs	Ninurta	4 (8)	1:i3, 3:5, 4, 101:2
qā'iš balāṭi	bestower of life	Ninurta	3 (6)	1:i9, 3:16, 4
qā'išat balāṭi	bestower of life	Ishtar	1 (2)	28:i7
qardu	heroic one	Adad, Ninurta	1, 7 (1, 29) = 8 (30)	148:18; 1:iii127, 17:i6, 17:i15, 26:35/4.1
qarrād Igigī	warrior of the Igigis	Ninurta	3 (6)	1:i2, 3:3–4, 4
qarrād Igigī u [Anunnakī]	warrior of the Igigis and [Anunnakis]	Ninurta	1 (1)	20:9/3.2
qarrādi^{o} *ilāni*	warrior of the deities	Ninurta	2 (2)	8, 17:i6/3.2
qarrādu šarhu gitmālu	splendid and perfect warrior	Ninurta	3 (6)	1:i1, 3:1–2, 4/3.2
rā'imat kināte	lover of righteousness	Sharrat-niphi	1 (2)	28:i5
rā'imūt šarrūtija	who love my kingship	Ashur, Ishtar	1, 1 (31, 31) = 2 (62)	40:39/4.1
rēšti šamê erṣeti	first in heaven and underworld	Ishtar, Sharrat-niphi	3, 1 (3, 2) = 4 (5)	8, 17:i10, 20:12; 28:i1/3.1
rubû	prince	Ashur	2 (6)	28:v15, 50:38
sāpin māt nakri	who flattens the enemy land	Ninurta	3 (6)	1:i7, 3:12–13, 4/3.2
ṣīru	exalted	Adad, Enlil, Ninurta	2, 3, 4 (2, 4, 7) = 9 (13)	17:i6; 17:i8, 20:3; 1:i1, 3:1/3.1
ša baluša ina Ešarra	without whom a judgement is not	Sharrat-niphi	1 (2)	28:i4

šipṭu ul immaggaru	agreed upon in Esharra			
ša [ina ekurrāti] siqirša kabitu	whose command is weighty [in the temples]	Sharrat-niphi	1 (2)	28:i1
ša ina puḫur ilāni siqrašu ilu mamma lāēnû	whose command none of the deities in the divine assembly can change	Ninurta	3 (6)	1:i8–9, 3:15–16, 4
ša ina tāḫāzi lā iššannanu tībūšu	whose attack in combat is unequaled	Ninurta	4 (8)	1:i1, 3:2, 4, 101:1–2
ša irammūni	who love me	"the deities"	1 (1)	32:11/4.1
ša kīma Šamaš kippat šamê [erṣeti] mithāriš tahīṭā	who like Shamash thoroughly has surveyed the circumference of heaven [and underworld]	Sharrat-niphi	1 (2)	28:i2
ša kippat šamê u erṣetim qātuššu paqdu	into whose hands is entrusted the circumference of heaven and underworld	Ninurta	3 (6)	1:i5–6, 3:10, 4
ša lā ēnû ištīššu	who never once changes	Ninurta	3 (6)	1:i7, 3:13–14, 4
ša lā ēnû mēlik[šu]	[whose] counsel can not be changed	Ea	1 (1)	100:2
ša lā ēnû qibīt pîšu	whose order of mouth can not be changed	Ninurta	3 (6)	1:i4, 3:7, 4
ša lā uttakkaru siqir šaptišu	whose pronouncement can not be altered	Ninurta	3 (6)	1:i5, 3:8–9, 4/4.2
ša paraṣ qardūti šuklulat	who perfects the rite(s) of warriorhood	Ishtar	3 (3)	8, 17:i10, 20:12–13/3.2
ša qurbūssaṭāb	whose closeness is pleasant	Ishtar	1 (2)	28:i7
ša rāḫiṣi	the flooder	Adad	11 (458)	1:iii120, 2:11, 3:34, 17:iv71, 19:73/3.2, 4.4
ša sīpušu ṭāb	to whom it is good to pray	Adad, Ninurta	1, 4 (1, 7) = 5 (8)	148:7; 1:i9, 3:16, 4, 169:5
ša siqrūšu […]	whose commands [are unalterable?]	Enlil	1 (1)	46:2

(continued)

title/epithet	translation	deity	quant	at/in
ša šamê erṣetim tahīṭa	who has surveyed heaven and underworld	Ishtar	1 (2)	28:i6
ša šangûtī irammū	who love my priesthood	Nergal, Ninurta	2, 4 (9, 18) = 6 (27)	2:40, 30:84; 2:26, 2:40, 9/4.2, 5.2
ša tību̅šu abūbu	whose attack is a flood	Ninurta	3 (6)	1:i7, 3:12, 4/3.2
ša tuqmātu ittallu	who extols in battles	Ninurta	3 (6)	1:i6, 3:11, 4/3.2
šadâni šapṣūte u malkī nakrīšu kīma qān api uhaṣṣiṣū	who cut down like marsh reeds difficult mountains and rulers hostile to him	Ashur, Shamash	3, 3 (6, 6) = 6 (12)	1:i22–23, 17:i17–18, 20:23/3.2
šadê šapṣūte u malkī nakrīšu kullat mātātišunu ana šēpēšu ušeknišā	who made the difficult mountains and the rulers of all lands hostile to him submit at his feet	Ashur, Ninurta	3, 3 (9, 9) = 6 (18)	1:iii128–129, 15, 27/3.2
šalummat kakkīšu melam bēlūtišu eli šarrāni ša kibrāt erbetti ušarrihūšu	who made him more splendid than any of the kings of the four quarters as for the aura of his weapons and the radiance of his lordship	"the deities"	3 (6)	1:i26–27, 17:i24–25, 20:31–32/4.1
šangûssu ina ekurrāti ana dāriš ukinnū	who established for all times his priesthood in the temples	"the deities"	3 (3)	17:i22–23, 20:29–30, 49:8/4.2
šaqû namrīri°	elevated luminary	Sin	3 (3)	8, 17:i4–5, [20:5]
šar [agê]	king [of the lunar disc]	Sin	1 (1)	20:5/3.1
šar Apzî	king of the Abzu	Ea	8 (41)	2:23, 17:i3, 20:4, 30:23, 32:8/3.1

šar gimrat ilāni rabûti	king of all the great gods	Ashur	4 (5)	8, 17:i1, 20:1, 47:1/3.1, 7.2
[*šar*] *Igigī u* [*Anunnakī*]	[king of] the Igigis and [Anunnakis]	Anu	1 (1)	20:2
šar šīmāti u gišḫurrī	king of destinies and designs	Enlil	1 (1)	98:1/3.1
šar tamḫāri	king of battle	Nergal, Ninurta	3, 2 (6, 2) = 5 (8)	8, 17:i8, 20:10; 1:i6, 3:10/3.2
šarrat kal ilāni	queen of all deities	Sharrat-niphi	1 (2)	28:i1/5.4.9
šarrat Kidmuri	queen of Kidmuru	Ishtar	1 (2)	99:1/5.4.9
šēmât ikribī	who listens to prayers	Sharrat-niphi	1 (2)	28:i5
šitarḫu	splendid	Ninurta	1 (1)	169:3/3.1
šulluṭu	triumphant	Ninurta	3 (6)	1:i6, 3:11, 4
šurbû	greatest	Ninurta	1 (1)	167:1/3.1
šurbût ilāni	greatest among the deities	Sharrat-niphi	1 (2)	28:i3/3.1
šūturtu	supreme	Ishtar	1 (2)	28:i6/3.1
talīmuša	her (Sharrat-niphi's) favourite brother	Shamash	1 (2)	28:i2
ummi ilāni rabûti	mother of the great gods	Ninlil	3 (3)	8, 17:i8, [20:12]
uršānat Igigī	heroine of the Igigis	Sharrat-niphi	1 (2)	28:i4
uznu rapaštu	extensively wise	Ea	2 (2)	30:23, 32:8
zīmu namru	shining appearance	Sharrat-niphi	1 (2)	28:i2/3.1

6 Divine titles and epithets in the texts of Shalmaneser III

Listing in alphabetical order of all the divine titles and epithets in the text corpus of Shalmaneser III. Quantifications (abbr. **quant**) indicate total number of attestations in "texts" and "exemplars" with the latter numbers within parantheses. If an epithet is shared by several deities, numbers first refer to those valid for an individual deity mirroring the order of the third column, and then to the total number of attestations, all deities combined. The final column (abbr. **at/in**, attestations/index) gives information on place of attestation in the primary sources and provides a complete index referring to the relevant (sub)sections in the book. The data concerning attestations and index respectively are separated graphically by "/". If an epithet is attested more than five times, a selection of the first, i.e. in their order in the SE-list, and "best", i.e. fully assigned and largely unreconstructed, attestations is given. When an epithet is shared by several deities, at least one attestation for each deity is provided, the respective data separated graphically by ";". The prefix SE is implicit. This appendix is referred to mainly in chapter 3.

title/epithet	translation	deity	quant	at/in
abu ilāni	father of the deities	Enlil	6 (21)	2:i1, 3, 4:3obv., 6:i2, 14:4/3.1
ālilū gitmālūtu	perfect heroes	Sibitti	1 (1)	95:1/3.2
apkal ilāni	sage of the deities	Marduk	3 (3)	10:i8, 14:9, 15/3.1, 7.3
ašarēd ilāni	foremost among the deities	Ninurta	2 (2)	10:i4, 19:2–3obv./3.1, 7.3
ašarēd ilāni šitarḫu	splendidly foremost among the deities	Ninurta	1 (14)	6:i6
ašaretti šamê u erṣetim	foremost in heaven and underworld	Ishtar	3 (3)	10:i5, 14:13, 15/3.1
ašarēdu	foremost	Shulmanu	RN	e.g. 2:i5/3.1, 4.1
[*āšib*] *Kalḫi*	[who dwells] in Kalhu	Ninurta	1 (1)	19:5obv.
āšib Kurba'il	who dwells in Kurbai'l	Adad	1 (1)	12:8
āšib Tarbiṣi	who dwells in Tarbisu	Nergal	1 (2)	96:1
āšibūt [*Ninua*]	who dwell [in Nineveh]	Sibitti	1 (1)	95:3–4
bābil [*ḫegalli*]	bringer of [abundance]	Adad	1 (1)	131:8
banītu	beautiful one	Ishtar	1 (1)	154:7rev.
bānû kullati	creator of all	Enlil, Ea	3, 1 (16, 3) = 4 (19)	6:i2, 14:4–5, 15; 2:i2*/3.1
bānû niklāti	creator of skills	Ea	3 (5)	2:i2, 3, 4:5–6obv.
bēl gimrī	lord of all	Shamash, Adad	2, 1 (14, 1) = 3 (15)	6:i5; 12:1/3.1
bēl ḫegalli	lord of abundance	Adad	2 (2)	14:7, 15/3.1
bēlī/šu	my/his lord(s)	Adad, Anu, Ashur, great gods, Nabu, Nergal, Ninurta, Sibitti	9, 2, 47, 2, 1, 3, 2, 2 (16, 9, 75, 4, 1, 3, 3, 2) = 68 (113)	12:8; 93:4; 1:27; 2:i33; 5:vi3; 94:1; 56:4; 95:4/3.1, 4.1/2/3, 5.3
bēl mātāti	lord of all lands	Anu, Ashur	6, 1 (21, 1) = 7 (22)	2:i1, 4:3obv., 6:i2, 14:3; 17:1/3.1, 6.3
bēl namrīri	lord of brilliance	Sin	1 (1)	10:i7

bēl nēmeqi ḫasīsu°	lord of wisdom and intelligence	Ea	2 (15)	6:i3, 10:i6/3.1
bēl qabli u tāḫāzi	lord of battle and combat	Ninurta	1 (1)	10:i4/3.2
bēl têrēti	lord of omens	Marduk	3 (3)	10:i8, 14:9, 15
bēlat qabli u tāḫāzi	mistress of war and combat	Ishtar	5 (20)	2:i3, 3, [4:8obv.], 6:i7, 38:2/3.2
bēlet Ninua	mistress of Niniveh	Ishtar	1 (1)	17:2
bēltī/šu	my/his mistress	Ishtar, Nana, Sharrat-niphi	1, 1, 3 (1, 2, 7) = 5 (10)	58:4; 5:vi3; 49:3, 50:4, 51:3/3.1, 4.1
bēltu rabītu	great mistress	Ishtar, Sharrat-niphi	1, 1 (1, 2) = 2 (3)	38:1; 49:2/3.1, 4.1
bēlu	lord	Adad, Ashur	1, 1 (1, 1) = 2 (2)	131:6′; 1:58′
bēlu [gitmālu]	[perfect] lord	Adad	1 (1)	131:1
bēlu īdû [...]	lord who knows [...]	Adad	1 (1)	131:7
bēlu rabû	great lord(s)	Adad, Ashur, Marduk, Ninurta, Sibitti	2, 27, 2, 3, 1 (2, 52, 4, 4, 1) = 35 (63)	12:8; 1:11; 5:v4; 19:6obv.; 95:4/3.1
bēlu uznu rapaštu	lord of wide understanding	Ea	1 (2)	56:6
dajjān kibrāti	judge of the (four) quarters	Shamash	3 (5)	2:i3, 3, [4:7obv.]/3.1
dajjān šamê u erṣetim	judge of heaven and underworld	Shamash	3 (3)	11:1′obv., 14:8, 15
dajjān šamê erṣetim šaqû	elevated judge of heaven and underworld	Shamash	1 (14)	6:i5
dandannu	all-powerful	Ninurta	2 (15)	6:i6, 19:2obv./3.1
eršu	wise one	Ea, Sin	3, 2 (5, 2) = 5 (7)	2:i2, 3, 4:5; [14:6], 15/3.1
etellu	pre-eminent	Sin	3 (5)	2:i2, 3, 4:7obv./3.1
eṭlu uršānu	heroic man	Adad	1 (1)	131:3
gešru	strong	Nabu, Ninurta	1, 2 (2, 15) = 3 (17)	5:vi2; 6:i6, 19:1obv./3.2
gešru šūturu	strongest	Adad	2 (2)	14:7, 15/3.1/2
gitmālu	perfect	Nergal	3 (3)	11:3′obv., 14:11, 15/3.1
gugal šamê erṣetim	canal inspector of heaven and underworld	Adad	3 (3)	10:i3, 12:1, 131:2

(continued)

title/epithet	translation	deity	quant	at/in
ḫā'iṭū šamê erṣeti	surveyors of heaven and underworld	Sibitti	1 (1)	95:1–2
ḫīrti Ellil	spouse of Enlil	Ninlil	3 (3)	11:5'obv., 14:12, 15
ilāni rabûti	great gods	Adad, Anu, Ashur, Ea, Enlil, Ishtar, Marduk, Nergal, Ninlil, Ninurta, Nusku, Shamash, Sibitti, Sin	8, 7, 12, 7, 7, 9, 3, 4, 3, 4, 3, 9, 1, 9 (25, 22, 44, 22, 22, 27, 3, 7, 3, 17, 3, 27, 1, 27) = 86 (250)	e.g. 2:i1–3, 14:14, 95:1/1.5, 3.1, 4.1
ilāni rēṣīšu	gods, his helpers	Ashur, Shamash	5, 5 (23, 23) = 10 (46)	1:7, 2:i9, 3, 6:i21, 8:16/4.1
ilāni tiklīšu	gods, his supporters	Adad, Shamash	2, 2 (2, 2) = 4 (4)	23:6, 24:2/4.1
ilī/ilānī	my god/deities	Ashur, the great gods	1, 5 (1, 5) = 6 (6)	17:58; 10:i26, 14:29, 14:70, 16:41/4.1
ilu dandannu	all-powerful god	Nergal	2 (2)	14:10, 15/3.1
ilu multālu	circumspect god	Nusku	3 (3)	11:4'obv., 14:12, 15/3.1
ilu rēmēnû	compassionate god(s)	Adad, Sibitti	1, 1 (1, 1) = 2 (2)	12:7; 95:3/3.2
ilu ṣīru	exalted god	Anu	1 (1)	10:i1/3.1
ilu ša nīš qāti	god of the hand lifting	Adad	1 (1)	131:6
Ištar Aššurītu	Assyrian Ishtar	Ishtar	1 (12)	43:10/5.4.6
Ištar ša [Ninua]	Ishtar of [Nineveh]	Ishtar	1 (1)	116:4
kāṣir urpēti	who assembles clouds	Adad	1 (1)	131:4
kaškaš ilāni	all-powerful among the deities	Adad	1 (1)	12:2
lēqû unnīnī	who take petitions	Sibitti	1 (1)	95:2
māḫirū teslītī	who receive supplications	Sibitti	1 (1)	95:2
mār Bēl	son of Bel	Nabu	1 (2)	5:vi2
mukanniš šapṣūte	who makes the obstinate submit	Ashur	1 (1)	25:44/3.2
mukīl mê nuḫši	who holds abundant water	Adad	1 (1)	12:4

mukinnū ešrēti	who establish shrines	Sibitti	1 (1)	95:2
muma"er gimrī	commander of all	Shamash	3 (3)	11:2′obv., 14:8, 15/3.1
muṣṣir eṣurāt šamê u erṣetim	who draws the designs of heaven and underworld	Enlil	3 (5)	2:i2, 3, 4:4obv./3.1
mušabriq berqi	who makes lightning strike	Adad	1 (1)	12:5
mušabšû urqēti	who creates greenery	Adad	1 (1)	12:5
mušamqitū zajjārī	who make enemies fall	Sibitti	1 (1)	95:3/3.2
[*mušamṣū*] *mal libbi*	[who comply with] the heart	Sibitti	1 (1)	95:3
mušarbū šarrūtija	who make my kingship great	the great gods	4 (17)	6:i8, 11:7′obv., 14:14, 15/4.1
mušarbū šumija	who make my name great	the great gods	1 (1)	21:3–4/4.1
mušaznin zunni	who creates rain	Adad	1 (1)	12:5
mušimmū šīmāti	who decree(s) destinies	Ea, Enlil, the great gods	2, 3, 5 (2, 5, 18) = 10 (25)	14:5; 2:i1; 6:i8, 10:i9, 15/3.1
muštēšir (*gimir*) *tenēšēte*	who guides aright (all of) humankind	Shamash	3 (5)	2:i3, 3, 4:7–8obv./3.1
mūtallikū sangāni	who roam about on mountain paths	Sibitti	1 (1)	95:1
nannār šamê ersetim	light of heaven and underworld	Sin	3 (5)	2:i2, 3, [4:6obv.]/3.1
nāši ḫaṭṭi ellati	bearer of the holy sceptre	Nusku	3 (3)	11:4′obv., 14:11, 15
nāši qinnanzi ellati mušanbi' tâmāte	who bears a holy whip which stirs up the seas	Adad	1 (1)	12:3
nēr multarḫi	slayer of the rebellious	Shamash	1 (1)	25:45/3.2
qardu šarḫu gitmālu	splendid and perfect warrior	Ninurta	1 (1)	19:3obv./3.2
qarrād Igigī u Anunnakī	warrior of the Igigis and Anunnakis	Ninurta	2 (2)	14:9–10, 15
qarrād ilāni	warrior of the deities	Nabu, Nergal	1, 1 (2, 2) = 2 (4)	5:vi2; 5:v4
rā'imūt ṣuṣē	who love marshes	Sibitti	1 (1)	95:1
rā'imūt šarrūtija	who love my kingship	the great gods	5 (7)	2:i3, 3, 4:9–10obv., 21:3, 22:2–3/4.1
rāḫiṣu	flooder	Adad	1 (2)	5:iii3/3.2, 4.4
rašubbu	terrifying	Adad	1 (1)	12:2/3.2
rē'û ša kal malikī	shepherd of all rulers	Ashur	1 (1)	17:1/3.1

(continued)

title/epithet	translation	deity	quant	at/in
rubû gašru	strong prince	Nabu	1 (2)	5:vi2
ṣābit kippat šārāni	who commands all the winds	Adad	1 (1)	12:4
ṣīru	exalted	Enlil, Ninurta	3, 1 (16, 1) = 4 (17)	6:i2, 14:4, 15; 19:2obv./3.1
ša bēlūtī kiššūtī u šāpirūtī šumu kabtu ušarbū	who made my lordship, power, leadership, and weighty name great	the great gods	1 (1)	22:3–5
ša bēlūtī kiššūtī u šāpirūtī ušarbū	who made my lordship, power and leadership great	the great gods	4 (19)	2:i4, 3, 4:10–11obv., 6:i9/4.1
ša ina rigmešu huršāni inuššū isabbu'ā tâmāte	at whose shout the highlands shake and the seas are stirred up	Adad	2 (2)	12:6, 131:5
[*ša*] *ina tāḫāzi lā iššannanu tībušu*	[whose] attack in combat is unequaled	Ninurta	1 (1)	19:4–5obv.
ša lā iššannanu dannūssu	whose strength is unequaled	Adad	1 (1)	12:2
ša mēlultaša tuqumtu	whose (cultic) game is battle	Ishtar	4 (19)	2:i3, 3, 4:9obv., 6:i7/3.2
ša nasḫuršu balṭu	whose favourable attention is life	Adad	1 (1)	12:7
ša paraṣ qardūti šuklulat	who perfects the rite(s) of warriorhood	Ishtar	2 (2)	14:13, 15/3.2
ša supûšunu ṭāb	to whom it is good to pray	Sibitti	1 (1)	95:3
ša šangûtī irammū	who love my priesthood	Nergal, Ninurta	2, 4 (15, 15) = 6 (30)	6:iv40, 16:341′; 5:ii1, 6:iv40, 16:34–35/4.2, 5.2
šadê dannūte ištu ṣīt šamši adi ereb šamši ušatmeḫā ana [*qātēšu*]	who have put in [his (Shalmaneser III's) hands] the mighty mountains from sunrise to sunset	Adad, Shamash	2, 2 (2, 2) = 4 (4)	23:7–9, 24:3
šaqû	elevated	Adad, Ishtar, Nergal	1, 1, 1 (1, 1, 2) = 3 (4)	12:1; 17:2; 5:v5/3.1
šaqû namrīri°	elevated luminary	Sin	3 (16)	6:i4, 14:6, 15
šar agê	king of the lunar disc	Sin	4 (17)	6:i4, 10:i7, 14:6, 15/3.1

šar Apzî	king of the Abzu	Ea	7 (22)	2:i2, 3, 4:5, 6:i3, 10:i6/3.1
šar gimrat ilāni rabûti	king of all the great gods	Ashur	6 (21)	2:i1, 3, 6:i1, 14:1–2, 15/3.1, 7.3
šar gimrī	king of all	Marduk	1 (2)	5:v6/3.1
šar Igigī u Anunnakī	king of the Igigis and Anunnakis	Anu	6 (21)	2:i1, 3, 4:2, 6:i1–2, 14:2–3
šar tamḫāri	king of battle	Nergal	3 (3)	11:3′obv., 14:11, 15/3.2
šēmû ikribī	who listen to prayers	Sibitti	1 (1)	95:2
šumī kabtu siqri ṣīra eli napḫar bēlē ma'diš iškunūninni	who have richly established for me my weighty name and my exalted command over all lords	the great gods	4 (19)	2:i4, 3, [4:11–12obv.], 6:i10
šurbû gitmālu	perfectly magnificient	Enlil	1 (11)	10:i2/3.1
ummi ilāni rabûti	mother of the great gods	Ninlil	3 (3)	11:5′–6′obv., 14:12–13, 15

7 Divine titles and epithets in the texts of the other kings

Listing in alphabetical order of all the divine titles and epithets in the text corpora of the other kings of the Early Neo-Assyrian Period. Quantifications (abbr. **quant**) indicate total number of attestations in "texts" and "exemplars" with the latter numbers within parantheses. If an epithet is shared by several deities, numbers first refer to those valid for an individual deity mirroring the order of the third column, and then to the total number of attestations, all deities combined. The final column (abbr. **at/in**, attestations/index) gives information on place of attestation in the primary sources and provides a complete index referring to the relevant (sub)sections in the book. The data concerning attestations and index respectively are separated graphically by "/". If an epithet is attested more than five times, a selection of the first, i.e. in their order in the relevant text list, and "best", i.e. fully assigned and largely unreconstructed, attestations is given. When an epithet is shared by several deities, at least one attestation for each deity is provided, the respective data being separated graphically by ";". The prefixes of each king (see "Abbreviations") are implicit. This appendix is referred to mainly in chapter 3.

Ad2-epithet	translation	deity	quant	at/in
abu ilāni rabûte	father of the great gods	Ashur	1 (2)	4:1/4.1
bēlī/šu	my/his lord	Ashur	14 (35)	1:9, 1:46, 1:47, 1:58, 1:59
dān	strong	Ashur	RN	e.g. 1:77/3.2
ilānī	my deities	"the deities"	1 (3)	1:52
ilāni rabûti	great gods	Ashur, Adad, Ishtar, Sin, Shamash	1, 1, 1, 1, 1 (12, 12, 12, 12, 12) = 5 (60)	3:18/1.5, 3.1, 4.1
ša šangûtī irammū	who love my priesthood	Ninurta, Nergal	1, 1 (3, 3) = 2 (6)	1:68

An2-epithet	translation	deity	quant	at/in
ālikat pānāt ummānātija	who marches ahead of my troops	Ishtar	1 (3)	2:97
apkal ilāni	sage of the deities	Marduk	2 (4)	2:2, 3
rēšti šamê u erṣete	foremost in heaven and underworld	Ishtar	2 (4)	2:4, 3
bēl kulūlija	lord of my crown	Shamash	1 (3)	2:102/4.1
bēl namrīri	lord of brilliance	Sin	2 (2)	2:1, 3
bēl têrēte	lord of omens	Marduk	2 (4)	2:2, 3
bēlī/šu	my/his lord(s)	Adad, Ashur, Ninurta	1, 10, 1 (3, 25, 3) = 12 (31)	2:92; 1:10, 1:17, 2:23; 1:4/5.3
bēlit qabli u tāḫāzi	mistress of war and combat	Ishtar	1 (3)	2:97
bēltī	my mistress	Gula	1 (3)	2:128
bēlu rabû	great lord	Ashur	4 (12)	1:10, 1:17′, 2:68, 2:97
dajjān šamê u erṣete	judge of heaven and underworld	Shamash	2 (4)	2:2, 3
gāmerūt purussê	who finalize decisions	the great gods	2 (4)	2:5, 3/3.1
gitmālu	perfect	Nergal	2 (4)	2:3, 3
ḫīrti Ellil	spouse of Enlil	Ninlil	2 (4)	2:4, 3
ilāni rabûti	great gods	Ashur, Enlil, Ishtar,	3, 2, 2, 2, 2, 2, 3,	e.g. 1:3, 2:5/1.5, 3.1, 4.1

		Marduk, Nergal, Ninlil, Ninurta, Nusku, Shamash, Sin	2, 2, 2 (7, 4, 4, 4, 4, 4, 7, 4, 4, 4) = 22 (46)	
ilu multālu	circumspect god	Nusku	2 (4)	2:3, 3
irammu šangûtī	who loves my priesthood	Shamash	1 (3)	2:103/4.2
muma"er gimrī	commander of all	Shamash	2 (4)	2:2, 3
mušimmū šīmāti	who decree destinies	the great gods	2 (4)	2:5, 3
nārārī	my (the king's) aid	Adad	RN	e.g. 1:1obv./4.1
nāši ḫaṭṭi ellate	bearer of the holy sceptre	Nusku	2 (4)	2:3, 3/5.4.4
qarrād Igigī u Anunnakī	warrior of the Igigis and Anunnakis	Ninurta	2 (4)	2:2–3, 3
ša paraṣ qardūti šuklulat	who perfects the rite(s) of warrior-hood	Ishtar	2 (4)	2:4, 3
ša šangûtī irammū	who love my priesthood	Ninurta, Nergal	2, 2 (4, 4) = 4 (8)	2:122, 12:6
šar agê	king of the lunar disc	Sin	2 (4)	[2:1], 3
šar tamḫāri	king of battle	Nergal	2 (4)	2:3, 3
ummi ilāni rabûti	mother of the great gods	Ninlil	2 (4)	2:4, 3

TN2-epithet	translation	deity	quant	at/in
abu ilāni	father of the deities	Enlil	5 (5)	1:3, 2, 3, 4, 23:1
apkal ilāni	sage of the deities	Marduk	4 (4)	1:8, 2, 3, 4
rēšti šamê u erṣete	foremost in heaven and underworld	Ishtar	4 (4)	1:13, 2, 3, 4
bēl ḫegalli	lord of abundance	Adad	4 (4)	1:6, 2, 3, 4
bēl mātāti	lord of all lands	Anu	4 (4)	1:3, 2, 3, 4
bēl namrīri	lord of brilliance	Sin	4 (4)	1:5, 2, 3, 4
bēl têrēte	lord of omens	Marduk	4 (4)	[1:8], 2, 3, 4
bēlat Ninua	mistress of Nineveh	Ishtar	1 (1)	2:9′
bēlī/šu	my/his lord	Ashur	5 (17)	5:4, [5:12], 5:24, 5:29, [23:1]
[*bēlu rabû*]	[great lord]	Ashur	2 (2)	[2:8′], [23:1]

(continued)

TN2-epithet	translation	deity	quant	at/in
dajjān šamê u erṣete	judge of heaven and underworld	Shamash	4 (4)	1:7, 2, 3, 4
Ellil Aššurî	Assyrian Enlil	Ashur	1 (1)	23:1/5.4.6
gāmerūt purussî	who finalize decisions	the great gods	4 (4)	1:14, 2, 3, 4/3.1
gešru šūturu	strongest	Adad	4 (4)	1:6, 2, 3, 4
gitmālu	perfect	Nergal	4 (4)	1:10, 2, 3, 4
ḫīrti Ellil	spouse of Enlil	Ninlil	4 (4)	1:12, 2, 3, 4
ilāni rabûte	great gods	Ashur, Enlil, Ishtar, Marduk, Nergal, Ninlil, Ninurta, Nusku, Shamash, Sin	4 x 10 = 40 (40)	1:1–14, 2, 3, 4/1.5, 3.1, 4.1
ilu multālu	circumspect god	Nusku	4 (4)	1:11, 2, 3, 4
muma”er gimrī	commander of all	Shamash	4 (4)	[1:7], 2, 3, 4
mušerbū šarrūt Tukultī-Ninurta	who make the kingship of Tukulti-Ninurta II great	the great gods	4 (4)	1:15, 2, 3, 4
mušimmu šīmāti	who decree(s) destinies	Ea, the great gods	4, 4 (4, 4) = 8 (8)	1:4, 2, 3, 4
nabnītī ana nabnīti bēlūti uštennū	who changed my figure to a lordly figure	“the deities”	4 (4)	1:19, 2, 3, 4/4.1
nāši ḫaṭṭi ellate	bearer of the holy sceptre	Nusku	4 (4)	1:11, 2, 3, 4
qarrād Igigī u Anunnakī	warrior of the Igigis and Anunnakis	Ninurta	4 (4)	1:9, 2, 3, 4
ṣīru	exalted	Enlil	4 (4)	1:3, 2, 3, 4
ša ina šassūr ummī kīniš [...]	who truly [took notice of me?] in my mother’s womb	“the deities”	4 (4)	1:18, 2, 3, 4/4.1
ša paraṣ qardūti šuklulat	who perfects the rite(s) of warriorhood	Ishtar	4 (4)	1:13, 2, 3, 4
ša šangûtī irammū	who love my priesthood	Nergal, Ninurta	2, 2 (5, 5) = 4 (10)	3:5′, [5:134]
ša tību šunu tuqumtu šašmu	whose attack imply battle and combat	the great gods	4 (4)	1:15, 2, 3, 4/3.2

šar agê	king of the lunar disc	Sin	4 (4)	1:5, 2, 3, 4
šar Apzî	king of the Abzu	Ea	4 (4)	1:4, 2, 3, 4
šar gimrat ilāni rabûti	king of all the great gods	Ashur	4 (4)	1:1, 2, 3, 4
šar Igigī u Anunnakī	king of the Igigis and the Anunnakis	Anu	4 (4)	1:2, 2, 3, 4
šar tamḫāri	king of battle	Nergal	4 (4)	[1:10], 2, 3, 4
tukultī	my (the king's) support	Ninurta	RN	e.g. 1:16/4.1
ummi ilāni rabûti	mother of the great gods	Ninlil	4 (4)	1:12, 2, 3, 4

SA5-epithet	translation	deity	quant	at/in
abi ilāni	father of the deities	Anu	1 (1)	15:3
ālali° *ilāni*	hero (?) of the deities	Ninurta	2 (3)	1:i8, 2
[*āliku*] …	[who marches] …	Zababa	1 (1)	[15:16]/3.2
apkal ilāni	sage of the deities	Ea	1 (1)	15:7
aplu ṣīru	exalted heir	Nabu	1 (1)	15:1/5.4.7
aplu šiplûṭu	hegemonic heir	Ninurta	2 (3)	1:i16–17, 2/5.4.7
ašarēd Anunnakī	foremost of the Anunnakis	Ninurta	2 (3)	1:i7, 2
ašarēdu šitarḫu	splendidly foremost	Nergal	1 (1)	12:1/3.1
āšib Kalḫi	who dwells in Kalhu	Ninurta	2 (3)	1:i23, 2
[*āšib*] *Tarbiṣa*°	[who dwells in] Tarbisu	Nergal	1 (1)	12:3
bēl gašri	strong lord	Ninurta	2 (3)	1:i1, 2
[*bēl šamê*]	[lord of heaven]	Sin	1 (1)	[15:10]
[*bēl*] *tukulti*	[lord of] support	Shamash	1 (1)	15:9/4.1
bēlassu	his mistress	Belat-parsi	4 (17)	5:1, 6:2, 7:2, 8:1
bēlu ṣīru	exalted lord	Ninurta	2 (3)	1:i10, 2
bēlī	my lord(s)	the great gods, Ashur, Marduk, Nergal	2, 6, 1, 1 (3, 9, 2, 1) = 10 (15)	1:i52; 1:ii43, 1:iii22; 1:iv6; 12:3
bēltu šinnat Anum° *u Dagan*	lady who is the like of Anu and Dagan	Kutushar	2 (3)	1:i18–19, 2/5.4.9

(continued)

SA5-epithet	translation	deity	quant	at/in
bēlu rabû	great lord	Marduk, Nergal	1, 1 (1, 1) = 2 (2)	15:16′; 12:3/3.1
binût Ešarra	creation of Esharra	Ninurta	2 (3)	1:i16, 2
bukur Enlil	child of Enlil	Ninurta	2 (3)	1:i15, 2
dajjānu rabû ša šamê u erṣetim	great judge of heaven and earth	Shamash	1 (1)	15:8
dandannu	all-powerful	Ninurta	2 (3)	1:i20, 2
dandannu ṣīru	exalted all-powerful	Nergal	1 (1)	12:1
etellu	pre-eminent	Ninurta	4 (6)	1:i2, 1:i23, 2, 2
gāmir emūqī gašrāti	consummate in great strength	Ninurta	2 (3)	1:i14–15, 2
gitmālum	perfect	Nergal	1 (1)	12:2
[*gugal šamê u erṣetim*]	[canal inspector of heaven and earth]	Adad	1 (1)	[15:13]
ilāni āšibūt Dēr	deities who dwell in Der	Anu-rabu, Burruqu, Gula, Mar-biti-sha-birit-nari, Mar-biti-shar-pan-biti, Nannai, Ner-e-tagmil, Sakkud, Sharrat-Der, Shukanija, Urkitu	1 x 11 = 11 (11)	2:iii47′–48′/1.5, 5.3
ilāni rabûti	great gods	Ashur, Marduk	1, 1 (2, 2) = 2 (4)	1:iv5/1.5, 3.1, 4.1
ilāni tiklīja	deities, my supporters	Adad, Ashur, Ishtar, Shamash	3, 3, 2, 3 (5, 5, 3, 5) = 11 (18)	1:ii14, 1:iii65
ilitti Kutušar	offspring of Kutushar	Ninurta	2 (3)	1:i18, 2
karaš niklāti	who understands skills	Ninurta	2 (3)	1:i22, 2/3.1
kaškaš ilāni	who is all-powerful among the deities	Ninurta	2 (3)	1:i23, 2/3.1
mālû …	full of …	Nergal	1 (1)	12:2
mālû pulḫāti	full of fearsomeness	Ninurta	2 (3)	1:i14, 2

mamlu	fierce	Ninurta	2 (3)	1:i5, 2/3.2
mūdê mimma šumšu	who knows everything	Ea	1 (1)	15:7/3.1
mukīl markas šamê erṣete	who holds the bond of heaven and underworld	Ninurta	2 (3)	1:i3–4, 2
muma”er gimrī	commander of all	Ninurta	2 (3)	1:i4, 2/3.1
mušīm šimāti	who decrees destinies	Enlil	1 (1)	15:3
[*muštēšir šiknat napištim*]	[who secures justice for all living beings]	Shamash	1 (1)	[15:8–9]/3.1
muttalli Igigī	prominent of the Igigis	Ninurta	2 (3)	1:i5, 2
nūr ilāni	light of the deities	Shamash	2 (3)	1:i11, 2
qarrād ilāni	warrior of the deities	Ninurta	2 (3)	1:i3, 2
[*qarrādu rabû*]	[great warrior]	Zababa	1 (1)	[15:16]/3.2
rākib abūbi	who rides the flood	Ninurta	2 (3)	1:i10, 2/3.2
rāš emūqī	acquirer of strength	Ninurta	2 (3)	1:i21, 2
ṣīru	exalted	Ninurta	2 (3)	1:i20, 2
ṣurru šumdulu	very wide of mind	Ninurta	2 (3)	1:i22, 2/3.1
ša amāssu ina maḫri illaku	whose command goes ahead	Marduk	1 (1)	15:16′
ša ina burūmî ellūtu šurruḫū	whose position is resplendent in the pure heaven	Ninurta	2 (3)	1:i17, 2
ša kīma Šamši ibarrū kibrāti	who, like Shamash, oversee the quarters	Ninurta	2 (3)	1:i11–12, 2/3.1
ša lā immaḫḫaru dannūssu	whose strength cannot be compared	Ninurta	2 (3)	1:i6–7, 2
ša lā šanān kaškaššu	whose all-powerfulness is without rival	Ninurta	2 (3)	1:i9, 2
ša lā uttakkaru ṣīt pîšu	whose word of mouth can not be altered	Ninurta	2 (3)	1:i19–20, 2
ša namrīri šitpuru	who is attired with brilliance	Ninurta	2 (3)	1:i13, 2/3.1
ša qibīssa ina [*Ekur kabtat*]	whose utterance [is weighty in Ekur]	Ninlil	1 (1)	15:5–6
[*ša qibīssa*° *lā uttakkaru*]	[whose utterance can not be altered]	Enlil	1 (1)	[15:4]
[*ša*] *šēressu ina ilāni šūpât*	[whose] punishing role is made apparent for the deities	Sin	1 (1)	15:10/3.2

(continued)

SA5-epithet	translation	deity	quant	at/in
ša šummuḫū mešrûti°	whose limbs are very luxuriant	Ninurta	2 (3)	1:i21, 2/3.1
šagapīru	majestic	Ninurta	2 (3)	1:i2, 2/3.1
šāgimu	thunderer	Adad	1 (2)	1:iii69/3.2
šamšī	my (the king's) sun	Adad	RN	e.g. 1:i26/4.1, 5.4.4
šitrāḫu	splendid	Ninurta	2 (3)	1:i6, 2
šūpû	famous	Ninurta	2 (3)	1:i8, 2/3.1
šurbû	greatest	Ninurta	4 (6)	1:i2, 1:i20, 2, 2/3.1
tukulti ilāni	support of the deities	Ninurta	2 (3)	1:i15–16, 2
ummu rabītu	great mother	Ninlil	1 (1)	15:5/5.4.9
uršanni° ilāni	hero of the deities	Ninurta	2 (3)	1:i12–13, 2
zar'ēšu	his descendants	"the deities"	2 (3)	1:i16, 2/5.4.7

An3-epithet	translation	deity	quant	at/in
abi ilāni	father of the deities	Ashur, Enlil	1, 2 (1, 3) = 3 (4)	6:28; 9:27rev., 34:3
āḫiz ṭuppi šīmāt [ilāni]	who has acquired the tablet of destinies [of the deities]	Nabu	1 (2)	34:6/3.1
āḫizu šukāmi	who has learnt the scribal art	Nabu	1 (2)	26:4
apal Nudimmud	heir of Nudimmud	Nabu	1 (2)	26:2
apkal ilāni	sage of the deities	Marduk	1 (2)	34:5
apkal niklāti	sage of skills	Nabu	1 (2)	26:3
ašarēd Igigī	foremost of the Igigis	Adad	1 (1)	6:2–3/3.1
ašaretti ilāni	foremost of the deities	Ninlil	1 (2)	34:13/5.4.9
āšib Dūr-Katlimmu	who dwells in Dur-Katlimmu	Shulmanu	1 (1)	42:1'/4.1
āšib Ezida	who dwells in Ezida	Nabu	1 (2)	26:7
āšib Ḫarran	who dwells in Harran	Sin	3 (3)	2:12, 2:17, 3:23/5.3

āšib Zamaḫi	who dwells in the city Zamahu	Adad	1 (1)	7:2
Aššurû/ītu	Assyrian	Enlil, Ishtar, Ninlil	1, 3, 1 (1, 4, 1) = 5 (6)	2:11; 9:29rev., 52:7′, 55:28; 2:12/5.4.6
azugallatu rabītu	great chief physician	Gula	1 (2)	34:7/3.1
bēl agê	lord of the lunar disc	Sin	1 (2)	34:7
bēl bēlē	lord of lords	Nabu	1 (2)	26:5/5.4.1
bēl mātāti	lord of all lands	Enlil	1 (2)	34:3/3.1
bēl šipṭi	lord of judgement	Nergal	1 (1)	9:28rev.
bēl šurbê	greatest lord	Adad	1 (1)	7:1/3.1
bēl têrēte	lord of omens	Marduk	1 (2)	34:5
bēlassu	his (the king's/an official's) mistress	Belat-parsi, Gula	2, 1 (17, 1) = 3 (18)	10:1, 11:1; 40:1
bēlat Ninua	mistress of Nineveh	Ishtar	1 (1)	9:22rev.
bēlat qabli [u] tāḫāzi	mistress of war [and] combat	Ishtar	1 (2)	34:7
bēlī/šu	my/his (the king's/an official's) lord	Adad, Ashur, Nabu, Shulmanu	2, 6, 2, 2 (2, 9, 15, 2) = 12 (28)	6:5; 5:7, 8:17; 14:4; 5:14/4.1, 5.4.7
bēltu	mistress	DN	1 (1)	44:7rev.
bēlu rabû	great lord	Adad, Ashur, Marduk, Nabu, Shulmanu	3, 10, 1, 1, 2 (3, 20, 1, 2, 2) = 17 (28)	6:5; 21:1; 9:17rev.; 26:8; 42:2′/3.1
bukur Anim	child of Anu	Adad	1 (1)	7:1
dajjān šamê u erṣetim	judge of heaven and earth	Shamash	1 (1)	6:30
dāpinu	martial	Nabu	1 (2)	26:1/3.2
ēdiššû	unique	Adad	1 (1)	7:1/3.1
eršu	wise	Ea	1 (2)	34:4
etel ilāni	pre-eminent among the deities	Adad	1 (1)	7:1/3.1
gešru rēštû	first of strength	Anu	1 (2)	34:2
gugal šamê u erṣetim	canal inspector of heaven and earth	Adad	3 (3)	6:1, 6:32, 7:2
ḫālip melammê ezzūte	who is bedecked with furious radiance	Adad	1 (1)	6:4
ḫīrat qarrād ilāni	spouse of the warrior of the deities	Gula	1 (2)	34:8/5.4.9
igigallu	wise one	Nabu	1 (2)	26:1

(continued)

An3-epithet	translation	deity	quant	at/in
ilāni rabûti	great gods	Adad, Ashur, Enlil, Ishtar, Marduk, Nabu, Nergal, Ninurta, Shamash, Sibitti	1, 2, 2, 2, 2, 2, 2, 2, 2, 1 (1, 2, 2, 2, 2, 2, 2, 2, 2, 1) = 18 (18)	52:8′–9′, 9:29rev./1.5, 3.1, 4.1
ilāni rabûti ša māt Aššur	great gods of Assyria	Adad, Ashur, Ber, Enlil, Ninlil, Sin	2, 2, 2, 1, 1, 2 (2, 2, 2, 1, 1, 2) = 10 (10)	2:11–13, 2:17/5.4.6
ilī	my god	Ashur	2 (2)	3:23, 5:7/4.1
mār Anim	son of Anu	Adad	1 (1)	6:1
mār Ellil gašri	strong son of Enlil	Ninurta	1 (2)	34:8
mār Esagil	son of Esagil	Nabu	1 (2)	26:1
mūdû mimma šumšu	who knows everything	Nabu	1 (2)	26:3
mugdašru	powerful	Adad	1 (1)	7:1/3.1
muma"er gimrī	commander of all	Marduk	1 (2)	34:5/3.1
munammir burūmê	who makes heaven bright	Sin	1 (2)	34:7
mušabriq berqi	who makes lightning strike	Adad	1 (1)	6:5
mušamqit lemutti	who causes the evil one to fall	Adad	1 (1)	6:4/3.2
mušarbû šarrūti	who makes kingship great	Enlil	1 (2)	34:3
mušaznin zunni	who creates rain	Adad	1 (1)	7:2
mušīm šīmāti	who decrees destinies	Ashur	1 (2)	34:1
muštālu	circumspect	Nabu	1 (2)	26:4
nannār [šamê erṣeti]	light [of heaven and underworld]	Sin	1 (2)	34:6
narām Ellil	beloved of Enlil	Nabu	1 (2)	26:5
nārārī	my (the king's) aid	Adad	RN	e.g. 1:1/4.1
[nāši] qinnanzi ellate	[who bears] a holy whip	Adad	1 (1)	6:5
pāqid kiššat šamê erṣetim	who is entrusted with all heaven and earth	Nabu	1 (2)	26:3

pētû uznī	opener of understanding	Ea	1 (2)	34:4
qardu šarḫu gitmālu	perfectly splendid heroic one	Adad	1 (1)	6:1–2/3.2
qarrād Anunnakī	warrior of the Anunnakis	Adad	1 (1)	6:3
qarrād ilāni	warrior of the deities	Ninurta	1 (2)	34:8
qarrādu	warrior	Ninurta	1 (1)	9:28rev.
rākib meḫāni rabûti	who rides the great storms	Adad	1 (1)	6:3–4/3.2
rapšā° uznī	wide of understanding	Nabu	1 (2)	26:4/3.1
rašubbu	terrifying	Adad	1 (1)	7:1
rē'ûssu kīma šamme balṭi eli nišē māt Aššur uṭibbū	who made his shepherdship as pleasing as a healthy plant to the Assyrians	the great gods	2 (2)	6:8–9, 8:2/5.4.6
rēmēnû	merciful	Nabu	2 (4)	26:4, 26:7/3.2
rubû kaškaššu	all-powerful prince	Nabu	1 (2)	26:2/3.1
sākipat ašṭūti	overthrower of the obdurate ones	Ishtar	1 (2)	34:7/3.2
sāniqu° mitḫurti	who brings about harmony	Nabu	1 (2)	34:6
ṣīru	exalted	Adad	1 (1)	7:2
ša balūššu ina šamê lā iššakkanu milku	without whom there can be no resolution in heaven	Nabu	1 (2)	26:6
ša ḫitlupū namrīri	who is clad in brilliance	Adad	1 (1)	6:3/3.1
[*ša ina*] *narî annê šumīšu-nu zakrū*	[whose] names are written [on] this stele	great gods of Assyria	1 (1)	2:18
ša lā iššannanu dannussu	whose strength is unequalled	Nabu	1 (2)	26:6/3.2
ša nasḫuršu ṭāb	whose favourable attention is good	Nabu	1 (2)	26:7
ša pungulū kubukkuš	whose strength is massive	Adad	1 (1)	6:2/3.2
ša qibīssu ṣīrat	whose command is exalted	Nabu	1 (2)	26:2
ša šuddû šušubbu bašû ittišu	who has with him (the ability to) depopulate and repopulate	Nabu	1 (2)	26:5/3.1
šadû rabû	great mountain	Enlil	1 (1)	44:5obv./3.1
šaqâtu ummi Ešarra	elevated mother of Esharra	Ninlil	1 (2)	34:13/5.4.9
šaqû	elevated	Nabu	1 (2)	26:1/3.1

(continued)

An3-epithet	translation	deity	quant	at/in
šar Apzû	king of the Abzu	Ea	1 (2)	34:4
šar Igigī	king of the Igigis	Ashur	2 (4)	1:3, 8:1
šar ilāni	king of the deities	Ashur	2 (4)	34:1, 55:30
šitrāḫu	splendid	Nabu	1 (2)	26:1/3.1
tajjāru	relenting	Nabu	1 (2)	26:7/3.2
tāmiḫ qan ṭuppi	who grasps the tablet stylus	Nabu	1 (2)	26:4
tiklīja	my supporters	Adad, Ashur, Ishtar, Marduk	1 x 4 = 4 (4)	6:16
tupšar Esagil	scribe of Esagil	Nabu	1 (2)	34:6
urappišū māssu	who has extended his (the king's) land	the great gods	1 (1)	6:9/3.2
ušaršidū kussâšu	who has established his throne	the great gods	1 (1)	8:3/4.1
zar'i ilāni rabûti	ancestor of the great gods	Anu	1 (2)	34:2/5.4.7

S4-epithet	translation	deity	quant	at/in
[*abi*] *ilāni*	[father] of the deities	Ashur	1 (1)	3:1
ašarēdu	foremost	Shulmanu	RN	e.g. 1:1/3.1
[*āšib Aššur*]	[who dwell in Assur]	"the deities"?	1 (1)	[3:7–8]
[*āšib Eḫursagkurkurra*]	[who dwells in Ehursagkurkurra]	Ashur	1 (1)	[3:2]
āšib Ḫarran	who dwells in Harran	Sin	1 (1)	1:20
[*āšibū Eḫursagkurkurra*]	[who dwell in Ehursagkurkurra]	"the deities"?	1 (1)	[3:4–5]
āšir Igigī u Anunnakī	who takes care of the Igigis and Anunnakis	Nabu	1 (1)	2:4
bēlē gešrūti	strong lords	the great gods	1 (1)	2:10/3.2

bēlī/šu	my/his lord(s)	the great gods, Ashur	1, 1 (1, 1) = 2 (2)	2:8; [3:4′]
bēlu rabû	great lord	Ashur, Marduk	1, 1 (1, 1) = 2 (2)	[3:2]; 2:1
dajjān kiššat ālāni	judge of all cities	Shamash	1 (1)	2:5/3.1
ilāni rabûti	great gods	Adad, Ashur, Inanna, Ishtar-kakkabi, Marduk, Nabu, Shamash, Sin	1, 1, 1, 1, 2, 1, 2, 1 (1, 1, 1, 1, 2, 1, 2, 1) = 10 (10)	2:8, 2:30/1.5, 3.1, 4.1
ilī	my god	Ashur	1 (1)	1:20/4.1
[*ilūtika rabûti*]	[your (the king's) great godhead]	Ashur	1 (1)	[1:11]/4.1
māḫirat suppē	who receives prayers	Inanna	1 (1)	2:7
mukīn māḫāzi	who establishes cultic centers	Marduk	1 (1)	2:2/4.3
mušēšib ālāni	who colonizes cities	Marduk	1 (1)	2:2/3.1
muttaddin kurmēti	who continually gives food rations	Nabu	1 (1)	2:4/4.3
namirtu	bright one	Ishtar-kakkabi	1 (1)	2:7/3.1
nannār šamê u erṣetim	light of heaven and underworld	Sin	1 (1)	2:6
nāši qarnī ṣīrūti	bearer of exalted horns	Sin	1 (1)	2:6/3.1
nāši ṭuppi šīmāt ilāni	bearer of the tablet of the destinies of the deities	Nabu	1 (1)	2:3
nūr mātāti	light of all lands	Shamash	1 (1)	2:5/3.1
pāqid ešrēt ilāni kalīša	who is entrusted with all the shrines of the deities	Marduk	1 (1)	2:2
qā'iš balāṭi	bestower of life	Nabu	1 (1)	2:4
rēṣīšu	his (the king's) helpers	the great gods	1 (1)	2:8
ṣābit qan ṭuppi elli	who holds the holy tablet stylus	Nabu	1 (1)	2:3
ṣulūl kibrāti	aegis of the (four) quarters	Shamash	1 (1)	2:5
ša litbušū namrīri	who is clothed in brilliance	Sin	1 (1)	2:6
ša ṭābat saḫirtīša?	whose overlooking is good	Inanna	1 (1)	2:7/3.2
šar ilāni	king of the deities	Marduk	1 (1)	2:1
šēmū taslītīšu	who listen to his (the king's) petitions	the great gods	1 (1)	2:8/4.1

(continued)

S4-epithet	translation	deity	quant	at/in
tāmiḫ kippat šamê u erṣetim	who grasps the perimeter of heaven and underworld	Marduk	1 (1)	2:1
tupšar ilāni	scribe of the deities	Nabu	1 (1)	2:3/3.1

Ad3-epithet	translation	deity	quant	at/in
dān	strong	Ashur	RN	e.g. 1:1/3.2

An5-epithet	translation	deity	quant	at/in
abi ilāni	father of the deities	Ashur	1 (1)	2:v5
ālik maḫri	who marches in the front	Palil	1 (1)	2:vi19/3.2
āšib Ḫarran	who dwells in Harran	Sin	1 (1)	2:iv4
bēlat Arba'il	mistress of Arbela	Ishtar	1 (1)	2:vi16
bēlat Ninua	mistress of Nineveh	Ishtar	1 (1)	2:vi15
bēlat sinnišūti	mistress of femininity	Ishtar	1 (1)	2:v12/5.4.9
bēlit° zikarūti	mistress of manliness	Ishtar	1 (1)	2:v12/5.4.9
bēlu rabû	great lord	Sin	1 (1)	2:iv4/3.1
gugal šamê u erṣetim	canal inspector of heaven and earth	Adad	1 (1)	2:iv8
nādin šarrūti	who gives kingship	Ashur	1 (1)	2:v5/4.1
nārārī	my (the king's) aid	Ashur	RN	e.g. 2:i13'/4.1
qardūtu	warriors	Sibitti	1 (1)	2:vi20/3.1
šar šamê u erṣetim	king of heaven and underworld	Ashur	1 (1)	2:vi6/3.1

8 Royal titles and epithets of Ashurnasirpal II

Appendix listing, in alphabetic order, all the royal titles and epithets of Ashurnasirpal II. Abbreviations refer to: **fr** frequency (total number of attestations), **se** sequence (attested in first position), (attested in) **A** Assur, **K** Kalhu (Nimrud), **N** Nineveh, **ic** the rest of the inner core (including Balawat), **oc** the outer core, **bf** the border areas or foreign lands, (attested in) **1** first regnal half, **2** second regnal half. (For the aspect of frequency, see also the list in app. 11.) Crosses indicate attestation, empty cell lack of attestation. Numbers in the second column refer to attestations in texts and exemplars respectively. The final column (abbr. **at/in**, attestations/index) gives information on place of attestation in the primary sources and provides a complete index referring to the relevant (sub)sections in the book. The data concerning attestations and index respectively are separated graphically by "/". If an epithet is attested more than five times, a selection of the first, i.e. in their order in the AE-list, and "best", i.e. fully assigned and largely unreconstructed, attestations is given. The giving of several attestations from the same text or of attestations from texts which lack information on columns and lines has been avoided whenever possible. This appendix is used mainly in chapters 4–9.

title/epithet	fr	se	A	K	N	ic	oc	bf	1	2	at/in
abūbu šamru (impetuous flood)	2 (32)		x		x					x?	40:13, [153:9]/4.1
(*kīma*) *Adad ša rāḫiṣi* ((like) Adad, the flooder)	16 (448)		x	x	x?	x		x	x	x	1:ii106, 2:11, 3:34, 4, 17:iv71/4.1/4, 5.4.2
agâ ṣīra [*ušatmeḫū* ...] ([into whose grasp they (Ashur, Ninurta) granted] the exalted crown)	1 (2)				x						47:14/4.1
āmeru° durgi u šapšāqi (who has seen innermost and rugged regions)	1 (31)				x					x?	40:5
ana ḫuribte taruṣu pānušu (whose face is turned towards the desert)	1 (4)			x						x	1:iii26/5.1
ana šitaprušu° ḫutennišu iṣaḫḫa libbašu (who rejoices in releasing his spear)	1 (4)			x						x	1:iii26
āpir šalummate (who is decked with aura)	9 (424)			x	x			x	x	x	1:i19–20, 2:18, 4, 17:i14, 23:13/4.1
ašarēd kalâ° malikī (foremost of all rulers)	2 (32)		x		x					x?	40:12, [153:8]/5.4.1
ašarēd tuqmāte (foremost in battles)	8 (29)			x		x			x	x	1:i35, 17: i40, 26:42, 54, 152:6/4.4
ašarēdāku (I am foremost)	6 (9)			x				x	x	x	1:i32, 4, 8, 13, 17:i35
bēl bēlē (lord of lords)	9 (43)		x	x	x			x	x	x	1:i21, 4, 17: i15, 40:13, 47:11/5.4.1
bēlāku (I am lord-like)	6 (9)			x				x	x	x	1:i32, 4, 8, 17:i34, 20:42/5.4.1
bilassunu imḫuru (who has received their tribute)	12 (442)			x		x			x	x	1:i16, 2:7, 3:28, 23:5, 26:13/5.4.3
bilta u maddattu elišunu ukinnu (who imposes upon them tribute and tax)	10 (31)			x		x		x	x	x	1:i27–28, 17:i26–27, 26:39, 54, 152:2–3/5.4.3
dā'iš kullat nakrī (trampler of all enemies)	10 (440)			x	x	x			x	x	1:i15, 2:5, 3:25, 23:4, 26:9–10/5.4.1
dā'iš mātāti nakrī (trampler of the lands of enemies)	2 (4)			x						x	1:iii116, 4/5.4.1

edû gapšu ša māḫira lā īšû (arisen flood wave which has no antagonist)	15 (463)			x		x			x	x	1:i13–14, 2:3–4, 3:23–24, 23:3, 26:6–7/4.1/4
edû gapšu ša lā iššannanu qablušu (arisen flood wave whose battle cannot be rivalled)	1 (1)							x	x		19:15/4.1/4
eršu/eršāku (wise/I am wise)	2 (9)	x		x						x	2:23, 29:8′/4.1, 5.4.7, 6.2
eṭlu (man)	1 (17)				x					x?	66:4/5.4.9
eṭlu qardu (heroic man)	28 (618)		x	x	x	x			x	x	1:i12, 2:2, 3:21, 23:2, 26:3/5.4.9, 7.2, 8.2/3
gešrāku (I am powerful)	2 (2)			x					x		13, 17:i34/4.1
gišginû dannu (strong clamp)	1 (1)							x	x		19:13/5.4.9
hasīsu (intelligent one)	1 (8)			x						x	2:23/4.1, 5.4.7, 6.2
ḫišiḫti Ellil (desired of Enlil)	2 (2)		x								171:6obv., 171:9rev./4.1
ḫišiḫtu° ilāni rabûti (desired of the great gods)	1 (1)		x								173:4rev./4.1
ḫuršāni pāṭ gimrišunu ipellu (who rules over the highlands in their entirety)	12 (443)			x		x			x	x	1:i16, 2:6, 3:27–28, 23:4–5, 26:12/5.4.1
ina malkī ša kibrāt erbetti šāninšu lā īšû (who has no rival among the rulers of the four quarters)	23 (565)			x	x	x		x	x	x	1:i12–13, 2:3, 3:22, 19:9–10, 23:2/5.4.1/9, 8.2
ina siqir Aššur u Ninurta ba'ūlāt Ellil [iltapru gimirta] (who by the command of Ashur and Ninurta [has full authority over] the population of Enlil)	1 (2)				x						47:12–13/3.1
(*kīma*) *iṣṣūri* ((like) a bird)	1 (4)			x						x	1:ii36/3.2, 5.2, 5.4.2
išippu na'du (attentive purification priest)	11 (36)			x	x	x		x	x	x	1:i21, 17: i15, 26:35, 47:11–12, 54/4.2, 6.2, 7.2, 8.2
iššak Aššur (vice-regent of Ashur)	28 (680)	x	x	x	x	x			x	x	2:1, 23:1, 30:1, 40:2, 41:1/4.1/2, 6.2, 7.2, 8.2
iššak Aššur u Ninurta (vice-regent of Ashur and Ninurta)	2 (4)			x					x		1:i33, 17:i37/4.1, 6.2, 7.2, 8.2
ištamdaḫu šadê u tâmāte (who has marched through mountains and seas)	1 (31)				x					x?	40:6/5.1

(continued)

title/epithet	fr	se	A	K	N	ic	oc	bf	1	2	at/in
ištu ṣīt šamši adi ereb šamši ana šēpēšu ušaknišu (who has made (all) from sunrise to sunset submit at his feet)	1 (2)					x					70:5–6/5.4.1
ittabbalu nišēšu ina šulmi (who governs his people in peace)	1 (31)				x					x?	40:16/5.4.2
kabtāku (I am important)	6 (9)			x				x	x	x	1:i32, 4, 8, 17:i35, [20:42]/5.4.7
kakku lā pādû mušamqit māt nakrīšu (merciless weapon which causes lands hostile to him to fall)	9 (30)			x		x		x	x	x	1:i34, 17:i38–39, 26:41, 54, 152:4–5/5.4.2, 8.2
kāšid ajjābīšu (conqueror of his foes)	4 (7)			x					x	x	1:i39–40, 4, 8, 17:i52–53/5.4.1
kāšid ajjābūt Aššur (conqueror of the foes of Ashur)	6 (9)			x				x	x	x	1:i28, 4, 8, 13, 17:i27/5.4.1
kāšid ālāni ḫuršāni pāṭ gimrišunu (conqueror of cities and the entire highlands)	15 (448)			x	x	x		x	x	x	1:i19, 2:17–18, 17:i12–13, 23:12, 26:33/5.4.1
kāšid ištu GN *adi* GN (conqueror from GN to GN)	9 (83)		x	x	x				x?	x?	39:4–6, 40: 19–20, 41:3–7, 42:2–3, 52:1′–2′/5.4.1, 8.3
kāšid GN *ana pāṭ gimriša* (conqueror of the whole of GN)	2 (57)		x		x				x?	x?	53:1–2, 66:6
kāšid mātāti kalîšina (conqueror of all lands)	1 (2)					x					70:4/5.4.1
kašūš ilāni rabûti (weapon of the great gods)	21 (461)			x	x	x		x	x	x	1:i11, 2:1, 3:19, 17:i16, 23:1/4.4, 8.2
lā ādiru ina tuqumte (fearless in battle)	25 (888)			x	x	x		x	x	x	1:i13, 2:3, 3:23, 17:i14, 19:11–12/5.4.9, 8.2/3
lā pādû (merciless)	5 (26)			x	x	x			x		1:iii127, 15, 26:34, 27, 54/4.1

labbāku (I am lion-like)	6 (9)		x				x	x	x	1:i33, 4, 8, 13, 17:i36/4.1, 5.2
le'âku (I am capable)	1 (1)		x							29:8′/4.1
liblibbi ša Aššur-dān (offspring of Ashur-dan II)	3 (6)		x				x		x	1:i30, 17: i31, [20:39]/4.1, 5.4.7
māḫir bilta° u maddatte ša kibrāt erbetta° (who receives tribute and tax from the four quarters)	1 (25)			x					x?	56:5/5.4.3
māḫir bilti u igisê ša kalîšina mātāti (who receives tribute and gifts from all lands)	2 (32)	x		x					x?	40:13, 153:9–10/5.4.3
malku (ruler)	1 (1)	x								173:13obv.
malku šūquru (very valuable ruler)	1 (1)	x								171:6obv.?
mār/apal Tukultī-Ninurta (son/heir of Tukulti-Ninurta II)	89 (1037)	x	x	x	x		x	x	x	1:ii125, 2:2, 4:1′, 9:1, 17:i28/4.1, 5.4.7
mār māri Adad-nārārī (grandson of Adad-narari II)	6 (39)		x	x			x	x?	x	1:i29, 17: i29, 19:24, 20:37, 40:18/5.4.7
māt Ḫatti ana siḫirtišu qāssu ikšudu (he whose hand has conquered the entire land of Hatti)	4 (63)			x					x?	40:21, 41:7–8, 42:3–4, 56:9/5.4.1
mātāti kalâšina [ana] šēpēšu ušeknišu (he who has made all lands submit [at] his feet)	1 (17)			x					x?	66:5/5.4.1
mātāti kalâšina qāssu ikšudu (he whose hand has conquered all lands)	13 (444)		x		x			x	x	1:i16, 2:6, 3:27, 23:4, 26:11–12/5.4.1
megir Ellil (favourite of Enlil)	2 (4)		x						x	1:i11, 3:20/4.1
megirka/ki (your (Ninurta's/Sharrat-niphi's) favourite)	2 (3)		x						x	29:4′, 28:i11/4.1
migir Anim (favourite of Anu)	10 (31)		x		x		x	x	x	1:i33, 17:i37, 26:40, 54, 152:4/4.1
mu'abbit dūrī nakrī/šu (who destroys the fortifications of (his) enemies)	2 (26)			x			x	x		19:19, 56:4

(continued)

title/epithet	fr	se	A	K	N	ic	oc	bf	1	2	at/in
mudīš targīgī (trampler of evildoers)	1 (31)				x					x?	40:6/5.4.1
mūdû (one who knows)	1 (8)			x						x	2:23/5.4.7, 6.2
muḫalliq zā'irīšu (destroyer of his enemies)	1 (26)				x					x?	56:4/5.4.1
mukabbis kišād ajjābīšu (who treads upon the necks of his foes)	12 (442)			x	x	x			x	x	1:i14–15, 2:4–5, 3:25, 23:3–4, 26:9/5.4.1
mukabbis kišād malkī (who treads upon the necks of rulers)	2 (32)		x		x					x?	40:12, 153:8/5.4.1
mukabbis rēšēte ša mātāte kalîš ḫuršāni (who treads upon the mountain peaks of all lands and highlands)	1 (31)				x					x?	40:3/5.1
mukabbisi° kišād malkī lā māgirūtešu (who treads upon the necks of rulers insubordinate to him)	1 (1)							x	x		19:14/5.4.1
mula"iṭ ekṣūte (controller of the brazen ones)	15 (448)			x	x	x		x	x	x	1:i19, 2:18, 17:i13, 23:12–13, 26:34/5.4.1, 8.2/3
munēr ajjābīšu (slayer of his foes)	8 (26)			x		x			x	x	1:i35, 17:i 40–41, 26: 43, 54, 152:7/5.4.1
muparriru° ḫuršāni šaqūti ša durugšunu lā etiqu (who opens elevated highlands of the innermost regions which not had been traversed)	1 (26)				x					x?	56:3/5.1
muparriru° kiṣrī multarḫi (who scatters the forces of the rebellious)	12 (442)			x		x		x	x	x	1:i15, 2:5, 3:26, 23:4, 26:10/5.4.1, 8.2
mupatti ṭūdāt šadê ša kīma šēlūt patri ana šamê ziqipta šaknū (opener of paths in mountains which rise perpendicularly to the sky like the tip of a sword)	2 (32)		x		x					x?	40:15–16, 153:12–13/5.1

murappišu° miṣir mātīšu (who extends the border(s) of his land)	1 (31)		x					x?	40:8/4.4, 5.4.6
murīb anunte (who requites with strife)	14 (447)	x	x	x		x	x	x	1:i20, 2:19, 17:i14, 23:13, 26:34/5.4.2
[*murīb*] *tuqumti* [*u*] *tamḫāri* ([who requites] with battle [and] conflict)	1 (1)					x	x		19:16–17/4.4
murtedû kalîš mātāti (leader of all lands)	1 (31)		x						45:7–8/5.4.1, 8.2
mušabbir kakkī malkī ša kalîšina kibrāti (who smashes the weapons of the rulers of all (the four) quarters)	1 (1)					x	x		19:19–20/5.4.1
mušakmeṣi° malkī lā kanšūtešu (who forces to bow down rulers unsubmissive to him)	1 (1)					x	x		19:17–18/5.4.1
mušekniš lā māgirūt Aššur ša pāṭāti eliš u šapliš (who makes those insubordinate to Ashur submit to the borders above and below)	1 (31)		x					x?	40:3–4/4.4, 5.4.1
mutēr gimilli māt Aššur (avenger of Assyria)	2 (32)		x					x?	40:7, 43:11′/5.4.2/5, 8.2
mutīr gimilli (avenger)	5 (8)	x					x	x	1:i21, 4, 8, 13, 17:i16/5.4.5
mutīr gimilli abbīšu (avenger of his fathers)	1 (4)	x						x	1:i21/5.4.7
muttallik šamgāni (who roams about on mountain paths)	2 (32)		x					x?	40:4, 43:5′/5.1
nabnītu ellutu (holy progeny)	1 (31)		x					x?	40:6/4.1, 5.4.7
nâdāku (I am celebrated)	6 (9)	x				x	x	x	1:i32, 4, 8, 13, 17:i34/5.4.7
nākirūt Aššur pāṭ gimrišunu eliš u šapliš ištananu (who has competed with every last enemy of Ashur above and below)	10 (25)	x		x		x	x	x	1:i27, 17:i25–26, 26:38–39, 54, 152:1–2/4.4, 5.4.1
namad Adad (loved one of Adad)	10 (31)	x		x		x	x	x	1:i33, 17:i37–38, [20:45], 26:40, 152:4/4.1, 8.2
napḫar malkī lā māgirīšu ikšudu rabītu qāssu (whose great hand onquered all rulers insubordinate to him)	4 (7)	x					x	x	1:i39, 4, 8, 17:i51–52/5.4.1

(continued)

title/epithet	fr	se	A	K	N	ic	oc	bf	1	2	at/in
napḫar nakrīšu ikšudu ešartu qāssu (whose just hand conquered all his enemies)	1 (31)				x					x?	40:8–9/5.4.1
narām Anim u Dagan (beloved of Anu and Dagan)	11 (427)			x		x		x	x	x	1:i10–11, 2:1, 3:18–19, 23:1, 28:i8/4.1, 8.2
narām libbija/ka/ki (beloved of my/your (Enlil's/Ninurta's/Sharrat-niphi's) heart)	5 (9)		x	x						x	1:i11, 3:19–20, 28:i10, 29:4′, 173:13obv./4.1
nibīt Ellil u Ninurta (designate of Enlil and Ninurta)	1 (8)			x						x	2:1/4.1
nibīt [ilāni] (designate [of the deities])	1 (2)				x						47:15/4.1
nibīt Ninurta qardi (designate of the heroic Ninurta)	10 (37)			x	x	x		x	x	x	1:i21, 17: i15, 26:35, 27, 54/4.1
nibīt Sîn (designate of Sin)	10 (31)			x		x		x	x	x	1:i33, 17:i37, 26:40, 54, 152:3/4.1
nišīt abiki Ellil (chosen of your (Ishtar's) father Enlil)	1 (1)				x						46:1/4.1
nišīt Ellil u Aššur (chosen of Enlil and Ashur)	1 (406)			x					x	x	23:1/4.1, 7.2
nišīt Ellil u Ninurta (chosen of Enlil and Ninurta)	13 (454)		x	x	x	x			x	x	1:i10, 2:1, 3:18, 23:1, 28:i8/4.1, 7.2, 8.2
nišīt īnē Ellil (chosen of Enlil)	2 (32)		x		x					x?	40:9–10, 153:3/4.1, 8.2
pāliḫ ilāni rabûti (worshipper of the great gods)	19 (463)			x	x	x		x	x	x	1:i18, 2:17, 17:i12, 20:15, 23:12/4.2, 8.2/3
parriku (overseer?)	1 (1)		x								173:4′/4.2
pēt uzni nēmeqi Ea išmāni ana jāši (open to understanding and wisdom which Ea destined for me)	1 (8)			x						x	2:23
qādid° *kal malkī* (who makes all rulers bow down)	1 (1)							x	x		19:11/5.4.1

qarrādu/qarrādāku (warrior/I am warrior-like)	10 (16)		x	x				x	x	x	1:i32, 1:ii35, 17:i36, [20:43], 154:15/5.1, 5.4.7/9, 6.2, 8.2
rē'û (shepherd)	4 (420)			x					x	x	2:19, 4, 23:13, 49:9/5.4.4, 7.2, 8.2
rē'û kibrāt erbetta° (shepherd of the four quarters)	2 (32)				x					x?	40:7, 43:10′/5.4.4
rē'û tabrâte° (amazing shepherd)	16 (464)			x		x		x	x	x	1:i13, 2:3, 3:23, 19:21, 23:2–3/5.4.4
rubû (prince)	7 (41)			x	x					x	1:i11, 3:20, 28:i10, 29:4′, 40:2/1.1, 1.4.2, 5.4.7, 7.2, 8.2/3
rubû kēnu (legitimate prince)	6 (9)		x	x				x	x	x	1:i24, 4, 8, 17:i20, [154:4]/5.4.7
rubû na'du (attentive prince)	22 (466)	x		x	x	x		x	x	x	1:i18, 2:17, 17:i12, 19–10–11, 23:12/4.2, 6.2, 7.2, 8.3
ṣābit līṭī (seizer of hostages)	14 (473)			x	x	x			x	x	1:i16–17, 2:7, 3:28, 23:5, 26:13/5.4.2, 8.2
ṣīrāku (I am exalted)	6 (9)			x				x	x	x	1:i32, 1, 4, 8, 13/5.4.7
ṣalūl kibrāti (aegis of the quarters)	3 (415)			x					x	x	2:19, 4, 23:13/5.4.4
ša ana šutēšur parṣī ekurrāti mātišu pitqudu kajjāna (to whom is perpetually entrusted the organization of the rites of the temples of his land)	5 (8)			x				x	x	x	1:i24, 4, 8, 17:i20–21, 20:26–27/4.2
ša ana tīb kakkīšu ezzūte gimir mātāti iḫillāma ultanapšaqā kīma kiškitte iṣūdā (at the attack of whose furious weapons all lands convulse, are constrained, and melt as though in a furnace)	1 (31)				x					x?	40:13–15/5.4.2

(continued)

title/epithet	fr	se	A	K	N	ic	oc	bf	1	2	at/in
ša arḫī pašqūte ittanallaku (who marches on narrow ways)	1 (31)				x					x?	40:5/5.1
ša biblat libbišu Ellil ušakšidušu (whose heart's desires Enlil helped him reach)	4 (7)			x					x	x	1:i39, 4, 8, 17:i50–51/4.1
ša bīt Ištar ša Ninua ēpušma° *arṣip*° (who made and repaired the temple of Ishtar of Niniveh)	2 (63)				x						111:4, 135:3–4/4.3
ša epšēt qātišu u nadān zībišu ilāni ša šamê u erṣeti irammū (whose deeds and giving of food offerings the great gods of heaven and underworld love)	5 (8)			x				x	x	x	1:i24–25, 4, 8, 17:i21–22, 20:27–29/4.2, 6.2
[*ša*] *ḫaṭṭa murte'ât nišē tušatmeḫu qāta* ([whose] hand you (Ashur) have granted the sceptre which herds people)	1 (1)		x						x?		154:3/5.4.4
ša ina ašri namrāṣi uparriru kiṣir multarḫi (who in harsh terrain scatters the forces of the rebellious)	4 (7)			x					x	x	1:i40, 4, 8, 17:i53–54/5.1
ša ina qitrub bēlūtišu šarrāni ekdūte lā pādûte ištu ṣīt šamši adi ereb šamši pâ ištēn ušaškin° (who by his lordly combat has placed under one command fierce merciless kings from sunrise to sunset)	4 (416)			x					x	x	2:20–21, 4, 23:14, 27/5.4.1
ša ina tukulti Aššur, Adad, Ištar, Ninurta rēṣīšu ittanallaku (who marches with the support of Ashur, Adad, Ishtar, Ninurta)	2 (42)				x					x?	56:7, 66:4–5/4.1, 7.2
ša ina tukulti Aššur ittanallaku (who marches with the support of Ashur)	22 (512)			x	x	x			x	x	1:i12, 2:2, 3:21–22, 23:2, 26:4/4.1
ša ina tukulti Aššur u Šamaš ittanallaku	2 (32)				x			x	x		19:7–9, 40:2/4.1

(who marches with the support of Ashur and Shamash)											
ša ištu GN *adi* GN [*qāssu*] *ikšudu* (whose [hand] conquered from GN to GN)	1 (25)				x					x?	56:8–9/5.4.1
ša kīma šarūr šamši andillašu° *eli mātišu šuparruru* (whose protection spreads like the rays of the sun over his land)	1 (31)				x					x?	40:16/5.4.4
ša mātāti kalâšina ištu ṣīt šamši [*adi ereb šamši ikšudu qāssu*] (whose [hand conquered] all lands from sunrise [to sunset])	1 (1)				x?					x?	33:18′/5.4.1
ša napḫar kiššat nišē ipellu (who rules all people)	18 (457)			x		x		x	x	x	1:i14, 2:4, 3:24–25, 17:i43–44, 19:18/5.4.1/4, 6.2, 8.2
ša napḫar kiššat nišē pâ ištēn ušaškinu (who has placed all people under one command)	1 (31)				x					x?	40:7/5.4.1
ša šangûssu eli ilūtika/ki rabûti/rabītu iṭibbu (whose priesthood satisfies your (Ninurta's/Sharrat-niphi's) great divinity)	4 (8)			x						x	1:i11–12, 3:20–21, [28:i11–13], [29:4′–5′]/4.2
[*ša*] *šuparruru* [*andillašu*° *eli mātišu*] ([whose protection] is spread out [over his land])	1 (1)		x							x?	153:6/5.4.4
[*ša* DN *ušatmeḫu kakka*] *ḫaṭṭa agâ u* [*šibirra*] ([who has been granted weapon], sceptre, crown, and [staff by DN])	1 (1)		x							x?	153:5/4.1
šagganakku° (governor)	1 (1)		x								173:14obv.
šāgiš ālāni u ḫuršāni (slaughterer of cities and highlands)	8 (29)			x		x			x	x	1:i34, 17:i39–40, 26:42, 54, 152:6/5.4.2
šaḫtu (reverent one)	4 (8)			x						x	1:i11, 3:19, 28:i9, [29:4′]/4.2
šakin Ellil (appointee of Enlil)	15 (223)	x	x		x				x?	x?	41:1, 57:1, 66:1, 67:1, 111:1/4.1

(continued)

title/epithet	fr	se	A	K	N	ic	oc	bf	1	2	at/in
šākin līte eli kalîšina mātāti (who achieves victory over all lands)	14 (450)			x	x?	x			x	x	1:i17, 2:7, 3:28–29, 23:5, 26:13–14/5.4.1
[*šākin*] *līte eli malkī ša kalîšina kibrāti* ([who achieves] victory over all rulers of the quarters)	1 (25)				x					x?	56:6/5.4.1
šakkanakki Aššur (governor of Ashur)	1 (31)				x					x?	40:9/4.1
šamšu (sun)	1 (1)							x	x		19:22/5.4.4
šamšu kiššat nišē (sun of all people)	8 (42)		x	x	x			x	x	x	1:i10, 3:18, 4, 28:i8, 40:1/5.4.4/6, 6.2, 8.2/3
šangû ellu (holy priest)	1 (1)				x						59:3/4.2
šangû ṣīru (exalted priest)	1 (1)				x						49:6/4.2
šāninišu° lā īšû (who has no rival)	1 (2)					x				x?	18:II2/5.4.9
šāpir kal nišē (commander of all people)	1 (1)							x	x		19:21/5.4.1
šar bēlē (king of lords)	13 (446)			x	x	x		x	x	x	1:i19, 2:18, 17:i13, 23:12, 26:33/5.4.1
šar kal malkī (king of all rulers)	11 (35)			x	x	x		x	x	x	1:i20, 4, 15, 17:i15, 26:34/5.4.1
šar kibrāt erbetti (king of the four quarters)	8 (26)			x		x			x	x	1:i35, 17: i40, 26:43, 54, 152:6/5.4.1, 6.1/2
šar kiššat kibrāte ša napḫar malkī kalîšunu (king of the totality of the quarters including all their rulers)	4 (7)			x					x	x	1:i35–36, 4, 8, 17:i42/5.4.1
šar kiššat nišē (king of all people)	1 (1)							x	x		19:22/5.4.1/4
šar kiššati (king of the universe)	69 (925)	x	x	x	x	x		x	x	x	1:i10, 2:1, 3:17, 9:1, 19:6/1.1/5, 5.4.1/6, 6.1/2
šar kullat kibrāt erbetti (king of all the four quarters)	10 (72)		x	x	x			x	x	x	1:i10, 3:17–18, 19:22, 28:i7–8, 40:1/5.4.1

šar lā šanān (king without rival)	6 (34)	x		x	x					x	1:i10, 3:17, 4, 28:i7, 29:2′/ 5.4.1/9, 6.2
šar māt Aššur (king of Assyria)	87 (974)	x	x	x	x	x		x	x	x	1:i28, 2:1, 9:1, 17:i27, 19:6/ 5.4.6, 6.1/2, 7.2, 8.2
šar mātāti šarḫu (splendid king of all lands)	1 (31)				x					x?	40:5/5.4.1
šar šarrāni (king of kings)	13 (65)			x	x			x	x	x	1:i21, 17: i15, 26:35, 40:9, 47:11/5.4.1
šar tanadāte (king worthy of praises)	3 (415)			x					x	x	2:19, 4, 23:13
šarḫu/šurruḫāku (splendid/I am splendid)	9 (42)		x	x	x			x	x	x	1:i32, 17: i35, 19:16, 40:13, [153:9]/4.1
šarru/šarrāku (king/I am king)	10 (16)	x		x				x	x	x	1:i32, 4, 8, 13, 17:i34/ 5.4.1/7
šarru ba"īt ilāni (king who is the desired one of the deities)	1 (31)				x					x?	40:9/4.1
šarru dannu (strong king)	64 (892)	x	x	x	x	x		x	x	x	1:i9, 2:1, 9:1, 17:i27, 19:6/ 5.4.9, 6.2, 7.2, 8.3
šarru dapīnu (martial king)	1 (31)				x					x?	40:6/4.4
(*šarru*) *lē'û qabli* (king/he who is capable in battle)	9 (27)			x		x		x	x	x	1:i34, 4, 17: i39, 26:42, 152:5/4.4, 8.2
šarru mušakmiṣ° lā kanšūtešu (king who forces to bow down those unsubmissive to him)	4 (7)			x					x	x	1:i36, 4, 8, 17:i43/5.4.1
(*šarru*) *mušakniš lā kanšūtešu* (king/he who makes those unsubmissive to him submit)	14 (472)			x	x	x			x	x	1:i14, 2:4, 3:24, 23:3, 26:7–8/5.4.1
(*šarru*) *mušḫarmiṭ kullat nakrīšu* (king/he who disintegrates all his enemies)	4 (7)			x					x	x	1:i35, 4, 8, 17:i41/5.4.1
šarru rabû (great king)	30 (356)	x	x	x	x	x		x	x	x	1:ii125, 9:1, 19:5, 26:1, 31:1/5.4.1, 6.2, 7.2, 8.2/3
šarru ṣīru (exalted king)	1 (1)				x?					x?	33:18′

(continued)

title/epithet	fr	se	A	K	N	ic	oc	bf	1	2	at/in
šarru ša biblat libbišu Aššur ušekšidušu (king whose heart's desire Ashur has caused him to reach)	1 (31)				x					x?	40:8/4.1
šarru ša ina qibīt pîšu ušḫarmaṭu šadê u tâmāte (king who disintegrates mountains and seas with his order)	3 (415)			x					x	x	2:19–20, 4, 23:13–14/4.4, 5.4.2
šarru ša ina tukulti Aššur u Ninurta mēšariš ittanallaku (king who marches justly with the support of Ashur and Ninurta)	5 (26)			x	x	x			x	x	1:iii128, 15, 26:36, 27, 54/ 4.1
šarru ša ina tukulti Aššur u Šamaš mēšariš ittanallaku (king who marches justly with the support of Ashur and Shamash)	5 (8)			x				x	x	x	1:i22, 4, 8, 17:i16–17, 20:21–22/4.1
(*šarru*) *ša ina tukulti ilāni rabûti ittanallaku* (king/he who marches with the support of the great gods)	13 (449)			x		x			x	x	1:i15–16, 2:5–6, 3:26–27, 23:4, 26:11/4.1
šarru ša ištu GN *adi* GN *ana šēpēšu ušeknиša* (king who made (all) from GN to GN submit at his feet)	19 (504)			x	x	x			x	x	1:iii121–22, 2:11–12, 3:34–37, 15, 23:8/5.4.1
šarru ša tanattašu^{o} *danānu* (king whose strength is worthy of praise)	1 (1)			x						x	30:22/5.4.9
šarru ša tanattašu^{o} *danānu kajjamānu* (king whose strength is constantly worthy of praise)	1 (4)			x						x	1:iii25–26
ṭiriṣ qāt [DN] (who is reached by [DN's] hand)	1 (1)		x						x?		154:2/4.2
tizqāru (prominent)	5 (26)			x	x	x			x		1:iii127, 15, 26:34, 27, 54
tušaršidu palâšu (whose reign you (Ninurta/ Sharrat-niphi) established)	4 (8)			x						x	1:i12, 3:21, 28:i14-ii1, 29:5′/4.1

uršānu/uršānāku (I am a hero/heroic)	10 (16)		x				x	x	x	1:i32, 4, 13, 17:i35, 20: 43/5.4.9, 6.2
uršānu lā pādû (merciless hero)	4 (417)		x	x				x	x	2:18, 4, 23: 13, 47:10
uršānu tizqāru lā pādû (prominent and merciless hero)	5 (8)		x				x	x	x	1:i20, 4, 8, 17:i14, [20:18]/5.4.9
ušumgallu ekdu (fierce dragon)	16 (456)		x	x	x		x	x	x	1:i19, 2:17, 17:i12, 19:12, 23:12/4.1/4, 8.2
utullu (chief herdsman)	6 (10)		x	x			x	x	x	1:i21, 4, 8, 17:i15, 47: 11/5.4.4, 6.2, 8.2
zānin nindabê ana ilāni rabûti (provider of food offerings for the great gods)	5 (8)		x				x	x	x	1:i23–24, 4, 8, 17:i19, 20:25/4.2
zikarāku (I am manly)	6 (9)		x				x	x	x	1:i33, 4, 8, 13, 17:i36/5.4.9
zikaru dannu (strong male)	12 (442)		x		x			x	x	1:i14, 2:4, 3:25, 23:3, 26:9/5.4.9, 8.2
zikaru qardu (heroic male)	1 (1)	x							x?	153:5/5.4.9, 8.2

9 Royal titles and epithets of Shalmaneser III

Appendix listing, in alphabetic order, all the royal titles and epithets of Shalmaneser III. Abbreviations refer to: **fr** frequency (total number of attestations), **se** sequence (attested in first position), (attested in) **A** Assur, **K** Kalhu (Nimrud), **N** Nineveh, **ic** the rest of the inner core (including Balawat), **of** the outer core, border areas, and/or foreign lands, (attested in) **1/2/3** first/second/last regnal phase. Crosses indicate attestation, empty cell lack thereof. Numbers in the second column refer to attestations in texts and exemplars respectively. (For the aspect of frequency, see also the list in appendix 11.) The final column (abbr. **at/in**, attestations/index) gives information on place of attestation in the primary sources and provides a complete index referring to the relevant (sub)sections in the book. The respective data concerning attestations and index are separated graphically by "/". If an epithet is attested more than five times, a selection of the first, i.e. in their order in the SE-list, and "best", i.e. fully assigned and largely unreconstructed, attestations is given. The giving of several attestations from the same text or of attestations from texts which lack information on columns and lines has been avoided whenever possible. This appendix is used mainly in chapters 4–9.

title/epithet	fr	se	A	K	N	ic	of	1	2	3	at/in
abūbāniš (like a flood)	2 (2)		x?	x					x?		[9:10], 12:18/4.1
(*kīma*) *Adad* ((like) the god Adad)	5 (12)			x		x	x	x			1:59′, 2:i46, 2:ii50, 2:ii 98, 3/4.1/4, 5.4.2
ālilu šamru (impetuous hero)	2 (3)			x		x		x		x	5:iv2, 16:48
āmeru° *durgi u šapšāqi* (who has seen innermost and rugged regions)	9 (27)		x	x			x	x	x		1:9, 2:i6–7, 3, 6:i15, 8:11/5.1, 8.2
āmir ēnāte ša Idiqlat u Puratte (who has seen the sources of the Tigris and the Euphrates)	1 (1)		x					x			25:12–13/5.1
[*āpir*] *šalummate* ([who is decked] with aura)	1 (2)					x		x			5:i3–4/4.1, 8.3
bāni Bāb-Tibira (builder of the Tabira Gate)	1 (1)		x						x?		101:5
bāni bīt Anim bīt Adad (builder of the temple of Anu and Adad)	1 (4)		x						x?		54:4–5/4.3
bāni dūr Libbi-āli (builder of the wall of the inner city (Assur))	1 (14)		x							x?	99:4
bānû kisal Aššur (builder of Ashur's courtyard)	1 (2)		x					x?			103:3/4.3
bēl kibrāt [*erbetti*] (lord of the [four] quarters)	1 (1)						x	x			17:43
bēlum° *šarrāni* (lord of kings)	1 (1)						x	x			17:28/5.4.1
bēlšu (his (an official's) lord)	3 (5)			x					x		[30:34], 31:19, 62
dā'iš kullat nakrīšu (trampler of all his enemies)	2 (2)			x					x		28:8–9, 30:10/5.4.1
edû gapšu [*ša māḫira lā īšû*] (arisen flood wave [which has no antagonist])	1 (2)					x		x			5:i3/4.1/4
ekdu (fierce)	1 (1)		x							x	40:i2
(*kīma*) *Erra* ((like) the god Erra)	1 (2)					x		x			5:iii2/4.4, 5.4.5, 8.3
eṭlu qardu (heroic man)	4 (5)		x?	x		x		x	x		5:i1, [9:4], 28:9, 30:10/5.4.9, 7.2, 8.2/3
(*kīma*) *Girru* ((like) fire/the god Girru)	2 (2)		x	x?					x	x	12:20, 40:i9/4.4, 5.4.2

iḫillū mātāte ina mēziz qardūtišu išdāšina (at whose warlike wrath the lands are convulsed down to their foundations)	2 (4)			x			x	x			2:i9, 3
[… *ilāni*] *ša šamê* [*u erṣeti haṭṭu*] *eširtu* [*qātuššu*] *umallû* ([whose hands the deities] of heaven [and underworld] filled with the just [sceptre])	1 (1)		x?						x?		9:15–17/4.1
ina šurrât šarrūtišu tâmtum elītum u tâmtum šupālītum qāssu ikšudu (whose hand at the beginning of his kingship conquered the upper and lower seas)	1 (1)			x				x			1:7–8/6.3
iššak Aššur (vice-regent of Ashur)	40 (112)	x	x	x	x	x	x	x	x	x	1:1, 2:i5, 3, 5:i5, 6:i11/4.1/2, 7.3, 8.2/3
*iššak Aššur pitqudu** (prudent vice-regent of Ashur)	1 (1)						x	x			2:i6*
iššakku° *Aššur šurruḫu* (splendid vice-regent of Ashur)	3 (3)			x					x		28:3, [30:4], 57:3
ištamdaḫu šadê u tâmāte (who has marched through mountains and seas)	4 (22)		x	x			x		x		2:i10, 3, 6:i23, 8:19/5.1
kakkēšu dannūte […] *šadê ināru* (who slew […] in the mountains with his mighty weapons)	1 (1)		x?						x?		9:8–9
kāšid GN/*ištu* GN *adi* GN (conqueror of GN/from GN to GN)	24 (39)		x	x	x		x	x	x	x	8:24–26, 12:11–13, 20:3–7, 21:6–8, 22:8–9/5.4.1
kašūš kal kibrāte (weapon (which smites) all the quarters)	2 (2)		x					x	x?		9:2–3, 25:3/5.4.2
[…] *kippat mātāti qātuššu ukinnū* ([into whose] hands (Ashur and the great gods) firmly established the circumference of lands)	1 (2)					x		x			5:i3/4.1
lā ādiru° *tuqumti* (fearless in battle)	1 (2)					x		x			5:i4/5.4.9, 8.3

(continued)

title/epithet	fr	se	A	K	N	ic	of	1	2	3	at/in
lā mupparkû zānin Ekur (ceaseless provider for Ekur)	1 (1)			x				x			1:5/4.2
lā pādû (merciless)	1 (2)					x		x			5:i2/4.1
lā pādû lā gāmil tuqunte (merciless and unsaving in battle)	2 (2)		x					x	x?		9:7, 25:6–7
lē'û (capable)	1 (1)		x							x	40:i3/4.1
māḫir bilti u igisê ša kalîšina kibrāti (receiver of tribute and gifts from all the quarters)	8 (26)		x	x			x	x	x		2:i7–8, 3, 6:i17, 8:12–13, 28:5–6/5.4.3
malku dannu itpēšu (strong and competent ruler)	1 (1)	x		x						x	16:1/5.4.1/7, 6.3
mār/apal Aššur-nāṣir-apli (son/heir of Ashur-nasirpal II)	72 (344)	x	x	x	x	x	x	x	x	x	1:10, 2:i11, 3, 6:i24, 8:20/4.1, 5.4.7
migir Ištar (favourite of Ishtar)	1 (1)		x								154:4rev./4.1
migirki (your (Ishtar's) favourite)	1 (1)		x								154:11obv./4.1
mūdû (one who knows)	1 (1)			x						x	16:2/5.4.7, 6.3
mukabbis kišād ajjābīšu (who treads upon the necks of his foes)	2 (2)			x					x		28:8, 30:8–9/5.4.1
mukabbis rēšēte ša šadê kalîš ḫuršāni (who treads upon the mountain peaks of all highlands)	9 (27)		x	x			x	x	x		1:9, 2:i7, 3, 6:i15–16, 8:11–12/5.1, 8.2
mukīl nindabê[ki] (holder of [your] (Ninlil's) food offerings)	1 (1)		x								154:1obv./4.2
[*mula''iṭ ekṣūte*] ([controller of the brazen ones])	1 (2)					x		x			[5:i3]/5.4.1, 8.3
munēr alṭūti (slayer of the obdurate)	1 (2)					x		x			5:i2/5.4.1
muparrir kiṣrī multarḫi (who scatters the forces of the rebellious)	2 (2)			x					x		28:8, 30:9/5.4.1

mupattû° *ṭūdāti ša eliš u šapliš* (who opens paths above and below)	8 (26)		x	x			x	x	x		2:i8, 3, 6:i18, 8:13–14, 28:6/5.1, 8.2
murtedû kalîš mātāti (leader of all lands)	11 (29)		x	x			x	x	x	x	1:2, 2:i6, 3, 6:i13, 8:7–8/5.4.1, 8.2
mušeknišu° [*lā kanšūte*] (who makes [the unsubmissive] submit)	1 (11)					x					41.1/5.4.1
mušte"û ašrāt ilāni ša qereb Ešarra (who frequents the shrines of the deities within Esharra)	4 (5)			x					x		28:4, 30:4–5, 56:2–3, 57:4/4.2
[*muštēšir?*] *kiššatu°* ([who directs] the universe)	1 (1)						x	x			17:4/5.4.1
nādin išqī u nindabê ana ilāni rabûti (who gives temple shares and food offerings to the great gods)	1 (1)			x				x			1:4/4.2
narām ilūtiki (beloved of your (Ninlil's) divinity)	1 (1)		x								154:5rev./4.1
nārāti šadê marṣūti ukabbisa šalṭiš (who triumphantly treads over rivers and difficult mountains)	2 (2)						x		x		23:12–13, 24:4–5/5.1
[*nišīt Ellil u Ninurta*] ([chosen of Enlil and Ninurta])	1 (1)			x						x	[16.1]/4.1, 7.3
nišīt īnē Ellil (chosen of Enlil)	11 (39)	x	x	x		x	x	x	x		1:3, 2:i6, 3, 4:16obv., 6:i14/4.1, 8.2
pāliḫ [*ilāni rabûti*] (worshipper [of the great gods])	1 (1)			x						x	16:3/4.2
perriku ṣīru (exalted overseer?)	1 (1)			x				x			1:6/4.2
qarrādu (warrior)	1 (3)						x	x			2:ii71/5.1, 5.4.9
rē'û kīnu (legitimate shepherd)	3 (4)	x		x		x		x		x	1:5, 5:i5, 16:3/5.4.4, 6.3, 7.3, 8.2
(*kīma*) *rīmi* ((like) a wild bull)	1 (3)						x	x			2:ii52/4.1/4

(continued)

title/epithet	fr	se	A	K	N	ic	of	1	2	3	at/in
rubû (prince)	21 (42)		x	x			x	x	x	x	1:1, 2:i5, 3, 6:i11, 8:3/1.1/5, 5.4.7, 7.3, 8.2
rubû na'du (attentive prince)	10 (29)		x	x			x	x	x		1:4, 2:i6, 3, 6:i14, 8:10–11/4.2
ṣābit serqiki (holder of your (Ninlil's) strewn offering)	1 (1)		x								154:1obv./4.2
ṣīt libbi ša Tukultī-Ninurta (offspring of Tukulti-Ninurta II)	1 (1)		x								154/5.4.7
ša ana tīb tāḫāzišu danni kibrāte ultanapšaqā (*iḫillū ālāni*) (at whose strong attack for combat the quarters are constrained (and cities are convulsed))	4 (22)		x	x			x	x	x		2:i8–9, 3, 6:i19–20, 8:14–15
ša ana ṭēmēt ilāni upaqqû (who heeds the orders of the deities)	1 (1)			x				x			1:6/4.2
ša arhī pašqūte ittanallaku (who marches on narrow ways)	4 (22)		x	x			x	x	x		2:i10, 3, 6:i22–23, 8:18–19/5.1
ša arki [*zā'irīšu*] *ittanallaku* (who marches after [his enemies])	2 (2)						x		x		23:10–11, [24:4]
[*ša*] *bēlūtišu šarrāni ekdūti u lā pādûti* [*ultu ṣīt šamše*] *adi ereb šamše iktašadu* ([whose] lordship has conquered fierce and merciless kings [from sunrise] to sunset)	1 (2)					x		x			5:i4–5/5.4.5/9
ša ina kibrāt erbette [*ittanallaku*] (who [marches] in the four quarters)	1 (2)					x		x			5:i1
ša ina malkī ša kibrāt erbetti šāninšu lā īšû (who has no rival among the rulers of the four quarters)	5 (23)		x	x			x	x	x		1:8, 2:i10, 3, 6:i21–22, 8:17/5.4.1/9

ša ina reṣūte ša Šamaš Adad lē'îš ittanallaku (who marches mightily with the help of Shamash and Adad)	2 (2)				x		x	23:4–7, 24:2
ša ina rēšti? idukku (who kills on the front line?)	1 (1)				x		x	24:4
ša ina šulme ittanarrû ba'ūlāt māt Aššur (who leads in peace the population of Assyria)	1 (1)		x			x		1:5–6/5.4.6, 6.3
ša ina tukulti Aššur mātāti kalîšina kīma kerṣappi ana šēpīšu ikbusu (who with the support of Ashur has trodden all lands under his feet as a footstool)	2 (2)		x				x	28:9–10, 30:10–12/5.4.1
ša ina tukulti Aššur u Šamaš ittanallaku (who marches with the support of Ashur and Shamash)	5 (23)	x	x		x	x	x	1:7, 2:i9, 3, 6:i20–21, 8:16/4.1
ša ina zikir bēlūtišu kibrāte ultanapšaqā iḫillū ālāni (at whose lordly command the quarters are constrained and cities are convulsed)	1 (1)		x				x	28:7
[*ša*] *kibrāti kalîšina qātuššu paqdā* (into [whose] hands are handed over all the quarters)	1 (2)			x		x		5:i2/5.4.1
ša kullat nakirīšu kīma ḫaṣbāte udaqqiqu (who has crushed all his enemies like potsherds)	2 (2)	x				x	x?	9:5–6, 25:4–6
ša tukultašu° *Ninurta* (whose support is Ninurta)	2 (3)		x	x		x	x	5:iv2, [16:48–49]/4.1, 7.3
šāgiš [*lā*] *kanšūt Aššur* (slaughterer of those [un]submissive to Ashur)	1 (2)			x		x		5:i2–3/4.4
šaḫtu (reverent one)	1 (1)		x			x		1:5/4.2

(continued)

title/epithet	fr	se	A	K	N	ic	of	1	2	3	at/in
šakin Ellil (appointee of Enlil)	11 (20)	x	x	x?	x			x	x?		26:2, 48:1, 50:2, 55:1, 93:2/4.1
šakkanakki ilāni rabûti (governor of the great gods)	1 (1)			x?					x		12:9/4.1
šakkanakku^{o} *Aššur pitqudu* (prudent governor of Ashur)	7 (24)		x	x			x	x	x		1:3, 2:i6, 3, 6:i14, 8:9–10/8.2
šakkanakku^{o} *Aššur šurruḫu** (splendid governor of Ashur)	1 (3)						x	x			2:i6*
šakkanakku pitqudu (prudent governor)	1 (1)		x								154:5rev.
šamšu kiššat nišē (sun of all people)	11 (30)		x	x		x	x	x	x	x	1:2, 2:i5, 3, 6:i12, 8:5–6/5.4.4/6, 6.3, 8.2/3
šangû ṣīru (exalted priest)	1 (1)		x						x		10:i13/4.2
šānin malkī ša kiššati rabûti šarrāni (rival of the great rulers of the universe and of the kings)	1 (1)		x							x	40:i3–4/5.4.1, 6.3
šāpir malkī ša kullate (commander of all rulers)	2 (2)		x					x	x?		9:3, 25:3–4/5.4.1
šaprû Aššur šurruḫu (splendid temple administrator of Ashur)	1 (2)			x							56:2/4.2
šar kibrāt erbetti (king of the four quarters)	3 (4)			x		x		x		x	1:2, 5:i3, 16:3/5.4.1, 6.1
šar kiššat nišē (king of all people)	23 (44)	x	x	x			x	x	x	x	1:1, 2:i5, 3, 6:i11, 8:2/5.4.1/4, 6.3, 7.3, 8.2/3
šar kiššati (king of the universe)	33 (230)	x	x	x	x	x	x	x	x	x?	5:i1, 9:1, 20:1, 21:5, 23:3/1.1/5, 5.4.1/6, 6.1/3
šar kullat kibrāt erbetti (king of all the four quarters)	12 (29)		x	x			x	x	x	x	2:i5, 3, 6:i12, 8:4–5, 10:i11–12/5.4.1, 8.2
šar lā šanān (king without rival)	2 (2)		x					x	x?		[9:2], 25:2/5.4.1/9, 6.3

šar māt Aššur (king of Assyria)	46 (273)	x	x	x	x	x	x	x	x	x?	1:1, 2:i5, 3, 5:v4, 5:vi5/ 5.4.6, 6.1/3, 7.3, 8.2
šar mātāti šarḫu (splendid king of all lands)	4 (22)		x	x			x	x	x		2:i10, 3, 6:i22, 8:18/5.4.1
šarru ba"īt ilāni (king who is the desired one of the deities)	10 (28)		x	x			x	x	x		1:3, 2:i6, 3, 6:i13, 8:8/4.1
šarru dannu (strong king)	34 (184)	x	x	x		x	x	x	x	x	1:1, 2:i5, 3, 5:i1, 5:ii2/ 5.4.9, 7.2, 8.3
šarru ekdu lā pādû (fierce and merciless king)	2 (2)						x		x		23:9–10, 24:3–4
šarru rabû (great king)	13 (105)	x	x	x		x	x	x	x	x	5:i1, 23:2, 24:1, 40:i1, 96:2/5.4.1/9, 6.3, 7.2, 8.3
šarūru (brilliant)	1 (1)			x				x			1:6/4.1
šitrāḫu (splendid)	1 (2)					x		x			5:i6/4.1
(*kīma*) *til abūbi* ((like) a flood mound)	12 (47)		x	x		x	x	x	x	x	5:ii2–3, 6:ii1, 6:iv36, 8:40, 31:16/4.4, 5.4.2
ušumgallu (dragon)	2 (2)		x					x	x?		9:2, 25:2/4.1/4
zānin išrēti[*ki*] (provider of [your] (Ninlil's) shrine)	1 (1)		x								154:11rev./4.2
zikaru dannu (strong male)	8 (26)		x	x			x	x	x		2:i9, 3, 6:i20, 8:15, 25:6/ 5.4.9, 8.2
*zikaru qardu** (heroic male)	1 (3)						x	x			2:i9*/5.4.9

10 Royal titles and epithets of the other kings

Appendix listing, in alphabetic order, all the royal titles and epithets of the other kings of the Early Neo-Assyrian Period. Abbreviations refer to: **fr** frequency (total number of attestations), **se** sequence (attested in first position), (attested in) **A** Assur, **K** Kalhu (Nimrud), **N** Nineveh, **ic** the rest of the inner core (including Balawat), **oc** the outer core, **bf** the border areas and foreign lands, (attested in) **1/2** first/second regnal phase. For the king abbreviations, see "Abbreviations". Crosses indicate attestation, empty cell lack thereof. Numbers in the second column refer to attestations in texts and exemplars respectively. (For the aspect of frequency, see also the list in app. 12.) The final column (abbreviated **at/in**, attestations/index) gives information on place of attestation in the primary sources and provides a complete index referring to the relevant (sub)sections in the book. The respective data concerning attestations and index are separated graphically by "/". If an epithet is attested more than five times, a selection of the first, i.e. in their order in the source code list (see app. 1), and "best", i.e. fully assigned and largely unreconstructed, attestations is given. The giving of several attestations from the same text or of attestations from texts which lack information on columns and lines has been avoided whenever possible. This appendix is used mainly in chapters 4–9.

Ad2-title/epithet	fr	se	A	K	N	ic	oc	bf	1	2	at/in
iššak Aššur (vice-regent of Ashur)	2 (5)		x								1:77, 4:2
mār/apal Tukultī-apil-Ešarra (son/heir of Tiglath-pileser II)	6 (25)		x			x					[1:5], 3:2, 4:3, 5:2, 6:2
nibīt Aššur (designate of Ashur)	1 (3)		x								1:1/4.1
[*ša* … *ana šarrūt*] *māt Aššur rabîš ukinnûšu* ([whom] Ashur greatly established [for the kingship] of Assyria)	1 (3)		x								1:4/4.1
[*ša* … *u*] *agâ ṣīru ušatmeḫu* ([into whose grasp] he (Ashur) granted the exalted crown)	1 (3)		x								1:3/4.1
[*ša* … *ultu*] *ullâ Aššur šumšu ibbû* ([whose] name Ashur called [since] earliest times)	1 (3)		x								1:2/4.1
šakan° Ellil (appointee of Enlil)	1 (2)	x	x								4:2
šar kiššati (king of the universe)	4 (19)		x			x					1:1, 3:1, 5:1, 6:1
šar māt Aššur (king of Assyria)	4 (20)		x			x					1:1, 3:1, 5:1, 6:1
šarru dannu (strong king)	4 (18)	x	x			x					1:1, 3:1, 5:1, 6:1
šarru rabû (great king)	1 (1)	x				x					6:1

An2-title/epithet	fr	se	A	K	N	ic	oc	bf	1	2	at/in
(*kīma*) *abūbe* ((like) the flood)	2 (6)		x							x	2:18, 4:5′
(*kīma*) *anḫulli* ((like) a storm)	2 (6)		x							x	2:20, 4:8′/4.4
ašarēdāku (I am foremost)	2 (4)		x							x	2:15, 3
ašṭāku (I am obdurate)	3 (7)		x							x	2:14, 3, 4
bēlāku (I am lord-like)	3 (7)		x							x	2:14, 3, 4
bibil libbi Aššur (select of Ashur)	1 (3)		x						x		1:2/4.1
bilta u tāmarta elišunu ukinn(*u*) (who imposed upon them tribute and audience gifts)	1 (3)		x							x	2:32/5.4.3

[(*kīma*) *būri*] ([(like) a bull calf])	1 (3)	x		x	[4:6′]/4.4
dabdâšu ṣābī ṣēri GN *šaknû* (who caused the defeat of the field troops of GN)	1 (3)	x		x	2:33
dabdâšu ša RN GN *ištu* GN *adi* GN *iškunu* (who caused the defeat of RN of GN from GN to GN)	1 (3)	x		x	2:26–27/5.4.5
dandannāku (I am all-powerful)	3 (7)	x		x	2:14, 3, 4
dannāku (I am strong)	3 (7)	x		x	2:14, 3, 4
dāpināku (I am martial)	2 (6)	x		x	2:19, [4:6′]/4.4
erbettešu ana GN *illiku* (who for a fourth time went to GN)	3 (7)	x	x	x	2:30, 4:22′, 5/5.1
eṭlu qardu (heroic man)	3 (7)	x	x	x	2:23, 4:13′, 5
eṭlu ša Aššur (man of Ashur)	1 (3)	x		x	2:77/5.4.9
gešrāku (I am strong)	3 (7)	x		x	2:14, 3, 4
(*kīma*) *Girru* ((like) fire/the god Girru)	2 (6)	x		x	2:18, 4:5′
GN *adi* GN *ana šēpēšu ušeknišu* (who has made GN as far as GN submit at his feet)	1 (3)	x		x	2:24–25
GN *ana pāṭ gimriša ipellu* (who rules over GN in its entirety)	3 (7)	x	x	x	2:26, 4:21′, 5
GN *ana miṣir mātišu uterru* (who brought GN within the border(s) of his land)	2 (6)	x		x	2:26, 2:34/5.4.6
GN *ana siḫirtiša kīma til abūbe asḫupu*[o] (who entirely overwhelmed GN like a flood mound)	1 (3)	x		x	2:32
GN *ikšud*(*u*) (who conquered GN)	1 (3)	x		x	2:31
GN *qāssu ikšudu* (whose hand conquered GN)	1 (3)	x		x	2:30
ḫitmuṭ raggi u ṣēni (who burns right up the wicked and evil)	2 (6)	x		x	2:17, 4:4′–5′/5.4.2
(*kīma*) *ḫuḫāri* ((like) a snarer)	2 (6)	x		x	2:21, [4:9′]
kabtāku (I am important)	3 (7)	x		x	2:14, 3, 4

(continued)

An2-title/epithet	fr	se	A	K	N	ic	oc	bf	1	2	at/in
kāšid GN *ana pāṭ gimriša* (conqueror of the entire GN)	1 (3)		x							x	2:26
labbāku (I am lion-like)	3 (7)		x							x	2:15, 3, 4:1′
līṭīšunu aṣbat° (who seized their hostages)	1 (3)		x							x	2:32/5.4.2
littu ellutu ša Aššur-rēša-iši (holy progeny of Ashur-resha-ishi II)	3 (7)		x							x	2:12, 3, 4
maddattu ša GN *maḫāri*° (who received the tax of GN)	1 (3)		x							x	2:33/5.4.3
mār/apal Aššur-dān (son/heir of Ashur-dan II)	8 (23)		x		x	x			x	x	1:5, 2:11, 6:2, 7:3, 8:3
*mār māri ša Tukultī-apil-Ešarra** (grandson of Tiglath-pileser II)	1 (1)		x							x	2:11*/5.4.7
mula"iṭ aštūtešu (controller of his obdurate resistance)	2 (6)		x							x	2:17, [4:4′]/5.4.2
munēr ajjābīšu (slayer of his foes)	2 (6)		x							x	2:16, [4:2′]/5.4.2
mušaḫmeṭi šadē ša mātāti (who sets the mountains of all lands on fire)	2 (6)		x							x	2:17, [4:3′]/5.1
(*kīma*) *nabli* ((like) a flash of fire)	1 (3)		x							x	2:66/4.4
nâdāku (I am celebrated)	3 (7)		x							x	2:14, 3, 4
namurrāku (I am awe-inspiringly radiant)	2 (4)		x							x	2:15, 3
(*kīma*) *patre šalbabe* ((like) a furious dagger)	2 (6)		x							x	2:19, 4:6′–7′/4.4
qarrādāku (I am warrior-like)	3 (7)		x							x	2:15, 3, 4:1′/6.4
rubû na'adu (attentive prince)	4 (10)		x						x	x	1:3, 2:5, 3, 4/6.4
sāpin ālāni (who flattens cities)	2 (6)		x							x	2:16, 4:3′/5.4.2
ṣīrāku (I am exalted)	2 (4)		x							x	2:15, 3
ša ina tukulti Aššur ištu GN *adi* GN *illiku* (who with the support of Ashur has marched from GN to GN)	3 (7)		x							x	2:23–24, 4:13′–15′, 5

ša ina tukulti Aššur u Ninurta ittanallaku (who marches with the support of Ashur and Ninurta)	1 (3)		x		x				x		1:3–4
(*kīma*) … *ša pāri* ((like) … of the skin)	2 (6)		x							x	2:20, 4:8′–9′
šadāni dannūtu ittatabalkitu (who continually crossed over mighty mountains)	1 (3)		x							x	2:31/5.1
šamšu kiššat nišē (sun of all people)	3 (7)		x							x	2:10, 3, 4/6.4
šar kibrāt erbetti (king of the four quarters)	5 (13)		x							x	2:10, 2:16, 3, 4, [4:2′]
šar kiššati (king of the universe)	5 (16)	x	x		x	x			x		1:1, 6:1, 7:2, 8:2, 10:3/6.4
šar kullat kibrāt erbetti (king of all the four quarters)	1 (3)		x						x		1:2/6.4
šar lē'û qabli (king capable in battle)	2 (6)		x							x	2:16, 4:3′
šar māt Aššur (king of Assyria)	12 (37)		x		x	x			x	x	1:1, 2:10, 4:2′, 7:2, 8:2/6.4
šarrāku (I am king)	3 (7)	x	x							x	2:14, 3, 4/6.4
šarru dannu (strong king)	9 (19)	x	x			x			x	x	1:1, 2:10, 4:2′, 6:1, 8:2
šarru mušerbû tanattīšu (king who makes his praise great)	1 (3)		x							x	2:78
šarru rabû (great king)	2 (4)	x	x			x			x		1:1, 8:1/6.4
šitmurāku (I am very wild)	3 (7)		x							x	2:15, 2:20, 3/4.4
(*kīma*) *šuburri* ((like) an end? (for the enemies?)	1 (3)		x							x	2:19
šurbâku (I am the greatest)	2 (4)		x							x	2:15, 3/5.4.7
šurruḫāku (I am splendid)	3 (7)		x							x	2:14, 3, 4/4.1
(*kīma*) *šuškalli* ((like) a net)	2 (6)		x							x	2:21, [4:9′]/4.4
(*kīma*) *tīb šāri* ((like) the beatings of the wind)	2 (6)		x							x	2:19, [4:7′]
uršānāku (I am heroic)	2 (4)		x							x	2:15, 3
ušamqitu gērīšu (who has felled his foes)	1 (3)		x						x		1:4/5.4.2
zikarāku (I am manly)	2 (4)		x							x	2:15, 3
zikaru qardu (heroic male)	2 (6)		x							x	2:17, 4:4′

TN2-title/epithet	fr	se	A	K	N	ic	oc	bf	1	2	at/in
ana mu"urūt kibrāt arba'i ana dāriš išquru šume kabta (whose weighty name he (Ashur) has pronounced forever for the four quarters)	4 (4)		x								1:24, 2, 3, 4/5.4.1
bēl bēlē (lord of lords)	4 (4)		x								[1:22], 2, 3, 4
bēlāku (I am lord-like)	4 (4)		x								1:28, 2, 3, 4
bibil libbišunu/ka (their/your (the deities'/ Ashur's) select one)	5 (5)		x								[1:17], 2, 3, 4, 23:3/4.1
… *ilūtika rabâte* (who … your (Ashur's) great divinity)	1 (1)		x?								23:3
išippu na'adu (attentive purification priest)	4 (4)		x								1:22, 2, 3, 4
iššak Aššur (vice-regent of Ashur)	5 (8)	x	x							x	[3:9′], 5:138, [7:1′], 23:2, 23:8
ištu GN *adi* GN *qāssu ikšudu* (whose hand conquered from GN to GN)	1 (1)					x?					6:5–10
mār/apal Adad-nārārī (son/heir of Adad-narari II)	20 (32)	x	x		x	x				x	5:138, 6:1, 9:3, 10:2, 11:3
muma"er kibrāt erbetti (commander of the four quarters)	4 (4)		x								1:34, 2, 3, 4/5.4.1
munnarbāku (I am swift)	4 (4)		x								1:30, 2, 3, 4/5.4.7/9
namad DN (loved one of DN)	4 (4)		x								1:33, 2, 3, 4/4.1
nišē ba'ūlāt Enlil ultašpiru gimirta (who had full authority over the people, Enlil's subjects)	4 (4)		x								[1:23], 2, 3, 4/5.4.6
palḫāku (I am fearful-inspiring)	4 (4)		x								1:29, 2, 3, 4/4.1
rašubbāku (I am terrifying)	4 (4)		x								1:31, 2, 3, 4/4.1
rē'û kīnu (legitimate shepherd)	4 (4)		x								[1:23], 2, 3, 4
rē'û narām° (beloved shepherd)	4 (4)		x								1:16–17, 2, 3, 4/5.4.4

rubû na'adu (attentive prince)	4 (4)	x	x					1:16, 2, 3, 4
rubû pāliḫka (prince who fears you (Ashur))	1 (1)		x?					23:2/4.1
ṣīrāku (I am exalted)	4 (4)		x					1:31, 2, 3, 4
ša Aššur kakkēšu ušaḫḫilu (whose weapons Ashur has worked on)	4 (4)		x					[1:24], 2, 3, 4/4.4
ša ina zikri Šamaš ḫaṭṭu ellutu nadnataššum (to whom by order of Shamash the holy sceptre was given)	4 (4)		x					1:22, 2, 3, 4/5.4.4
ša zikrišu eli malikī nebû° (whose name was called over the rulers)	4 (4)		x					1:23, 2, 3, 4/5.4.1
šakin Ellil (appointee of Enlil)	2 (2)	x	x?					23:2, 23:8
šalummāku (I am radiant)	4 (4)		x					1:30, 2, 3, 4/4.1
šamšu kiššat nišē (sun of all people)	4 (4)		x					[1:25], 2, 3, 4,
šāpirāku (I am commander)	4 (4)		x					1:32, 2, 3, 4/5.4.1
šar kal malkī (king of all rulers)	4 (4)		x					[1:22], 2, 3, 4/5.4.1
šar kibrāt erbetti (king of the four quarters)	5 (5)		x					[1:22], [1:25], 2, 3, 4
šar kiššati (king of the universe)	9 (18)	x	x		x	x?	x	9:2, 13:2, 14:1, 15:1, 16:1
šar kiššati lā šanān (king of the universe without rival)	4 (4)		x					[1:21–22], 2, 3, 4/5.4.9
šar māt Aššur (king of Assyria)	17 (26)	x	x		x	x	x	9:2, 11:2, 13:2, 14:1, 15:1
šar šarrāni (king of kings)	4 (4)		x					[1:22], 2, 3, 4
šarrāku (I am king)	4 (4)	x	x					1:28, 2, 3, 4
šarru dannu (strong king)	11 (14)	x	x		x			1:21, 2, 3, 13:2, 15:1
šarru rabû (great king)	1 (1)	x			x			12:1
šarru ša ištu GN *adi* GN *iṣbat(u)* (king who seized from GN to GN)	1 (1)					x?		6:2–5/5.4.1
šatammu ṣīru (exalted (temple) administrator)	4 (4)		x					1:23, 2, 3, 4
šurbâku (I am the greatest)	4 (4)		x					1:29, 2, 3, 4
uršanāku (I am heroic)	4 (4)		x					1:29, 2, 3, 4
utullu (chief herdsman)	4 (4)		x					[1:22], 2, 3, 4

SA5-title/epithet	fr	se	A	K	N	ic	oc	bf	1	2	at/in
(*kīma*) *Adad šāgimi* ((like) Adad, the thunderer)	2 (3)		x	x	x					x	1:iii68–69, 2/4.4
(*kīma*) *arâni* ((like) an eagle)	2 (3)		x	x	x					x	1:ii52, 2/4.4, 5.2
iššak Aššur (vice-regent of Ashur)	1 (9)		x?								5:2
mār/apal Šulmānu-ašarēd (son/heir of Shalmaneser III)	7 (32)		x	x	x					x	1:i34, 5:3, 6:3, 8:3, 9:3
mukīl parṣī Ekur (who upholds the rites of Ekur)	2 (3)		x	x	x					x	1:i31, 2/4.2
muma"er gimrī (commander of all)	2 (3)		x	x	x					x	1:i28–29, 2/5.4.1
murtedû kalîš mātāti (leader of all lands)	2 (3)		x	x	x					x	1:i28, 2
nāši ḫaṭṭi ešrete (bearer of the just sceptre)	2 (3)		x	x	x					x	1:i27–28, 2/5.4.4
rē'û ašrāti (shepherd of shrines)	2 (3)		x	x	x					x	1:i27, 2/4.2
(*kīma*) *sapāri* ((like) a net)	2 (3)		x	x	x					x	1:ii6, 2/4.4
ša ana šipri Eḫursagkurkurra ekurrāti mātišu gummur libbašuma bašâ° uznāšu (who has dedicated heart and mind to, and being at hand for, the work of Ehursagkurkurra and the temples of his land)	2 (3)		x	x	x					x	1:i32–33, 2/4.3
ša ultu ullâ ilāni ibbū zikiršu (whose name the deities called from earliest times)	2 (3)		x	x	x					x	1:i29–30, 2/4.1
šakin Ellil (appointee of Enlil)	2 (10)	x	x								5:2, 6:2*
šangû ellu (holy priest)	2 (3)		x	x	x					x	1:i30, 2
šar kiššat lā maḫri (king of the universe without equal)	2 (3)		x	x	x					x	1:i26–27, 2/5.4.9
šar kiššati (king of the universe)	1 (15)		x		x					x	9:2
šar māt Aššur (king of Assyria)	6 (24)	x	x	x	x					x	6:2, 7:3, 9:2, 10:1, 11:3
šar māt Šumerî u Akkadî (king of Sumer and Akkad)	1 (15)		x		x					x	9:2/5.4.1/5

šarru (king)	2 (2)			x?					x?		15:4′, 15:14′
šarru dannu (strong king)	3 (18)	x	x	x	x					x	1:i26, 2, 9:1/7.4
zānin Ešarra lā mupparkû (ceaseless provider for Esharra)	2 (3)		x	x	x					x	1:i30–31, 2/4.2
zēr šarrūti dārû (eternal royal offspring)	2 (3)		x	x	x					x	1:i29, 2/5.4.7

An3-title/epithet	**fr**	**se**	**A**	**K**	**N**	**ic**	**oc**	**bf**	**1**	**2**	**at/in**
apal Šulmānu-ašarēd (heir of Shalmaneser III)	1 (3)			x							1:9
ardu (servant)	1 (1)		x?								43:2/4.1/2
bēlī/šu (my/his (an official's) lord)	4 (5)			x		x	x		x?	x?	6:28, 7:20, 26:8, 42:7′
ipēlma kal gimrī (he who ruled over everything)	1 (3)			x							1:8–9
iššak Aššur (vice-regent of Ashur)	3 (26)		x		x						14:1, 15:1, [21:1]
iššakku ṣīru (exalted vice-regent)	1 (1)						x			x?	6:7/4.1
ištu tâmtim rabīti ša napḫa° šamši adi tâmtim rabīti ša šulmu° šamši qāssu ikšudu (he who conquered from the eastern to the western Great Sea)	1 (3)			x							1:5–8/5.4.1
kāšid ištu GN *adi* GN (conqueror from GN to GN)	1 (1)			x						x	8:5–11/7.4
liblib ša Ilu-kapkapi (offspring of Ilu-kabkabi)	1 (3)			x							1:23–24
liblibbi Tukultī-Ninurta (offspring of Tukulti-Ninurta I)	1 (3)			x							1:19
liblibbi ša Šulmānu-ašarēd (offspring of Shalmaneser I)	1 (3)			x							1:21
malkī ša kibrāt erbetti ušeknišu ana šēpēšu (who has made the rulers of the four quarters submit at his feet)	1 (1)			x						x	8:4–5/5.4.1

(continued)

An3-title/epithet	fr	se	A	K	N	ic	oc	bf	1	2	at/in
mār māri ša Aššur-nāṣir-apli (grandson of Ashurnasirpal II)	1 (3)			x							1:14
mār Sammurāmat (son of Sammuramat)	1 (1)							x	x?		3:2–3/5.4.7/9, 6.4
mār/apal Šamšī-Adad (son/heir of Shamshi-Adad V)	27 (76)		x	x	x		x	x	x?	x	1:9, 2:2, 3:2, 5:1, 6:9/5.4.7/9, 6.4
māršu (his (Shamshi-Adad V's) son)	1 (4)				x				x?		13:4
mukīl parṣī Ekur (who upholds the rites of Ekur)	1 (1)			x						x	8:3/4.2
pāliḫ ilūtika rabûti (who fears your great divinity (Ashur))	1 (1)		x?								43:2/4.1
pir'i Adad-nārārī (descendant of Adad-narari II)	1 (3)			x							1:15–16
rē'û tabrâte° (amazing shepherd)	1 (1)						x			x?	6:6
ša ina tukulti Aššur ittanallaku (who marches with the support of Ashur)	1 (1)			x						x	8:4
ša nīš qātīšu nadān zībīšu iḫšuḫū ilāni rabûti (whose ritual gesture and food offerings the great gods desired)	1 (1)						x			x?	6:7–8/4.2
šakin Ellil (appointee of Enlil)	5 (31)	x	x		x				x	x	14:1, 15:1, 21:1, [55:1], 56:1
šangû ellu (holy priest)	2 (2)	x	x?	x						x	8:3, 43:1′
šar kiššati (king of the universe)	13 (19)	x	x	x	x		x	x		x	1:2, 2:1, 5:1, 6:6, 7:3
šar la šanān (king without rival)	1 (1)						x			x?	6:6
šar māt Aššur (king of Assyria)	36 (67)	x	x	x	x	x	x	x	x?	x	1:2, 2:1, 3:1, 5:1, 6:6/6.4
šarru (king)	5 (5)	x		x?	x		x			x	6:28, 9:10, [9:11], 9:19′, 52:3′/5.4.7
šarru dannu (strong king)	8 (10)	x		x	x		x	x	x?	x	1:1, 2:1, 3:5, 5:1, 6:6/7.4

šarru rabû (great king)	6 (8)	x		x	x		x	x		x	1:1, 2:1, [5:1], 6:6, 8:1/6.4, 7.4
šarru ša ina ṣeḫrūssu Aššur uttûšuma malkūt lā šanān umallû qātuššu (king in whose youth Ashur conceived and bestowed with a rulership withou rival)	2 (4)			x						x	1:2–5, 8:1–2/4.1
waklu (overseer)	9 (14)	x	x	x?					x	x	45:2, 52:2, 53:2, 54:2, 55:1/4.1
zānin Ešarra lā mupparkû (ceaseless provider for Esharra)	1 (1)			x						x	8:3/4.2

S4-title/epithet	**fr**	**se**	**A**	**K**	**N**	**ic**	**oc**	**bf**	**1**	**2**	**at/in**
[*ardu*] ([servant])	1 (1)		x?						x		[3:10]/4.1/2
mār/apal Adad-nārārī (son/heir of Adad-narari III)	1 (1)							x		x	1:2
[*pāliḫ ilūtika rabûti*] ([who fears your great divinity (Ashur)])	1 (1)		x?						x		[3:10]/4.1
šangû ellu (holy priest)	1 (1)	x	x?						x		3:10
šar māt Aššur (king of Assyria)	2 (2)						x?	x		x	1:1, [2:9]
šarru dannu (strong king)	1 (1)	x						x		x	1:1

Ad3-title/epithet	**fr**	**se**	**A**	**K**	**N**	**ic**	**oc**	**bf**	**1**	**2**	**at/in**
iššak Aššur (vice-regent of Ashur)	1 (1)		x								1:1
mār/apal Adad-nārārī (son/heir of Adad-narari III)	1 (1)		x								1:2
šakin Ellil (appointee of Enlil)	1 (1)	x	x								1:1

An5-title/epithet	**fr**	**se**	**A**	**K**	**N**	**ic**	**oc**	**bf**	**1**	**2**	**at/in**
šar māt Aššur (king of Assyria)	11 (11)			x?					x?		1:7′, 2:i13′, 2:iii25′, 2:iv1, 2:iv18/8.4

11 List of the most common royal titles and epithets I

This appendix, which draws on appendices 8–9, lists the most frequently attested royal titles and epithets in the inscriptions of Ashurnasirpal II and Shalmaneser III. The abbreviation **fr** refers to frequency. Numbers without parantheses are based on counting attestations in "texts", those within parantheses on counting attestations in "exemplars". The two concluding epithets of Shalmaneser III in the list below were selected (among equally frequent epithets) simply on alphabetical grounds. Presence or absence in the much attested (having 406 exemplars in RIMA2) Standard Inscription (AE23) accounts for the high and varying numbers in the second column. A fair list of the most common titles and epithets of Ashurnasirpal II based on exemplars needs to be presented otherwise, since around 15 royal titles or epithets with between 400–500 attestations are not represented in the list below. Rather than making an additional list, I refer the reader to the titulary sections in AE23. This appendix is mostly used and referred to in chapter 8.

epithet of Ashurnasirpal II	fr	epithet of Shalmaneser III	fr
mār/apal Tukultī-Ninurta (son/heir of Tukulti-Ninurta II)	89 (1037)	*mār/apal Aššur-nāṣir-apli* (son/heir of Ashurnasirpal II)	72 (344)
šar māt Aššur (king of Assyria)	87 (974)	*šar māt Aššur* (king of Assyria)	46 (273)
šar kiššati (king of the universe)	69 (925)	*iššak Aššur* (vice-regent of Ashur)	40 (112)
šarru dannu (strong king)	64 (892)	*šarru dannu* (strong king)	34 (184)
šarru rabû (great king)	30 (356)	*šar kiššati* (king of the universe)	33 (230)
iššak Aššur (vice-regent of Ashur)	28 (680)	*kāšid ištu* GN *adi* GN (conqueror from GN to GN/of GN)	24 (39)
eṭlu qardu (heroic man)	28 (618)	*šar kiššat nišē* (king of all people)	23 (44)
lā ādiru ina tuqumte (fearless in battle)	25 (888)	*rubû* (prince)	21 (42)
ina malkī ša kibrāt erbetti šāninšu lā īšû (who has no rival among the rulers of the four quarters)	23 (565)	*šarru rabû* (great king)	13 (105)
ša ina tukulti Aššur ittanallaku (who marches with the support of Ashur)	22 (512)	*kīma til abūbi* (like (the effects of) a flood mound)	12 (47)
rubû na'du (attentive prince)	22 (466)	*šar kullat kibrāt erbetti* (king of all the four quarters)	12 (29)
kašūš ilāni rabûti (weapon of the great gods)	21 (461)	*nišīt īnē Ellil* (chosen of Enlil)	11 (39)
šarru ša ištu GN *adi* GN *ana šēpēšu ušekniša* (king who made all lands from GN to GN submit at his feet)	19 (504)	*šamšu kiššat nišē* (sun of all people)	11 (30)
pāliḫ ilāni rabûti (worshipper of the great gods)	19 (463)	*murtedû kalîš mātāte* (leader of all lands)	11 (29)
ša napḫar kiššat nišē ipellu (who rules all people)	18 (457)	*šakin Ellil* (appointee of Enlil)	11 (20)
rē'û tabrâte° (amazing shepherd)	16 (464)	*rubû na'du* (attentive prince)	10 (29)
ušumgallu ekdu (fierce dragon)	16 (456)	*šarru ba"īt ilāni* (king who is the desired one of the deities)	10 (28)
kīma Adad ša rāḫiṣi (like Adad, the flooder)	16 (448)	*āmeru*° *durgi u šapšāqi* (who has seen innermost and rugged regions)	9 (27)
edû gapšu ša māḫira lā īšû (arisen flood wave which has no antagonist)	15 (463)	*mukabbis rēšēte ša šadê kalîš ḫuršāni* (who treads upon the mountain peaks of all highlands)	9 (27)
kāšid ālāni ḫuršāni pāṭ gimrišunu (conqueror of cities and the entire highlands)	15 (448)	*māḫir bilti u igisê ša kalîšina kibrāti* (receiver of tribute and gifts from all the quarters)	8 (26)
mula"iṭ ekṣūte (controller of the brazen ones)	15 (448)	*mupattû*° *ṭūdāti ša eliš u šapliš* (opener of paths above and below)	8 (26)

šakin Ellil (appointee of Enlil)	15 (223)	*zikaru dannu* (strong male)	8 (26)
ṣābit līṭī (seizer of hostages)	14 (473)	*šakkanakku°* *Aššur pitqudu* (prudent governor of Ashur)	7 (24)
(*šarru*) *mušakniš lā kanšūtešu* (king/he who makes those unsubmissive to him submit)	14 (472)	*ša ina malkī ša kibrāt erbetti šāninšu lā īšû* (he who has no rival among the rulers of the four quarters)	5 (23)
šākin līte eli kalîšina mātāti (who achieves victory over all lands)	14 (450)	*ša ina tukulti Aššur u Šamaš ittanallaku* (who marches with the support of Ashur and Shamash)	5 (23)
murīb anunte (he who requites with strife)	14 (447)	(*ša*) *ana tīb tāḫāzišu danni kibrāte ultanapšaqā* (*iḫillū ālāni*) (at whose strong attack for combat the four quarters are constrained (and cities are convulsed))	4 (22)
nišīt Ellil u Ninurta (chosen of Enlil and Ninurta)	13 (454)	*ištamdaḫu šadê u tâmāte* (who has marched through mountains and seas)	4 (22)

12 List of the most common royal titles and epithets II

This appendix, which draws on appendix 10, lists the ten most frequently attested royal titles/epithets for each of the other Early Neo-Assyrian kings. The abbreviation **fr** refers to frequency. Numbers without parantheses are based on counting attestations in "texts", those within parantheses on counting attestations in "exemplars". The final epithets of Adad-narari II, Tukulti-Ninurta II, and Shamshi-Adad V respectively were selected (among equally frequent epithets) simply on alphabetical grounds. Empty cells denote lack of any further epithet. This appendix is mostly used in chapter 8.

epithet of Ashur-dan II	**fr**	**epithet of Adad-narari II**	**fr**
mār/apal Tukultī-apil-Ešarra (son/heir of Tiglath-pileser II)	6 (25)	*šar māt Aššur* (king of Assyria)	12 (37)
šar māt Aššur (king of Assyria)	4 (20)	*šarru dannu* (strong king)	9 (19)
šar kiššati (king of the universe)	4 (19)	*mār/apal Aššur-dān* (son/heir of Ashur-dan II)	8 (23)
šarru dannu (strong king)	4 (18)	*šar kiššati* (king of the universe)	5 (16)
iššak Aššur (vice-regent of Ashur)	2 (5)	*šar kibrāt erbetti* (king of the four quarters)	5 (13)
nibīt Aššur (designate of Ashur)	1 (3)	*rubû na'adu* (attentive prince)	4 (10)
[*ša … ana šarrūt*] *māt Aššur rabîš ukinnûšu* ([whom] he (Ashur) greatly established [for the kingship] of Assyria)	1 (3)	*aštāku* (I am obdurate)	3 (7)
[*ša … u*] *agâ ṣīru ušatmeḫu* ([into whose grasp] he (Ashur) granted the exalted crown)	1 (3)	*bēlāku* (I am lord-like)	3 (7)
[*ša … ultu*] *ullâ Aššur šumšu ibbû* ([whose] name Ashur called [since] earliest times)	1 (3)	*dandannāku* (I am all-powerful)	3 (7)
šakan° Ellil (appointee of Enlil)	1 (2)	*dannāku* (I am strong)	3 (7)

epithet of Tukulti-Ninurta II	**fr**	**epithet of Shamshi-Adad V**	**fr**
mār/apal Adad-nārārī (son/heir of Adad-narari II)	20 (32)	*mār/apal Šulmānu-ašarēd* (son/heir of Shalmaneser III)	7 (32)
šar māt Aššur (king of Assyria)	17 (26)	*šar māt Aššur* (king of Assyria)	6 (24)
šarru dannu (strong king)	11 (14)	*šarru dannu* (strong king)	3 (18)
šar kiššati (king of the universe)	9 (18)	*šakin Ellil* (appointee of Enlil)	2 (10)
iššak Aššur (vice-regent of Ashur)	5 (8)	(*kīma*) *Adad šāgimi* ((like) Adad, the thunderer)	2 (3)
bibil libbišunu/ka (their/your select one)	5 (5)	(*kīma*) *arâni* ((like) an eagle)	2 (3)
šar kibrāt erbetti (king of the four quarters)	5 (5)	*mukīl parṣī Ekur* (who upholds the rites of Ekur)	2 (3)
ana mu"urūt kibrāt arba'i ana dāriš išquru šume kabta (whose weighty name he (Ashur) has pronounced forever for the four quarters)	4 (4)	*muma"er gimrī* (commander of all)	2 (3)

bēl bēlē (lord of lords)	4 (4)	*murtedû kalîš mātāti* (leader of all lands)	2 (3)
bēlāku (I am lord-like)	4 (4)	*nāši ḫaṭṭi ešrete* (bearer of the just sceptre)	2 (3)

epithet of Adad-narari III	**fr**	**epithet of Shalmaneser IV**	**fr**
šar māt Aššur (king of Assyria)	36 (67)	*šar māt Aššur* (king of Assyria)	2 (2)
mār/apal Šamšī-Adad (son/heir of Shamshi-Adad V)	27 (76)	[*ardu*] ([servant])	1 (1)
šar kiššati (king of the universe)	13 (19)	*mār/apal Adad-nārārī* (son/heir of Adad-narari III)	1 (1)
waklu (overseer)	9 (14)	[*pāliḫ ilūtika rabûti*] ([who fears your great divinity (Ashur)])	1 (1)
šarru dannu (strong king)	8 (10)	*šangû ellu* (holy priest)	1 (1)
šarru rabû (great king)	6 (8)	*šarru dannu* (strong king)	1 (1)
šakin Ellil (appointee of Enlil)	5 (31)		
šarru (king)	5 (5)		
bēlī/šu (my/his (an official's) lord)	4 (5)		
iššak Aššur (vice-regent of Ashur)	3 (26)		

epithet of Ashur-dan III	**fr**	**epithet of Ashur-narari V**	**fr**
iššak Aššur (vice-regent of Ashur)	1 (1)	*šar māt Aššur* (king of Assyria)	11 (11)
mār/apal Adad-nārārī (son/heir of Adad-narari III)	1 (1)		
šakin Ellil (appointee of Enlil)	1 (1)		

13 Visual representations of Ashurnasirpal II

Below is a thematically ordered list of all the visual representations of Ashurnasirpal II, comprising 131 attestations, presented. The abbreviations stand for: **A** Assur, **K** Kalhu (Nimrud), **N** Nineveh, **ic** the rest of the inner core (including Balawat), **oc** the outer core, **bf** the border areas or foreign lands, **1** first regnal half, **2** second regnal half. Crosses indicate attestation, empty cell signals lack of attestation. (For the aspect of frequency, see also the list in app. 15.) The final column provides an index whose numbers refer to (sub)sections. Only direct references to the royal visual representation in question are included in the index. The idea of this appendix is partly taken from Magen (1986) who lists royal motifs in a similar way. Numbers within parantheses regarding AI23-motifs refer to the ordering of Magen. The appendix conveyed here is mainly used and referred to in chapters 4–9.

motif	source	A	K	N	ic	oc	bf	1	2	index
king in battle	AI4: B18t.		x					x		5.4.1/9, 7.2
king in battle	AI4: B11t.		x					x		3.2
king in battle	AI4: B3t.		x					x		3.2, 4.4, 5.4.2
king in battle	AI4: B5b.		x					x		4.4
king in battle	AI4: WFL21t.		x					x		2.1, 3.2, 4.4
king in battle	AI13: 9–10				x				x?	5.2, 7.2
king in battle	AI13: 11–12				x				x?	
king in battle	AI13: 19–20				x				x?	
king in battle	AI13: 27–28				x				x?	
king in battle	AI14: 59–60				x				x?	
king in battle	AI14: 75–76				x				x?	
king in battle	AI14: 85–86				x				x?	
king in battle	AI36		x							4.1/4
king on march	AI4: B5t.		x					x		7.2
king on march	AI4: WFL19b.		x					x		5.1, 7.2
king on march	AI4: B9b.		x					x		5.1
king receiving captives	AI4: B18b.		x					x		5.4.6, 7.2
king receiving captives	AI4: B7b.		x					x		5.4.7
king receiving captives	AI13: 17–18				x				x?	5.4.3/7/9
king receiving captives	AI13: 21–22				x				x?	7.2
king receiving captives	AI13: 23–24				x				x?	5.4.3/7/9
king receiving captives	AI13: 37–38				x				x?	5.4.2
king receiving booty?	AI4: WFL24b.		x					x		7.2
king receiving tribute	AI4: D2		x					x		2.1, 5.4.1, 7.2
king receiving tribute?	AI4: WFL16t.		x					x		
king receiving tribute	AI13: 7–8				x				x?	
king receiving tribute	AI13: 33–34				x				x?	8.2/3
king receiving tribute	AI13: 35–36				x				x?	5.4.4, 7.2

king receiving tribute	AI14: 57–58			x		x?	3.2
king receiving tribute	AI14: 67–68			x		x?	4.1
king receiving tribute	AI14: 73–74			x		x?	5.4.4, 7.2
king receiving tribute	AI14: 79–80			x		x?	5.4.3
king receiving tribute	AI14: 81–82			x		x?	5.4.1/3
king receiving tribute	AI14: 83–84			x		x?	5.4.3/7
king receiving tribute?	AI15: 95	x			x		5.4.3
king receiving tribute?	AI15: 96	x			x		
king receiving tribute?	AI26	x					5.4.1/2
king receiving tribute	AI29	x					5.4.3
king receiving tribute?	AI30		x				5.4.7
king receiving tribute?	AI28	x					5.4.4
king receiving tribute	AI16: 138 A1	x				x	4.4, 5.4.1
king receiving tribute	AI16: 138 A3	x				x	4.4, 5.4.1
king receiving tribute	AI23: P2 (49a)	x			x		4.1/4
king as tree feller?	AI27	x					5.4.3
king as hunter	AI4: B20t.	x			x		2.1, 5.2, 6.2
king as hunter	AI4: B19t.	x			x		2.1, 5.2, 6.2
king as hunter	AI4: WFL13b.	x			x		2.1
king as hunter	AI4: WFL14b.	x			x		2.1
king as hunter	AI13: 13–14			x		x?	5.2
king as hunter	AI13: 15–16			x		x?	5.2, 8.3
king as hunter	AI13: 29–30			x		x?	5.2, 5.4.7, 7.2
king as hunter	AI1: 86		x			x?	5.2, 7.2
king as hunter	AI35	x?					5.2
king as hunter	AI37	x?					4.1, 5.2
king as hunter	AI23: G8 (31a)	x			x		7.2
king as hunter	AI23: G11 (33a)	x			x		
king as hunter	AI23: G16 (36a)	x			x		5.2
king as hunter	AI23: P2 (49b)	x			x		4.1, 5.2

(continued)

motif	source	A	K	N	ic	oc	bf	1	2	index
king as hunter	AI23: P4(49c)		x					x		4.1
king as hunter	AI23: S3 (50a)		x					x		5.2
king as venerating priest	A14: B23l.		x					x		2.1, 3.1/2, 4.2
king as venerating priest	AI4: B23r.		x					x		2.1, 3.1/2, 4.2
king as venerating priest	AI4: B13l.		x					x		2.1, 3.2, 4.2
king as venerating priest	AI4: B13r.		x					x		2.1, 3.2, 4.2
king as venerating priest	AI23: G3 (29a)		x					x		4.2
king as venerating priest	AI23: G3 (29b)		x					x		4.2
king as venerating priest	AI19		x					x		4.1/2/4
king as venerating priest	AI18						x	x		4.2, 8.3
king as venerating priest	AI17						x	x		4.1, 6.2, 7.2
king as venerating priest	AI32: l.		x?							4.2
king as venerating priest	AI32: r.		x?							4.2
king as venerating priest	AI33: l.					x				4.2
king as venerating priest	AI33: r.					x				4.2
king as venerating priest	AI34									
king as priest (statue)	AI12		x						x?	3.1, 4.1/2/3, 5.4.4
king as libating priest	AI4: B20b.		x					x		2.1, 5.2, 6.2
king as libating priest	AI4: B19b.		x					x		2.1, 5.2, 6.2
king as libating priest	AI4: G8		x					x		6.2
king as libating priest	AI4: G10		x					x		
king as libating priest	AI4: G13		x					x		
king as libating priest	AI4: G16		x					x		
king as libating priest	AI4: G25		x					x		
king as libating priest	AI4: G29		x					x		2.1
king as libating priest	AI4: C7		x					x		
king as libating priest	AI4: H2		x					x		

king as libating priest	AI4: H4	x		x		
king as libating priest	AI4: H9	x		x		
king as libating priest	AI4: [H13]	x		x		
king as libating priest	AI4: H16	x		x		
king as libating priest	AI4: H19	x		x		
king as libating priest	AI4: [H26]	x		x		
king as libating priest	AI4: H29	x		x		
king as libating priest	AI4: H31	x		x		
king as libating priest	AI4: H33	x		x		
king as libating priest	AI25	x				3.1, 4.2, 5.4.4
king as libating priest	AI22	x				5.4.4
king as libating priest	AI1: 214–220		x		x?	5.2, 7.2
king as libating priest	AI23: G (40a)	x		x		7.2
king being ritually purified	AI4: F4	x		x		7.2
king being ritually purified	AI23: C7 (27a)	x		x		4.1
king being ritually purified	AI23: C7 (27b)	x		x		4.1
king being ritually purified	AI23: G8 (31b)	x		x		
king being ritually purified	AI23: G8 (31c)	x		x		
king being ritually purified	AI23: G11 (33c)	x		x		
king being ritually purified	AI23: G11 (33d)	x		x		
king having his weapons ritually purified	AI4: G6	x		x		4.4, 6.2, 7.2
king having his weapons ritually purified	AI4: G11	x		x		
king having his weapons ritually purified	AI4: G14	x		x		5.4.1
king having his weapons ritually purified	AI4: G23	x		x		
king having his weapons ritually purified	AI4: G31	x		x		
king having his weapons ritually purified	AI4: N6	x		x		
king having his weapons ritually purified	AI23: G3 (29c)	x		x		
king having his weapons ritually purified	AI23: G3 (29d)	x		x		
king having his weapons ritually purified	AI23: G3 (29e)	x		x		
king having his weapons ritually purified	AI23: G3 (29f)	x		x		

(continued)

motif	source	A	K	N	ic	oc	bf	1	2	index
king having his weapons ritually purified	AI23: G3 (29g)		x					x		
king having his weapons ritually purified	AI23: G3 (29h)		x					x		
king having his weapons ritually purified	AI23: G3 (29i)		x					x		
king having his weapons ritually purified	AI23: G3 (29l)		x					x		
king having his weapons ritually purified	AI23: G2 (29k)		x					x		
king having his weapons ritually purified	AI23: G3 (29m)		x					x		
king having his weapons ritually purified	AI23: G3 (29n)		x					x		
king having his weapons ritually purified	AI23: G11 (33b)		x					x		
king as shepherd	AI4: B14		x					x		3.1, 5.4.4, 7.2
king as shepherd	AI4: B12		x					x		3.1, 5.4.4
king as shepherd	AI4: S3		x					x		2.1
king as shepherd	AI20		x						x	4.2, 5.4.4
king banqueting	AI4: G3		x					x		5.4.4/7
king banqueting?	AI31		x							4.2
king receiving submissive Assyrians	AI24: 22b.									4.1, 5.4.1/6
king being crowned by deities	AI24: 22t.									4.1, 5.4.1/6

14 Visual representations of Shalmaneser III and the other kings

Below is a thematically ordered list of all the visual representations of Shalmaneser III (60) and of the other kings (10). The abbreviations stand for: **A** Assur, **K** Kalhu (Nimrud), **N** Nineveh, **co** the rest of the inner core (including Balawat), **oc** the outer core, **bf** the border areas and foreign lands, **of** the two latest mentioned areas combined, **1/2/3** first/second/third regnal phase. Crosses indicate attestations, empty cells denote lack of attestations. (For the aspect of frequency, see also the list in app. 15.) For the abbreviations in the second column, see "Abbreviations". The final column provides an index. The numbers in the index column refer to (sub)sections. Only direct references to the royal visual representation in question are included in the index. The idea of this appendix is partly taken from Magen (1986) who lists royal motifs in a similar way. The appendix conveyed here is mainly used in chapters 4–9.

motif	source	A	K	N	ic	of	1	2	3	index
king in battle	SI10: 1b.				x		x			4.4, 5.4.1, 6.3
king in battle	SI10: 2t.				x		x			
king in battle	SI10: 2b.				x		x			
king in battle	SI10: 3b.				x		x			6.3
king in battle	SI10: 7t.				x		x			4.4, 5.4.1
king in battle	SI10: 9t.				x		x			
king in battle	SI10: 12t.				x		x			5.2
king in battle	SI10: 12b.				x		x			5.2
king in battle	SI10: 13t.				x		x			
king in battle	SI10: 15b.				x		x			
king in battle	SI10: 16t.				x		x			
king in battle	SI10: 16b.				x		x			7.3
king observing battle	SI10: 4t.				x		x			4.2, 5.4.3/7, 8.3
king observing battle	SI10: 4b.				x		x			4.2, 5.4.3/7, 6.3, 8.3
king observing battle	SI10: 8t.				x		x			5.4.4/7
king observing battle	SI10: 8b.				x		x			5.4.3/4/7
king observing battle	SI10: 10b.				x		x			5.4.3
king observing battle	SI10: 15t.				x		x			7.3
king on march	SI10: 11b.				x		x			6.3, 7.3
king receiving captives	SI10: 3b.				x		x			6.3
king receiving captives	SI10: 13b.				x		x			7.3
king receiving booty	SI10: 9b.				x		x			4.4, 5.4.1/3/7, 6.3, 7.3
king receiving booty	SI11: A1		x						x	2.1, 4.1/4, 5.4.1/2/3/5/7/9
king receiving tribute	SI10: 3t.				x		x			
king receiving tribute	SI10: 5t.				x		x			5.4.3/7, 8.2/3
king receiving tribute	SI10: 5b.				x		x			5.4.3/7, 8.2/3
king receiving tribute	SI10: 6t.				x		x			
king receiving tribute	SI10: 6b.				x		x			

king receiving tribute	SI10: 7b.				x		x			4.1, 5.4.1/3/7
king receiving tribute	SI10: 11t.				x		x			
king receiving tribute	SI11: A2		x						x	2.1, 4.1/2, 5.2/3, 5.4.1/3/5/7
king receiving tribute	SI14: 4b		x				x?			4.1/4, 5.4.1/3/5/7, 7.3
king receiving tribute	SI14: 6a		x				x?			5.4.3/7/9, 6.3
king receiving tribute?	SI22		x							
king receiving tribute	SI23		x							5.4.3
king receiving tribute	SI24		x							4.2, 5.4.3
king receiving timber?	SI10: 14t.				x		x			
king as hunter	SI26			x?						5.2, 7.3
king as venerating priest	SI18: 9l.		x							3.2, 4.1/2/4, 5.4.4, 7.3
king as venerating priest	SI18: 9r.		x							3.2, 4.1/2/4, 5.4.4, 7.3
king as venerating priest	SI13					x	x			4.2, 7.3, 8.3
king as venerating priest	SI15					x	x			4.3
king as venerating priest	SI16					x	x			4.1/2/3
king as venerating priest	SI17					x		x		4.1/3
king as venerating priest (stele image)	SI10: 1t.				x		x			4.2/4
king as venerating priest (stele image)	SI10: 10b.				x		x			4.2, 5.1, 7.3
king as venerating priest (stele image)	SI10: 14t.				x		x			4.2, 6.3
king as priest (statue)	SI5		x					x		4.1/2/3, 7.3
king as priest (statue)	SI6	x							x	4.2/4, 5.4.4/9, 7.3
king as priest (statue)	SI7		x						x	4.2, 7.3
king as priest (statue)	SI8	x								4.2, 7.3
king as libating priest	SI10: 1t.				x		x			4.2/4
king as libating priest	SI10: 10b.				x		x			4.2, 5.1, 7.3
king as libating priest	SI19		x							4.2
king as libating priest	SI20		x							4.2

(continued)

motif	source	A	K	N	ic	of	1	2	3	index
king banqueting	SI21		x							5.4.4/7, 7.3
king banqueting	SI25		x?							5.4.4
king meeting another ruler	SI14: 7c		x				x?			5.4.5, 6.3, 7.3
king receiving submissive Assyrians	SI10: 10t.				x		x			5.4.1/6
king as master builder? (statue)	SI4	x					x			4.3

motif	source	A	K	N	ic	oc	bf	1	2	index
king as venerating priest	SA5I1		x						x	2.1, 4.1/2, 5.4.7, 8.4
king as venerating priest	SA5I2				x				x	2.1, 4.1/2
king as venerating priest	An3I2					x			x?	2.1, 4.1/2, 7.4, 8.4
king as venerating priest	An3I3					x			x?	2.1, 7.4
king as venerating priest	An3I4					x				2.1
king as venerating priest?	An3I6						x		x?	2.1, 5.4.5/7, 6.4, 7.4
king as venerating priest	An3I7						x			2.1
king as hunter	An3I11			x?						2.1, 5.2
king as venerating priest	An3I12									2.1, 5.4.5/7
king as venerating priest	An3I13									2.1, 4.1/2

15 List of the most common royal visual representations

This appendix lists, drawing on appendices 13–14, all the visual representations attested for Ashurnasirpal II (131), Shalmaneser III (60), and the other Early Neo-Assyrian kings (10) according to frequency (abbreviated **fr**). Numbers refer either to the total number of attestations of a particular motif, or motif corpus (see the numbers in the last rows of the two tables), or to the relative proportion, given in percentage, of a particular motif within a certain motif corpus. This appendix is a part of the discussion in chapter 8.

Ashurnasirpal II-motif	fr	Shalmaneser III-motif	fr
Libating priest	23 (17,6 %)	Receiving tribute	13 (21,7 %)
Receiving tribute	20 (15,3 %)	In battle	12 (20,0 %)
Having his weapons ritually purified	18 (13,7 %)	Venerating priest	9 (15,0 %)
Hunter	16 (12,2 %)	Observing battle	6 (10,0 %)
Venerating priest	14 (10,7 %)	Priest (statue)	4 (6,7 %)
In battle	13 (9,9 %)	Libating priest	4 (6,7 %)
Being ritually purified	7 (5,3 %)	Receiving captives	2 (3,3 %)
Receiving captives	6 (4,6 %)	Receiving booty	2 (3,3 %)
Shepherd	4 (3,1 %)	Banqueting	2 (3,3 %)
On march	3 (2,3 %)	On march	1 (1,7 %)
Banqueting	2 (1,5 %)	Hunter	1 (1,7 %)
Receiving booty?	1 (0,8 %)	Meeting another ruler	1 (1,7 %)
Felling tree?	1 (0,8 %)	Receiving submissive Assyrians	1 (1,7 %)
Priest (statue)	1 (0,8 %)	Master builder (statue)?	1 (1,7 %)
Receiving submissive Assyrians	1 (0,8 %)	Receiving timber?	1 (1,7 %)
Being crowned by deities	1 (0,8 %)		
	= 131		= 60

motif of the eNA I-kings	fr	motif of the eNA III-kings	fr
–	–	Venerating priest (SA5, An3)	9 (90,0 %)
–	–	Hunter (An3)	1 (10,0 %)
	= 0		= 10

16 Early Neo-Assyrian state ideology in history

This appendix places the identified Early Neo-Assyrian state ideology into a wider historical-ideological context. All royal visual representations (1), the most common royal titles/epithets as counted from "texts" (2), and the textual narrative themes covering the whole study (3), of all the rulers are listed, and the presence or absence of these ideological features in other time periods are noted by the use or lack of a cross. Quantifications give the total number of attestations, all Early Neo-Assyrian sources combined. Abbreviations stand for: **quant** quantification of attestations, **sect** (sub)section of the book, **OA I** Old Assyrian Period *excluding* Shamshi-Adad I, **OA II** Old Assyrian Period *including* Shamshi-Adad I, **MA I** Middle Assyrian Period before Tiglath-pileser I, **MA II** Middle Assyrian Period from Tiglath-pileser I onwards, **eNA** Early Neo-Assyrian Period (934–745 BCE), **lNA I** Late Neo-Assyrian Period before Sennacherib, **lNA II** Late Neo-Assyrian Period from Sennacherib onwards. This appendix is centred on in chapter 9.

royal visual representation, eNA	quant	OA I	OA II	MA I	MA II	lNA I	lNA II
receiving tribute	33				x	x	
venerating priest	32			x	x	x	x
libating priest	27				x	x?	x
in battle	25				x	x	
weapon cleansing	18					x	
hunter	18				x	x	x
receiving captives	8					x	x
ritually purified	7					x	x?
observing battle	6					x	
priest (statue)	5						
banqueting	4			x?	x	x	x
on march	4			x?	x	x	x
shepherd	4				x	x	x
receiving booty	3					x	x
receiving Assyrians	2						
felling tree	1						
being crowned	1						
meeting a ruler	1						
master builder?	1						x
receiving timber?	1						

royal epithet, eNA	quant	OA I	OA II	MA I	MA II	lNA I	lNA II
mār/apal RN	231	x	x	x	x	x	x
šar māt Aššur	219			x	x	x	x
šar kiššati	135		x	x	x	x	x
šarru dannu	134		x	x	x	x	x
iššak Aššur	80	x	x	x	x	x	x
šarru rabû	53		x	x	x	x	x
rubû na'du	40			x	x	x	x
šakin Enlil	37		x	x	x	x	x
kāšid ištu GN *adi* GN	35			x	x	x	x
eṭlu qardu	35			x	x	x	(x)
šar kiššat nišē	31			x			
rubû	28	(x)	(x)	x	(x)	x	(x)
ina malkī ša kibrāt erbetti lā šāninšu īšû	28						
lā ādiru° tuqumte	26					x	(x)
ša ina tukulti Aššur ittanallaku	26						
šamšu kiššat nišē	26			x			x
šar kibrāt erbetti	24			x	x	x	x
šarru/šarrāku	24			x	x	x	x
kīma Adad	23				x	x	x
šar kullat kibrāt erbetti	23			(x)	x	(x)	(x)

textual theme, eNA	sect	OA I	OA II	MA I	MA II	lNA I	lNA II
deities as masters	3.1			x	x	x	x
deities as conquerors	3.2		x	x	x	x	x
divine choice	4.1	x	x	x	x	x	x
priest	4.2	x	x	x	x	x	x
master builder	4.3	x	x	x	x	x	x
warrior	4.4		x	x	x	x	x
difficult path	5.1			x	x	x	x
hunter	5.2				x		x
respecting foreign deities	5.3		x		x	x	x
king over every land	5.4.1			x	x	x	x
king over all peoples	5.4.1			x	x	x	x
booty	5.4.2			x	x	x	x
deportations	5.4.2			x	x	x	x
tribute	5.4.3		x	x	x	x	x
fetching resources	5.4.3			x	x	x	x
paternalism	5.4.4	x		x	x	x	x
Babylonia emphasis	5.4.5	x	x	x	x	x	x
Assyria	5.4.6			x	x	x	x
royal line references	5.4.7	x	x	x	x	x	x
heroic priority	5.4.7	x	x	x	x	x	x
identity/alterity	5.4.8	x	x	x	x	x	x
gendered imagery	5.4.9	x	x	x	x	x	x